Adventure Guide™ *to the*

Yucatán
Cancún & Cozumel

3rd Edition

Bruce & June Conord

HUNTER

HUNTER PUBLISHING, INC,
130 Campus Drive, Edison, NJ 08818
732-225-1900; 800-255-0343; fax 732-417-1744
hunterp@bellsouth.net

Ulysses Travel Publications
4176 Saint-Denis, Montréal, Québec, Canada H2W 2M5
514-843-9882, ext. 2232; fax 514-843-9448

Windsor Books
The Boundary, Wheatley Road, Garsington, Oxford, OX44 9EJ England
01865-361122; fax 01865-361133

ISBN 1-58843-370-6
© 2004 Hunter Publishing, Inc.

This and other Hunter travel guides are also available as e-books through our online partners, including netlibrary.com, Amazon.com and BarnesandNoble.com, as well as directly from the publisher.

This guide focuses on recreational activities. As all such activities contain elements of risk, the publisher, author, affiliated individuals and companies disclaim any responsibility for any injury, harm, or illness that may occur to anyone through, or by use of, the information in this book. Every effort was made to insure the accuracy of information in this book, but the publisher and author do not assume, and hereby disclaim, any liability for any loss or damage caused by errors, omissions, misleading information or potential travel problems caused by this guide, even if such errors or omissions are the result of negligence, accident or any other cause.

Cover photo: *Serpentine Heads, Chichen Itzá Ruins*
(© Gibson Stock Photography)

Maps by Kim André & Toni Carbone, © 2004 Hunter Publishing, Inc.

Chac Mool logo © 2001 Bruce & June Conord; on spine
design by Judy Mazziotti (judymazz@bellatlantic.net)

All other images © 2004 Bruce & June Conord

Acknowledgments

As anyone might imagine, writing an in-depth travel guide – even to such a terrific place as the Yucatán – requires a great deal of work. Lots of fun, but lots of work. Although there are far too many people to thank each one individually for their kindness and consideration, we are overly indebted to the following people whose help made this book possible: Michael Hunter, our long-time publisher and editor for this edition, as well as Toni Wheeler and Kim André and all the friendly folks at Hunter Publishing. A big *gracias* to Ana Mari Irabién who does a fabulous job for the Cancún Convention and Visitor's Bureau, and her assistant, Lizbeth Santoyo; Ana Argaez of the Yucatán State Tourist Board, a tireless advocate for her home state; and Alejandro Serrano López, from the beautiful State of Campeche Tourism Board, who gave up his Christmas Eve to help us. Thank you too to Maite Weitzman Hernández from AeroMexico, our favorite airline south of the border; and Wilbert Ventura Canul at Localiza Car Rentals. We must also thank Lisa Blau at Lisa Adams PR, Victoria Pratt at Victoria Pratt PR, Jorge Macari C., Marissa Setien, and Gabriel Escalante, for their generous assistance. Thanks as well to Ben and Matt Hill for house sitting while we gallivant around the world.

Additionally, we wish to thank our readers and others who offered us compliments, criticisms, and helpful suggestions, including "Bush," whom everyone in Puerto Morelos knows by that name, Erik Mendicuti, Miriam Wyman, Bob Katz, Karn & Bob Weigel, Bob Haneveld, Erika Holm, Margareta Horiba, Alma Duran & Stephan Merk, Marjorie Stone & Jack Rogers, Sheila Boyce, Raul LiCausi, Angela Beathard, Alyshia & Carlos Galvez, Peter Helby, Bruce Rogers, and especially Freddie L. Heitman from Fort Worth, Texas, who obviously loves the Yucatán as much as we do. Last, but not least, we give a warm *gracias* to Silvia González Rosado, who does such a wonderful job on our laundry at Burbujas Lavandería in Tulum Pueblo.

■ ■ ■

Dedication

This book is dedicated to the ones we love. We hope that life offers them many adventures full of wonder and delight.

He that loves reading has everything within his reach.
~ William Godwin

About the Authors

The Conords have been traveling and writing about their journeys for years. They enjoy adventure and ecological travel, as well as historical and cultural forays in foreign lands. Their other Hunter titles, *Adventure Guide to Costa Rica* and *Cancún, Cozumel & the Riviera Maya Alive!*, garnered critical acclaim.

Bruce went to Rutgers University and has written biographies of John Lennon, Bill Cosby and Cesar Chavez. He has worked as an import manager, teacher, advertising executive, copywriter and publisher's representative. Writing, photography, soccer and travel are his passions.

June grew up in southwest England and went to Plymouth Art College. Whenever she gets near the ocean, she feels happy. Her professional credits include numerous newspaper and magazine articles and stock photography. She has edited, photographed and worked alongside Bruce in many of their joint efforts to eke out a living and travel more. For relaxation, she could happily spend all day on a pebble beach, poking a stick in rock pools and collecting shells.

Their individual work is represented by a stock photography agency and their photographs of Mexico have been featured at an exhibit in the New York Arts Club.

■ ■ ■

Contents

Yucatán

Maps

Introduction

Don't be a tourist.
~ Travel Channel, 1997

This book is about adventure, excitement and fun in a vibrant land alive with natural wonders and contemporary culture amid fragments of departed grandeur. You don't have to speak Spanish to enjoy the superb attractions – English is welcome everywhere. We know of few destinations that offer more all-round pleasure.

Whether your definition of adventure is lying on the beach and sipping margaritas, or hiking into the jungle to explore the spectacular ruins of the lost Maya civilization, this book has you covered. We give first-hand evaluations of hundreds of hotels and restaurants, plus the absolute best values in lodging, meals and shopping, so you can get more for your money.

We'll show you where to enjoy the best of Cancún's glitzy resorts at a fraction of the regular cost. Sit and eat a delicious fish dinner under the shade of a palapa (Yucatán's natural beach umbrella) at a hard-to-find seaside restaurant where only "insiders" go. Stay in a Spanish Colonial hotel with 18-foot-high ceilings and walls more than one foot thick. Sling a hammock in a 200-year-old hacienda where time has stood still. Or sleep in beachfront bungalows so close to the Caribbean that the waves lap gently against the front porch. Savor white sandy beaches and turquoise seas, or be thrilled by the unearthly sound of howler monkeys echoing through miles of unbroken rainforest.

It's a countryside whose legacy is intricately involved with the past – including magnificent ruined Maya cities with temples, ballcourts and giant pyramids where humans were once sacrificed. Follow us to deserted antiquarian sites and climb above the jungle canopy with only the ghosts of warrior kings to keep you company.

Visit Colonial buildings that housed the barons of the lucrative henequen trade and Spanish forts built to keep away the likes of Blackbeard the Pirate. Walk around grand Colonial churches and monasteries in tiny towns or enjoy Spanish haciendas and abandoned plantations.

The Yucatán is also a nature lover's paradise. Swim in an underground *cenote* – filled with crystal-clear water – where the only natural light filters through a hole in the roof of an immense cavern.

Float down a forgotten stream past elegant blue herons, snowy egrets and roseate spoonbills standing guard over a mangrove savanna in one of the largest protected biospheres in the Americas. Dive into the warm Lagoon of Seven Colors, where the Maya believed the rainbow began, or take a boat to an *ojo de agua* – an "eye of water." Get close to brilliant pink flamingos by the thousands, spider and howler monkeys in the trees and iguanas sunning on the rocks of a deserted beach.

Bike or hike for hours along a shell-covered coastline without meeting another soul. Snorkel a spectacular reef alive with exotic fish that are as curious about you as you are of them. Dive to an underwater cavern where schools of sharks "sleep," suspended in the current, oblivious to your passing. Pilot a boat to a deserted island to see the wild capybara or sail to an island bird sanctuary with Captain Ricardo on the last wooden boat built on Isla Mujeres (pronunciation MOO-herez).

Wrestle a six-foot crocodile into your boat for nighttime tagging and identification by a biologist. Lie back and admire the Southern night sky – bright enough to read by and streaked with the traces of falling stars. Shop in local *mercados* and rub shoulders (if you're very short) with Maya women in ancestral huipil dresses. Interested in traditional crafts such as hammocks, wood carvings and pottery? See them being made in villages off the beaten trail. Catch a ride in a Victorian horse-drawn hansom to a renowned local restaurant that serves delicious authentic Yucatecan cuisine. All that and more you'll find here in our new *Adventure Guide to the Yucatán, Cancún & Cozumel*. We hope you enjoy it.

By the way, we've included a Maya phonetic phrase glossary at the end of this book to stun your friends and amaze the people you meet in the countryside. Have fun!

> *Happy trails to you.*
> ~ Roy Rogers theme song

Using This Guide

> *Travelers are fantasists, conjurers, seers – and what they finally discover is that every round object is a crystal ball: stone, teapot, the marvelous globe of the human eye.*
> ~ Cynthia Ozick in *The New York Times*, March 1985

■ The Three Main Travel Routes

 Nearly everyone who comes to the Yucatán flies into Cancún, a busy international airport. For those staying in Cancún itself, combi buses or taxis take you to your hotel, to one of the fabulous beaches or downtown. If you are exploring the delightful countryside, there are three basic theme journeys *Adventure Guide* readers can take, depending on available time and personal priorities.

- The first is a **Sea and Sun** route, which heads south along the "Riviera Maya" coast of the state of Quintana Roo, covering Playa del Carmen, Cozumel, Tulum, Bacalar and Chetumal.

- The second goes west, directly into **Maya and Colonial history**. It highlights such towns as Valladolid, Chichén Itzá, Izamal, Mérida and Uxmal.

- The third way combines the first two and is known among travelers as **"the circuit,"** a complete loop of the peninsula, including Campeche state. Our problem in writing about things along the way is our readers' direction of travel in the circuit – clockwise or counterclockwise. If you're traveling north from Chetumal rather than south from Cancún, for example, the beaches will be in reverse order. In that case, try holding the book upside-down in a mirror.

We end the first section with the ruins of southern Quintana Roo, then we pop back to the Yucatán for the second section because so many travelers go that way – west from Cancún toward Mérida. The last section covers Campeche, the peninsula's least-visited state, plus Palenque in Chiapas. See the map of page 11 for locations of states.

UNITED STATES OF AMERICA

MEXICO

Gulf of Mexico

N

Mexico City •

Mérida •   Cancún •

Pacific Ocean

Caribbean Sea

© 2003 HUNTER PUBLISHING, INC.

■ Contact Information

Websites & E-Mail: Nearly every major establishment now has e-mail and a website, so we've included the Internet address after the phone number. In the interest of space, however, we give only the website when you can use that to send them an e-mail.

Internet Cafés: Because so few people have Internet connections in their home, public Internet cafés have sprung up everywhere. They charge between $1 and $3 per hour. We can testify that they are a great way to access your e-mail and keep in touch with friends while on the road, but some are slow as molasses if you use them to surf the Web.

On the Street: Addresses in Cancún's Hotel Zone are given as the kilometer number, e.g., Km 9.5. The 47 km Paseo Kukulcán begins downtown and ends on the way to the airport. The higher the kilometer number, the farther it is from downtown.

■ Pricing

Although we made every effort to be as thorough, complete and accurate as possible, things change in Mexico – *muy rapido*. New establishments pop up overnight, places that are good go bad, formerly lousy restaurants clean up their act, and hotels remodel. If you find things have changed since this writing, please let us know. You can reach our editor at kim@hunterpublishing.com; we can be reached at brucewrite@aol.com or junioc@aol.com. Same goes if you've found something good that we didn't include – let us know! The following chart shows the price brackets we have used. They reflect a relative comparison using dollar-sign symbols.

PRICING CHARTS			
HOTELS		**RESTAURANTS**	
NOTE: Often, one shared bed in a room is cheaper than two. Prices based on cost per night, for two.		*NOTE: Prices are based on a typical entrée for one person. They do not include beverage.*	
[No $]	Less than US $20	–	–
$	US $20 - $40	$	Less than US $5
$$	US $40 - $80	$$	US $5 - 10
$$$	US $80 - $125	$$$	Over US $10
$$$$	US $125 - $200	–	–
$$$$$	Over US $200	–	–

AUTHORS' TIP: *Be sure to read our* Handy Hints *on page 91. And, if you plan to rent a car, please read our* Driving Tips *on page 66.*

■ We Love to Get Mail About Our Book!

Hunter Publishing makes every effort to ensure that its travel guides are the most current sources available to travelers.

If you have any information that you feel should be included in the next edition of *The Adventure Guide to the Yucatán, Cancún & Cozumel*, please write to us at 130 Campus Drive, Edison, NJ 08818. Feel free to include your opinion or experiences of the places you've visited, as well as price updates and suggestions for ways in which we could improve this book for future readers.

If you'd like to contact the authors, Bruce and June Conord, directly, e-mail brucewrite@aol.com or junioc@aol.com. They welcome your comments and suggestions.

A tourist sits under a palapa, the Yucatán's natural beach umbrella.

The Yucatán Peninsula At A Glance

On a Clear Day You Can See Forever
~ 1965 musical

WHEN TO VISIT: The high tourist season in the Yucatán is in the dry winter months from **December through April**. Cancún and Cozumel are most popular during Christmas and Spring Break. The weather averages a comfortable 80°F year-round.

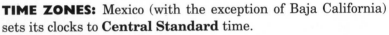

MONEY: Mexican money is the **peso.** It floats against the dollar and can be exchanged at banks and change booths. American dollars are accepted almost everywhere, except in remote areas, at a variable exchange rate. Credit cards are accepted mainly in bigger cities.

PEOPLE: The population of the Yucatán is a combination of Maya and Spanish/Indian *mestizos*.

VISA: No visas are required, but **tourist cards** are a necessity and you will be given one on the plane before you land. The total allowable length of stay indicated on your tourist card, is up to 180 days. To stay longer you can either obtain a card from an embassy before traveling, or renew the standard one before it expires. This can be done in any of the major cities around the peninsula.

CLOTHING: Pack light.

ELECTRICITY: 110 volts.

TIME ZONES: Mexico (with the exception of Baja California) sets its clocks to **Central Standard** time.

FLIGHT TIMES TO Cancún (hours): New York (3.5); Miami (1.5); Los Angeles (4.5); Vancouver BC (6); Toronto (4.5); Denver (4); Europe (12).

HEALTH: No shots are required. The **water** in Cancún and major cities is safe and most hotels and restaurants offer purified tap water. You might prefer to drink bottled water (*agua purificada*) or seltzer (*agua mineral*). Qualified **English-speaking doctors** are available for health emergencies.

CRIME: Crime in the Yucatán is limited to rare instances of pickpocketing or overcharging for drinks.

LANGUAGE: Spanish, Mayan and English are spoken in the major cities.

SMOKING: There's far too much in bars, but **Cuban cigar** smokers will be pleased: they're legal here.

THINGS TO BUY: Silver and gold jewelry, pottery, hammocks, honey, embroidered dresses, Panama hats, men's *guayabera* shirts, wood carvings and blankets.

DRIVING/CAR RENTAL: Rental cars are expensive. You should buy all the insurance offered – and then some. Roads are excellent but night driving is very dangerous for a variety of reasons. Buses are a good alternative and are very reasonably priced.

THINGS TO DO & SEE: Swim in *cenotes*, lie on fabulous beaches, snorkel and dive to colorful reefs, windsurf, get tanned, drink margaritas and beer (not necessarily in that order), read a book, explore the ruins, go down into caves, hike, bike, camp and just generally have a wonderful, exciting vacation.

■ 20 Things Not to be Missed

There are many things to do and see all over the peninsula. We have arranged our top choices by interest. They are not necessarily listed in order of preference, so pick and choose, combine – you can't go wrong.

Maya Ruins

Our picks from the 1,620+ archeological sites on the peninsula.

1. TULUM: This is a ruined post-Classic walled city about two hours south of Cancún. It sits perched on a bluff overlooking the breathtaking turquoise-blue Caribbean Sea. The spectacular view is one good reason Tulum is now Mexico's most-visited archeological site. See page 227.

2. CHICHÉN ITZÁ: The Yucatán's most famous ruin is one of the legendary "lost cities" of the Maya. No one knows why the ancient civilization that created the magnificent El Castillo pyramid simply walked away leaving the huge stone structures to the encroaching jungle. Features a ballcourt and sacrificial altars. See page 326.

3. EK BALAM: Until late in 1999, Ek Balam was a fairly minor site thought to be post-Classic. But when archeologists uncovered the first of the three pyramids that surround a central courtyard, they discovered fabulous freizes, paintings and sculpture now believed to be Late Classic and possibly earlier. This site, just north of Valladolid off the highway, is well worth a visit if you want to see magnificent architecture without any crowds. See page 339.

4. UXMAL: This very impressive large site boasts the dazzlingly detailed Chenes architectural style. Much less crowded with tourists than Chichén, Uxmal was an abandoned city, "found" by a Spanish clergyman around 1562, then fortunately ignored by all until the mid-1800s. It has a fascinating nighttime light show. See page 370.

5. EDZNÁ: These impressive ruins boast more of the intricate carvings associated with Classic Maya architecture than any other site. The northern Maya culture was at its zenith when Edzná was suddenly deserted, not to be reclaimed from the jungle again until 1927. See page 406.

6. DZIBANCHÉ: This recently opened Maya city lies in the jungles of southern Quintana Roo. It is not well known by tourists, and its huge pyramids and temples are whisper-quiet except for the calls of forest birds and the ghosts of Maya kings. See page 272.

Colonial Cities

Colonial cities are peppered throughout the Yucatán. Here's a selection of our favorites.

7. MÉRIDA: The center of culture in the Yucatán, Mérida is a fascinating mix of a strong Colonial heritage and ancient Maya culture, and features celebrations seven days a week. Centuries ago, when it was the ceremonial city T'Ho, Maya from rural areas started to meet at its market, a practice that continues today. See pages 276-310.

8. CAMPECHE: Time has stood still for this walled city that once withstood the attacks of Caribbean pirates. Narrow streets, brightly painted homes and thick walls distinguish this traditional Colonial gem on the Gulf of Mexico. It's the best place to spend Christmas. See pages 391-434.

9. VALLADOLID: In the heart of the Yucatán Peninsula, Valladolid has a tragic history that began with the Conquest and continued through the Caste War and Mexican Revolution. Quaint and quiet, but near everything. See pages 314-325.

Nature & Ecology

The peninsula has numerous natural attractions, many of which are unique.

10. CENOTE AKTUN CHEN: This fabulous underground cavern features untouched stalagmites and stalagmites along with a brilliant green *cenote*. Tastefully hidden spotlights illuminate its large, non-claustrophobic caverns. See page 223.

11. SNORKELING OR DIVING: A ring of spectacular reefs surround the island of Cozumel and line the shore from Puerto Morelos to Xcalak. Divers come here for the great drift diving. Snorkelers are just as happy with the colorful fish near the shore. See page 185.

12. FLAMINGOS AT CELESTUN/RIO LAGARTOS: In either of these two nature preserves you can take a boat out to see thousands of brilliant pink flamingoes feeding in the shallow lagoons. See pages 341 and 354.

13. SIAN KA'AN BIOSPHERE: EcoColors Nature Tours offers a guided boat tour into this huge nature preserve. They specialize in one- , three- and seven-day tours. See page 238.

14. ISLA CONTOY: A nature and bird preserve off the coast, north of Cancún, this island is accessible only by boat. It offers a fun and educational day trip. See page 156.

15. CENOTE X-KEKEN/CENOTE SAMULA: Go here, but don't tell anyone else. These underground caves have holes in their roofs so shafts of sunlight beam down into their blue-green water pools. Swimming in them or just seeing them is magical. See pages 319-20.

Fun

Of course, Cancún is known as a party town with plenty to do around the clock, but the region has a few other fun surprises too.

16. CANCÚN: What is there to say? Cancún is famous for being itself. Enjoy the pure white beaches but don't miss downtown Cancún. The strip of restaurants, flea markets and shops along Avenida Tulum is as close to Mexican as you can get in the resort.

17. ISLA MUJERES: This little island was once a fishing village long before they built the ritzy resort of Cancún across the bay. Even though it's now a shopping mecca for day-trippers, it's still an ideal choice for a laid-back beach vacation.

18. COZUMEL: Cozumel has everything going for it, whatever your vacation goals. Shopping, diving, snorkeling, pristine swimming beaches, golf, rocky coasts, and much more.

19. PLAYA DEL CARMEN: Don't worry, be happy. Playa has grown from a tiny village at the dock of the ferry to Cozumel to a hip and happening spot filled with Europeans and adventuresome North Americans. It's the fastest-growing city on the continent.

20. XCARET, XEL-HA, XPUHA & TRES RIOS: Different by design, these four snorkel, swim and entertainment parks are very popular with fun-loving vacationers. The largest "eco-park," Xcaret, is served by colorful buses from the Hotel Zone and boasts many water-related activities. All of them offer an entertaining day-trip with plenty of things to do.

A visit to at least one of these recreational parks adds to any Cancún, Playa or Cozumel vacation. See pages 218, 223, 221 and 202, respectively.

■ Travel with Kids

The Yucatán is an ideal vacation spot for children of all ages. There are beaches and swimming pools for the wet-set, archeological ruins to climb around for the energetic, and many ecological and historical places for the thinkers. We have marked in our book the sights, places, and activities that would appeal to children up to teens. Look for the symbol shown here.

Land of the Maya

... For, lo, the winter is past, the rain is over and gone;
The flowers appear on the earth;
the time of the singing of birds is come,
and the voice of the turtledove is heard in our land.
~ Song of Solomon, Isaiah 2:10-12

Geography

The Yucatán Peninsula sticks out of Mexico's land mass and into the Gulf of Mexico like a big hitchhiking thumb. Its broad width provides a natural division between the warm waters of the Gulf and the Caribbean Sea. Because it borders the Central American countries of Guatemala and Belize, most people think of the area as being Mexico's southernmost point. Yet where Mexico narrows at its border with Guatemala, the Yucatán curves north and therefore, geographically, the entire peninsula is farther north than Acapulco. The cities of Cancún and Mérida are at more northern latitudes than Mexico City, and Miami is a mere 1,102 km (684 miles) away.

So why is the Yucatán considered so remote? Like many regions around the world, its development (or lack thereof) can be traced to its geography. It has been – and in some ways, still is – not easily accessible by land. Thick jungles and high mountains in Chiapas, the southernmost state in Mexico, and swampy lowlands in neighboring Tabasco always limited overland routes. Decent roads into the area were not built until the 1970s. Before that, most commerce and travel was by ship and then by air. Much of what the Spanish Conquistadors found physically on the peninsula in the 1500s you can still find there today. (Sorry, but as they found out the hard way, there's no gold – unless you count the jewelry worn by the guests at Cancún's expensive resorts.)

■ Thumbnail Sketch

The Yucatán's name may have derived from a classic New World misinterpretation. When Spanish adventurers put ashore and asked the native Maya to tell them the name of the land, they replied "u'y than, u'y than," meaning:

"We don't understand, what are you saying?" What resulted is the corrupted pronunciation: "Yucatán."

The three Mexican states that comprise the peninsula – **Yucatán**, **Quintana Roo** and **Campeche** – are part of a huge (84,900-square-mile) limestone platform that also includes the country of Belize and parts of the states of Tabasco and Chiapas. Millions of years ago it rose from the sea bottom like a giant submerged turtle.

 MYSTERIOUS MAYA: Ironically, in some myths, the ancient Maya conceived of their land exactly that way – as the back of a turtle.

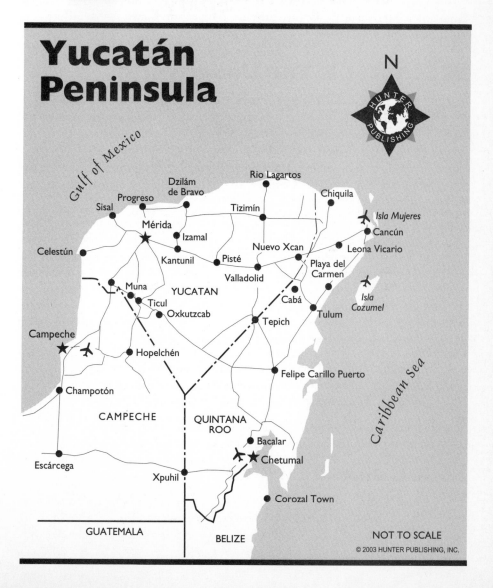

Yucatán Peninsula

N

Gulf of Mexico

Rio Lagartos
Dzilám de Bravo
Progreso
Sisal
Tizimín
Chiquila
Isla Mujeres
Mérida
Izamal
Cancún
Celestún
Nuevo Xcan
Leona Vicario
Kantunil
Pisté
Playa del Carmen
Valladolid
Muna
YUCATAN
Isla Cozumel
Ticul
Cabá
Oxkutzcab
Tepich
Tulum
Campeche
Hopelchén
Champotón
Felipe Carillo Puerto
Caribbean Sea
CAMPECHE
QUINTANA ROO
Bacalar
Escárcega
Chetumal
Xpuhil
Corozal Town
GUATEMALA
BELIZE
NOT TO SCALE

Introduction

The soil layer is shallow and, because the underlying limestone is porous, there are only a handful of streams (mostly in southern Campeche) and several scattered lagoons around the peninsula. But under the sea, the offshore shoals make the Yucatán perfect for watersports, such as snorkeling and diving, and the entire region is a rich fishing ground. The surrounding seas are clear and sparkle in typical Caribbean turquoise or Gulf blue.

Inland, the terrain is mostly pancake-flat and rises to mountains only in Guatemala, southern Belize and in Chiapas. The lowland exceptions are some conical limestone hills in the remote **Rio Bec** area and some other parts of Campeche, and a series of small rolling ridges, known as the **Puuc Hills**, which stretch southeastward from just south of Mérida. Because the land is so flat, these hills can provide panoramic views, especially along Yucatán's Highway 184.

■ Cenotes & The Underworld

 The Yucatán makes up for its lack of altitude with **sinkholes**. Deep ones. These form when underground water carves a cavern in the porous limestone. After millions of years the roof collapses, forming a large, steep-walled open well. These are called **cenotes** (say-NO-tays). Cenotes are found in large numbers throughout the peninsula. One of the most famous is the **Sacred Cenote** at the ancient Maya ruins of Chichén Itzá (see page 331).

The Classic Maya civilization grew up around these water sources and even today they provide a source of fresh water to some interior communities. Because of the lack of surface water, the Maya could not irrigate crops in the north. They relied on cenotes for drinking water, and some cities also built cisterns, called chaltuns, to trap and hold rainwater. The long dry season enhanced the importance of **Chac,** the rain god. He was an all-important deity who nourished the fields and sustained life. Virtually all towns and small Maya villages throughout the peninsula have a cenote.

 MYSTERIOUS MAYA: Folklore considered cenotes as the source of the wind as well as openings into the underworld.

In many scattered lagoons, updrafts of fresh water from underwater springs and cenotes bubble to the surface to form an ***ojo de agua*** (eye of water, pronounced "oh-ho day Ah-Gua"). The gently swirling water, as clear as a windowpane, is sediment-free.

Grutas (GREW-tass) or caves, are another fascinating feature of the Yucatán. Only four large caverns are open for escorted tours – Aktun Chen, Balankanche, Xtacumbilxunán, near Bolonchén, and Loltún. In general, spelunking and cave exploration is still a largely undeveloped resource for tourism. If you'd like to explore the bowels of the earth for yourself, see the section on Calcehtok, page 356-67. You can hire an excellent private guide there and go spelunking at your own speed.

Underwater *cenote* **cave diving** requires special dive skills and nerves of steel. Clear water and interesting rock formations make this a special thrill for experienced divers. Maps of the underground rivers and cenote tunnels are available to certified cave divers from the National Association of Cave Diving in Florida, www.safediving.com.

■ Life's a Beach

The long peninsula shoreline runs about 1,600 km (1,000 miles). The eastern Caribbean shore has pure white beaches and boasts three offshore islands: **Cozumel, Isla Mujeres** and **Isla Contoy**. The beachside resort city of Cancún didn't even exist until developers in the early 1970s figured out that the location's warm climate and long sandy Caribbean beaches were ideal for tourism. Now it's the most popular tourist destination in all of Mexico, surpassing even the old Pacific coast favorites of Acapulco and Puerto Vallarta. The Quintana Roo shoreline, which faces the Caribbean, is acknowledged to have some of the best beaches in the country, if not the entire world.

South from Isla Mujeres, a sliver of an island off Cancún, the second-longest **coral reef** in the world stretches down to the Bay of Honduras, over 250 km (156 miles) away. Reef diving is spectacular around **Cozumel** and **Xcalak,** southeast of Chetumal, and on the quays off the **Belize coast**.

The coastal terrain varies from sandy beach to mangrove to rock. The eastern end of Isla Mujeres has an impressive view of the sunrise from its rocky cliffs into the rough surf below. And between Champotón and Campeche City, along the western Gulf coast, erosion of a natural ridge has produced the only coast with cliffs on the Gulf of Mexico. The highest elevation there is approximately 75 meters (246 feet). The southwestern coast of Campeche also has a complex of freshwater marshlands more extensive than the Florida Everglades. Along the rest of the coast up from Campeche and Yucatán and down through Quintana Roo, you'll find mangrove swamps, inviting sandy beaches and brackish lagoons, the combination of which make for a rich and diverse wildlife habitat.

Climate

*The extinction of the dinosaurs may have begun in the Yucatán –
when the impact of the Chicxulub comet changed the
world's climate 65 million years ago.*

■ Weather

The Yucatán's weather is the reason why birds and people go south for the winter. Sunny and warm, the peninsula enjoys a temperate climate year-round. Instead of four seasons, it has only two: a mild dry season in winter (November-April) and a hot rainy season in summer (May-October). The most popular time for vacationers from North America runs from December through March. In Cancún, the Christmas holiday season and Spring Break are the most heavily booked.

But the entire area has much to offer throughout the year. Don't let the words "rainy season" conjure up images of deluges that limit you to watching Mexican soap operas on TV while trapped in your room for days on end. Although you may have that unfortunate experience, the Yucatán's rains often come and go rapidly. And if you're in Progreso, in the north, you'll be lucky to see rain at all. Two diverging trade winds cut the peninsula in two: the northernmost part is much drier than the southern. In July and August, vacationing Mexicans fill Progreso.

SEASONAL TEMPERATURES		
Month	High (°F/°C)	Low (°F/°C)
January	80/27	64/18
February	86/30	68/20
March	90/32	72/22
April	95/35	77/25
May	99/37	81/25
June	99/37	77/25
July	99/37	77/25
August	99/37	77/25
September	91/35	73/23
October	95/35	73/23
November	88/31	72/22
December	80/27	65/19

The Yucatán's warm temperatures average 29°C (85°F) during the day, cooler in the evening. Occasionally, ***nortes*** (NOR-tays) occur in the winter. These are cold fronts, dips in Arctic air that come down from Canada, cooling things off considerably for a day or more. Generally, however, the Yucatán has a sunny clime with distinctive high cumulus clouds speckling the sky. The temperature and humidity vary by location – inland and southern are warmer and more humid. On our first trip, we left behind 13 inches of snow and 20°F in New York and were greeted by Cancún's bright sunlight and 80°F. That wasn't hard to take.

Hurricanes

Travel agents sometimes lump Cancún and Cozumel together with other "Caribbean" destinations, such as Jamaica and the Virgin Islands, because both Mexican locations are favorite ports of call for cruise ships. And the Yucatán is subject to the same furious forces of nature that plague other idyllic Caribbean settings farther east – hurricanes.

HURRICANE CATEGORIES		
Atlantic hurricanes are ranked by the Saffir-Simpson hurricane intensity scale to give an estimate of the potential flooding and damage. Category Three and above are considered intense.		
Category	Winds (mph)	Sustained Damage
One	74-95	Minimum: Damage primarily to shrubbery and trees.
Two	96-110	Moderate: Considerable damage to shrubbery and foliage; some trees blown down. Some damage to roofing materials.
Three	111-130	Extensive: Foliage torn from trees; large trees blown down. Some structural damage to small buildings. Mobile homes destroyed. Flooding along the coastline.
Four	131-155	Extreme: Shrubs and trees blown down. Complete failure of roofs on small residences. Major beach erosion. Mass evacuation of homes within 500 yards of shore required. Hurricane Andrew that smashed into South Florida in 1992 was a Category Four.
Five	155+	Catastrophic: Complete building failures. Small buildings overturned or blown away. Low-lying escape routes inland cut by rising water three to five hours before the hurricane's center arrives. Hurricane Camille, a Category Five, struck Mississippi and Louisiana in 1969.

The peninsula lies smack in the main path of any hurricanes and tropical storms that track through the Gulf of Mexico and the western Caribbean Sea.

The entire coast is vulnerable, but the most storm-prone area is the biosphere reserve of Sian Ka'an near Tulum. Meteorologists have been compiling records since 1886 and have found that hurricanes strike most often between August and October, with September having the highest probability. On September 13, 1988, **Hurricane Gilbert** struck just south of Cancún. The damage to the resort area was staggering, totaling over US $10 billion. We met a man on Isla Mujeres who described floating on a wooden door as waves washed away his home. He saved himself by holding onto a neighbor's TV antenna. He later showed us what was left of his house – two walls and a great view of the sea. Tragically, the hurricane also smashed to rubble the ancient lighthouse/temple perched high on the rocky bluffs at the east end of the island. Before that, the structure had survived hundreds of years of use by Maya priests, Spanish Conquistadors and camera-toting tourists. It was partly rebuilt in time for the 2000 millennium celebration.

A hurricane's winds have to be over 74 mph to distinguish it from a tropical storm. Most of the destruction is due to what's called a **storm surge**, a powerful wall of water forced up by the strong winds.

Hurricanes begin as a cluster of thunderstorms that organize and rotate around a low pressure center. Their potency increases over warm ocean waters, where thermal energy is converted into kinetic energy. The addition of moisture (evaporated from the sea's surface) powers them like giant heat engines. At the center of the storm is an "eye," a cloud-free area of calm around which circulates a wall of the most powerful winds. Amazingly, an average hurricane releases enough power in a single day to supply many industrialized nations with energy for a year. Because of their destructive impact, the hurricane names Camille and Andrew have been retired.

Hurricanes are nothing to take lightly, so if you're on the coastline and one is on the way, move inland immediately.

Ecology & Environment

Land of the Pheasant and the Deer
~ Mayan name for the Yucatán

■ Environment

 For a relatively small geographic area, the mostly dry-forested Yucatán Peninsula has an amazing variety of ecosystems that nurture a multiplicity of plants and wildlife. The flat landscape changes from the thorn forest of the northern coast to more luxuriant jungle vegetation in the wetter southern interior. Major tracts of wilderness are now dedicated for preservation in the Yucatán, Belize and Guatemala, although their management is not always well funded. In the state of Quintana Roo there's the **Reserva de la Biósfera Sian Ka'an**, south of Tulum; **Reserva Ecológica El Edén** in the interior; **Laguna Chankanab Parque Nacíonal**, on Cozumel; and the **Isla Contoy Bird Sanctuary,** near Cancún. The state of Yucatán boasts **Rio Lagartos Parque Nacíonal** (and the nearby **San Felipe Parque Nacíonal**) and **Parque Natural del Flamenco Mexicano de Celestún**. All three are known as bird sanctuaries, with flamingos especially prominent. The state of Campeche has the **Laguna de Terminos Reserve** and the **Reserva de la Biósfera de Calakmul**, which extends into Guatemala. Adjoining Calakmul to the east is Belize's **Rio Bravo Conservation Area**. The reef that runs down the Quintana Roo coast to Belize is also being protected by new Mexican environmental laws and, in some circumstances, active enforcement (armed Park Rangers in boats near Isla Contoy in Quintana Roo, for example) guard the delicate reef against vandalism.

EARTHWATCH

Tired of watching the world go by and not having an impact? The Earthwatch Institute recruits paying volunteers to help scientists with field work on research expeditions. The theme can be anything from archeology to zoology. A recent project aimed to photographically document Colonial and pre-Hispanic architecture in the Yucatán. For information about volunteering in Mexico or any of the 56 countries in which Earthwatch operates, write to the Earthwatch Institute, 680 Mount Auburn, PO Box 9104, Watertown, MA 02272, ☎ 800/776-0188, www.earthwatch.org.

Flora

Stingless bees, native to the Yucatán, collect nectar from two million flowers to make one pound of honeycomb.

■ Forests

The thorn forest of the northern Yucatán is similar to others in dry parts of Mexico. The area has thin soil cover and little rainfall, but an abundant amount of scrub grows from every crevice. After the first blush of excitement in seeing a new country, however, the flat Yucatecan landscape can be monotonous, especially on long drives. The scrub is a mixture of thorny leguminous trees and cactus. Greenery is subdued in the dry season, but the landscape comes alive in spring and summer with abundant flowers and green leaves. The profusion of flowers encourages domesticated beekeeping to make **honey**, or *miel* (me-EL), a vital food source and a major crop since pre-Columbian times.

MYSTERIOUS MAYA: People worshipped Hobnil Bacab, god of bees and beekeepers, reflecting the importance the liquid gold played in their lives.

If you have a sweet tooth, don't go home without having tried Yucatecan honey. We always buy a bottle in the countryside or in a *mercado* and haul it home with us.

The Yucatán's forests, from north to south, are called thorn (also known as scrub), deciduous, evergreen-seasonal and rainforest. The area covering parts of the extreme south of the Yucatán, Chiapas and Tabasco, is the only true **tropical rainforest** in Mexico. Over 1,500 different plant species have been identified here to date, even though botanical research has barely scratched the surface.

The **evergreen and seasonal forests** contain large ceiba, breadnut, mahogany and palm trees; plus guaya, papaya, mamey and chico zapotes, all of

 which bear edible fruit. Mamey zapote has a light cocoa-brown skin and soft, sweet, rose-colored fruit pulp, while the chico zapote has a brown potato-colored skin and a fruit described as tasting like "pears with brown sugar."

As you drive in the Yucatán you may see **zapote trees** with their bark cut in a criss-cross pattern. By cutting them this special way locals were able to extract the sap, which was in high demand in the early 1900s. The sap, called chicle, was the latex originally used for chewing gum. An inevitable consequence of this demand was the need for the Maya chicle workers to push farther and farther into the unexplored jungle to find fresh trees. When they did so, they found many of the lost cities of their Classic ancestors.

Criss-cross scars on the zapote tree, a sign that it has been tapped for sap.

DOUBLE YOUR PLEASURE, DOUBLE YOUR FUN

Chewing gum was introduced to North America, indirectly, by the "villain" of the Alamo, Mexican General Antoñio Lopez de Santa Ana. The General chewed the rubbery but tasteless chicle as a habit. When he visited the States in 1839, inventor Thomas Adams saw great potential in the General's obsession. Over years he perfected the recipe, adding sugar and flavoring, and by 1871 "Adams New York Gum" appeared in a Hoboken, NJ drugstore. The rest is history. One of the earliest chewing gums sold in the United States was called "Yucatán."

Medicinal Rewards

Thankfully, in some circles the value of the staggering biodiversity in rainforests is no longer being ignored. Worldwide efforts to halt rainforest destruction have resulted in increased awareness among governments that the forest has more value standing than cleared.

Besides being important watersheds, rainforests hold secrets that can benefit mankind. More than 70% of the plants known to produce compounds with anti-cancerous properties are tropical. Cures for malaria (quinine) and amoebic dysentery (ipecac) are only two of the hundreds of medicines derived from botanical sources. Cortisone is another, and so is diosgenin, the active agent in birth control pills, developed from Mexican and Guatemalan wild yams.

Since time began, man has used plants as medicine. Indigenous peoples around the world, including the Maya, still use plants and home remedies medicinally with great effect. Not only is the rainforest medically valuable, but it also provides commercial and edible products, such as rubber, vanilla, coconuts, resins, starch, thatch, dyes and bananas. And there are potentially thousands of new medicines waiting to be found in the rainforest.

Development

A corrupt previous government moved the boundaries of Sian Ka'an Biosphere to allow more development along the fragile Punta Allen peninsula. The decision benefitted at least one politician, but definitely not the ecology. One new hotel that opened there in 2000 bulldozed all the trees and undergrowth along the dunes, built 50 air-conditioned units powered by a diesel generator, and then proclaimed itself a "Mayan Ecological Hotel." In some circles in Mexico the standard for using the word "ecological" involves either one living tree or some green paint, whichever is more convenient.

It's easy, however, to be an ecological advocate in more financially secure regions such as Western Europe, Canada or the US than it is for the people struggling to live in what is often called a Third World country. Sometimes, the exploitation of the rainforest provides subsistence living for the poor. In other cases, such as the hotel we described above, it's the greed of rich individuals and corporations attempting to get richer. Efforts by private organizations and educational institutions are now in top gear. Their goal is to educate the people and the Mexican authorities on the need for funding environmental protection, and the financial rewards of doing so. Environmental advocates in the government agree "eco-political" progress is being made – and ecotourism can take some of the credit. Although, like the word "organic," ecotourism has become a cliché, the responsible use of low-impact tourism can make the difference between preservation and destruction of natural resources. (For example, hotel owners along the Boca Paila Road banded together to restrict the hours of electricity use, which now cuts out by 11 pm on most nights.)

One of the bigger environmental concerns in the Yucatán is the oil drilling offshore of Campeche. Pemex, the federal monopoly gas and oil behemoth, has a miserable record in other oil-producing states, and the pressure is on to insure a clean and environmentally safe operation. So far, it's comparatively successful.

Conservation

On a grassroots level there are several organizations working and encouraging ecotourism in the Yucatán. Two private, non-profit groups, **Amigos de Sian Ka'an** and **Pronatura Peninsula de Yucatán**, work diligently to preserve the region's precious ecological balance. They have the expertise to share the responsibility for the parks' and biospheres' long- and short-term operations and have raised much needed funds to do so. Other private efforts have also encouraged responsible agricultural land use and a reduction in pesticides and fertilizers.

Unfortunately, as time and "progress" marches on, so does the destruction of the native forests. Since Colonial days, lumber harvesting and agricultural clearing have made their mark on the peninsula and the booming population growth in recent years is accelerating that pressure. But it's also clear that conservation efforts have made inroads in the Yucatán. Besides Sian Ka'an (1.5 million acres), Rio Lagartos (118,000 acres) and Celestún (15,000 acres), nearly two million acres of evergreen jungle forest was set aside in the extreme south of Campeche and Quintana Roo in the new **Calakmul Biosphere Reserve**. Flowing into neighboring Guatemala, Calakmul is the largest rainforest park in all North America.

■ Flowers, Fruit & Fragrance

 It has always intrigued us to find plants that barely survive on our kitchen windowsill at home growing wild and abundant in the jungle. **Philodendron** and **caladium** become huge and show stunning colors in the jungle. **Hibiscus** thrive here, as do exotic herbs and the fragrant frangipani (*plumeria*). One of our favorite semi-tropical flowers is the ubiquitous **bougainvillea**. Its large red, orange and pink blossoms appear in every garden, framing Colonial courtyard arches. The plants also grow wild along the road.

Bananas, oranges, coconuts and limes are the big fruits of the countryside. **Limes**, called *limones* (lee-MON-ehz), are an important ingredient in Yucatecan cooking. If you're not aware of what they can do to enhance the taste of food, spend a week in the country and we guarantee you'll become addicted to the unique flavor.

Despite the yellowing disease that has devastated coconut groves throughout Central America, Florida and Mexico, cold **coconut juice** (*cocos frios*) is a popular drink. It's sold like lemonade at roadside stands.

Oranges are especially sweet and juicy in the Yucatán. Known as *naranjas* (na-RAHN-hass) in Spanish and *chinas* (CHEE-nas) in Mayan, they are often sold by vendors on the street with the skin already peeled. Antique American hand-crank apple peelers find a new life in Mexico, where they're used to peel the bitter skin of the orange, leaving the white pith to hold in the juice. (This peeling method cleverly eliminates stinging lips!) For an incomparable experience, eat an orange as the locals do – cut in half and dipped into red chili powder. Wow! Sweet and hot.

An essential stop on any adventure itinerary is the town *mercado* (market) for a sampling of regional fruit and vegetables. Check out the red radishes as big as plums, carrots the color of orange crayons, beans and nuts of every size

and description and big bunches of fresh flowers. Try *jícama* (HE-cama), a delicious root vegetable that tastes like a cross between an apple and potato. It's peeled, sprinkled with lime juice, chili and salt, then eaten raw. You'll also find plastic cups of sliced *jícama* and other fruits sold by vendors in the square or on street corners.

Since pre-Columbian times, local inhabitants have learned to make the most of their natural resources. Wild and cultivated gourds, for example, are a useful part of rural life. A Maya at work in his field will probably have a hollowed gourd, plugged by a piece of dried corn cob, holding his drinking water. This device is called a ***Chu*** (chew) in Mayan and is designed so that the

Ceiba tree, the sacred tree of life.

water slowly seeps through to the exterior surface and evaporates, keeping the inside liquid cool.

The **ceiba tree**, which is almost sacred to the Maya, is rarely cut down, even if it takes root in an inconvenient place – like the middle of a farm field. This tall tree has a thick, arrow-straight trunk and perpendicular branches. The younger trees grow sharp spikes to protect their bark.

MYSTERIOUS MAYA: In Maya folklore, the majestic ceiba tree is the center support that holds up the world's sky.

Besides commercially harvested hardwoods, such as mahogany, many forest trees offer benefits, sometimes in the form of edible fruit. The **mamey tree** provides both pleasing shade and a sweet snack fruit that tastes much like a yam or sweet potato. The fruit of the **guaya**, a member of the lichi nut family, is another local favorite. In summer, the flaming orange-red flowering trees that line so many sidewalks are the beautiful *flamboyanes* (royal poinciana).

Henequen

Henequen, or sisal, is the rope fiber produced from one of the more than 300 varieties of the **agave** plant, which thrive in warm arid and semiarid regions. Agave plants have long, stiff evergreen leaves that splay out from the center, forming a rosette that resembles the top of a gigantic pineapple. Fibers taken

Sisal changed the course of history in the Yucatán.

from the plant leaf are used primarily to make rope, although certain varieties are used in the making of soap, food and the alcoholic drinks pulque and tequila.

In the late 1800s, the peninsula was the sole source of the natural fiber. The invention of synthetic fibers brought a sharp reduction in the demand for natural fiber rope. The word "sisal" (pronounced see-SAL) comes from the name of the old Yucatán port from which the fibers were first shipped.

Orchids

Exotic orchids are the largest family of flowering plants in the world. They thrive in warm, humid climates. The many varieties have different styles of flowers, from tiny delicate petals running along the stem to bold blossoms and thick green leaves. The Yucatán claims over 100 different varieties, 75% of which are epiphytes (from the Greek for "upon plants"). Epiphytes attach to host trees and gain their nourishment from airborne dust and rain. These are not parasitic relationships because they do not feed on their hosts. In the amazing world of nature, many tree orchids make use of variety-specific pollinators – bees, ants, hummingbirds, wasps and moths – for fertilization. Ground-dwelling epiphytes are known as bromeliads, named for Swedish botanist, Olaf Bromel. The best-known bromeliad is the pineapple.

Fauna

A wonderful bird is the pelican,
His bill will hold more than his belican.
He can take in his beak
Food enough for a week,
But I'm damned if I see how the helican.
~ The Pelican by Dixon Lanier Merritt, 1879-1954

Until recently, the isolation of the Yucatán has meant that birds and animals continued to thrive here when development pressures pushed them out elsewhere. A huge number of animals use the region as the tourists do, visiting when it gets too cold up north. The peninsula is a prime spot for winter migrating birds and butterflies. According to Pronatura Peninsula de Yucatán environmentalists, almost a third of the bird species in the ancient land of the Maya are migratory, including most of the neo-tropical species whose sudden declines have caused worldwide alarm. The "Land of the Turkey and Deer" features such exotic natives as peccaries, tapirs, manatees, iguanas and jaguars. All told, 147 species of vertebrates, not including fish, are native to Yucatán's forests.

■ Lions & Ocelots & Jaguars, Oh My!

Not so very long ago, the wild cats of the jungle could almost be termed "common," especially in Campeche and southern Quintana Roo. No longer. Civilization has driven them deeper into the shrinking forests. The four species native to the peninsula are the jaguar, jaguarundi, ocelot and the puma. It's unlikely you'll ever get to see one of these mostly nocturnal carnivores in the wilderness, but they are still out there.

The king of the jungle is the **jaguar,** the largest of the New World cats. A male jaguar may reach over six feet in length and can weigh in at 300 lbs. Its short coat, spotted much like a leopard, ranges from grayish gold to reddish tan with spots grouped in small circles, known as rosettes. Unlike the leopard, however, the jaguars' rosettes sur-

Because of the dwindling habitat, the jaguar is vulnerable to extinction in Mexico and Central America.

round solid spots. Occasionally, jaguars are black all over. These large cats feed on tapirs, peccaries, foxes, turtle eggs, rodents, even deer, but rarely man. They breed once a year with no fixed breeding season. After birthing one to four kittens, the mother raises her young for about a year until they can hunt on their own. If you're dying to see one up close, read page 419, where we tell you where to go.

 MYSTERIOUS MAYA: In Maya culture, the jaguar is the form taken by the sun as it descends to the underworld at night. Its image symbolizes power and strength.

The **jaguarundi** is the smallest cat. It comes in a variety colors, ranging from brown to gray. The low-slung body of the jaguarundi is like that of a weasel, and it is slightly larger than a household cat, standing up to 14 inches at the shoulders and weighing as much as 20 lbs. Its sinuous tail takes up nearly half of the cat's 35- to 55-inch length. Already a rare animal, the jaguarundi is becoming more rare as its natural habitat in wild thickets and lowland forests is cut and burned for ranching. We were lucky enough to photograph one outside its den in the brush near the salt mountains of Coloradas.

The **ocelot** is one of Latin America's most beautiful and rare cats, noted for its creamy tan fur and dark spots with open centers. An ocelot weighs from 20 to 32 lbs and grows to about 37 inches in length. Like most wild cats, it maintains territories marked by scent. The ocelot is a solitary ground hunter, but is agile enough to climb trees if threatened. Their main predator is man, who values their fur. They are a protected endangered species, so the only hunting is done by poachers.

The **puma**, which is also native to the United States and Canada, is otherwise known as the cougar or mountain lion. A full-grown male puma may be nearly as big as a jaguar and weigh 200 lbs. Its soft fur coat runs from reddish to gray to brown. This big cat is an amazingly agile climber, able to leap a distance of 12 meters (40 feet) and an astounding four meters (15 feet) high. The puma can successfully drop from a height of 18 meters (60 feet).

Land of Pheasant & Deer

 Yucatán's **deer** are very much the same as deer found throughout North America, but the pheasant of the old Mayan saying is really an **ocellated turkey**, which looks more like a peacock. If you have it on a menu you'll find it slightly stronger-tasting than the native bird that has been fattened up for Thanksgiving in the States.

TURKEY TALE

According to one theory, turkeys got their common name in England after the birds were picked up in the Colonies and the Yucatán and later transferred to ships returning to England from Turkey and the Near East. Hence the English public thought of them as "Turkey" birds.

Peccaries, Tapirs & Armadillos

Some of the strangest looking animal natives are peccaries, tapirs and armadillos. The **peccary** is the wild boar of the Yucatán and is related to the hog. Collared peccaries travel in packs of two to 15, while white-lipped peccaries move in herds of 100 or more. The collared variety, found in woodlands and dry forests, gets its name from the strip of white fur around its shoulders. The larger white-lipped peccary has white fur near its mouth and roams mainly in the tropical rainforest. They both boast two solid, sharp tusks protruding from their jaws.

The **tapir** is shy and nocturnal, so there is little chance of seeing one in the wild. A strict herbivore, it usually lives near water and is very clean. The tapir's principal predator is the jaguar. When threatened away from a water escape route (the first choice), tapirs lower their head and blindly crash through the jungle, smashing into bushes and even trees to get away.

Armadillos are found most frequently in the north, where they are trapped for food by Maya villagers.

The **armadillo** is common to the southwestern United States and all of Mexico. This armor-plated, dinosaur-like animal has a keen sense of smell and an elongated snout used to root out insects and grubs from underground. Its long, razor-sharp claws are used to dig up grubs or burrow into the ground to make their homes. Once, while driving near Chichén Itzá, we saw a young boy on the roadside holding one up by its long tail, for sale. We bought the hapless creature with its dangerously sharp claws and drove a mile or two, then pulled over and released it into the bush. What can we say? We're softies.

■ Crocodiles

An armadillo would win the beauty contest if competing with the authentically prehistoric crocodile. The long leathery-scaled crocodile has beady eyes that stare blankly from its head as it skims the surface of the water hunting for frogs, fish, birds and small mammals. It hunts at night, eyes glowing red in the beam of a flashlight. During the day, crocs sun themselves along the riverbanks and in mangrove swamps. A crocodile can grow as long as six meters (20 feet).

Your chance of seeing a crocodile during the day in the wild is very remote. However, you can see plenty of them at Croco Cun (see page 123), south of Cancún, which is devoted to the study and preservation of the species. Croco Run is an interesting side-trip from the resort town.

■ Feathered Friends

The Yucatán is prime real estate for birds – and for bird lovers. The peninsula's rich wetlands provide feeding grounds for flocks of both. Carry a pair of good binoculars if you're off into the bush or heading down the coast. Amateur birdwatchers thrill to the sight of native birds, such as the **orange oriole, yellow-lored parrot** or the **black catbird**, as well as a wealth of migratory varieties. Ornithologists working with the Amigos de Sian Ka'an estimate there are 6-9,000 varieties of birds in the protected wetlands.

Even neophytes like us can appreciate the mesmerizing sight of a sharp-winged **frigate bird** floating effortlessly on the sea breeze; the unexpected thrill of a flock of bright-green **parrots** rising from trees; or the spectacular dive of a **cormorant**, splashing into the water at one spot only to pop up somewhere else. Stroll in the main plaza in Valladolid at dusk and listen to the loud cacophony of bird calls as a flock settles in for the night. See the majestic flight of a huge white-tipped black bird as it circles and lands – only to realize that up close it is an ugly **vulture**. Or sit on the beach and watch the animated **pelican,** gracefully diving into the surf for fish, then bobbing on the water and grinning back at you. Pelicans are fun to observe as they jockey for position to eat scraps alongside

Parrots are an eye-catching spectacle.

the fishing boats on Isla Mujeres, Ciudad del Carmen, Isla Contoy and Champotón.

*Mid-November marks the week-long **Annual Yucatán Bird Festival**, organized by ecological groups on the peninsula. A recent festival featured a competitive "xoc chi'ch" – bird marathon – at Celestún, Rio Lagartos,Yaxuná, and Kiuic, with community guides, park rangers, national and international experts competing to identify rare species. There were also workshops and conferences. Contact **Ecoturismo Yucatán** (☎ 999/920-2772) for details and e-mail Barbara MacKinnon (a founder of Amigos de Sian Ka'an) at barbaram@sureste.com to register for the marathon.*

Flamingos

But it is the flamingo that attracts scores of tourists to the Yucatán. The biospheres at Celestún and Rio Lagartos are home to huge flocks of these one meter (three feet) and taller birds. The large wading flamingo has long spindly backward-bending legs and a thin curved neck and beak. It comes in colors ranging from a soft pinkish-white to a stunning salmon-pink. Local guides take tourists out in boats to the feeding grounds, where huge flocks contain thousands of the colorful birds. It's a breathtaking sight.

Flamingos feed standing on mud banks in estuaries and lagoon shallows. They force muddy water through the serrated edges of their bill, straining the edible animal and vegetable matter for nourishment. The mineral salt content of the muddy water is what affects the coloring of the flamingo – and the Yucatán's salts make for spectacular colors.

Life Undersea

The sea has many voices.
~ T.S. Eliot, 1888-1965

■ Reefs

You could say the entire Yucatán Peninsula is one gigantic limestone reef forced up from the bottom of the sea in one of the earth's endless tectonic plate clashes. The material that forms all reefs is essentially the same as the substrata on the peninsula: limestone. On the dry land the limestone is formed by untold generations of tiny sea crustaceans, mollusks and polyps that died eons ago. But on the underwater shelf that runs down Quintana Roo's eastern Caribbean coast, those sea creatures are alive and growing in one of nature's strangest combinations: coral. The reefs that coral form are home to a million or more different aquatic species – perhaps more variety of life than in tropical rainforests.

Coral is the common name for several species of **coelenterates**, a large group of invertebrate animals. The class has over 6,000 living species and scientists have identified 6,000 different extinct species. The phylum include jellyfish, hydras, sea cucumbers and sea anemones. What they all have in common is a cylindrical shape, a gastrovasular cavity and a "mouth" surrounded by tentacles. **Coral polyps** (the living organism) extract calcium from sea water and create calcium carbonate "skeletons" that offer physical support and protection when they're threatened.

Most coral live in colonies, attaching themselves first to limestone on the sea bed, then to each other. As polyps die, leaving hard stony limestone skeletons as a base, new living coral builds upon them. In time, this forms the enormous underwater structures we know as reefs. Coral reproduce either asexually from buds or with a larval polyp, called a planula, which floats away and settles elsewhere to begin a new reef colony.

To form and grow, coral reefs need four critical environmental factors.

- Sea **water temperature** between 23° and 27°C (73-80°F). The warmest temperature that coral will endure is 30°C (86°F).

- Water shallow enough to allow **sunlight** to penetrate. Symbiotic algae (zooxanthellane) lives in the tissues of the living coral and photosynthesizes nutrients and oxygen used by the coral. These algae provide "stony" or hard coral with a brown or yellow color. Other colors found in coral – red, pink, orange, black and purple – come as a result of colored calcareous spicules. (Got all that? There will be a test at the end of the book.)

- **Salinity** should be between 30 and 40 parts per thousand. If the sea water is either too saline or not saline enough – perhaps due to freshwater runoff from the mainland or to heavy amounts of rainfall – coral will not grow.

- Coral thrives in areas of strong **wave action**, which aerates the water. Along the Yucatán coast the Caribbean Sea, unlike the Gulf of Mexico, has some active surf. Waves help prevent silt from accumulating in the reef and suffocating the living coral.

Reef Threats

In response to environmental stresses – such as higher water temperatures – coral will expel their algae, thus **bleaching** the reef and leaving it ghostly white. Without its beneficial algae the reef begins to die. A reef can come back from occasional mild periods of bleaching, but a sustained warming of the water will kill it completely. Scientists, marine biologists and zoologists are still unsure how global warming is affecting the oceans, but it appears that the rise in water temperature is a major contributor to bleaching. In addition, oil spills, water pollution, damage from ships and attacks of the coral-eating starfish known as the "crown of thorns" have placed many of the world's reefs under additional threat.

The reefs off Quintana Roo, known collectively as the **Belize Reef**, have battled some bleaching in recent years. Another threat comes from **divers and snorkelers**, usually amateurs, who break off pieces and touch or stand on the reef, killing the fragile living organisms. If you're underwater, look but do not touch.

Reef Types

The Yucatán has all three reef types: **fringe reefs**, located close to the shore in very shallow water, like El Garrafón Park on Isla Mujeres; **barrier reefs**, which lie farther offshore and are separated from the land by lagoons or water generally no deeper than 10 meters (about 30 feet), such as at Akumal; and **atolls**, ring islands that form a natural lagoon in the middle. Atolls are often associated with extinct underwater volcanoes and are found mostly in the South Pacific, but Quintana Roo's **Chinchorro coral atoll** sits only 22 km (14 miles) off Xcalak. Its inner lagoon varies in depth from two to eight meters. Beyond the reef, the ocean floor drops away to depths of 150 to 200 meters (450-600 feet).

The name "Chinchorro" is derived from the Spanish for "fisherman's net," a reflection not of the rich marine life there, but of the many vessels snagged and sunk in its deceptively shallow waters.

■ Something's Fishy

 Since pre-Hispanic times, fishing has been an important economic activity. Along the coast entire communities earn their livelihood catching fish, lobster and shrimp. As you might imagine, the seas surrounding the Yucatán teem with life. The reefs and depths of the Caribbean, as well as the warm shallows of the Gulf of Mexico, provide the perfect habitat for hundreds of fish, shellfish, invertebrates, reptiles and amphibians.

Turtles

The beaches from Tulum south and along the stretch from Campeche to Carmen are the breeding grounds for **sea turtles**, who come ashore to lay their eggs in the sand. The loggerhead is the most common turtle, along with the green, the hawksbill and sometimes the leatherback varieties. **Loggerheads**, with their massive bird-jawed skulls, have short fins and grow to about four feet in length. **Green** turtles lay their eggs every two to three years, storming the beach in large groups. The black, narrow-finned **leatherback** (aptly named because of the leathery hide it has in place of a shell) grows as large as six feet and weighs as much as 1,500 lbs. The **hawksbill** is one of the smallest marine turtles, measuring in at three feet or less and only 200 lbs. Because of its highly valued spindle-shaped tortoise shell, it has been hunted to near extinction.

If you're lucky enough to be in Mexico during summer nesting season, hire an experienced guide to take you to a turtle beach. To huddle on the deserted sand late at night with only the brush stroke of the Milky Way to illuminate your world is quite an experience. Turtles return to the same beach each year and lay their precious eggs by digging a shallow hole in the sand with their flippers. Once covered over, the hatchlings emerge about 60 days later and crawl toward the surf. Hopefully. Any type of unnatural light or noise will disturb the giant lumbering females and can cause them to abort their nest. And between wrong turns and predators – sea gulls, large fish, raccoons, foxes and human poachers – only 4 or 5% of the eggs develop into fully mature turtles. Isla Mujeres has a turtle research station that makes for a pleasant and educational visit. Mexican laws severely restrict the harvesting of sea turtles, so if it's ever on a menu, please don't order it.

Shellfish

Walk the beaches of Campeche, Yucatán and Quintana Roo and you'll see plenty of sea shells by the seashore. **Conch**, of course, is the largest (sometimes as big as two feet) and one of the most beautiful. *Caracol*, as conch is known in Spanish, also provides a delicious meat that Maya people have eaten for hundreds of years. The meat is extracted by drilling a small hole in the shell top and forcing out the muscle. It's commonly served in ceviche, a dish that uses lime juice to "cook" the meat. Vendors line the dock area on Cozumel selling conch shells. They're a popular souvenir.

Other shells with great names include the whelk, alphabet cone, banded and true tulips, egg cockle, calico scallop, angel wing, sunrise tellin, sunray venus, zebra ark and the pearl oyster.

At the Table

It's said that sea air spurs the appetite. That may explain the large numbers of restaurants serving delicious lobster and shrimp caught in the Yucatán's waters. Fresh lobster is on the menu nearly everywhere along the shoreline and shrimp is especially popular in Campeche, where they have a particularly delicate variety. These fishy delights cost a fraction of what is usually charged in Canadian and US restaurants.

> *All men are equal before fish.*
> ~ Herbert Hoover, 1874-1964

Below the Water

If it's fish you want – to see or to eat – then you've found a home in the Yucatán. Put on a snorkel mask and get into the excitement. **Barracuda**, with their long snouts and razor teeth, grin at you. **Stingrays** bury themselves in the sand and **sand sharks** slide away. And the colors are amazing. Spanish and French grunts, yellowjacks, queen triggerfish, blue tangs, banded butterfish, damselfish, red snappers, sergeant majors, angelfish and spotted drums are just a few of the colorful, edible inhabitants.

People of the Yucatán

*The forces of the past live on and exert influence on us,
though we may not be consciously aware of this... We are all
imbedded in the flux of generations, whose legacy of
thought and feeling we irrevocably carry along with us.*
~ Kurt W. Marek, *Gods, Graves and Scholars*

*Maya woman selling her wares
in the* mercado *at Mérida.*

The Yucatán is home to some of the friendliest folks in the world. Whether in Cancún's lively restaurants, Mérida's fashionable Paseo de Montejo, Campeche's old walled forts or Valladolid's *mercado*, you can be sure of a warm welcome from everyone.

A large percentage of the population is Maya, descendants of the original glorious civilization that stretched from the peninsula into the Mexican state of Chiapas, Guatemala, Belize and parts of El Salvador and Honduras. Generally small of stature, with facial structures that resemble the American Indian, most Maya speak their own native tongue as well as Spanish, which is now required in school.

The largest proportion of inhabitants is **mestizo**, the term used to describe Mexican people whose Spanish bloodline is mixed with that of the indigenous population. An influx of Lebanese merchants into the Yucatán during henequen's heyday also added to the gene pool. Additionally, recent job opportunities in Cancún have attracted many workers from all over Mexico, especially the Federal District (Mexico City). Many of the newcomers have intermarried, blending into the population.

It's the way the Yucatecan people got to where they are today – both histori-cally and culturally – that makes the story of the region so very fascinating. Tragedy, peace, bloodlust, sacrifice, gore, romance, glory, pain, triumph, love, ignorance, enlightenment, lost opportunities, treachery, greed, friendship and intrigue fill the history of the Maya, the Spanish and Mexico as a whole. And that's just the beginning.

The Maya

Our days upon earth are a shadow.
~ The Bible, Job 8:9

█ Meaning of Maya

 Astronomers, mathematicians, agronomists, philosophers, artists, architects, sculptors and warriors – the Maya of old were a rich, com-plex society. Their stunning accomplishments are still evident today, fascinating anyone who learns of them. It was the Maya who first cultivated chocolate, chili peppers, vanilla, papayas and pineapples. The Maya built causeways and reservoirs, created great works of sculpture and art, carved fantastic jade masks and wove rich colorful textiles. They also developed so-phisticated mathematical systems; complex, accurate calendars; and per-fectly proportioned buildings of immense size and beauty. Much of this while Europe remained in the Dark Ages.

In the modern world, observers pronounce that Maya culture will soon disap-pear. Roads and cars have made their world smaller; seaside resorts such as Cancún attract hoards of camera-clicking foreign day-trippers; and Mexican and North American TV programs are beamed into remote villages. But the Maya people have always been resilient. Their history has reinforced a pat-tern of community-based culture – with pride and respect for tradition. Their communal society has adapted modern means to preserve the Maya culture and language. Besides, they've had centuries to practice survival skills under pressure.

█ The Beginning

The Maya civilization waxed and waned during three long periods archeologists have distinguished as Preclassic, Classic and Post Classic. The rise of the first civilizations in Mesoamerica took place in what's called the **Preclassic period** (ca. 1500 BC-AD 250), with several different peoples in different areas of Mexico and Central America. There were the Zapotec of Oaxaca, the Olmec on the Gulf Coast, and the Maya in the lowlands and high-lands of Guatemala and Mexico.

Powerful kings who were both rulers and high priests had direct responsibility for the ordered world of the Preclassic Maya. The success and power of their rule was in a direct relation to the kingdom's military strength. Inter-city rivalries were common and the high-living royalty often met ignominious sacrificial ends if defeated.

Sketch by Campeche artist Alejandro Serrano. © Alejandro Serrano

By AD 400, complex writing and regional trade had developed and some impressive capital cities had been built. **El Tigre**, the largest single Maya temple ever, was constructed at El Mirador, an important Preclassic city a few kilometers south of the Mexican border in the Petén region of Guatemala.

The end of the Preclassic period may have come about with the AD 250 eruption of a volcano in El Salvador, which spewed ash over much of the southern highland Maya area. Loss of agriculture and commerce in the south increased the importance of the lowlands of the Yucatán in the north, thus begetting new power bases and new glory days of Maya civilization.

■ Classic Splendor

The apex of Maya growth and prosperity occurred from AD 250 to 900. The **Early Classic period** (AD 250-600) saw the rise of city states of Tikal and Calakmul, who struggled with each other for control of the lowlands. Calakmul eventually defeated Tikal, but was unable to exert power over more territory, losing its chance to rule the world. The Early Classic period gradually slid into the **Late Classic period** (AD 600-800).

During the Classic age, the Maya developed advanced building styles and carved stone records called stelae. Large ceremonial city centers were built that included massive stone pyramids, ballcourts and platform temples.

Tikal reemerged as a powerful city with as many as 40,000 people over six square miles – a population density comparable to an average city in modern Europe or America.

But for reasons not fully understood – drought and overpopulation are two theories – the Classic kingdoms began to lose their luster. The last hundred years of this time are known as **Terminal Classic period** and, as the name implies, marked the demise of the era. Maya kings' influence over the population declined, indicated by the halt of ceremonial construction, and by AD 900, with no more dated stelae carved in Tikal, it was a clear end of the epoch.

The great mystery is why. That question lured the Yucatán's first tourists, **John Lloyd Stephens**, a

Detailed stonework at Uxmal.

self-taught American archeologist, and **Frederick Catherwood**, an English sketch artist experienced in architectural drawing, to explore the ruins of southern Mexico. They set out in the midst of social and civil war and recorded 44 abandoned ruins. Stephens wrote two books, *Incidents of Travel in Central America, Chiapas and Yucatán* (1841) and *Incidents of Travel in Yucatán* (1843), which launched the archeological search for the Maya past.

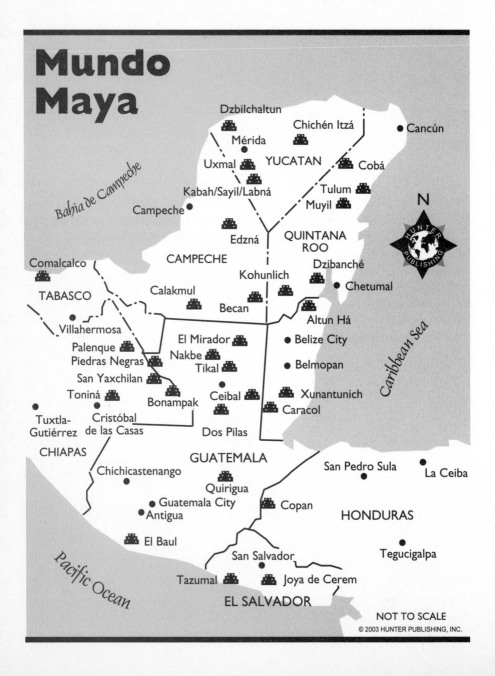

NOT TO SCALE

© 2003 HUNTER PUBLISHING, INC.

Spider monkey, Quintana Roo

Above: Green iguana, Playa del Carmén

Below: Maya women

Maya women and huipiles, Valladolid

Of his first visit to Uxmal he wrote: "... emerging suddenly from the woods, to my astonishment came upon a large open field strewed with mounds of ruins and vast buildings on terraces and pyramidal structures, grand and in good preservation, richly ornamented, without a brush to obstruct the view, in picturesque effect almost equal to the ruins of Thebes." Stephens was one of the first who correctly surmised that the ancient cities of the Maya world were built by the native people still living there and not some mysterious Egyptian or lost European race.

Cities that reached their prime during the Classic period – **Palenque, Tikal, Uxmal, Cobá, Edzná** and **Copan** – are often thought of as the cities of the "lost" Maya civilization. No one knows exactly why these great metropolises were suddenly abandoned – forfeited to the jungle – beginning in the ninth century. However, the beginning of the end of the Classic period did not mean the complete end of Maya culture. Other cities rose to take their place.

■ A House Divided

Into the vacuum caused by the demise of the Classic kingdoms came outside invaders to the land. The lowland Maya were partly integrated and perhaps partly conquered around AD 850 by the **Itzá**, a Mexicanized Chontal-Maya tribe from Tabasco. The grand capital they built with a mixed architectural style was centrally located Chichén Itzá in northern Yucatán. The foreigners brought with them their fierce warrior ways, blended religion and influences from central Mexico such as the Toltec cult of the **Feathered Serpent** (Quetzalcóatl or Kukulcán).

A serpent's mouth reaches for the sky at Mayapan.

KUKULCAN, IF YOU CAN

No other deity-personage created a deeper impression on the Mesoamerican people than Quetzalcóatl ("Snake of Precious Feathers" or "Plumed Serpent"). The Maya origins of the legend begin with the Toltec civilization in Mexico's central valley around the mid-900s. Topiltzin, a young Toltec prince, entered the priesthood of the ancient god of civilization and fertility, Quetzalcóatl. As was the custom, he assumed the name of the deity. He became a great leader and spurred the Toltec to new heights of civilization. His name became inseparable with the legend. But a power struggle with other lords forced him into exile. Maya records indicate that Quetzalcóatl, or Kukulcán as they called him, invaded the Yucatán and may have ruled at Chichén Itzá. Legends of his "death" vary, but all state that he would return to vanquish his enemies. The vague date indicated was 1-Reed, the anniversary of his birth in the cyclical calendar. This was the sword of Damocles that hung over the Aztec, the civilization that had succeeded the Toltec by the time Cortéz landed in 1519, the year of 1-Reed.

The most beautiful bird of Central America is the quetzal. It's very rare, and not a native of the Yucatán. The bird's long, brightly colored tail feathers were plucked to be worn only by Maya royalty. The quetzal was then released to grow new plumage. Killing a quetzal was forbidden.

The Yucatecan Maya despised the Itzá Maya and referred to them in surviving Maya chronicles with such epithets as "foreigners," "tricksters and rascals," "lewd ones," as well as "people without fathers or mothers." The Itzá intermarried and ruled the Yucatán from their capital until the city fell to warriors from a rival city, **Mayapan**, in 1221. In what may sound like a plot from Shakespeare, the ruler of Chichén kidnapped the wife of the king of Izamal. Izamal's main ally at that time was the opportunistic king of Mayapan. His warriors drove the Itzá from Chichén and the victorious city of Mayapan became the new center of civilization.

But Mayapan was in turn sacked and abandoned in a civil uprising around 1440 after a later king in Mayapan's Cocom family lineage apparently tyranized the people. A prince of the **Xiú family** led a revolt that slaughtered the ruling Cocom king and his entire family. Only one son, away on a trading mission, survived. In an ironic twist of fate, one of that son's direct descendants would inadvertently wreak a terrible revenge on all the Maya people nearly 100 years later.

In 1536, after the Spanish had been initially driven out of the Yucatán, the ruler of the Xiú at Maní decided it was a good time to offer thanks to the gods at the Cenote of Sacrifices in Chichén Itzá. Nachi Cocom, the great grandson of the surviving Cocom son, granted the Xiú ruler safe passage through his province on the way. He entertained the 40-man traveling court for four days until, at a banquet on the last evening, he and his warriors suddenly turned and butchered their Xiú guests. This treachery caused a civil war between the two most powerful kingdoms in the Yucatán. Luckily for the Spanish, when they returned in 1540 they found a Maya empire divided against itself.

There's an interesting sidelight to the fall of Chichén Itzá in 1221: surviving Itzás fled south and settled on an island in the middle of Lake Petén in Guatemala. They founded a city known as Tayasal, now named Flores. This isolated Itzá kingdom remained intact until 1697 – over 450 years after their defeat at Chichén and 150 years after the Conquest – when a Spanish naval force finally destroyed the last of over 3,000 years of Maya high civilization.

So much of our future lies in preserving our past.
~ Peter Westbrook

■ Heaven Help Us

The ancient Maya had a large number of gods in their complex religion, each with clearly defined characteristics and purposes.

TOP FIVE MAYA GODS OF ALL TIME

Itzamná (or Zamná). Itzamná, the big cheese overall and lord of the heavens as well as night and day, could be called upon in hard times or calamities. Who says nice guys finish last? Itzamná was always benevolent.

Chac. Although second in power, Chac was first in importance as the god of rain, and by association, the weather and fertility.

Ah Mun was the corn god and the god of agriculture. He was always represented as a youth, often with a corn ear headdress.

Ah Puch, the god of death, ruled over the ninth and lowest of the Maya underworlds. He was always in a bad mood.

Ek Chuah. Ek was the god of war, human sacrifice and violent death. Defintely not the kind of god you'd want to meet in an alleys.

In addition to these, there were **patron gods**, 13 of the upper world and nine of the lower, plus numerous **calendar gods** who posed for glyphs. Others, such as Kukulcán and Chac Mool, came in as the society changed in Post Classic times. The religious hierarchy became so bewildering that it was beyond the comprehension of the average Maya, who relied on priests to interpret the religion (what's new?). To the common man, who lives or dies by the cycle of rain and drought, Chac remains the god most involved in daily life.

God is not all that exists; God is all that does not exist.
~ Remy de Gourmont, French philosopher, 1858-1915

The Spanish

Nothing remains but flowers and sad songs,
In Tlatelolco and Mexico,
Where once there were warriors and wise men.
~ Cantares Mexicanos, Aztec poems (ca. 1523)

■ Something Old, Something New

The Americas came as a complete surprise to **Christopher Colum-bus**, who was convinced that he had found a new route from Europe to the Far East. He thought the Caribbean islands were barrier islands of India, hence the name "Indian" used to describe Native Americans. His first contact with the Maya came on July 30, 1502 when he encountered sea traders near the Bay Islands off the coast of Honduras. Their canoes were filled with textiles, grains, cacao beans and a fermented liquor. Columbus the explorer was soon followed by Spanish military expeditions looking to conquer and colonize this "New World."

The first European footprints on Maya territory came in 1511, when 17 passengers from a Spanish shipwreck came ashore in the Yucatán. Captured by Maya warriors, most were killed or sacrificed. Two survived, however, and each took opposite views of their captors. The religious cleric, **Brother Gerónimo de Aguilar**, couldn't wait for rescue from the heathen barbarian. The simple sailor, **Gonzalo Guerrero**, grew to love the Maya so much he led their warriors in battle to try to stop the Spanish invasion.

That invasion began in 1517 when **Fernando Hernández de Córdoba** accidentally, but officially, "discovered" Mexico when he landed on Cape Catouche near present day Isla Holbox on the tip of the Yucatán. After small skirmishes with the natives, he and one hundred of his men sailed on to Campeche and Champotón, where they were again attacked by Maya warriors. Hernández, mortally wounded, lost half his men in the battle and died shortly after returning to his base in Cuba. The ambush was purportedly arranged by none other than Gonzalo Guerrero. However, Hernández's report of large cities with stone houses – plus exaggerations of Maya gold – convinced the Spanish that Mexico might be the India they'd been searching for.

In 1519 a well-armed expedition led by **Hernán Cortéz** landed on the island of Cozumel, a Maya religious and trading center. He and his men pillaged the village and the temples at San Gervasio and the smaller El Cedral, where the Conquistadors celebrated the first Mass in present-day Mexico. When Cortéz heard of the two Spanish shipwreck survivors, he offered to buy their freedom from local Maya lords. Brother Géronimo was anxious to return to "civilization," but Gonzalo Guerrero refused to go back. By then, he had married a

Maya princess and fathered the first "mestizo" (mixed race) children of the New World. Nothing is certain of Guerrero's ultimate fate but legend indicates that he proved to be a thorn in the side of his former countrymen by organizing fierce Maya resistance.

Guerrero may have succeeded in thwarting the initial Spanish invasion, but it was Brother Gerónimo who had the most impact on Mexico's history. During his captivity he learned the Yucatec Mayan language and his linguistic skill proved to be critical in the conquest of the rest of Mexico. Aggressive Maya resistance prevented Cortéz from establishing a foothold on the Yucatán mainland so he and his men, with Brother Gerónimo aboard, sailed around to the Gulf to land at present-day Veracruz. The inhabitants there, believing the Spanish to be gods attached to their horses, surrendered, giving Cortéz a valuable lesson he would not forget. In tribute, he received gifts of food and 20 young girls. One of these girls was Malintzin, or Malinche, a captive of the Maya who spoke both the Mayan language and Nahuatl, the language of the Aztec. Cortéz, through Malintzin and Gerónimo, could now communicate and negotiate with Mexico's militarily strongest indigenous people – at the height of their civilization – the **Aztec**. The Aztec ruled all of central Mexico from their floating capital city, Tenochtitlán, where they nervously awaited the return of the avenging god, Quetzalcóatl.

Thus began a two-year conquest of the powerful Aztec empire by Cortéz's small band of battle-hardened soldiers. Superior steel weapons and invaluable alliances with rivals of the Aztecs – plus the prophecy that predicted their downfall at the hands of the avenging Quetzalcóatl – allowed Cortéz, a consummate warrior and ruthless tactician, to succeed. A thousand-year-old civilization of millions fell to a force of 500 men.

Ironically, the first Mexican civilization Columbus encountered in 1502 was the last native Mexican civilization to be conquered.

■ New Spain

While Cortéz and Spanish Viceroys exploited Mexico and the lands as far south as Panama and Peru, the subjugation of the Maya in the Yucatán was left to **Francisco de Montejo**, a captain under Cortéz. Employing the medieval concept of the *adelantado* ("one who pushes forward"), Montejo had to recruit his own army and pay them in order to subdue the native inhabitants. In return, the Spanish crown offered him the title of Adelantado Governor and Captain General. Marriage to a wealthy widow financed his initial expedition of three ships and 250 men.

Unfortunately for Montejo, the Maya were not the Aztec. To conquer the 16 autonomous Maya provinces, he began a bloody, cruel and bitter struggle that lasted 20 years. His first forays into the land in 1527 were disastrous. Even in the long run it must have seemed hardly worth the terrible trouble. The Maya had no stores of gold so there was little in the way of booty for

Conquistadors. And the dry brush and rough rocky terrain of the Yucatán took away the advantage of Spanish fighting methods and weapons. Worst of all for the would-be conquerors, Maya resistance was fierce. After a while, the elder Montejo passed the repulsive work on to his son, also named Francisco de Montejo. Holed up in a narrow enclave in Campeche, the soldiers renewed their attacks in 1540, fighting their way up the peninsula.

Montejo the Younger founded the city of **Mérida** in 1542, at the holy Maya city of T'Ho (pronounced "Hoe"). In a fateful alliance with the Xiú, he defeated most of the large-scale resistance by the Cocom Maya. In a last-ditch effort to unseat the Spanish, the Cocom-led Maya attacked Mérida on the night of November 8th, 1546, the date of "Death and the End" in the traditional Maya calendar. The warriors slaughtered not only Spaniards and Indians who had accepted Christianity, but, in a complete rejection of the foreign culture, they also killed horses, cattle – anything that the invaders had brought with them, even fruit trees. In the end, however, they failed to completely dislodge the Spanish Conquistadors from the city.

The fighting in the "Great Maya Rebellion" lasted five months and was finally suppressed in 1547. But Spanish control over the land and its people was incomplete at best and sporadic warfare continued for centuries. In some sense the resistance didn't end until the 1930s, when Quintana Roo's Cruzob Maya finally made peace with the Mexican government. The conquered Maya lamented their loss in the book *Chilam Balam de Chumayel*, in which they complain:

> *There was no sin...*
> *No illness afflicted man,*
> *Aches did not hurt the bones,*
> *Fevers were unknown,*
> *There was no smallpox...*
> *All that ended with the dzules (strangers)*
> *They taught fear....*

Disease rather than war became the big threat to the Maya after the Conquest. Smallpox and other illnesses to which Europeans had resistance decimated the native population. In all of Mexico, the indigenous population plummeted from over 11 million in the 1520s to only one million by 1650.

Introduction

Colonial Days

[The Conquest] was neither a victory nor a defeat;
it was the painful birth of the Mexican nation, the Mexico of today.
~ 1964 Inscription on Tlatelolco Square, Mexico City

■ Dirty Business

Almost immediately after the Conquest, the Yucatán became a Colonial backwater compared to the rest of Mexico and South America. To the great disappointment of the Spanish, there was no gold in its limestone flatlands. The precious metal ornaments they saw when they first landed at Cozumel were all imported from the highlands. The only exploitable economic resource was the land, so Montejo gave away large parcels in exchange for service in battle. As a result, a feudal nobility of prominent families came to control large cattle ranches. The labor pool was the Maya, who were exploited mercilessly.

The clergy – Catholic missionaries hell bent on converting the Maya to Christianity – further consolidated the conquest. Franciscan brothers were key players in the peninsula's political structure. Into the religious-political mix came **Friar Diego de Landa**, named the first provincial minister in 1559. He was a zealous missionary who, responding to rumors of sacrilege and sacrifice by the Maya, held an inquisition (auto-de-fé) at the monastery in Maní, where he gained confessions to heresy by harsh torture. Some hapless Indians took their own lives rather than suffer torture. At the same time Landa was determined to rid the Maya of their "books of the devil." He ordered the burning and destroying of all Maya books, codices and artifacts, effectively erasing most of their written records. Ironically, Landa went on to write his own book called *Relacíon de las Cosas de Yucatán*, which may be the most important contemporary single source on Maya culture and history we have today. Despite his torture of Indians accused of pagan rituals, Landa championed an end to their secular abuse by wealthy landowners and crown officials (see pages 384-85).

■ Building Boom

Like their Maya predecessors, the Spanish went on a building boom during the long Colonial era, this time constructing churches rather than pyramids and temples. The Spanish settlers tore down many of the abandoned Maya temples and used the stones in the construction of their own houses of worship. Stones from Zaci helped build Valladolid's Church of San Bernardino de Siena in 1552. The massive Mannerist-style Cathedral de San Ildefonso was built on the square in Mérida in 1598 with some of the ruins of the Maya pyramids of T'Ho. Others followed, including the Franciscan convent, La Mejorada, in 1640 and a church in virtually every village under Spanish control. The architecture is distinctly Colonial.

Abandoned church ruins in Kikil, near Tizimin.

Eventually, a population boom of non-Indian settlers and a recovery in the number of Maya after the devastating famine of 1769-1774 increased the demand for food. The land holdings of the elite, formerly cattle ranches, were now used to grow food as prices escalated. Maya left their villages to settle on haciendas, converting the estates into commercial units. These were effectively "company towns," in which the worker was no more than a legalized serf. The haciendas were the financial, political and social base for the privileged class until well into the late 20th century. Rigid racial class structures developed among Creoles (whites born in Mexico), *mestizos* (a racial mix of Caucasian and Indian) and the native American Maya.

Despite royal attempts from Spain to rein in the abuse of Indian labor, the Yucatán's elite continued their exploitation of the natives. Eventually, in 1761, **Jacinto Canek**, a Jesuit-educated Indian, called for a rebellion. He declared himself the king that the books of Chilam Balam promised would drive the foreigners out. But a Spanish force attacked the poorly armed rebels and killed 600 of them. Jacinto was captured, tortured and executed, gruesomely drawn and quartered in the plaza of Mérida. Eight companions were garroted and 200 were flogged and had one ear cut off to mark them as rebels. One result of the crackdown by conservatives was the expulsion of the

Jesuit order, who had been rivals of the Franciscans. This impaired the peninsula's educational system, further retarding social progress.

■ Independence Day

 On September 28, 1821 three centuries of Spanish Colonial rule ended and Mexico, a free nation, was born. By then, the Yucatán reflected the turmoil that was going on back in Europe, where the French had overthrown the Spanish monarchy; and in Mexico, where elements of liberalism agitated for civil rights. Soon blood spilled. Traditional rivals, Campeche and Mérida fought for power while the entire peninsula ignored the rest of Mexico, which was embroiled in a series of continuing revolutions. Unhappy with centralism and liberal land reforms, the powerful families in the Yucatán declared the region's independence from Mexico in 1838. Facing economic realities, it came back into the fold in 1843, but that made no difference to the Indian community, which was still under the yoke of Hispanic oppression. In early 1847 the Yucatán seceded again after secessionists armed the Maya to serve as soldiers against the Mexican garrisons. With the federal government preoccupied by the Mexican-American War and Campeche and Mérida still bickering over independence, the Maya themselves rebelled. Only this time they were well armed.

■ Blood from a Stone

 In 1847 a seemingly bottomless pit of barbarism opened in the Yucatán – into which the blood of thousands flowed. The chilling precursor of the violence that would soon engulf the land occurred in January of that year when the Maya were called to arms by Creoles in the name of their Yucatecan **independence movement**. The revolutionaries stormed **Valladolid**, an old Colonial town laden with aristocratic pretensions and naively confident in its racial superiority. The moment Maya soldiers entered the city, years of pent up anger exploded and they ran amuck.

Most of the city's non-Indian population who had not yet fled were massacred. The defending garrison's colonel was dragged from his office and hacked to death, a paralyzed curate was attacked with a machete in his hammock and young girls of wealthy families were raped, then tied to the iron grilles of the windows and mutilated. Aware now that whites were not invincible, a fierce spirit of independence awoke in the native soldiers, but their simmering sentiments went unnoticed by the succesful Yucatecan secessionists.

Several months later, an informer named a young Maya, **Antonio Ay**, in a plot for another revolution, this time to reduce taxes on the Indian population. To set a stern example and to avenge the January atrocities, a firing squad shot young Ay against the wall of Valladolid's Santa Ana chapel on

July 26, 1847. His death was the catalyst that ignited the **Caste War** – so called because of the complex racial levels, or "castes," that the Spanish had developed to differentiate the mixed bloodline of the Mexican people. It was an uprising of such magnitude and violence that soon vengeful Maya armies drove the remaining white citizenry behind the thick walls of Campeche and barricades in the narrow streets of Mérida. The fighting devastated the countryside and most haciendas were sacked and destroyed. Except for a few desperate pockets, the Yucatán was now back in the hands of its original inhabitants. They were poised to push their oppressors back into the sea within a matter of a week or two, but what happened next can be explained only by the religious significance of the land – and maize – to the Maya.

The entire army packed up and went home to plant corn.

"The day was warm and sultry," recalled Leandro Poot, son of the Maya leader. "All at once the sh'mataneheeles (winged ants, harbingers of the first rain) appeared in great clouds to the north, to the south, to the east and to the west, all over the world. When my father's people saw this they said to themselves and to their brothers: *The time has come for us to make our planting, for if we do not we shall have no Grace of God to fill the bellies of our children.*"

The Yucatecan Creoles used the reprieve to reinforce themselves with Mexican federal soldiers available after the end of the Mexican-American War and offered in exchange for renewed support of a united Mexico. Barbarous counter-attacks on the dispersed Maya regained much of the land the Yucatecans had lost.

Interestingly, 938 American volunteers, primarily men of the Thirteenth Infantry Regiment who had been mustered out of the US Army in Mobile, Alabama after the end of the war with Mexico, came to the Yucatán to fight on the side of Mexico as mercenaries. Their first encounter with the Maya resulted in 40 casualties and an unanticipated defeat. Again Leandro Poot: "It was easy to kill the strange white men, for they were big and fought in a line.... Their bodies were pink and red in

Rural Maya boy carries firewood home to his family.

the sunlight and from their throats came a strange war cry 'Hu Hu!' [Hurrah!]. They were brave men and shot keenly.... Some died laughing and some with strange words in their own tongue, but none died cowardly." Many of the gringo officers resigned and went home, others remained and fought well. The bayonet charge was their speciality.

In 1850, the strange cult of the **"Speaking Cross"** emerged in the village of Chan Santa Cruz (present-day Felipe Carrillo Puerto, see page 245) in Quintana Roo. Next to a small dark cenote, superstitious and religious Cruzob Maya worshipped a series of crosses that spoke to them in Mayan and directed a continued campaign against *dzules* (foreigners). Not coincidentally, one of the Cruzob holy men was a ventriloquist. The war dragged on, with the fighters from the cult of the Speaking Cross continually harassing the Yucatecans and defeating any expeditions that tried to tame the wild state, now separated from Yucatán's control and called the "frontier." In one battle, the Maya used biological warfare. By soaking the clothing of a cholera victim in water and leaving hollowed out logs of poisoned water next to a well, they infected the Yucatecan soldiers who drank from it.

The incredibly brutal battles continued through 1855, when a semi-stalemate became apparent. The Yucatecans held the cities and countryside in the west and north, while the Maya held the inland in the south and eastern province of Quintana Roo. During this time, Yucatecans began the despicable practice of selling captured Maya to Cuba as slaves ($45 a head for men and $25 for women, children free).

> *Whenever I hear anyone arguing for slavery, I feel a*
> *strong impulse to see it tried on him personally.*
> ~ Abraham Lincoln, 1809-1865

Though sisal production provided a new source of wealth and stability to the Yucatecans in the north, anarchy reigned in the east well past the official end of the Caste War in 1855. Skirmishing continued off and on until the very early 1900s when the Maya were finally subdued by repeating rifles and years of starvation and disease. In 1901, the frontier became the Federal Territory of Quintana Roo and official statehood finally came in 1974.

■ Sisal, The Green Gold

 Though Montejo and the Spanish Conquistadors found no gold in the Yucatán, their descendants did. They found green gold – henequen or sisal – which was used to make rope. The semi-arid tropics of the Yucatán proved to be an ideal growing region for the plant. The name "sisal" came from the port of the same name east of Mérida from where it was exported.

Commercial production of sisal began around 1830 in the peninsula, which immediately had a virtual monopoly on the market. The existing hacienda system, with its built-in labor pool, provided the means to grow and harvest the slow-maturing plant. By the turn of the century, the world's demand for rope fiber had skyrocketed due to its use in agricultural harvesting and baling machines. The Yucatán went from one of Mexico's poorest states to one of its richest. Unfortunately for the *campesinos* (working rural poor), that prosperity remained mostly with those families who had land grants generations before.

Narrow-gauge railways carried tons of leaves from the fields to the hacienda's processing plant where steam engines stripped the fiber for drying. With an insatiable demand spurred by World War I, henequen reached its pinnacle in price and production between 1916 and 1918. Mérida built its opulent baronial homes on the Paseo de Montejo, paved its streets and installed electric street lights – far in advance of Mexico City – with the proceeds of henequen sales.

Following the Armistice, the price of sisal fell precipitously. Aggravating the fact was the wartime introduction of competing henequen plantations in Africa. Richer soils overseas meant a higher quality product could be grown cheaper outside the Yucatán. With the later invention of synthetic fibers, demand fell further. The green gold that had fueled the peninsula's economy so richly now led it on a long, slow decline, from which it has never fully recovered.

Grand houses, such as this one on Paseo Montejo in Mérida, were paid for with the profits from sisal production.

Introduction

Modern Times

Progress, therefore, is not an accident, but a necessity....
It is a part of nature.
~ Herbert Spencer, 1820-1903

■ Love Story

Alma Reed, an American journalist, gazed into the intense green eyes of the man who sat opposite. She was a 33-year-old tough investigative writer who could hold her own in a man's world; and he, **Felipe Carrillo Puerto**, was the charismatic new revolutionary governor of the Yucatán. The electrical spark between them could have lit the street lamps of Mérida. The adventuresome Alma was in the Yucatán on assignment for *The New York Times* to cover the Carnegie Institute archeological study of the ruins at Chichén Itzá. Yet the social reforms ushered in by the new Governor Carrillo piqued her reporter's sense for news. The Mexican Revolution had ended only three years before and Carrillo was making an impressive name for himself as a reformer.

There were as many facets to Felipe Carrillo as there were to Alma Reed and both were intrigued by each other's intellect. He claimed to be a descendant of the Mayapán king who drove the Itzás from Chichén 700 years before. Under his liberal leadership he gave women the right to vote, organized Feminist Leagues, and placed women in governmental posts. He legalized birth control and established the first family planning clinics in the Americas. He supported land reform by forming *edijos*, communal farming groups. He built schools and roads and encouraged cottage industries for the poor. Most memorably, however, he was a vocal proponent of civil rights for the Maya.

She was an accomplished writer, strong willed, intelligent and very beautiful. At five feet seven, she towered over the Maya men and women among whom she and Felipe walked. When she returned to the Gran Hotel in Mérida after that first meeting she wrote in her dairy: "He is a miracle of goodness and beauty."

They both knew it was love at first sight, but Carrillo was married, with grown children. Nevertheless, the two spent every available minute together. Like a modern Romeo and Juliet, they stood watching while Carnegie archeologists poked around the breathtaking ruins of Chichén Itzá, when Alma asked why the Maya built such a fantastic city, only to desert it.

"Perhaps one day you, little peregrina, will discover the answer to that riddle," Felipe replied.

"Peregrina?"

"Pilgrim – is that not what you are? – a wanderer who will all too soon return to your own far off land."

After a brief intense affair, in which the two made no secret of their love for each other, Alma returned to New York with a ground-breaking story about American Edward Thompson's pillage of Maya artifacts from the Sacred Cenote at Chichén, which Harvard University had cached in their Peabody Museum. Her revelations allowed the Mexican government to reclaim some of the stolen treasures – though not until 1958. They are now on display in Mexico City, as well as the Peabody.

Alma's stories were so insightful that *The Times* decided to make her "their man in Mexico." Once she returned to Mérida, Felipe swept her heart away again when he visited with the news that he had made divorce legal in the Yucatán and had become the first to make use of it. He asked her to marry him and surprised her with a love song, *La Peregrina*, written and composed at his request. Its lyrical melody and heartfelt words remain popular to this day in Mexico. He also bestowed on her a Mayan name, "Pixan-Halal." Pixan means soul and Halal is the word for a water reed.

Their love for one another was so strong that it forever changed their lives. In October, Alma returned to her native San Francisco to prepare for their wedding, scheduled for January 1924. But a power struggle on the federal level gave the powerful hacienda interests, who had bridled under Carrillo's reforms, a chance to get rid of him. Late in 1923, Mexico and the Yucatán were plunged into a revolutionary bloodbath. Carrillo, three of his brothers, and six lieutenants were arrested and imprisoned. His pleas for the lives of his family and friends were ignored. On the morning of January 3, 1924, he and his party were marched to the Cemeterio General in Mérida and lined up against a high stone wall. Felipe gave one of the nervous soldiers the ring that was to be Alma's wedding band. "Please see that Pixan-Halal gets it," he asked.

La Peregrina (The Wanderer)
The Ballad of Alma Reed

Wanderer of the clear and divine eyes,
And cheeks aflame with the redness of the sky,
Little woman of the red lips,
And hair as radiant as the sun,
Traveler who left your own scenes – the fir trees and the snow,
the virginal snow – And came to find refuge in the palm groves,
Under the sky of my land,
My tropic land, The little singing birds of my fields,
Offer their voices in singing to you – And they look at you,
And the flowers of perfumed nectars
Caress you and kiss you on lips and temples.
When you leave my palm groves and my land,
Traveler of the enchanting face,
Don't forget, don't forget, my land,
Don't forget, don't forget, my love.

Introduction

Felipe Carillo's family mausoleum in Mérida.

The first volley from the firing squad hit the wall above their heads. The soldiers refused to kill the brave governor who had acquired the nickname of the "Abraham Lincoln of Mexico" for what he had done to free the Maya from virtual slavery. Incensed, the infamous military commander, Colonel Ricardo Braco, had the firing squad shot by other soldiers before executing Carrillo, his brothers and their supporters.

Felipe's grave, near the wall that still bears the bullet holes, is a large crescent moon-shaped family monument in the crowded cemetery. Poignantly, only a few feet away, under the quiet shade of a cedars of Lebanon pine, the grave containing Alma Reed's ashes watches over the man whom she remained in love with until her death at age 77 in 1966. Sometimes, in the early evening, visitors to the cemetery claim to hear the faint strains of La Peregrina on the warm breeze.

■ Life Story

 The Yucatán's past – desperate and bloody, rich and grand, glorious and shameful – has been replaced with a present that offers much promise. Sporadic confrontations with the Maya fizzled out by the 1930s after the elections of Governor Felipe Carrillo Puerto and President Carlos Lázaro Cárdenas, who distributed land to the peasants and nationalized the oil companies in 1938. Between the 1930s and the 1970s, socialism had a strong voice in federal government and the worst Indian abuses were addressed. During this time the Maya gradually converted their economy from barter to a monetary base. Those changes accelerated in the 1970s with improved roads, the development of Cancún and the statehood of Quintana Roo – all of which boosted the peninsula's economy. But the Maya do not represent all the workers in Cancún; immigrants from all over Mexico have flocked to the city by the thousands in search of work.

Najs *are seen even in larger towns, where modern buildings have been erected around them.*

Outside of the resort, many Maya still live in thatch-roofed oval huts called *otoch* (oh-toech) or *naj* (pronounced nah). Made of vertical sticks tied together, which can then be plastered, a *naj* is the timeless house in Maya culture. You can see identical ones depicted on bas-reliefs of the 1,000-year-old Nun's Quadrangle in Uxmal, one of the Yucatán's more famous archeological sites.

In rural areas, the Maya grow their traditional food staples – corn, beans, chilis, tomatoes and squash – using a slash and burn cultivation technique. Individual families often surround their home with lime, orange, banana and papaya trees. The most traditional of the Indian communities on the Yucatán Peninsula are found in the **Zona Maya**, an isolated area of central Quintana Roo (but you'll easily be able to visit villages on side roads or along the free road from Cancún to Mérida).

Current estimates put the total Maya world population at between four and six million; divided into different ethnic groups that speak about 30 distinct indigenous languages. Many of them are bilingual, learning Spanish to communicate with the *ladinos* (the non-Maya inhabitants of the area), especially in the marketplace. It is still possible, however, to venture into villages where not a word of Spanish is spoken by many adults, even though Spanish language is now required in school.

On New Year's Day, 1994, Maya in the highlands of Chiapas (calling themselves, Zapatistas, after the revolutionary hero, Emiliano Zapata) led an effective and deadly series of armed attacks against the Mexican government. Although their grievances are long founded, the revolt was ignited by the prospect of further economic hardships as a result of the NAFTA Treaty, a free trade agreement signed among Mexico, the US and Canada. Traditional *edijos*, small plots of communal farming land, are threatened by the need for market efficiencies. The violence included a series of criminal attacks on buses, trains and cars. The rebellion was not duplicated in the Yucatán, but the government's attention was drawn again to the plight of all Mexico's indigenous peoples. Tension in Chiapas remains high. However, a large police and army presence ensures most of the state is safe for tourism.

The ups and downs of Mexico over the years include the painful devaluation of the peso in the mid-1990s (which, combined with inflation, cut the average Mexican's buying power nearly in half) and continual scandals at the highest governmental levels concerning election fraud, drug trafficking and corruption. Although not insulated from these problems, sometimes the Yucatán seems a world apart, progressing at its own pace.

The people of the Yucatán are hard-working and peace-loving. We love to stop in small towns and chat with the locals, who are always pleased to meet us, giggling at our bad Spanish and even worse Mayan. In fact, everyone we met in the Yucatán welcomed us with genuine hospitality and eagerness to show the very best of the land they call home. We stopped by one Maya family and asked permission to take a photo of their children. In response, they invited us into their simple home to celebrate Christmas dinner. How could we not feel this is a special place?

The Yucatán is a treasure trove of attractions – historical and contemporary, natural and phenomenal. So put away any fears of banditos or getting lost in the wilderness and being eaten by wild animals, and come down for the adventure of a lifetime.

The greatest discovery of any generation is that human beings can alter their lives by altering the attitudes of their minds.
~ Albert Schweitzer

Get Ready, Set, Go!

For my part, I travel not to go anywhere, but to go. I travel for travel's sake.
~ *Travels with a Donkey* by Robert Louis Stevenson

Travel Essentials

So you're off to the Yucatán for a vacation adventure. Good choice. You'll be a *gringo*, a non-offensive term for someone from north of the border, or a *Norteamericano* or *Canadiense*, as distinguished from Mexicans, who are "Americans" too.

If this is your first experience south of the border or if you're planning to leave the Cancún Hotel Zone to explore the real Yucatán, here's some more practical information you'll find handy for your trip.

■ Information Sources

i To get general information and brochures, call the **Mexico Hotline** in the US, ☎ 800/44-MEXICO (800/446-3942); in Canada, ☎ 800/2MEXICO (800/263-9426). Or visit **www.cancun.com** and **www.mexico.com**. You can also e-mail for information to welcome@Cancun.com.

Tourist Offices

■ MEXICO/CANCÚN

Mexico Government Tourist Office
Avenida Cobá & Avenida Carlos Nader, Cancún, ☎ 998/884-3238, 884-3438
Mexico Quintana Roo State Tourism Office
26 Avenida Tulum, Cancún, ☎ 998/884-8073

■ CANADA

Mexico Government Tourist Offices
☎ 800-2MEXICO, toll-free from anywhere within Canada
Mexico Government Tourist Office
2 Bloor St. West, Suite 1801, Toronto, ON M4W 3E2, ☎ 416/925-0704
Mexico Government Tourist Office
1 Place Ville Marie, #2409, Montreal QC, H3B 3M9, ☎ 514/871-1052
Mexico Government Tourist Office
999 W. Hastings St., Suite 1610, Vancouver BC, ☎ 604/669-2845

■ ENGLAND

Mexico Government Tourist Office
60161 Trafalgar Square, 3rd Floor, London, WCN 5DS, ☎ 0171/859-3177

■ UNITED STATES

Mexico Government Tourist Offices
☎ 800/44-MEXICO, toll-free from anywhere within USA
Mexico Government Tourist Office
1911 Pennsylvania Ave., Washington, DC 20006, ☎ 202/728-1750
Mexico Government Tourist Office
70 E. Lake St., Ste 1413, Chicago, IL 60601, ☎ 312/565-2778 , fax 312/609-0808
Mexico Government Tourist Office
Epcot Center, Ave. of the Stars, Lake Buenavista, FL 32830, ☎ 407/827-5315
Mexico Government Tourist Office
405 Park Ave., Ste 1401, New York, NY 10022, ☎ 212/755-7261, fax 212/753-2874

■ Measurements

 The Yucatán is in the Central Time Zone. Weights, measures and temperatures are in metric. Gasoline is sold by the liter and distances are measured by kilometers. Dates are expressed with the day first, followed by the month. For example, Christmas Day is written

25/12. Often, hours are posted in military time – a 24-hour format. Two in the afternoon is 14:00, 10 at night is 22:00.

Going Metric

To make your travels in Mexico a little easier, we have provided the following chart that shows metric equivalets for the measurements you are familiar with.

GENERAL MEASUREMENTS

1 kilometer = .6124 miles

1 mile = 1.6093 kilometers

1 foot = .304 meters

1 inch = 2.54 centimeters

1 square mile = 2.59 square kilometers

1 pound = .4536 kilograms

1 ounce = 28.35 grams

1 imperial gallon = 4.5459 liters

1 US gallon = 3.7854 liters

1 quart = .94635 liters

TEMPERATURES

For Fahrenheit: Multiply Centigrade figure by 1.8 and add 32.
For Centigrade: Subtract 32 from Fahrenheit figure and divide by 1.8.

Centigrade	Fahrenheit
40°	104°
35°	95°
30°	86°
25°	77°
20°	64°
15°	59°
10°	50°

■ Customs

 Rules on the possession of **firearms and drugs** are simple: Don't have any, period. Drug possession penalties in Mexico (even for the smallest amount) include harsh prison terms, and your embassy can do little to help. It's just not worth it. Mexico is making a serious effort to curb drug trafficking. If you drive in the countryside, expect to be stopped several times by Army anti-drug patrols.

You can carry into Mexico two bottles of any liquor and two cartons of your favorite coffin nails. Supposedly, there is a limit of 12 rolls of film, but we've carried well over 60 rolls in a clear plastic bag and nobody raised an eyebrow, even when we were searched on their green light/red light system. The system works as follows: you punch a button at inbound Customs and if the traffic light goes green, you pass through unhindered. If it flashes red, you are subject to either a cursory or complete luggage search.

On your return to the United States you can bring in US $400 of duty-free goods per person, including only one litre of alcoholic beverages. Canadians are allowed Canadian $300 with a written exemption or $100 without. US citizens cannot bring back Cuban cigars. Archeological artifacts or items made from endangered species are strictly forbidden exports.

■ What to Take

Everyone does it. It starts with "what if?" – "What if it rains?" "What if it's cold?" "What if we go out to a fancy place?" "What if you spill ketchup on your shirt and my dress gets caught in a taxi door?" Then we wind up packing too much.

So here's the scoop – pack light, then take all your stuff back out and cut the quantity in half. The idea is to bring only enough clothes and necessities to last until you get to a laundromat or store. Clothing and shoes are relatively cheap in Mexico. There's always an inexpensive laundromat (*lavandería*) close by. Try to take no more than four to five days' worth of clothes, no matter how long your trip. And take older clothes that you won't miss if you stain them or the laundry fades or shrinks them. You can always buy what you need.

Toiletries necessarily depend on what you're doing and where. The better hotels have shampoo and soap and just about everything else is readily available in stores and supermarkets, so don't bring a gallon. Leave any open toiletries and unwanted clothes in Mexico.

> *Americans have always been eager for travel, that being how*
> *they got to the New World in the first place.*
> ~ Otto Friedrich, *Time* magazine, April 22, 1985

PACKING LIST

CLOTHING

- [ ] comfortable walking shoes with non-skid soles – wear a pair of slip-offs on the plane to make it easier when they check your shoes on boarding
- [ ] several pair of cotton socks
- [ ] underwear
- [ ] sandals
- [ ] one/two pair of no-iron slacks. Slacks are suitable for men and women in towns (jeans are too heavy).
- [ ] two pair of shorts
- [ ] women: two modest lightweight dresses and/or skirts
- [ ] two shirts or blouses
- [ ] three T-shirts
- [ ] swimsuit (carry with you everywhere)
- [ ] sleepwear
- [ ] light cotton sweater or sport coat
- [ ] water-resistant windbreaker
- [ ] hat and sunglasses

TOILETRIES

- [ ] fanny pack and money belt
- [ ] shampoo
- [ ] toothpaste and toothbrush
- [ ] prescription medicine
- [ ] comb/brush
- [ ] women: make-up as desired
- [ ] personal hygiene products
- [ ] sunscreen lotion, UVA/UVB protection, SPF 30+ (sunscreen takes 30 mins. to become effective after application)
- [ ] good insect repellent, a must for back country travel
- [ ] aloe gel for sunburn
- [ ] Immodium AD and aspirin
- [ ] triple antibiotic cream
- [ ] band aids
- [ ] facecloth

If you're roughing it, also bring:

- [ ] bar soap
- [ ] hand towel
- [ ] toilet paper (buy there)
- [ ] small size sink stop
- [ ] candle and matches (buy there)

OTHER ITEMS

- [ ] resealable plastic freezer bags (have multiple uses)
- [ ] antiseptic towelettes
- [ ] hand-held calculator
- [ ] small flashlight
- [ ] sharp penknife
- [ ] notebook and pen
- [ ] camera, film and extra batteries
- [ ] compact umbrella (good for shade in the hot sun at the ruins as well)
- [ ] flip-flops for slippery bathroom floors

- [ ] Spanish-English dictionary or phrase book
- [ ] sports watch
- [ ] earplugs
- [ ] passport, ID, driver's license
- [ ] paperback reading book (exchange for others at many hotels)
- [ ] sewing kit with small scissors
- [ ] laundry bag
- [ ] address book
- [ ] credit cards, travelers checks
- [ ] phone card
- [ ] this book (very important)

■ Entry Requirements

To enter Mexico, Americans and Canadians need proof of citizenship, such as a passport or certified birth certificate and a photo ID. (Canadians can use a Canadian Identification Card as proof of citizenship.) UK citizens need a passport.

Passports

Passport applications for United States citizens can be obtained from regional and government authorities at major post offices, courthouses or federal passport offices in larger metropolitan areas. You can also download an application online at **http://travel.state.gov**. Apply two or three months before your trip. A passport carries more authority with bureaucratic Mexican officials, so it pays to have one.

To replace a lost passport in Mexico, contact the nearest embassy or consular office (see *Just in Case*, below). The State Department website offers tons of additional information, including a very useful **Consular Information Sheet** that contains special safety or health alerts. You can get the CIS automatically faxed to you by calling ☎ 202/647-3000, or dial 202/647-5225 and press #1.

> *I was well acquainted with the gag that if you look like your passport picture you need a vacation. But I was unprepared for the preponderance of thug-like pictures I found in the course of processing them.*
> ~ Frances G. Knight, Director US Passport Division

US Passport Agencies

If you didn't leave it to the last minute, it might be better to apply for an American passport through a local Clerk of Court or Post Office. Passport Agencies tend to have long lines during the busiest months.

■ BOSTON
Thomas P. O'Neill Federal Building
10 Causeway Street, Suite 247, Boston, MA 02222-1094; 9 am-4 pm
Region: Maine, Massachusetts, New Hampshire, Rhode Island,
Upstate New York, Vermont.

■ CHICAGO
Kluczynski Federal Building
230 S. Dearborn Street, Suite 380, Chicago, IL 60604-1564; 9 am-4 pm
Region: Illinois, Indiana, Michigan, Wisconsin.

■ HONOLULU
First Hawaiian Tower
1132 Bishop Street, Suite 500, Honolulu, HI 96813-2809; 9 am-4 pm
☎ 808/522-8283
Region: American Samoa, Federated States of Micronesia,
Guam, Hawaii, Northern Mariana Islands.

■ HOUSTON
Mickey Leland Federal Building
1919 Smith Street, Suite 1100, Houston, TX 77002-8049; 8 am-3 pm
Region: Kansas, Oklahoma, New Mexico, Texas.

■ LOS ANGELES
Federal Building
11000 Wilshire Blvd., Suite 13100, Los Angeles, CA 90024-3615; 8 am-3 pm
Region: California (all counties south of and including San Luis Obispo, Kern
and San Bernardino) and Nevada (Clark County only).

■ MIAMI
Claude Pepper Federal Office Building
51 SW First Avenue, 3rd Floor, Miami, FL 33120-1680; 9 am-4 pm
Region: Florida, Georgia, Puerto Rico, South Carolina, US Virgin Islands.

■ NATIONAL PASSPORT CENTER
31 Rochester Avenue, Portsmouth, NH 03801-2900; 9 am-4 pm
Handles applications for passports by mail (form DSP-82)

■ NEW ORLEANS
Postal Services Building
701 Loyola Avenue, Suite T-12005; New Orleans, LA 70113-1931; 9 am-4 pm
Region: Alabama, Arkansas, Iowa, Kentucky, North Carolina, Louisiana, Mississippi, Missouri, Ohio, Tennessee, Virginia (except DC suburbs).

■ NEW YORK
Rockefeller Center, 630 Fifth Ave., Suite 270, New York, NY 10111-0031;
7:30 am-3 pm
☎ 212/399-5290
Region: New York City, Long Island
*Note: New York Passport Agency accepts only emergency applications from
those leaving within two weeks.*

■ PHILADELPHIA
US Custom House
200 Chestnut Street, Room 103, Philadelphia, PA 19106-2970; 9 am-4 pm
Region: Delaware, New Jersey, Pennsylvania, West Virginia.

■ SAN FRANCISCO
95 Hawthorne Street, 5th Floor, San Francisco, CA 94105-3901; 9 am-4 pm
Region: Arizona, California (all counties north of and including Monterey,
Kings, Oulare and Inyo), Nevada (except Clark Co.) and Utah.

■ SEATTLE

Henry Jackson Federal Building, 915 Second Avenue, Suite 992, Seattle, WA 98174-1091; 8 am-3 pm
Region: Alaska, Colorado, Idaho, Minnesota, Montana, Nebraska, North Dakota, Oregon, South Dakota, Washington, Wyoming.

■ STAMFORD

One Landmark Square, Broad and Atlantic Streets, Stamford, CT 06901-2667; 9 am-4 pm
Region: Connecticut and Westchester County (New York)

■ WASHINGTON

1111 19th Street, NW, Room 300, Washington, DC 20522-1705; 8 am-3 pm
Region: Maryland, northern Virginia (including Alexandria, Arlington and Fairfax Counties) and the District of Columbia.

Tourist Cards

No visa is required to enter Mexico, but you will need a Tourist Card, usually obtained from the airline before you land or at the travel agency where you buy your ticket. This is an important document, so look after it. Tourist cards are valid for up to 180 days. If you plan to stay longer, get your card from the Mexican Embassy or Consular Office nearest you before leaving home. Otherwise, you'll have to extend it at an office of *migración* in one of the peninsula's larger cities (see *Servicios Migratorios* in the *Just in Case* section below). A law passed late in 1999 established a fixed charge of about $16 to extend the tourist card in a Mexico-based office. Failure to extend your card before the expiration date results in aggravation and a fine.

■ Honeymoons & Weddings

 Mexico is now the number one foreign destination for honeymooners. Cancún's Judge Veronica Lopez de Arriaga marries about 150 couples per month. "I love my job because I get to know the world through the marriages of many foreign couples," she claims. In an average year, she officiates at ceremonies for over 400 American couples, plus 300 other nationalities, including Japanese, Canadian, German, Austrian and Italian. In total, more than 1,600 foreign couples marry each year in Cancún.

An archeologist is the best husband any woman can have:
The older she gets, the more interested he is in her.
~ Agatha Christie, English author, 1890-1976

Planning

Many hotels can make all wedding arrangements for you. Or you can do it yourself. Bakers and photographers downtown are experienced and dependable. The Justice of the Peace charges US $400 to perform the ceremony at a location other than their offices; many couples choose to tie the knot on a beach.

A variety of companies can help with your Mexican wedding arrangements, from booking the Justice of the Peace to arranging the florist to meeting with a baker. **Weddings on the Move** is one such organization. They can be reached at ☎ 800/444-6967, www.idoweddings.com. Located in Cancún is the all women-run **Caribbean Cancún Weddings** (☎ 998/881-7307, fax 881-7308, www.caribbean-cancunwedding.com) who offer nuptial planning for the Riviera Maya as well. Be sure to check with your travel agent for honeymoon packages. Many of the resort hotels also offer wedding ceremony packages, allowing for a romantic tropical affair at your hotel.

Marriage Documents

It's easy to arrange a civil or religious ceremony in Mexico. The legal requirements and regulations are minimal and mirror what a couple would need to provide in the United States. You'll need the following:

- ❑ Tourist card
- ❑ Birth certificate
- ❑ Blood test certificate
- ❑ Valid passport
- ❑ Divorce certificate (if applicable)
- ❑ Marriage Application Form (available one week in advance from the civil registry on Av. Tulum, near the shopping center, Plaza 2000, in Cancún).
- ❑ Four witnesses with details of their name, address, age, nationality and tourist card number.

■ Travel Deals

 Cancún has a very busy international airport served by numerous major airlines and a fair number of charter companies. If you're the kind of person who prefers the security of staying in one hotel, check your newspaper's travel section. Advertised package trips that include airfare can be hard to beat and they offer a choice of accommodations from luxury to moderate. A good travel agent should be able to offer a selection and might also know about bucket shops or wholesalers for airfare-only deals. We once flew Apple Vacations "air only" on a Mexicana flight at a good discount. Another big Cancún package vacation company is **Vacation Express** (☎ 800/309-4717, www.vacationexpress.com). They are especially good from

Atlanta. See the *Way to Go* section, below, for details about cheap stand-by tickets from Air Tech.

■ Escorted & Custom Tours

For organized adventures, **Trek America** (☎ 800/221-0596, www. trekamerica.com) offers flexible travel packages that involve camping and hiking. **Backroads Tours** (☎ 800/245-3874, www. backroads.com) has escorted biking and hiking tours to the Yucatán and elsewhere in Mexico. London-based **Exodus Adventure Holidays**, with offices all over Europe, offers more of the same. Their website is www.exodustravels. co.uk. **Holbrook Travel** (☎ 800/451-7111, www.holbrooktravel.com) is excellent, reputable and experienced – plus they're into ecotourism. **Far Horizons** (☎ 800/552-4575, www.farhorizon.com) are known for cultural and historical adventures, and **Maya Tour** (☎ 800/392-6292, www.mayatour. com) specialize in archeological tours.

Packages include visits to Colonial cities and ruins in Mundo Maya (Mayan World), either solely in the Yucatán or including Chiapas, Belize, Costa Rica, Honduras or Guatemala. Some contain naturalist itineraries such as birdwatching or a visit to a cenote and all claim qualified and experienced guides.

Ken Johnson's little Cancún-based **EcoColors** company (☎ 998/884-9580 & 884-3667, www.ecotravelmexico.com, info@ecotravelmexico.com) specializes in arranging tours with ecology and adventure as their theme. They cover Quintana Roo, Yucatán, Campeche, Chiapas and the countries of Belize and Guatemala. Explore the countryside as a small group or with your family, accompanied by a trained archeological guide from **Mayasites Travel** (in Mexico, ☎ 916/345-0307, www.mayasites.com), a full-service agency. A Mérida tour operator is **Ecoturismo Yucatán** (☎ 999/925-2187, www.ecoyuc.com). Canadian Denis LaFoy offers group and individual tours from Mérida at his **Yucatán Trails Travel** (☎ 999/928-2582, yucatantrails@hotmail.com). Adventure tourism is the speciality of English-speaking Carlos Sosa at **Balam-Beh Expeditions**, ☎ 999/924-1871, balambeh@prodigy.net.mx. There are numerous day tours offered out of Cancún, available from any travel agent.

You'll come across many free tourist information booths at the airport and in downtown Cancún, as well as booths and storefronts that advertise free trips to Isla Mujeres, discounted tours or car rentals, gifts or Jungle Tours, etc. These are mostly time-share promotions that require what is euphemistically called "an hour" of your time. It often turns out to be very much longer and there's strong sales pressure to buy at the property you tour. Unless you're an old pro and seriously thinking of an interval ownership, just say no.

■ Way to Go

Flying to Mexico

Our favorite airline into Cancún is **Aeromexico** (☎ 800/237-6639, www.aeromexico.com). Their service and schedules are first-rate, with very competitive prices.

Other major carriers include **Continental** (☎ 800/231-0856, www.continental.com), **American** (☎ 800/433-7300, www.aa.com), **Mexicana** (☎ 800/531-7921, www.mexicana.com), **US Airways** (☎ 800/428-4322, www.usairways.com), **Delta** (☎ 800/221-1212, www.delta.com), **KLM/Northwest** (☎ 800/225-2525, www.nwa.com), and **United** (☎ 800/241-6522, www.ual.com). Some direct flights are available to Cozumel and also Mérida; check with your travel agent or online.

Exit according to rule, first leg and then head.
Remove high heels and synthetic stockings before evacuation.
Open the door, take out the recovery line and throw it away.
~ Emergency instructions of the Rumanian National Airlines, 1984

Students and faculty might do well phoning **Council Travel** (☎ 800/226-8624, www.counciltravel.com). A ticket consolidator that offers great last-minute deals on charter flights from major cities in the USA is **Air-Tech, Ltd.,** (☎ 212/219-7000, www.airtech.com).

Flying Within Mexico

A good regional airline that flies on from Cancún to Cozumel, Chichén Itzá, Mérida, Chiapas and other major cities is **Aerocaribe/Aerocozumel** (☎ 998/886-0083 or 884-2000, www.aerocaribe.com). Any of the numerous travel agents in Cancún can arrange flights for you.

Sailing to Mexico

An exciting new way to get back and forth from Mexico is the **Yucatan Express** (☎ 866/670-3939, www.yucatanexpress.com), which sails weekly during the high season from Tampa, Florida to Progreso. It's a combination passenger cruise ship and car ferry that features an onboard casino, games, night club, music, and other amenities of a small cruise ship. Departures from Florida, as of press time, are 5 pm on Fridays, arriving in Progreso on Sunday morning. It returns on Sunday evenings at 6 pm. Passenger prices start at $150 round-trip and a little more than twice that for vehicles. If you're staying long-term or driving on to Chiapas, Oaxaca, Belize, or Guatemala, it's a great way to avoid renting a car. Day-trippers can make the round-trip for less.

Driving to Mexico

If you're coming by car from the US, it takes a good four or five days of steady driving from the border to reach Campeche. In place of a tourist card you'll get a combination tourist card/vehicle permit for you and your car. Foreign auto insurance is invalid in Mexico, so you'll need to get some from an agency such as **Sanborn's Mexico Insurance**, PO Box 310, 2009 South 10th St., McAllen, TX 78505-0310 (☎ 800/222-0158, fax 210/686-0732, www.sanbornsinsurance.com), or online from **Drivemex** (www.drivemex.com). They shop rates for you among three insurance companies. Very convenient. You need a copy of your title, a major credit card and a notarized letter from any lease or lien holders. Note: You must be in the car every time it's driven. If you try to leave the country without your vehicle, it will be a bureaucratic and financial nightmare.

Car Rentals

The best way to tour the Yucatán is by car and they are easily rented in Cancún and other major cities. The disadvantage is the cost, as there are no bargains. Shop around the major car companies in the US and be sure to ask if their rates (weekly is cheaper) include insurance, tax and/or mileage. Compare apples to apples. Often – but not always – you can negotiate a better deal with the local office rather than through the 800 numbers. We got a very good deal negotiating directly with Mastercar rental in Cancún's Hotel Zone.

Mexican driving **insurance** is required and costs almost as much as the rental rate. Zero deductible insurance – which runs as much as $5-15 extra per day – is a definite plus when driving on foreign soil with foreign rocks kicked up by foreign cars. We can't stress enough how important getting zero-deductible full coverage can be. Unlike Europe or the States, your credit card doesn't effectively pick up the Collision Damage Waiver. If you have only regular Mexican insurance and are involved in an accident where the car is wrecked, you could be responsible for 10% of the car's value, at least $2,500 or more.

You have to be at least 23 (some require age 25) to rent a car and must have a major credit card. The cheapest cars for rent are VW Beetles, or their equivalent, with standard shift and no radio or air. (Air-conditioning is cool but not necessary.) The highest prices are for four-wheel-drive Jeeps and SUVs.

> **AUTHORS TIP:** *If you haven't prepaid, ask about paying with cash instead of credit card when you return the car. We once put our car rental on a card and saved 10% on the insurance by paying for it at the end in cash. One friend claims he received a 20% discount by paying the whole thing in cash.*

We used **Localiza** (☎ 998/886-0248, www.localizarentacar.com) for our last long-term automobile rental and were very pleased with their rates. They also have offices in Mérida, Puerto Morelos, Playa del Carmen, and Cozumel. International car rental companies with offices in Cancún include **Avis** (in US ☎ 800/331-1084, in Cancún 998/886-0221), **Alamo** (in US ☎ 800/327-9633, in Cancún 998/886-0505), **Budget** (US ☎ 800/472-3325, in Cancún 998/886-0026), **Dollar** (US ☎ 800/800-4000, in Cancún 998/883-0133), **Hertz** (US ☎ 800/654-3001, in Cancún 998/886-0045), **National** (US ☎ 800/227-7368, in Cancún 998/886-0152), and **Thrifty** (US ☎ 800/367-2277, in Cancún 998/883-2525). These and other local companies, such as **Caribetur** (☎ 998/883-1071), have offices downtown, as well as at the airport. Check for their ads in *Cancún Tips*. Most car rentals have opened offices in Playa del Carmen as well. Check your car thoroughly for all its parts and condition. Rental cars are required by law to have a good spare tire, jack, seatbelts and a fire extinguisher.

Driving Mexico-Style

With some cautions, driving in the Yucatán is a breeze. The main roads are in excellent shape. Cancún is a big city and anyone experienced driving in heavy traffic will feel right at home. Parking, however, is another thing, with the downtown offering only a limited number of spaces. If you're staying locally, don't bother renting; the bus service is excellent. The other congested city is Mérida. Most of its streets in the center are alternating one-way and there's a vigilant traffic cop on every corner.

The peninsula's main roads are surprisingly straight, level and well marked. Intrepid travelers may run into some rough pavement – or none at all – only on secondary roads, especially in the wet season. All-in-all, very few people have problems driving in the Yucatán.

If you do have a flat or break down, Mexico has an amazing roadside assistance group known as the **Green Angels** that regularly patrols main roads. The Green Angels offer a free service, although generous tips are greatly appreciated. A pile of branches or brush in the road indicates a disabled car ahead. If you break down, try to do this so cars will pass with caution. Use the emergency flashers and keep to the side of the road. To signal for help, raise the

Green Angels to the rescue!

hood. You can dial "066," similar to our 911, for emergencies. Fortunately, we never had to test this service.

■ CALLING ALL GREEN ANGELS

Cancún & the Riviera Maya . . . . ☎ 998/884-1107
Campeche . . . . ☎ 981/816-6068
Mérida. . . . . ☎ 999/924-9542
Valladolid . . . . ☎ 985/856-2065

Magna sin is the unleaded gasoline in Mexico, sold from the green pump. Be sure to read our *Driving Tips*, below.

Driving Tips

Check your car thoroughly before you leave the rental agency, especially the windscreen fluid, wipers, spare tire and jack. Bugs and dust (*polvo*) just love to hang out on windshields. Check the signals, windows, lights, seat belts, brakes and fire extinguisher. If you don't have a 100% deductible policy, mark every little nick and ding on your inspection sheet. Also, be sure you have a gas cap and check it again when you fill up just before returning the car. We were in a rental office once when they charged a tourist US $45 for a missing gas cap. As he left he grumbled about the possibility that the station he had just filled up in and the rent-a-car agency were in collusion. If you're not satisfied with your car, insist on one in better condition. You might also consider having an extra key made in town. We learned that lesson the hard way. We highly recommend that you buy zero deductible insurance, or full coverage, even though the rental car company may not offer it at first. It's worth the extra moola.

- Watch your speed in Cancún's Hotel Zone; the speed limit changes suddenly from 70 kph (45 mph) to 40 kph (25 mph) and there are lots of Transit Police using radar to catch speeders.

- Don't drive in the countryside at night – it's dangerous. Roads are relatively narrow, totally dark, and have wild animals, bicyclists and pedestrians wandering around on them. In addition, oncoming trucks and buses with high-beam headlights are a real pain. Even more exciting are the cars and trucks that don't have lights at all.

- Outside Cancún, left turn signals are used constantly but their meaning varies dramatically. They can mean the car, bus or truck in front of you is turning left – but that would be too obvious. They could also mean that it's okay for you to pass because there is no oncoming traffic ahead. Or else they're saying hello to the oncoming traffic, another truck or bus approaching in the other direction. Or perhaps the right signal is out and the signal is really half of the emergency light signifying the car is slowing down. Of course, the driver could have forgotten to turn off the signal altogether. Take your pick, but proceed with lots of caution.

■ Keep in mind that many automobiles on the road don't have working directional signals and sometimes not even working brake lights. Always drive defensively and slow down; you're on vacation.

■ Left turns are not too common in Mexico unless it's into a small road. At busier intersections, left turns are made from a right-hand pull over, much like a jug-handle. On a four-lane road, pull over on the right and let any traffic pass. Cross only when traffic is clear. We found this a very hard rule to follow.

■ It's a good idea to fill your gas tank every chance you get when traveling in rural areas. In some very remote villages your tank is filled from a gas can or siphoned directly from a barrel. If you're running low and you come into a tiny village, tell someone you need a few liters of gasoline (*necessito gasolina*) and most places have someone who can help.

TOPES

Topes. Remember that word. If you see it on a sign, slow down or you may leave your car's undercarriage behind you in the road. *Topes* (toe-PAYS) are speed bumps that slow traffic to a crawl before every school building, bus stop and before entering and exiting each small town. Your first experience with a *tope* may be in downtown Cancún, where pedestrian crossings are giant *topes* (always yield to pedestrians there). *Topes* litter the free road to Mérida, so be patient and enjoy the scenery. Remember too, that some will appear in the road without any warning signs. Frequently, little refreshment stands or people selling fruit or handicrafts sprout up at the speed bumps.

■ Carry a cleaning rag or paper towels with you and, if you're doing much traveling, buy a small bottle of window cleaner. Young boys will clean your windshield at most gas stations; the meager tips you give are often split with the pump attendant.

■ Any fraction of a peso when you fill up your tank is customarily rounded up to the next peso. You can tip the attendant a few pesos if you wish.

■ Pedestrians have the right of way, so stop for them in crosswalks.

■ Never drink and drive, anywhere, any time.

■ Wear a seatbelt when driving yourself or inside a taxi – it's the law.

■ Gas stations do not repair cars in Mexicof. If you're having mechanical problems, ask for a *taller mecanico*, an auto repair shop.

If you get a flat tire, which rental insurance does not cover, look for a tire hanging on a tree or some such sign in the countryside signifing a tire repair shop. Tires are called *llantas* (YAN-tas). Cities have large tire repair shops. Mexico roads are hard on tires if only judged on the number of repair places you'll pass.

■ Parking in the cities can be a problem. Red curbs mean don't park, yellow ones may be okay, although on Cozumel they're supposedly reserved for motorbikes. If your hotel doesn't have secured parking, look for signs that read *Estacionmiento* (parking lot). Don't leave valuables in plain sight, even though many lots are guarded 24 hours. Parking prices are reasonable and a tip to the attendant upon departure is customary.

■ Ask the rental agent how many liters it takes to fill the tank (our Bug took about 40). It's an unfortunate truth that some gas station attendants try to cheat you. See our section on scams, page 83.

■ Getting Around

 Unless transportation is included in your hotel price, the only way to get anywhere from the airport is either by a rental car or by buying a ticket at one of several airport booths for a taxi or shared combi-bus. For the frugal, there is a public bus service to the downtown only. See pages 95-96 for complete information on arrival and departure. Pick up a copy of *Cancún Tips* and any other magazines or brochures at Cancún's modern airport and look for discount coupons and special offers.

Buses

If you're staying downtown, pushing on to Playa del Carmen, or anywhere on the peninsula, buses are an excellent alternative to the high price of renting a car. Cancún's spanking new bus terminal is behind the circle (*glorieta*) of Av. Tulum and Av. Uxmal. Buses are reliable and surprisingly inexpensive. Mexico has two classes of bus service. First class offers the more modern, comfortable and air-conditioned buses, with bathrooms, that make fewer, or even no, stops between points. They run full-length movies and shorts for entertainment. Second class offers more of a local route, often with well-worn buses, and takes much more time. From Cancún you can get frequent service on either, south to Playa del Carmen and Chetumal, or west to Valladolid, Chichén Itzá and Mérida (four hours). Long distance buses can also carry you direct to Campeche, Villahermosa, Veracruz or even Mexico City.

The principal inter-city long distance carrier in Mexico is **ADO** (Autobuses del Oriente). Other companies that cover the peninsula from Cancún are **ATS** (first class) and **Oriente, Noreste, Dorado, Mayab** and **Playa Ex-**

press, all second class. Book through travel agents or at the ticket booths in bus stations.

Service within Cancún is excellent. Buses marked *Zona Hoteles,* Hotel Zone, ply up and down the strip and run frequently between downtown and the hotel area. The fare is about 60¢. A change on Av. Tulum will take you up to Puerto Juárez and the ferry to Isla Mujeres (a trip on the ferry is much more fun than taking the Hotel Zone's shuttle boat).

If your itinerary is reasonably set, completely flexible, or your

Bus travel is inexpensive and comfortable.

budget is limited, seriously consider travel by bus. It will save money and is a great way to meet fellow travelers as well as local people.

Hitchhiking

A thing of the past in the States, hitchhiking is alive in the Yucatán. If you're thinking of hitching, take all the common-sense precautions, such as not accepting a ride with someone who has been drinking or, if you're female, not accepting a ride from a carload of guys. It's always best to travel in pairs, but expect a long wait: *gringos* are in the habit of passing you up and some Yucatecans might think you're rich enough to take the bus which, given the low cost and safety, is probably a much better idea.

Picking up locals is another thing. If you drive extensively, you may see people sitting in the shade along the side of a road as if they're waiting for a bus. They may hold up a hand as if to say hi. Chances are they'd like a ride. If you're not comfortable with stopping, wave hello and keep driving. We sometimes pick up people to practice our Spanish or Mayan until the next village. When you let them off, it's a custom – at least among older folk, who may be as poor as church mice – to dig their hand into a well-worn pocket and ask, *Cuanto cuesta?* How much?

Simply smile and reply, *Por nada.* Nothing.

What to Expect

*If you reject the food, ignore the customs, fear the religion
and avoid the people, you might better stay home.*
~ James A. Michener

■ Culture & Customs

Siesta!

Zᶻᶻ ᶻ The siesta is still a part of Mexico's lifestyle and one of the reasons impatient North Americans talk of a Mexican *mañana* attitude. While it's true that the lifestyle in Mexico is slower, why would you go on vacation to a place that requires more work from you than you do at home? The image of a lazy Mexican asleep under a sombrero is just not true, especially not in the Yucatán. For example, you'll see men working in the blazing sun with machetes clearing brush from the sides of highways. We watched welders and construction workers labor all day and into the following morning to finish the roof of the Flamingo Plaza Sanborn's restaurant in Cancún, which was due to open soon. Things may proceed at their own pace in Mexico, but it's not from lack of effort.

Because the heat of the day comes in the afternoon, it is customary to close shops and offices for long lunches or naps, then open again at four or five in the afternoon and remain open until seven or eight at night. Because of the pressure of tourists who, like mad dogs and Englishmen, go out in the noonday sun, not as many shops or restaurants close down in Cancún. But siestas are still a part of the culture, so pace yourself accordingly.

Local Mores

Cancún differs from the rest of the Yucatán because of the overwhelming influence of North American culture. People speak English everywhere and the city's Mexican hotels, stores, restaurants and workers cater to American tastes. Two embarrassed patrolmen used to walk the north beach of Isla Mujeres once or twice a day and ask women to please not go topless. That particular beach is frequented mostly by *extranjeros* (foreigners), so they were really just going through the motions. It's definitely not acceptable to sunbathe topless where local families go, nor to wear revealing clothes or bathing suits in the shopping malls, on the bus or in the streets downtown. Mexicans are mostly Catholic and conservative, but they can party with the best of them too. We'd like to think that users of this guide would be sensitive to local mores.

What's very positive about the society south of the border is its emphasis on the family. It's a real pleasure to stroll in a public park on Sundays and holidays and see so many families out enjoying themselves – a valuable example to take back home.

■ Sports

The ancient Maya played a kind of basketball/soccer game in which the players could not touch the ball with their hands or feet, but propelled it instead with their hips. You'll see stone rings that served as goals on the ceremonial ballcourt at Chichén Itzá. Losers (or maybe the winners) lost their lives in sacrifice. A nightly match (without the sacrifice) is held at Xcaret's reproduction ballcourt.

Today's Yucatecans enjoy organized sports such as soccer, basketball and baseball. But you may be surprised to learn that **baseball** has taken over soccer as Yucatán state's favorite sport. Baseball fields share space with soccer fields in villages throughout the peninsula.

Bullfighting goes on year-round every Wednesday in Cancún's bullring downtown. Be forewarned that they kill the bulls. During small town or village festivals in the countryside, bullfights are an entirely different experience, with matadors who travel a circuit.

Resort sport activities include diving, snorkeling, windsurfing and swimming. There are several fishing tournaments and you can also take a fishing trip any day of the week. Cancún has a nighttime marathon in September, which draws mostly Mexican runners. A more international race is held in December, attracting world-class competitors as well as amateurs. People with buns of iron can compete in a triathlon on Playa Langosta in September.

> *To many, holidays are not voyages of discovery,*
> *but a ritual of reassurance.*
> ~ Philip Andrew Adams, Australian writer

■ Holidays, Festivals & Local Cultural Events

Most of Mexico's festivals and holidays have religious significance. Catholicism is the country's predominant religion, although evangelist faiths have made some inroads. Local villages have annual bashes tied to the patron saint of their town.

These aren't solemn occasions, but spirited celebrations that, in some cases, blend Maya rituals and culture with the Catholic religion. People dress up and enjoy dancing, music, feasts and fireworks.

If you're planning to attend any major special events, it might pay to make hotel reservations in advance. Remember, some of the dates below change slightly with the calendar.

Calendar of Events

■ JANUARY

Jan 1: New Year's Day. Agricultural fairs in the country. Look for scarecrows on porches and roofs, holding a bottle of booze. These represent *burrachos*, drunks celebrating a new year.

Jan 6: Día de los Reyes Magos, Day of Three Kings. Christmas gifts are exchanged in memory of the three wise men who brought gifts to the infant Jesus. At many parties a *rosca*, a ring-shaped cake with a miniature doll baked inside, is served. The person whose slice contains the doll must throw another party on February 2, Candlemas. In Campeche there's a religious ceremony called a **Cock Dance**, where 12 men perform a complicated ritual dance known as the Olk Kekén.

Jan 25 - Feb 2: Town Fair in Candelaria, Campeche. Includes the blessing of long wax candles used when someone dies.

Last Sunday in Jan: Día de la Immaculada Concepcíon. A lively festival is held after nine days of religious services, highlighted by a dance that features a pig's head covered with offerings of ribbons and flowers, including cigarettes and liquor.

■ FEBRUARY

Feb 1-5: San Felipe Festival in San Felipe (near Rio Largartos).

Feb 2: Candeleria. Many villages celebrate Candlemas with candlelight processions. **Corn Fair** in Tzucacab, Yucatán.

Traditional dancing.

Feb 5: Constitution Day. Legal holiday.

Feb 24: Flag Day

Feb/Mar: Carnival. Festive carnivals are held in Mérida, Chetumal, Isla Mujeres, Cozumel, Campeche and many towns around the countryside the week before Ash Wednesday. It's a last blast before the somber season of Lent. Parades with decorated floats, fancy costumes, fiestas and sporting events are featured throughout the Yucatán. Cozumel has a huge community party in the downtown. Mérida has parades, floats and traditional dancing. Chetumal hosts a Caribbean-style affair with folk dancers. Carnival's festivities end on Fat Tuesday, the day before Ash Wednesday and the first of the 40 days of Lent before Easter.

■ MARCH

Mar 16-21: Spring Fair in José Maria Morelos, a small town about 85 km (53 miles) east of Felipe Carrillo Puerto in Quintana Roo.

Mar 21: Vernal Spring Equinox. The shadow of a serpent appears to undulate down the steps of the pyramid of Kukulcán at Chichén Itzá. The Maya perfectly positioned the pyramid so that as the sun strikes the steps during the two times of the Equinox a unique pattern of light and shadow creates the illusion of a slithering serpent. Packed with spectators. Advance tickets are sold through Ticketmaster.

Mar 21: Birthday of Benito Juárez (1806). The first Indian-blood President of Mexico and leader of the reform movement, La Reforma.

Mar/Apr: Easter Sunday. Perhaps the most holy day in Mexico. Religious processions are held throughout the countryside. The week preceding is called La Semana Santa (Holy Week). Dramatizations of the crucifixion of Christ occur on Good Friday in Mérida and Anaceh, among other towns in Yucatán state.

■ APRIL

Apr 3: San Ildefonso in Izamal.

Apr 13-17: Honey Fair held in Hopelchén, Campeche. Bees and honey have their own diety in the ancient Maya religion.

End of Apr/beginning of May: International yacht races are held in the Bahia off Isla Mujeres. There's a deep-sea fishing tournament there around the same time. In Cozumel, the **El Cedral Fair** occurs at the end of April and lasts for one week.

May 1: Labor Day. Legal holiday.

May 1-7: Theater Festival in Mérida.

May 2-3: International Deep-Sea Fishing Tournament, Cozumel. Seybaplaya, Campeche, celebrates its **patron saint**.

May 3: Day of the Holy Cross. Fiestas at Celestún, Felipe Carrillo Puerto and Hopelchén.

May 5: Cinco de Mayo. This holiday – also celebrated in Mexican restaurants and bars throughout the States – commemorates the Battle of the Puebla (1862), in which the Mexican Army defeated invading French troops. The victory proved temporary and the naive Franco-Austrian Archduke, Maximilian, was installed as the ill-fated "Emperor of Mexico." He was left to his own devices when the French withdrew their troops at the demand of the US. In Cancún, tourists celebrate by drinking yards of beer.

Early May: The Corona Cup is held, with four categories of sports car racing.

Second week May: Jazz Festival. Cancún's jazz festival attracts some big names and not-so-well-knowns to a popular celebration of music.

May 12-18: Immaculate Conception. Maya music, bullfights and religious processions honor the Virgin in Chankah Veracruz (near Felipe Carrillo Puerto).

May 20: Hammock Fair. A good time to buy a hammock in Tekom, south of Valladolid on Higway 295.

May 20-30: Jipi Festival in honor of the palm plant jipijapa (HEE-pee-HAA-pah), from which Panama hats are made. Held in Becal, Campeche.

■ JUNE

June 4: Festivities in Valladolid. Music and dance as well as historic re-creations.

June 22-Aug 4: Saint John the Baptist in Campeche.

June 29: Saints Peter and Paul get their due in local fiestas.

■ JULY

Early July: Ticul Festival. A week-long fiesta celebrates the founding of Ticul, Yucatán.

July 16-31: Festival in Ciudad del Carmen includes nautical events and cattle drives. These festivities are repeated for Carnival when the town fills up.

July 25: Saint James the Apostle is celebrated in Rio Lagartos.

■ AUGUST

Aug 15: Our Lady of Izamal. This is the scheduled festival day in a town known for its religious parties, but friends who were there on the 15th were told that it was the following week – or the week before.

Aug 16: Chetumal and Bacalar sponsor a motorboat race and regatta, to honor **Saint Joaquín** on the Chaac Inlet on and around this date.

Aug 17: Cruz de la Bahia on Isla Mujeres. A bronze cross weighing about a ton (39 feet in height and nearly 10 feet wide) was set into the Manchones Reef between Isla Mujeres and the coastline in 1994. The "Cross of the Bay" is the island's tribute to all the men and women of the sea. Scuba divers celebrate with a mass dive.

Aug 20: Traditional Fair occurs in Maní, Yucatán.

■ SEPTEMBER

Sept 14: Festival of San Román, Campeche. Celebrates the arrival of the Black Christ, carved in ebony. When Captain Juan Cano de Coca Gaitan brought it to Campeche from Veracruz in 1565, he sailed through a hurricane that sank another ship whose captain had refused to carry the cross.

Sept 15: Independence Day. Legal holiday.

ca. Sept 22: Autumnal Fall Equinox at Chichén Itzá's archeological zone. Reenactments of Maya rituals and dancing. The two equinoxes occur when the sun is vertically above the earth's equator. Less crowded than the first equinox.

Sept 27, first two weeks in Oct: Procession de Cristo de las Ampollas (Christ of the Blisters), a religious holiday, occurs in Mérida. This statue of Christ was carved from a tree struck by lightning that, legend has it, burned all night without any sign of fire damage. Its fiesta includes fireworks, music and folk dances.

Sept 29-Oct 9: Saint Miguel Archangel gets his own celebration in San Miguel, Cozumel.

■ OCTOBER

Oct 4: Feast Day of San Francisco de Asis. Maya villages near Mérida (Conkal, Hocaba, Pueblo, Telchac Puerto and Uman) celebrate a week-long fiesta that ends on this day.

2nd weekend Oct: Isla Mujeres Music Festival. An eclectic array of talented musicians rock the island.

Oct 12: Columbus Day. Legal holiday.

Oct 18-28: A fiesta honoring **El Cristo de Stilpech** features a procession with the image of Christ carried on foot from Stilpech to Izamal. Religious services, fireworks and a grand fiesta on the 25th. Spirited *jaranas* (regional folk) dances are featured.

Oct 31: All Souls' Eve. Beginning of an eight-day memorial observance. Flowers and candles are placed on graves of relatives. Boo!

Last week Oct-first week Nov: Orange Festival in Oxkutzcab, Yucatán.

Gift shop skeletons.

■ NOVEMBER

Nov 1-2: All Souls' Day/All Saint's Day/ Day of the Dead. Graveside and church ceremonies honor the memory of departed loved ones. Instead of a somber occasion, the Day of the Dead is a happy celebration with a fiesta atmosphere highlighted by sugar skulls and candy skeletons. A family meal is eaten at the gravesites and favorite food is left for the departed souls. A haunting experience.

1st week Nov: X'matkuil Fair is hosted at a former henequen hacienda eight kms (five miles) north of Mérida. Local arts and crafts, bullfights, rodeo competitions and lots of food.

Nov 20: Día de la Revolucíon commemorates the Revolution of 1910.

End of Nov/beginning of Dec: Expo-Cancún is a big city fair held outdoors near the bullring downtown. Arts and crafts exhibits and folk dancing.

■ DECEMBER

Dec 4-8: A fair occurs in Campeche and Champotón.

Dec 8: Feast of the Immaculate Conception. Festivities are held in many locations in the Yucatán, but there's a particularly notable fiesta in Izamal. In Celestún and Champotón boat processions carry a statue of the Virgin Mary in the lead. Champotón also features a waterskiing show and other aquatic events and a fair.

Dec 12: Our Lady of Guadalupe. Mexico's patron saint and a big holiday. All over the Yucatán young people run or bicycle from town to town with a torch in her honor. They're everywhere on the roads, so drive carefully. Children begin their off-key Christmas caroling carrying a decorated tree of ribbons and plastic flowers. Contributions are graciously accepted.

Dec 15: International Marathon is run in Cancún. Begun in 1996.

Dec 16-24: The Mexican custom of *Posadas*, celebrated by parties and restaurant meals with friends, family and co-workers. There are processions and children break piñatas. Christmas Eve is an important family night.

Dec 25: Christmas Day.

Dec 31: New Year's Eve. Partytime. In the Yucatán look for stuffed dummy people on porches and roofs, holding bottles of booze. These are *burrachos*, drunks celebrating a new year.

■ Food & Drink

The Yucatán also differs from the rest of Mexico in its food. Two types of *comidas tipicas*, typical food specialties, are fish or meat flavored with a spicy (but not hot) anchiote paste; and meats, marinated in a rich sauce, then steam-baked in earthen pits.

Despite their habañero pepper, 20 times hotter than the jalapeño of northern Mexico, Yucatecans prefer their heat on the side, rather than cooked into the food. Always ask if the dish of salsa offered contains habañero before scooping some up on a chip. Otherwise you'll be drinking liquids and eating tortillas till the cows come home.

Regional Specialties

Each Yucatecan state has its own culinary claim to fame – as well as the Mexican stand-by of tacos and burritos. Thinly sliced pork, marinated in sour orange and vinegar, then grilled and served topped by pickled onion, is **poc chuc**, a dish made famous by Los Almendros restaurants. **Sopa de limon** is a chicken soup with tortillas and a squeeze of lime juice; **cochinita pibil** and **pollo pibil** are flaky, tender pieces of pork or chicken, spiced and marinated in a rich sauce and baked in banana leaves; and anything called "a la Yucateca" is spiced in a wonderful anchiote paste and grilled. Fish done that way is called **tikin-xic** (Tick-IN-shick).

Valladolid has its own sausages, called *longanizas*; Campeche invented fresh shrimp cocktails; and Mérida has incorporated Lebanese cooking into its cuisine. In addition, Cancún boasts some of the best international cooking around. If you see **barbacoa** on the menu, it is lamb prepared like pibil (above).

One thing you may want to remember is that waiters in the hinterlands consider it rude to offer you your bill before you ask for it, so be sure to say *la cuenta, por favor,* when you're close to being finished. Also realize that it sometimes seems that your service varies depending on how much of a hurry you're in – the more hurry, the more wait.

A *comida corrida* is a fixed price complete meal that includes everything but your drink. It's low priced and not necessarily the best dish on the menu, but generally tasty and filling. Another dish that fills you up without costing much is *molletes*, grilled open-faced rolls with refried beans and melted cheese. The soups in Mexico are very flavorful and they seem to go well with the warm climate.

Yucatecan Recipes

■ Ceviche (SAY-beach-AY)
Ingredients: 2 cups of assorted seafood, 2 seeded jalapeño peppers (fresh), 2 cloves of garlic, sea salt to taste.

Mexican fishermen often prepare this pleasurable snack at the water's edge from their fresh catch. It's usually eaten with crackers, together with some tequila or beer. A variety of seafood can be used to make ceviche, so each batch is unique. Start with a small amount at first, adapting the proportions of ingredients.

Cut skinned and boned raw fish plus shrimp, oysters, clams (whatever you have available) into tiny bite-size pieces until you have about two cups' worth. Place in a ceramic bowl and cover with the juice of two limes. Add sea salt to taste. Stir and set aside.

Chop very finely all other ingredients and add them to the seafood. Marinate at least 10 minutes before serving, longer if you have the patience. Ceviche is customarily eaten with toothpicks.

Optional: a dash of bottled hot sauce, pepper, cilantro (dried or fresh), even oregano or parsley flakes can add an interesting flavor.

■ Pollo Pibil (Chicken Pibil)

Ingredients: 1 large chicken cut into serving-size pieces (leg, breast, etc.), 3 banana leaves (if not available, we used a "brown and serve" bag with great success; aluminum foil can also be substituted), 1 cup of vinegar, 1 cup of bitter orange juice, 1 white onion (medium-size, roasted), 4 garlic cloves, 8 black peppercorns, 10 grams achiote (hard to find in powdered form in many parts of the US; substitute "Sazon" seasoning with achiote packaged by Goya Foods, available in most supermarkets), 1 cup oil, salt to taste.

Blend roasted onion, crushed garlic cloves, peppercorns and orange juice. Pour mixture into bowl together with the oil and achiote, previously dissolved in vinegar. Marinate the chicken pieces in the mixture for 10 minutes. Wrap them in a bed of banana leaves (or substitute). Bake in a medium oven (375°) for 30 minutes or until steam escapes when bundles are pierced. Usually served topped with pickled red onions. Makes about six servings.

■ Pampano en Verde (Pompano in Green Sauce)

Ingredients: 6 large pompano fish fillets; 9 garlic cloves; 2 tomatoes; 1 onion; 2 chiles xcatic – not generally available in the US (substitute 2 Italian peppers, seeded and cut into thick strips); 1 cup of vinegar; oil; small bunch parsley; juice of 3 or 4 lemons; peppercorns; oregano; cumin; salt to taste.

Blend the parsley, oregano, peppercorns, cumin, 6 crushed garlic cloves, vinegar and salt. Pour lemon juice over the fish fillets and marinate them in the blended sauce. Finely chop the remaining garlic cloves, slice the onion and tomatoes. Cook the fish in a frying pan, adding the chopped garlic cloves, tomatoes and onions, together with the chiles. Allow this to simmer slowly, adding water if necessary, until fish is flaky. Makes six servings.

■ Camarones de Coco (Coconut Shrimp)

Ingredients: 24 peeled shrimp, deveined, with tails on; juice of one lime; salt; 1½ cups crushed cornflakes; sweetened desiccated coconut; oil for frying; 3 whole coconuts, cut in half. For the paste, 200 grams of flour; 2 eggs; milk. For compote, 3 sour apples, peeled and cubed; ½ cup sugar; 1 stick cinnamon.

Apple compote: Cook apples with the sugar, cinnamon and a small amount of water until soft and thick. Remove the stick.

Paste: Mix the eggs and flour, adding only enough milk to make a thick sauce.

Cut open the backs of the shrimp ¾ of the way, steep them for a few seconds in the lime juice, drain and place in paste. Mix coconut and cornfalkes together and coat shrimp. Fry them in hot oil, taking care not to burn. Drain. Fill the coconut shell with compote and place the shrimp around it. Serves six. This is a specialty of Restaurante La Pigua (see page 410).

Drinks

 Favorite alcoholic drinks (*bebidas*) in the nation include margaritas and tequila. And nothing beats Mexican tequila. Try Don Julio Reposado or Herradura Reposado. Those who appreciate complex tastes should try "añejo" – aged tequila. It's very much like a single malt.

You can buy Heineken or American beer in Cancún, but why would you? Mexico's beers are excellent. **Sol, Dos Equis** and **Corona** brands may be familiar to you, but **Superior** and **Victoria** are very good Mexican beers. Two great local brews from Mérida are **Montejo** (our all-time favorite) and **Leon Negra**, a dark amber brew. A refreshing light-alcohol drink is **chelada**, a glass of limeade with a little beer added.

> **NOTE:** Tourists and residents alike should appreciate the connection between trouble and alcohol. Stay out of situations where you or other people drink too much; Mexico is not the place to lose control.

Coca-Cola and **Pepsi** are ubiquitous, of course, but other flavors in Mexico's soda (*refrescos*) line-up include orange, grapefruit and apple. *Licuados,* fresh fruit juice drinks, are available plain or mixed with milk. Our favorite is *Horchata*, a refreshingly delicious drink made from rice and milk and flavored with cinnamon and cane sugar. Or try *Jamaica* (ha-MY-ka), a wonderful red fruit drink made from flowers.

■ Shopping & Bargaining

There are plenty of designer clothes and gift stores in the large shopping malls of the Hotel Zone. Prices are lower, but sales pressure is higher in downtown Cancún, where indoor markets are located on Av. Tulum.

Haggling & Hassling

"Señora, Señor, where are you from?" "Like to look at some blankets?" "Best price, cheaper than Kmart," vendors call out to entice you into shopping at their stalls. This constant come-on is a source of irritation to those more accustomed to searching for sales help at home. In Cancún, you will never be left alone.

It may help if you realize just how hard things are economically for people in Mexico. Most of the vendors can't afford to stock the stalls they sell from, so most have their goods on consignment, which can be tough, especially in a country where the wage averages only US $25 per week and *gringo* dollars can mean the difference between just being poor and abject poverty. And with hundreds of competing places to shop, perhaps you could learn to be more tolerant of the high pressure and accept it gracefully as part of the shopping ritual. Usually a firm, "no, gracias" discourages further patter.

We're less inclined to be hard bargainers because much of what we buy is already cheaper than it would be at home. A seasoned negotiator offers about half of what's asked and settles for a price somewhere in between. We still bargain in the markets and even at hotels, but our realization of the economic inequities between most tourists and the average worker in the Yucatán tempers our desire to bicker for a quarter of an hour just to save a dollar. But we never allow vendors or taxi drivers to cheat us. Always shop around or ask the cost first – a good habit anywhere.

Local Goods

What we do buy in the Yucatán are things not readily available at home. We'll buy some ground chili powder, anchiote paste and a bottle of honey on every trip. There are also unique gift items we can't pass up.

Silver and gold jewelry are cheaper in Mexico so we always look for the unusual. Large **hammocks**, hand woven of string, are the traditional bed, couch and crib in the Yucatán. Made of nylon, cotton, silk or sisal, mostly in the state of Yucatán, they are extremely comfortable once you get used to sleeping in them. In Campeche, hand-crafted **wooden model ships** are featured in a great arts and crafts store in the Centro. Chetumal has an artisans' shop with carvings and crafts that combine Maya and Caribbean influences from Belize. **Pottery** is always a good bet (the Maya were known for their skills). **Tree of Life candelabras**, made in central Mexico, are elaborate and beautiful. Frequently used at Christmas, they depict the fall of Adam and Eve and are decorated with a snake, angels, leaves and flowers in bright colors. Also check out hand-painted **lacquerware** and **woven baskets**.

Once you leave Cancún you will see Maya women dressed in their traditional white cotton shift dresses called *huipiles* (WE-peels). They're colorfully embroidered around a square neckline and hem. A white cotton lace-trimmed underskirt (*ternos*) peeks out demurely below the hemline. The embroidery on the huipiles of Quintana Roo is geometric and abstract, while in the Yucatán it is done in cross-stitched floral. Silk or cotton shawls (*rebozos*) are also part of the traditional dress.

Men's business dress includes short-sleeved embroidered and pleated light shirts, called *guayaberas* (guy-ya-BEAras), that are worn outside the pants. This traditional shirt is common throughout Hispanic America, where it's generally too warm to wear ties or jackets. They usually come in pastel colors and white. A good place to buy these is in the *mercados* and stores in Valladolid and Mérida. There are several shops in Mérida where you can also have them made to your size.

Panama hats are made in the state of Campeche from the fibers of the jipijapa palm. They offer good protection against the strong Yucatecan sun and their fibers breathe, allowing the air to keep your head cool. Types of fiber, closeness of weave and suppleness determine the quality. The best ones are *fino*, a fine weave of thin palm fibers. The middle and fine grades are durable, pliable hats that, once flattened, tightly rolled and stuffed in a suitcase, can be ready to wear again with a sprinkle of water. If you're not going to Campeche, street vendors and shops in Mérida will be happy to sell you one. Buy the best you can afford for both comfort and long life.

■ Money Matters

The Mexican money is the **peso**, sometimes called the new peso after a drastic devaluation late in 1994. It floats against the dollar (the more pesos per dollar, the better the rate of exchange for you). Throughout Mexico, most prices are quoted in pesos (written with "$" signs), but make sure before you buy. A careless Mexican businessman took one of the glamorous suites in Casa Turquesa in Cancún thinking that the 3,200 price was in pesos (when it was eight pesos to the dollar). The next day he was presented with a $24,000 bill – US $3,200. Good morning, Señor!

Credit Cards

Don't count on using credit cards anywhere but in the cities, and even then only in the larger establishments. In some cases, a surcharge is added to your bill to cover an additional fee Mexican banks tag on to transactions. Before you go, inform your credit card company that you'll be in Mexico. That will prevent them from denying purchases for fear your card has been stolen.

Credit Card Contacts	
American Express	☎ 800/502-0600
MasterCard	☎ 880/247-4623
Visa	☎ 410/581-9994

Traveler's Checks

Banks exchange cash or traveler's checks, usually without commission, during limited hours everywhere but in the smallest towns. They require a passport as ID. In Cancún and tourist destinations, such as Playa del Carmen, exchange booths will change cash or traveler's checks at a slightly lower rate than banks, but they are open longer hours and offer convenience. You'll need a copy of your passport, although sometimes another ID, such as a photo driver's license, will do.

Shop around because the rates vary between change booths and even banks – and they change daily. Ask about the rate before you commit. The worst place to convert money is your hotel, where the rate is generally lower than anywhere else. The change booths with the best rates in Cancún are downtown, as opposed to the Hotel Zone, and of those, the best rates are often found at the two on the south side of Av. Cobá, before you get to Av. Tulum, near the Plaza America. There are several banks downtown and in the shopping centers.

ATMs

Be sure to tell your bank that you'll be in Mexico. That way they'll not be suspicious of any overseas use and will approve your bank card for ATM withdrawals. Most larger cities have ATMs in shopping malls and banks. Any credit card charges or cash withdrawals go through at the official exchange rate, so we prefer them over traveler's checks.

■ Safety & Crime

 In the many times we've been to the Yucatán we've rarely had a problem and are completely comfortable traveling everywhere there. But because it's a new environment, be aware of the possibility of danger. Safe traveling involves basic common sense. Inform yourself about where you're going and what to expect.

"Pedestrian Beware" seems to be the unofficial slogan when it comes to walking on the streets and sidewalks of Mexico. Cancún's Hotel Zone is an exception, of course, but elsewhere potholes, broken curbs and head-bashing sidewalk awnings are the norm. Be careful too, climbing around the thousand-year-old Maya ruins. Don't be embarrassed to use your hands or the rope aid and go slowly. Always think safety first. Be sure to wear good non-slip sandals or walking shoes and carry a flashlight after dark. Be aware of your surroundings. As Carl Franz, another Mexico aficionado, put it: "Expect the unexpected, underfoot, overhead, from ahead or behind."

Ever wake up in the middle of the night and not know which hotel you are in or where the bathroom is located? Imagine if there were a **fire**. As any frequent traveler should do – at home or abroad – make sure you familiarize yourself with the emergency exits and escape routes at your hotels.

Besides charging too much for the drinks in the Hotel Zone restaurants, crime in the Yucatán is mostly limited to **pickpocketing** or lifting of things left unattended or in an unlocked automobile. Simple precautions lessen your chances of being victimized. Even if you are a victim, you can make sure your vacation is not completely ruined. Carry only enough money with you to cover expenses for the day and leave the rest with your valuables in the hotel's safe. Leave your expensive watch and gold jewelry home.

A good defense against street crime – as well as getting separated on the beach or in the woods – may be wearing a referee's whistle on one of those popular neck lariats. A loud whistle should scare away petty criminals.

It's rare that valuables or cash left in your hotel room are stolen, but it does happen. If your hotel offers a **lock box safe** it's worth using. Just don't lose the key, which can cost US $50 to replace. Keep traveler's check numbers separate from the checks in case the latter are lost or stolen. We've become addicted to fanny packs as a relatively secure way to carry a wallet. They're difficult to pickpocket and, in addition, relieve the pain of sitting with a lumpy wallet in the back of your pants.

We once fell prey to the old "drop some coins in front of a naive tourist so they watch – or even help – you pick them up while your accomplice nicks their camera" routine. Though we've never had another instance and have returned several times, we were suckers for that one in a crowded *mercado* a few years ago. Be aware of getting bumped or distracted by anything unusual. If you have a camera, keep your camera bag closed and secured between pictures.

For Women Travelers

It's not a secret that women traveling alone, or even together, have special considerations and concerns. We know of no major problems for female travelers anywhere in the Yucatán, but apply the same precautions you might take when going out for an evening at home.

Women are most often vulnerable when they have been drinking. This is especially true during Spring Break when a disturbing number of "date rapes" and sexual attacks occur.

One of the not-so-good things about Mexican culture is **machismo**. Women may have doors opened for them, seats offered and, in general, be put on a pedestal. Then again, attractive young women are also treated to little sounds, low whistles or veiled propositions in public. The good thing is that it happens much less in Cancún than in the rest of Mexico and even less in rural Yucatán. It should not be a big problem to you, even if you're traveling alone. However, you might handle it the way Mexican women do by avoiding eye contact on the street, ignoring the occasional harmless strutting, and by walking or sitting with other women. Despite limited opportunities in Mexico's male-oriented coporate economy, more and more small businesses are women-owned, especially in the hospitality and service industry. A high percentage of the hotels and restaurants we reviewed are owned or managed by women (a female owner is a *dueña*, "dwAYN-ya").

Bribes & Scams

Although we're giving this section much coverage because people worry about it, problems involving bribes or being scammed happen infrequently in the Yucatán. When something does happen it's annoying, but seldom serious. If something should happen to you, try not to let it spoil your vacation.

Tipping taken to its extreme in Mexico is the ***mordida***, a small bribe paid to an official to "expedite" matters. Tourists rarely encounter the "bite," as it translates, because they seldom have to deal with Mexican authorities. There is no need, for example, to bribe anyone at the *migracíon* office to extend your tourist card.

The most common instances of *mordida* involve driving and the police. When you're stopped for a minor traffic violation, as we were once in Mérida and once in Chetumal (both times for driving the wrong way on an unmarked one-way street), you can expect a stern lecture and perhaps a fine. Don't be cowed or intimidated and be sure to maintain a respectful attitude. Wait to hear the policeman's lecture before you apologize for your honest mistake. If you're not sure, make him explain exactly what it is he thinks you've done wrong.

In Chetumal the policeman gave us an on-the-spot lecture about paying attention to signs that weren't there and the need to be law-abiding tourists. After carefully explaining all the laws in great detail, he let us go. The two policemen in Mérida who stopped us one Easter Sunday were not as accommodating. We had turned right, realized it was a one-way and immediately made a U-turn. Not fast enough. The policeman signalled us over and got out of his car when we parked. We waited patiently through a lecture about the severity of the transgression until the subject of a fine came up. When it did, it came with an invitation to go to the stationhouse. It was a cue to say something like "Officer, we're on our way to (wherever) so would it be possible for you to pay our fine for us?" (Usually about US $5.) It's the fastest and easiest way to handle things and it's even quasi-acceptable.

Policemen must know what terror it strikes in the heart of tourists to think they have to go to a stationhouse to resolve such a simple matter. If you're adamant about not having done anything wrong, you can agree to follow him there, at which point he may backtrack and let you go with a warning. Always allow him to save face – this is not a one-upsmanship contest you need to win. No matter which course you choose, you can chalk the experience up to a complete appreciation of the idiosyncrasies of travel in Mexico.

An alternative angle is to feign total ignorance of even the most obvious words in the Spanish language. Never be impolite or snicker or you'll regret it. An attentive face that struggles to understand the complete depth of all your wrongdoings, as related in your lecture, followed by a *"lo siento pero no entiendo"* (I'm sorry, I don't understand) may exasperate the officer until he finally gives up in disgust at your ignorance. This is a delicate game and you don't want to aggravate or insult him. If you're somewhat fluent in Spanish you could try not quite getting his point. We told the officer a long involved story about another policeman who directed us up that wrong way in our effort to find a store to buy flowers to put on the grave of Felipe Carrillo, a national hero. We were going the wrong way? Which way should we go? Was he now directing us on the correct route? Where was the graveyard that everyone told us was so beautiful in his wonderful city?

If the officer is on foot and waves you over for something minor you could always develop instant cataracts and keep driving. Few foot patrolmen have radios to call ahead so high-tailing it out of there avoids the inconvenience of a traffic stop. Good luck. Don't try that in a crowded area like Mérida's *mercado* where the traffic crawls and the policeman's whistle alerts the cop on the next corner. Nor at any of the numerous Army or agricultural checkpoints along the highway or side roads. You're usually waved through these stops, although you may also be questioned and asked to open your trunk. The Army is making an effort to control any drug or arms smuggling that may pass through the Yucatán's many miles of deserted coastline. If you try to outrun an Army checkpoint there's a soldier down the road in a sand bag foxhole who might shoot you. In rural areas you may see an open truck on the side of the road filled with soldiers dozing against their weapons. Don't worry. Besides drug and arms eradication, this is Mexico's way of reassuring tourists that they are safe and secure.

Americans want to be liked – it's part of their psychological make up. Unless you're a paranoid schizophrenic, chances are you travel, as we do, in wide-eyed wonder and complete openness. It brings out the best in us as well as the people we meet. But there's always the one person who looks at your innocence and says, "sucker." The only time anyone ever tried to take advantage

Two little Maya girls

Hacienda Uayamon, outbuilding (see page 103)

of us with a "scam" (other than the distraction ploy used to lift our camera) was at two gasoline stations. Considering the number of times we've been in the Yucatán, that's not a bad average.

The simplest "fill 'er up" scam happened to us on the western outskirts of Valladolid, where the city's one-way street continues as Highway 180. At the Pemex on the left heading west, several boys stood in front of the pump as we pulled up. As the overly attentive attendant quickly pushed the nozzle into our tank, two boys came to our windows with questions about how we liked Mexico and so forth. We chatted away until it came time to pay the bill, which was twice what it should have cost. The scam works by having someone screen your view of the pump to keep you from noticing that it was not cleared back to zero before pumping your gas. The solution? Make sure you have a clear view of the pump before saying how much gas you want. Especially effective is to step out of the car and look. If in doubt, wave him away as if you don't want gas, just directions. If you want to avoid this particular station there's another Pemex in town. Head east, and after 180 becomes Calle 41, it's on your left. If you're heading west on Calle 39 toward Chichén, look for the Pemex sign on the side of a building with a driveway on your left, near the Super Maz shopping center. Of course, last time we filled up at that one, the attendant tried to short-change us. Just our luck.

It's hard to avoid the gas station on the Chetumal-Escárcega highway, near Xpujil (sometimes spelled Xpuhil), just east of the Calakmul biosphere's border. It's a long run between cities and most cars need to fill up here (although there is a new Pemex station between Xpujil and Escarcega at Km 51, west of Laguna Silvituc). The attendants here tried to overcharge us when they still had the old fashioned pumps that showed only liters. We got out of the car to make sure the pump was cleared and were engaged in a friendly conversation with two other men and the attendant. When the tank was full the attendant showed us the price on his hand-held calculator, about twice what it should have been.

Since we knew we needed half a tank in our Bug, about 20 liters, the 25 liters the pump showed was probably correct. So we took out our own calculator and punched in the pump's 25 liters, then multiplied that by the cost per liter we had paid in Chetumal. "There must be something wrong with your calculator, here's what it should be," we told him. Realizing we weren't going to fall for his sleight of hand he responded: "Gasoline is more expensive this far from the city." It was, but only by a peso or so, so we agreed on our price. Later we met a Canadian couple who had felt intimidated by the men hovering around them as they discussed the high price. They paid it without arguing. Before filling up anywhere, know how many liters your car should take. And don't feel intimidated!

Now that all Pemex stations are using new pumps that show both liters and price, the Xpujil bandits have developed a new method of cheating. Reader

Peter Helby from Denmark wrote to us about his experience: "As you suggested, I was careful to notice that the pump started from zero. I kept an eye on it to see that it was actually running and that the pesos and liter figures were roughly progressing as they should be. Then the attendant started to involve me in friendly chatting. A little later two or three of his colleagues also came along, starting to joke. They had some huge bugs that they wanted to show me, put in my hand, etc... Pretty nice ploy for diverting attention. I was quite relaxed and joined a bit in their game, as I could not see what might go wrong. Suddenly the pump stopped. Before I could see the result, it was set back to zero, and run up a liter or two again. So even with the modernized equipment, we were back in the type of situation you describe, where it is impossible to see what you should actually pay. The attendant wanted 160 pesos. I negotiated it down to 120. The last number I remembered seeing on the pump was 85 pesos."

It's a game now between *Adventure Guide* readers and those artful attendants, so be sure not to let them win. We're counting on you!

Last but not least, pay attention to those decimal places when you sign a charge slip.

■ Health & Happiness

 The first time we came back from Yucatán, we extolled the virtues of Cancún to a friend who was getting married. "Did you get sick?" he worried. "No, not at all," we replied honestly. "We spent two weeks wandering around the interior, eating what and where we pleased. The only precaution we took was to drink *agua mineral* or *agua purificada*." Our ever-cautious honeymooning friends Rich and Gail never left the Hotel Zone, drank only bottled water and ate only in the fancy restaurant in their hotel. Regardless of their precautions, both of them got sick with *tourista*, a digestive disorder caused by bacteria foreign to your system. Since that time Cancún and all the major cities in the Yucatán have improved their purified drinking water system, so tap water should not cause problems. Most ice in restaurants is made from purified water (*agua purificada*), but if you're in doubt, ask for your drink *sin hielo* (without ice).

We eventually learned, firsthand, that drinking bottled water does not offer fail-safe prevention. Nothing does. Some medical sources even suggest *tourista* can be caused by a combination of other factors. Its symptoms, which mimic salmonella poisoning, may include any or all the following: nausea, diarrhea, vomiting, stomach cramps and low-grade fever. Purists suggest waiting it out for three or four days, but that's hardly realistic if you've got only a week's vacation and a gazillion things to do. So here's our tried and true treatment.

If we're in a budget hotel, the first thing we do when we start feeling bad (and it comes on very quickly) is upgrade to a hotel with air-conditioning – maybe even cable TV – and a comfortable bed. A couple of aspirin and plenty of sleep is called for. If we suffer frequent diarrhea and stomach cramps, we take the recommended dose of Imodium AD. Pepto Bismol relieves the symptoms as well, but takes longer. It's necessary to drink plenty of bottled water or Coca-Cola with lime or, in severe cases, rehydration fluids such as Pedialyte, available at a local drugstore. We often also drink *manzanilla* (chamomile) tea, with honey, a helpful folk remedy. Then we crank up the air-conditioner, curl up and go to sleep. We repeat the Immodium if the diarrhea returns. In about 24 hours we're usually feeling well enough to get back out and enjoy the sunshine. But you may still feel a little weak, so take it easy. For a few days you may also experience mild stomach cramps after eating. Eat light and cut out liquor and hot spices.

The US Public Health Service does not recommend taking any prophylactic medicines before becoming ill, but there are other ways to aid in prevention. Besides drinking bottled water, use it when you clean your teeth. Peel fruit before eating and avoid salads outside large towns (or at least ask if it was washed in purified water). In addition, we theorize that much of the

Girl washing her hands in the mercado.

bacteria that gives problems can be eliminated with frequent hand washings. The sensory delights of the Yucatán include touching new things, so a good hand scrub every chance you get is a good idea. You should have a fair number of chances because many restaurants offer a sink right in the dining room and it's considered polite to wash before eating. Alternatively, use the antiseptic towelettes we suggest you pack or consider taking along one of the new anti-bacterial sanitizing liquids, such as Purell, available in the US.

One tends to be preoccupied with one's bowels in Mexico, with entire conversations revolving around the subject. That's because the other side of the coin is "**travelers constipation**." Our "killer" cure is plenty of fresh fruit in our diet and tons of liquid.

If you should have a severe medical problem, most hotels will arrange for an English-speaking doctor to make a house call. Mexico's doctors are well trained. If you're really sick, don't wait until you get home to have someone look at you. Go to a hospital, rather than a private *clinica*, for treatment. Malaria and cholera are extremely rare in the Yucatán, but they're not to be fooled with. Use mosquito repellent to aid in malaria prevention. If you're traveling on to more remote sections of Central America, such as Guatemala,

Two girls on a pay phone in Playa del Carmen.

El Salvador or Honduras, a vaccination against hepatitis A is recommended. (A shot of immune globulin gives temporary protection.) Hepatitis A is thought to be contracted through contaminated water. A doctor friend of ours, who has vacationed in Mexico for the past 20 years, recommends a hepatitis vaccine for all travelers regardless of where they go: England, France, or Mexico.

You might check with your **medical insurance** company to see if they cover expenses outside of the country. Most do, but very few will pay for emergency medical evacuations, sometimes called air ambulances. See a list of companies that provide travel medical insurance at www.travel.state.gov/medical.html.

■ Telephones

Phone service in Mexico has improved a great deal in the last few years, but it can still be quite confusing. Here are some guidelines that should help:

- To call Mexico from the US, dial 011 for an international line, then 52 for the country code, then the 10-digit number. We list the area code first, separated from the phone number by a slash (/).
- To phone numbers in another area code within Mexico (such as to Cancún from Playa), dial 01, then the 10-digit number.
- To phone the US or Canada from Mexico, dial 001 and then the area code and number.
- To call the US or Canada from Mexico collect or to charge to an ATT card, dial 090 for an international operator.
- To call anywhere else in the world, dial 00 plus the country code and number.

If you phone from your hotel, make sure the connection charges are not exorbitant; otherwise use a phone company calling card or dial **Telmex** at ☎ 01-800/728-4647. Small towns offer a central location for telephone service called a Larga Distancia. These offices are also good for local calls within the Yucatán if you want to pay cash.

Public telephones marked "**Ladatel**" can also be used to call the States directly. Charge your call to your phone card or use a Ladatel phone card. These prepaid cards are available from any of the many vendors that display the blue and yellow Ladatel logo. They're commonly sold in values of 30, 50 and 100 pesos. With a card, you can direct dial or reach an overseas operator. While it may be inconvenient to stand at a phone box, the Ladatel card offers a good rate for calls overseas (50¢ per minute).

Also look for **Ladafon** cards, which have a code to punch in. Their per-minute rates, especially to the US, are a little lower than Latadel's.

To reach **AT&T Direct Service**, you can dial either ☎ 001/800/288-2872 or 001/800/462-4240. **MCI WorldPhone** says to dial ☎ 001/800/674-7000. **Sprint International** is at ☎ 001/800/877-8000. Good luck!

PRESS *I NOW!

If you can avoid it, do not place your call home on phones that tell you to punch *01, or 95, to charge your call to a major credit card. These phones are conveniently located everywhere in Cancún and charges are upwards of US $25 per minute! It's a rip-off aimed at those who don't have major phone company cards. Get a Ladatel card!

Prepaid calling cards, sold in stores, are also a good cheap way to make calls within Mexico. Dial 01 before the area code to call long distance within Mexico.

On various trips we took our US cell phone, with an overseas roaming rate of US $1.50, but only the AT&T phone worked outside of the major cities, as they have a relationship with Telemex. On our latest trip we bought a prepaid Telcel phone (available at many stores or at the Telcel office on Av. Tulum next to the Hotel Calinda America) for US $66 with $300 pesos worth of minutes. Replace the fast-disappearing minutes (domestic calls are 5 pesos per minute) by buying prepaid cards and putting the coded numbers in. The good thing about them is the generally good coverage (all over Mexico) and that you don't pay for incoming calls, making it useful as an emergency phone for your relatives overseas to get in touch. Taxi drivers are known to buy used cell phones for approximately US $20.

■ Tipping & Begging

% Many restaurants add a 10% tip (*propina*) to your bill along with the tax. If you have good service, don't hesitate to leave another 5-10%. Tips are often the major source of income for service workers, as their salaries are well below North American standards and sometimes even below Mexican standards. Tipping is customary in situations where a service is given; otherwise it's at your discretion. We drove to a remote Maya village to find a ruined hacienda. When we stopped to ask directions of a man on a bicycle, he insisted on leading us there (although it was only one block more). Despite telling him we didn't need a guide, he led – or was it followed? – us around and provided details about the history and family that we would never have known. We tipped him US $2. In Campeche, when we parked, men would come out from the shade of a tree and wash our car. It wasn't necessary to have our rental car washed, although it got dusty every day, but it provided them with meager employment so we paid US $2 each time. Tip rates for maid service in hotel rooms should also be about US $2 per day. Taxi drivers don't usually get tipped unless they perform a special service.

When you buy things in larger stores that charge a sales tax for convenience they sometimes round up or down any fractions of a peso. Children (12 years or older) bag your groceries or purchases and it's customary to tip them a peso plus any fractions that come as change.

If you drive in the Yucatán, you'll see men with rags near every parking area or lot. They'll direct you into your space, signal you when you're backing out – sometimes conveniently blocking traffic for you – and reasonably guard the cars in their territory. A tip is called for.

In general, it's probably worth bringing a big stash of dollar bills and an understanding attitude just for gratuities. That way, if you're at all confused over the value of pesos or don't have the right change, a dollar or two is always handy and very welcome.

Begging is a problem that vexes us in New York as well as in Mexico. A number of old Maya women and men will beg on the street in the larger cities of the interior, especially on Sundays at the churches. They may have obvious infirmities, but many are just old and somehow out of the traditional Maya family care. Sometimes we give, sometimes we don't.

In Valladolid, a sign cautions tourists not to tolerate children begging. Sometimes they ask to "watch your car," which they pronounce in English as "wash your car." Instead, refuse and encourage them to go to school. Valladolid seems to be the only town where this happens, but children selling handicrafts, such as hand-embroidered hankies, Barbie doll huipiles and woven friendship bracelets, are everywhere in the Yucatán. Some are up late at night working the outdoor restaurants. It's an unfortunate fact of life.

We try to make a habit of taking along small gifts and/or something to contribute to countries where we travel. We bought new and used baseball caps at flea markets and garage sales for 50¢ to US $2 and used them as additional "thank-yous" to our guides or anyone who was helpful to us. We also carried a big bag of pens and pencils that we gave out to children (we even stopped at a rural school and gave a supply to the teacher). Other easy-to-carry gifts are packets of seeds, especially vegetables, that you can give to adults in rural areas.

Being There

Poor Mexico, so far from God, so close to the United States.
~ Porfirio Diáz, 1830-1915

■ Handy Hints

Here's an assortment of hints and ideas – culled from years of trial-and-error experience and in no particular order – to make your travel easier, safer and more fun.

- We make much use of resealable plastic bags in which to carry or store things.
- Bring lots of single dollar bills for tipping.
- Don't bring much jewelry, and don't pack it in checked luggage. Why not wear one pair of earrings and buy a second and third pair in Mexico?
- We met an intrepid couple with backpacks who used plastic pull-tight seals, insuring that their bags couldn't be opened without cutting. They kept a supply and resealed the luggage after each packing. Now we do the same.
- If you're a water-lover and have packed light, consider taking a tube and face mask for snorkeling rather than paying US $6 rental each time you go. Better yet, you can buy a fairly good set at Chedraui store in downtown Cancún for about US $10.
- Lost documents can be a hassle, so make a photocopy of your tourist card in a hotel or copy shop as soon as you can and put it with your passport. A copy will help in replacing it if it's lost or stolen. If you haven't already, copy your passport and carry the photocopy, rather than the passport, with you. Leave your passport in the hotel safe.
- Colorful woven plastic mesh shopping bags, sold inexpensively in *mercados*, make a great carry-on bag for all those gifts you swore

you weren't going to bring back. You can reuse them to do grocery shopping at home.

■ Faucet handles are marked "C," meaning Caliente, which translates as Hot.

■ Bathrooms are usually marked *Caballeros* (Men) and *Damas* (Women).

■ We discovered the hard way that the plastic bucket next to the toilet in hotels is used for dirty toilet paper. The problem occurs in the countryside outside of the resort hotels, where the plumbing can't handle paper and could get blocked. The maid will empty and wash the bucket daily. This really takes a bit of getting used to.

■ Wrinkles in slacks, jackets and tops can sometimes be lessened by carefully folding and placing them under your mattress at night. Whenever you drop off laundry to be cleaned, be sure to specify that you want your whites and colors *separado*, washed separately.

■ Free refills of your coffee are uncommon in Mexico and not automatic when your cup is empty. Sanborn's is a notable exception. A drink in a bar or restaurant should be accompanied by *bocas* or *botanas*, appetizers or ceviche. These are sometimes not automatically given to *gringos*, so you might have to ask.

■ Find a skink (*iguanita*) in your room and find good luck. People-shy skinks eat mosquitos.

■ If you live in a cold-weather city such as Minneapolis, there may be some low-priced specials on charters or regular airlines to get you down to Mexico in the middle of winter. We met more Minnesotans in Cancún than there are in St. Paul. Ask your travel agent to watch out for you. Prices are lower in the off-season, that's obvious, but there's also a bit of a lull in Cancún and Cozumel in early January so there's more room to negotiate. It never hurts to ask for a discount or a promotional rate.

■ Hotels just a block off the waterfront are generally cheaper than those right on it. Because electricity is expensive, rooms with air-conditioners (*con clima*) frequently cost more. Try a night or two with a ceiling fan and see how you like it.

■ Bakeries (*panaderias*) are a good resource for inexpensive snacks or breakfasts and a great place to try new taste sensations. Many of the pastries and breads are dry, so get a coffee or tea somewhere to wash them down. Things to go are sold *para llevar* (para yea-bar) and if it's a soda or beer in a recyclable bottle you'll pay a little extra.

■ Free concerts are common on weekends and holidays in city parks and plazas. Special events abound. Stop in the tourist office at each new city and ask what's happening. Mérida, a cultural gem, has events nearly every night. Museums and archeological sights are free on Sundays for Mexicans, but foreigners have to pay admission. Many close on Mondays. All of the Maya sites have a fee to enter. How much depends on several factors, but Chichén is the area's most expensive. Flash photography is hardly ever allowed and tripods are also forbidden without a permit bought in advance from INAH (Instituto de Historia y Antropología). Contact the appropriate state's Tourism Office and they can arrange permission. All sites charge extra if you want to use a video camera.

■ It's a good idea to ask permission to photograph the Yucatán's indigenous people. More often than not, a smile or nod allows an absolutely perfect memory to be captured on your film. Although we rarely will pay for a photo (the Yucatecan Maya are not as demanding as those in Chiapas), sometimes we tip afterward. We also give out pens or a packet of seeds. If a person refuses permission, please respect his or her wishes.

■ Always count your change. It's good practice until you get used to the different monetary system and it prevents misunderstandings. A good way to know what a taxi should cost is to ask someone at your hotel, or check the front page in *Cancún Tips* magazine. Agree on a price before you drive off.

■ If you need some more time on your tourist card and you're in the south and not able to find Chetumal's obscure Immigration office, take a quick trip into Belize. When you return you automatically get a new 30-day tourist card – if you're lucky. You're supposed to be out of the country at least 72 hours in order to get a new card. To circumvent that, try to cross in a crowd and don't stand out. Wear a different hat or something on your return so they won't remember you later in the day. We made a mistake by crossing on a quiet Christmas Day and chatting up the officer. The friendly guy gave us our old expiring cards back when we returned. Ho, Ho, Ho.

■ Several of the hotels we mention are in fairly remote areas of the countryside, beyond telephone – and in some cases electric – lines. Most hotels have either cellular phones or at least shortwave radios in case of emergencies.

■ If a Mexican mentions Mexico, chances are they're speaking of the capital city (Districto Federal), not the country.

■ The term *gringo* is not derogatory.

■ In an elevator, "PB" means Planta Baja, the first floor in Mexico. What we think of as the second floor is considered the first floor and is usually marked "1."

- The crowded little VW combi, or *colectivo*, buses you see running around take passengers for a slightly higher price than regular buses. They can be flagged down anywhere, but it's hard to know if they're going your way. *Colectivos* cover some areas that are not touched on regular bus routes.

- If you're wandering the Yucatán, many hotels have storage lockers where you can leave your extra stuff rather than lugging it around. Even if they don't, they may be willing to hold it for you.

- A special edition of *The Miami Herald* is published for Mexico daily and many Cancún hotels also offer *USA Today*. Newsboys ply the morning restaurants on Isla Mujeres, Playa del Carmen, Cozumel and Cancún.

■ Just in Case

Embassies

If you lose your passport or have need of consular services such as lists of qualified medical doctors or *abogados* (lawyers), or you just need advice and empathy, you can turn to your embassy. You should know that the embassy won't, however, give you money, fly you home or get you out of jail.

The **Embassy of the United States** is in Mexico City, ☎ 555/211-0042. There is a US Consular Agency in Plaza Caracol, 3rd floor, in Cancún's Hotel Zone, ☎ 998/883-0272, and another in Mérida on Paseo Montejo near the Fiesta Americana Hotel, ☎ 999/925-5011.

The **Austrian Consulate** is downtown in Mexico City at #4 Calle Cantera, ☎ 998/884-7505.

Canadians can reach their embassy in Mexico City, Monday through Friday, from 9 am to 5 pm (closed for lunch from 1-2) at ☎ 555/724-7900. In Cancún there's a Canadian consul in the Plaza Caracol, 3rd floor, Monday-Friday, 9-5, ☎ 998/883-3360. For emergency help outside office hours, ☎ 800/706-2900.

Cancún's **French Consul**, located at the corner of Bonampak and Uxmal in Edificio la Marina, Suite 311, Mexico City, will see people only by appointment, ☎ 998/884-8848.

The **German** offices are open 9-2 every day, including Saturday, at 36 Punta Conoco, downtown, ☎ 998/884-1898.

The **British Consulate** in Cancún is in the Royal Sands, ☎ 998/881-0100. Off-hour emergencies can try calling ☎ 998/845-1398. Reach the **Embassy of the United Kingdom** in Mexico City by dialing ☎ 555/207-2569 between 9 am and 2 pm; in Mérida the consul can be reached at ☎ 999/921-6799.

Italy's busy Cancún consul is at 39 Alcatraces, ☎ 998/884-12-61, and the **Spanish** equivalent is at the Oasis on Kukulcán, ☎ 998/848-9918. **Switzer-**

land's bureaucrats are in the Venus Building, Av. Coba #2, ☎ 998/884-8486, ext 8013, and **Netherland's** consul shares space with Martinair at the airport, ☎ 998/886-0070. The **Japanese** have no consul in Cancún, but do have an Embassy in Mexico City at ☎ 555/511-0028.

Emergencies

All emergency services – police, fire, ambulance – can be reached by dialing 066, the equivalent of 911 in the US or 999 in England. Police emergencies are 060, while medical emergencies are 065.

Police in downtown Cancún are at ☎ 998/884-1913; the highway police are ☎ 998/884-1107. On Isla Mujeres, you can phone the police at ☎ 998/877-0458.

See each town's section for local police, emergency, and medical phone numbers.

The big hospital in Cancún is **Hospital Americano** (☎ 998/884-6133) on Av. Uxmal opposite the side of the Chedraui. Downtown, the private American-style medical centers are **Total Assist** (☎ 998/884-8082), next to Bancomer on Av. Tulum, and the large **Ameri-Med** (☎ 998/881-3434), next to Plaza Americas, Av. Bonhampak and Nichupté. In the Hotel Zone, the Ameri-Med office (☎ 998/883-0985) is next to La Boom's and the **American Medical Center** (☎ 998/883-1001, www.americanmedicalcenter.com), owned by an American doctor, is in Plaza Quetzal, across the the Presidente Hotel and next to a Dominos Pizza.

In Mérida, there is the **Hospital General O'Horan** (☎ 999/924-4111) or the **Instituto Médico Qurúgico del Sureste** (☎ 999/925-8164).

> *My traveling companions are ghosts and empty pockets.*
> ~ Paul Simon, *Graceland*

Arrivals & Departures

> *If we do not change our direction, we are likely to end up*
> *where we are headed.*
> ~ Chinese proverb

■ Arrivals

 Unless you're being picked up by the hotel, the preferred choices of transportation upon arrival in Cancún are either taxi or combi (*colectivo*) bus. One-way tickets for each are sold at several kiosks in the airport arrivals area. Taxis are the quicker of the two, and they are also the most comfortable and the most expensive. Combi buses cram eight people plus baggage and a driver into an air-conditioned van. If you're going downtown rather than to the Hotel Zone, you have time to relax. The combi works its way along the long, resort-lined beach before heading downtown. A one or two dollar tip for luggage is reasonable.

Buy your ticket in pesos; it's cheaper than the dollar rate. If you don't need to change any money, you can buy a ticket at either of the two kiosks before Customs. If you need to change some money, go through Customs and stop at the change booth there (which has a better exchange rate than the ones before Customs). You can then buy your transportation ticket outside the terminal at a third kiosk. You'll also pass car rental desks along the way.

The less common choice of transport directly to the downtown only is by public bus, which you can catch across the parking lot from the airport entrance next to the Budget Car Rental office. The trip runs about US $2. It's cheaper than a taxi and faster than a combi. There is direct service to the bus terminal downtown.

If you're on a charter flight, you'll probably arrive at the new South Terminal, which has the same transportation options. If you're taking the public bus into town, there is a free shuttle between terminals.

Going to Playa or Cozumel? The cost of getting there has gone down. You can buy a ticket at the kiosks for a new official bus service for about US $18. But if you walk out of the terminal past the car rental desks you'll find the desk for the **Riviera Express** bus; it costs only US $15 round-trip. Same road south, just not such fancy buses.

To get to Isla Mujeres from downtown, take any bus marked "Puerto Juárez" or "Punta Sam" north on Av. Tulum from in front of the Comercial Mexicana supermarket. It's a short ride on Av. Lopez Portillo to the ferries. Driving from the Hotel Zone, turn right on Av. Bonampak and turn right at the light. Otherwise, take one of the shuttle boats from Playa Linda in the Hotel Zone.

■ Departures

If transportation wasn't included as part of the hotel cost, you have to take a taxi from the Hotel Zone to the airport for departure. Or perhaps you can make a deal with a van driver at one of the hotels who pick up for the package vacation crowd. Taxi rides to the airport were around US $16 at writing. Agree on the fare before you leave the curb. Average taxi prices are printed in the large *Cancún Tips* magazine.

From downtown, you can take a taxi or the second-class public bus that runs passengers with luggage to the airport. The bus stops on Av. Tulum near the pedestrian crosswalk on the northern corner across from the bus station and south of the Chedraui in front of the Hotel Handall. As far as we know, it won't pick up passengers on Tulum between Avenidas Coba and Uxmal.

Hacienda Hotels

People don't see the writing on the wall
until their back is up against it.
~ Adlai Stevenson

The feudal hacienda (self-contained ranch) system flourished in the Yucatan like no other place in Mexico. First of all, the peninsula was considered remote from the rest of the country. The land was divvied up among the Conquistadors in the mid-1500s and then to the powerful families that came to the New World from Spain. Most haciendas began as cattle and horse ranches and later, when henequen proved so profitable, they became huge farms with processing plants on the grounds.

HOTEL PRICE CHART	
NOTE: Often, one shared bed in a room is cheaper than two. Prices based on cost per night, for two.	
[No $]	Less than US $20
$	US $20 - $40
$$	US $40 - $80
$$$	US $80 - $125

Maya workers lived and died on the hacienda land, a misfortunate built-in labor pool. Haciendas were little fiefdoms unto themselves with the owner's family ruling a strict racial, socio-economic class (*casta*) system. Some owners were so rich and powerful they even minted their own coins.

Regardless of whether their buildings have the Colonial, Moorish or Neoclassic architectural styles, haciendas generally follow the same layout. Virtually all of them situated their main house, *casco*, reserved for the landowner's family, next to the main well, *noria*. Each had a Catholic chapel for the family and often a second for the peons. All haciendas were given a patron saint and many used his name as part of theirs.

Most large haciendas had a store, plaza, corrals and an arched gate that proclaimed the hacienda's wealth and status. By the 1950s that wealth had completely dried up and only the richest families maintained their properties. With more than 360 haciendas around Mérida – in various states of restoration and ruin – haciendas are seeing new life as unique hotels. The former workers housing is often being restored as high-class private quarters for guests as "hacienda hotel fever" has struck the peninsula.

■ In the Yucatán

Mérida

Hacienda Katanchel *(Km 26, Route 180, US ☎ 888/882-9470, Mexico ☎ 999/923-4020, fax 923-4000, www.hacienda-katanchel.com, 39 rooms &*

Hacienda Katanchel peeks out from behind lush foliage.

suites, pool, restaurant, telephones). Turn into the white stone driveway under a red Colonial arch along the highway and slip back in time. The bright white lane slices through 740 acres of green forest as straight as an arrow for several kilometers, toward the sprawling red hacienda. When architect Aníbal Gonzalez and his wife, Mónica Hernández, bought the abandoned 350-year-old property, they discovered 33 workers' quarters that the jungle had almost reclaimed. The casitas follow the line of a narrow gauge train track that was used to transport henequen until the 1950s. These have now been converted into luxury "pavilion" suites, with individual mineral water pools and private gardens. Six suites are part of the original main hacienda. Today, the train track carries guests in a mule-drawn carriage to the former machine house – where the henequen was once worked – now a delightful common area, bar and dining room. The food here is strictly gourmet with a Yucatecan flair, and coffee or tea is discreetly delivered outside your door every morning. Guests are pampered in every way, right down to the exquisite bed linens. Nightlife in the countryside is all natural; the stars overhead are brilliant. Ironically, a pre-Classic third-century Maya observatory was also discovered on the grounds because "Katanchel" in Mayan means "under the Milky Way." $$$$$

Hacienda Xcanatún *(Km 12 Hwy. 261, US ☎ 877/278-8018, Canada 866/ 818-8342, Mexico 999/941-0213, www.xcanatun.com, 18 suites, 2 pools, spa, air, restaurant).* Reconstruction began in 1995 and was completed early in 2000, when Xcanatún, which means "stone house" in Mayan, held a much-heralded opening. Built in the mid-1700s, this elegant hacienda has been meticulously transformed into a beautiful luxury hotel only minutes from the convention center. The fully modernized suites are spacious, with high ceilings. Bathrooms are also grand. The hotel is about one kilometer east of the highway on 7½ acres of grounds, half of which are gardens. Their restaurant, Casa de Piedra, features fine French and Caribbean dining. $$$$$

Hacienda Temozón *(Km 182 Hwy. 261, US ☎ 888/625-5144, Europe 353-21-4279-200, Mexico 999/923-8089, fax 999/923-7963, www. haciendatemozon.com, 26 rooms & suites, restaurants, air, telephones, in-room safe, tennis).* President Clinton helped put the fabulous Hacienda Temozón on the map when he met there for a summit with Mexican President Ernesto Zedillo in February 1999. They signed several agreements, including a conservation defense fund to prevent disasters like the forest fires in Chiapas in 1998. The huge 150-foot swimming pool at the belle époque-style hacienda is situated so that it mirrors the hacienda from one end, Taj Mahal-style. Open gardens and a jogging/walking path are surrounded by a high red wall. Bicycles are available. Spacious rooms are decorated in 19th-century style with 21st-century taste; tile floors and pastel color walls. On the road from Mérida to Uxmal, Temozón is the epitome of country luxury. $$$$$

Hacienda Teya *(Km 12.5 Route 180, ☎ 999/928-1989 or 988-0800, www. haciendateya.com, restaurant open noon-6 pm, 6 rooms, honeymoon suite, air, gift shop).* Considered to be one of the finest restaurants around, the Hacienda San Ildefonso Teya (built 1683) will soon expand their accommodations, adding 20 more all-suite rooms with jacuzzis. For now, their six large, pleasant Colonial-style rooms usually house the many wedding parties that take place in their pretty chapel and on the beautiful grounds. The historic hacienda, just outside Mérida, has hosted Queen Sofia from Spain, the Duke and Duchess of Luxembourg, as well as First Lady Hillary Clinton. The dining room upstairs features watercolors of haciendas by Sergio Gual Aguilar, linen tablecloths, wooden chairs and tables. Large bright windows that overlook the garden have stained glass arched tops. Lunch time attracts business people, locals out for a special occasion, and tourists or expats searching for a fine meal. $$

Izamal

Hacienda San Antonio Chalante *(Sudzal, ☎/fax 988/954-0287, www. macanche.com, info@macanche.com, 9 rooms & suites, 2 pools, horseback riding, bar).* In 1997 the owner of Macan Ché, along with an archeologist partner, purchased this ruined hacienda in Sudzal and has worked hard to restore it. The principal family home now contains a common living room and three large bedrooms with private baths. Like Macan Ché, each of the hacienda's rooms has a themed décor, such as "Frida Kahlo," "El Greco," and even the risqué "Lady Chatterley." The master suite features a bathroom with a big bay window. The cenote-like deep swimming pool boasts a Temazcál sauna built underneath. The 16th-century property also has an overseer's house that has four private bedrooms with bath, living room and the original kitchen. Two former workers' cottages, restored as private bungalows, are also available to rent. From Izamal go, south toward Kantunil and turn left at the church in Sudzal. The hacienda is 2.7 kilometers east. $-$$

Hacienda San José *(Km 30 Tixkokob-Tekantó Rd, Tixkokob, reservations ☎ in US 888/625-5144, in Mexico 999/910-4617, fax 999/923-7963, www. luxurycollection.com, 15 rooms & suites, restaurant, pool).* At last, a blue hacienda instead of the predominant gold and brick red colors! This full-service luxury hotel hacienda is outside Mérida near the hammock-making town of Tixkokob. All the suites and rooms are housed in the former plantation house, now restored to a sophisticated private hide-away. One of the Starwood luxury properties. $$$-$$$$

Valladolid/Chichen Itza

Hacienda San Miguel *(outside town on road to Uaymá, Tinúm & Dzitas, ☎ 985/858-1539, http://dyred.sureste.com/sanmiguel/index.htm, 8 cabañas with fans, pool, includes breakfast).* This old hacienda is still a working ranch, so their cattle graze right up to the front porch – just as in the old days – and drink from a trough that catches rainwater run-off. The owners are still restoring the main building, but down the walk, among lovely gardens, all-new accommodations are available in large individual stone casitas, topped with palapa roofs. Each casita had a porch, two queen-size beds and a modern tile bath. Hiking, nature walks, biking and horseback riding available. They opened to the public in early 2000 and are hopeful the working aspect of the hacienda will appeal to guests and groups who seek an unusual experience while still staying in comfort. $$

Hacienda Chichén Resort *(Hotel Zone, US ☎ 800/624-8451, Mexico 985/ 851-0045, www.haciendachichen.com, 19 rooms, 7 suites, air, pool, restaurants, safety deposit, babysitting).* A stay here combines three different periods in Mexico's history. The oldest period is Post-Classic, borrowed from the nearby Chichén Itzá Maya ruins. Some of the ruins' stone blocks were used to build the main hacienda house and they are still visible in the interior's west wall. The hacienda was originally built as a cattle ranch in the 1500s, during the Spanish Colonial period, and it became a henequen plantation in the mid-1800s. The modern period began in the early 1900s when American Vice-Counsel Edward Thompson bought the hacienda and began archeological work on the nearby ruins. In 1923 the cottages that are now individual guest rooms were built for Carnegie Institute archeologists. Completely remodeled inside, they are period with wood-beam ceilings and wrought-iron headboards, but have all the modern necessaries, including large bathrooms. The lovely terrace restaurant has seating inside or out, looking over lush gardens and the swimming pool. The hacienda's grounds are ripe for exploring the old henequen works, ruined outbuildings and an ancient church. And any stay features an incredible amount of song birds who live in its lovely gardens. Anytime of the year is good for bird watching, but the best time is in March, when more migrating birds stop to rest here. Hacienda Chichén has tons of atmosphere and is close to the ruins. $$$

Oxkintoc

Hacienda Santa Rosa *(Km 129 Hwy 180 near Maxcanu, ☎ in US 888/625-5144, in Mexico 999/910-4852, fax 923-7963, www.luxurycollection.com, air, pool).* This small luxury hacienda hotel is elegant yet intimate, its ambience like a private home. Close to Oxkintoc ruins and the wild natural western coast of the Yucatán. It's also a good stop for lunch or dinner in their patio dining area. $$$$+

Oxkutzcab/ Ruta Puuc

Hacienda Tabí *(Calle 58 between 47 & 45, Barrio Sta. Ana, Mérida)* is being restored by the **Foundation Cultural Yucatán** (☎ 999/923-9453), a non-profit organization that is hoping to create a cultural center on the 3,900-acre site (10% of its original size). Donations are graciously accepted. The stunning 17th-century hacienda has a big, red-flowering bougainvillea gracing the front; some sections around back need structural repair. Its history began with growing corn, cotton and tobacco in the good soil of the area. Spared by the violence of the Caste War, around 1850, it began sugarcane production which developed into an excellent business. By 1900, Tabí had been transformed into the spectacular home we see today. As many as 2,500 workers lived on the hacienda property during that time and many of the nearly 500 household and ground servants were Chinese. Eulogio Duarte, the strong-willed *hacendado* who ran the place at its zenith in a style reminiscent of times gone by, died in 1905. His family was unable to cope with the fall in sugar prices

An old sugarcane plantation, Tabí offers unique overnight accommodations.

combined with the stresses of the Mexican Revolution. A few years after his death, they abandoned it as a working plantation.

John Lloyd Stephens, Edward Thompson, Henry Mercer and many other early travelers stayed at this impressive family home, although as recently as the 1950s there was no access road, only a jungle path. It changed owners several times until the Foundation picked up the property in 1992. The kitchen looks as if the last owner had just left, and the Maya caretaker, Abelardo Marin, is particularly proud of the library. Modern bathrooms have been installed in the upstairs bedrooms, where the floors are beautifully tiled in intricate and colorful floral designs and the ceilings are a lofty 16.5 feet. For under $10 you can join the ghosts of the past and sleep overnight in a hammock – a real adventure! There are some rooms with beds.

Few visit here and that's both a blessing and a shame. It's a fabulous place to explore, one that still breathes history. If you visit, the caretaker will show you the property with its ruined chapel (a massive brown beehive hangs in the wooden eaves), a tall furnace chimney you can walk inside, and old sugar cane machinery. Please remember to tip. There is also a cenote and a small ruin down a cattle trail in the back. Tabí is an experience not to be missed.

■ In Campeche

Hacienda Blanca Flor *(reservations ☎ 999/925-8042, www.ccecamp.com. mx/blancaflor.htm, 14 jr. suites, 6 casitas, pool, includes breakfast)*. Find this well-known hacienda hotel when coming from Mérida by turning off Rt. 180 at the sign for Pocboc. From Campeche, go through Hecelchakán, take the road toward Santa Cruz and watch for the ruined church on the left; the hacienda is opposite. The 17th-century main house is set back from the road under great Ceiba trees. Its large rooms with marble tile floors surround a beautiful central courtyard garden with parakeet aviaries that keep the yard full of song. The furniture in the 12 large rooms and five casitas is not Colonial, but the ambiance of the hacienda is. The garden that provides veggies for the kitchen is the same one tended by the monks who once lived here. By reservation only. $$

WHITE FLOWER

Blanca Flor means "white flower," an idyllic-sounding name. However, the hotel's history is anything but idyllic. It was built in 1588 by Fray Pedro Peña, as a Franciscan monastery. During the Caste War, the Spanish successfully defended the house against Maya insurgents. The former monastery and henequen plantation hosted Empress Carlota on her Yucatán tour, just before she fled the country and her husband was executed. The hacienda's ruined chapel on a hill across the street saw fierce fighting during Mexico's 1915 Revolution. When the well-equipped revolutionary army of General Alvarado marched up the Camino Real for Mérida to force federal authority over the Yucatán, which had threatened to secede from the Republic, hastily organized volunteers from Mérida set up a defensive position in the hacienda's chapel. Outnumbered and outgunned, the Yucatecans held off the Mexican army for 12 hours, inflicting heavy casualties with machine guns mounted on the roof. The main house fell early in the fighting and one young Yucatecan survived the slaughter of the occupants when a "coup de grace" did not kill him. Finally dislodged from the now ruined church, the heroic surviving volunteers retreated, only to be captured up the road in Pocboc. Weeds and scrub brush now surround the chapel's graceful Ionic porch, and its roof is long gone.

Edzná

Hacienda Uayamón *(Km 20, off the road from China to Edzná, ☎ in US 888/625-5144, in Mexico 981/829-7526, www.luxurycollection.com, 12 rooms, pool, restaurant).* Refined and luxurious, Hacienda Uayamón features a grand main home surrounded by manicured gardens. Exclusive and tasteful, each guest room is in a separate casita and boasts a terrace and private garden. There's a cool pool in the middle of ruins. Secluded on a quiet sideroad, the hotel is only a few minutes drive from the magnificent Edzná ruins and about a half-hour outside the Colonial city of Campeche. $$$$-$$$$$

Quintana Roo

The Maya of interior Quintana Roo live much as their forefathers did – still preserving many of their ancient traditions.

At A Glance

NAME: The state of Quintana Roo (keen-TANA ROE) was named after Andrés Quintana Roo, Yucatán's first poet. Born in Mérida on November 30, 1787, he died in Mexico City in 1851. In a fateful paradox, this was the first landfall of the Spanish Conquistadors (1517), but the last land in Mexico to be conquered. Quintana Roo was once a part of the states of Yucatán and Campeche. It was designated a federal territory on November 24, 1902, but it was not until October 8, 1974 that it became a full-fledged Mexican State – just in time to build the Cancún resort.

CAPITAL: Chetumal.

MAJOR CITIES: Cancún, Chetumal, San Miguel Cozumel, Felipe Puerto Carrillo, Isla Mujeres and Playa del Carmen.

POPULATION: 650,000 indigenous Maya and Spanish descent.

CLIMATE: Hot and humid inland, ocean breezes cool the coastline. Rain in the summer.

VEGETATION: Jungle, mangroves and some savanna.

GEOGRAPHY: Lowland, cenotes, Caribbean beaches, islands.

SIZE: 50,843 square kilometers (20,337 square miles).

WILDLIFE: Spider monkeys, deer, jaguars, tapirs, water birds, crocodiles and armadillos.

ECOLOGICAL RESERVES: Sian Ka'an, Punta Laguna, El Edén, Cozumel Reefs National Park, Isla Contoy.

MAJOR ARCHEOLOGICAL SITES: Tulum, Cobá, Rio Bec, Kohunlich, Muyil, Dzibanché (also spelled Tzibanché), San Gervasio.

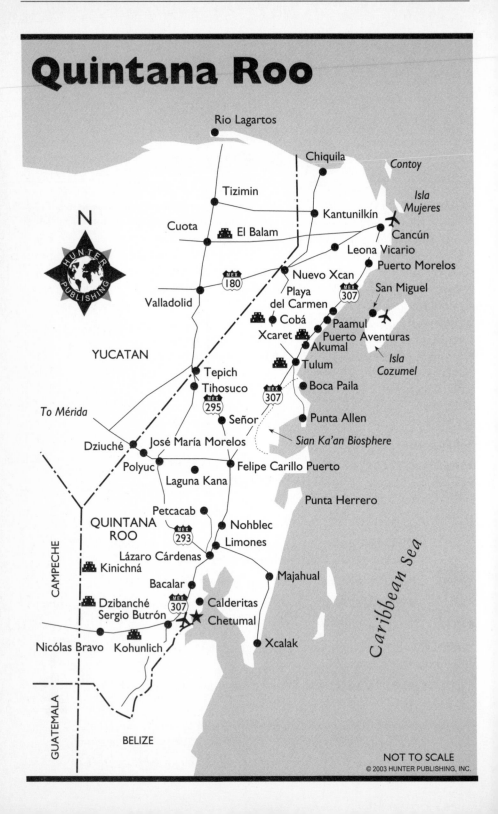

Quintana Roo

Rio Lagartos

Chiquila

Contoy

Isla Mujeres

Tizimin

Kantunilkín

Cuota

El Balam

Cancún

Leona Vicario

Puerto Morelos

Nuevo Xcan

San Miguel

MEX 180

Playa del Carmen

MEX 307

Valladolid

Cobá

Paamul

Xcaret

Puerto Aventuras

Akumal

YUCATAN

Tulum

Isla Cozumel

Tepich

Tihosuco

Boca Paila

MEX 295

MEX 307

To Mérida

Señor

Punta Allen

Dziuché

Sian Ka'an Biosphere

José María Morelos

Polyuc

Felipe Carillo Puerto

Laguna Kana

Punta Herrero

Petcacab

Nohblec

QUINTANA ROO

MEX 293

Limones

Lázaro Cárdenas

Kinichná

Majahual

Bacalar

Dzibanché

MEX 307

Calderitas

Sergio Butrón

Chetumal

CAMPECHE

Nicólas Bravo

Kohunlich

Xcalak

Caribbean Sea

GUATEMALA

BELIZE

NOT TO SCALE
© 2003 HUNTER PUBLISHING, INC.

Cancún

*I never expected to see the day when girls would get
sunburned in the places they do now.*
~ Will Rogers, American humorist, 1879-1935

The sandy strip of Cancún's Hotel Zone, packed with luxury hotels hugging the shore, forms the shape of a lucky number seven, wedged between the turquoise surf of the Caribbean and the calm waters of the Nichupté Lagoon. The name Cancún in Mayan means "Golden Snake" and it aptly describes the slender slither of its powdery golden sand beaches. Squeezed along the 27-km (43.5-mile) causeway are 25,000 hotel rooms in a mix of architectural styles, which welcome sun-worshippers and vacationers from all over the world. Last year, some 2.5 million visitors touched down at the resort's modern airport, most bound for the luxury and pampering of the famous Hotel Zone.

Cancún's hotel zone is surrounded by clear seas.

Unlike Acapulco or Puerto Vallarta, which were idyllic little villages until tourism replaced fishing as the major source of income, Cancún is a made-to-order resort, built specifically for tourism where the wild jungle met a deserted shore. One creation legend claims that in 1968 a computer was programmed to select the ideal spot for a major resort. It was fed vital statistics from all over Mexico, and the place it churned out was Cancún. The statisti-

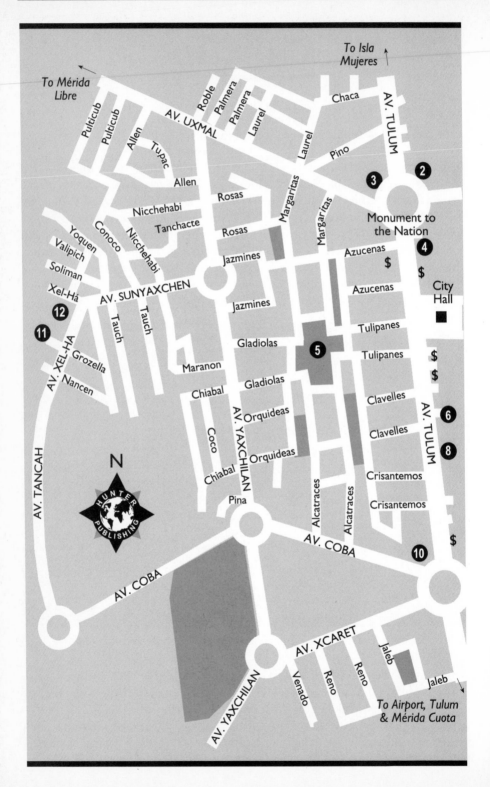

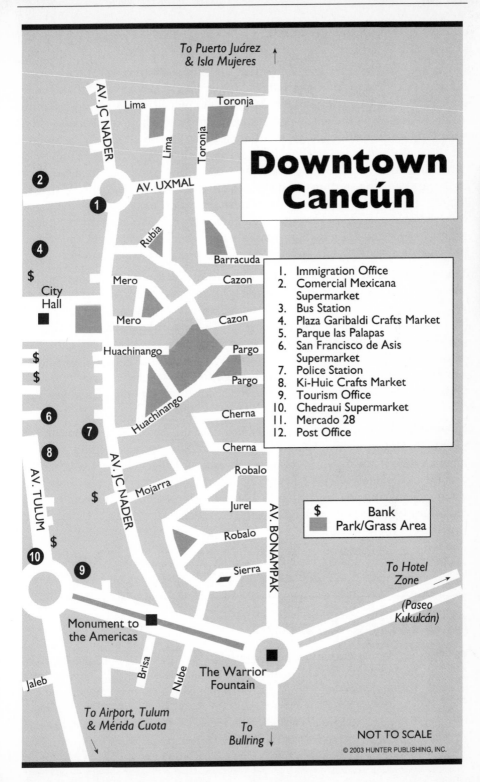

To Puerto Juárez & Isla Mujeres

Downtown Cancún

Quintana Roo

1. Immigration Office
2. Comercial Mexicana Supermarket
3. Bus Station
4. Plaza Garibaldi Crafts Market
5. Parque las Palapas
6. San Francisco de Asis Supermarket
7. Police Station
8. Ki-Huic Crafts Market
9. Tourism Office
10. Chedraui Supermarket
11. Mercado 28
12. Post Office

$ Bank
Park/Grass Area

AV. JC NADER
Lima
Toronja
Lima
Toronja
AV. UXMAL
Rubia
Barracuda
Mero
Cazon
City Hall
Mero
Cazon
Huachinango
Pargo
Pargo
Huachinango
Cherna
Cherna
Robalo
AV. TULUM
AV. JC NADER
Mojarra
Jurel
AV. BONAMPAK
Robalo
Sierra

To Hotel Zone

(Paseo Kukulcán)

Monument to the Americas

Brisa
Nube
The Warrior Fountain

Jaleb

To Airport, Tulum & Mérida Cuota

To Bullring

NOT TO SCALE

© 2003 HUNTER PUBLISHING, INC.

cal parameters included climate, beach conditions and proximity to the United States. Whether the rumor is true or not, we do know that nothing much was here before the development, just some small ruins of the ancient Maya civilization out on the barren dunes and scrub brush. Only Puerto Juárez and the tiny island of Isla Mujeres supported minor Mexican fishing villages. John Stephens, the American adventurer who toured the world of the Maya in the 19th century, mentioned that, "In the afternoon we steered for the mainland, passing the island of Kancune, a barren strip of land with sand hills and stone buildings visible upon it." See what's left of those stone buildings near the southern end of the hotel zone in San Miguelito, half a kilometer north of El Rey, and Yamil Lu'um, on a hill next to the Sheraton. It didn't take long for bankers and government officials to realize that Cancún's reliable sunshine (240 days per year), warm weather and sparkling waters provided the perfect place to build a new world-class seaside resort.

The other Cancún – inland from the waterfront – is the Mexican town built to supply housing and community for the hospitality workers in the Hotel Zone. While some of it is not of particular interest, the downtown (El Centro) has become a tourist destination all its own. We suspect that if the buildings in the Hotel Zone sank into the sea, Cancún downtown would stay on, living and working much as it does now – a gumbo of Yucatecan, Maya, Mexican and North American lifestyles. It's a pleasant and lively place to be, close enough to the shore and the diversions of the Hotel Zone, but far enough away so that the feeling is quite different.

No matter what your vacation needs, between the two Cancúns you can satisfy them. Get-away-and-relax-on-the-beach vacationers will find Cancún is all it's cracked up to be. More adventuresome, lower-budget travelers can find the best of both worlds downtown. Cancún's easy-going but cosmopolitan ways make it an easy transition to a Mexican "vacation mode." And Cancún makes a good base from which to begin your exploration and enjoyment of adventures in the Yucatán.

Orientation

■ Getting Around

The international airport is outside the city in the dry jungle. Most flights pass over the brilliant sand beaches and bright blue water of the shoreline before setting down, which whets your appetite for getting right to the beach. Buy your tickets for the colectivo buses or taxis into the Hotel Zone or town at booths in the airport, which offers set prices and prevents any rip-offs (see *Arrivals & Departures*, pages 95-96).

Cancún (population 325,000) is divided into two zones, the **downtown** and the **Hotel Zone**. The Hotel Zone sits alongside the clear Caribbean Sea and is the Cancún you see in all the brochures and ads. Hotels here are more expensive than those downtown. The beaches have it all for sun and fun vacations. The downtown is inland, connected to the Hotel Zone by the **Paseo Kukulcán** and reached by inexpensive (80¢) public buses or taxis. Distances are marked along the 27-km Paseo Kukulcán in the Hotel Zone, beginning downtown. Clearly marked "Zona Hoteles," the Ruta (Route) #1 and #2 buses take you downtown and back (Ruta #1 turns up Av. Tulum, Ruta 2 crosses it on Av. Cobá). A fun way to get around the Hotel Zone is by **Water Taxi** (☎ 998/883-3155), which plies the lagoon hourly from 9 am to 11 pm. It stops at major marinas and sites, allowing you to get out and shop or dine. It's a relaxing, enjoyable way to get around town without clogging the roads. A weekly pass is about US $35, a day-pass is US $15, and one-way trips are US $3. Children are half-price. For the **Isla Mujeres** ferry from downtown, walk north on Av. Tulum across Av. Uxmal to the supermarket, Comercial Mexicana (look for the pelican logo), and catch the bus marked "Puerto Juárez" at the bus stop there. It goes right to the ferry dock.

The main drag downtown is **Av. Tulum**, which runs north and south perpendicular to Av. Cobá. Cobá becomes **Paseo Kukulcán** (also spelled Kukulkán) in the Hotel Zone. Most of the downtown attractions – stores, hotels and restaurants – cluster around the three parallel avenues of **Nader, Tulum** and **Yaxchilán**. The bus station is behind the circle of Av. Tulum and Av. Uxmal. City blocks in Spanish are *manzanas* and groups of blocks are *super-manzanas* or SM. The heart of the downtown is a rhomboid-shaped area surrounded by Avenidas Tulum and Yaxchilán, Uxmal and Cobá.

Practicalities

EMBASSIES: A US Consular Agency is located in Plaza Caracol, 3rd floor, in the Hotel Zone, ☎ 998/883-0272, open 9-1 daily. In the case of an emergency, ☎ 999/925-6366 in Mérida or 555/211-0042 in Mexico City. **Canadians** can reach their embassy in Mexico City, Monday through Friday, from 9 am to 5 pm (closed for lunch from 1-2) at ☎ 555/724-7900. In Cancún there's a Canadian consul in the Plaza Caracol, 3rd floor, Monday-Friday, 9-5, ☎ 998/983-3360. In the event of an emergency outside office hours, ☎ 01/800/706-2900. See pages 94-95 for other countries' consular representatives in Cancún.

LAUNDROMAT: A laundromat that does a good job of washing, drying and folding clothes is **Lavanderia Tulum**, between the Comercial Mexicana and the big McDonalds on Av. Tulum. It's open Monday through Saturday, 7 am to 8 pm, and on Sunday from 9 am to 6 pm. Full-service laundry runs about 80¢ per kilo. **Alborada** is a much larger self-service or drop-off laundromat located closer to downtown on Av. Nader, No 5. A third, low-cost choice operates from the basement of a building on Av. Bonampak, one block north from the corner of Av. Uxmal. One of the least expensive options is **Lavanderia Las Palapas**, next to Cairo Furniture on Calle Alcatraces alongside Palapa Park, which has excellent service.

MEDICAL FACILITIES: The **Red Cross** is open 24 hours a day on Av. Labna No. 2 (☎ 988/884-1116). The big hospital in Cancún is **Hospital Americano** (☎ 998/884-6133) on Av. Uxmal opposite the side of the Chedraui. Downtown, the private American-style medical centers are **Total Assist** (☎ 998/884-8082), next to Bancomer on Av. Tulum, and the large **Ameri-Med** (☎ 998/881-3434), next to Plaza Americas, Av. Bonhampak and Nichupté. In the Hotel Zone, the **Ameri-Med** office (☎ 998/883-0985) is next to La Boom's and the **American Medical Center** (☎ 998/883-1001, www. americanmedicalcenter.com) is in Plaza Quetzal, across from the Presidente Hotel and next to a Dominos Pizza.

MONEY MATTERS: The **American Express** office (☎ 998/884-1999) is open weekdays, 9-6, and Saturdays 9-1 on Av. Tulum near the Hotel America.

PHARMACIES: There are several pharmacies in the Hotel Zone malls and plazas, two in Plaza Caracol and several downtown. The **Farmacia Canto** (☎ 988/884-4083), a drugstore on Av. Yaxchilán and Sunyaxchen, is open 24 hours.

POLICE: You can reach the police at ☎ 998/884-1913 or 884-2342. For emergencies, dial 060.

POST OFFICE: The post office is on the corner of Av. Sunyaxchen and Av. Xel-Há and is open Monday through Friday, 8 am to 7 pm, and Sunday 9 am to 1 pm.

RELIGIOUS SERVICES: Church services are held in many hotels for Roman Catholics. There's a RC church in the Hotel Zone called the **Resurrection of the Lord** at Km 3. Services are held Monday-Friday, 8 pm; Sunday, 10:30 am, noon, 6:30 and 8 pm. Another RC church is downtown at Calle Margaritas No 15. **Cristo Rey** holds services Monday-Friday at 7 am and 7 pm, and on Sunday at 8 and 10:30 am, 5, 6:30 and 8 pm. Episcopalians have a mass at the **Marriot Casa Magna**, Sundays at 10 am.

STORES/GIFTS: Papelería de Cancún is a large office supply and gift store tucked up Calle Margarita near the Parque Palapa. It sells all kinds of office supplies, makes copies and has an impressive line of souvenirs and gifts.

SUPPORT GROUPS: There's a **Narcotics Anonymous** meeting in Spanish every night from 8:30 to 10 pm at Parque Margaritas (41 Norte between 50 and 51) and one in English every Monday, downtown at Plaza Centro (3rd floor) on Av. Nader at 7:30 pm. English-language meetings of the **Friends of Bill W** (AA) also assemble at Plaza Centro, 3rd floor, on Av. Nader every day

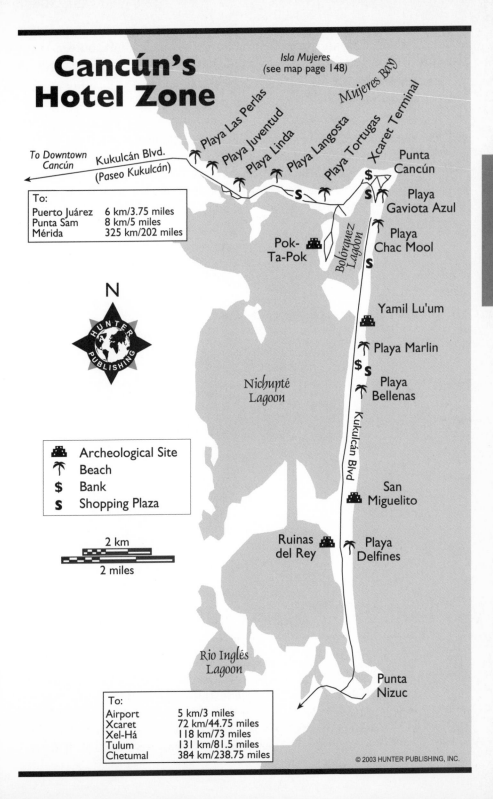

Cancún's Hotel Zone

Isla Mujeres (see map page 148)

Mujeres Bay

Playa Las Perlas
Playa Juventud
Playa Linda
Playa Langosta
Playa Tortugas
Xcaret Terminal

To Downtown Cancún

Kukulcán Blvd. (Paseo Kukulcán)

Punta Cancún

Playa Gaviota Azul

To:
Puerto Juárez   6 km/3.75 miles
Punta Sam   8 km/5 miles
Mérida   325 km/202 miles

Pok-Ta-Pok

Bolórquez Lagoon

Playa Chac Mool

N

Yamil Lu'um

Playa Marlin

Playa Bellenas

Nichupté Lagoon

Kukulcán Blvd

Archeological Site
Beach
Bank
Shopping Plaza

San Miguelito

2 km
2 miles

Ruinas del Rey

Playa Delfines

Rio Inglés Lagoon

Punta Nizuc

To:
Airport   5 km/3 miles
Xcaret   72 km/44.75 miles
Xel-Há   118 km/73 miles
Tulum   131 km/81.5 miles
Chetumal   384 km/238.75 miles

Quintana Roo

from 6:15 pm for an hour. They can be reached at ☎ 998/884-2445 or 884-3375 or an emergency group number at ☎ 998/874-3082. Unfortunately, these times and numbers may change, so call ahead.

TOURIST INFORMATION: Find tourist information in the office of Convention & Visitors Bureau on Av. Cobá and Nader (☎ 998/884-6531, www.gocancun.com).

WATER TAXI: Every hour the **Aqua Bus Water Taxi** (☎ 998/883-5649) plies the lagoon around the Hotel Zone. A weekly pass is US $35, a daily pass, US $15, and one-ways are US $3 (children half-price). The canopied, wide-bottom boat has adequate safety features (we checked) and is a relaxing way to travel.

Cancún's beachfront.

Beaches

A series of 11 public beaches along the Paseo allow access to the sea. All beaches in Mexico are free, although some hotels are not anxious for you to know it. The beaches on the leeward side (the long part of the number seven shape), protected by Isla Mujeres, are better for swimming. The windward Caribbean beaches are more picturesque, with broad sand, warm waters and strong surf. The south beach farthest from the downtown, **Playa Delfines**, is a favorite of locals partly because this stretch of sand against the brilliant turquoise sea is free of hotels. **Playa Tortugas**, with its soft sand and gentle surf, is the most popular spot for tourists staying downtown.

Events

Bullfights abound at Avs. Bonampak and Sayil each Wednesday at 3:30 pm. Get your tickets through travel agents or at the bullring. **Carnival festivities** take place before Lent and there's a delicious **Gastronomy Fair** in November. Ironmen can enter the **Madman Race** in mid-October or the **International Triathlon**, November 1-2. **Feria Cancún** runs through the month of May. Call the Cancún tourism office for more information on any of these events, ☎ 998/884-631.

Gay Travel

The gay community numbers about 300 locals plus a large number of international travelers, many of whom visit regularly. Additionally, a fair number of Mexicans are bi-sexual. The local gay scene includes **Picante Hot Bar**, in the Plaza Galeria shopping mall on Av. Tulum near the Tulum Cinemas, and **Karumba**, a night club that welcomes cross dressers and lesbians as well. Karumba (☎ 998/884-0032, www.karambabar.com) is upstairs above a restaurant on Av. Tulum. Open Tuesday-Sunday from 10:30 pm to 6 am. A gay-friendly travel agency in the US is **Cancún Beach Express** (☎ 757/380-0943).

Shopping

A strong dollar combined with high-quality goods, fascinating folkart, handicrafts and fun souvenirs, make Mexico a shopper's paradise. The problem is not so much *what to buy* among Cancún's shops, malls and flea markets, but *where to begin*. There are shopping plazas and North American-styled malls conveniently located in the Cancún Hotel Zone. In addition, the downtown offers several flea market groupings along with fine shops and grocery/department stores. Don't be afraid to enter the warren of close shops in the flea markets. You won't get lost, but might leave with an unexpected bargain.

Enjoy a traditional Mexican shopping experience at Plaza Garibaldi.

■ Downtown

Ki-Huic. The biggest market downtown is in the center of Av. Tulum between two banks. Open daily from 9 am to 10 pm (some stores take a siesta), this streetfront and indoor labyrinth of stalls is the city's oldest, with 100 vendors selling gifts and crafts. Strike some good bargains here, but be prepared to haggle if you like what you see. You'll be "eagerly invited" to enter each shop.

Plaza Garibaldi. This market on Av. Tulum, at corner of Av. Uxmal, contains streetside stalls with serapes, tablecloths and traditional clothing, gifts and crafts. More shops are located inside.

Plaza Mexico. The market at Av. Tulum No. 200 is a cluster of 50 handicraft shops.

Plaza Bonita. On Av. Xel-Há, near the post office. This attractive outdoor mall looks like a little village street, right next to Mercado 28. This is a favorite shopping and eating area of local residents, with upscale goods and some great prices.

Find the store in the complex where you can buy all kinds of herbs and scents, including aromas in spray cans, to attract money or a mate. We bought copal, the ancient incense used by the Maya for thousands of years (see page 301). Get a charcoal burner to ignite the sticky crystals. Don't miss the **Pewter Mexicano Factory** (☎ 998/888-4357, www.pewtermexicano.com) facing the parking lot off Av. Sunyaxchen, which has some real bargains. Buy a case of Cuban cigars cheaper than duty-free, or have a cup of java at the tiny cigar store next door, **Smokers Stylish** (☎ 998/884-0309, angyval@hotmail.com). They'll ship home for you.

Mercado 28. Maybe more people read our book than we think. We wrote up this market back in 1998, long before it was discovered by Hotel Zone tourists. Now it's a super-popular stop for gift bargain hunters and a fun shopping experience as it's not as claustrophobic as some of the downtown flea markets. Sit in one of the tiny eateries and watch the people go by. To avoid *gringos*, there's the less-appealing **Mercado 23**, located about three blocks northwest of the bus station downtown. Better prices but a smaller selection.

Supermarkets downtown are the **San Francisco de Asis,** in the middle of Av. Tulum; the **Comercial Mexicana**, at the circle of Av. Tulum and Uxmal; and the **Chedraui**, at the corner of Av. Tulum and Cobá. They're good places to stock up on water, food and miscellaneous necessities. All three double as department stores. Chedraui has the largest selection and a good bakery called La Hogaza. Take an aluminum pizza tray and some tongs and pick what you desire from the open racks. The sales clerk will add it up and bag it at the register. Bakery goods are very inexpensive. Another large Chedraui is located in the Plaza Las Americas mall about a kilometer south on Av. Tulum. This mall also features a **JC Penney's** and movie theaters. All the Chedrauis have recently installed cafeterias, which are good, cheap places for a bite.

There's a large **Ace Hardware** on Av. Tulum south of the city center. A **Sam's Club** (the US-based members-only store) is tucked behind Av. Yaxchilán and Av. Labna, near the Telemex microwave towers. Inside, you'll find a list of stores and restaurants that offer discounts with a Sam's card. If your annual membership at Sam's is expiring soon, think about renewing here – it could be a little cheaper.

Next to Sam's is a large **Walmart** (open 24 hours) and down the street is a giant **Costco** at Av. Kabah and Av. Yaxchilán. *Cancún Tips* magazine often has a coupon for one-day membership with a 5% surcharge over Costco member's prices.

If you wander downtown to Parque Palapas, look for **Cairo Furniture** on Alcatraces (☎ 998/884-7024). This quality furniture store features some very interesting casual wood furniture that they can ship home for you.

■ Hotel Zone

KID FRIENDLY

Forum by the Sea, Km 9.5 Paseo Kulkulcán, one of the newer shopping mall complexes in Cancún is also the hardest to miss, although you may not realize it's a mall at all. The massive guitar of the Hard Rock Café is cemented into the sidewalk out front, and one half the building looks as though it's made of huge boulders where jungle animals, such as King Kong, scamper. The cliff wall is part of the Rainforest Café, located on the second floor. The Forum features a huge open atrium with 65 shops and attractions wrapped around it.

Plaza Flamingo, Km 11 Paseo Kukulcán, is a pleasant, air-conditioned mall with a good variety of shops. The small fast food court has a wide selection and is very clean and open. A paved walk follows the Paseo behind this mall along the lagoon – very scenic. This is our favorite mall in the Hotel Zone, quiet and laid back.

Plaza Kukulkan at Km 13. This is the largest indoor, all-American-style shopping mall in Cancún, with over 200 upscale shops. An upstairs food court offers 16 fast food choices and there are good restaurants downstairs, too.

> The mall at Plaza Kukulkan is home to one of the Hotel Zone's two English-language cinemas, **Telecines** (☎ 998/885-2022), playing first-run Hollywood movies. The mall is also home to a video and laser-game center and a bowling alley.

Plaza Caracol, Km 8.5, across from the Convention Center. Plaza Caracol is centrally located in the busy Convention Center area that is often mistakenly referred to as "downtown." The large white mall rests on an island where Paseo Kukulcán divides and turns south. It features nearly 200 shops, including designer specialty stores and some of the best restaurants in the Hotel Zone.

Plaza Maya Fair, Km 8.5. This small eye-pleasing plaza was known as Mayfair until a remodeling in 1998 put a Maya-inspired façade on the building, including a huge Chenes-style archway at one end. Now, it's known as Maya Fair. It's being billed as an ecological mall because of its greenery, waterfalls and exotic indoor gardens. Other plazas (Terramar, Lagunas) connect with Maya Fair and there is much outdoor shopping and eating here. Sidewalk spray paint artists draw a big crowd in several of the outdoor malls at night. Their paintings are quite clever and very cheap.

Coral Negro Mercado de Artesanias, Km 9 almost opposite the Hard Rock Café, is a Mexican-style artisans' *mercado* with a fancier outdoor handicraft gift section that imitates a village square. The 65-shop market covers both sides of Kukulcán, with more next to Italianni's Restaurant. This is a popular stop for Americans who want a taste of real *mercado* shopping without leaving the Hotel Zone. Prices are reasonable.

La Fiesta, Km 9.5 on the lagoon side, advertises itself as having the best prices in the Hotel Zone for a myriad of gifts and souvenirs. It's a large pinkish building next to TGI Friday's on the southern bend of Kukulcán. Rows and rows of handicrafts and clothes and typical gift merchandise at reasonable prices. This Mexican market that's inside and air-conditioned is well worth a look.

Plaza Nautilus, Km 3.5 on the lagoon, is a favorite of many shoppers. It has 70 assorted stores.

 La Isla Shopping Village, Km 13.5, is Cancún's newest and most ambitious shopping area, located along the lagoon in the Hotel Zone. Not fully opened until spring of 2000, La Isla features a city street-like "downtown" full of upscale shops and restaurants that line its traffic-free walkways. Huge canvas roofs attached to massive metal poles protect pedestrians in inclement weather. Covered parking for 1,000 and ATMs available. Upscale and unusual shops are featured, along with restaurants and a multiplex cinema.

> **AUTHOR TIP:** *La Isla mall features* **Cinemark** *(☎ 998/883-5603), another multi-screen English-language movie house in the Hotel Zone. It has the most screens, so check local listings for first-run movies.*

Mexican Folk Art Museum, Km 4, is a treasure trove of folk arts and crafts from all over Mexico. The gift shop entrance is almost as mind-bogglingly colorful as the large, one-room museum. High quality knick-knacks.

The Hotel Zone has a tiny convenience store on the lagoon side past the ruins and before you reach Club Med.

 Isla Mujeres. If lunch is provided on the boat ride over to Isla Mujeres, you'll miss out on some inexpensive and delicious dining opportunities in town. Isla Mujeres is virtually crime-free and the shops are generally cheaper than in the Hotel Zone.

Night Spots

> *As always on this boulevard, the faces were young, coming*
> *annually in an endless migration from every country,*
> *every continent, to alight here once in a long journey of their lives.*
> ~ Brian Moore, author

There is so much demand for late-night entertainment, a half-dozen clubs stand within walking distance of each other at the center of the Hotel Zone near the Convention Center. For an unusual movie house experience, see the *Flicks* section below.

■ Clubs & Discos

 Our all-time favorite nightclub in Cancún is **Azucar** (☎ 998/848-7000, www.eelio.com), located next to the Camino Real on Punta Cancún, Kulkulcún Km 9. This hip hotspot features live music and a

Quintana Roo

jumping dance floor, plus a friendly crowd (minus drunken teenagers). Hot salsa and merengue bands from Cuba appear regularly and nobody sits when they get rocking. On one unforgettable evening an all-girl salsa band from Havana kept us out until 4 am, well past our bedtime. A best bet for a fun evening, with free salsa dance lessons nightly from 9:30 to 10:30 pm, so you have no excuse.

For pulsating palpitations, try **CoCo Bongo**, one of the hottest Hotel Zone nightclubs, attached to the Forum by the Sea shopping plaza. It packs them in every night from after 10 pm until the wee hours.

Dady'O, across the street at Km 9.5, is another "in" disco in town where you'll come across long lines, especially on the weekends. It throbs with nightlife in its cavern-like décor with projection screen TV. A sister bar and grill is **Dady Rock**, where they party just as well.

Ma'ax'O, the newest and hippest entrant in the night scene, rocks and rolls in La Isla shopping village, Km 13.5. It's very popular. And a **Pasaje del Terror** fun house opened there in early 2000, with live interactive entertainment that will strike terror in your heart. The multi-media terror experience uses sound effects and up to 18 actors in creepy roles as you make your way single file through a labyrinth filled with horrors beyond description. At least, beyond our description. The show, which began in Spain and is now performed worldwide, has been visited by nearly one million people so far.

The **Hard Rock Café** is in the center of the Forum mall. Look for the huge Fender Stratocaster guitar. A large **Planet Hollywood**, the California-style restaurant/club, is in the Plaza Flamingo. **La Boom**, with a live rock band, and **Tequila Boom** next to it, boom their high-tech music out at Km 3.5. Singles and video bar. **Up & Down**, in the Oasis Hotel, Km 17, combines a restaurant (Up) with an ultra-modern disco that can host 2,000 gyrating bodies (Down).

The **Royal Bandstand** at Kulkulkán, Km 13.5, is a dinner/nightclub in the vein of the old Rainbow Room at Rockefeller Center, but with a much livelier beat. Whether it's a Cuban band knocking out contemporary Latin music, Michael and Lilly performing American standards, or Barry Ivan White singing Mo-town soul, this should not be-missed. The kitchen closes at 11, but the music lasts until 1 am. Reservations recommended (☎ 998/848-8220.

Cancún's newest, much-anticipated nightclub is **The City**, a tri-level complex with restaurant, lounge, beach club and disco at Km 9 (www.thecitycancun.com). In the tradition of New York dance clubs, The City offers VIP areas, pulsating lightshows and a large, energetic dance floor. The building has been made to look like a city skyline and the beach club in the rear boasts a waterslide, artificial wave machine, competitive watersports and more partying outdoors. It's the "in" place to be.

Péricos, on Av. Yaxchilán No. 61 downtown, is one of the last "happening" places downtown. It's an eatery and bar with live Mexican music from

7:30 pm to midnight. Its party atmosphere makes a festive night out. Bar stools here are saddles.

Late night downtown consists mostly of restaurants and bars along Av. Tulum, including **La Tosca**, a popular restaurant open until 11:30 pm. On the next block you'll find the **Karumba Disco**, open at 11, located over the Casa Italiana restaurant on Av. Tulum. Karumba hosts a lively gay scene.

Late night music lovers should flock to **Barry's Place**, a live entertainment dinner nightclub downtown on the second floor of the old "Fama" building, almost directly across Av. Tulum from city hall. It attracts some fabulous musicians and singers, including the owner, Barry Ivan White, a member of the Platters. Barry's is the place musicians and singers go for their own fun. Standards, jazz, Latin and soul from 11 pm to sunrise. Reservations ☎ 044-998/125-1746. Also ask about his nightclub opening in the hotel zone.

■ Traditional Folk Dances & Museums

Monday through Friday there's a nightly show called **Voces y Bailes de Mexico** (Songs and Dances of Mexico), with up to 80 performers in a rousing tribute to Mexico's diverse culture. It starts at 7 pm at the **Teatro de Cancún** (Embarcadero, Paseo Kukulcán Km 4, ☎ 998/849-4848, www.embarcadero.com). Drinks are included in the pricey price, but it's a very entertaining and professional show. Then, at 9 pm, **Traditions of the Caribbean** brings its tropical rhythms and interpretive dance to the same theater.

You can't miss the Embarcadero; it's where the **Sightseeing Tower** (see *Adventures in the Air*, page 128) is located, but our best bet there is the upstairs corner Mexican Folk Art Museum. The variety of colorful folk art on display in the small **Museo de Arte Popular Mexicano** is absolutely mind-boggling. If you are not familiar with the rich heritage of art in Mexico, then this museum is a must. Examples of traditional costumes, fine arts and local handicrafts – both stunningly elaborate and surprisingly simple – were collected to offer viewers a treasure trove of folk art. Even the 42 realistic mannequins, some of whom can appear unattractive at first glance, were created from latex masks of living indigenous people from all over Mexico. Set aside enough time to absorb the complex displays which are fascinating, but not suitable for kids who touch. Signed artwork and wonderful handicrafts are for sale in the well-stocked gift shop. Discount combination tickets available for the Sightseeing Tower. About US $10.

Ballet Folklórico Nacional de Mexico features traditional Mexican music and folk dancing at the Convention Center at the turn opposite Punta Cancún. Dinner and show or just show tickets are available (☎ 998/883-0199). Several upscale hotels also do a dinner show with another Ballet Folklórico performance.

■ Dinner Cruises

The sternwheel paddle steamer that plies the lagoon with twinkly lights on its railing is the **Cancún Queen**, which offers a three-course meal, open bar, live band and dancing. The *Queen* departs from Aquaworld Marina, Km 15.2, nightly at 6 pm. Casual dress is also the style on the **Columbus Lobster Dinner Cruise** (☎ 998/849-4621), which offers a lobster or steak dinner under more twinkly lights in its rigging, plus dancing and open bar. It runs twice daily at 6 pm and 8 pm from the Royal Mayan Marina at Km 16.5. ***Pirate's Night*** cruises the Bahia de Mujeres to its own "Treasure Island" for a buffet dinner. Don't wear heels; you may have to walk the plank! Departs daily, except Sunday, from the Playa Langosta Dock, Km 5.5, at 6:30 and returns at 11:30 pm.

■ Gambling

Luckily, there are no gambling casinos in Cancún. Sports betting is allowed in the **L.F. Caliente Restaurant-Bar,** open 11 am to midnight in the Fiesta Americana Hotel in the Hotel Zone, and in the **Plaza Caribe Hotel,** downtown.

■ Flicks

There is a movie theater in Plaza Kukulcán called **The New Telecines** (☎ 998/885-2022) and another large **Cinemark** multiplex movie house (☎ 998/883-5603) has opened in La Isla shopping center along the lagoon. There are several more downtown: **Espectaculos del Caribe** on Av. Tulum No. 44, with dialog in English and subtitles in Spanish; **Cinemas Tulum** has five screens on northern Av. Tulum; and **Cines Cancún** on Av. Cobá, No. 112.

The most fun we've had in a movie house in long time was the **Cinépolis VIP** cinema (info ☎ 998/884-1410, reservations ☎ 892-2103) in the Plaza Las Americas shopping mall downtown, south on Av. Tulum. There's also a regular Cinépolis movie house in the mall but we enjoyed the classy VIP, located upstairs above the JC Penney's. There's a big lounge waiting area with food concessions and a bar, and the movie seats are like large Stratocaster recliners. Just before the movie begins young girls come and take orders for sodas, popcorn, even Japanese food. Then they'll deliver them to your seat while you're watching. This was the best US $6 we spent (seniors and children are only US $4). They take credit cards.

Every Monday night at 8 pm, bohemian moviegoers can go to the **Casa de Cultura** (Prolongacion Yaxchilan, near Sam's Club, ☎ 998/884-8364), where they show art films, mostly in Spanish, for under US $2.

Adventures

There was a young lady named Bright,
Whose speed was far faster than light;
She set out one day in a relative way,
And returned home the previous night.
~ Professor Arthur Buller, 1874-1944

If you're based in Cancún or Isla Mujeres and want to see it all in day-trips or short overnight jaunts, there's no lack of ways to get wherever you're going.

◼ Nearby Sights & Attractions

 A "must see" is **Tulum**, a Post-Classic ruined walled city, set high upon a bluff with spectacular views of the turquoise Caribbean below. Tulum is now the most-visited archeological site in all of Mexico, with millions of visitors each year. Bring your swimsuit.

Chichén Itzá is a much more impressive archeological site because of its size and architecture. The giant pyramid El Castillo, where human sacrifices occurred, dominates the fascinating abandoned city. On the way, a stop or overnight stay in the historic Colonial city of **Valladolid** gives a sense of the Yucatán not found in the modern streets of Cancún. From there you can visit the impressive **Ek Balam** ruins, the **Xke'ken** and **Samula** cenotes near Dzitnup, or the **Balankanché Caves** near Chichén.

Of course, **Isla Mujeres** should be more than a quick shopping trip. Its quaint personality survives the hordes of daytrippers that shuttle over from the mainland. A wonderful snorkel and nature trip from there is to **Isla Contoy**, a bird sanctuary.

 Croco Cun (☎ 998/850-3719, US $15), about 45 minutes south of Cancún near Puerto Morelos, is a crocodile research zoo that offers a fascinating glimpse of the prehistoric beasts up close. It's a good kid spot.

 The caves and cenote **Aktun Chen**, near Playa, opened in 1999. A visit here involves a one-hour guided tour of the incredible underground caverns with plenty of stalactites and stalagmites and a beautiful emerald green cenote. No phone.

Five miles north of Tulum, **Xel-Há** (shell-HA) is a natural aquarium in a lagoon that offers commercialized snorkeling and swimming in an attractive park-like setting. The clear lagoon is lined with coral

Quintana Roo

caves and a sunken Maya altar. A cool snorkel and swim after visiting Tulum is their big selling point.

 Xcaret (ish-car-ET) is a large-scale "eco-archeological" park that has walking and horseback riding trails, a recreation of a Maya village, an underground river that runs through a sacred cave, a recreated Maya ballcourt, and several beaches with soft white sand. It attracts busloads of water-lovers and fun-seekers. Dolphins perform in the lagoon and there's an aquarium, an aviary and a zoo. Brightly painted buses leave from the Xcaret terminal building Plaza Caracol, next to the Coral Beach Hotel, at 9 and 10 am everyday. No reservations are needed, but be there at least 30 minutes before departure. Less elaborate but lots of fun and very beautiful is the **Tres Rios** park, the nearest of the parks to Cancún, just south of Puerto Morelos.

 Xpu-Há (ish-pu-ha) is a newly opened totally all-inclusive "eco-park" that will also attract tourists interested in enjoying themselves on the beach and in the woods without the guilt of heavy environmental impact.

The ancient lost city of **Cobá** is within reach, as is the **Gran Cenote** (where you can swim) near Tulum Pueblo, or take exciting educational trips into the **Sian Ka'an Biosphere**, a 1.3 million-acre nature reserve.

Playa del Carmen is the haunt of European travelers and **Cozumel** is a diver's and snorkeler's paradise. Both are much different experiences than Cancún, especially Playa.

ADVENTURE TRAVEL

For some people, just going to Mexico – much less leaving the Hotel Zone on a public bus – is an adventure. Our definition of "adventure" includes activities for the first-timer because every journey begins with the first step. That's why we mention golf (yes, even miniature golf) in the same breath as we tell of tagging crocodiles in the Biosphere or visiting the deserted jungle cities of the Classic Maya culture. Excitement is as much a matter of your attitude as what you do. As you'll see, we're always on the lookout for unusual, non-touristy places and activities, as well as exploring life off the beaten trail. So kick back and enjoy – you're going to love it! While you're here, try to use your elementary Spanish and Mayan at every opportunity. Mexicans will appreciate your effort and go out of their way to be helpful and friendly.

■ Adventures on Water

 SWIMMING: Naturally, a beach resort should offer good swimming spots and Cancún's chalk-white beaches are no exception. And the Hotel Zone's pools are renowned. When you're tired of splashing around in the Hotel Zone, you'll find no shortage of popular nearby places that are doubly attractive because they combine water activities with natural beauty and active entertainment. See our reviews (and pronunciation!) of Xcaret, Xel-Há, Xpu-Há and Tres Rios parks in the Maya Riviera section, pages202, 218-23.

SNUBA: For those who love to snorkel but aren't up to scuba diving, local eco-parks now feature a very cool new sport called snuba. It's the latest craze for water-lovers and is now offered at major seaside resorts around the world. Not limited to swimming on the surface with a snorkel, snubers are free to dive up to 20 feet around a central raft that houses their automatic breathing apparatus. Unencumbered by a lot of equipment,

A Sunfish plying the waters in Cancún.

participants can dive to the shallow reefs, attached only to a seven-meter-long (20 feet) air hose and weight belt. Snuba is currently offered at **Xcaret, Xel-Há** and **Cozumel**.

DIVING: Local dive spots are **Chital**, north of Hotel Presidente, with shallow depths and clear visibility to 33 meters; **Cuevones Reef**, three km north of Punta Cancún, with a 45-meter visibility; and **Manchones Reef**, off Isla Mujeres. **Playa Linda** is the headquarters of many of the specialty cruises, fishing and sightseeing boats.

ORGANIZED TOURS: The "**Jungle Tour**" that you'll be offered everywhere involves boarding either a one- or two-person personal watercraft, such as a jet ski or small speedboat, and heading into the mangrove lagoon. This is less a tour of the jungle than a chance to zoom around and get wet. Some operators offer snorkel stops. **AquaWorld** (Km 15. 2, ☎ 998/848-8300) is a big supplier of jungle tours and it also offers underwater sightseeing tours in a nautical bus. **Nautibus** (☎ 998/983-35-52) runs a similar underwater sightseeing adventure in a vessel they describe as a floating submarine. **Isla Discovery** ships you over to La Isla to swim with dolphins (☎ 998/849-4621).

Water-themed tours, including the ones above, are available from travel agents and can include diving and snorkeling – as close as Isla Mujeres or as far away as Isla Contoy. Snorkeling is best at Punta Nizuc, Punta Cancún and Playa Tortugas (watch the strong currents here). Also try offshore at Chital, Cuevones and Manchones Reefs.

CRUISES: You can catch any of many cruises to **Isla Mujeres** (US $15 and up) from the Hotel Zone. A more adventuresome (and cheaper) way is to take the bus on Av. Tulum (north of Av. Uxmal) to Puerto Juárez and catch one of the speedy cruisers (15 minutes; US $4) or the slower people ferry (40 minutes; US $1.50).

WATERSKIING: Waterskiing is available with other watersports at most marinas, but you get great service and instruction at **Waterski Cancún** (☎ 998/880-6087).

WATER PARK: Though it may seem like carrying coals to Newcastle, the Hotel Zone has a watersports complex. **Parque Nizuc** (☎ 998/881-1300, www.parquenizuc.com) is the euphemistic name for the 17-acre, US $20 million **Wet n' Wild** amusement park on the edge of a protected mangrove wetland. The warm-water slip-and-slide funnery is found south of the Hotel Zone at Km 25. The 2003 admission prices were US $30 adults, US $20 for children. Swim with Dolphins can be reserved by calling ☎ 998/881-3030.

PARASAILING: Some beachfront hotels offer parasailing, an activity in which you are pulled by a motorboat above the sea or the lagoon while attached to a parachute. If yours doesn't offer it, inquire at **Lorenzillo's Restaurant** (☎ 998/983-3007). Be aware that this is a dangerous sport and injuries are not unheard of.

WINDSURFING: Sailboarding also has its fans here. At Playa Tortugas, Km 7 (distances are marked along the 27-Km Paseo Kukulcán in the Hotel Zone, beginning downtown), there's the **International Windsurfer Sailing School** (☎ 998/984-2023). It has rental equipment and lessons. A local **National Windsurfing Tournament** (☎ 998/984-3212) is held here every year. Pedro Silvera organizes an annual **Windsurfing Tournament** in Progreso (☎ 999/944-3537 or e-mail pedros@sureste.com).

SAILING & FISHING: You can sail from any number of lagoon marinas. A Sunfish is ideal for the calm lagoon. Fly fishing and deep-sea fishing lure many Cancún sportsmen. April through September draws the best varieties of fish to local waters, but the sport is good year-round. Several marinas in Cancún and over on Isla Mujeres will arrange charters of four, six or eight hours. Charters include captain, first mate, gear, bait and beverages. And a boat.

Never a ship sails out of the bay,
But carries my heart as a stowaway.
~ Roselle Mercer Montgomery

■ Adventures on Wheels

 RECREATION PATH: A smooth 14-km (8.7-mile) serpentine path for bicycling, inline skating, jogging and walking weaves among flowers and topiary bushes along the zone's Paseo Kukulcán from downtown to Punta Cancún. It continues again in parts all the way out to Wet & Wild. Young vacationers with hard bodies get a workout here, especially in the morning hours.

GO-KARTING: Go-kart racing is very popular. Cartwheel over to **Karting International Cancún**, open daily from 10 am to 11 pm, south of town. Some special vehicles reach speeds of 80 mph on a competition standard track. Other karts putter along at 15 mph maximum. When we passed they were advertising rebates or free taxi rides from downtown (one-way).

■ Adventures on Foot

 GOLF: Golfers can enjoy the **Pok-Ta-Pok Club**, open 6 am-6 pm, along the lagoon at Km 7.5 (☎ 998/883-1277). Designed by Robert Trent Jones, the 18-hole course incorporates Maya ruins and sand traps, restaurant, bar, pro shop, rentals, a pool, tennis courts and driving range. The **Hilton Beach and Golf Resort** (formerly Caesar's Park, ☎ 998/881-8000) boasts its own championship 18-hole, par-72 course, designed around the Ruinas del Rey archeological site on the Nichupté Lagoon.

 There's a **Mini Golf Palace** at the Cancún Palace, Km 14.5, featuring 36 holes of mini-golf around pyramids, waterfalls, a river and a lagoon.

MAYA RUINS: Cancún's Hotel Zone contains two minor Maya ruin sites, the largest of which is **El Rey** (Kukulcán, Km 18.5, ☎ 998/883-2080, www.elreycancun.com). These ruins, mentioned by John Stephens in his 19th-century explorations, contain a few small surviving buildings, a three-story pryamid, some columned ruins, and a *sacbé* (a ceremonial road). And to bring more tourists into the site they have recreated pre-Columbian Maya life in an exhibit and opened a dinner restaurant known as the King's Palace. Dinner features Yucatecan cooking and ceremonial rites, music and dances. Call for information or book at your hotel. The other ruin, **Yamil Lu'um**, is written up under the Sheraton Hotel (see page 131).

BOWLING: There's a bowling alley in **Kukulcán Plaza**, open from 10 am to 1:30 am (☎ 998/885-3425) and one downtown called **Wol-Há** on Av. Tulum (☎ 998/887-2616).

TENNIS: Many hotels offer tennis courts for their guests, but there are no public courts in Cancún. Either sneak on to one of the hotel courts or take a temporary membership at Pok-Ta-Pok Club, whose courts are well maintained.

■ Adventures on Horseback

Horseback riding is a popular pastime for visitors. The largest ranch, **Rancho Loma Bonita** (☎ 998/887-5423), is located at Km 313 on Highway 307. A shuttle leaves from OK Maguey restaurant (at Km 13.5 on the Hotel Zone) twice a day. Rides on the American owners' 987 acres can be booked through travel agents, or you might save 10% by calling and arranging the trip yourself.

■ Adventures in the Air

DESTINATION CUBA: You can fly direct from Cancún to **Havana,** Cuba for one-night shopping sprees or longer vacations without having your passport stamped by Cuban officials. (Although it is legal for US citizens to visit Cuba, it is illegal for them to spend any money there, so the omission of a stamp avoids trouble.) Contact any travel agency to find out about the pricey junkets. Any not-so-pricey junkets tend to be on Cuban planes, in which we are not overly confident, so ask first.

FLIGHTSEEING: AeroCosta (☎ 998/884-0383) offers private charters for flightseeing and charter air tours along the coast or inland to archeological sights and Colonial cities. They fly a big new Cessna 206. Licensed pilots might have some luck renting general aviation planes from **Cancún Air** (☎ 998/986-0183) at the airport.

KID FRIENDLY

See a panoramic view of the Hotel Zone from the **Sightseeing Tower** (Embarcadero, Blvd. Kukulcán Km 4, ☎ 998/849-7777, www. embarcadero.com). A brief narrative accompanies the enclosed platform ride that offers a 360-degree view of that part of the Hotel Zone and lagoon mangroves. The pretty Calinda Beach Hotel opposite should get a lot of business as a result of the 100-foot-plus tower. Tower tickets are either for one ride (adults US $9) or an all-day and night pass ($14). Children under 12, half-price. Combination tickets are available for the Mexican Art Museum.

Accommodations

Compare hotel and restaurant prices in Cancún with those in major North American cities and you'll see what a bargain Mexico is. Not because it's cheaper in Cancún – you'll pay about the same price as you would in New York – but when you walk out the door you're on a magnificent beach. And you're on vacation! That said, there's no sense in paying more than you have to. Find a freebie called *Cancún Tips* magazine and look for some good discount coupons, including some for hotels. They're available at the airport in shops and booths, as well as your hotel.

> **AUTHORS' TIP:** *Be wary of the "free info" booths, where vendors will offer you a free trip to Isla or elsewhere if you visit a time-share or similar property. Just get the "tips" – free – and go. Some of the sales pitches are aggressive.*

If you're planning to stay only in Cancún's beachfront Hotel Zone, a good travel agent in your hometown should be able find several inexpensive packages – perhaps one that includes air and hotel – to fit your budget. Even adventure travelers can begin or end a Yucatán adventure in comfort. Here are some of our personal favorites in the Hotel Zone, several of which are all-inclusive.

■ Cancún's Hotel Zone

Villas Tacul *(Kukulcán Blvd Km 5.5, ☎ 998/849-7060, fax 998/849-7070, in US 800/842-0193 or 877/278-8018, in Canada 866-818-8342, www.villastacul.com.mx & www.mexicoboutiquehotels.com, 23 villas, air, cable TV, restaurant, pool, tennis courts).* This hidden treasure of a hotel, behind a long, undulating white wall, began its life as a private retreat for visiting government VIPs and dignitaries when Cancún was first being developed. The low-rise design is a throw-back to the original idea of having smaller, Caribbean-style hotels line the resort's soft white sands. Too bad everyone didn't follow Tacul's vision. Twenty-three Spanish-inspired villas – each containing one to five bedrooms or studios – are scattered around 12 acres of manicured gardens. Their large freeform swimming pool is shaded by palm trees planted in mini tropical islands. Nine of the villas face the sea (our choice), each with a small sand beach in an individual cove of limestone rock or swim at the larger, white sand beach at the west end. Villas Tacul maintains an "oasis in paradise" reputation. $$$$

HOTEL PRICE CHART	
NOTE: Often, one shared bed in a room is cheaper than two. Prices are per night, for two.	
[No $]	Less than US $20
$	US $20 - $40
$$	US $40 - $80
$$$	US $80 - $125
$$$$	US $125 - $200

Sina Suites *(Calle Quetzal, Blvd Kulkulcán Km 7.5, ☎ 998/883-1017, fax 883-2459, www.cancunsinasuites.com, 36 suites & a few rooms, restaurant, air, pool, dock).* Serene Sina Suites is a perfect hide-away for travelers who want to stay in the Cancún Hotel Zone but don't need the busy beach or an impersonal pressed-flesh resort atmosphere. Suites featuring full kitchens are oversized, with a view of the lagoon and the Cancún skyline, and are a definite good value. A large blue pool wraps around a sunken little restaurant that's centered in beautifully manicured gardens. It is situated on Calle Quetzal, a quiet residential cul-de-sac side street that borders the golf course on one side and the lagoon on the other. Turn at the parking lot entrance to Ty-Coz, before you get to the Presidente hotel. Spotlessly clean, Sina Suites have a charm you won't find in other places. A personal favorite. $$$

Also nearby on Calle Quetzal are **Grand Royal Lagoon** *(☎ 998/883-2899, in Mexico toll-free 800/552-4666, www.grlagoon.com)* and **Imperial Laguna Cancún** *(☎ 998/883-3448, www.mexhotels.com)* are both suite-style hotels that feature more hotel-like rooms with added kitchenettes. The excellent **La Palapa Restaurant** *(☎ 998/883-5454)* is the best feature of the Imperial; check out our review in the dining section.

Casa Turquesa *(Kukulcán Km 13.5, ☎ 998/885-2924 or 885-2925, fax 998/ 885-2922, in US 877/278-8018, in Canada 866/818-8342, www. casaturquesa.com, 31 suites with air, big pool, cable TV, ensuite jacuzzi, 2 restaurants, tennis court, fitness center, safe, mini-bar, wet bar, massage, free in-room musical CDs & VCR movies).* Walk to your room along a warren of marble-floor hallways and sitting areas, past original works of art, and you may just run into Bruce Willis or Demi Moore. Or perhaps Sly Stallone or Reba McEntire. That's because the Casa's small number of opulent suites and its renowned, but overpriced, restaurant – appropriately named **Celebrity** – attract notables (including the President of Mexico) who cherish their privacy and comfort. It's a member of Boutique Hotels of the World. Rooms are very large, with king-size beds, couch, cocktail table, dining table with chairs and private balcony or patio facing the beach, complete with a two-person jacuzzi and built-in day bed. The honeymoon suite sits high above the hotel with panoramic private balconies. As long as you're "roughing it" in the Hotel Zone – why not go deluxe? $$$$$

Hotel Flamingo *(Kukulcán Km 11, in US ☎ 800-544-3005, in Mexico ☎ 998/ 883-1544, fax 998/883-1029, www.flamingohotels.com, 220 rooms & jr. suites with air, 2 pools, balconies, safe deposit, wet bar).* The Flamingo is ideally located on a white Caribbean beach in the center of the *Zona Hoteles*, midway from the airport to the center of town, across from the Flamingo Plaza shopping mall. The rooms, beds and décor are attractive and comfortable. All rooms feature balconies. The hotel's restaurant, **La Frente**, is open to the poolside, with sliding glass windows overlooking the sea. The all-you-can-eat buffet (US $15 per person) offers a different theme every night: Yucatecan, Mexican, Italian, etc. Across the street, the Flamingo Plaza is a good source of inexpensive Hotel Zone food. It has Sanborn's, Dunkin' Donuts, McDonald's and our Mexican food favorite, Checándole. $$$-$$$$

Calinda Beach *(Kukulcán Km 4.5,* ☎ *998/849-4510, 470 rooms with air, telephones, pool, hot tub, restaurant, watersports, cable TV).* This Quality Hotel property, one of two in the Hotel Zone, is situated on one of the area's prettiest and best swimming beaches, adjacent to the inlet of the lagoon. The rooms all have balconies facing the soft surf. Ask for a special rate that includes breakfast. $$$-$$$$

Club Las Velas *(Kukulcán Km 5.8,* ☎ *998/849-7393, 89 rooms with air, 2 restaurants, nautical center, TV).* An all-inclusive resort facing the picturesque Laguna Nichupté. The rooms and two-level suites here are located in white adobe-style buildings scattered around colorful garden-filled courtyards. The effect is pleasantly reminiscent of a Colonial Mexican village. One courtyard, surrounded by cool plants and shade trees, boasts a huge green pond with several giant freshwater turtles and many fish. Las Velas, which means "sails" in Spanish, has a sandy beach on the lagoon. For those who prefer the ocean, the resort's own boat ferries guests to seaside beaches, or you can walk across the road to a public beach. Some rooms could use a few more comforts (such as table/reading lamps) in the ensuite sitting areas. Las Velas is very popular with travelers from England. Quiet and secluded, it offers a taste of Mexico. $$$$

El Pueblito Beach Hotel *(Kukulcán Km 17.5,* ☎ *998/881-8800, pueblito@ infosel.net.mx, 240 rooms with air, 3 restaurants, 5 pools, safe, TV, tennis court).* Only a few all-inclusive hotels in the zone try to create their own Mexican atmosphere and El Pueblito – which means "small village" – does it very well. Twenty-one multi-unit guest houses, clustered around courtyards that are woven with greenery and flowers, overlook a fine sand Caribbean beach. The reception and dining area are housed in a Colonial-style hacienda. The rooms are large, with simple furnishings that invoke an "Old Mexico" feeling. Small, enchanting terraced pools cascade down to the seafront. Recently renovated, the property is located on the quieter, southern end of the Hotel Zone, across from El Rey Maya ruins. A good buy, especially if you are not into the larger resorts. Popular with European and South American vacationers. $$$$-$$$$$

Sheraton Resort and Towers *(Kukulcán Km 12.5,* ☎ *in US 800/325-3535, in Mexico* ☎ *998/891-4400, fax 998/865-0204, www.sheraton.com, 471 rooms, 2 pools, health club with jacuzzi, TV, tennis, 4 restaurants).* The older, but super-clean-inside Sheraton is housed in a pyramid-style building and an adjacent tower next to some small Maya ruins. All are set on a bluff above a good beach. Back from the road, the hotel features several acres of manicured jungle gardens in the middle of which is a huge figure-eight pool. The large L-shaped lobby has a cool fountain garden under a skylight. Medium-size rooms have stone tile bathrooms and either two double beds or one king-size. Standard oceanfront rooms have wonderful views, but no balconies. Tower rooms all have private balconies and ocean views, and breakfast is included in the price. Oceanfront and garden suites have a large balcony with jacuzzi and two bathrooms. The nearby Maya ruin (Yamil Lu'um) includes the Temple of the Hand Print, so named because a hand print of a man was discovered in the stucco of an inside wall, along with the impression of the tail and backside of a cat. $$$$-$$$$$

Hilton Beach & Golf Resort *(Kukulcán Km 17, ☎ in US 800/445-8667, in Mexico ☎ 998/881-8000, fax 998/881-8080, www.hilton.com, pools, 426 rooms, 5 restaurants, phone, TV, golf course, health club, lighted tennis courts).* Late in 1999, Hilton bought this property, formerly Caesar's Park, located in the south end near the bottom of the island's "7" shape, on one of Cancún's best beaches. The Hilton commands a spectacular, unobstructed view of the Caribbean and its own 18-hole championship golf course next to the lagoon. It's the largest piece of land of any Cancún property (250 acres). The pyramid-shaped, nine-story hotel houses 426 oceanview rooms with computer ports, dual jacks on phone lines and voice mail (handy for us travel writers, but who wants to work on vacation?). Rooms have a soft beige and pink décor with marble tiles, pastel Mexican cotton bedding, pottery lamps, light wood and rattan furnishings and large combination bathrooms, but very small balconies. On the side of the main building, lovely low-rise villas, called Royal Suites, weave down to a perfect white beach. These suites are considerably larger than regular suites and boast amenities equivalent to concierge floors, including continental breakfast, hors d'oeuvres, and separate check-in. Ask about their golf packages and specials. $$$$$

Presidente Inter-Continental *(Kukulcán Km 7.5, in US ☎ 800-327-0200, in Mexico ☎ 998/848-8700, fax 998/883-25-15, www.intercontinental.com, 299 rooms, 2 pools, 4 restaurants, tennis, air, cable TV, kids club).* The Presidente is the grande dame of Cancún. It was one of the (if not *the*) first hotels built in the Hotel Zone. All the rooms were tastefully remodeled in 1999. The lobby's reflecting pool is particularly intriguing and the lobby bar features nightly live entertainment. The comfortable rooms have one king-size or two queen beds, dining table and chairs, and tiled bathrooms. They face ei-

ther the lagoon or the beach and are in the tall tower or the lower wing. The breakfast buffet is outrageously good. Presidente guests don't pay greens fees at Pok-Ta-Pok golf course. $$$-$$$$

Westin Regina *(Kukulcán Km 20, ☎ in US 800/937-8461, in Mexico 998/848-7400, fax 885-0296, www.starwood.com, 293 rooms on 6 floors, pool, restaurant, air, coffee makers, cable, babysitting).* If there's one Cancún property that knows what comfort means, it's the Westin. What a class hotel! We got lost in the soft king-size bed with six pillows and 300 count cotton sheets – and if we hadn't had to leave the room to swim in the pool, we would have never left. Shades of Willie Wonka. Evening turndown service features super-rich chocolates on the bed. The room's white walls and tile floors understate its elegance with a pleasant extra of floor-to-ceiling lattice sliding

Cenote Aktun Chen, Quintana Roo (see page 123)

Pool at Casa de los Sueños, Isla Mujeres (see page 166)

window shutters that allow diffused natural light if you desire. Each over-sized superior accommodation includes a large bathroom with top-shelf toi-letries and a welcome coffee machine. The Westin may be located at the far end of the hotel zone, but it's high on the list of Cancún's best hotels. $$$$-$$$$$

Youth Hostel *(Kukulcán Km 3.2, ☎ 998/983-1337, beach)*. The only "hotel" that qualifies as budget in the Hotel Zone is this youth hostel, which sleeps men and women in separate rooms with bunk beds. Rather than a hostel, it should be called a "hovel" because of its run-down condition. Years of neglect have taken their toll on this once-attractive motel-style building. Paint is peeling and the blinds are torn. You need to bring your own toilet paper to the communal bathroom because there are no rolls in the stalls, only the one on the wall several feet away. Pull up your pants first, you may trip!

The hostel, however, is on the beach and it is very cheap – about US $10 per night, plus a US $6 refundable deposit in case you steal the threadbare sheets. A few tolerable private cabañas that sleep two or more are available at US $30 per night. Tent camping spaces on the beach run around US $5. The sandy shore is picture-perfect, making this a great spot, provided you have considerate camping neighbors. Sometimes they allow RVs. Ask the caretakers if you need to rent a hammock.

Hotel Ríu *(all-inclusive, www.riu.com)*. You can't miss this hotel – its gran-diose design casts an unwelcome shadow over a popular corner of the Hotel Zone opposite Plaza Caracol. Despite owning attractive properties down in Playacar, the Ríu hotel chain must have thought they were building a resort in East Berlin instead of Cancún. The huge, wing-shaped hotel is crowned on each end with guard towers that look like they could hold machine guns to cut down escaping guests. In a Hotel Zone that boasts some architecturally notable designs, the Soviet, Lubianca-like Ríu stands out like a sore thumb. $$$$$

■ Cancún City

The downtown area of Cancún provides the best opportunity for bargains in hotels and restaurants. But it is also a great experience. Unfortunately, it's not on the beach. Many tourists are concerned about possible dangers, rip-offs or trouble outside of the protected cocoon of the Hotel Zone, but the crime rate is no higher (and probably lower) than that of many US cities. The down-town area is full of both Mexicans and tourists. We've selected a series of ho-tels in safe areas of the downtown with reputations for customer satisfaction.

Moderate Hotels

Radisson *(Av. Nader No 1, in US ☎ 800-333-3333, in Mexico ☎ 998/987-4455, fax 884-7954, 246 deluxe rooms, air, fitness center, cable TV, 2 restau-*

Quintana Roo

rants, pool, bar, breakfast included). The Radisson is a little out of the way, one block north of Av. Uxmal on Av. Nader, but it is the downtown's premier hotel and a bit of an upgrade from its previous life as a Holiday Inn. Located next to a school on a bend in the road of a quasi-residential neighborhood, it is quiet and secure. The atrium lobby has overstuffed furniture and through its glass doors is the central courtyard containing the long irregularly shaped blue pool, with a waterfall at one end, and an inviting snack palapa bar. The four-story Colonial-style wings, whose comfortably-sized rooms feature two beds and tile bath, surround the sunny courtyard. When there is business done in Cancún, it's usually done here – in comfort. The staff is attentive. $$$

Hotel Antillano *(Av. Tulum & Claveles, ☎ 998/884-1132, fax 998/884-1878, www.hotelantillano.com, 48 rooms with air, TV, pool, telephones, continental breakfast included).* The hotel is as bright, fresh and spotlessly clean as it was the first time we stayed here many years ago. But the price has gone up to a point that makes it hard to call this a real bargain anymore – unless you compare prices to those in the Hotel Zone. Still, it's an excellent choice in downtown for quality and a perennial favorite. The floors are all polished terra-cotta tile and the rooms are stucco-white with rosewood trim. In larger rooms the feeling is intimate, with curved walls and bathrooms and closets set back into niches. Smaller rooms are a little on the cramped side. Free storage lockers are available, which is handy if you want to wander the peninsula. $$

El Rey del Caribe *(Av. Uxmal near the corner of Nader, ☎ 998/984-2028, fax 998/984-9857, www.reycaribe.com, 24 rooms with air, pool, jacuzzi, parking, cable TV, kitchenettes, transportation from airport).* The Rey del Caribe is a gold hacienda-style building with a green central courtyard garden and red terra-cotta tile floors. Just off the busiest part of town, the Rey is one of the best values in the moderate category. The rooms are clean and bright and have something of a Colonial feel. They are modern and well-equipped, with kitchenettes and room safes. A jacuzzi and tiny pool are nestled among the flowering plants, as well as their new al-fresco all-purpose breakfast and relaxation gazebo. The Rodríguez family has added spa services, including massage and a meditation area, and they complement that in-town serenity with ecological contributions such as a solar panels and composting toilets. Seven rooms in the back are especially pleasant – we like #25, both big and bright. On the third floor in the front are two very appealing rooms, but we don't recommmend them if you're carrying a lot of luggage. One is a single and the other, #18, has a balcony with a good city view. $$

Suites Cancún *(Calle Alcatraces No. 32 opposite Palapas Park, ☎ 998/884-23-01, fax 998/884-7270, www.suitescancun.com.mx, 30 suites with air or fans, pool, TV).* Suites and rooms in this hotel, tucked away in a quiet section of town, rent by the day, week or month. Each suite faces a central outdoor courtyard and has tiled floors, small but pleasant bathrooms, an open, fully-equipped kitchen area, dining and sitting sections, bedrooms with two twin and one king bed each and generous closets. Suites Cancún offers a very good rate for long-term stays. $$

Xbalamqué *(Av. Yaxchilan, ☎ 998/887-7853, www.kim-ek.com, 80 rooms & suites, air, cable, gym, health spa, pool, parking).* Be prepared to be surprised by the elaborate décor, comfortable rooms, appealing pool, inviting cantina restaurant, and in-

HOTEL PRICE CHART	
NOTE: Often, one shared bed in a room is cheaper than two. Prices are per night, for two.	
[No $]	Less than US $20
$	US $20 - $40
$$	US $40 - $80
$$$	US $80 - $125
$$$$	US $125 - $200

teresting health spa in this downtown hotel (pronounced ish-bawl-am-KAY). We expected a hokey faux resort when we entered the giant Maya mouth doorway, but the hotel's painted mural public areas were of high quality and set the mood for discovering a charming back-yard pool and hidden health spa. The spa offers massage, new-age homeopathy, beauty treatments, and a natural products store. One of the most interesting features is a brick, sauna-like "Temazcal," the ancient indigenous American ceremonial sweat lodge that incorporates essential herbs and aromatherapy. A thermal bath and massage cost only about US $50 for 45 minutes. The poolside restaurant has a Mexican cantina atmosphere, and there's a really great café and bookstore out front featuring live music. Most importantly, the accommodations are very pleasant. You'll wonder why anyone would bother going to the Hotel Zone if you stay here. $$

Suites El Patio *(Av. Bonhampak #51 at corner Cereza, ☎ 998/884-3500, fax 998/884-3540, www.cancun-suites.com, air, cable TV, breakfast included).* Suites El Patio was obviously built with a Colonial ambiance in mind. Enter through the heavy black wrought-iron gate (secured after dark) into a small, pleasant, Mexican-tiled courtyard with patio furniture nestled among the abundant greenery. The upper rooms are accessed through an outside stair-way that has an additional small sitting area built in. Each comfortable room has either a queen or two twin beds and super-clean bathrooms. The furnishings are Colonial Spanish, with carved wood armoires and leather chairs. Very popular. The owners succeed in delivering a different, more authentic, Cancún experience. $-$$

Budget Hotels

Punta Allen Guest House *(Calle Punta Allen, ☎ 998/884-0225 or 884-1001, 18 rooms with air, TV, breakfast).* The Punta Allen, an intimate, family-owned hotel, has a large salon for sitting and dining that was once the downstairs of this three-story former private home. Rooms facing the side street have balconies and there's a locked entrance gate of wrought iron. Rooms in the back are a tad small. The Punta Allen will appeal to travelers who appreciate their privacy and security, as well as a friendly atmosphere. Its low price, charm and location – on a quiet street only two blocks from downtown – make this Colonial-styled gem a genuine best value. $

Novotel *(Av. Tulum,* ☎ *998/884-2999, fax 998/884-3162, www. novotelcancun.com, 43 rooms with air or fans, pool, restaurant, TV).* Located near the circle of Av. Tulum and Uxmal, the modern Novotel is reminiscent of an old Colonial building. There's heavy wood furniture in the sitting area and an indoor courtyard dining area. The "superior" rooms are in this building and are so-called because they offer cable TV, air-conditioning and a tiny balcony. Out back, next to the tiny pool, there are two Caribbean-style wooden buildings that house the "standard" rooms. Except for television and air-conditioning, these rooms are the same and are even slightly larger than the superiors. We think these newer, quieter rooms are the better buy. $$

Maria de Lourdes Hotel *(Av. Yaxchilan,* ☎ *998/884-4744, fax 998/884-1242, www.hotelmariadelourdes.com, 51 rooms with air, TV, phones, pool).* The Maria is known as a perennial good value in "close-to-it-all" downtown hotels. It's pleasant and friendly, and has an outdoor patio and pool. A small restaurant here is open Monday-Saturday 7-11, for *desayuno* (breakfast) and 4-8 pm for *cena* (dinner). Each respectable-size room has two queen-size beds. $$

Parador *(Av. Tulum No. 26,* ☎ *998/884-1043 or 884-1310, fax 998/884-9712, 66 rooms with air, pool, TV, restaurant, private parking).* This budget hotel is starting to show some wear around the edges, but the guest rooms are clean and neat. The Parador features a small, odd-shaped swimming pool and a children's wading pool in the back. Located right in the heart of the downtown. It sees lots of repeat customers. $

Hotel Hacienda *(Av. Sunyaxchen,* ☎ *998/884-3672, fax 998/884-1208, 35 rooms with air, pool, restaurant, TV).* This family-owned hotel has a small eating area for high-season breakfast next to its blue sparkling swimming pool in the center courtyard. Located just two blocks from downtown. The brightly painted rooms are relatively small. It has the same owner as the Hotel Berny on Isla Mujeres. We met several Americans who stayed here long-term. Limited private parking in front. $$

Hotel Colonial *(Tulepanes,* ☎ *998/884-1535, fax 998/884-4861, 50 rooms with air or fans, TV).* Recently reconditioned, the Colonial has stepped up its Colonial appeal to make it well worth considering. The rooms, surrounding a large and airy courtyard located just steps off Av. Tulum, boast new beds, tile floors and big bathrooms. $-$$

Hotel Maria Isabel *(Calle Palmeras, ☎/fax 998/884-9015, 10 rooms, air, TV, overhead lights, 3 floors).* On a quiet side street off Av. Uxmal, the Maria Isabel is a small hotel popular with budget travelers, especially Europeans. Smallish rooms have good bathrooms. Bills itself as Cancún's original hostel. $

Hotel Posada Lucy *(Calle Gladiolas No. 25, ☎ 998/884-4165, TV, 19 rooms with air, 5 have little kitchens).* The posada is a well-known stop among bargain travelers to Cancún, but some better values have come along since the Lucy made a name for itself. Its largish rooms are a little dark but comfortable (one smaller room has a fan only). Getting a room with a kitchenette might be worthwhile, especially if you're spending some time in town. $-$$

Villa Maya Cancún *(Av. Uxmal No. 20 on the corner of Rubia, ☎ 988/884-2829, fax 988/884-1762, 15 rooms with air, TV, phones, pool).* Nestled on the corner of a dead-end street (Rubia) and across from the Howard Johnson's, the Villa Maya is quiet and clean with pleasing rooms and a friendly staff. This is a good choice for an inexpensive stay in town without sacrificing comfort or cleanliness. Upstairs rooms are brighter. It was the first economy hotel we stayed in the downtown and is a sentimental favorite. $

Mecoloco Trailer Park *(between Puerto Juárez & Punta Sam, ☎ 998/843-0324, trailerparkmecoloco@hotmail.com, showers, laundry & food store).* The Meco has full hook-ups for RVs or trailers and spaces to pitch a tent. Most tenting spots are out in the open, but there are some shaded spots. The beach across the street is OK, but the public one down the road is better. Internet service is available inside the popular convenience store. Close to ferries for Isla Mujeres, the park has surprisingly good rates. There's regular, inexpensive bus service to downtown or the beaches, making this a real bargain. $

Hostels

Soberanis Youth Hostel *(Av. Cobá, ☎ 998/884-4564, www.sobranis.com.mx, air, Internet, breakfast included).* Also known as Cancún Hostel, the Sobranis has the advantage that the Ruta #2 bus, to and from the beaches in the Hotel Zone, stops in front of their door. Private rooms as well as typical dorm style. They are affliated with Hostelling International. Look for a building like a hotel, just around the side of the Chedraui, in the middle of everything, downtown.

Mexico Youth Hostel *(Andador Palmera behind the Tapatio Restaurant off Av. Uxmal, ☎ 998/887-0191, www.mexicohostels.com, fans, lockers, continental breakfast included).* Meet world travelers up close and personal in the Hostelling International-affliated Youth Hostel, located four blocks from the the bus station. While you're trying to think in Spanish, you can practice your German, French, and Italian. This dormitory-style hotel offers other amenities beyond just privacy – locker rentals, self-service laundry, communal bathrooms, Internet access, bike rentals, TV lounge, full kitchen and bunk beds. There are crowded dorm quarters for men, women, and mixto. The coolest – but most crowded – sleeping is under the roof-top palapa.

Mayan Hostel *(Calle Margaritas,* ☎ *998/892-0103, www.cancunhostel.com, fans, lockers, Internet, kitchen).* While all the sweaty bodies jam the other hostels in town, sneak over to the open and airy little rooftop Mayan Hostel, run by a Mexican family of Arabic and German extraction. Two palapa-roofed traditional Maya wood huts provide secure dorm sleeping for only 10. Bath and shower, free lockers and clean linen, kitchen, TV, Internet access, laundry and more. We found it cuter, cooler, and much more comfortable than the cattle-car sleeping of other hostels. At night the rooftop tables and soft lighting make this hostel one of the most inviting we've seen for a long time. Highly recommended.

Dining

Part of the secret of success in life is to eat what you like and let the food fight it out inside.
~ Mark Twain, 1835-1910

What's a vacation for if not to eat out? In Cancún, there's a whole range of choices for meals – Mexican, continental, Italian, Chinese, Japanese, seafood, fast food, BBQ. It's all there and in every price range, so you're sure to find something to meet your taste and budget. Naturally, the Hotel Zone's prices are higher and ambiance richer. It's best to make reservations during high season.

DINING PRICE CHART	
NOTE: Prices based on a typical entrée, per person, and do not include beverage.	
$	Less than US $5
$$	US $5 - 10
$$$	Over US $10

■ Cancún's Hotel Zone

Expensive

Casa Rolandi *(Plaza Caracol, Km 8.5,* ☎ *998/883-1817, www.rolandi.com).* Among diners-in-the-know, there is little argument that Casa Rolandi is the best Italian and seafood restaurant in the Hotel Zone. Loyal customers (like us) come back year after year to its corner location on the lagoon side of Plaza Caracol. Behind stained glass windows, Rolandi's presents a Mediterrean, bistro-like atmosphere, with soft music and soft lighting, pressed linen tablecloths, and an intimate setting. Unlike restaurants that depend on an artificial ambience to please patrons, Casa Rolandi allows its menu to speak for itself – and the dining is delightful. Choose your lobster from their tank, peruse the fresh seafood bar, or sit down and relax at your table and order something delicious à la carte. Say hello from us to Mirko, Casa Rolandi's long-time manager. $$$

Hacienda El Mortero *(Kukulcán Km 9.5, across from the Convention Center,* ☎ *998/883-1133)*. The ambiance of El Mortero is one of the most intriguing in Cancún. Built in the style of its 18th-century namesake, the hacienda displays curved arches, hanging plants, soft lighting, adobe walls, Spanish tile and beveled glass windows. The traditional menu features steak, prime rib and authentic Mexican dishes with such touches as homemade tortillas and sauces. The bar offers 15 types of tequila and all guests are offered a cocktail on the house. Mariachis play nightly at 7:30, 9 and 10, and a romantic guitar trio serenades on Saturday. There is a non-smoking section. A unique experience. Open from 6:30 to 11:30 pm. $$$

Plantation House *(Kukulcán Km 10.5,* ☎ *998/883-1433)* This fancy seafood restaurant is housed in a Caribbean version of Tara – as if *Gone with the Wind* had been about a Caribbean restaurant. Lots and lots of polished wood in a beautiful veranda dining room overlooking the Mississippi – actually the Nichupté Lagoon. The menu features fine food and dinner here is a special night out. Ya'll come back now, ya hear? $$$+

Mango Tango *(Kukulcán Km 14.2,* ☎ *98/85-03-03)*. Caribbean is the style and the flavor of Mango Tango, a huge, stand-alone restaurant facing Nichupté Lagoon. The menu's best dishes are seafood, and they also serve up steaks and beef shish kabobs. The calypso atmosphere pulsates when the Caribbean Festival show begins at 7 pm and 9:30. Although Cancún has little culture in common with Caribbean islands such as Jamaica (of course, they do share great white beaches and warm tropical weather), the folklore show is both fun and festive. The food and atmosphere at Mango Tango is good enough to keep diners coming back. If you like sweet dishes, try the mango chutney shrimp. Open from noon to 2 am. $$$

La Palapa *(Calle Quetzal, Imperial Laguna Hotel, off Blvd Kukulcán, Km 7.5,* ☎ *998/883-5454)*. It's been said that the finest of French food is best prepared by Belgian chefs, and at La Palapa that seems to be true. Who would have thought to have a gourmet restaurant on a rustic wooden dock behind a two-star hotel facing the lagoon? Most of the diners who find their way here find it by word of mouth – and the word is good! The menu changes nightly and comes written on a blackboard brought to your table. It's a very romantic setting. Our most recent meal included creamed soup, a mouth-watering pork loin with a mustard sauce, garlic mashed potatoes, and a cheesecake for dessert. It also boasts a good wine list. Next time, go where the hordes of tasteless tourists don't go – La Palapa. $$$

La Dolce Vita *(Av. Kukulcán Km 14.6,* ☎ *998/885-0150)*. After years of luring customers downtown to its pretty garden setting, La Dolce now sits on the edge of the lagoon in the Hotel Zone. They retained the same attentive staff and superb regional Italian cuisine. One of the house specialties is beautifully presented lobster medallions and shrimp simmered in white wine and herbs over green tagliolini (US $17). The manager, Juan, has been with the restaurant for over 15 years and he stops and greets customers at every table. La Dolce reeks of casual elegance, with terrace dining, soft lighting, romantic live music and luxurious table settings. We never miss dinner here on a trip to Cancún. Reservations are suggested. $$$+

Budget/Moderate

Local families come for lunch and a swim at Rio Nizuc.

Rio Nizuc *(south end of the Zona Hoteleria, Kulkulkán Blvd, no phone).* There's a small sign among the mangroves, easily missed, that announces the location of the Rio Nizuc restaurant. Fortunately, few tourists find this gem, although hundreds of them pass by on jet skis as they enter the Laguna Nichupté on a Jungle Tour. You can sit in the cool shade and watch them watch you with envy as you enjoy this very special mostly seafood restaurant. To get here, pass the Westin, turn left just over the bridge on the edge of the Hotel Zone and park in the dirt parking lot. Follow the path among the mangroves to this rustic, water's-edge restaurant for an afternoon rendezvous. One of the dishes they're famous for is Tikin-xic, fresh fish cooked in Maya anchiote spice and limes. Absolutely delicious. Bring your swimsuit and snorkel for an after-lunch dip. Have a beer or two and spend the day. Open for lunch 11 am-6 pm. $$

Sanborn's Café *(Plaza Flamingo and Maya Fair, no phone).* Sanborn's is a chain of restaurants similar to an American diner/restaurant, perhaps with a touch of pancake house thrown in. In fact, they serve breakfast 24 hours a day on linen tablecloths, with cups of good coffee and free refills. For lunch and dinner they feature Mexican cooking at reasonable prices. The waitresses dress in colorful long cotton skirts and give attentive service. Sanborn's also offers a non-smoking area, a rare feature in this region. Very dependable and pleasing, with a downtown location at Av. Uxmal and Tulum, across the street from the bus terminal. $-$$

Ty-Coz *(Kukulcán, angled across the street from El Presidente hotel and a larger one at Km 7).* With only three patio tables in front, this little place defies the odds in the "bigger-is-better" Cancún Hotel Zone. It serves deliciously strong cappuccino and fresh-brewed coffee and makes fabulous sandwiches on crusty French bread. A second sit-down restaurant has opened at Km 7 and there's always the original one, downtown. Daily specials. $

Checándole *(Flamingo Plaza, no phone).* A fast-food offshoot of a popular Mexican restaurant in Cancún City. The food here is tasty and well prepared. Hot spices are on the side. Specials often offer two-for-one beers. Right next to a McDonald's and a row of food stalls – but Checándole is the best of the bunch. $

■ Cancún City

The experience of eating downtown is very different from the Hotel Zone, perhaps because the atmosphere is more authentically Mexican, or maybe because it's so much cheaper. Take a bus into town and look around. We review a wide range of dining delights. Calling ahead to reserve is not necessary at many of these places, the majority of which do not have business phones.

Budget

Los Amigos Restaurant *(Av. Tulum).* Colorful painted ladder-back chairs fill the sidewalk under tables with umbrellas, next to several similar downtown restaurants. All Tulum Ave. restaurants have barkers to lure customers with the offer of a free drink, and Los Amigos is no exception. For dinner they display plates of grilled steaks and fresh seafood that they guarantee will be just as appetizing and generous when served to you. We paid under $10 for a large filet mignon, potato, green salad and a margarita. With prices like that it's hard to go back to the Hotel Zone and spend the same or more for a sandwich and soda. $-$$

Los Huaraches de Alcatraces *(Claveles No. 31, no phone, open Tuesday through Saturday, 7 am to 10 pm).* Ever wonder where the locals eat in a resort town like Cancún? Many of them eat here, only one block off touristy Tulum Ave. Inexpensive food is offered à la carte cafeteria-style in this clean walk-through restaurant. The word Huaraches (oua-RACHES) means "sandals" and the food item with the same name is an oval-shaped tortilla filled with refried beans *(frijoles)* that you can have topped with chicken, beef, more beans or anything that catches your fancy. It's an excellent value. If you're not familiar with the dishes, the staff will patiently describe each one, even as the line builds in back of you. Evening meals are served tableside. $

Gory Tacos *(Tulipanes No. 26).* Simple décor and relatively cheap fast food make Gory a popular spot with young tourists and locals. The Mexican menu includes quesadillas, tortas and, of course, tacos. Or you can order complete meals of chicken, beef or fish that come with ample side dishes. Daily specials. $

Quintana Roo

Ty Coz *(☎ 998/884-6050, Av. Tulum, on the north side of the Comercial Mexicana, closed Sundays).* See our review of their smaller Hotel Zone eatery, above. This downtown location is much larger, with appealing café dining, French movie star posters, photos on the wall, and a somewhat larger menu. A Frenchman from Brittany with a penchant for Scots bagpipes owns the two Ty Coz sandwich shops where we eat every time we're in Cancún. Great coffee and sandwiches on crusty bread. Who could ask for a better meal? $

D'Pa *(Alcatraces, ☎ 998/884-7615).* D'Pa is a romantic sidewalk café featuring a menu of fine French crêpes – both sweet and savory. It's located on the edge of Parque las Palapas; clients dine al fresco on sidewalk tables or in the small interior, reminiscent of an intimate Paris bistro. Great for desserts or a light dinner. With soft French music in the background, dining at D'Pa puts you in the mood. Pedestrian house wine. Opens at 5 pm, closed Mondays. $$

El Café *(Av. Nader No. 5).* Only one block from crowded Av. Tulum, this clean and cool outdoor café serves up coffee or tea and fresh-baked *pan dulce* (sweet rolls) both mornings and afternoons. This is where the local business people come to have those too-long lunches. El Café offers a varied menu from breakfast through dinner, all of it good and served under drooping flamboyante trees. Unusually fast service, tasty food and reasonable prices are why we eat here often. $-$$

Pizza Rolandi *(Av. Coba & Tulum).* Cool and private, this out-of-the way pizza joint features excellent brick oven pizza and tasty Italian food in a romantic setting. It is less crowded than its sister Rolandis on Isla Mujeres and Plaza Caracol in the Hotel Zone. $-$$

Los Bisquets *(Av. Nader, ☎ 998/887-6876).* One of our favorite breakfast and lunch places is Los Bisquets Obregón, on Av. Nader halfway between the circle at Uxmal (where there's a big California restaurant) and the Radisson hotel. Los Bisquets is a chain of eateries that feature home-baked biscuits and pastries in a full-service restaurant. Delicious coffee, breakfast, lunch, dinner – all behind big glass windows. Friendly and welcoming atmosphere, plus a large menu. Small non-smoking area. $-$$

Moderate

Meson de Vecindario "La Baguette" *(corner of Av. Uxmal & Nader).* Open for lunch and dinner, this neat and tidy French bistro began life as a bakery and sandwhich shop but has grown into a trendy eatery. Set back from the road under a dark green awning with a palm tree wrapped in romantic twinkling lights, the Meson offers inside or outdoor dining. The restaurant serves wine, cappuccino, and good food at brightly hand-painted tables. If you're tired of Mexican food, stop here. C'est magnifique. $$

La Habichuela *(Av. Margarita No. 25, ☎ 988/884-3158).* Capturing a quiet corner of old Yucatán with its lush garden and Maya artifacts, La Habichuela (string bean) is a legend among locals and select tourists. Since 1977, the Pezzotti family has run this almost-secret restaurant, serving fine cuts of meat and seafood with a Caribbean flavor. Their specialty is *cocobichuela*, lobster and shrimp cooked in a mild curry sauce and served in a coconut shell with fruit (US $30). The romantic courtyard ambiance includes beautiful table settings of linen and crystal, soft lighting and outdoor dining to the gentle sound of a fountain. Not easy to find, but worth every effort. Next door, Labna restaurant is owned by the same family. $$$

Perico's Restaurant *(Av. Yaxchilán)*. Perico's continues to attract diners with an extensive menu of Mexican food, steaks and seafood. The colorful bar, with huge murals of Mexican heroes and American movie stars, makes use of saddles atop its bar stools. There's always a party atmosphere here from 1 pm to closing at 1 am, with much music and an infectious conga line. This is one of the downtown's most festive places; happy hour here is just that. It's worth a visit just to see. $$-$$$

La Parilla *(Av. Yaxchilan, ☎ 998/884-5398)*. Back when Cancún was young and innocent, La Parilla, "The Grill," opened as a street-side spot for Arabic/Greek-style pork tacos. They must have done it right because over the years La Parilla grew into a large, friendly Mexican restaurant that now seats a hundred hungry diners. Look for the big black and white bull on the sidewalk and that tiny original grill, left intact as a reminder of more humble beginnings. By offering generous helpings at reasonable prices, La Parilla has become a mini-chain, with restaurants in Playa, Campeche and Mérida, plus the popular La Parranda restaurant in the Hotel Zone. They offer a huge seafood buffet every Friday evening, and mariachis play every night. If you're in the mood for Mexican, think La Parilla. Open from 12:30 pm to 4 am. $$

Villarica Restaurant *(Av. Yaxchilan at the circle)*. Bamboo walls and an upstairs palapa roof mark this seafood restaurant, one big block over from the town's center. Very popular with locals. Excellent menu and good food draws repeat customers every evening. $$

Los Almendros *(Av. Tulum, two blocks north of the bus terminal)*. If you're not heading out into the Yucatán, a stop at this Cancún restaurant is an absolute must. This was once the premiere Yucatecan restaurant in Mexico, and is famous for introducing Poc Chuc, a dish of delicious thinly sliced, grilled pork fillets marinated in orange and served with onions. Other locations include Ticul and Mérida. Typical Yucatecan dishes are illustrated in photos on the walls as well as on the menu, so be adventuresome – it's a taste adventure. You can't say you've been to the Yucatán without eating here – or in their other locations in Ticul and Mérida. Next door to Restaurant El Arabe, a good place for Middle Eastern food. $$

La Placita *(Av. Yaxchilan, ☎ 998/884-0407)*. In downtown Cancún, some of the best eateries have concentrated on Av. Yaxchilan – and La Placita is one of the best of those. It's a restaurant dicotmy – facing the street is a relaxed outdoor dining area where you can eat informally under beer-logo umbrellas. Inside, however, starched linen napery and crystal glasses promise a surprisingly delicious formal dinner at a very reasonable price. La Placita has been around since Cancún began, and for good reason. There's a fine wine list and don't miss the intriguing bathrooms upstairs. It has a second smaller location at the Plaza de Toros. $$

El Pescador *(Tulipanes,* ☎ *998/884-2673).* Since its opening in 1980, the Pescador has steadily competed with **Carrillo's Lobster House**, the other premier seafood restaurant downtown on Av. Claveles. Carrillo's has a charming budget hotel in back of the restaurant. Both serve great seafood and each has its loyal fans, but El Pescador is slightly more popular. The heavy wooden tables are works of art in themselves, with individual hand-painted scenes on their tiled tops. $$$

*Maya children in front of white-washed stone walls,
which are often seen in small villages.*

Quintana Roo

Leaving Town

Not all those that wander are lost.
~ JRR Tolkien, *Fellowship of the Ring*

See *Departures* on page 96 for airport departure information.

■ Heading South

To go south toward **Playa del Carmen** or **Tulum** from the Hotel Zone, drive south on **Paseo Kukulcán** and take the marked exit over the bridge. This is **Highway 307 South** that goes all the way to **Chetumal**. A divided highway has replaced the old two-lane road, at least as far as Tulum Pueblo. Traffic travels rather fast. If you're downtown, go south on Av. Tulum, which turns into 307 South.

■ Heading West

Following Horace Greeley's directions into the Yucatán offers a choice of two routes, both shown on maps as **Highway 180.** The first is the **Mérida Cuota,** the only road west that's easy to find from

Cancún. It's a toll road with very few exits and two collection booths, one east of Valladolid and one west of Piste. It's relatively expensive (US $14 from Cancún to Chichén Itzá; US $23 total from Cancún to Mérida), but this new road allows cars to zip along at a very fast clip. If you're going from one place to another – such as Valladolid, Chichén Itzá or Mérida – the Cuota's shortcut through the jungle makes life much easier. Access the Cuota from Highway 307, just south of the turn for the airport. Head toward Playa/Tulum for a few kilometers then follow the signs for Mérida and Valladolid.

It takes only 3½ hours on the Cuota to reach Mérida.

DISTANCES FROM CANCÚN	
Aktun Chen . . . . 84 km/52 miles	Progreso . . . . 341 km/212 miles
Akumal . . . . 105 km/65 miles	Puerto Aventuras . . . . 98 km/61 miles
Campeche . . . . 494 km/307 miles	Puerto Juárez . . . . 2 km/1.2 miles
Chemuyil . . . . 109 km/68 miles	Puerto Morelos . . . . 36 km/22 miles
Chetumal . . . . 379 km/236 miles	Punta Sam . . . . 7 km/4 miles
Chichén Itzá . . . . 192 km/119 miles	Tres Rios . . . . 40 km/25 miles
Cobá . . . . 96 km/60 miles	Tulum . . . . 131 km/81 miles
Cozumel . . . . 93 km/58 miles	Uxmal . . . . 382 km/237 miles
Isla Mujeres . . . . 10 km/6 miles	Valladolid . . . . 152 km/94 miles
Mérida . . . . 306 km/190 miles	Xcaret . . . . 72 km/45 miles
Playa Del Carmen . . . . . . 68 km/42 miles	Xel-Há . . . . 122 km/76 miles

The alternative route is **Mérida Libre**, a two-lane road through the heart of Maya country. It offers the great advantage of being able to see the "real" Yucatán, and we've had a special adventure of one sort or another every time we've been on it. The road is always interesting, wandering through villages passed by time, but it does require some patience. *Topes* (speed bumps) guard each village and they make for a slower journey. But there's more to life than driving fast, especially in the Yucatán. Handicrafts, gifts and bottles of honey are sold from private homes along the way.

To find Mérida Libre from downtown, take **Av. Uxmal** west for a few blocks and turn left at the Mérida sign on **Av. Lopez Portillo**, which becomes **Route 180**. Same results apply when taking **Cobá** west to **Av. Kabah** (turn right to Portillo, then left for Mérida). If you're in the section of the Hotel Zone that is closer to the downtown, follow the directions above. Otherwise, head south on 307 (toward Playa/Tulum) and turn right at the big Pemex station on your right. Follow that to a left turn (Av. Lopez Portillo) marked for Mérida. That becomes Route 180 and you're on your way.

See the chapter titled *East - Red (Lakin Chac)*, pages 311-352, for information on the numerous attractions along the way. If you change your mind or find the road too slow, there is an opportunity to get on the Cuota when it crosses under the free road about 15 minutes west of town.

■ Heading North

To get to **Isla Mujeres** from downtown, take any bus marked "Puerto Juárez" or "Punta Sam" north on Av. Tulum from in front of the Comercial Mexicana supermarket. It's a short ride on Av. Lopez Portillo to the ferries. Driving from the Hotel Zone, turn right on Av. Bonampak and make another right at the light. Otherwise, take one of the shuttle boats from Playa Linda in the Hotel Zone. Punta Sam, the departure point for the large car ferry to La Isla, is north of Puerto Juárez. The road used to end there but no longer. Now some condominiums and private homes have sprung up along the bumpy road that follows the fine white sand seafront.

If the weather changes, I'm out of here.
~ Neil Young in an interview

Isla Mujeres

A woman is a citizen who works for Mexico. We must not treat her differently from a man, except to honor her more.
~ Adolpho López Mateos, former President of Mexico

If your fantasy is a vacation on a small peaceful island where time passes at its own slow pace, then we have the place for you. Eleven km (6.8 miles) off the Cancún shoreline rests an island with a name right out of a 1950's grade-B movie – the "Island of Women," Isla Mujeres. It's close enough to Cancún for

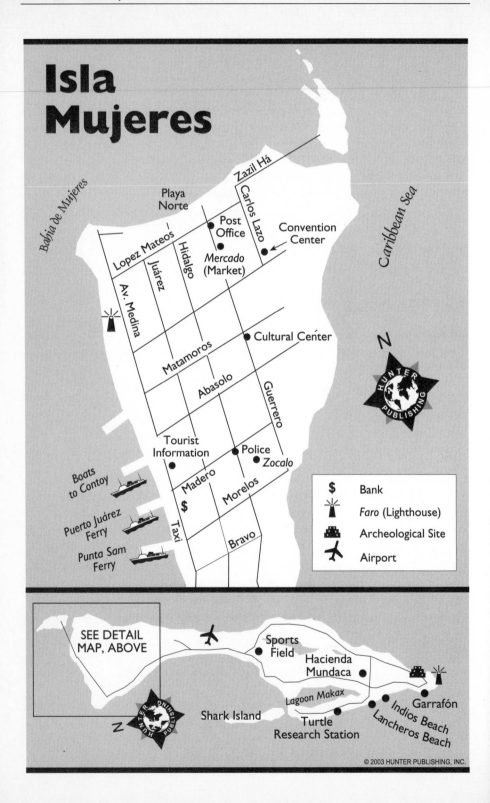

Isla Mujeres

Bahía de Mujeres

Zazil Há

Playa Norte

Carlos Lazo

Post Office

Convention Center

Caribbean Sea

Lopez Mateos

Juárez

Hidalgo

Av. Medina

Mercado (Market)

Cultural Center

Matamoros

Abasolo

Guerrero

N

Tourist Information

Police

Zocalo

Boats to Contoy

Madero

Morelos

Puerto Juárez Ferry

$

Taxi

Punta Sam Ferry

Bravo

$ Bank

Faro (Lighthouse)

Archeological Site

Airport

SEE DETAIL MAP, ABOVE

Sports Field

Hacienda Mundaca

Lagoon Makax

Garrafón

Shark Island

Turtle Research Station

Indios Beach

Lancheros Beach

N

HUNTER PUBLISHING

© 2003 HUNTER PUBLISHING, INC.

easy access but far enough away to offer a taste of real Mexico. The sandy slip of land – only 1.5 km (one mile) at its widest and eight km (five miles) end to end – is a lower-priced, low-key alternative to the shopping-mall atmosphere of Cancún itself. While many Cancún-based tourists take advantage of the lower shopping prices by commuting from the mainland on party boats, by the late afternoon they've upped anchor and the island comes alive.

Although there are no bikini-clad Amazons here, the Spanish coined the name "Isla Mujeres" after they found some stone idols of bare-breasted women, believed to be Ixchel, goddess of fertility. If the Conquistadors returned today, they could find live women with bare breasts on the North Beach. The Maya temple-lighthouse on the rocky southeastern tip provided an important link in the chain of lookout signals around the peninsula. After a thousand years of guard duty, Hurricane Gilbert reduced the structure to rubble in 1988 (it was partly rebuilt in time for the millennium celebration). But there's still a working lighthouse here and, for a *propina* (tip), you can go up to the top. From the dramatic rock cliff headlands, early risers can watch the sun come up over the Caribbean. You'll be standing on one of Mexico's most easterly points, where the first warm morning rays of sunlight strike the land. This was a special place to the Maya.

Isla Mujeres is washed by the Caribbean Sea on one side and cradled by the turquoise Bahia de Mujeres on the other. The island is casual and relaxed with a blended Mexican-Caribbean feel. Its only town is the fishing village where shops and low-rise hotels are located in a basket weave of narrow

Sailboat drifts at sunset off the coast of Isla Mujeres.

cobblestone and sand streets. During the day, those streets fill with daytrippers and shoppers, but in the early morning and evening the local population comes out to play. A sizable number of expatriate North Americans and Europeans run funky little cafés and trendy eateries here.

Despite the inevitable conversion from fishing to tourism as its main income, La Isla has managed to retain much of its native charm. A white and red lighthouse rises above the palms to welcome home fishermen to the island's clapboard and stucco houses – painted in whites and blues and pinks and turquoise – that lean helter-skelter in an easy-going tropical attitude. It's a fantastic place to enjoy the sea, around which life on this ancient fishing island still revolves.

Isla Mujeres' nightlife pales in comparison to Cancún's, except when the whole island has a celebration. Unless it's a holiday, most nightlife is bar action, often with dancing. Online tourist information is available at **www. isla-mujeres.net**.

Orientation

■ Getting Around

Our favorite method of arriving on Isla Mujeres is by way of the old people ferry (US $1.50), a brightly painted white wooden boat. *Beatriz Blanca* looks a little like Humphrey Bogart's *African Queen*. Our shipmates, passengers too poor to pay the extra few pesos for the faster cruiser ferries that also serve the island, are good-natured and chat away in Spanish. On one journey (40 minutes), a broad-faced Maya woman dressed in a traditional *huipil* (a cotton dress embroidered around the collar and hem) held a live chicken that poked its head out from her shopping bag. It looked right at us, questioning our future enjoyment of chicken fajitas. Laden with a load of timber and cinder block someone brought aboard as baggage, our slow boat chugged across the strait while we acclimated ourselves to an unhurried lifestyle.

Yet even troglodytes like us see the advantage in the new high-speed boats that zip across the blue-green waters between Puerto Juárez and La Isla in only 15 minutes every half-hour or so for just US $4. Unless you're patient or just lucky, chances are you'll take the faster boat, which departs more frequently from the same dock. There is also an even larger car ferry that leaves and returns to Punta Sam, only a kilometer or two north of Puerto Juárez.

There's no sense in taking a car over to the island unless you're living there. To get to either ferry from Cancún, take cab or catch a bus marked "Puerto Juárez" from in front of the Comercial Mexicana supermarket (look for its Pelican logo) on Av. Tulum, north of the *glorieta* (circle) with Av. Uxmal.

When you arrive on Isla Mujeres you'll be docking at a wooden pier in a quaint harbor, home to fisherman, yachtsmen and pirates for generations. Pink Colonial-style arches straddle the ends of narrow streets facing the waterfront. This is the north end of town, where all the shops, the best beaches and most of the hotels on the half-mile-wide island are situated. There's a taxi stand to the right of the pier, although most of the hotels are within walking distance. People mill about the pier as each boat arrives, some selling handicrafts or offering rides, others just hanging out people-watching. On the street are some yellow tricycles (*triciclos*), large bicycles built with one wheel in back and a freight cage and/or seats over the two front wheels. They are common in the Yucatán and offer an interesting way to arrive at your island hotel – like Sydney Greenstreet in a rickshaw. Have them carry your luggage; the rates are inexpensive.

You can easily walk the entire village. The town's energetic youth can be found at the basketball court in the plaza near the end of the *malecón*, the red brick pedestrian walkway along the Caribbean. The commercial heart of the city clusters in the north, but most residents live in the suburbs in the center of the island. To go somewhere on the south end, such as El Garrafón Park or Maria's, take a cab.

To see the entire island with the wind in your hair and the sun on your back, rent a motorbike or a gas-powered golf cart, the most popular form of transportation on the island. Wave to the policeman directing non-existent traffic and head south for **El Garrafón Park** ("The Jug"), a coral reef underwater national park. The Caribbean island's southern end is less populated and its rolling hills are covered by scrub brush and punctuated by an occasional house.

Perhaps less thrilling – but much cheaper – is to rent a bicycle and explore the mostly flat, lightly traveled streets. The main road follows the southern shoreline in a big loop past a Naval base, small airport, the pirate Mundaca's place, El Garrafón Park, Ixchel lighthouse and then back along the rocky deserted Caribbean side. The road takes several sharp turns, and at one there's a soccer pitch of white limestone dirt rather than grass. At Mundaca's house a road to Sac Bajo branches off along the peninsula between the sea and the lagoon.

Practicalities

COMMUNITY CENTERS: The **Cultural Center** (no telephone) farther east on Av. Guerrero hosts frequent activities for children and has a paperback library where you can trade English-language books from the open shelves. In back of the *mercado* is the **Centro de Convenciones**, which has a popular indoor basketball court.

FERRY SCHEDULE: The Express boats from Puerto Juaréz to Isla Mujeres leave every half-hour from 8 am to 8 pm. The return trips depart every half-hour, beginning at 7 am, with the last boat at 7:30 pm. The car ferry from Punta Sam sails at 8 and 11 am, 2:45, 5:30, and 8:15 pm. The returns are at 6:30 and 9:30 am, 2:45, 4:15, and 7:15 pm. These schedules can change.

HEALTH CLUB: Good living is good health. Discover **Isleños' Gym** on Av. Hidalgo, north end (no phone). After a hard work-out (without air-conditioning) *los Isleños* head for the showers – or in this case, the beach. The **Women Only Gym** is for women only. It's open from 7:30 am to 7 pm every day, on the second floor of a building on Guerrero, just off the corner of Matamoros.

LANGUAGE SCHOOL: Learn Spanish in paradise on Isla Mujere's first Spanish language school, **Ixchel Institute**, at Madero and Av. Guerrero (☎ 998/939-1218, www.stormpages.com/ixchel). Small classes and individual attention. Ask for Emily or Laura.

LAUNDROMATS: Two laundromats compete for business in town, but there's no question that **Wash Express** is hands-down cheaper than the more established **Tim Phó's**. Both are located on Av. Abasolo, and both do a good job washing and folding, but Tim charges more to separate whites and colors.

MARKET: The *mercado* is next door to the post office on Av. Guerrero. For the Super Maz supermaket, see page 155.

MEDICAL FACILITIES & DOCTORS: There is a decompression chamber at the **Hospital de la Armada** on Medina (☎ 998/877-0001). Several doctors on the island speak English. In fact, one is English. **Dr. Greta Shorey** came for a vacation after doing volunteer work in Africa and met and married an American yachtsman. Now her GP skills are available at the **Cruz Roja Mexicana** (Red Cross, ☎ 998/877-0443), near Mundaca's Hacienda. **Dr. Antonio Salas** also speaks English and makes house calls. He practices general medicine on Calle Hidalgo (☎ 998/877-0477).

MONEY MATTERS: The only bank in town for changing money (9 am to 2:30 pm, Monday through Friday) is the **Bital Bank**, opposite the docks downtown.

POLICE: Police headquarters is near the basketball court in the main *zócalo* (☎ 998/877-0082 or 060 for emergencies).

POST OFFICE: The post office is on Av. Guerrero at Lopez Mateos.

TOURIST INFORMATION: Find tourist information on Av. Medina in the tourist office (☎ 998/877-0316, www.isla-mujeres.net).

AUTHOR'S TIP: *If you're returning to Cancún airport from the island, don't agree to a taxi ride from the guys that hang out on the dock in Puerto Juárez. They count on your not knowing the right fare (about US $20). Pick up a taxi in the parking lot in front of the ticket office. Negotiate the fare before leaving. Check in the large Cancún Tips for the current average prices.*

Beaches

Calm water and gentle surf mark the idyllic western and northern beaches, while clashing Caribbean currents make swimming dangerous on the spectacular eastern shore. **Playa del Norte** (North Beach) is a pristine white sandy beach with a warm shallow surf. **Playa Lancheros** has a more secluded location toward the southern end near El Garrafón Park, where waters are good for beginner snorkelers. It features a good beach restaurant and palapa gift shops. Local families favor the beach near the dock downtown. The best for young children is the beach and inlet past the **Na Balam Hotel**, where the water is warm and shallow. In 1999, a sand bar formed in front of the Na Balam and the shallow water between it and the beach is only a couple of inches deep. Kids love it.

North Beach.

All major beaches have a beach chair and/or umbrella rental concession; rentals start at about US $5 per day.

Events

Boating and sailing **regattas** are organized by the **Club de Yates** for the last week of April or first week of May. For specific information, ☎ 998/877-0173. A **fishing tournament** runs February through May, and the waters surrounding La Isla are good year-round for bonito, grouper, mackerel, kingfish and amberjack. For information on events, call the Tourism Office at ☎ 998/877-0307.

Shopping

The shops of La Isla offer better deals than those in the Hotel Zone and that's why boatloads of sunburned shoppers descend on the island daily. Remember, many stores close for siesta during the hottest times of the day. There are many shops from which to choose, but noteworthy are the following:

Casa Isleño II is a custom-painted T-shirt and shell shop run by Henrietta Morris de Avila on Guerrero next to the hospital. She is a talented artist and long-time resident.

Artesanias El Nopal sells Mexican folk art and women's co-op crafts at the corner of Guerrero and Matamoros. The **Gladys Galdamez** shop on Hildalgo (☎ 998/877-0302) offers designer dresses and sports clothes, accessories and beach wear, many designed and created on the island. You can order quality women's fashions, made to measure in 24 hours. Tailoring done on premises. **Boutique Elenita**, on Av. Hidalgo No. 13, has attractive gifts and crafts, but their ad for leather pocketbooks in the newspaper loses something in translation: "Wallets and Bags of Skin."

Van Cleef & Arpels jewelry is on Av. Morelos at Juárez.

Buy stunning papier-mâché masks and sculptures, a traditional craft, from **Emilio Sosa Medina**, a true artist, at his workshop-showroom on Av. Lopez Mateos, next to the cemetery. All are originals.

Paulita's, on Av. Morelos in front of the police station, will lure you in with their large collection of arts and crafts and wide variety of incredible collector's masks. On Juárez, the owner of **Artesanias Arco Iris**, Alejandro Trejo, comes from an area in central Mexico known for its hand-woven blankets and wall-hangings colored with natural dyes.

A real treat is **Aztlan**, a crowded little shop on Av. Madero between Hidalgo and Juárez. The charming owner, Ana Silva, features crafts from all over Mexico as well as her own creations. Aztlan is an Aztec word meaning ceremonies or place of gods.

Cosmic Cosas (☎ 998/860-3495, cosmiccosas@yahoo.com) is a used bookstore, with Internet access, and a popular Av. Matamoros hang-out. They take paperbacks in trade. Genevieve, the owner, is instrumental in an effort to get the island's cat and dog population under control by offering adoption services plus free neutering and spaying. We admire her work, so stop in and say hello.

The modern **supermarket** is a Super Maz, located on Av. Madero, on the Zocálo, and it's open late. The traditional mercado is next to the Post Office on Av. Guerrero.

Adventures

I collect experiences the way others like to collect coins...
~ Michael McGuire, adventurer

The laid-back attitude on La Isla's doesn't mean there isn't plenty to do, it just means you can do nothing at all. When you're ready to get up and go, read on.

■ Attractions

TURTLE RESEARCH STATION: The western shore north of Playa Paraiso is home to Centro de Investigaciones, a turtle research station funded by the government and private donations. This is a fascinating and popular educational stop for some of the party boats over from Cancún. They usually drop off punters who walk along the beach to reach the station. Isla Mujeres was an ancestral hatching ground for giant sea turtles, who lumbered ashore from May through September to lay their eggs in the silky sand. Many turtles were captured by local fishermen and killed for their meat and shell; the eggs were dug up for food. Finally, a concerned fisherman convinced his brethren to spare the eggs. His efforts led to the founding of the research station where turtles are now bred for release. In an effort to educate and sensitize locals about the turtles' plight, local school children participate in the annual releases. Take the guided tour. Donations welcome.

Educational programs teach children how to protect turtles.

■ Adventures on Water

BOAT/SWIM TOURS TO ISLA CONTOY: How could you not go swimming on an island? Check out the beaches we listed above, but avoid the strong undertow on the eastern shore. We took Captain Ricardo Gaitán's six-hour cruise to the uninhabited Isla Contoy (US $50) for a day of nature hiking and birdwatching, plus snorkeling and beachcombing. His boat, the *Estrella del Norte*, a 36-foot motor sailboat, was the last one to be built on the island, christened in 1968. The coral island of Isla Contoy is a bird sanctuary for 70 species, including some large nesting colonies. During the summer, female sea turtles lay their eggs along its sandy bays. After snorkeling on a colorful coral reef on the way over, we spent lots of our time beachcombing among the rock pools while the others in the group sunbathed and swam. There's a small museum and a climbable lookout tower for a panoramic view. Included are gear and lunch – grilled grouper, deliciously spiced à la Yucateca, caught by the mate on the way over. (Just in case you don't catch a fish, they bring one along for you.) Buy your tickets or make reservations directly at the Capitán's office on Av. Madero (☎ 998/877-0434). Alternatively, you can take a fast launch from the Fisherman's Coopertiva, north of the ferry dock. It's a bit cheaper and much faster (as long as seas aren't too rough), but you can't beat the romance of a journey under a red sail in wooden-hulled ship.

Looking out from the bow of Estrella del Norte.

Another trip offered by Capt. Gaitán is an exciting but rugged explorer's adventure to **Boca Iglesia**. The ghostly church (*iglesia*) is all that stands in a colony established by the earliest Spanish Conquistadors in the mangrove jungle north of Contoy. It was wiped out in a massacre by the Maya in the early 1500s. You'll be walking in historic footsteps near Cabo Catoche, the first land fall of the Spanish in 1517, where there's also a little explored Maya ruin, Ecab (Gran Cairo). A very real *Adventure Guide* trip. Groups only.

EL GARRAFÓN NATIONAL UNDERSEA PARK: On the east end of the island, this is a great place for beginning snorkelers to float near a colorful reef, teeming with fish. The reef itself is now roped off – off-limits to snorkelers and swimmers. Due to prolonged damage to the reef, among other reasons, the operation of the park has been taken over by the people that run Xcaret and Xel-Há. They've made it a day destination (entrance US $8), upgrading the facilities to include a locker rooms with US $2 towel rental and showers, two big restaurants, hammock and beach area, and a gigantic gift shop. You can rent snorkel equipment (lifevests are free) or buy a ticket (US $6) for the Zip Slide. The Zip Slide is a wire strung from a platform to the cliff face, then from there out to a platform in the bay. You are hooked into a harness and slide along the line. These are common in Costa Rica (see our *Adventure Guide to Costa Rica*) and lots of fun. For those who want to dive like an experienced snorkeler, try the **Snuba** rental. That's when your snorkel gear is hooked up to a fresh-air line, so you can snorkel or even shallow-dive attached to the air hose. It costs about US $40. Across the street from Garrafon Park is the 100-foot **Scenic Tower**, identical to the one in Cancún. On an island that has only one high-rise hotel – and that with only seven stories – the Scenic Tower is an affront to our sensibilities.

If you're looking for a beach without the bells and whistles of Garrafón, try the full-service **Beach Club at Garrafón de Castillo Hotel**, a short distance before the Park, or **Playa Lancheros**, a less formal and less well-equipped beach near Mundaca's.

FISHING CHARTERS: To go fishing or snorkeling is easy, just visit the Cooperativa and ask to be set up with a qualified fisherman. **Capitan Gaitán** offers light tackle, big game fishing charters (see above) in a trimaran or 30-foot twin-engine speed boat, *Afrodita*. Two captains, also in demand for deep-sea charters, are partners – **Ruben Peña** and **Anthony Medillo, Jr.** Call them at ☎ 998/877-0759. They are experienced in salt water fly fishing.

DIVING & SNORKELING: In the late 1950s, Carlos Garcia, a young island lobster diver, discovered a deep-sea cave. He saw some sharks enter the cave, but they didn't come out the other side. Curious, he went inside only to find sharks asleep in the current with their eyes wide open. The cave is now known as the **Cave of the Sleeping Sharks**. Dive shops, such as **Coral Dive Center** (Av. Matamoros, ☎ 998/877-0763, www.coralscubadivecenter.com), **Bahia Dive Shop** (☎ 998/877-0340), and **Sea Hawk Divers**, on the north beach (☎ 998/877-0296), will take certified divers on this popular professional-grade 65-foot scuba dive. The slumbering sharks became world-famous when Jacques Cousteau and his crew, in collaboration with Mexican diving legend Ramon Bravo, filmed them for one of his television specials.

Other snorkel and dive spots are the **Cuevones Reef** at 10.5 meters deep (35 feet) and the **Manchones** and **Banderas Reefs**, coral reefs one kilometer long by 700 meters wide (1,093 x 764 yards), at a depth of about 10 meters (33 feet). A bronze cross weighing approximately one ton, 39 feet high and 9.75 feet wide, was planted into the Manchones Reef between Isla Mujeres and the coastline in 1994. The **Cruz de la Bahia** is the island's tribute to all men and women of the sea. Divers celebrate the founding of Isla Mujeres in 1854 with a mass dive on August 17.

Snorkelers can float among the fish that swim around the lighthouse at the entrance to the harbor or the launches will take you out to the reefs stretching toward Isla Contoy.

> *Then there were no people, nor animals, nor trees.*
> *There was only the deaf silence of the waters.*
> ~ Popul Vuh, a surviving Maya text

■ Adventures on Wheels

 To putter around town, rent a gas-powered golf cart or motorscooter. There are plenty of vendors (the slightly cheaper ones are back away from the dock area). Try **Motorenta Kankin** on Calle Abasolo; **Pepe's** on Hidalgo; **Ciro's** (which has the best golf carts) on Guerrero; or **Zorro's**, also on Guerrero. If there are two of you, make sure your scooter is a two-person model. Of late, some rental places are offering only single-seaters and they're damn uncomfortable for two.

Bicycles are for rent at several hotels and some of the moto/golf rental places, such as Zorro's.

■ Adventures on Foot

 BEACHCOMBING: The **northeastern beach** is great for beachcombing. It's rocky and rough and the sand is littered with shells and bits of colorful coral. Pools of water host small fish and shrimp.

SPORTS: Hoopsters can join in pick-up **basketball games** at the Municipal Court in the main plaza (volleyball is also played here) and soccer heads can show off their skills at the sports field south of the airport.

HIKING: From El Garrafón Park it's a short walk up to **Ixchel lighthouse** and the **rock headlands** of the island. Check out the spectacular dawn! At the other end, crowds gather for the sunset on the northern beach. The deserted Caribbean eastern shore makes a great walk for beachcombers into exploring rocky pools and washed up coral and shells.

Mundaca's Hacienda (see below) is a park-like area with cement paths that weave through the former gardens, and oh how we wish it had been restored with more ambiance. Mundaca's romantic/tragic tale would attract more tourists with a better site, perhaps one with restored gardens. Nevertheless, it's worth a quick stop. Another one of our favorite stops on the island is the **cemetery** along the north beach on Av. Lopez Mateos. Mexicans build shrines to their dead and leave personal objects on them as a celebration of their life. We wept over a little girl's tiny pink slippers left on her grave. You'll find Mundaca's grave marker there too, complete with skull and crossbones. (He's not supposed to be under there because he died in Mérida.)

Pirate's Treasure

Fermin Mundaca de Marechaja lived life as a pirate and slave trader, getting rich at the expense of others who paid with their lives for his greed. For many years he plied the seas from Africa to Cuba with human cargo destined to labor as slaves and die in the sugarcane fields. By 1860 the British Navy's campaign against slavery cramped his style, so he furled his sails and retired to the sheltered harbor of

Skull and crossbones decorate Mundaca's grave marker.

Quintana Roo

Isla Mujeres. Once there, he fell in love with an 18-year-old girl, famous on the island for her beauty, called La Trigueña, "The Brunette." But the young girl rejected him. Determined to win her love, he built a whimsical hacienda surrounded by gardens filled with exotic plants, entered by arches carved with her name. But instead of changing her mind, La Trigueña married a young island fisherman whom she loved. She bore her husband child after child while Mundaca slowly went insane. He died in Mérida but the grave marker he had carved for himself is located in the island's sandy cemetery (approximately two rows in the front center to the right of the gate). His ruined hacienda and former gardens – a tragic example of "love's labor lost" – makes an interesting short visit.

> *As you are, I was. As I am, you will be.*
> ~ words on Mundaca's grave

Accommodations

La Isla's hotels run the gamut from budget to moderate and plain to fancy. Because of the laid-back lifestyle and proximity to the beach, staying anywhere on the island is a delight. We have always gloated in our ability to find good bargains here. The jewels of the island for most travelers are the moderately priced hotels on or near the beach. Some have impressive accommodations or locations even by Cancún standards.

■ Budget Hotels

South End

Mar y Sol (☎/*fax 998/877-0004, www. sundreamers.com/mim/marysol.htm*). Janet McCammon, a delightfully deep-tanned woman, is one of the pirate island's secret treasures. She lives life to its fullest most of the year on Isla Mujeres, but when she gets bored she hops a cargo ship for exotic ports around the world. When she's in town she rents out small housekeeping studios on a good swimming beach just south of Playa Lancheros, heading out toward El Garrafón Park. The weekly rent averages only US $35 per day and an even better rate for longer term. $-$$

HOTEL PRICE CHART	
NOTE: Often, one shared bed in a room is cheaper than two. Prices based on cost per night, for two.	
[No $]	Less than US $20
$	US $20 - $40
$$	US $40 - $80
$$$	US $80 - $125

Maria's Kan Kin (*near El Garrafón Park,* ☎ *998/877-0015, 8 rooms with air, kitchenettes, suite plus cabaña*). As of press time, Maria was renting her darling rooms for the week or month only, at very reasonable rates. If you've read previous editions of our guide you'll know how much pleasure we've had vacationing at her lovely garden beach hotel – but times have changed for the venerable French woman, whom we much admire, and the hotel has slowed down with her. Things could change back very quickly – and probably will have by the time you read this, but stop by and see. Say hello from us. $$

In Town

Poc Na (*Matamoros,* ☎/*fax 998/877-0090, 10 dorm rooms with beds & fans, 2 private rooms with air, rec room, continental breakfast included*). Late in 2002, some savy Argentinians took over the management and made great improvements to the island's only official youth hostel. They put in new beds, kept the women's-only dorm – two others are co-ed – added more secure lockers, built new bathrooms, opened a kitchen (8 am to 11 pm) that offers dinner specials good enough to attract diners who aren't staying there, and they moved the camping area to a walled sandy backyard. The beach bar stays open long hours in high season and the lounge shows movie videos twice a week (and every time it's rainy). They also built two Japanese-style bunk sleeping rooms (take a top bed with the window for the breeze) and added a rec room with pool tables. Good value for a hostel and much improved.

Vistalmar *(Medina,* ☎ *998/877-0209, fax 998/877-0096, 36 rooms with air or fans, cable TV).* The best rooms – the three back apartments around a friendly little terrace – at this perennially popular place are next to impossible to get. They are rented long-term all year. But the front rooms' balconies and the hotel roof are good hangouts. Regular guests gather here to watch the beach-goers across the street or the crowd that comes off the ferry. Ideally located both downtown and near the waterfront. The rooms here are simple and clean. $-$$

Hotel Carmelina *(Guerrero,* ☎ *998/877-0006, 20 rooms, most with fans).* A favorite with very budget-minded travelers because each large room has two queen-size beds, one single bed, good-size closets and hot water. It's also clean. On the down side there are no dressers. Painted an unmistakeable white, with lavender trim. The hotel offers bicycles available for rent, a good way to see the island. $

Las Palmas *(Guerrero across from the* mercado, *no phone, 14 rooms with fans).* This is a very basic hotel with two beds and a low ceiling in each room. It's nice and clean, but an overhang above the windows makes the rooms a little dark. Upstairs rooms may be more appealing. Only a block from the north beach and across the street from the local *mercado* and several inexpensive luncheonettes. $

Xul-Há *(Hidalgo,* ☎ *998/877-0075, 9 rooms with fan or air, cable TV).* The inside of this hotel is plain, and the rooms are very clean. Within the last few years it was remodeled and had a paint job. Usually filled with European tourists. Xul-Há means the end or "bottom of the water." $

Marcianito *(Abasolo,* ☎ *998/877-0111).* This 13-room hotel is easy to miss because it's squeezed between two storefronts. Each freshly painted, average-size room comes with a fan, closet and one queen-size and one single bed. Completely remodeled in 2000, the rooms are good and clean. $

Maria José *(Madero near the ferry dock,* ☎ *998/877-0245).* Only the third floor has a view of the sea from the hallway, but the older rooms in this well-known but basic budget hotel are medium in size, clean and simple. A good location just opposite the pier. $

Apartments Trin Chan *(Carlos Lazo, next to the IMSS office,* ☎ *998/877-0856, atrinchan@prodigy.net.mx, 5 apartments, fan, kitchen).* These apartments rent for a night if they're available, but since there are only a few, guests tend to stay a week at a time. Four larger apartments that sleep as many as four people are simply furnished – with all modern conveniences – but we liked the additional end unit, the smaller "Casa Gilligan," made of wood with a palapa roof. Just steps to the beach. $

María Leticia *(Juarez, ☎ 998/877-0394, 5 rooms plus 5 apartments, air, cable TV, safes).* When we stay downtown for more than a day or two, Nibardo Fernández' intimate little apartment complex is one of our favorite choices. It's very appealing, Mediterranean-white throughout, with a sandy shady little courtyard embraced by the two-story buildings. The cute private accommodations include basic rooms, efficiency studios, and medium-size, one-bedroom apartments that sleep up to four. Fully equipped kitchenettes and well decorated. Very clean, very safe. Stay for two weeks or more and get a big discount. $

■ Moderate Hotels

In Town/North Beach

Playa Media Luna *(on the beach behind the Centro de Convenciones, in US ☎ 800/223-5695, in Mexico ☎ 998/877-0759, www.playamedialuna.com, 18 rooms, air, pool, includes continental breakfast).* Opened just in time for the turn of the millennium, the Playa Luna is owned by the same hard-working hotel family as the Maria del Mar. Rooms in the four-story, two-wing hotel are offset from each other, and feature verandas or patios with hammocks. Each has a view of the Caribbean. Two twin beds are in the smaller size rooms, which also have a refrigerator and a plentiful bathroom. Its half moon beach – the hotel's name – offers a protected cove to go wading or swimming in a surf that is too rough in other spots. There's also a small pool with wet bar. $$$

Casa Isleño II Apartments *(Guerrero, ☎/fax 998/877-0265, air).* These are owned by long-time Isla resident Henrietta Morris de Avila, who hand-paints custom tee-shirts. In her large home, one street from the Caribbean, she has made small apartments with fans and complete kitchens that rent by the week or month. Very sweet, secure and quiet, the rooms have a "built-above-the-garage-at-a-beach-house" feel to them. We found them homey and appealing. $$

Roca Mar *(Bravo, ☎/fax 998/877-0101, pool & patio, 22 rooms with fans plus one suite in a beach house).* Perched on the edge of the Caribbean where it meets the town center, the Roca Mar hotel is one of the island's oldest, although it doesn't look it. The smallish rooms, with two queen-size beds and thick wooden window shutters, have been remodeled; each has an absolutely spectacular ocean view from its balcony. The lone suite has two bedrooms (a single and a double) and a kitchenette so it's a good value for families. It's also a popular honeymoon suite, right next to the pool (US $120). Perfect hotel for roar-of-the-surf sleepers and those who love the sea. $$

Francis Arlene *(Guerrero, ☎/fax 998/877-0310, hfrancis@prodigy.net.mx, 26 rooms with air or fans).* This soft peach-colored family-run establishment has guests who return each year for the homey atmosphere. It's no wonder:

the beds are comfortable and the showers hot. The Arlene has been completely remodeled and redecorated within the last few years, and all rooms have small terraces or balconies, one block from the beach. Three rooms have kitchenettes and a "suite" on the top floor has a king-size bed. A good value with high standards. $$

Meson del Bucanero *(Hidalgo, upstairs from the popular restaurant of the same name & across the street from the Belmar,* ☎ *998/877-0210, www. bucaneros.com).* This hotel is clean and bright, with 14 attractive small rooms with fans. During our visit they were completing an additional eight new rooms that will have air-conditioning, TV and fan. Colonial style, with stained glass windows in some of the bathrooms, the bedrooms are a soft cream color with natural wood trim. The bathrooms also boast rare full-size bathtubs and white tile floors. The restaurant serves very good food at moderate prices. Between it and the Pizza Rolandi across the street, this portion of Av. Hidalgo is tough to pass if you're hungry. $$

Maria del Mar *(Lazo,* ☎ *in US 800/223-5695, in Mexico 998/877-0179, fax 998/887-0213, www.cabanasdelmar.com, 73 rooms with air or fans, pool, restaurant, bar, continental breakfast included).* On the north beach of the island. There are 18 attractive rooms which the hotel calls its "castle" over their Buho's restaurant/bar and a main hotel building styled like an old hacienda. Upstairs rooms with dressers, wardrobes and balconies are comfortable and offer a good view. Near the new pool there are also 24 upstairs/downstairs cabañas with large rooms and big palapa-covered front terraces – great for shade when it's hot or to entertain on the odd rainy day. One of the island's most established hotels. $$

Posada del Mar *(Medina,* ☎ *998/887-0044, fax 998/877-0266, 49 rooms & 15 bungalows, pool, restaurant, bar).* Across the street from the beach and close to all the shops and the ferry, the posada is a long-time favorite. It was one of the island's first hotels, greatly expanded and remodeled in 2003. Each room in the main building faces the shore and has a balcony and air-conditioning. Upstairs rooms are much better than those downstairs. Penguinos is the hotel's palapa-covered restaurant and bar. It got its name many years ago when a slightly inebriated customer happily remarked that his beer was "as cold as a penguin." Order a "penguin" today and you'll get an ice cold Superior beer. $$

Southeast/El Garrafón

Su Casa *(Laguna, Sac Bajo,* ☎*/fax 998/877-0180, lostoasis@lostoasis.net, 9 casitas, fans, kitchenettes).* You would think Miriam and Yussey should have lost their New York accents by now, after all this time on Isla Mujeres. The couple came to dive the warm waters nearly 40 years ago and decided to set up a life here. They rented a boat to circle the island and when they found the best beach, they landed, approached the owner and bought it. It

HOTEL PRICE CHART	
NOTE: Often, one shared bed in a room is cheaper than two. Prices based on cost per night, for two.	
[No $]	Less than US $20
$	US $20 - $40
$$	US $40 - $80
$$$	US $80 - $125

now features Su Casa, a series of small cottages that make for great beach vacations an an ideal location for family reunions or group retreats. Nothing fancy, two beds and a studio kitchen. Vell, if it's beach you vont, it's beach ve got. $$

Villas Punta Sur *(Km 6 near El Garrafón Park, ☎ 998/877-0572, fax 998/887-0371, www.coralscubadivecenter.com, 12 rooms in 6 villas, pool).* These lovely one- and two-bedroom apartment villas are set on a wooded hill overlooking the bay, but not on the beach side of the road. They are Colonial in style, yet modern, large and airy, with fully equipped kitchenettes. The villas attract many repeat customers, especially families or two couples sharing. There's a quiet little pool. The owners run the Coral Dive shop downtown. $$

Garrafón del Castilla *(next to El Garrafón Park, ☎/fax 998/877-0019 or 887-0508, 12 rooms with air or fans plus 2 bungalows).* Small but pleasant hotel rooms here look out to the bay from the steep bluff next to El Garrafón Park. Each has a balcony, big closet, dresser with mirror, in-room refrigerator and a marble bathroom counter. You can negotiate rates if they're not full. Better yet, check out the bungalow rooms, which are separate from the newer hotel building. They're nearly as nice and also cheaper. Hoping to attract people who don't want to pay the high price of El Garrafón Park, the hotel has now opened a beach club that charges US $3 for entrance. $$

Suites Playa Gaviotas *(Km 4.5 near El Garrafón Park, ☎/fax 998/877-0216, 10 suites and bungalows, air, includes continental breakfast).* The attractive railroad-style suites at this pleasant hotel are located in a big white building on a hill above a broad white beach. They are very economical. Each suite has a veranda with a good seaview, two queen-size beds, big closets and a kitchenette. A beachside bungalow has two older apartment suites. $$

■ Luxury Hotels

Avalon Reef Club *(north tip of the island, in US & Canada ☎ 888/497-4325, in Mexico 998/848-9300, www.avalonresorts.net, 90 rooms, six suites with jacuzzis, & 56 individual casita rooms, pool, air, restaurant, bar, spa).* For well over a decade this wedge-shaped hotel stood alone on the far tip of the island – a mute reminder of the force of the hurricane that wrecked its short reign as the king of Isla Mujeres' hotels. Finally in 2002, high-class hotel chain Avalon Resorts spent a fortune remodeling the distinctive tower and added 14 inviting attached villas that either zig-zag along the craggy shoreline, hard against the Caribbean or softly touch the protected sandy bay beach. You need to cross a wooden bridge over turquoise waters to reach the Avalon, adding to its exclusivity – yet it's only a short walk to the downtown attractions. The tower rooms are average in size and all offer fabulous views. The villas, however, are worth the extra bucks. There's a really cool swim spot located on the Caribbean side of the villas – a rock pool where the waves crash over the reef, creating a foam waterfall into the sheltered water.

Na Balam *(at the end of the north beach,* ☎ *998/877-0279, fax 998/877-0446, www.nabalam.com, 31 rooms with air, pool, dive shop, master suite with jacuzzi, restaurant and bar, optional meal plans).* All the attractive rooms here feature terraces or balconies, large beds and bathrooms decorated in Maya motif. The deluxe Na Balam has expanded in recent years to include new cabañas, a small pool and yoga meetings, which attract a gentle crowd of cosmic-conscious travelers. Second-floor beachside rooms are vine-covered and look over palm trees to the fine sand *playa*, where topless sunbathing is common. The happy hour's two-for-one drinks pack the beach bar with friendly folks who chat while the sun sets. The adjacent indoor-outdoor Zazil-Há restaurant is one of the island's finest. $$$$

Cristalmar *(Laguna Mar Macax, Sac Bajo,* ☎ *in US & Canada 888/571-3239, in Mexico 998/877-0390, http://cristalmarhotel.com, 38 suites with air & kitchenettes, very large pool, restaurant).* This is one of the few hotels on the slender slip of land between the lagoon and protected waters of the Bahia Mujeres. It's set along a road populated with the private homes of wealthy North Americans. Each large suite has a kitchenette, one or two bedrooms, dining room and sitting area. Inviting and pleasantly apportioned, the hotel is worth considering because of its fabulous beach (right next to a sea turtle research area), large pool and the advantage of kitchenettes. It's about US $4 for a taxi ride into town. This all-suite facility offers full or partial meal plans. $$$$

Villa Rolandi *(Laguna Mar, Sac Bajo,* ☎ *998/877-0700, fax 998/887-0100, www.villarolandi.com, 20 suites, air, pool, piano bar, cable TV, all-inclusive, includes transportation from Cancún).* From humble beginnings at Pizza Rolandi's restaurant – and years of experience with the the moderately priced, downtown Hotel Belmar (☎ 998/877-0430, www.rolandi.com) – the owner opened this super-luxury hotel, restaurant and beach club. The hotel, which rests on white sands, is Colonial style with a Mediterranean influenced. An opulent lobby boasts arched Catalana Boveda brick ceilings, as do the top-level rooms. The deep blue pool overlooks the Cancún skyline, and all suites face the Bahía Mujeres. Suites feature huge bathrooms with double sinks, as well as beautiful marble showers for two. Each individual balcony has a private jacuzzi. The walls are wired with hidden speakers for music and the TV, and there are also computer phone plugs and cordless phones. Guests are transported to the hotel by private yacht from Cancún. Continental breakfast may be served through an access in the wall, for intimate privacy.

Your choice of lunch or dinner at Casa Rolandi, the Northern Italian cuisine restaurant on the large veranda, is included. The price may be Cancún-like, but the luxury and personal attention far exceed what those large hotels across the bay offer. $$$$+

Casa de los Sueños B&B *(near El Garrafón Park, US* ☎ *800/551-2558, Mexico* ☎ *998/877-0651, fax 998/877-0708, 9 rooms & suites, air, cable TV, credit cards, no smoking).* The "House of Dreams" is a dream house built on a bluff overlooking the Bahía Mujeres, a short distance from El Garrafón Park. Behind a tall wall with large wooden doors is Casa's hidden courtyard, fronted by a fountain pond. Ahead, the house is divided by an open-air, sunken living room protected by a second-story causeway. Beyond the living room is a picture-perfect infinity pool looking onto the bay and the hurried life of Cancún. La Casa delivers relaxation with an adults-only atmosphere. The master suite features a jacuzzi and one junior suite has a kitchen. Morning juice and coffee are brought to your room while the full American breakfast is served in the dining area. $$$$+

Hotel Secreto *(Playa Media Luna,* ☎ *in US 800/223-5695, in Mexico 998/877-1039, fax 877-1048, www.hotelsecreto.com, 9 rooms, air, pool, fridge, cable, CD players in rooms).* The ultra-modern Hotel Secreto is the million-dollar creation of a Boston native who married into a Lima hotelier family. He and his wife built the perfect honeymoon hotel. Rooms are minimalistic in décor, with colorful original art emphasizing a virginal, white-upon-white theme. There are glass French doors, stylized wooden Arts and Craft headboards, and either two queens or one king-size, four-poster bed in each room. With a freeform infinity pool facing the sea, the hotel shares the little half moon bay with its sister (literally) hotel. A Caribbean diamond. $$$$

Dining

This tiny island has nowhere near the huge variety of restaurants that feed Cancún's appetite. But just because there are fewer choices, it doesn't mean the dining here is of a lower quality; it's just less expensive. Again, reservations are not necessary and many of these places do not have a business phone. Naturally, fresh seafood is the specialty of

DINING PRICE CHART	
NOTE: Prices based on a typical entrée, per person, and do not include beverage.	
$	Less than US $5
$$	US $5 - 10
$$$	Over US $10

most restaurants in the village, where residents have always been seafarers. Some island women joke that their sons could sail before they could walk.

Miramar *(Av. Medina, next to the ferry dock, no phone).* This small and personal restaurant sits beneath a palapa roof, unchanged and undiscovered by the crowds of tourists that disembark the nearby ferry and charter boats arriving from Cancún. The Miramar is an idyllic spot to spend hours over a few beers or a delicious meal while watching the local fishing launches bring in their catch. Close your eyes and listen to the melodic sound of fishermen talking or the hypnotic rhythm of boat owners who scrape barnacles from their beached boats with handfuls of sand. Sit and watch the daily pelican show as the fisherman throw scraps from their cleaned catch. (If you have a room with a kitchenette, buy your fresh fish near the Miramar as the boats come in.) Open for breakfast through dinner with a complete menu that includes beef, chicken and pork as well as fresh fish. $$

Café Cito *(Matamoros, no phone)*. The influx of residents who have chucked the rat race for the slow pace of the island has spawned many new restaurants that combine an artistic ambiance with creative cuisine. One of these surviving the test of time is Café Cito. A black and white cat purrs lazily on one of the open-shuttered, streetside windows, beckoning you into this neat breakfast and dinner café. Painted blue and white, it has a custom-made, stained glass wave separating the connected dining areas, and there are beach scenes under each small, glass-topped table. $$

Brisa Mexicana *(Matamoros & Hidalgo)*. Chen Huaye, La Isla's long-time Yucatecan restaurant, closed its old doors, only to reincarnate as a traditional seafood and meat restaurant on a corner in the middle of the downtown. A legacy of good food at good prices. $$

Bistro Francais *(Matamoros)*. Open from 8 am till noon, then again from 6 to 10 pm for dinner, the Bistro is one of the island's larger charming storefront restaurants. It does a good business because of the reasonable prices, colorful ambiance – the menu is painted on the walls – and excellent presentation. The restaurant's rare-in-Mexico bottomless cup of coffee is delicious and refilled often. The French toast for breakfast is "oo-la-la" and includes a fresh fruit plate. A friendly and relaxed atmosphere. Surprisingly economical. $$

Café El Nopalito *(at the corner of Matamoros & Guerrero, closed Wednesdays)*. This breakfast and brunch health food restaurant (open 6 am) is combined with a folk-art gift shop called El Nopal. Delicious homemade breads, granola and good service makes this a popular spot to sit at its great painted tables and chat. The gift store carries clothes from some classy Mexican designers – and many local women's co-op crafts. $$

*People, like wines, have their moods and no restaurant is suited
to every mood and every occasion.... There are days when one
does not feel like making love. There are days when I don't like
to shave and I have a favorite restaurant for these non-shaving days, which are
not necessarily non-love-making days.*
~ David Schoebruen, *Esquire*, February 1961

Chiles Locos *(Av. Hildago; dinner only from 7 pm, two-for-one cocktails).*
Jorge learned his cooking in Campeche, where food is an art form. Here on La
Isla, he operates this storefront restaurant that features sidewalk dining under a red clay tile roof. One evening we ordered Chiles en Nogada, a regional
dish from Puebla that contains the three colors of the Mexican flag – green,
white and red. It's a green poblano pepper, stuffed with a meat and fruit filling, covered by a white cream sauce made with ground cashews and sprinkled with red pomegranate seeds. What a delightfully delicious experience!
Excellent Chiapas coffee in glass mugs at breakfast. We'll be back. $$

Pizza Rolandi *(Hidalgo, across the street from Meson del Bucanero).*
Rolandi is the island's most popular eatery featuring Italian and Mexican
cooking and excellent brick oven pizza. Its open dining porch extends out into
the shopping avenue in front. Its good-time atmosphere can be warm and in-
viting, and the place is often full of diners. See page 138 for details about the
Casa Rolandi in Cancún. $$

Mirtita's Restaurant and Bar *(Medina, across from the Punta Sam ferry
dock).* A local watering hole for fisherman and islanders. Good prices make
up for its plain atmosphere. $-$$

Cazuela M&J *(Bravo).* The Cazuela is a little treasure of a restaurant
tucked into a corner behind the Roca Mar hotel. It offers a great view of the
pounding surf. Owners Marco and Julie named it after the popular egg dish
they developed, cooked in a ceramic chafing dish called a *cazuela*. The dish
comes with a variety of fillings and is a cross between an omelet and soufflé.
The hand-colored menus reflect the care and consideration that makes the
M&J popular with both expatriates and visitors. $-$$

Fredy's *(Hidalgo).* Fred bought the old Mano de Dios restaurant – which was
kind of a local bar but still one of our favorite cheap eateries on Isla Mujeres –
and brightened it up both inside and out. With a new and improved menu,
Fredy's is a bargain restaurant that offers good homemade Mexican cooking
and fresh fish tastefully prepared. It is next door to the Red Eye Café, across
the street from a Crystal stand that sells cold water, soda and beer. $$

Manolo's *(Matamoros).* Garden dining out back, with twinkly lights in the
evening, a jungle scene painted in front and bright, multicolor furniture
distinguish this mainly seafood restaurant on a quiet part of Av. Matamoros.

Tonyno's *(Hidalgo)*. Exposed brick walls covered by clay suns and moons and masks create the atmosphere in this narrow storefront dinner restaurant down the street from the fancier and pricier Pizza Rolandi. Tonyno's offers delicious Italian food – such as a meat lasagna with a béchamel sauce or wood oven-baked pizza – at very reasonable prices. If you're enjoying the nightly live music you may be handed a bongo or tambourine and invited to join in, though of late the place next door has been loud enough to drown out the music. Free tequilas arrive at your table as they deliver your bill. During the day, Tonyno's is a gift shop. $-$$

Caribbean Café *(Hidalgo)*. Mostly known for its romantic evening ambiance, this little backyard, open-air restaurant welcomed its first customers in 2002 with a sand floor, live music nightly, twinkly lights in the trees, candles on the tables, and a varied menu that includes veggie dishes. Great place for a date. $-$$

Casa O's *(near El Garrafón Park)*. The house of the O's, its name taken from the staff's predominance of first names that begin with "O," has managed to attract many upscale diners to its pretty palapa restaurant overlooking the bay and Cancún. The staff and renowned chef came over wholesale from Maria's next door when the American owner is said to have offered them a piece of the pie. It's a good restaurant with a reputation for fine dining. $$$

Loncheria El Poc Chuc *(Juárez)*. Six tables squeeze into this narrow little restaurant on the corner of Juárez. The Mexican menu offers some of the best prices in town from breakfast to dinner. Sandwiches come on toasted kaiser rolls. Try the Torta Loca, or crazy sandwich, for about US $2. It's filled with chicken, ham, eggs, sausage, refried beans, salad – just about anything but the kitchen sink. $

Playa Lancheros *(near Mundaca's Hacienda at the turn for Sac Bajo)*. We mentioned it earlier, but it bears repeating here. The open air beach bar and restaurant at Playa Lancheros is king of the laid-back lunch places. Famous for Tikin xic – or some such spelling – grilled fish with that wonderful secret Maya spice, anchiote. It's not a hot spice, but it adds a delicious taste to your grilled fish. This is the place to bring your swimsuit, grab a beer, order a fish, and relax the day away. Lots of locals and tourists in the know hang out here.

Zazil-Há *(at the Na-Balam hotel, ☎ 998/877-0279)*. When islanders and tourists are up for a fancy night out with friends, an intimate dinner, or just a great meal, they often choose Zazil-Há. The outdoor/air-conditioned indoor palapa-covered restaurant Zazil-Há has a superb atmosphere and gourmet cooking at relatively moderate prices. There's wonderful dining on the upstairs veranda. The beachfront bar, packed with people to its palm-topped rafters around sunset, serves bar food and drinks all day. $$-$$$

Quintana Roo

Isla Holbox

Better to be a free bird than a captive king.
~ Danish proverb

Isla Holbox (OL-bosh), like Cancún, is more of a sandbar peninsula with a large lagoon/river forming a barrier between the mainland and the Caribbean Sea. Located well north of the Isla Contoy Bird Sanctuary, the village of Holbox remains tiny a fishing community on the northernmost tip of the Yucatán Peninsula. But perhaps not for too much longer.

The attraction of Holbox has always been its fishing, long deserted beaches, and remote untamed natural wilderness. And until recently, the island was visited by only an adventurous few. Now, enough boutique hotels have been built to make a vacation here comfortable as well as pleasurable. This is your chance to see Mexican seaside village life that's fast disappearing from the Yucatán, thanks to mega-resorts and package tours. If you'd like to vacation where the beaches are wonderful and the prices are low, make haste for Holbox – a beach place that hasn't yet been discovered by hordes in Hawaiian shirts. Beachcombers rejoice: the beaches here are packed with seashells of incredible beauty. Holbox is a destination ripe for ecotourism. Local boats are now taking visitors out among the endangered whale sharks when they migrate offshore during July and August. Absolutely incredible. The tip of the island is aptly named "Punta Mosquito," so pack plenty of insect repellent, but don't miss it.

The tranquil harbor at Isla Holbox.

Orientation

It is possible to visit Holbox in a very long day trip from the Cancún area, but we think you'll be happier staying overnight. If you have only one day to spare, you could hire a boat from Isla Mujeres, but it's good three-hour trip. By car, head west from Cancún on Mérida Libre, Rt. 180, and just before Nuevo Xcan turn right at the sign for Chiquila. This tiny fishing village offers a painfully slow twice-a-day car ferry (9 and 6) that runs across the large lagoon out to Holbox. Everyone who is not taking a car (you shouldn't) parks it under the big palapa (look back to the right as you come to the pier) that serves as a parking garage (under US $2 day) and travels on the passenger launch. The scheduled launch (US $3) zips across the lagoon from Chiquila five times per day at 6 and 8 in the morning, noon, and 2 and 5 pm. Return trips (remember, all of this is weather permitting) leave Holbox at 5, 7 and 11 am, and at 1 and 4 in the afternoon.

If you arrive too late for the island launch (and don't want to hire a private one, available for around US $20), the only place to stay in Chiquila is the so-so Hotel Puerto del Sol. Back in the village of Kantunil Kin, 44 km (27 miles) south, you could stay in the Posada Letí or perhaps the Posada del Parque in the center of town. If you have time, explore the unexcavated Maya ruins nearby.

Once on Holbox, head for the beach across the sandy street that passes as the main drag. We rented a golf cart from **Rent-A-Car Holbox** (no reservations needed). It got us around nicely for about US $60 day, or US $10 per hour. The company also rents motor scooters for half the price. Holbox has no bank or change booth yet, but there is a larga distancia (**telephone exchange**) on the square.

When you get to the beach, look out for sailboats bobbing in the waves. You're standing not far from where Maya warriors first saw Spanish ships in 1517. The Maya promptly drove the landing party away, but you'll be a welcomed guest.

The official island website is **www.islaholbox.com.mx**.

Accommodations & Dining

Fish should smell like the tide.
Once they smell like fish, it's too late.
~ Oscar Gizelt, food & beverage manager, Delmonico's restaurant, NY

Restaurants in town serve – you guessed it – delicious fresh fish. Locals agree the best in town is **Restaurant Zarabanda** (☎ 984/875-2194), one block off the main plaza. Second-best is the **Restaurante Edelin** (no reservations), which serves pizza and lobster on the square. A number of Italian restaurants have opened recently; many near the square are worth checking out.

■ Hotels

Posada d'Ingrid (☎ *984/875-2070, 10 rooms, 4 with air & 2 double beds, 6 with double bed & fan).* The Ingrid's basic motel-like accommodations feature two beds in each clean room and hot and cold water in the bathroom. Straight to the beach, make a left, one block. $

HOTEL PRICE CHART	
NOTE: Often, one shared bed in a room is cheaper than two. Prices based on cost per night, for two.	
[No $]	Less than US $20
$	US $20 - $40
$$	US $40 - $80
$$$	US $80 - $125

Faro Viejo *(on beach, ☎ 984/875-2217, www.faroviejoholbox.com.mx, 10 rooms, 3 two-bedroom suites with kitchenettes, air, TV, video bar, restaurant).* The three suites are below the 10 upstairs rooms in this refreshing beachfront hotel called the "Old Lighthouse," named after the fragile-looking structure on the beach that served as a warning of danger to fishermen. The hotel was built in 1997. Its rooms were upgraded in December 1999 and it now promises to be one of Holbox's most popular hotels. $$-$$$

Villas Los Mapaches *(on beach, ☎/fax 984/875-2090, 4 villas, air, kitchenettes).* These comfortable palapa villas and rooms, owned by a European expat, rent for the day, week or month. All have refrigerators and kitchenettes. The largest suite is beautifully decorated and well apportioned, a perfect place for longer stays or families. It runs about twice the cost of the lower bungalows. Tropical garden landscaping behind a gate on the beach. $-$$

Villas Delphines *(on beach, ☎ 984/875-2196, www.holbox.com, 10 cabañas, restaurant, bar).* Villas Delphines represent Holbox's premier "eco" hotel complex. Each round, palapa-roofed villa is built above the sand on stilts, with local materials, and they use alternative solar energy water heaters. The rooms are decorated in bright Mexican colors against natural woods – very inviting. We thought the prices a little steep for the area, but other hotels will not be too far behind. $$$

Posada Los Arcos de Dinora *(on main plaza, ☎ 984/875-2043, 10 rooms, fans).* On the other end of the spectrum is this pleasant but spartan little hotel run by the ever-smiling dueña, Dinora. Rooms behind white Colonial arches surround a garden courtyard. They have very basic beds and bathrooms.

Posada La Palapa *(on beach, ☎ 984/875-2121, 5 rooms, restaurant/bar).* If you're thinking different, think about this huge circular *naj* (traditional hut), with overhanging palapa roof, originally built as someone's home. Enter an open central hallway where five private bedrooms spin off. One of the quarters is very large, with three beds and a sitting area. We took the first room on the right, a double with a cute bathroom, and fell asleep to the sea wind blowing against the palapa roof. Bed and breakfast rate available. There's a tiny Mex-Italian restaurant on the sand, open for three meals, weather permitting. $

Cozumel

Not bound to swear allegiance to any master,
wherever the wind takes me I travel as a visitor.
~ Horace 65 - 8 BC

The kaleidoscope of colors here is amazing. Sergeant major fish striped in bright yellow and black. Parrotfish shine as if under a dayglow lamp. French grunts with blue-green shimmering stripes dart among white angelfish as two schools mingle to avoid the human swimmers ogling them. The garlands of reef around Cozumel were discovered many years ago by divers and snorkelers who flocked here for the indescribable beauty of life undersea and a visibility reaching 250 feet. Later, cruise ships began an annual migration like huge pregnant white ducks to the docks of Cozumel. Now both the

A cruise ship drops a daily dose of tourists at Cozumel's dock.

reefs and the seafront downtown become crowded with divers and cruise passengers making the most of their time here.

Positioned somewhere between the resort atmosphere of Cancún and the laissez-faire attitude of Isla Mujeres, Cozumel casts a magical spell over anyone who sets foot on shore. The island somehow manages to absorb a daily dose of tourists and still maintain a charm all its own; it is only about 5% developed. Beyond the tourist mecca are spectacular natural wonders and a relaxed lifestyle. The ancient Maya called the island Ah Cuzamil Peten, "Place of Swallows."

MYSTERIOUS MAYA: Maya women made a pilgrimage to Cozumel to honor Ixchel, goddess of fertility and the moon.

It was here that Spanish warrior Hernando Cortéz landed in 1518 in an expedition that would develop into the conquest of the continent. He found friendly natives – as do tourists who disembark nearly 500 years later. Cozumel became a port of call for Caribbean cruise ships after Jacques Cousteau filmed its amazing reefs in the 1950s. Now, an average of 600 cruise ships visit the island annually. It's also a favorite hop-over for tourists from Cancún.

After diseases brought by Europeans decimated the Maya population, Cozumel was virtually abandoned except by pirates, such as Jean Lafitte, who used its sheltering waters as a base to attack passing cargo ships. Refugees from the Caste War repopulated the island in the mid-1800s.

You can "do" Cozumel in a day or spend a month and still not "do" everything. The reasons for the island's popularity are obvious: sparkling emerald waters that hold a coral coat of many colors and a population of warm and friendly Cozumeleños make the island a natural place to be.

The island's official website is **www.cozumel.net**.

Orientation

■ Getting Around

San Miguel (population 69,000) is the only city on Mexico's largest island at 47 km (28 miles) long and 15 km (11 miles) wide. With a maximum elevation of 45 feet, the island sits 18 km (11 miles) offshore from Playa del Carmen. Two **ferry services** – a car ferry from Puerto Morelos and a people ferry from Playa del Carmen – serve Cozumel from the Yucatán mainland.

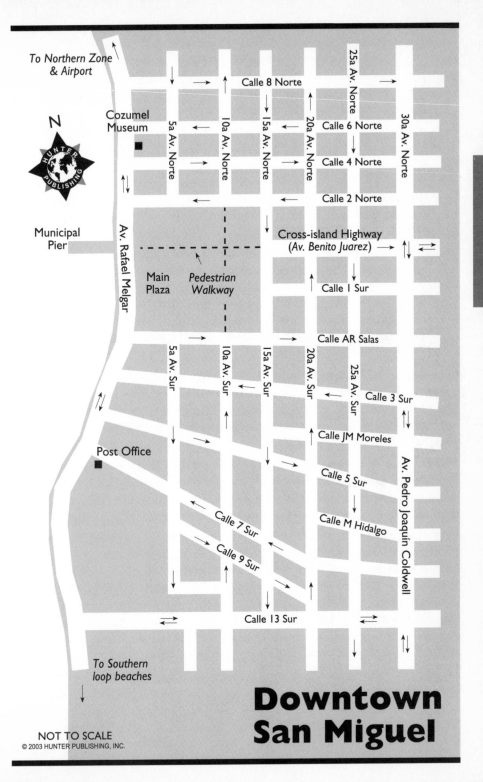

To Northern Zone & Airport

Cozumel Museum

N

Calle 8 Norte

25a Av. Norte

5a Av. Norte

10a Av. Norte

15a Av. Norte

20a Av. Norte

30a Av. Norte

Calle 6 Norte

Calle 4 Norte

Calle 2 Norte

Municipal Pier

Av. Rafael Melgar

Cross-island Highway
(Av. Benito Juarez)

Main Plaza

Pedestrian Walkway

Calle 1 Sur

Calle AR Salas

5a Av. Sur

10a Av. Sur

15a Av. Sur

20a Av. Sur

25a Av. Sur

Calle 3 Sur

Calle JM Moreles

Post Office

Calle 5 Sur

Calle 7 Sur

Calle M Hidalgo

Av. Pedro Joaquín Coldwell

Calle 9 Sur

Calle 13 Sur

To Southern loop beaches

Downtown San Miguel

NOT TO SCALE
© 2003 HUNTER PUBLISHING, INC.

> **AUTHORS' TIP:** *Buy your ticket for the ferry from Playa to Cozumel (US $9) from several ticket booths near the dock. The ticket booth on Cozumel is at the dock entrance. The boat runs frequently and takes about a half-hour. In windy weather, take a Dramamine beforehand. See* Practicalities *on page 179 for the schedule. Don't fall for the "free ticket" that's offered by hawkers near the dock in Playa. You'll spend a good three hours getting pressured to buy a timeshare if you do.*

San Miguel also has an international **airport** with some direct flights landing from the States and several 15-minute connecting flights from Cancún (call Aerocozumel, ☎ 998/884-2000). The airport is on the island's north end.

The scrub brush jungle covers the northern half of the island, which is virtually uninhabited. The southern portions, the interior and the entire windward east coast also have few inhabitants. A road loops the entire southern part along the sea, then cuts back into town, dividing the island in half, while a coastal road follows the northern shore to its end. The concentration of population in San Miguel makes for some interesting expeditions and explorations far from the madding crowd.

Chankanaab National Park, south of town, may have some crowds but is a great place to snorkel, sun and see a botanical garden. The western shore beaches – both north and south of the main pier – are very beautiful. The northern section is mostly hotels and private homes of the wealthy; to the south are the "public" beaches.

Unlike other Mexican towns, Cozumel has no public buses. Besides taxis (a good choice when going direct from one place to another), three types of personal transportation are available: **motorbikes, bicycles** and **cars**, including four-wheel-drives. Taxis have no meters so negotiate your fare first.

Many major hotels rent motorbikes or cars and every street corner downtown near the dock has men hawking rentals. Cozumel's excellent roads combined with long stretches of wilderness make a motorbike ideal – and they even come with automatic shifts. The prices on vehicles are pretty much the same between companies, especially near the dock, but you could try going direct to some of the shops in town or waiting until the ferry is empty and the crowd disbursed before negotiating. It's illegal to ride a scooter/moped without a helmet. Also, a rental vehicle may not come with insurance, so check first.

If you are already a crowd, or want to really see every detail of Cozumel's wilderness, try getting a good deal on a Jeep. Only a four-wheel-drive vehicle can handle the arduous northeast coast road (in the dry season only) to El Castillo Real ruin, a minor Maya ruin overlooking a good snorkeling spot. Farther along is the dramatic picturesque **Punta Molas lighthouse** warn-

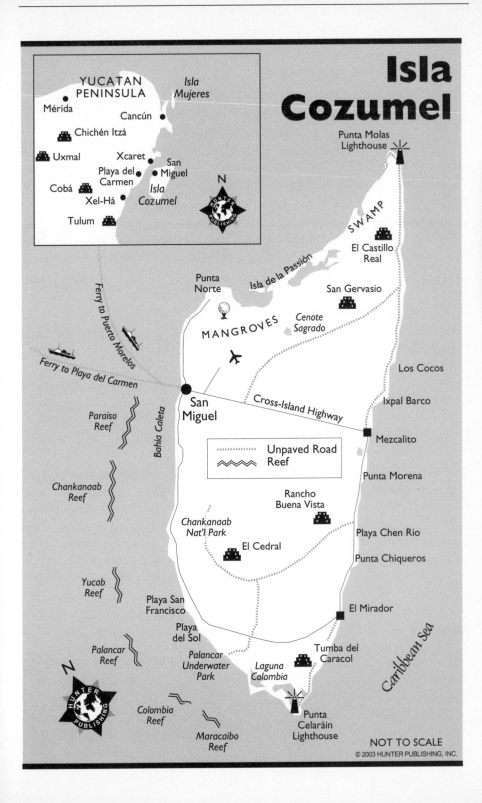

Isla Cozumel

YUCATAN PENINSULA

Isla Mujeres

Mérida

Cancún

Chichén Itzá

Uxmal

Xcaret

Playa del Carmen

San Miguel

Cobá

Isla Cozumel

Xel-Há

Tulum

N

HUNTER PUBLISHING

Punta Molas Lighthouse

SWAMP

El Castillo Real

San Gervasio

Punta Norte

Isla de la Passión

MANGROVES

Cenote Sagrado

Los Cocos

Ferry to Puerto Morelos

Ferry to Playa del Carmen

Cross-Island Highway

Ixpal Barco

San Miguel

Paraiso Reef

Bahía Caleta

Mezcalito

Unpaved Road

Reef

Punta Morena

Chankanaab Reef

Rancho Buena Vista

Chankanaab Nat'l Park

El Cedral

Playa Chen Rio

Punta Chiqueros

Yucab Reef

Playa San Francisco

El Mirador

Playa del Sol

Palancar Reef

Palancar Underwater Park

Laguna Colombia

Tumba del Caracol

Caribbean Sea

N

HUNTER PUBLISHING

Colombia Reef

Maracaibo Reef

Punta Celaráin Lighthouse

NOT TO SCALE

© 2003 HUNTER PUBLISHING, INC.

ing ships of the reefs – then you have to turn around and bounce back. Take note – Jeeps carrying more than five people are subject to a moving violation ticket and impoundment of the car.

The rest of Cozumel has excellent roads and enough to see and do to keep occupied, even if it's nothing more than floating around in the warm Caribbean waters.

If you're staying in town, a bicycle is handy on the more lightly traveled side streets. For longer hauls down to southern beaches or to do the island loop you'd have to be very fit. Bikes are available for rent at several of the car rental agencies.

TRANSPORTATION RENTALS (A PARTIAL LIST)		
Company	Telephone, location	Available vehicles
Aguila Jeep & Moto	☎ 987/872-1190, Av. Rafael Melgar south of ferry	Motorcycles, bikes, Jeeps, cars
Budget Jeep & Auto	☎ 987/872-0903, Av. 5 @ Calle 2	Jeeps, cars
Masha	☎ 987/872-1096, 5ta Av. @ 3 Sur	Motorcycles, bikes
Localiza	☎ 987/872-2111	Cars
Avis	☎ 987/872-0099, airport	Cars
Rentador Cozumel	☎ 987/872-1120, Hotel Flores	Motorcycles, bikes
Less Pay	☎ 987/872-4744, Hotel Barracuda	Jeeps, cars
Auto Rent	☎ 987/872-0844, La Ceiba Hotel	Jeeps, cars

The street layout in Cozumel makes it easy to know where you are... once you get used to it. **Av. Rafael Melgar** is the main road running along the western waterfront. There you'll find La Caleta, a new state-of-the-art lighthouse built to guide cruise ships. Roads running north and south, parallel to the water, are *avenidas* and those running perpendicular to the sea, east and west, are *calles*. The sole exception to this is **Av. Benito Juárez**, which cuts San Miguel and the island into northern and southern halves and should be a calle, but is not.

Streets north of Juárez are marked *norte* and have even numbers (2, 4, 6, etc.). All the *calles* south of Juárez are *sur* and are given odd numbers (3, 5, 7, etc.). Vehicles traveling north and south are supposed to have the right of way, while those traveling east and west are required to stop on every corner. Drive very carefully and look before you go.

> ## PARKING PROBLEMS
>
> Parking can sometimes be scarce in town. Don't park by red curbs – they're "No Parking" zones. Your car or moto could be towed or the license plate removed (so that you pay a fine at the rental agency).

Practicalities

COMMUNICATION: There are several **Internet cafés**. Those closer to the ferry dock are more expensive. You can phone home, send e-mail or fax from the **Calling Station**, ☎ 987/872-1417, on Av. Melgar at Calle 3 Sur, open until at least 10 pm daily.

CONSULATE/IMMIGRATION: There's a new US consulate office on Cozumel, located on the Plaza Principal (☎ 987/872-4574 or 872-6152). To extend your tourist card here, visit the *Migracíon* office in the Palacio Municipal (☎ 987/872-0226).

FERRY SCHEDULE: (Playa to Cozumel) 6, 8, 9, 10, 11 am, 1, 3, 5, 6, 7, 9, 11 pm. (Cozumel to Playa) 5, 7, 8, 9, 10 am, noon, 2, 4, 5, 6:30, 8, 10 pm.

GROCERIES: A good **bakery** is **Panificadora La Cozumeleña** on Calle 3 Sur and Av. 10 a.

LAUNDROMAT: **Laundromat Margarita** is on Av. 20, near Calle 3 Sur.

MEDICAL FACILITIES & DOCTORS: There are several English-speaking doctors on the island. Try **Dr. Lewis** on Av. 50 (☎ 987/872-1616). There's the **Medical Center** on Av. 20 Norte No. 425 (☎ 987/872-2929). There's also a tourist **Medical Service**, open 24 hours, on Av. 50 between Calles 11 and 13 Sur (☎ 987/872-0912). Call an **ambulance** at ☎ 987/872-0639. A diver's **decompression chamber** is on Calle 5 Sur off Melgar, ☎ 987/872-2387.

MINI GOLF: The cute **Cozumel Mini Golf** has 18 holes up and down a little hill at the corner of Calle 1 Sur and Av. 15, US $6, kids $4.

MONEY MATTERS: There are several **banks** around offering money exchange (usually in the mornings) and two money change booths are located on the square. The **American Express** representative is at the Fiesta Cozumel, Av. Melgar No. 27 (☎ 987/872-2262).

PHARMACIES: There are several pharmacies in town, including one on the plaza, another at the *zócalo* near the Hotel Lopez and a 24-hour one at the **Medical Center** on Av. 20 Norte No. 425 (☎ 987/872-2929).

POLICE: The police are reached at ☎ 987/872-0092 or 987/872-0409 in the Palacio Municipal on Calle 11 Sur. For English service, ask for James Garcia.

POST OFFICE: The post office is on Av. Rafael Melgar at Calle 7 Sur.

SHOPPING: Cozumel and shopping are synonymous. Your first stop should be downtown in the shopping area around the main square. In the **Plaza del Sol** facing the square are a number of flea market gift and souvenir shops that offer good prices with bargaining. Then the **open-air flea market** has long been a staple for people getting off the cruise ships and is a fun place to shop. It's located across the street from the old cruise ship dock, the southern-most pier. A brand new shopping plaza, **Punta Langosta**, has been built like an American mall across from the new cruise ship dock almost in the middle of downtown. Over 75 upscale shops and restaurants are there. One of them is **Los Cinco Soles**, whose more established store is to the north of the ferry pier on Av. Melgar. See our review of Pancho's Backyard restaurant, page 192, for a brief history and description of all the goodies you can buy. It has the best quality and overall selection for gifts. And of course, all along the waterfront and Av. Melgar are other stores that cater to cruisers, some of which offer very interesting things.

SPA: Did someone say pampered massage? **Caribbean Massage**, Av. 5 South between Calles 3 and 5, offers everything soothing. Swedish massage, aromatherapy, mud wraps, facials, manicures, waxing, haircuts and styling, even a sunburn treatment are given in a spotlessly clean parlor. Make appointments at ☎ 987/872-5068. Open 9-8 pm. Around the block on Calle 5, between Melgar and Av. 5 Sur, is **Spa del Sol** (☎ 987/869-1194), which offers relaxation and therapeutic massage, aromatherapy, and beauty treatments in their facility or at your hotel.

SUPPORT GROUPS: English-language **Alcoholics Anonymous** and **Narcotics Anonymous** group meetings are held Sunday, Monday, Wednesday and Friday at 6 pm at the Hotel Colonial on the corner of Av. 5 and Calle 7 Sur (☎ 987/872-1007).

TOURIST INFORMATION: This can be obtained from the **Tourism Office** (☎ 987/872-7585, www.cozumel.net). Climb the less-than-clean stairway in the middle of the Plaza del Sol building that faces the central plaza. We were more pleased with the help provided by the **Hotel Association** (☎ 987/872-3132) on Calle 2 Norte, between Avenidas 10 & 15.

Pyramid at Cobá, Quintana Roo (see page 242-43)

Beaches

For thousands of years the seekers have come....
And they still come to Cozumel.
~ Legends of Old Mexico, Father Oveido Hernandez, 1847

The windward eastern beaches are rocky, dramatic, impressive, gorgeous and – with a few exceptions – too rough and dangerous for swimming. These are best suited to beachcombing and shell collecting. The leeward western beaches feature picture-book white sand, gentle lapping waves, warm emerald-green water and a series of vibrant living reefs. These are the beaches for good swimming, snorkeling and diving.

■ Along the Leeward Shore

 The beaches north of the pier downtown on the leeward side of the island are also sublime, especially around **Playa Azul**. They are less accessible because of all the private homes and hotels. The strange unfinished lighthouse-looking structure near the marina is part of a mansion, connected with the main house by a tunnel under the road. Rumor has it (as told to us by a grinning security guard) the eccentric owner killed his family and himself there.

 Following the leeward loop about nine km (5.5 miles) south of town brings you to **Chankanaab National Park**, a lagoon and botanical garden set along the shore. The garden features over 400 plant species. The lagoon used to be connected to the sea through underground passages. Those waterways have now collapsed, creating a living aquarium with over 60 different aquatic species. Sand beaches, restaurants, a museum, plus snorkel and dive areas with rental and lessons are available in the park. In the water, fish hang out waiting for food scraps and the snorkeling among them is wonderful. The park is also a marvelous place to relax in the sun or shade in picnic areas. Chankanaab boasts the new Dolphin Discovery, an exciting half-hour interactive swim with dolphins (see below, page 185).

The beach just before Chankanaab is **Playa Corona**, with a fresh fish and Mexican food restaurant and snorkel rental. **Playa San Francisco**, the beach south of Chankanaab, is very popular with cruise tourists who stop for lunch and a swim. It's one of the best beaches in Cozumel. **Playa Sol**, (☎ 987/872-9030, www.playasol.com.mx), a bit farther south, has become a big-time tourist destination from its more humble beginnings. It now boasts a huge, beachside palapa restaurant with Mexican buffet, a zoo and lots of gift-buying opportunities. Snorkeling, diving (to their own imitation sunken Maya city), swimming, and most watersports are available. Exaggerated entrance fee. **Playa del Cedral** is opposite the turn

Quintana Roo

for the inland village and small El Cedral ruins. It's a public park with a tiny seafood restaurant. **Playa Palancar** is opposite the famous reef of the same name. It features a restaurant and good swimming. There are a number of these beautiful beach spots and restaurant combinations along the east coast road.

■ Along the Windward Shore

After a long ride through the jungle bush you come to the **Paradise Café**, a reggae bar along the rough, west-coast windward side. A right leads to the **Punta del Sur**, a recently created nature preserve and park around the secluded beaches at the **Punta Celerain Lighthouse**. The lighthouse is now the **Museo de Navigacion**, with displays themed to ships and the sea. A comfortable bus takes visitors from the information center on a guided tour of the natural area, providing binoculars to see the wildlife and vistas from *mirador* towers along the road. The Late Postclassic Maya ruins at the southernmost tip, **El Caracol**, while small, are quite charming. Embedded with rows of conch shells that call in the wind, the diminutive building is one-of-a-kind in Maya architecture.

 MYSTERIOUS MAYA: Some historians theorize the Maya architects arranged the conch shells to "sing" when the wind blew across the building.

In a conservation effort, the beaches here are guarded by local soldiers during turtle egg-laying season. Admission to Punta Del Sur is around US $10, which includes the tour. A large restaurant is planned.

Just north of the sharp turn at the Paradise Café is a **blowhole** in the rock, a great place to get wet and a fun photo op if the tide is in. The road runs north from here along the rugged rocky windswept coastline.

The next site of interest is **El Mirador snack bar**, a tiny place with outdoor tables among the dunes. You might spot a guy with a huge iguana here. He hopes to get a US $1 tip for photos. As you drive the road there are plenty of herons and pelicans to be seen in the wild.

Pretty **Playa Bonita** has an eatery and allows beach camping. Farther along, the **Chen Rio beach**, with an excellent little seafood restaurant, is shielded by rock formations that form a cove and break up the waves. It's great for swimming and snorkeling and a peaceful place to stop and eat, swim or just hang a hammock. A left turn at the end of the long road is required to return to San Miguel, past the San Gervasio ruins. To continue north on the dirt road to Puntas Molas requires a four-wheel-drive and stamina.

Events

Carnival, the Sunday before Ash Wednesday, is a hugely festive holiday bash with masquerades and dances. The island comes alive for this, by far the biggest event of the year, with some parties running all night long. Floats, prepared by hotels, restaurants and clubs, give the parade a Mardi Gras style. Street dancing competitions occur during the entire week. The "Comparas" groups are judged on originality, style, color and execution. All the balls and fiestas are open to the public, but you must buy tickets ahead of time on the square above Chico's.

A free open-air **concert** is held every Sunday from 7-10 pm in the main square.

In May is the **Feria de Cedral**, when Cozumeleños celebrate the first Catholic mass in Mexico, said at the El Cedral ruins. Contact Cozumel Tourism at ☎ 987/872-7585. "Everyone, including Chaplain Juan Diaz, participated in the simple ceremony," wrote one of the chroniclers of the event. "This was done in a way to avoid insulting the local pagan priest and designed to make no enemies among the natives."

After the Cedral Fair, everyone goes fishing. There are three big tournaments during May and June. June also hosts the **Pedro and Pablo Festival** (Peter and Paul Festival). In order to travel so much, we often have to rob Pedro to pay Pablo.

Night Spots

Come a little bit closer, you're my kind of man
So big and so strong.
Come a little bit closer, I'm all alone
and the night is so long.
~ sung by Jay and the Americans

A large number of island visitors return to their cruise ships by the early evening. After the ships weigh anchor and light up their rigging as they sail off, the nightlife in Cozumel begins. Although it is not quite as much a party town as Cancún – perhaps because alcohol and diving don't mix well – it still swings.

The hottest eating, dancing, "ass-kicking," but touristy, party place is **Carlos and Charlie's** roof dance and grill restaurant, near the ferry dock on Av. Melgar. It's up a steep set of stairs that guarantee a problem coming back down after a few drinks! Dine on the terrace overlooking the harbor and the main drag below. When Carlos closes at 1 am the sleepless from Seattle may wander over to find you at **Joe's**, a crowded bar and live-music super party place on Av. 10 between 1 & 3 South; or at **Raga**, the live reggae, salsa and rock music Caribbean restaurant and bar, on Av. Salas between 10 and 15. It opens at 10:30 pm. The oceanfront drive boasts a popular **Hard Rock Café** and a **Planet Hollywood**, both smaller and more intimate than their Cancún counterparts.

Follow the sounds of singing to **Tony Rome's** (Calle Adolfo Rosado Salas near Av. 5 Sur, ☎ 987/872-0131), where Tony Rome himself croons relaxing music with two shows nightly at 7:30 and 9:30. Tony's is a required stop for any true Cozumel experience. With open-neck shirt and gold chains, he looks like a caricature of a lounge singer – perhaps because that's what he was in the States, headlining for years in casinos in Las Vegas and Atlantic City. Smile at his style if you must. When the South Jersey native begins to sing, you'll fall over at his wonderful voice and you'll find yourself singing along with the standards. Tony's offers good ribs, good times and loaded drinks. Say hello from us.

Black and White, a restaurant/piano bar/nightclub that draws a hip local crowd, is near the central downtown area. Head east on Juárez four blocks from the plaza and turn right at the Pemex on Av. Pedro Joaquin (30 a). Go four blocks more to the happening bar. Cool, baby.

The disco dance floors can become very crowded in Cozumel. **Neptuno Disco**, five blocks south of the plaza along the water, fills with a good mix of locals and tourists who love to dance and mingle. They have huge TV screens and a sharp laser light show.

Adventures & Attractions

There is a third dimension to traveling,
the longing for what is beyond.
~ Jan Myrdal, *The Silk Road*

■ Attractions

 The **Cozumel Museum** opened in 1987 in an airy building along the seafront, 2½ blocks north of the main plaza. It presents local archeological history in four *salas*, exhibition halls, on two floors. The well-arranged museum is open 9 am to 8 pm daily. No flash photography is permitted. It has a good **coffee shop** upstairs.

■ Adventures

WATERSPORTS: It's a no-brainer to guess that adventure activities on Cozumel island center around the water. If you're an experienced diver with PADI certification, there is no end of opportunities. Numerous dive trip operators will take you to the 17 major dive spots offshore, which include a sunken airplane near the La Ceiba Hotel. For a list of approved providers, stop by the **Cozumel Dive Association** on Av. 15 between 2 and 4, ☎ 987/872-5955, www.cozumel.net/diving/anoaat.

Snorkelers can find paradise at **Chankanaab National Park** (www.cozumelparks.com.mx) or off the shores of the beachfront hotels. Either persuasion can rent a boat and guide at the marina near the airport. The park also offers **Dolphin Discovery**, a supervised, hands-on swim with the lovable sea mammals. They are offered at 9 and 11 am and 1 and 3 pm. Make reservations ahead of time, ☎ 987/872-6604, 05, 06, or 07. Cost is about US $130, for everyone ages eight and up.

FISHING: You can charter fishing boats from **Cozumel Anglers Fleet** (☎ 987/872-0118), **Cozumel Adventures** (☎ 987/872-0489), or **Sportel** (☎ 987/878-0214).

HIKING & BIKING/MAYA RUINS: Hikers and bikers might also like to go to the main Maya ruins, **San Gervasio**. The trails between the sites follow the ancient *sacbeob* (plural of *sacbé*) under the shade of trees. (*Sacbeob* were raised causeways built by the Maya.) It's as much fun to walk around as it is to see the ruins. In 2000 the restoration of the El Ramonal section of the ruins was completed with the help of 40 local Maya families and a grant from American Express.

HORSEBACK RIDING: There are several ranches offering guided horseback trips into the bush. Look for signs at the end of the north beaches, near the Presidente Hotel, and on the leeward side.

GOLF: With a $200 million investment, the new **Cozumel Country Club** (☎ 987/872-9570, www.cozumelcountryclub.com.mx) is setting world-class standards with

Girl on horseback.

its 18-hole championship course set among the mangroves on the island's north end. Bring a handicap and some insect repellent. Find it north of town, past the airport.

Accommodations

The areas north and south of the town of San Miguel house the more expensive, but generally gorgeous, beachfront hotels. If you're on a budget, don't despair – the island is small enough that everywhere is close to the beach. Staying in one of the downtown hotels is a good way to save money, but we've also found some excellent values beachside.

■ Budget Hotels

Hotel Cozumeleño Inn *(Calle 4 North #3, ☎ 987/872-0314, air or fan)*. The Cozumeleño makes the most of what it has: good, very clean, basic rooms in a bright white three-story downtown hotel. Rooms facing the street are larger than those facing the tiny square courtyard with a pool. $

HOTEL PRICE CHART	
NOTE: Often, one shared bed in a room is cheaper than two. Prices based on cost per night, for two.	
[No $]	Less than US $20
$	US $20 - $40
$$	US $40 - $80
$$$	US $80 - $125

Hotel Flores *(Calle Rosado Salas No. 72, ☎ 987/872-1429, fax 987/872-2475, 33 rooms with fans or air)*. Situated above dive shops and car rental places, the Flores is an exceptionally economical place to stay in the downtown center. Half a block east of the waterfront, up the street from Pepe's Grill. $

Maya Cozumel *(Calle 5 Sur, between 5a and Melgar, ☎ 987/872-0011, www. hotelflamingo.com, 38 rooms with air, small pool, telephones)*. The neat and attractive Maya Cozumel has several Maya statues, paintings and artifacts filling its lovely gardens, rooms and lobby. Definitely worth checking out. We find it to be a comfortable, popular place to stay. $

Hotel Flamingo *(Calle 6 Norte, between 5a and Melgar, ☎ 987/872-7060, 22 rooms with fan)*. The relatively modern Flamingo is a three-story budget hotel with aspirations of luxury. Bright-white tile floors and street-view balconies in the larger second- and third-floor rooms enhance the value. Often considered the best value downtown. $

Hotel Del Centro *(Av. Juarez & Av. 25, ☎ 987/872-5471, 14 rooms, TV, air, pool, continental breakfast included)*. This is a bit off the water – and on a busy corner – but it features an attractive courtyard, hand-painted doorways to each medium-size room, a small pool, and cheap prices. It's up Av. Juárez several blocks from the water.

■ Moderate Hotels

B&B Caribo *(Av. Juárez, ☎ 987/872-3195, 10 rooms with air, including 3 kitchenette suites).* The American owners of this bed & breakfast know what pleases *norteamericanos* – pleasant, spotlessly clean rooms and a welcoming, very American atmosphere. There's a shady screened-in porch and cable TV in the communal sitting room and dining areas. A former doctor's residence, it's no surprise that his bedroom at the back of the first floor is the best. Also ask about the rooftop rooms. $$

Tamarindo B&B *(Calle 4 between 20th & 25th, ☎/fax 987/872-3614, 5 rooms, security, safe).* Native Frenchwoman and former language teacher Elaine Godement met her husband, Mexican architect Jorge Ruiz Esparza, in San Francisco before settling in Cozumel and opening this magnificent but hard to find bed and breakfast. Two bright and airy upstairs rooms are in the white stucco main building. These inviting rooms have French doors, narrow balconies, a circular staircase to a little patio, hidden skylights in the bathrooms and Elaine's continental decorating touch. Two brand new attractive rooms with air conditioning and kitchenettes are located in a separate stucco building at the back of the fruit-tree garden. Then there's one palapa Maya hut, with a private bath, also in the garden. The separate palapa room is the best value at the same price as the upstairs rooms. The Tamarindo is worth finding. There's a shared kitchen off the upstairs patio and a generous European-style breakfast included in the price. Child care and French lessons are also available. Don't worry if they're full; they've opened a second B&B nearby. $$

Amigo's B&B *(Calle 7 between 25 & 30, ☎ 987/872-3868, www.bacalar.net, 3 cabañas, air, kitchenettes, continental breakfast included).* It is everyone's dream to come to Cozumel, stay, and open a charming B&B to help finance their new lifestyle. Well, Bob and Kathy Kopelman's small "Amigo's B&B" is one such dream. Their family- and kid-friendly thatch-roof hogar hotel – with a maximum occupancy of only eight – faces a large yard with a tropical garden and big freeform pool. The central communal area, where morning breakfast (hot option available) is served, contains TV, furniture, magazines and games. A separate gated entrance and lovely shrubbery add to the privacy, despite Amigo's in-town location. It has twin beds only, which can be pushed together to make a king. The Kopelmans have another B&B on Bacalar Lake. $$

Hotel Barracuda *(Av. Melgar, ☎ 987/872-0002, fax 987/872-1243, 51 rooms with private terraces).* This is an old favorite of scuba divers who flock to the island for the incredible sites available in the surrounding waters. Despite an energetic clientele, the rooms themselves are somewhat tired. $$

Suites Elizabeth *(Calle Rosado Salas No. 44,* ☎ *987/872-0330, fax 987/ 872-0781, 19 rooms with air, TV).* Dated furnishings don't detract from the convenience of this functional accommodation, only a hundred feet or so from the downtown waterfront. The large upstairs balconies don't offer much of a view, but if they did, you'd pay more. Comfortable and clean. $$

Safari Inn *(Av. Melgar south of the ferry dock,* ☎ *987/872-0101, fax 987/ 872-0661, 12 rooms with air).* Facing the busy street that runs along the sea, this second- and third-floor hotel is a downtown divers' favorite. The attraction is the excellent dive shop downstairs and very large rooms with built-in couches. If you're on the island to dive, ask about their package deals. $$

Club del Sol *(Southern Coastal Road Km 6.8,* ☎ *987/872-3777, 41 rooms with air).* The Club del Sol – not nearly as pretentious as its name – is painted a deep sunflower gold. Well south of the downtown, it sits across the street from a tiny beach that rents scuba and snorkel gear. Each room in the two-story building that runs back from the road has a table with two chairs and faces a pretty garden. Some rooms are available with kitchenettes (US $7 extra) that include fridge, stove, pots and plates. This is an excellent value for so close to the beach. $$

Caribe Hotel *(Calle 2 between 15th & 20th,* ☎ *987/872-0225, fax 987/872-1913, pool, 14 rooms with fan).* This pink motel, built in 1992, has rooms and a small L-shaped pool centered around a pretty garden in a peaceful section of town. The medium-size rooms in this one-story establishment are painted bright Caribbean blue, which makes them slightly dark with the door closed, but they're very clean and appealing. We liked it here. $$

Villas Las Anclas *(Av. 5 Sur,* ☎ *987/872-1403 or 872-6103, fax 987/872-5473, cozumel@lasanclas.com, all suites).* Although this small hotel of staggered attached upstairs/downstairs villas was built in 1988, it looks new. What has matured nicely is the tiny green garden along the villas' doorways. Downstairs quarters contain a well-equipped kitchen and sunken living room with comfortable furniture, day bed, attractive artwork and a large picture window. The upstairs sleeping loft, accessed by a wrought-iron spiral staircase, features a queen-size bed, tiled bathroom and huge closet. A stay here is very much like staying in someone's apartment, someone with good taste. $$$

Hacienda San Miguel *(Calle 10, between Av. 10 & Melgar,* ☎ *987/872-1986, fax 872-7043, www.gotocozumel.com, 10 rooms plus large townhouse, cable TV, kitchenettes, safe, air, continental breakfast included).* This classy hacienda-style hotel, hidden on a quiet side-street, opened in 1999 and established a new high standard for downtown accommodations. It is one of our favorite places to stay. "Hacienda style" usually means a central garden courtyard, Moorish-influenced Colonial architecture, wrought-iron balconies and tile floors throughout – and the San Miguel has all of the aforementioned. An added bonus is that each room has a tiny balcony or patio, and lots of closet space. Special rates are available for the week or longer; the townhouse rents for about US $130 per night. Beach club affiliated. $$

Posada Lety *(Calle 1, between Av. 10 & 15, ☎ 987/872-0257, 8 rooms, fans).* This *posada*, which translates as cheap place to stay, offers basic Caribbean-style accommodations with big wooden-shuttered windows. The large rooms have simple décor and are clean. Across the street from the wonderful Diamond Bakery. $

HOTEL PRICE CHART	
NOTE: Often, one shared bed in a room is cheaper than two. Prices based on cost per night, for two.	
[No $]	Less than US $20
$	US $20 - $40
$$	US $40 - $80
$$$	US $80 - $125

■ Luxury Hotels

Occidental Grand Cozumel *(Km 17.5 near San Francisco Palancar, ☎ in US 800/907-9500, in Mexico 987/872-9730, fax 872-9745, 255 rooms, air, pool, cable TV, restaurants, kids' club, all-inclusive).* This beachside hotel is a step above the typical all-inclusives, with luxurious Colonial hacienda-style architecture and a beautiful beach. Four restaurants, two pools, bars and a dance club. Opened in 2003, it's the newest on the island. $$$$$

Playa Azul Hotel *(Northern Coast Rd, Km 4, ☎ 987/872-0199, fax 987/872-0110, www.playa-azul.com, 50 rooms, balconies or terraces, pool, restaurant/bar, safe deposit box, telephone).* The name, "Blue Beach," refers to the turquoise water in front of a bright-white sand. The hotel was completely remodeled, with a new addition, in 2000, and all rooms face the sea. Despite the spacious quarters, the hotel maintains an intimate, relaxed feeling and the staff is especially attentive. It is family run, offers a high standard of service, and is one of our island favorites. Martha and Fernando traded their Mexico City teaching careers for the soft sand of Cozumel – you might be tempted to do the same if you stay here. The pool is small, but the hotel's beach is one of the island's finest, with a natural cove, ideal for children. Playa Azul lucked out when the Cozumel Country Club opened across the street. Now they are the first hotel on the island to offer "Golf Inclusive" packages. $$$

La Ceiba *(Coastal Rd South, near the cruise ship dock, in US ☎ 800/437-9609, in Mexico ☎ 987/872-0844, fax 987/872-0065, big pool, jacuzzi, tennis, gym, sauna, restaurant & bar, 113 rooms with air).* La Ceiba, named for a type of tree indigenous to the Yucatán and sacred to the Maya, is a regular re-

Quintana Roo

sort hotel very popular with divers. There's a small beach – with optional top-less sunbathing – within sight of the giant cruise ships that anchor offshore. Just beyond the wooden pier in back of the hotel is a large Convair 40-passenger plane, sunk in the crystal-clear water for a disaster movie by a Mexican film company. Now it's a frequent dive and snorkel spot that you can swim to even if you're not staying here. Del Mar aquatic shop on the beach runs frequent trips to the wreck and the reefs and the hotel offers dive packages. $$$

Presidente Inter-Continental *(Southern Coast Rd, Km 6.5, in US ☎ 800/ 327-0200, in Mexico ☎ 987/872-9500, fax 987/872-9528, www.intercontinental.com, pool with jacuzzi, 2 tennis courts, scuba & snorkel rental, 2 restaurants and bar, 253 rooms & suites with air, cable TV, telephones).* We can't think of a hotel in the Yucatán we have enjoyed more than the fabulous El Presidente. Yes, it's expensive, but its location on 100 acres along a crescent-shaped beach is absolutely perfect for swimming and snorkeling. Schools of colorful fish provide great underwater photo ops and there are attractive gardens all over the property. The most expensive rooms (other than suites) are beachfront, but we loved ours, a superior (#2125), whose patio – surrounded by a flowering hibiscus hedge – faced the little beach and the sunset. Rooms in the main building are attractive inside but, if you can, spend the extra $50 or so to get a superior. $$$$-$$$$$

Dining

Courage is walking naked through a cannibal village.
~ Leonard Louis Levinson

It's a universal truth that virtually everything on an island costs more than it does on the mainland. Even fish – go figure. But there are still plenty of places on Cozumel where you can get a meal for a bargain price. If you're looking for good food at a good price, we've selected a number of sit-down restaurants that are well worth visiting.

DINING PRICE CHART	
NOTE: Prices based on a typical entrée, per person, and do not include beverage.	
$	Less than US $5
$$	US $5 - 10
$$$	Over US $10

If you're broke, the absolute cheapest places to eat are those limited-menu fast-food *loncherias* near the *mercado* and the central plaza.

El Moro *(75 Bis Norte #124 between Calle 2 & 4, ☎ 987/872-3029, closed Thursday).* Most tourists have a hard time locating this place and often give up looking. They just don't know what they're missing. Get a cab or go west on Av. Juárez until you get to the large new Pemex station on the left. Make a left just before Pemex, then make the first right and the first left onto a bumpy dirt street. This is the place for hungry diners in the know. El Moro, or "The Moor," offers an extensive menu (in both English and Spanish) of Mexican regional dishes and fresh seafood. Once you try any of the varied menu choices, you'll wonder why you bothered to eat anywhere else on the island. With giant drinks and excellent food, it's an unbeatable value. $

Jeanie's Waffle House *(Calle 11 & Melgar – through the parking lot of the Acuario Restaurant).* We could only love a place called "Waffle House." It's the kind of place we can relax our "going native" façade and chow down on what we haven't had for awhile – feel-good food such as hotcakes and ice cream, plus waffles and crêpes to crow about. Semi-open-air dining until 2 pm. $-$$

La Choza *(Calle Rosado Salas at Av. 10 Sur,* ☎ *987/872-0958).* La Choza has a big Maya palapa roof over its corner dining area and large, open windows. Its reputation is for the best *comida tipica,* or typical Yucatecan-Mexican food, on the island. We can't argue too much about that, because our pork stew and beefsteak in pepper sauce was well prepared and quite tasty. If it's too crowded, right next door is **La Mision**, where an equally delicious meal can be had. $$

Casa Denis *(Calle 1 Sur,* ☎ *987/872-0067).* The yellow wooden house on the right as you walk up Calle Uno is Casa Denis. A few tables are set out front in the pedestrians-only street. There are two small dining parlors inside and some more tables in the shady back garden patio. The mamey tree you see has grown there since 1880. Check out the tons of old photos on the interior walls and amaze your friends by knowing that Jackie Onassis, Lee Radziwell and Truman Capote have all dined here. Casa Denis offers tasty light or full Mexican home-style meals. $$

Las Palmeras *(at the ferry pier,* ☎ *987/872-0532).* When it comes to location, location, location, Las Palmeras has got it, got it, got it. Certainly not the cheapest nor even the best restaurant on Cozumel, this cool and breezy palm-planted open-air corner spot is nevertheless very tempting. Its décor is appealing, it's right at the ferry dock, and the food smells good. We find it awfully hard to get off the ferry hungry and pass by without at least a look at their menu. Sea breezes and oversized awnings keep it cool inside. Best time is off hours and the best seats are those that allow unrestricted gawking at the crowds coming and going on the *malecón.* $$

Casa Maya *(Av. 5 Sur, near Calle 3,* ☎ *987/872-3511).* An assortment of magazines and artwork line the walls of the Casa Maya and classical music replaces the ubiquitous Mexican music of most restaurants. It's open for three meals daily, with an especially delicious breakfast. Super clean. $

La Veranda *(Calle 4 North between 5 & 10,* ☎ *987/872-4132).* The Veranda boasts a relaxed atmosphere, classy ambiance and fine fusion cooking. Tucked on a side street in a typical Caribbean house with a small front garden and long porch, the wooden beams and hardwood trim dominate the air-conditioned interior dining and bar area. The menu is creative and appetizing, a pleasant change. Seafood dishes are the specialty. Their signature dinner is a mixed platter of fish, shrimp, octopus, lobster and squid (US $36 for two). More to our tastes was the jerked chicken, served hot and spicy with rice. For the most romantic setting, try the back porch – la veranda – where tables overlook a softly lighted tropical garden patio. A few wrought-iron tables are also available in the garden that contains a fountain and antique lamp post. Opens at 6 pm. $$$

La Parroquia *(Av. 10 between 1 & Juárez)*. This rooftop restaurant/bar is not the cleanest, but it is a fun place full of mostly locals who provide as much if not more of the atmosphere than the palapa roof and fishing/nautical decorations. Good food and cold beer. Serves lunch and a crowded late-night dinner. $

Tony Rome's *(Calle Adolfo Rosado Salas near Av. 5 Sur, www.tonyrome. com,* ☎ *987/872-0131)*. See our review of Tony's in the Night Spots section, page 184. As to food, we can sing his praises. Tony's features Kansas City steaks, good barbecue ribs and tasty Mexican standards in a Mexican village setting. Tony personally visits your table to ask how everything is – everything was fine with us when we ate there. Furthermore, he'll pick up your cab fare if you come for dinner. $-$$

El Abuelo Gerardo *(Av. 10 Norte #21,* ☎ *987/872-1012)*. Grandfather Gerardo's is another local favorite eatery that specializes in seafood and home-cooked Mexican meals. Bright open dining room with colorful table-cloths and an *al fresco* dining area under umbrellas in the back. No cruise shippers here, so the food is authentic and the prices are excellent. Check out the old photos of Cozumel. $-$$

Diamond Bakery Café *(Av. 1 Sur near the corner of Av. 15,* ☎ *987/872-5782, dcbakery@dicoz.com)*. Since the Diamond moved from its corner location next door (now a pharmacy), it is more of a café eaterie than a bakery. But they still offer baked goodies from a small display case. Homemade ice cream and excellent coffee are dispensed from the stand-up coffee bar and their intimate seating is under a celestial ceiling, and with walls painted like a jungle. The menu is larger and the food and service are still excellent, but we miss their old spot. $-$$

Pancho's Backyard *(corner of Av. Melgar & Calle 8, behind Los Cinco Soles mall,* ☎ *987/872-2141)*. In the rear of Los Cinco Soles, Cozumel's most famous shopping store, hides Pancho's Backyard, a lovely courtyard restaurant under Colonial arches and loads of greenery. In the early 1900s the building was a warehouse that stored bales of dried resin from the chicozapote tree, the basic ingredient of chewing gum and Quintana Roo's main export. In 1960 it became a hotel. In 1990, after four years of extensive renovations, Pancho and his wife, Sharon, opened the large store, art gallery and restaurant. The charming atmosphere is matched by delicious food – generous servings of Mexican and seafood dishes, cappuccino and expresso coffees. Beautiful custom-painted dinnerware and hand-blown glassware used in the restaurant are certified lead-free and sold up front in the store. You can also shop in the clean, well-organized store for metal works from Jalisco, enamel painted animals, tablecloths, onyx and silver jewelry, embroidered clothing, papier-mâché fruit, high-quality reproductions of Maya artifacts and gifts from all over Mexico. The store is kind enough to supply public restrooms, thank you! $$-$$$

El Capi Navegante *(Av. 10 between 3 & 5,* ☎ *987/872-1730)*. Capi Navegante serves up some of the best fresh fish and seafood dinners on the island. It's a favorite of locals – as well as for tourists seeking an upscale evening meal. They offer a varied menu for lunch and dinner. This is the best place to guarantee a good meal. $$-$$$

Chen Río *(the windward side of the island)*. Think of an informal island restaurant of plastic tables under palapas on the beach, the surf crashing against the rocks offshore. Then think lunch, beer, a swim, fried fish. That's the menu – today's catch. Speak some Mayan from our glossary and then ask about the price. We have spent some unforgettable afternoons there – we'd really hate to have a real job. Take a taxi or rent a car and follow the coast road across or around the island's shore. Bring a swimsuit and sun lotion. This place is worth the trip. $

There are a few very welcome coffee shops on the island offering light foods and rich cappuccino. Try **Café Caribe** *(Av. 10 between Adolfo Salas & 3 Sur)*, or **Café Europa** *(Av. 5 corner of Calle 1)*. Other options are the **Coffee Bean** *(3 Sur between Melgar & Av. 5)* or the bright pink and mocha **Café Chiapas** *(Calle 2 Norte)*. And don't forget the **Diamond Bakery Café** and **Coffeelia** *(Calle 5 between Melgar & Av. 5 Sur)*.

Riviera Maya, Cancún to Playa

Good travel books are novels at heart.
~ Jonathan Raban, author

This section of shore was formerly known as the "Turquoise Coast" because of its brilliant blue Caribbean Sea colors and fine white sand. But shoreline development has galloped ahead since the government pegged the Quintana Roo coastline as the "Riviera Maya" and opened it to hotel builders. The proliferation of resorts is not a surprise because the coastline south from Cancún offers long stretches of sugar-white, palm-fringed beaches, secret

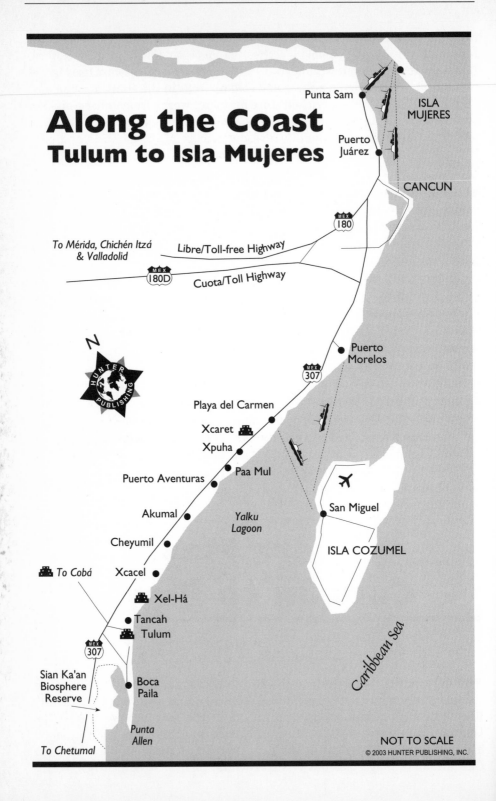

Along the Coast
Tulum to Isla Mujeres

Punta Sam

ISLA MUJERES

Puerto Juárez

CANCUN

MEX 180

To Mérida, Chichén Itzá & Valladolid

Libre/Toll-free Highway

MEX 180D

Cuota/Toll Highway

N

HUNTER PUBLISHING

Puerto Morelos

MEX 307

Playa del Carmen

Xcaret

Xpuha

Paa Mul

Puerto Aventuras

Akumal

Yalku Lagoon

San Miguel

Cheyumil

ISLA COZUMEL

To Cobá   Xcacel

Xel-Há

Tancah

Tulum

MEX 307

Sian Ka'an Biosphere Reserve

Boca Paila

Caribbean Sea

Punta Allen

To Chetumal

NOT TO SCALE

© 2003 HUNTER PUBLISHING, INC.

grottos, tropical coves, Maya ruins and deep clear cenotes speckle the craggy limestone shoreline. We list attractions and destinations in order (*mas o menos*) heading south from Cancún, with the km distances indicated in most cases. The entire coastline is 379 km from Cancún to Chetumal.

Puerto Morelos

Puerto Morelos is the first town south of Cancún and the embarkation point for the car ferry to Cozumel island. Visitors who stay are more likely to be here for a month than a week, and Americans and Canadians dominate the part-time population. The beaches are a magnificient white and the town is a very low key suburban development. Fortunately, the high-volume building and tourism frenzy bypassed this location for Playa del Carmen and resorts farther south, leaving Puerto Morelos to provide a quiet vacation spot only 30 minutes south of Cancún. The town is also home to a very active environmental group who successfully stopped one of the big hotel chains (whose Cancún properties we no longer include in this book) from bulldozing the mangroves to build yet another mega-resort.

A major attraction is the **Croco Cun Zoo** crocodile farm preserve (☎ 998/850-3719, see page 123). This area and inland in the present state of Quintana Roo, all the way down to the Belize border, was where *chicleros* used to harvest chicle sap, a major turn-of-the-century export.

CHICLE

Chicle, the sap from the native chicozapote tree, provided the original base for chewing gum. Quintana Roo saw a boom then bust in chicle in the 1920s. Any trees you might see along the roadway with criss-crossed scars as if a strangler vine once wrapped the trunk are actually the marks of chicle tapping.

Orientation

 There is regular bus service between Puerto Morelos and Cancún's main bus terminal from the highway. Look for the ticket office near the light. Taxis from there to downtown PM cost US $2. If you're taking the ferry to Cozumel, reach the terminal by turning right as you enter town and it's one kilometer or less down the road. It's not really worth taking your car over – US $60 plus US $8 per person on a three- to four-hour trip. Turn right at the town square to reach the **Artisans Hunab-Ku Market**, a large hut built to showcase local craftspeople.

Adventures

JUNGLE HIKING: An adventure provider that has taken Puerto Morelos by storm is **Goyo's Adventures** (☎ 998/871-0189, goyosjungle@excite.com), run by Goyo Morgan, a colorful character who has lived in the area since 1976. Despite his town location on the beach, Goyo's specialty is jungle hiking – fascinating guided tours that include Maya ruins, chicle villages, hiking and cenote swimming. Ask about his healing center, "Temazcal," a Maya herbal-sauna experience. Regular trips leave Tuesday and Friday at 9 am. You can visit the chicle villages and explore the cenotes on your own quite easily; get on the service road along the highway just south of the Puerto Morelos traffic light and hang a right at the huge sign for the tiny village (eight families) of **Central Vallarta**. The drive is under 20 km (13 miles) inland. Ask for Cenote Lucero Verde (Green Star), where there's also a non-excavated Maya site. Wear long pants for the hike in the fields. Farther down the road is Tres Bocas, which offers camping and a small restaurant.

WATERPSORTS: For watersports, try **Wet Set Water Adventures**, ☎ 998/871-0198, www.wetset.com, a dive and snorkel shop run by *gringo* Paul Hensley. He has locations the Caribbean Reef Club and the Casita del Mar. Sea kayak and mountain bike rentals are available at **Rancho Libertad Hotel**.

Eco-divers rejoice. There's a new **artificial reef** just off the Acamaya Hotel's beach, put down to protect the natural reef. Lots of colorful fish and a growing coral colony.

ADVENTURES FOR YOUR BRAIN: We always considered reading as an adventure, so in keeping with that, look in at Rob and Joann's **Alma Libre Bookstore** (☎ 998/871-0713, www.almalibrebooks.com) on the square. They are the hub of social and educational activity in town, and, being Canadians, they're sooo nice, eh? They offer a tremendous selection of used and new titles, plus free local recommendations and advice. Buy our other books, *Cancún, Cozumel & the Riviera Maya Alive!* and the *Adventure Guide to Costa Rica* there. But be aware the "Free Soul" bookstore is closed during the summer.

Accommodations

The development rush ignored the little port town of Puerto Morelos. Consequently, it attracts easy-going tourists who stay longer, often in rooms with kitchenettes. Puerto Morelos' great appeal – besides its wonderful beach – is that it's quiet, both day and night.

You can book ahead in the following places or a ton more of newly opened small hotel, apartment, condo and B&Bs that are springing up everywhere lately in popular Puerto by contacting English-speaking Martha or Andres at **Marand Travel** (☎ 998/871-0332, www. puertomorelos.com.mx), a helpful travel agency next to the church on the square. They can do it all, and have done it all with their fabulous Puerto Morelos website and you can pick up a **free map** of the town if you stop by. Find the town's popular **ATM** in front of the grocery store on the square.

HOTEL PRICE CHART	
NOTE: Often, one shared bed in a room is cheaper than two. Prices based on cost per night, for two.	
[No $]	Less than US $20
$	US $20 - $40
$$	US $40 - $80
$$$	US $80 - $125

■ Budget Hotels

Posada Amor *(one block in from the beach, ☎ 998/871-0033, fax 998/871-0178; 18 rooms with fans, but only 8 have private bathrooms, restaurant).* This eclectic jumble of rustic bungalow cabañas became known as "House of Love" after two children in the Fernandez family – who own and manage the hotel – married Canadian guests they had met there. The hotel's "typical" Maya accommodations run from modern plain to rustic primitive. The Robinson Crusoe adventure atmosphere and the friendly Fernandez family make this a popular stay, but check the rooms to make sure this is your kind of quarters. Definitely not for everyone. Mosquito repellent required. See the popular restaurant of the same name, below. $+

Motel Eden *(Av. Andres Quintana Roo, no phone, reservations at the owner's house, ☎ 998/871-0015, 19 rooms with fans, kitchenettes).* With its back to the mangrove savanna and three blocks from the beach, the Eden is the best bargain in town, if you like basic. The two stories of white cement contain rooms that are almost suite-like. The kitchen and dining areas are separated from the bedroom by partition walls. The bedroom has one queen-size and one twin-size bed, plus a big closet and bathroom. Friendly fellow guests and decent rooms invite longer stays, and many folks book by the month. Remember to keep some mosquito repellent handy if you're out on the terrace. $

Amar Inn *(Av. Javier Rojo Gomez, beachfront, ☎ 998/871-0026, 3 bungalows, 6 rooms with fans).* Funky and strange, the Amar is an experience as much as a hotel. The three rooms that face the beach are large and clean with one queen-size and one twin-size mattress (you can ask for a different configuration). A wood stairway spirals to the second floor around a tree. Three bungalows attach to each other and face a jungle-like center courtyard with statues randomly placed among the banana and palm trees. The rustic

Quintana Roo

cabaña quarters have thatched palapa and stick and plaster construction, but come with all the necessities, including hot water. Sleeping lofts save space and each has simple cooking facilities. This is a family hotel and one can feel quite at home here. Ask for a discount on weekly stays. $$

Hotel Inglaterra *(Av. Niños Heroes, ☎ 998/871-0418, michaelobrien7@ ntlworld.com, 10 rooms, air or fans).* A country isn't a real country unless at least one person settles there to represent the former British Empire, where the sun never sets. Just ask Michael, the owner of this basic hotel two blocks from the beach. Free coffee. $

■ Moderate Hotels

Rancho Libertad *(beachfront, south of the car ferry, ☎ 998/871-0181, www. rancholibertad.com, 13 rooms with fans, prices include breakfast).* Six duplex, palapa-roofed, octagonal-shaped cabañas are set back among the palms here on a broad, bright-white sand beach. The airy second-floor guest rooms cost more, but all the rooms have comfortable beds suspended from the ceiling and spacious bathrooms. A huge sand-floor, beachside palapa with a tiled dining area and kitchen serves as a common room for guests. The kitchen dishes up a big buffet breakfast (included in the room price) and guests can use the facility to store food or cook. The unusually large common room is like a giant screened-in sand box with such toys as a swing, stereo, lounge chairs and books. Co-owner and manager Ginny Hill, a certified instructor, offers dive lessons and the room price includes the use of snorkel gear and bikes. Don't bring the kids, it's adults only. Good karma. $$+

Posada El Moro *(Av. Rojo Gómez, 50 meters north of park, ☎ 998/871-0159, morelos-roths@att.net, eight rooms, air, TV).* Only a half block north of the square, the two-story white stucco Posada El Moro is a handsome but basic hotel, trimmed with appealing natural wood inside and out. The clean, simple rooms are large and airy and close to everything. $$

Hacienda Morelos *(beachfront, a block south of the main square, ☎ 998/ 871-0015, pool, 12 rooms, air, terrace, kitchenettes, restaurant).* The sparkling clean Hacienda hotel overlooks the water, and the upstairs rooms have an especially pleasing view of the Caribbean. Each fair-size room has a small kitchenette with refrigerator. Chip's Bar, a *gringo*-run bar and grill, has moved into the Hacienda and is offering a Sunday BBQ. Bring your taste buds. $$

Acamaya *(☎/fax 998/871-0132, acamayareef@avantel.net beachfront, 7 cabañas, 2 with air, 4 with private baths, full trailer hook-ups).* The husband and wife team of Daisy and Denis Urbain – he's French, she's Salvadorian – own this tiny campground/cabaña combination hard against some modern condos and an old fishing port. Trees shade the spots available to trailers and RVs or tenters. From the outside, the cabañas are primitive looking, but they have bright and cheerful bedspreads, kitchenettes and a couch that could be used as a bed for a child or small adult. Shared bathroom and showers. Intimate, pleasant and far away from the madding crowd – this is a great place to do nothing. The guest-only restaurant serves inexpensive dishes with very generous portions, family style. To get here, make the turn just before Croco Cun along the highway or snake your way back north from Puerto Morelos along the beach road that passes Motel Eden. Deserted beach. $$

Ojo de Agua *(Av. Javier Rojo Gomez, beachfront, ☎/fax 998/871-0027, www.ojo-de-agua.com, 36 rooms with air, TV, pool, restaurant, dive shop).* This popular spot hasn't changed much since its opening in 1970 – it's still a great place. The Ojo boasts a charming odd-shaped small swimming pool, a sun deck lined with flowers and a restaurant that overlooks the sea. The rooms are large with good-size closets and modern bathrooms. Twelve studios with fans have kitchenettes and are very popular with families. $$+

 Ojo de Agua means "eye of the water," a phenomenon caused by underground water rising into a lagoon or shallow sea and causing a change of water color.

Cabañas Puerto Morelos *(Av. Javier Rojo Gomez, ☎/fax 998/871-0199, www.cancuncabanas.com, 3 rooms with fans & kitchenette, tiny pool).* Gringo owners Roger and Teresa offer three very attractive one-bedroom suites that they call "cabañas," completely furnished with all the amenities North Americans expect. This is a home away from home. The three downstairs suite/rooms have complete kitchens (plus a personal coffee brewer, a rarity in Mexico) and sleeping couches with either one king-size, one queen, or two twins. $$

Casita Del Mar *(Av. Javier Rojo Gomez, ☎ 998/871-0301, www.hotelcasitadelmar.com, beachfront, 19 rooms with air, pool, restaurant, breakfast included).* This Caribbean-colored, hacienda-like beachfront hotel opened in January 1997. Small handsome rooms with either one king-size or two twin beds face the pretty beach. The custom-made stick furniture is very appealing, as are the color-matched drapes and bedspreads. Not the cheapest in town, but an intimate, pleasing place. The hotel's lovely little poolside restaurant is inexpensive. $$

Villas Playasol (Av. Javier Rojo Gomez, www.adventureguides.com). We liked this small, beachside condo complex with a huge swimming pool so much that we bought a two-bedroom unit on the top floor. If you're staying a week or more why not rent from us? Our condo features a full kitchen, 1½ baths, air conditioning, ocean view, balcony, Internet, washer and dryer, and cable TV. King-size bed in the master bedroom plus two twins in the second. Very appealing. $$.

Quintana Roo

■ Luxury Hotels

Ceiba del Mar Resort & Spa *(1.5 km north of downtown Puerto Morelos, ☎ in US 877/545-6221, in Mexico 998/872-8060, fax 872-8061, www.ceibadelmar. com, 120 rooms, air, cable, pool, restaurant, spa).* The Ceiba is the kind of boutique hotel and spa that should define the Riviera Maya, instead of those ugly mega-resorts and their impersonal, pressed-flesh housing units. This five-star luxury villa hotel sits on a rise, from which its Maya-inspired white buildings spill down to the sea. A freeform pool surrounds a sunken swim-up bar and restaurant, open for lunch, and a larger gourmet restaurant sits along a central pond planted to look like a cenote. The very comfortable Mexican-contemporary rooms boast soft pleasing décor – highlighted by tile floors and natural wood trim – and each offers a private balcony with sea view. The bathrooms feature a big folk-art sun mirror, bath and shower, and hairdryer. As part of the spa experience, a temazcal – ancient American herbal sweat lodge – can be arranged. Personalized service makes the Ceiba a luxury favorite. $$$$

HOTEL PRICE CHART	
NOTE: Often, one shared bed in a room is cheaper than two. Prices based on cost per night, for two.	
[No $]	Less than US $20
$	US $20 - $40
$$	US $40 - $80
$$$	US $80 - $125

Dining

The number of food offerings in Puerto Morelos has gone up exponentially, with the opening of several new quality eateries. The little town is attracting diners from Cancún as well as farther south on the Riviera Maya.

DINING PRICE CHART	
NOTE: Prices based on a typical entrée, per person, and do not include beverage.	
$	Less than US $5
$$	US $5 - 10
$$$	Over US $10

John Gray's Kitchen *(Av. Niños Heroes, ☎ 998/871-0665).* It's a cook's dream to not only build his own restaurant, but to design his own kitchen as well. So John Gray – who made a well-deserved name for himself as executive chef in Ritz Carlton kitchens around the world – logically named the restaurant he designed and built himself "John Gray's Kitchen." He will introduce himself at your table, set in an intimate dining room with a modern décor, and answer any questions you might have about the food. The dinner-only menu changes every night to reflect what's fresh at the market and what pleases the chef. And, based on the loyal following of local residents and visitors, what pleases John Gray is bound to please his customers. Tucked away on a back street, this is the kind of gourmet food you would never expect to find in little Puerto Morelos – or Cancún for that matter. Very highly recommended and worth finding. $$$

Don Pepe *(Av. Rojo Gómez, 50 meters north of park, ☎ 998/871-0602).* Don Pepe wandered over to Puerto Morelos from Andulusia, Spain, for "no particular reason," and opened a brightly painted bar and restaurant because he couldn't find a good paella. Now he can get some anytime at his own place. Most dining is on the covered terrace along the street, where the delicious fish and meats on the menu are cooked on a grill. The bar portion inside offers additional seating and a pool table in a palapa-roofed second room. Open 1 pm to 2 am. $$

The friendly owner at Don Pepe offers a 10% discount to Adventure Guide readers who carry this book, so look him up – the food is excellent.

Hola Asia *(on the square, no phone).* Completely remodeled in 2002. Say hello to some great food at this expanded restaurant that specializes in unexpectedly gourmet Chinese and Asian food. The friendly place has a large local ex-pat following. Ah-so. $

Mama's Bakery *(Av. Niños Heroes, ☎ 998/845-6810, stickybunsmx@yahoo. com).* Breads in Mexico just can't compare to the artisan breads of Europe and the States. That's why Dianne's bakery and little breakfast shop is so popular with the town's expats. Pick up a loaf of bread if you have a kitchenette or, better yet, hang around until the sticky buns come out of the oven. Delicioso! Open from 7 to 4, Wednesday through Saturday. $

There's an AA Open Meeting (☎ 998/871-0575), Tuesday and Friday, 6-7 pm, at Mama's Bakery, first left in town, then about three blocks. In English.

Pelicanos *(☎ 998/871-0014, beachfront, opposite the park).* Pelicanos has the best location, atmosphere, service and menu in Puerto Morelos. You'll find it opposite the park, under a huge palapa dome roof, overlooking the beach. Ocean breezes keep it cool and comfortable. The restaurant serves up Mexican food, fresh fish and seafood at moderate prices. $$

Posada Amor *(Av. Javier Rojo Gomez).* This family-run restaurant in front of the hotel of the same name is the favorite meeting and eating place for Canadians staying in Puerto Morelos. The service is impeccable, the food is very good and the prices are reasonable. Worth a stop, especially for the Sunday buffet breakfast. $

Good regional eats can be had at **El Tio's**, a little hole-in-the-wall luncheonette just off the northeast corner of the square along the waterfront. A real old-time Mexican fishing village experience can still be had down the street from El Tio's at **Petita**, a local no-name restaurant with shady palapas and a sand floor behind a shack. Gringos are scare here but we always take friends for the freshest and cheapest fish around. The family that serves it, caught it. In front of Pelicanos is a very popular little eatery called **Caffe del Puerto**, serving great coffee, pizza, and sandwiches. Everybody knows it and everybody goes there.

South from Puerto Morelos

■ Playa Secreto - Km 312

KID FRIENDLY Just south of Puerto Morelos is this secret little beach lined by Mediterranean-style condos and private homes. One of them is the secret, but not-so-little house, **Casa del Secreto** (Km 312, ☎ 998/874-4286, www.casadelsecreto.com). Doy Cooper from Texas opens her magnificent home to welcome guests for weekly or monthly stays. Most families rent the entire upstairs apartment of three separate bedrooms with three private baths, kitchen, dining and sitting rooms. Check out the painted ceilings, a Riviera does Michelangelo combo. Appealing, coordinated Mexican décor. A veranda overlooks the warm Caribbean and a little pool is available on the patio. Cable TV, phones, video library, and a children's playground. Reservations required. $$$$

■ Punta Maroma - Km 306

Punta Maroma *(Km 306, ☎ in US 866/454-9351, in Mexico 998/872-8200, fax 872-8220, www.maromahotel.com, pool, air, restaurant, spa)* is such an exclusive hotel, there's no sign for it along the highway. Oh sure, there's a sign for Playa Maroma at the Venta Club Resort, but nothing indicates this wonderful smaller luxury property next door. Make a U-turn there and enter at a little guard house just 20 meters (65 feet) north on the highway. The lack of advertising helps keep the riff-raff out of a 58-room luxury hotel that often hosts Hollywood celebrities and rock stars in private villas. The magnificent property is surrounded by a 500-acre private nature reserve and faces the ocean on a stunning, mile-long powder white beach. $$$$$

■ Tres Rios Park - Km 301

This new entertainment and recreational park proclaims itself a "Tropical Reserve" because of its natural setting and activities in nature. Not as elaborate or established as Xcaret or Xel-Há, Tres Rios features a rather unusual ostrich petting and riding area, bicycle rides in the forest, snorkeling in a cenote or the beach, sea kayaking on the rivers or the ocean, swimming, horseback riding in the forest or on the beach and fishing. It was opened late in 1999, and they've added attractions as they've grown; there's now a guided "Sensorama" walk. Hikers concentrate on their other senses besides sight.

The all-inclusive entrance fee (including buffet lunch) in 2003 was about US $80. That price incorporates transport from Cancún, but prices with rides from Playa are cheaper. A semi-inclusive entrance fee (US $22) offers the use of canoes, kayaks, life vests and bicycles, and everything else requires an additional fee. Drive, catch a bus, or make arrangements with a travel agent in your hotel. They also offer a half-day excursion (10 am to 2 pm), including transportation from Cancún. The park is at Km 301; www.tres-rios.com. Book in advance through a local Mexican travel agency or check *Cancún Tips* magazine for the Tres Rios ad.

Tres Rios

■ Punta Bete - Km 295.5

This isn't a town, but rather a superb beach about three miles long, stretching north above Playa del Carmen. With the explosive growth of Playa there may someday be no distinction between it and Punta Bete. So enjoy it now, while it's natural and gorgeous. Punta Bete features a series of several rustic camping and cabaña beachfront hotels. Despite pressure to expand or sell out to big hotel interests, the property owners at Punta Bete treasure their peace and quiet. With one noteable exception. There's a luxury boutique, the Ikal del Mar, that has so much hubris they built an offensively huge wall around their property and have a guard to keep people away from their guests on the beach. Who wants to stay in a prison, even if it is luxurious?

The turn for the beach is off the highway on the south side of the Coca-Cola/Cristal bottling plant. Pass a housing development of little boxes along the road. Don't be discouraged, it's worth the effort. The road splits a couple of times to form a maze, but don't worry, you can get there from here.

Los Piños *(on the beach, Km 295.5, no phone, 8 rooms with fans)*. The serene beach at Xcalacoco was named after the coconut plantation that was there when Juan Fernando Rejon Cardana's grandfather started this little campground and restaurant in 1971. New rooms have just been built back from the beach. They are big and comfortable with tiled bathrooms (and toilet seats), closets and screened windows. They now have electricity. Camping is beachfront under palapa huts (US $4). The tiny restaurant's specialty is *tikinchik*, Maya-spiced fish. Breakfast runs about US $6. Daily snorkel tours cost US $20; five-hour deep-sea fishing trips are US $150. $-$$

Coco's Cabañas *(on the beach, Km 52, no phone, www.yucatanweb.com, 5 bungalows)*. Swiss national Helmut and his Mexican wife Sylvia built this intimate little cabaña hotel right behind Los Piños. Each darling round palapa contains a queen-size bed, closet, terrace, private bathroom. Great restaurant and bar, with a cool little pool in front. It's not directly on the beach, but has the most individual charm of all the properties here and is our top choice. $$

Qualton *(on beach, Km 295.5, ☎ 984/877-4000, 30 rooms, pool, air, restaurant)*. The Qualton is the only traditional hotel on Punta Bete, but it's appealingly decorated, with comfortable, clean rooms and a blue pool, plus a nice beach. Very reasonable and a good value. $$

Playa Xcalacoco *(on beach, Km 295.5, ☎ 984/877-5400)*. This used to be Frederico's (he's moved to Bacalar, we hear). Not much of a place to stay, but good eats in the pretty little restaurant. $

Camping Xcalacoco *(on the beach, no phone)*. Its name says it all. Camp under an open palapa roof or under the stars.

Paradise Point *(on the beach, Km 295.5, 9 rooms).* Darlene and Richard, a couple from the Lake Wobegon area (aka Minnesota), fell in love with this neighborhood and bought Paradise. The rooms in their cement buildings, right on the shore, are painted in bright Caribbean colors inside, with private bathrooms and solar power. There's a rocky beach, but you can swim a little way away at Los Piños. $-$$

Bahia Xcalacoco *(on beach, Km 295.5, no phone, restaurant).* There's a great view from the top apartment/suites of the rental building here at Bahia. Rosa, a Philadelphia native, and her husband, Ricardo, offer two-bed units with a shared kitchen. Very serene. $$

Playa del Carmen

You don't watch for potholes around here,
you watch for the little roadway between them.
~ Raza Manji quoted in a *New York Times* article,
The Pothole: A Source of Civic Pride

The once sleepy village of Playa del Carmen doubled twice in population, then doubled again, and doubled again in the last few years. Its development has been fueled by European visitors who discovered the alabaster-white beaches, gentle surf, coral reefs and slow lifestyle were the equal of the more expensive island of Cozumel just across the straits. According to the World Bank, in 2000 Playa del Carmen became the fastest-growing city in the Americas.

Playa's dock is the pier for the "people ferry" to Cozumel, and it's only a short trip over to snorkel or dive on Cozumel's incredible coral reefs.

The strong Italian and German influences here have created a unique vagabond traveler ambiance. Numerous outrageously de-

It was Europeans who put Playa del Carmen on the tourist map.

licious Italian restaurants provide sustenance and several German-owned hotels raise the standards of service to exacting levels. Combine that with a relaxed Mexican-Caribbean feeling and a sprinkling of American free-spirits and you've got Playa. It's definitely not the place to "get away," but it is a place to enjoy marvelous beaches by day and a lively nightlife in the evening. The mix of backpackers, students, well-heeled tourists, archeological buffs and New Age sun worshippers makes Playa very interesting and worth some time.

Orientation

■ Getting Around

To reach Playa, 68 km (42 miles) south of Cancún, take a **bus** from the station downtown (about one hour). If you're in the Hotel Zone, you could negotiate a fare with a Cancún **taxi** driver to scoot you down. We did, and paid only about US $15 more than the bus and saved quite a bit of time. Most fortunate is the bus service from the airport (see *Arrivals*, page 96).

Playa's unusual lighthouse.

The main road into town, **Av. Juárez** or **Av. Principal**, depending on whom you ask, leads you right to the ferry dock and the pedestrian-only **5th Avenue**, running perpendicular to the beach. This street boasts many of the town's hotels, stores and restaurants. The Playa Riviera bus station (☎ 984/873-0455) at the end of Av. Juárez offers express service to and from Cancún leaving every 10 minutes or so. They also serve Tulum, Xcaret, Xel-Há, Cobá, and Chichén. A new long-distance terminal has been built eight blocks away on Av. 20 and Calle 12, where you can connect to Chetumal, Valladolid and Chichén, Mérida, or other Mexico destinations. Most hotels are within easy walking distance from the Playa bus terminal and the avenue in front is full of men on large yellow tricycles (*triciclos*), who will ride you and/or your luggage cheaply to your hotel in a Mexican version of a rickshaw.

A stroll on the beach leads to Playa's attractive **lighthouse** (*faro*), now part of the beautiful "boutique" El Faro Hotel, where you may still be able to climb its exterior circular cement staircase to the top. The view is excellent and provides a great photo op.

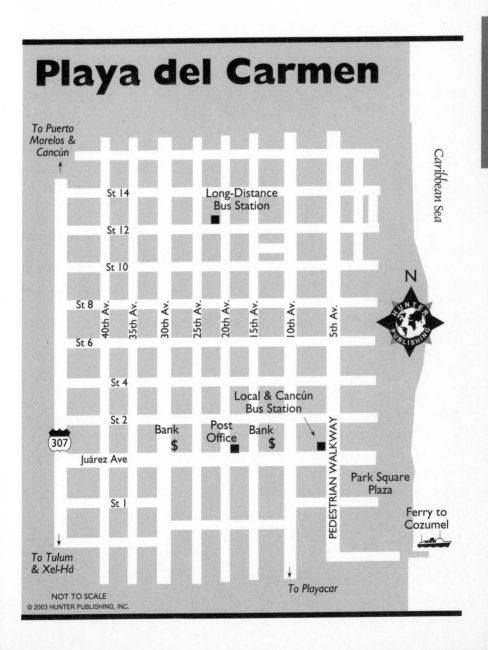

Practicalities

BIKE RENTALS: Several hotels rent bicycles, but get a mountain bike to dodge the water-filled cenote-like potholes in the sandy streets.

FERRY TICKETS: Buy your ticket for the ferry from Playa to Cozumel (US $9) from any of several ticket booths near the dock. It runs frequently and takes about a half-hour. In windy weather, take a Dramamine beforehand. See page 179 for the schedule. Don't fall for the "free ticket if you visit our property" booths that litter the dock area. If you do, you'll spend three hours getting pressured to buy a time-share.

GYM: Get fit at **Body Works Fitness Club**, open 7 am to 10 pm, Monday through Friday, 9 to 5 on Saturday, closed Sundays, on Calle 8 between 5 & 10. Guest fees begin at US $8, but you can buy packages of visits for less. Gym, yoga, and aerobics.

LANGUAGE SCHOOLS: Learn Spanish at **El Estudiante Academy** (☎ 984/873-0050, www.playaspanishschool.com) on Av. 5 between 14 & 16. This respected school offers immersion learning with a homestay or hotel packages, breakfast included. There are only three students per teacher. Cost is about US $600 for a two-week course. Another school is **Playalingua del Caribe** (Calle 20, between 5 & 10, ☎ 984/873-3876, www.playalingua.com), which offers half-day classes at their facility that includes 10 double and 10 single rooms and a pool. An average two-week stay, with bed and breakfast included, costs around US $575.

MEDICAL FACILITIES: A pharmacy and the Centro de Salud Medical Center (☎ 984/873-0314) are by the post office on Av. Juárez. The Red Cross is at ☎ 984/873-1233.

MONEY MATTERS: There are two banks downtown on Juárez and the **Bancomer** has an ATM.

PARKING: Park at a public parking lot on Av. 10 N at the corner of 2. Cost is US $1 per hour, US $6 overnight. A second lot is a block north on Av. 10.

POLICE: The police (☎ 984/873-0291 or 873-0110) have set up a tourist help kiosk on 5th Ave (Av. 5) near the central plaza. Emergency, ☎ 060.

POST OFFICE: Located three blocks back from the beach on Av. Juárez.

SHOPPING/GIFTS: The stores of Playa's 5th Ave and surrounding side streets offer an eclectic assortment of handmade pottery, arts and crafts – both local and from all over Mexico – gifts and New Age paraphernalia. In addition, a wonderful array of brilliant *pareos* are made in Playa.

TOURIST INFORMATION: The Tourist Office can be reached at ☎ 984/873-1001. You can also get information on the Web at **www.playadelcarmen. com.**

TOUR OPERATORS: For local adventure tours, try **Alltournative**, in Plaza Antigua, Playacar (☎ 984/873-2036, www.alltournative.com). They run climbing, rappelling, archeological and cultural trips, as well as hiking, cenote snorkeling and more.

Adventures

WATERSPORTS: Most of Playa's activities involve the water – the beaches are fabulous for swimming, snorkeling, or diving. There are numerous dive shops around. Try the **Tank Há** (*Há* means water in Mayan) dive shop at the Maya Bric Hotel (5th Ave between Calles 8 and 10, ☎ 984/873-0302, or check www.tankha.com). Others with high PADI marks include the **Phocea Caribe** (on beach 5th Av. between 12 & 14, ☎ 984/873-1024, www.phoceacaribe.com), **Dive Mike Diving** (Calle 8 & 5th Av., ☎ 984/803-1228, www.divemike.com), **Abyss Dive Shop** (Blue Parrot Inn, ☎ 984/873-2164, www.abyssdiveshop.com), and **Phantom Divers** (Av. 1 & Calle 14, ☎ 984/879-3988, www.phantomdivers.com). Well south of town is the well-known **Hidden Worlds Dive Center** (at Dos Ojos Cenote, ☎ 984/877-8535, www.hiddenworlds.com).

ADVENTURES ON WHEELS: A lot of tours leave from Playa, as does public transportation to the many ecoparks nearby. Car rentals are available everywhere. A place just south of Playacar on the main highway offers rides through the bush on a motorcycle or ATV. It's not good for mother nature, so we don't mention it here.

ADVENTURES IN AIR: For sightseeing or touring, **Aero Saab** offers flights in a six-cylinder Cessna 182. They're based at the Playa del Carmen Airport on Av. 20 between Playa and Playacar. Reach them at ☎ 984/873-0804 or www.aerosaab.com.

ADVENTURES ON FOOT: There's a challenging golf course in Playacar, the hotel, condo, and residential resort community south along the beach from Playa del Carmen. **Playacar Golf Club** (Paseo Xaman-Há, ☎ 984/871-6088, teetimes@palaceresorts.com), owned by Palace Resorts, offers a great, rambling par 72 course with plenty of beautiful scenery that includes sand traps and lots of water hazards. The surrounding green jungle swallows errant shots forever. We loved playing the first nine holes at the reduced afternoon rate (US $90), but Tiger Woods and Annika Sorenstam need not worry about us. This is a much more interesting and challenging course than Cancún's. Green fees in 2003 for 18 holes were US $150, including cart, snacks and drinks.

Accommodations

Slumber not in the tents of your fathers.
The world is advancing.
~ Giuseppe Mazzini

Between the time you plan your trip and the time you arrive in Playa del Carmen, chances are there will be another new hotel or restaurant. We gave up trying to keep count after the number of hotels exceeded 150. The former sleepy little fishing village is seeing phenomenal growth, thanks mostly to European vacationers who discovered that Playa is more laid back than Cozumel, and totally unlike Cancún. Although it's not the same village it was only a few years ago, tourism has created a busy atmosphere that still caters to an off-beat, almost bohemian crowd. This is a fun place to stay. If you take one of the many good hotels on 5th Ave – in the absolute middle of things – remember the stores and bars stay open late, so if you want to sleep, choose a room toward the back. Prices have skyrocketed in recent years so if you need cheap, think well away from the beach. In many cases the price difference between some of the budget and moderate hotels in Playa was nearly insignificant so check in both categories.

HOTEL PRICE CHART	
NOTE: Often, one shared bed in a room is cheaper than two. Prices based on cost per night, for two.	
[No $]	Less than US $20
$	US $20 - $40
$$	US $40 - $80
$$$	US $80 - $125

AUTHOR'S NOTE: *If any of the web pages we list here have changed, you can search for many hotels' e-mail addresses at www.playadelcarmen.com.*

■ Budget Hotels & Hostels

Maya Bric *(5th Ave between Calles 8 & 10, ☎ 984/873-0011, www.mayabric. com, 24 rooms with air or fans, pool, dive shop).* This is everyone's favorite hotel in Playa. Well, perhaps not everyone – it's a little too reserved for the party-animal crowd. And perhaps not really budget either (it barely falls into this category). The pleasing and airy rooms cluster around a landscaped flower garden and small pool. Each plain guest room has two queen-size beds and the reputable beachside dive shop runs snorkel and dive trips daily. The family-run hotel is very quiet and locks its gates at night, so it's also private and secure. $$

Cabañas Las Ruinas *(beachfront, Calle 2,* ☎ *984/873-0405).* This is the only authorized beach campground in Playa. As the name implies, it's not exactly high living – in fact, it's downright dirty and dingy. But the name actually refers to a tiny Maya ruin within the grounds. You have a choice of small cabañas with bath, tent spaces or hammock sleeping under a palapa. Lockers and safety boxes, available for rent, are strongly recommended. $-$$

Posada Marina "Backpackers" Youth Hostel *(5th Ave & Calle 24, no phone, dorms plus 6 private rooms, pool).* Playa's popularity has meant that prices have risen substantially in the last few years. Now "Backpackers" Posada Marina is offering much needed low-cost accommodations just one block from the beach. It is affiliated with Hostelling International and has dorm sleeping under a palapa-topped cabaña as well as small private rooms with kitchenettes. Owner Tony Burwell claims they speak Spanish, English, German, French, Russian and Portuguese. Two other in-town hostels opened in 2002 are the **Urban Hostel** *(Av. 10 between 4 & 6,* ☎ *984/879-9342, urbanhostel@yahoo.com, 24 beds)* and the more expensive **Hostel El Palomar** *(Av. 5 & Juárez,* ☎ *984/803-2606, hostelpalomar@hotmail.com).* $

Posada Sian Ka'an *(Calle 2 between Av 5 & beach,* ☎ *984/873-0202, fax 873-0204, mayarooo@prodigy.com.mx, 16 rooms fans or air, two with kitchenettes).* Sian Ka'an means "Birth of the Sky" in Mayan, referring to the sun rising in the east across the blue Caribbean sea, just steps from this pleasing posada. And there is probably no more "Mayan" hotel in Playa del Carmen – just say "Bash kawa leek" (What's happening?) to the workers and you'll get a friendly "Mish ba'a" (Not much) in return. The entrance to the posada faces a rolling green grass garden with a large cenote on one side. Small cabañas face the cenote and garden on ground level, while the main hotel features large front rooms upstairs. Behind a wall cut off from the busy world outside, a stay here is serene. No TV or dressers, but comfortable rooms, clean bathrooms, and free coffee in reception. $-$$

Hotel El Acuario *(Av. 25 between 2 & 4,* ☎ *984/873-2133, www. elacuariohotel.com, 12 rooms, pool, fridge, air).* This two-story hotel is a good five blocks from the beach, but has a lot to recommend it. Each colorfully decorated room has a little porch or balcony surrounding an attractive garden with a small pool. A pleased reader described it as warm, friendly and very welcoming. $

Hotel La Estancia *(Calle 12 between 10 & 15, no phone, 12 rooms).* A basic motel with six rooms with double beds and private bathrooms. Negotiate for long-term rentals. Quiet, with outside hammocks. $

Pension San Juan *(5th between 6 & 8,* ☎ *984/873-0647, fax 879-3990, www.pensionsanjuan.com, 16 rooms, air or fans, refrigerator).* This is an especially attractive 5th Ave property, personally managed by its owner, Raul Torres. It features yellow and blue Mexican décor in the generally cheerful bedrooms. Choose one away from the street, upstairs. A cute little terrace, with tables and chairs, overlooks the avenue below. Complimentary coffee or tea every morning on the terrace. $-$$

Mom's *(Av. 30 at Calle 4, ☎/fax 984/873-0315, www.momshotel.com, 20 rooms with air or fans, 3 apartments, bar/restaurant with satellite TV, room rates include breakfast).* Although nothing to look at from the outside, Mom's is quite an attractive, Colonial-style hotel inside. There's a small pool tucked into the corner of the open center courtyard and a bulletin board near the entrance that's frequently used as a communal message center. They rent bicycles here, a good way to get around the town. American owner Ricco Merkle is a jovial host and experienced travelers flock to his comfortable medium-size rooms with bedside table lamps and original artwork on the walls. There's a steak house restaurant/bar. Five blocks off the beach. Open since 1982. $$

Posada Las Flores *(5th Ave between 4 & 6, no phone, 12 rooms with fans).* Las Flores is set back from 5th Ave. Enter through a metal gate past an original Maya *otoch*. The welcome gate is locked at night for added security. Colonial arches in buildings that surround a little colorful garden courtyard with caged song birds. Small but pleasant basic rooms with two singles or one double bed are clean and very popular. This is one of Playa's better buys. $

Hotel Molcas *(Av. 5, up from ferry dock, ☎ 984/873-0070, www.molcas.com. mx, 36 rooms, air, pool, cable).* The venerable Molcas, one of Playa del Carmen's first hotels, received a much-appreciated remodeling in 2001, which has restored it to its former place among Playa hotels worth consideration. A large, lovely rooftop breakfast restaurant and sun-bathing area with a central pool makes it much more pleasant, as do the rooms with two double beds and refrigerators. Moorish design; rooms that face the street have tiny balconies. Clean, with new low prices. $

■ Moderate Hotels

La Ziranda *(Calle 4 between 15 & 20, ☎ 984/873-2476, www.hotellaziranda. com, 15 rooms, fans).* The enticing Ziranda, which features a leafy ceiba tree as its symbol, boasts modern Mexican architecture to host guests on a quiet Playa side street. It opened in December 1999. All the double rooms have small verandas or patios, some facing the backyard garden. The color scheme is soft gold and adobe red and bathrooms have exhaust fans (which many more expensive places lack). Owner Nora Quiroz, who fled the chaos of Mexico City for the relative quiet life of Playa, built her outside hallways in such a way that some of the trees rise right through both floors, with openings to accommodate the trunks. A nice place and a great value. $-$$

Tree Tops Hotel *(Calle 8, ☎/fax 984/873-0351, www.treetops.com, 3 private bungalows, 12 rooms & 3 suites in hotel, pool, fans, includes breakfast).* Tree

Tops is one of Playa's before-discovery-by-the-hordes hotels and a perennial favorite. Originally it was only a rustic bungalow hotel, preserving a piece of the Quintana Roo jungle behind a big wall, a half-block off the beach. These days, long-time expat Bill and Sandy Dillon have built a comfortable modern hotel around that bit of primal jungle, with a teeny-tiny pool next to their bar and a small restaurant out front. Suites offer kitchenettes, but long-time repeat guests come back for the nostalgic, rustic cabañas under cool vegetation. $$

Casa de las Flores *(Av. 20, between 4 & 6,* ☎ *984/873-2898, www. hotelcasadelasflores.com, 15 rooms, air or fans, cable, kitchenettes, pool).* We have heard nothing but good things from readers about Casa de las Flores, a quiet hotel a few blocks back from the beach. Although it is relatively new, owner Beatriz Salazar styled it like a restored Colonial hacienda, emphasizing arches and angles. She also built a small pool and one suite. Upstairs rooms don't offer kitchenettes and are about US $10 less. Breakfast is available for an extra US $5. An excellent value and very pleasing. $-$$

Hotel Los Itzaes *(Av. 10 & Calle 5,* ☎ *984/873-2397, fax 873-2373, www. itzaes.com, 14 rooms, 2 junior suites, air, cable, beach club, parking, restaurant, breakfast included).* The Itzaes were the tribe who made Chichén Itzá famous and, although their namesake hotel is not as grand as those ancient ruins, it is a lot more comfortable and worth a visit if you're looking for traditional repose. The public area contains a solarium terrace filled with greenery, and the individual rooms are casually elegant and well-appointed. The roof offers an impressive view of the city from the sundeck, while in the street are several economical eateries and a daily flea market. $$$

Hotel Delfin *(5th Ave at Calle 6, US* ☎ *800/601-7285, Mexico* ☎ *984/873-0176, hoteldelfin.com, 14 rooms with fans, surf shop, refrigerators).* Americans Dan and Miriam Shore built the Delfin on the pedestrian walkway that once overlooked the sea. The ivy-covered hotel has a European flavor. It has good-size rooms, and is reasonably priced. $$

Hotel Alejari *(Calle 6, beachfront,* ☎ *984/873-0372, fax 984/873-0005, www.xaac.com/playacar/alejari.htm, 28 rooms & studios with air or fans, restaurant).* The garden path weaves through a labyrinth of hibiscus bushes and flowers and leads to duplex rooms and studios, some with air and some with kitchenettes. Choose a good room and you'll never want to leave. Rates are reasonable in the beachfront restaurant, where you can eat in the dining room or under individual palapa shades. $$

Las Ondinas *(Av. 10 at 14,* ☎ *984/873-1013, ondinas3@prodigy.net.mx, 13 rooms, air or fan, restaurant).* Fascinating, close-knit casitas in a green garden distinguish the "Mermaids" posada. A winding path weaves to the stick-walled *otochs* with palapa roofs. In back there is a building with two suite/apartments where bathrooms are ensuite but kitchen facilities are shared. $$

Albatros Royale *(Calle 8 beachfront, US ☎ 800/538-6802, Mexico ☎ 984/873-0001, www.mexicoholiday.com, 31 rooms with fans, safety boxes surf shop, rates include breakfast).* These modern interpretations of Maya *naj* homes are romantic, absolutely clean, and pleasant. Rooms on the top have palapa roofs and balconies; downstairs, all have porches and all come with hammocks for lounging or sleeping outside. A stone walkway leads from the white-tiled rooms and winds through lush flowering bushes out to the beach. This is a well-designed hotel. $$-$$$

HOTEL PRICE CHART	
NOTE: *Often, one shared bed in a room is cheaper than two. Prices based on cost per night, for two.*	
[No $]	Less than US $20
$	US $20 - $40
$$	US $40 - $80
$$$	US $80 - $125

Pelicano Inn *(Calle 8 beachfront, US ☎ 800/538-6802, Mexico ☎ 984/873-0997, www.mexicoholiday.com, 38 rooms with fans, restaurant, rates include breakfast).* The rooms of this appealing Pueblo-style hotel have red-tiled roofs and private balconies or patios that surround a village-like courtyard. Completely rebuilt within the last five years, the hotel knows what guests like and offers it. The rooms are either beachfront, garden-view or ocean-view and the ambiance is like that of a small apartment in the center of town. Behind huge glass windows facing the beach, Ronny's Steakhouse specializes in fine cuts of beef. $$-$$$

Jungla Caribe *(Calle 8 near 5th Ave, ☎ 984/873-0650, www.jungla-caribe. com, 25 rooms & suites with air, TV, pool, restaurant/bar).* This four-story corner hotel houses a fine bar and restaurant called Jaguar. The tables in this second-floor eatery overlook either the street or the lush jungle garden. The hotel entrance is inviting and the service is impeccable. In the middle of the courtyard there's an attractive, though narrow, figure-eight swimming pool. The rooms are all very large with a fancy Spanish Mediterranean décor. The ultra-modern tiled bathrooms even have a bidet, a rare luxury in Mexico. High quality throughout. Ask about a discount for stays of more than one night. The owner also has four furnished apartments that rent for about US $800 per week. $$-$$$

■ Luxury Hotels

Shangri-La Caribe *(Av. 38 on the beach, US ☎ 800/433-0885, Mexico ☎ 984/873-0584, www.cancun.com/hotels/laspalapas, 72 cabañas, air, 2 pools, 2 restaurants, bar, all-inclusive).* The Shangri-La is famous among long-time Playa del Carmen visitors. Once located well north of the downtown, the "downtown" has now moved up to it. But the Shangri-La retains its private club feeling and great beach location. The palapa-topped housing units are furnished with two queen-sized beds and bathrooms with wonderful hand-painted porcelain basins and tile. Verandas with hammocks are ubiquitous. Rooms do not have TVs. Breakfast and dinner included. Located next to a great public beach. $$$$

Hacienda del Caribe *(Calle 2, between Av. 5 & 10, ☎ 984/873-3130, fax: 873-1149, www.haciendadelcaribe.com, 34 rooms, air, pool, cable, jacuzzi).* Just a half-block off Av. 5, the Hacienda del Caribe is one of Playa's most interesting hotels. With the deliberate ambiance of a Colonial-era hacienda, this bright gold hotel offers beautiful rooms facing an intriguing courtyard that contains a postage-stamp-size pool with lots of greenery and art all around. Third-floor rooms have brick catalan ceilings with skylights and balconies over the street. We must confess to being charmed by its recreation of hacienda-style living and attention to detail. Its high-season prices are in line with other hotels of its quality. If the ambiance pleases you as it does us, you won't be disappointed with a stay here. $$$

Mayan Paradise Hotel *(Av. 10, ☎ 984/873-0933, 40 rooms with air, 4 suites, kitchenettes, TV, restaurant, pool, bicycle rental, rates include breakfast).* Expensive and off the beach, this is nevertheless the best place to splurge in Playa del Carmen. The small hotel is probably the most attractive and luxurious of anything in town, with high palapa roofs and polished woods that give its cabaña rooms an almost Polynesian feel. The luxurious quarters all have kitchenettes and lovely shaded terraces. With an owner named "Palacio," how could you not expect palatial accommodations? One-bedroom suites have a jacuzzi and steam bath. The pleasing pool is a figure-eight shape, but if you prefer the sand, the hotel offers its own beach club. You'll find this gem three blocks off the beach to the north of the ferry dock. $$$$

Hotel Lunata *(5th Av. between Calles 6 & 8, ☎ 873-0884, www.lunata.com, 10 rooms, cable, breakfast included).* The Lunata hotel may be downtown Playa's most romantic luxury hideaway, right in the middle of 5th Avenue. Each large room, with wood beams and hacienda décor, features big closets, Mexican tile floors, and small balconies that face a lovely garden in the back. Each pretty tile bathroom has its own private little garden. $$-$$$

Capitan Lafitte *(Hwy. 307, US ☎ 800/538-6802, Mexico ☎ 984/873-0212, www.capitanlafitte.com, 57 rooms, air or fans, pool, bar, TV room, playground, restaurant, all-inclusive).* Though not technically in Playa del Carmen, Capitan Lafitte's location just north of the spreading city qualifies it here. Immensely popular with vacationers for many years, Lafitte's posada rooms are located in duplex, triplex and quad buildings, spread out on a broad wide beach with coconut palms. Pleasing bedrooms, lots of activities and amenities – horseback riding, playground, a beautiful beach – contribute to a high rate of repeat patrons. All-inclusive package. $$$$-$$$$$

Want to go where every North American goes? Try the **Blue Parrot**, the kind of place Jimmy Buffet might write a song about. Very busy bawdy beach bar, bungalows, hotel rooms and villas at the end on Calle 12 *(☎ 984/873-0083,* *www.blueparrot.com, $$-$$$).* Or for a special B&B experience, try **Baal Nah Kah**, on Calle 12 between 5a and 1a. It has only five deluxe rooms (☎ *984/873-0040, www.mexicoholiday.com, $$-$$$).* It's a Turquoise Reef property, as is **Chichan Baal Kah** *(☎ 984/873-0040, Calle 16 between 5 and 4, www.mexicoholiday.com, $$-$$$),* an intimate and romantic little apartment-hotel with maid service and an appealing small private pool.

Playacar

Often considered an upscale part of Playa del Carmen, Playacar is a combination hotel, condominium, and residential gated resort development along the shore south of downtown Playa. There are two brick driveway entrances along the highway and one from downtown 5th Av. Most of the hotel properties in Playacar are all-inclusive. We don't often stay at all-inclusives but enjoyed a long respite at **Club Viva Azteca** *(Paseo Xaman-Há, ☎ 984/877-4100, www.vivaresorts.com, 234 rooms, air, pool, cable, tennis, gym, $$$$)* in the center of Playacar, almost across from the Playacar Golf Course. The standard rooms, with two queen-size beds, were comfortable and cool and surrounded a huge pool and jacuzzi. The white-sand beach along the coast here is fabulous and the advantage (or not) of an all-inclusive like Viva is the opportunity to eat as much as you want at a variety of restaurants within the complex. Nightly entertainment and organized sports make it a good place to relax. An added appeal for us is their concerted efforts to gain a "Green Globe 21 Certification." The Green Globe is an international effort to comply with hotel environmental standards defined by the World Tourism Organization and agreed to at the Earth Summit.

Dining

You're never too old to become younger.
~ Mae West

 Restaurants and gift shops jostle each other for space along the pedestrian walkway part of 5th Avenue (as even many locals call Avenida Cinco). There are so many places here – beachside, or within a few blocks – that we selected only a sampling of delicious restaurants in the lower price range and a few exceptional eateries in the moderate range. Most do not require reservations. Try any place – eat well and enjoy.

El Chino *(Calle 4 between 10 & 15, ☎ 984/873-0015).* Despite its name it doesn't offer Chinese food, but specializes in Yucatecan cuisine. We found the spotlessly clean El Chino offers delicious regional food at excellent prices – it's the best value in Playa. It's set under a palapa roof, with wooden chairs and tables, big arched windows on either side, and an extensive Mexican menu. The *dueña*, Reyna Beltrán, supervises the staff personally so service is impeccable, and the cook is a chef. Open from 7 am to 11 pm. $-$$

Karen's Grill & Pizzas *(5th Ave between Calles 2 & 4, ☎ 984/873-0179)*. More fun than gourmet, Karen's fills up and up and up with a boisterous crowd watching TV, music videos or listening to live music. Italian and Mexican menu. Don't bother to ask for Karen – she ain't here.

DINING PRICE CHART	
NOTE: *Prices based on a typical entrée, per person, and do not include beverage.*	
$	Less than US $5
$$	US $5 - 10
$$$	Over US $10

Limones Restaurant *(5th Ave at Calle 6, ☎ 984/873-0848)*. This highly romantic restaurant set down in a hollow right on the pedestrian mall features international and French cuisine. Soft candlelight, numerous plants and a terraced dining area enhance the amorous atmosphere. There's live music in their Red & Black Bar. Daily specials. $$

Da Gabi Restaurant *(Calle 12 at Av. 1, ☎ 984/873-0048)*. This is one of the best in the plethora of Italian restaurants in Playa. We had a delicious gourmet meal for only a few dollars more than we would have spent at a less-interesting sidewalk café on the pedestrian walkway. The evening ambiance is romantic as diners sit in a giant palapa decorated in twinkly lights. Delicious Italian and Mexican cooking. $$

There are some fine dining restaurants along the beach, usually associated with hotels, with excellent food but fairly high prices – **Ronny's Steak House** is a tasteful example. However, many little seafood restaurants and bars, such as **La Tarraya** between 2 and 4, also set up on the beach looking across the strait to Cozumel. They don't offer much in the way of fancy ambiance – except for the Caribbean sea a few feet away – but they do serve tasty food at good prices.

There are more eateries worth mentioning in the mix of dining choices, for example, **Spaghetteria** offers pasta and more on Calle 12 and Av. 1. **Media Luna** (5th between Av. 8 and 10) also features excellent vegetarian fare. **Yaxche** (Calle 8 between Av. 5 and 10) dishes up wonderful regional dishes, and tender Argentine grilled meats can be found at **Buenos Aires**, located in the Plaza Playa (Calle 6 between Av. 5 and 10). And for people-watching there's no better than **La Parilla** (see our review of their Cancún restaurant on page 143), which sits above 5th Av. at Calle 8.

The many Europeans in Playa means there are good coffee shops aplenty to feed our caffeine need. **Hot Bakery** is a really great place on Calle 10 between 5th and 10th, as is the famous **Coffee Press**, Calle 2 between 5th and the beach. We stopped by on their wedding day at **Cafe Reunion** (Calle 6 between 5th and 10th) on the corner of a small shopping alley. **Java Joe's** is on 5th Av. between 10th and 12th, along with **Cafe Sasta** and **Cafe Tropical**, both between 8th and 10th. Most offer breakfast and lunch and some are open late, so have a latté on us.

Riviera Maya, Playa to Tulum

The waves echo behind me. Patience – Faith – Openness is what the sea has to teach us. Simplicity – Solitude – Intermittency.... But there are other beaches to explore. There are more shells to find. This is only the beginning.
~ Anne Morrow Lindbergh, *Gift From the Sea.*

Xcaret - Km 282

KID FRIENDLY Promoted as an "eco-archeological" park, Xcaret (ISH-car-et), ☎ 998/883-3143, is a resort playground that combines Maya ruins with tranquil coves, inlets, grottos, natural wells and an underground river. Originally known as Polé, meaning "Place of Trade," it was the pre-Hispanic port for Maya canoes to the sacred island of Cozumel. It offers excellent swimming (available with dolphins for big bucks extra), good but crowded restaurants, snorkeling and sunbathing. There's a wild bird aviary, gift shops, a rotating scenic tower, a small museum, scale models of some of the Yucatán's more famous Maya ruins, a botanical garden and a saltwater aquarium. You can horseback ride or enjoy the shade of palm trees in one of their hammocks.

Xcaret is a few kilometers south of Playa and 72 km (45 miles) south of Cancún. Colorful funky buses run from the Hotel Zone every morning and return late in the day. They've added a fascinating night-time light show (starts at 5 pm) with festive dancing and folk activities, all included in the admission price of about US $70, with transportation from Cancún for the day (under 11 years, US $20). Price is about US $40 without transportation. The evening festivities feature a game in their recreation of an ancient Maya ballcourt – fascinating to watch and, fortunately for the participants, the losers are not beheaded nowadays.

Bring your snorkel equipment or rent it at the park. Don't bother renting flippers for the underground river snorkel, they only obstruct others and a strong current pulls you along anyway. The underground river is an interesting trip, but not for the claustrophobic (some caverns are quite dark) and is not all that great when it's very crowded. When there are many people,

Traditional Maya sports are played at Xcaret.

choose the Maya river run, which is less jammed but also with dark tunnels. Both offer different snorkel fun.

SNUBA

For those who love to snorkel but aren't up to scuba diving, Xcaret features a very cool new sport called "snuba." Instead of swimming only at the surface with a breathing snorkel, snubers are attached to a long air hose, wetsuit and a weight belt. Unencumbered by a lot of equipment, participants are free to shallow dive to 20 feet from a central raft that houses their automatic breathing apparatus.

For an extra fee, qualified divers can dive to a sunken 90-foot shrimp boat, the *Mama Viña* (at a depth of 27 meters, 90 feet), and explore the cabin and living quarters complete with a full bar built of fine wood.

Though Xcaret, like any building project, had an inevitable negative impact on the natural area it encompasses, those in charge work hard to promote local ecology. They have a nursery for reforestation and several projects that promote sea turtle and endangered bird survival, plus educational programs for local school children. Open daily from 8:30 am to 9 pm and Sunday from 8:30 to 6 pm. Buses depart daily from the Xcaret terminal in the Cancún Hotel Zone (Blvd Kukulcán, Km 9) at 9, 10, and 11 am.

Paa Mul - Km 273

Paa Mul, which means "Destroyed Ruin" in Mayan, has a crescent-shaped beach and a storybook location on the Caribbean south of Xcaret.

Paa Mul Cabañas and RV Park *(Highway 307, Km 85, ☎ 984/875-1053, www.paamulcabanas.com, 22 rooms with fans, restaurant, bar, dive shop, $$)*. About 10 km south of Xcaret lies this simple little gem of a place on an isolated bay that only Canadians seem to have discovered. Step out of one of the 10 bungalows and you're nearly in the surf. Each large room, completely remodeled in 2002, has two queen-size beds with bent wood headboards, clean tiled bathrooms, hooks for hammocks and broad front porches. The sound of the waves lapping against the shore will rock you to sleep. The half-moon swimming beach is about 50 meters (165 feet) away. Above that cove they've built 12 lovely rustic cabins that either face the sea or a pretty jungle garden. But they could use mosquito netting, so bring your repellent. The oceanfront bar and restaurant now sambas to a Brazilian beat with a grilled menu and seafood prepared by the chef, Kalu. The fine dining area overlooks the beach and exposed reef. Many of the RVs are here long term under giant, custom-built shade palapas. Annual space rental is around US $4,000, and they'll move your rig inland if there's a hurricane. Located just north of the fancy Puerto Adventuras resorts, Paa Mul has been around since 1961. $$

The **Scuba Max** dive shop *(☎ 984/875-1066, www.scubamex.com)*, part of the RV park, features computer dives that allow you to guage precisely how much time you have in the water. The jovial owner, John, runs snorkel or dive trips for just US $25-35. This is one of the best dive shops – and one of the best places to dive from – on the Riviera Maya.

■ Cenotes

As you continue south on 307 there is a series of cenotes just off the road, all but one managed by local Maya familes: **Chikin-Há**, **Kantunchi**, **Cenote Crystallino**, and **Cenote Azul**. Azul and Crystallino are best for swimming. Katunchi has become an "Eco Park" with a US $10 entrance fee. It boasts four cenotes in caves, a small Maya ruin, a new cavern that is open for exploration after swimming across some cold water, and a palapa reception area with snack bar. Wash off any sunscreen before swimming in cenotes as it damages the marine life. The cenote park is owned by the people who own Hul-Ku Hotel *(Av. 20 between Calle 4 and 6, ☎ 984/983-0021)* in Playa del Carmen.

Puerto Adventuras

Puerto Adventuras is a self-contained 90-acre resort around a protected bay. The Museo CEDAM, a diving museum (see page 222), is the most adventuresome attraction, although there is now a golf course and raquetball club. Adventuras features an absolutely fabulous beach that is very popular with Americans who stay for weeks at a time and snorkel or dive the fabulous offshore reef. In fact, many people have second homes here. But some food for thought is that there are two Puerto Adventuras, the beachside one and the Mexican village built across the highway to house the workers who build the buildings, feed and clean up after the tourists. The disparity between the two is shocking. Apparently, few of the thousands of dollars taken in daily at the resort manage to cross the street. You can't miss this place. Watch for the huge sign on Hwy 307.

The big salmon color building a kilometer north of Puerto Adventuras is the **Lapis Jewelry Factory** (☎ 984/803-2078), a sprawling outlet priced destination for Cancún and cruise ship shoppers. It's a place where jewelry is made and showcased, as the name suggests, but it also features imported oriental carpet, mostly from craftsmen in Turkey. Rugs are priced for shipping home.

Xpu-Há - Km 263

Imagine buying a 91-acre chunk of some of the best beach in the world, so pristine that manatees frequent the lagoon. Then you get development permits based on the fact you're building an "eco-park." Once the park is open, you wait a year or two, then build a massive, all-inclusive, you-can't-get-near-our-beach resort. You are Palace Resorts and your eco-park is an echo of its former self. An ecological disappointment.

But part of the lovely Xpuha Beach just south of the former ecological park is still accessible – it may be the best bit of beach you'll ever see. The separate entrances to Xpuha are marked with "X"s. X-1 through X-3 are all private homes, while X-4 leads to the lovely beachfront hotel, **Villas Caribe** (☎ 984/ 876-9945, info@xpuhahotel.com, 24 rooms with fans, refrigerator, restaurant, $$). It has the same owner as Hotel Flores on Cozumel. The rooms are large and airy and the hotel's darling little seaside restaurant is the best place around to eat. Twelve rooms are in the two-story hotel, while 12 others are in bungalows along the beach. A super value at the low end of the $$ range.

Next door, the Copacabana Hotel stretches from the highway all the way to X-5 beach, crowding the property edge on each side. We have photos of them bulldozing down mangroves to build the 200-room-plus all-inclusive resort.

Now, after the damage is done, they advertise as a resort with "priority to the environment and living species inhabiting the area." What species are left – lounge lizards? Pass it by.

Playa Bonaza, aka Xpu-Há, is at X-6, opposite the Pemex station. It contains a daily beach club called La Playa and features two restaurants, one on the beach, and a dive shop. Finally, **Camping X-7** is a beachcomber's delight, with primitive campsites under seagrape trees and limited RV parking. They also have some rustic casita rooms. Stop for a visit and say hello to the laid-back owner, Samuel Meso Díaz.

Akumal – Km 257

The fame that Cozumel and the Mexican Caribbean has for incredible dive spots first spread from Akumal in 1958 when a group of ex-WW II Mexican frogmen salvaged the Spanish galleon, *Mantanceros*, sunk against the Palancar Reef in 1741. They called their group **CEDAM**, the Club de Exploracíon y Deporte Acuáticos de Mexico. In 1968 they donated Xel-Há and over 5,000 acres of their coconut-palmed land around Akumal as a national park. Before Cancún, Akumal (Mayan for "Land of Turtles") was the only resort along the Quintana Roo coast. Since then the shoreline has been built up to a point where condos, villas and hotels line the formerly deserted half-moon-bay beach. It's a fine place to stay if you're after the amenities of the Cancún Hotel Zone without the crowds. Several small boutique hotels and guest houses are available for vacationers and those who love to dive. One of our favorites is **Que Onda Posada y Restaurante** (☎ *984/ 875-9101, www.queondaakumal. com*), with seven boutique rooms and an Italian restaurant, next to Yalku Lagoon. A road trip for food could take you back down the highway to Chemuyil, where Akumalers sneak over for good pizza at **Pizza Leo's** (☎ *984/875-4000*). Follow the signs.

Cenote Yal-Ku, Akumal.

Our favorite destination in Akumal is **Yal-Ku**, a lagoon in a locally owned picnic park where the lagoon's fish-filled canals of emerald-green and turquoise water provide wonderful snorkeling. It's at the north end of the road that loops Half Moon Bay in Akumal. US $6 entrance fee. There is also a teeny tiny Maya building here.

Aktun Chen – Km 250

Sand-strewn caverns, cool and deep,
Where the winds are all asleep.
~ Matthew Arnold, 1822-1888

Back in 1984, the Ancona family from Mérida bought the 988 acres that surrounds these spectacular underground caves and cenote and began to make them more accessible. The labyrinth caverns, discovered by chicle workers who used the caves for shelter in bad weather, were un-desecrated by human hands. The one-hour guided tour in Spanish or English covers 600 meters, about half a mile, underground. It is a trip through fascinating caverns with plenty of dramatic but slow-growing stalactites and stalagmites. The lighting is cleverly hidden so that it appears as natural as possible. In general, the caverns are large and open and not claustrophobic to most people, but the incredible natural cave walls are close enough so that you can appreciate their delicacy. The tour climaxes at an amazingly beautiful shallow green cenote, so peaceful and still, with an *ojo de agua*, an eye of water. This is a breathtaking natural wonderland underground and above, an ecological preserve of native trees and animals (including deer, spider monkeys, badgers, wild boars, wild turkeys, iguanas, and lots of birds). The exit is at a different end than the entrance so you and your group can eat or relax at their snack bar then walk back on a road through the jungle. There's a hard-to-miss sign on Hwy 307, from which you drive 3.5 km (two miles) up a dirt road. Admission around US $18; open 9 am to 5 pm; www.aktunchen.com.

Xel-Há – Km 245

Mayan for "Clear Water," Xel-Há (Shel-ha) is aptly named. The park (☎ 998/884-9422 or 984/873-3588, www.xelha.com.mx) is a series of interconnected clear-water lagoons that form a natural aquarium for angelfish, lobster, barracuda, parrotfish, French grunts and many others. Wash off your suntan lotion before entering the water, as it harms the marine life.

Snorkeling and swimming are the predictable big pastimes here, or you can drop into one of the comfortable Yucatecan hammocks strung in a sandy grove of coconut palms. For those who love to snorkel but aren't up to scuba diving, Xel-Há features "snuba." See page 219 for details about this cool new sport. It's a great way to explore the shallow reefs up close.

Xel-Há also boasts five restaurants, 11 different shops, lockers, walking trails, showers and changing rooms.

A few hundred feet before the inlet are several cenotes and some small Classic and Post-classic Maya ruins with painted murals. The ruins are small, but their location was once a very important site. A good walking path through the jungle offers a close-up of the typical vegetation, including bromeliads, orchids and ferns, while swallows fly overhead. The park is a com-

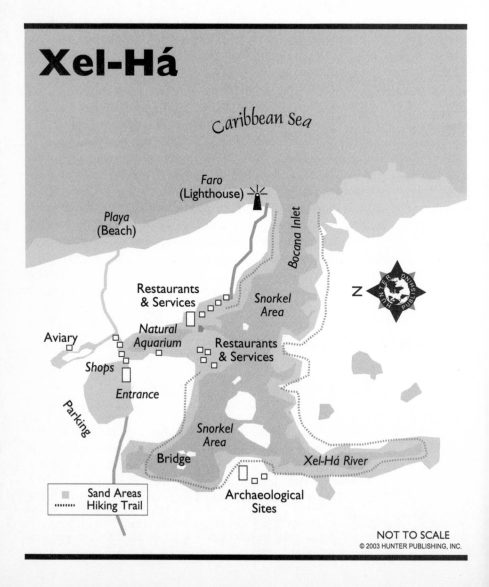

Xel-Há

Caribbean Sea

Faro
(Lighthouse)

Playa
(Beach)

Bocana Inlet

Restaurants
& Services

Snorkel
Area

N

Aviary

Natural
Aquarium

Restaurants
& Services

Shops

Entrance

Parking

Snorkel
Area

Bridge

Xel-Há River

Archaeological
Sites

Sand Areas
Hiking Trail

NOT TO SCALE
© 2003 HUNTER PUBLISHING, INC.

mon stop with bus tours heading to Tulum from Cancún so it can become crowded. Still, it's a big place. Admission is US $20, open 8:30-6 pm.

About one km (.62 mile) south on the right-hand side is **Dos Ojos Cenote**, with a large dive shop that offers saltwater or open freshwater diving as well as cave diving for those qualified.

Two kilometers south on the right side is **Hidden Worlds Cenotes Park** (☎ *984/877-8535, www.hiddenworlds.com.mx*), a cavern diving and snorkeling park. Housed just south of the Dos Ojos Cenote, the underwater adventure tour is unlike the artificially enhanced water parks. This is the real McCoy. They offer tours for diving or snorkeling, with all equipment, into a unique natural world so incredible the IMAX film, *Journey Into Amazing Caves*, was filmed there. Cavern Dive and Snorkel Tours depart at 9 and 11 am, and 1 pm. Water temperature averages 24° C (75° F).

Playa Soliman – Km 241.5

There's only a small sign for this secluded series of beautiful bays at Punta Soliman. Miss it and you'll miss the kind of Caribbean beach experience you've always dreamed of. Follow the sand road to the end and turn left for **Restaurante Oscar y Lalo's** – a laid-back seaside eatery and romantic hideaway. The shady palapa-covered restaurant offers ice-cold beer, delicious seafood and Mexican dishes at a very reasonable cost. Order a cold Montejo and a fresh fish for two and you'll think you're in heaven. Bring your gear, because beach use is free and there's a great snorkeling reef protecting the tranquil bay. Be energetic and rent sea kayaks or swim in the clear cenote nearby, or be lazy and sleep in a hammock under coconut palms. Stop here and you may not want to leave – this is a very special place and a treasure.

Tankah Cenote – Km 238.5

The only sign for this magical sinkhole, nine km (5.5 miles) south of Xel-Há, is for the **Casa Cenote Restaurant** (*www.casacenote.com, $$*). Perched on a rise above a gorgeous beach, the Casa serves up Texas-style pricey Mexican food. The owners have built a couple of studio rooms for rent. Very attractive.

This is a prime spot to while away hours, stopping occasionally to sunbathe (ocean swimming is best a short walk up the beach) or dip in the clear blue-green cenote across the street. This is a great swimming and snorkeling cenote and scuba divers love to explore its deep caves. The Tankah cenote is one of the largest in the Yucatán. Stand on the edge and look straight down where the walls slip deep into the abyss. The shallowest part looks to be about 15 feet deep. Snorkelers will relish looking at the many fish that swim by in these clear waters.

Before you come to the restaurant and unmarked cenote, there are a few houses scattered along the beach, one of which is a B&B, **Tankah Inn** *(tankahdiveinn@mailcity.com)*, managed by an American couple, Jim and Shelah. Jim has developed a very clever solution to the perennial wastewater problem that affects places on the beach – he filters it then evaporates it. The good rooms are popular with divers. About US $120 a day.

Just north of the Casa Cenote Restaurant there's a fabulous place to stay, **Blue Sky** *(Tankah, ☎ 984/801-4004, in Canada 250/342-2834, www. blueskymexico.com)*. It's a small, modern, bright white, junior-suite hotel with beachfront rooms running about US $100. Very inviting.

Tulum, Punta Allen & Sian Ka'an

A proverb is a short saying based on long experience.
~ Miguel de Cervantes

Tulum, like Cancún, is actually two cities: the ancient abandoned Tulum ruins and Tulum Pueblo, two km (1.25 miles) south of the archeological zone. In addition, Boca Paila, the Punta Allen peninsula, and the Sian Ka'an Biosphere are all accessed through Tulum.

The **Gran Cenote** is not far outside Tulum Pueblo, four km (two miles) down the road toward Cobá. A small admission fee (US $3) entitles you to climb down some steep steps into an open sinkhole, where the bright blue water of the Gran Cenote flows under a cave to an open area beyond. This is a fabulous place for snorkeling. On the other side of the cavern is deep water where only the brave can dive from a rock ledge. To prevent damage to marine life, do not wear suntan lotion when going into the water.

Another cenote worth a visit is **Cenote Crystal**, a short distance south of Tulum Pueblo on 307. This cool clear languid cenote, surrounded by trees, is great for swimming and snorkeling and is a hot spot for cave divers. It has an extensive network of underwater caves, including one that leads under the road to Cenote Escondido on the other side. Other nearby cenotes good for swimming or viewing are **Casa Cenote** (north of Tulum), **Dos Ojos** and **Car Wash** (on the road to Cobá).

*The end of the human race will be that it will
eventually die of civilization.*
~ Ralph Waldo Emerson, 1803-1882

Tulum Ruins

KID FRIENDLY

For a bunch of old stone buildings, Tulum ("wall") is a particularly impressive site, perched as it is high on top of limestone cliffs that spill down to the turquoise waters of the Caribbean below. The first time we entered the modest walled city, it took our breath away. **El Castillo**, a large temple, is the site's biggest structure. Regrettably, it is now off-limits to climb, although the nearby **Temple of the Descending God** is still accessible. If there are not too many people around it's a wonderful feeling to sit in the sun on the temple's platform with the waves crashing below and imagine what it must have been like a thousand years ago.

AUTHOR'S TIP: *If you time your visit for early morning or late afternoon, you'll be blessed with fewer crowds. Bring your swimsuit and walk down to the secluded beaches below.*

Tulum looks out over a turquoise sea.

Tulum is not a particularly important city to archeologists, though it was inhabited for a relatively long time and was occupied at the time of the Conquest. Facing east as it does, it is no wonder the Maya called it Zamá, "City of the Dawn." Sunrises here are spectacular. It's a Late Post-classic city, which means that the style of architecture is nowhere near the complexity of the Classic period. By this time in history, the building arts and stone-cutting skills of the Maya had degraded so they used much heavy stucco to cover the rough spots. But what Tulum lacks in architectural style it more than makes up for in location. It is now the most-visited archeological site in all of Mexico, with busloads of tourists coming from Cancún and cruise ships docked at Cozumel or Playa. Even its first tourist, John Lloyd Stephens, American author and adventurer who toured the Yucatán in the early 1840s, was impressed: *Besides the deep and exciting interest of the ruins themselves, we had around us what we wanted at all the other places, the magnificence of nature.... We had found this one of the most interesting places we had seen in our whole exploration of ruins.*

The walls on three sides enclosing the city may have been defensive, as they average 18 feet thick and are between nine and 15 feet high, but many think it is just as possible they were symbolic. Entrance is through one of the original five tunnels through the wall. Guides are available outside at the large new visitor's center that is complete with restaurants, snack bars, and *mucho* gift shops. A troop of brightly dressed Los Olmecas Ototonacos de Veracruz Native Americans perform ceremonial twirling dances while hanging upside-down from a huge flagpole. (Nothing to do with Tulum or the Maya, but entertaining and worth the US $1 tip they request.) A word of caution if you're driving. The parking lot has odd-angled stone walls that, if you're not careful, can scrape the car as you maneuver.

 *If you're serious about appreciating the details of many of the Maya ruins in your journeys around the Yucatán, we recommend **An Archeological Guide to Mexico's Yucatán Peninsula**, by Joyce Kelly (University of Oklahoma Press), available in paperback.*

I have a trunk containing continents.
~ Beryl Markham in a PBS interview, 1986

Tulum Pueblo

Tulum Pueblo is an undistinguished community that straddles Highway 307 before it's swallowed up by the jungle along the long southern portion down to Chetumal. We used to call it "Pollo Town" because of the many stops on either side of the divided road that grill chickens, *pollo asado* or *pollo carbon*. The thick mouth-watering smoke hovers across the road, making it impossible to drive through without getting hungry. Furthermore, it's a very long haul down to the next major town, Puerto Felipe Carrillo.

There are still a fair amount of grills, but the Italian restaurants may soon crowd them out. A sizable influx of European immigrants, mostly Italians, have discovered Tulum Pueblo's proximity to the fabulous beaches of the Punta Allen peninsula and the convenience of its 24-hour electric and low living costs. As a consequence, there are several new eateries (see the *Dining*

Mercado, Mérida

section) and the town is sprucing itself up because of increased tourism. Tulum is improving so much that a dive center, **Aktún** (☎ 984/871-2081, www.aktundive.com) has opened in El Meson, an eight-room hotel that caters to divers. For nightlife, you can try **La Gruta Disco**, in the middle of town.

The hotel and restaurant choices near the Tulum ruins are in three close but distinct areas: the pueblo of Tulum itself, including a few hotels near the ruins; a stretch of the Boca Paila Road along the beach south from the ruins; and the Boca Paila Road farther along the shore south into the Punta Allen peninsula. They offer very different experiences, so your choice may depend on what you like and what your plans are. Check out the local hostel's website, **www.intulum.com**, or, better yet, the Tulum Hotel Association's site, **www.hotelstulum.com**.

An excellent new laundromat, **Lavanderia Burbujas**, has opened on Calle Jupiter, a side-street near the south end of town. It's well worth finding, as the congenial owner does an excellent job – plus the place is neat and clean. We save up our dirty laundry just to drop it here.

■ Accommodations

Hotel Acuario *(Hotel Zone,* ☎ *984/871-2081, 26 rooms with air, pool, TV, restaurant).* The Acuario is a bulky pink hotel along Highway 307 at the beginning of the old road to the Tulum ruins, now a dead-end. It's a Colonial-style building wrapped around a deep swimming pool in the courtyard. The rooms have stone-tile floors and modern bathrooms, comfortable beds but paper-thin sheets. Our TV got two hazy channels. Its redeeming features are a good restaurant and a small convenience store. Within walking distance of the ruins. $$

HOTEL PRICE CHART	
NOTE: Often, one shared bed in a room is cheaper than two. Prices based on cost per night, for two.	
[No $]	Less than US $20
$	US $20 - $40
$$	US $40 - $80
$$$	US $80 - $125
$$$$	US $125 - $200

Andrea's Palapas *(Hotel Zone,* ☎ *984/871-2256, restaurant).* Andrea's consists of adjoining rooms in a large rectangular building, each one clean but spartan. Private bathrooms and showers. The restaurant out front is good and quite economical. $

Weary Traveler Hostel *(middle of town,* ☎ *984/871-2390, www.intulum. com, restaurant, communal kitchen, tiny breakfast included).* For travelers, weary or otherwise, this is a great place to hang out or get yourself oriented, network, and hook up with others. The busy streetfront entrance is filled with Internet users and curious passersby. They offer tours and services for travelers. As in most hostels, sleeping is dorm-style and can get quite noisy with all the activities that the hostel sponsors. Their restaurant, with Indian and vegetarian food, is called Hell's Kitchen and features a Tex-Mex BBQ (meats) every Sunday evening, beginning at 6 pm. Flamenco and belly dancers join in at 8 pm. If you can't live with cold-water showers and shared baths, look next door to the **Hotel Maya**, where you can get a decent room with private bath for US $12-18.

Chilam Balam Hotel *(middle of town,* ☎ *984/871-2042, chilambalam@ hotmail.com, 28 rooms, air or fans, TV, restaurant, $-$$).* A very basic but clean Mexican hotel on the main drag. Choose an upstairs room. At the back, there is an inexpensive, family-style restaurant that's open for three meals. Across the street is a more intriguing small hotel, **L'Hotelito** *(*☎ *984/871-2061, hotelito@tulumabc.com, 10 rooms, air, fans, $-$$)* with a big palapa entryway. Not too fancy, but pleasing.

Kin-Há *(Calle Orion,* ☎ *984/871-2321, www.hotelkinha.com, beach club).* The side street downtown hotel Kin-Há, "Good Water," offers attractive large suites with double beds and an apartment with a kitchenette. All rooms face a private garden. Turn between the *papeleria* and the *farmacia* on the main drag. $$

Villa Tulum *(Entrance road to the Boca Paila & Tulum Ruins Roads* ☎ *984/ 871-2418, www.hotelvillatulum.com, 18 rooms, air, pool, restaurant).* A huge palapa Mexican restaurant sits alongside the road to the beach, Av. Cobá South, and this attractive hotel is right behind it. New in January of 2000, it features an irregularly shaped blue pool and inviting rooms in a building facing a grassy knoll. This should prove popular, especially the big restaurant with its wooden chairs carved with sun and moon. Great bargain, and prices can be negotiated. $$

■ Dining

Besides the restaurants in the hotels on the Boca Paila Road, there are some good eateries in the little village of Tulum Pueblo. It's hard to even drive through the town without getting hungry – the smoky smell of delicious *pollo carbon*, grilled chicken, drifts across the road from charcoal grills on both sides of the street. Try some, you'll like it. But an increasing *extranjero* population here and on the Boca Paila Road has meant there are a few more cosmopolitan restaurants to choose from.

DINING PRICE CHART	
NOTE: Prices based on a typical entrée, per person, and do not include beverage.	
$	Less than US $5
$$	US $5 - 10
$$$	Over US $10

Il Giardino di Toni y Simone *(*☎ *984/879-6664, up a side street near where the concrete road divider begins).* To get to Il Giardino as you're heading south, make the first right at the beginning of town. A short but bumpy bit of road leads to this lovely garden restaurant on the right. It is run by Carmela (Simone is Carmela's daughter) and features fine Italian cuisine and wine. The large kitchen is behind stone walls. Dining is either under a palapa over-hang on the porch or under individual palapa umbrellas on an artificial beach. Very welcome are their spotlessly clean bathrooms. The food here is beautifully presented and absolutely delicious. If you've just discovered the ruins nearby, this is a good place to celebrate the experience. Don't leave without having cappuccino with cream, after the pasta with garlic oil and fresh-ground black pepper, and please say hello from us. $$

Don Cafecito *(no phone, middle of town)*. The most popular restaurant in the downtown also has the best coffee and food. Is there a connection? It opens early for breakfast – uncommon in Mexico – and the tables under the overhang and out on the front patio fill with the many expats who live here, plus Mexican locals and hungry tourists. Clean and cheap. We really liked it and went back often. $

Doña Tina's *(no phone, at the southern edge of town)*. Doña Tina has been running this little restaurant since 1979. It's located right at the end of the divided road through downtown Tulum Pueblo. There's not much atmosphere in her palapa-covered, stick-walled open dining area, but it's a good place to get homemade Mexican food at a price that's well below your budget. $

Que Fresco! *(at Zamas Cabañas, Boca Paila Road)*. Although we note its flavors in our review of Zamas, we want to reiterate just how popular this beachfront restaurant is. The food is so tasty, it's been voted one of the top 10 places to eat on the Riviera Maya, but you need to judge for yourself. Tell them we sent you. $-$$

La Nava *(middle of town)*. This little sit-down pizzeria arguably makes the best pizza in Tulum. We didn't argue, however, we just ate. $

Restaurante Il Basilico *(middle of town, ☎ 984/876-3352)*. This quaint Italian restaurant opened in 2002 and immediately gained a well-deserved reputation for good food among the Italian community. It specializes in brick-oven pizza and fine pasta dishes. The appealing interior of white walls and dark wood features intimate cubicle seating illuminated with candles. At-tractive from the outside and romantic on the inside, the Basilico's wine list and fine dining menu (around US $9 per entrée) make it a popular place for dinner. Open daily except Tuesdays, 5-11:30 pm. $$

Punta Allen Peninsula

Naturae enim non imperatur, nisi parendo.
(Nature cannot be ordered about, except by obeying her.)
~ Francis Bacon 1561-1626

If you close your eyes and imagine paradise – complete with blinding white sand beaches, warm deep blue water, swaying palms and romantic palapa cabañas – you're imagining the northern coast of the Punta Allen peninsula. Despite its natural beauty, this little piece of paradise will not suit everyone.

Beginning at the Tulum ruins, the coast curves southeast, forming a narrow peninsula that serves as a barrier between land and sea. Boca Paila is a section of the peninsula where a narrow causeway crosses the road. At the end of the long sand peninsula, with its bone-jarring rutted road, lies the undisturbed Maya fishing village of Punta Allen. No longer as remote as it once was, the shores north of Boca Paila seem to sprout new beachside accommodations. Fortunately, future development is limited, thanks to the Sian Ka'an Biosphere, a 1.3 million-acre nature reserve that begins along the road and continues for 95 km (60 miles) south.

Development is also limited by the lack of electricity, which is currently generated only during the day. The caveat to these positive ecological considerations is increased unsupervised tourism into Sian Ka'an, the reduction of the Biosphere's physical boundary by a corrupt former government, and the ensuing seashore development, including one hotel, Los Lirios, that bills itself as "ecological," but runs its diesel generator 24 hours to supply air conditioning. That said, this area features some of the most exquisite and peaceful beaches we've ever seen.

■ Accommodations

 The list of hotels is divided by either a turn left (north), or a turn right (south), when you reach the Tulum Ruins-Boca Paila Road.

Tulum Ruins Road

A series of rustic and not-so-rustic beachfront cabañas have been attracting adventuresome tourists for a good number of years. The road to them is unmarked; you'll find it opposite the turn for Cobá, just south of the Tulum ruins. Go east for

HOTEL PRICE CHART	
NOTE: Often, one shared bed in a room is cheaper than two. Prices based on cost per night, for two.	
[No $]	Less than US $20
$	US $20 - $40
$$	US $40 - $80
$$$	US $80 - $125
$$$$	US $125 - $200

two kilometers to where the road ends in a "T." A left there will take you back north along the beach toward the ruins. A right leads to the Sian Ka'an Biosphere and, eventually, to the fishing village of Punta Allen at the end of the long peninsula. The beaches both ways are some of the most beautiful in the Yucatán. All the cabañas' electricity comes from generators, which are turned off between 10 and 11 pm. This routine suits both hotel owners and guests alike because it limits new construction, at least for now.

If you make a left on what we're calling the "Tulum Ruins Road," here's what you'll find:

Diamonte K *(Tulum Ruins Road,* ☎ *984/871-2376, 21 cabañas, hammock dormitories, veggie restaurant).* The coffeehouse feeling of this popular European destination gives it a laissez-faire feeling. The overall décor follows a safari theme, with a shady restaurant, communal area and individual palapa cabañas. Cabañas are set on a rough rocky seafront, but walk a few hundred feet and you'll come to a long, flat, sandy beach nook. This was once called Gatos. The new owners have changed the name and made many improvements, but retained its eclectic-without-electric ambiance. $$

New El Paraiso *(Tulum Ruins Road,* ☎ *984/871-2007).* Motel-style rooms with double beds and not much more. It's set back from a fine beach on a rolling bluff. Cleaned up and painted since it became "new." Ask if they've got any new rustic cabañas on the shore. Restaurant and swim club on the beach. $

Mar Caribe *(Tulum Ruins Road, no phone, 10 cabañas, communal bath & showers).* This large and open beachfront establishment is owned and run by the Colectivo de Pescadores (Fishing Cooperative) in Tulum Pueblo. That means the local fishermen beach their boats and unload their catch here. We suspect you've got be young and unencumbered to appreciate the primitive hut accomodations here. They've opened a restaurant/bar in the former dorm sleeping palapa.

Cabañas Don Armandos *(Tulum Ruins Road,* ☎ *984/871-2417, 35 cabañas, dive shop).* Don Armandos has long been a favorite place to stay near the Tulum ruins. We found the spartan rooms on the fabulous flat beach only for the hardy and suggest you bring your own soap, towels, toilet paper, candles and bottled water. Very disappointing. However, the English-speaking owner runs a very good family-style restaurant serving from 7 am to 9:30 pm. Within walking distance of the ruins.

El Mirador & Cabañas Santa Fe *(Tulum Ruins Road, no phone, restaurant).* The road north to the Tulum ruins is blocked to cars just past these two sandy, primitive camping and cabaña crash pads. Beautiful broad Caribbean beachfront. The new restaurant has a great view from the top of a big bluff. Camping and cabaña rooms are snuggled into the sand. The ruins are a five-minute walk away.

Boca Paila Road

A right turn back at that "T" intersection leads south toward the Sian Ka'an Biosphere, the Boca Paila Bridge and finally to Punta Allen. Almost immediately you'll encounter paradise. The accommodations listed below are in order as you will pass them heading south. We review virtually every hotel here and wonder if that really helps or hinders your choice. Please let us know if we should be more selective. Give us some feedback. By the way, your vehicle may be stopped and searched by anti-drug military patrols on this road.

Papaya Playa *(Boca Paila Road, 29 cabañas & beach huts, camping, small restaurant, no phone, sertrapote@hotmail.com).* A great place for a romantic, secluded getaway along a magnificent beach. Opened in December of 1996, it's the kind of place Marlon Brando goes all the way to Tahiti for. The cabañas are large and cheery and feature floor-to-ceiling wooden doors with louvers that swing vertically to let in the breeze. Set down in a tiled drain area, one room's shower hangs from a tall piece of driftwood, mounted upright to make it look like a tree. The beach huts are primitive but appealing, with suspended beds over the sand floor. Safe, shallow swimming is down the bluff on a sandy, white, deserted beach. These are the first cabañas you see on the left after turning south. $-$$

Cabañas Copal *(Boca Paila Road,☎ 984/871-2000, www.cabanascopal. com, 36 cabañas, 4 with private bath).* This interesting beachfront cabaña complex was squeezed into this space in 1998. It used to be like a hostel, but is now upscale. Beachfront units cost more than the ones in the woods. Negotiate when not full. $$$

Beach along Boca Paila Road.

Cabañas La Conchita *(Boca Paila Road,* ☎ *984/871-2092, www. differentworld.com, 8 bungalows, breakfast included).* In 1999, Jorge Rosales Rodríguez, the Californian owner of this picture-perfect beach location, built a charming little hotel that remains one of our favorite spots to stay on the Boca Paila Road. The palapa-roofed bungalows are upstairs/downstairs, facing a sandy courtyard garden and only steps to the bright white beach. His wife decorated the rooms in stunning, Mexican-modern taste. La Conchita, which means "the seashell," boasts remarkable ambiance, quality, and especially location. It offers a delicious seaside breakfast. $$$

Cabañas Punta Piedra *(Boca Paila Road,* ☎ *984/871-8483)* has basic accommodations with traditional *naj* construction and palapa roofs. There's a new communal bath and shower building. The large rock formation that juts into the water along the beach is great for sunbathing and watching the iguanas. You can rent snorkeling equipment and bicycles. A new money exchange building is on the road in front and a small grocery across the street. $

Cabañas Nohoch-Tunich *(Boca Paila Road,* ☎ *984/871-2092, 18 rooms, restaurant).* Two attractive two-story peach and white stucco buildings offer new rooms with two queen-size beds each. The upstairs rooms are more appealing because they have a wraparound balcony that overlooks the big rock crowding the beach. New cabañas with bathrooms and showers have been built back against the rock. Three other cabañas, without private bathrooms, front the *playa.* All-in-all, a good value. At the entrance is a restaurant with Mexican and Italian selections as well as fresh seafood. $-$$

Piedra Escondida *(Boca Paila Road,* ☎ *984/871-8155, www. piedraescondida.com, 8 rooms, restaurant).* The lovely rooms in this up and down palapa villa hotel on the shore are light and airy with attractive bedspreads, Mexican décor and private baths. Outside wash basins and hammocks hung on tile porches, with a cozy sitting area next to reception and the bar. Excellent restaurant with candlelit tables. No credit cards. $$-$$$

Cabañas La Perla *(Boca Paila Road,* ☎ *984/871-2382, 2 cabañas & 6 rooms, restaurant).* Lazy hammocks hang in a small grove of palms nearby La Perla's bar and palapa restaurant overlooking the beach. The cabañas are rustic, but a new stucco-and-stone two-story building is very attractive and also worth a look. It's Spanish-styled and nicely decorated, including curtains. The best room is number four, which has a tiny balcony and sea view. RV and camping spots. $$-$$$

Zamas Cabañas *(Boca Paila Road,* ☎ *US 415/387-9806, Mexico 984/877-8523, www.zamas.com, 15 bungalows, restaurant, bar).* Watch pelicans divebomb for fish in the surf at this bend-in-the-road beachfront cabaña complex. American owners Susan Bohlken and Dan McGettigan bought a part of deserted paradise in 1986 and built appealing, rustic bungalows in 1993. Across the street from the beach they recently built three large palapa-roofed buildings that house two suites in each. The huge bathrooms are a special treat that outsize most hotel bedrooms. The hotel's restaurant, **Qué Fresco!** (How Fresh!) is a local favorite, with international fame, and, not surprisingly, fresh seafood. They have just installed a wood-burning pizza oven. Some of the beachfront cabañas share a bath and the ecological owners engage solar batteries for the lights. Snorkeling and diving are available. The name Zamá was the original name of the ruined city of Tulum, meaning "City of the Dawn." The paved road ends in front of Maya Tulum at the former entrance to Sian Ka'an Biosphere Preserve (a questionable government land deal moved the boundary three km farther down). Anything farther is slower going over pot-holed packed earth as the road bumps and grinds. There's no need for concern because it's not that bad all the way to the bridge – well past Cabañas Tulum – but gets rougher past Boca Paila. Every once in a while the holes are filled, but that doesn't last. $$-$$$

Maya Tulum *(Boca Paila Road, US* ☎ *888/515-4580, Mexico 984/871-2067, www.mayatulum.com, 20 rooms, 10 with private bathrooms, restaurant).* This retreat offers accommodations in three categories of deluxe and was formerly well known as "Osho Oasis" to beachcombing travelers. If the isolated seaside life isn't enough to soothe the wild beast in you, they offer yoga, meditation, massage and a vegetarian restaurant. Very attractive cabañas and lovely communal areas are decorated with Japanese simplicity. $$$

Los Arrecifes *(Boca Paila Road,* ☎ *984/871-2092, www.losarrecifestulum. com, 23 cabañas, 11 with private bathrooms, restaurant).* Pull the rope on a sea-bell to attract the manager from somewhere among the palms on this flat-beach part of paradise. The cabañas, with two queen-size beds, whitewashed walls and mosquito netting, are pleasant. The attraction for beach bums of all types are Los Arrecifes' round, very primitive *najs* (sand floors and hanging beds) right on the beach. But over the huge sand dune are six modern rooms facing the sea. Check out the trampoline on the beach! $-$$

Restaurant y Cabañas Ana y José *(Boca Paila Road,* ☎ *984/871-2477, www.anayjose.com, 14 rooms with fans, 1 honeymoon suite, pool, restaurant).* Extremely popular, Ana y José's is a landmark along the rough road to Punta Allen. It continues to be the standard by which other places are measured. Its picturesque white stucco two-story buildings are set back from the stunning beach and house well-decorated rooms on both floors. Upstairs rooms with palapa roofs are, naturally, in higher demand. Ana and José offer an excellent, comfortable restaurant overlooking the water with inside or outside dining. The new pool has a grotto at one end. The suite above the restaurant/bar is more rustic than the rooms, but has a great view of the surf. Everybody knows Ana y Jose's. $$-$$$.

Cabañas Tulum *(Km 7 Boca Paila Road,* ☎ *984/871-2092, fax 879-7395, www.hotelstulum.com, 33 rooms, restaurant, bar, rec room).* In 1972, this was one of the first accommodations on the Boca Paila Road and, until 1997, it was the furthest along of the cabaña hotels strung along the upper edge of the

Sian Ka'an Biosphere. Cabañas Tulum's stucco bungalows, with a design reminiscent of a New Jersey shore motel, line the high ground above a long gorgeous beach shaded by palm trees. Painted in bright Caribbean colors, each has a tiled front porch with wooden chairs and private baths. An informal, relaxed atmosphere prevails. Wide wonderful beach. $$

Tita Tulum *(Km 8 Boca Paila Road, ☎ 984/877-8513, fax 871-2033, www. titatulum.com, 6 rooms, restaurant).* Friends know Esther as "Tita," and the delightfully friendly owner of this small cabaña hotel makes everyone feel they are friends. Small, side-by-side stucco casitas, with palapa roofs and hammocks hung on the porch, face the beautiful bright white Boca Paila beach. Generous-size rooms feature big clean bathrooms, full-size beds, and individual porches. Across from her cute restaurant specializing in seafood, there is a small room, without a sea view, available for frugal travelers. Charming accomodations in an intimate setting. $$$

Nueva Vida *(Km 8.5 Boca Paila Road, ☎ 984/877-2092, 3 bungalows, restaurant, includes breakfast).* Nueva Vida means "New Life" and it refers to the new life lead by Ramiro, the son of the owners, Gea and Oscar. Ramiro was seriously injured and nearly died in a bad motorcycle accident – "don't drink and drive," he reminds everyone – so his new life is a constant struggle to overcome his injuries. His parents' therapy included creating this perfect little hideaway on the beach. The bungalows are built of all natural material and sit on stilts two meters off the jungle floor (so as not to damage the dunes). Each has a veranda, two beds, private bathroom and big closets, hot water and electricity powered by solar panels.

Las Ranitas *(Boca Paila Road, ☎ 984/877-8554, fax 984/873-0934, www. lasranitas.com, 18 rooms, pool, restaurant, tennis).* Mix a cup of luxury with three cups of beauty and add a dash of ecology and you have Las Ranitas, "The Frogs." Everything about this former private home converted to villa hotel is appealing, from the visually stunning art and impeccable décor right down to the solar panels and recycling plant for water hidden under the tennis courts. Yannick and his wife, Leïla, own and operate this hidden gem and they take great pride in the ecological innovations incorporated into the construction. Suites are built in a half-moon shape with individual verandas or patios facing the sea and bathrooms with custom Mexican tilework. Everywhere you look Leïla has tastefully combined her favorite colors of soft yellows and blues in the décor. Las Ranitas name is a play on the nickname the English have for the French, "Frogs." Where else would you find a bidet in a Mexico? Reservations recommended, but be aware that their cancelation policy is needlessly onerous. $$$$

HOTEL PRICE CHART	
NOTE: Often, one shared bed in a room is cheaper than two. Prices based on cost per night, for two.	
[No $]	Less than US $20
$	US $20 - $40
$$	US $40 - $80
$$$	US $80 - $125
$$$$	US $125 - $200

Posada Dos Ceibas *(Km 10 Boca Paila Road, ☎/fax 984/877-6024, www. dosceibas.com, 8 rooms, restaurant).* You're already in the Sian Ka'an Biosphere if you stay at Dos Ceibas. This intimate little hotel specializes in eco-spiritual accomodations, including a meditation bungalow known as El Nido, "The Nest." The rooms are in colorful, circular, two-story casitas scattered up garden paths behind the very pretty beach. A serene favorite for yoga retreats. $$$

Be warned if you're driving south from here, the road is bone-jarring all the way to the end of the peninsula. If you venture down to the fishing village of Punta Allen, look for the rustic Cruzan Guest House, below, or ask around for any of the posadas in town that rent rooms.

Cruzan Guest House *(Punta Allen, ☎ 984/877-0358 in Felipe Carrillo Puerto, 8 rooms, 6 with bathrooms, restaurant).* For a long time this was the only "hotel" in the sleepy little Maya fishing village of Punta Allen. One room is in the main house and there are also some rustic cabañas. Transplanted Californian owner Sonja Lilvik arranges deep-sea fishing trips, diving, boat tours or birdwatching excursions from the Cruzan. $$

We think there are some alternatives to the Cruzan. A new **hotel** a half-mile north of the village has opened on the beach (it hadn't selected a name when we visited, but is a good buy at around US $40). American **Sirena** has rooms in two houses she rents in town (posadasirena@tulum-mexico.com) and her neighbor has fixed up his **house** to take guests. Adventuresome travelers can go without reservations and ask around.

Sian Ka'an Biosphere

People into eco-tourism really don't want things made too easy for them, they are generally travelers who eschew anything like mass tourism.
~ Barbara MacKinnon, one of the founders of Amigos de Sian Ka'an

The bus we catch for the wilderness area known as Sian Ka'an leaves the Cancún terminal at 6 am. By the time we reach Tulum Pueblo the tourist contingent is down to the two of us and an American doctor, who is kicking around Quintana Roo on a two-week vacation. At 9 am we catch a cab down the beautiful beach along the Boca Paila Road to Ana y José's cabañas, where our biologist guide, Manuel Galindo, greets us

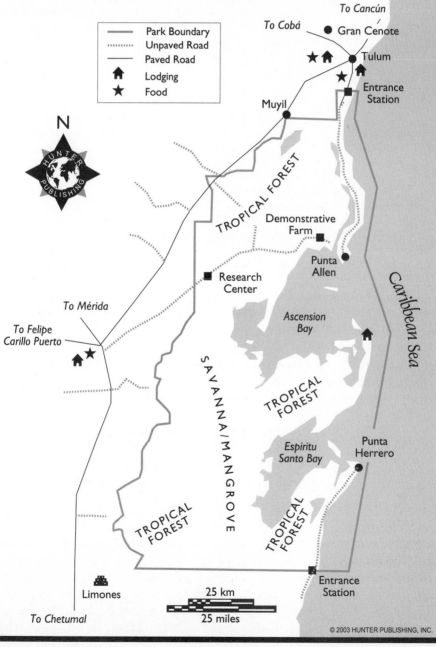

Sian Ka'an Biosphere Reserve

To Cancún

To Cobá

Gran Cenote

- Park Boundary
- Unpaved Road
- Paved Road
- Lodging
- Food

Tulum

Entrance Station

Muyil

N

TROPICAL FOREST

Demonstrative Farm

Punta Allen

Research Center

To Mérida

Ascension Bay

To Felipe Carillo Puerto

Caribbean Sea

TROPICAL FOREST

SAVANNA/MANGROVE

Espiritu Santo Bay

Punta Herrero

TROPICAL FOREST

TROPICAL FOREST

Limones

25 km

Entrance Station

To Chetumal

25 miles

Quintana Roo

A lazy crocodile at Sian Ka'an.

enthusiastically. "The Sian Ka'an Biosphere was set aside as a protected natural reserve in January 1986," he tells us. The site was named from the Mayan, Ziyan Caán, meaning "Birth of the Sky." The biosphere was the first large-scale attempt by the government to actively safeguard one of Mexico's last undeveloped areas.

The unique reserve covers 1.3 million acres of land, savannas, salt marshes, beaches and three lagoons. The protected area also includes 110 km (69 miles) of coral reef. Fewer than 1,000 people live in the zone, most of them lobster fishermen in Punta Allen. Manuel drove us to Boca Paila while he told us about the flora and fauna of the area – 1,200 species of animals in 17 different classifications. We joined with others for a boat ride into two of the large lagoons. The best part comes when we entered twisting channels that connect lagoons. These are lined with reed and mangrove and the banks are alive with birds – roseate spoonbills, blue and white herons, wood storks, kingfishers, diving cormorants, king vultures. We kept an eye out for any of the two species of crocodile, 12 kinds of snake, five types of iguana, wild pheasants, pelicans, flamingoes, jungle cats, manatees, several kinds of marine turtles and Amazonian dolphins that make their home here.

 *Birdwatchers should pick up Barbara MacKinnon's book, **100 Common Birds of the Yucatán**, published by Amigos de Sian Ka'an. Helpful descriptions and even more helpful color photos aid in identification.*

After seeing some *ojos de agua* in the lake, we re-enter the canal and dock at an overgrown Maya ruin, a customs house that checked cargo and collected fees from trading canoes nearly 1,000 years ago. The highlight of the trip occurs when Manuel goes ahead in the boat while we jump in the strong current of the channel and float downstream, joking about the two types of crocodiles.

Along the road is the ranger station and Colonial arch that signifies the official entrance to Sian Ka'an on the way down to the fishing village of Punta Allen. In 2003 the Amigos de Sian Ka'an, and environmental groups such as the Nature Conservancy, bought the 64 acres of shoreline called Pez Maya, near the Boca Paila Bridge. Because they need to focus their energies on protecting the shore from further overdevelopment, they have stopped offering tours to the Biosphere from Tulum. At press time, details had not been finalized, but they promised a place where tourists, students and scientists could study and enjoy the biological diversity of this precious area. Info from Amigos de Sian Ka'an, ☎ 998/849-75540, www.amigosdesiankaan.org.

Our second venture into the wilderness came on a Thursday night when we took a cab from Tulum Pueblo to the Muyil ruins to meet Carlos, a working biologist. We piled into a launch and set out into the black lagoon, led only by the glare from Carlos' coal miner's helmet and the light of a billion stars. The lagoon's water was warm and shallow, ideal for the prehistoric nocturnal-hunting crocodile. Carlos explained the counting and tagging research is to ascertain if the crocodile population can be sustained with selective harvesting by the local Maya families. If it can – and they can make money at it – it will take some of the ecological pressure off other resources and lessen the need for slash-and-burn agriculture.

When Carlos saw the red dots of a croc's eyes, he turned on a spotlight that eerily illuminated the mangrove trees along the bank. The crocodiles slid back into the tangled web of roots. We missed out on the thrashing and rolling of the beasts along the boat as they're marked with metal tags. It will be for someone else, another week. Meanwhile the southern sky put on a show of twinkly lights and shooting stars that boggles the senses, while little fish jumped in front of Carlos' light, in a dance of silver. We lie back in the boat, watching the moon glisten in the warm water and pretend we're Maya traders, slicing across the night lagoon. Never to be forgotten.

> *England-based Coral Cay Conservation has begun an environmental project in Sian Ka'an to survey the region's terrestrial environments and provide training and education for local people. The coral reefs, coastal dunes, lagoons, mangrove swamps, seasonally flooded marshlands and lowland forest provide habitats for diverse terrestrial and aquatic species. But there's room for more. Contact* **Coral Cay Conservation**, *The Tower, 125 High Street, Colliers Wood, London SW19 2JG, UK,* ☎ *011-44-208/545-7722, www.coralcay.org.*

Trips into the biosphere are run by Ken Johnson's **EcoColors** (☎ 998/884-9580 & 884-3667, www.ecotravelmexico.com, info@ecotravelmexico.com). They offer experienced English-speaking guides and transportation out of Cancún, Tulum or Playa del Carmen. Or try **Uyo Ochel Maya** (☎ 983/809-4468, caamaltours@hotmail.com), a local tourism cooperative 100 meters (328 feet) from the second *tope* in Chunyaxche, just north of the Muyil ruins, south of Tulum. There's a sign nailed on a tree, where you turn into the Maya *naj*, half-hidden in the woods. Ask for Ismael Caamal; he speaks English. To go on a nighttime crocodile tagging, call the biologist, **Carlos Navarro** at ☎ 998/880-6024, or maybe convince Ismael to take you. Expect to pay US $60 and up for a guided visit. Because of the biosphere's fragile environment, we definitely discourage you from taking one of the Jeep tours to Punta Allen from Playa del Carmen or any of the other less-than-careful tours.

A new NGO, **Centro Ecológico Sian Ka'an** (☎ 984/871-2491, www.CESiak. org), now offers eco-tours, eco-study, fly-fishing, and pretty accommodations on 15 acres deep in the biosphere. A good tourism/education effort.

Amigo De Sian Ka'an Membership: Become an Amigo de Sian Ka'an yourself. Memberships include a biannual, bilingual bulletin, car sticker, discounts on tours and merchandise and the knowledge you are a contributor to the preservation of an important ecological treasure. Contributions begin at US $25. Send your check to Amigos de Sian Ka'an, Apartado 770, 77500 Cancún, Quintana Roo, México. Donations of US $100 or more are tax-deductible. Send the larger amounts to Sian Ka'an Project, Friends of Mexican Development Foundation, 165 East 72nd St, Suite 1B, New York, NY 10021.

Sian Ka'an Visitors Center: This small ecolodge offers comfortable rooms and ecotours in the reserve, It is on Tulum-Boca Paila Road, nine km after the Mayan Arch. The site has an observation tower as well as a museum, a system for treating wastewater, solar panels for energy and a compost sytem for garbage. For more information, contact EcoColors at ☎ 998/884-9580 & 884-3667, www.ecotravelmexico.com, info@ecotravelmexico.com.

Cobá

What is a ruin but time easing itself of endurance?
~ Selected Works, Djuna Barnes, 1962

The Maya civilization may have grown around Cobá due to its group of five lakes (rare in the Yucatán), scattered as if by chance around the nearby jungle. Cobá, meaning "Ruffled Waters," was mentioned in the Chilam Balam de Chumayel, a chronicle of Maya history told in Mayan but written in Spanish. Occupied from the Classic through the Post-Classic periods, it was a rival of Chichén Itzá during the latter's apex.

The Ruins

The large site spreads out over several square miles, and its ruins are not well preserved. The most interesting of the structures are the massive **Nohoch Mul temple** and the **Iglesia**, a nine-tiered pyramid with broad steps. From the base of the tall Nohoch Mul pyramid, a *sacbé*, a sacred white road, runs some 100 km (62 miles) to the minor city of Yaxuná, near Chichén Itzá. Cobá is also the place to see standing **stelae**, carved with incredibly long date glyphs. Most are badly weathered. Climbing any of the structures takes you above the tree line, where a cooling breeze may provide relief from the hot and humid jungle. If you need a break, check to see whether you can use the Villas' pool (see below) if you buy a drink at their bar.

Practicalities

The little town has improved itself on the east side of the lake near the bus station where there are several restaurants. The other side of the lake is the residential village, without services except for a small local crafts store and *gasolinera* where fuel is dispensed from steel drums.

Cobá can be included in your itinerary from either Valladolid, Tulum or Nuevo Xcan, a town halfway between Cancún and Valladolid on Highway 180. If you're coming from Tulum, there are a fair number of cenotes now made accessible by local Maya entrepreneurs – you'll see their signs. A new road runs northwest from Cobá to Chemax, cutting the time to Valladolid and Mérida. For travelers heading west, it eliminates the need to drive north past the Monkey Reserve to Nuevo Xcan.

Several of the shops along the pot-holed road from Tulum to Cobá feature some high-quality, locally made handicrafts that warrant a look, especially if you're into folk art or need gifts to take home. It's cheaper than Cancún by far. Or check out **Alfredo Gonzalez** in the little village of U-Hmay, Km 22. He and his son, Glen, make magnificent museum-quality reproductions of Classic Maya art in their thatched roof *otoch* workshop. You can see some of his work at www.artenasaniasqroo.com.

Spider Monkey Reserve

North of Cobá 18 km (11 miles) on the road to Nuevo Xcan is the **Reserva de Areania Mono**, a spider monkey reserve. Serapio Canul Tep, a Maya elder who realized the population of local monkeys was endangered by fellow villagers who hunted them for food, founded the reserve a number of years ago. His efforts led to the large reserve, now managed by local families from the town of Punta Laguna. A US $4 admission gets you a guide (Spanish or Maya) who will walk with you on the paths that lead into the thick jungle. Besides spider monkeys, the reserve also houses the howler monkey, a cousin of the spider monkeys who can swell its larynx to form a natural amplifier – allowing its cry to be heard as far as 9-10 km (five-six miles) away. You may also see wild turkeys or deer on the path past a small Maya ruin to the cave also see wild turkeys or deer on the path past a small Maya ruin to the cave where the monkey colony lives. A couple of hundred feet down a dirt road is a large natural lake, Lago Punta Laguna. Wear plenty of insect repellent.

Accommodations & Dining

 Villas Arqueológicas *(Cobá, ☎ US 800/258-2633, Mexico 955/ 858-1527, www.clubmed.com, 40 rooms with air, pool, restaurant, shops, tennis)*. A mirror image of its sister hotels in Uxmal and Chichén, Villas is on the large lake, just a few minute's walk from the ruins – it even has its own tiny ruins in back by the tennis courts. From the small front porch, the sunset over the water and into the jungle is quite beautiful and guests tend to congregate there to watch. Along the reed-covered bank is a small pier with a palapa-covered gazebo at the end, where a sign says no swimming. As we approached it during an evening stroll, a Maya woman came up to us and told us a crocodile had just caught a small dog at the water-line, not two minutes before our walk. Now that's adventure travel!

But not to worry, swimming in the pool is perfect and the rooms that surround it are comfortably intimate. And because Cobá is not on the beach, the price is very reasonable for the high quality – an excellent value. $$

Nichte Há *(no phone, next to Villas)*. Open at 6 am, this little restaurant on a hill overlooking the lake offers relief from the high price of Villas dining next door. Excellent Mexican and Yucatecan cooking. $

Posada Bocadito *(no phone, next to the bus stop, 12 rooms with fans)*. Cold water and basic rooms. Cheap. The Bocadito is next to the quiet bus station, which has a restaurant of the same name. It's a popular spot with bus travelers but we were disappointed with the food. $

At the end of town, to the left along the road around the lake to the ruins, there are several gift shops and Mexican restaurants that cater to visitors.

Costa Maya

There is nothing so good for the human soul as the discovery that there were ancient and flourishing civilized societies which have somehow managed to exist for many centuries and are still in being though they have had no help from the traveler in solving their problems.
~ Walter Lippman, 1889-1974

Muyil

South from Tulum Pueblo one enters a sparsely inhabited 98-km stretch (61 miles) of jungle bordered on the east by the Sian Ka'an Biosphere and on the west by a trackless jungle. But it wasn't always without big cities. The rather geographically large Maya ruin of Muyil, "Place of Rabbits," is hidden on the left as you pass near the minuscule village of Chunyaxche. Most of the ruins, covered by brush, are badly weathered and only archeological freaks will find more than a quick look worthwhile. However, birdwatching is excellent here.

The ancient Classic-age city is connected to the Caribbean through a series of lagoons and canals but is not thought to have been a shipping port. Today, that water route is within Sian Ka'an Biosphere. To birdwatch, kayak, canoe, hike or just visit with an English-speaking trained guide, stop in at **Uyo Ochel Maya** (☎ 983/809-4468, caamaltours@hotmail.com), a local tourism cooperative 100 meters (328 feet) from the second *tope* (speed bump) in Chunyaxche, just north of the Muyil ruins. There's a sign nailed on a tree; turn there into the Maya *naj* (shelter), half-hidden in the woods. Ask for Ismael Caamal, who speaks English. Water tours are available in kayaks or launches, or they also offer birdwatching and hiking tours. These are the guys you might convince to take you on a nighttime crocodile photo safari.

About halfway to Felipe Carillo, just south of Chumyil, are some rustic furniture makers who sell their chairs and tables from roadside workshops.

Felipe Carrillo Puerto

Civilization is a movement and not a condition;
a voyage and not a harbor.
~ Arnold Toynbee, historian, 1889-1975

This dusty crossroads market town was named for the assassinated hero who governed the Yucatán and worked for the liberation of the grossly exploited Maya. Ironically, the city was one of the last bastions of the Maya independence movement and is still the unofficial capital of Zona Maya. The brutal War of the Castes (see page 46) drove the Maya into the remote Quintana Roo countryside. A settlement grew here called Chan Santa Cruz (Small Holy Cross) after a wooden cross was erected at a cenote and "spoke" to the people in their native tongue, extolling the Cruzob Maya Indians to renew their resistance to the oppressive Spanish-Yucatecan rulers. The cross, in a mix of ancient Maya religion and Christianity, directed Maya holy men to run a campaign against the *dzules*, "foreigners." Perhaps it is no surprise that one of the leaders of the bizarre cult of the talking cross was a ventriloquist. The Maya traded for weapons with the

The settlement of Chan Santa Cruz grew around the "speaking" cross.

English loggers in British Honduras, now Belize, and brought the arms in canoes up the Rio Hondo along the border. See page 46 for a brief overview of the fierce Caste War and Chan Santa Cruz's major role.

■ Sights

To visit the muddy little cenote and cross that started it all, turn west at the Pemex station in the downtown (just past the circle at the *mercado*) and go about five blocks. Ask someone to point out the **Sanctuario del Cruz Parlante**. In the park, steeped in bloody Maya history, you'll find the small cenote, a tiny museum, and a brick shrine containing the famous painted cross. Also of interest in town is the **Templo Balam Nah**, "House of the Jaguar God," on the town square, two blocks southwest from the *mercado*. The fortress-like Colonial-style church was built by white slaves – captured hacienda families and soldiers – a century and a half ago. For a while it housed the Speaking Cross. To its right is what looks like a dry well with a wrought-iron arch over it. This is **La Pila de los Azotes**, the "whipping fountain," where the Cruzob elders hung the white slaves by their arms and beat them. On the left side of the church is the **Cultural Center**, with a permanent display of famous, rather dark painter, Jorge Corona.

The *mercado* in town is typical of traditional shopping and gathering spots for the Maya living in rural areas. It is worth visiting if only to absorb the sights and cacophony of sounds, including blasting music, of life as it was before Cancún changed society.

Few tourists find the town worth an overnight – although, if it's late, the **Faisán y Venado Hotel** is very good, and its restaurant serves up excellent Yucatecan fare and is very inexpensive. But there are a ton of **eco-tourism** opportunites in the area. A little guide co-op group called **Mots Maya** (Calle 75, between 78 & 80, ☎ 983/809-4881, www.motsmaya.com.mx) is great for that. The tri-lingual guides offer cultural and historical tours in town and the surrounding villages, as well as kayak explorations of local lagoons, nature walks, and bike rides. Lodge in Caste War General Francisco May's Hacienda or visit Vigía Chico, the entrance to Sian Ka'an recognized by birders and ornithologists as one of the best routes for sighting many of the 350 endemic and migrant bird species that stop in Yucatán. If you're a kayak purist, you're in luck. Mots Maya is the only builder of handmade wooden kayaks that we know of in Mexico – certainly the only one in all the Yucatán. Buy one and take it home. Find Mots Maya buy turning east after a big billboard as you come into town from the north. It's four blocks down on the left. Or phone them and they'll meet you at the *mercado* or bus station.

Into the Maya World

Two roads to the right in the center of town lead into the heart of the Maya world. The first, **Route 295**, takes you back north through the most traditional Maya area past Tixacal and on to Valladolid. A Maya general and supreme council still possess a sister cross to the original in a Tixacal sanctuary. Every two years the **Quich Kelen Yum Tata**, a celebration offered to the Trinity, takes place there. This is a solemn occasion that ends with the Holy Cross procession around May 3. In an attempt to preserve traditions, tourists are sometimes turned away from this celebration. If you wish to photograph or speak with an elder, ask permission.

Farther north is **Tihosuco** ("Place of the Copal Tree"), the historic hometown of Jacinto Pat, one of the Caste War leaders. Here you can find the **Caste War Museum**. The former Maya town was captured by Montejo the Younger in 1542. To defend their faith and their lives the Franciscans built the fortress church of San Agustín there. In 1686 it withstood attack from the infamous Dutch pirate Lorencillo and his band of buccaneers based in Bacalar. In 1849 the town's residents held off a fierce Maya attack, but the fortress fell to a later siege in 1866 and was gutted by the vengeful Maya.

Next comes **Tepich**, the birthplace of Ceclio Chi, a famous Caste War leader, who is buried in the local cemetery.

Quintana Roo

Two km (1.25 miles) south of Tixcacalcupul and 22 km (14 miles) south of Valladolid you'll cross the **Cobá to Yaxuná** *sacbé*. A sign says "Mirador," meaning a sight, but there really isn't much to see. The ancient raised white roadway looks like a clearing in the trees, but if you look closely in the weeds you'll see the outline of the *sacbé*, made of limestone boulders. Tixcacalcupul was the base of the Cupul Maya during the Spanish Conquest. The plaza features a statue of Juan Cupul who lead his people's resistance against Montejo. The rifle slits on the roof parapet of the town's church were cut and used for frequent defense during the Caste War. The last village before Valladolid is **Chichimila,** the home of Antonio Ay, whose execution started the Caste War.

The second way inland from Puerto is northwest along Ruta Maya, **Highway 184**, along the Puuc Hills through the historical Maya communities of Tzucacab, Ticul, Muna and finally Mérida. It's a fascinating trip back through time. If you're continuing on to Bacalar and Chetumal, keep straight on 307. Fill up with gasoline in Felipe Carrillo, no matter where you're going from there.

■ Accommodations & Dining

For dining, one the best choices in surprisingly restaurant-rich Puerto is the **Mayob Turquesa Restaurant**, less than a kilometer north of downtown on 307. The impressive paintings hanging on the wall are by local artist Marcelo Jimenez, who is the director of the Cultural Center in town. Master painter Jorge Corona once lived in the center's Colonial building and the school he founded there for Maya artists has made an impact on local and regional arts. Beneath the Mayob Turquesa's big cool palapa you can stop for a rest and have a good inexpensive meal under one of their six overhead fans. If it's hot, take a dip in one of their two swimming pools before passing through the crowded town ahead.

However, we almost always eat at the **Faisán y Venado**, an excellent and clean Yucatecan restaurant with generous, well-prepared servings that are unbeatably inexpensive. The well-known dining establishment is located in town, on the left if you're heading south. Heartliy recommended. Even the toilets in the clean bathrooms are worth a visit. They were made for the tiny Maya women.

Down the block is **Restaurant 24 Horas**, across from the bus station. Two doors away is **Hamburger Maya**, worth a stop just for its name. Both places are clean, tasty and cheap. If you want to spend a night in town, try the **Hotel Faisany Verado**. Rooms are clean and inexpensive.

Xcalak Peninsula

The land mass south of the Sian Ka'an boundary and east of Highway 307 inland contains a flat limestone shelf of mangrove, savanna and low rain-forest, long accessible only by sea. A wide paved road from just south of Limones now allows the long drive to **Majahual** (pronounced ma-who-AL). The once-small village there has become popular with Chetumal families as a vacation spot and summer homes dot the shore. But people are snapping up beach real estate like crazy. Look for this area to become very popular for vacationers. The road east to Majahual from 307 goes for a long time through trackless mangrove lagoons along the southern boundary of Sian Ka'an.

After a long drive you'll come to where the army maintains a drug checkpoint at the turn south for Xcalak. They don't usually search, but ask you where you are going or where you've been. Sometimes they look in the trunk. From the intersection, it's just a short drive straight ahead to Majahual, where a new pier for cruise ships, known as Puerto Maya, has opened the area to more tourism. Besides walking around the little village – which comes alive with plenty of cute gift kiosks when a ship is in – the majority of cruisers are bused down to the Maya ruins of Chacchoben and Kohunlich. It's a day-trip for them.

The town of Majahual itself is laid-back, in a bohemian kind of way, and set right on the bay. In the downtown (reminiscent of Puerto Viejo in Costa Rica) you can stay or eat at **Hotel Mahahual** (☎ 983/832-8111), the town's only real hotel. It's a standard Mexican hotel, with a good restaurant. To the north is the cruise ship pier and to the south is the rutted road that follows the shore for 60 km down to Xcalak. It's along this road that some charming little beachfront hotels and cabañas have opened to divers, snorkelers and beach-combers. Two of our favorites, for good reasons, are the following.

Balamku *(Km 5.7 south, Canada* ☎ *416/233-5393, no phone, www.balamku. com, 6 rooms, restaurant, meditation palapa, pool).* Balamku's Canadian owners are adventuresome types. Alan once sailed across the Atlantic in a 17-meter cement-hulled sailboat he built himself. On a whim, he and his wife, Carol, wandered down the pot-holed sand road south of Majahual until they stumbled across an ideal location for this upscale small hotel. There is nothing like Balamku in Majahual – luxury accomodations in a self-contained village of individual or duplex rooms and a restaurant serving international foods (including our favorite, curry). Groups are welcome. They offer a small pool if you aren't into diving the reefs offshore. A great deal of effort was put into the comfortable modern room décor and every use was made of available ecological engineering, including composting toilets. Yoga-friendly, peace and love. $$

Kohunbeach *(Km 7 south, three cabañas, no phone, kohunbeach@hotmail.com).* Janet gave up the beach of Cape Cod, Massachusetts and Guillermo the hub-bub of Mexico City for this wonderful little spot on a bend in the coast road. The name of their place is a clever play on words referring to the Maya ruins of Kohunlich (it rhymes). Three Maya-inspired palapa-roofed cabañas line a picturesque beach, each featuring white walls, screened windows, Caribbean shutters, private bathrooms with hot water and comfortable beds. Ours contained a rare-in-Mexico queen-size bed with carved wood headboard, plus a cushioned couch and chairs. Its simple attraction includes the gentle sound of lapping surf and a view of the offshore reef. Janet has transplanted her love of gardening with colorful tropical plantings among the cabañas and along the winding sand paths. A great get-away. $

The peninsula's most architectually interesting hotel has to be the **Maya Há Resort** *(Km 20 south, ☎ 983/831-0065, www.mayaha.com, air, dive packages, restaurant).* An easier way to get to it is to skip going into town and take the road toward Xcalak and look for a side-road to Punta Herradura. The office is in a four-story pyramid complete with a full staircase to the observation deck cum temple on the roof. Rather than ancient tombs, the pyramid's interior houses an air-conditioned restaurant and bar with game room. Auxiliary buildings such as the dive shop are also modeled after Maya structures, as are the 18 guest villas. Dive packages average US $200 per day, including lodging and trips.

If you turn left at the military drug checkpoint – toward the Majahual airport and Uvero, rather than south toward Xcalak – the road extends about 60 km to the north, ending at Tampalam. The Majahual airport is two km down the road. Currently no scheduled airlines offer service but private planes and charters land periodically. At Km 9, you can exit the inland paved road and travel along the bumpy beach road. Along this stretch are various little houses and shacks. Three kilometers after leaving the paved road is **KaiLuumcito** *(12 km north of Majahual on the beach road, 8 units, no phone, info@turqreef.com www.mexicoholiday.com, from $100 per night in summer to $140 per night in winter – breakfast and dinner included).* It's an offshoot of the popular KaiLuum II eco-resort in Playa del Carmen. The accommodations are "tentalapas" – fully furnished canvas-wall tents under thatch roofs. Each has two hammocks on the porch ideally situated for watching the waves. The property is lit exclusively with torches, candles and lanterns. Quite romantic! The staff and chefs are Mayan locals and dinners are typically traditional Mayan fare with a flair. Scott, the manager, an American ex-pat, was formerly a tour guide to ruins throughout Central America. He's a wealth of knowledge about Mayan architecture and history.

■ Xcalak

From the Majahual checkpoint to Xcalak (ISH-calak), the road, repaved in 1998 and sometimes down to one lane from the encroaching jungle, stretches a long way south past dark forests and sunny savannas. Please don't drive too fast. The birds here are incredible, but they have a habit of flying into your path, smashing against the windshield and littering the road with their sacrificed bodies.

The road ends at the fishing village of Xcalak, where most of the tourists are die-hard divers or fishers or a new generation of beach bum hippies. The divers are here for the three-tank **Chinchorro Banks**, a 42-km (26-mile) atoll two hours offshore by boat. Strewn with shipwrecks and crowded with colorful coral, the dive area is protected as a no-fishing national park. The Nature Conservancy calls it "the most biologically diverse reef of the Mexican Caribbean."

CHINCHORRO

The name Chinchorro is derived from the Spanish for "fisherman's net," a reflection not of the rich marine life there, but of the many vessels snagged and sunk in its shallow waters.

From here, you're a short boat ride (9 or 10 km) from the better-known cayes of Belize, namely Ambergris Caye, and there are enough underwater sights nearby to wrinkle your skin for weeks.

The village itself is even more low-rise and Caribbean laid-back than Majahual. Its hotels cater mostly to divers and snorkelers who have discovered the offshore delights, fishermen, or just beach bums like ourselves. We first met the owners of **Casa Carolina** *(4 km north, ☎ 983/831-0444, www. casacarolina.net, breakfast included)*, at an eco-tourism conference in Princeton. Bob and Caroline built a wonderful little four-room modern hotel, plus a two-bedroom house and a large palapa restaurant, on a wide-open stretch of white sand beach. There are full kitchenettes in bright and large, airy rooms with queen beds. Idylllic. Bob is a dive master who runs daily trips to the reef offshore, with instruction available. $$

A long-established dive and fishing specialty hotel is David and Ilana Randall's **Costa de Cocos** *(2.5 km north, ☎ 983/831-0110, www. costadecocos.com, restaurant, breakfast, MAP available)*. On a beach with swaying coconut trees and 16 small individual cabañas, this sprawling property remains the most popular spot for good dives and good times. Look for the windmill; the Randalls are very into preserving the ecology. $$$

Marina Mike's *(north end of town, ☎ 983/831-0063, www.xcalak.com)* has expanded to offer four new deluxe hotel suites and a well-appointed palapa

Quintana Roo

cabaña. The fully equipped dive shop up the street, **XTC Dives**, is one of the few with hard-to-get permits to dive the Chinchorro Reef. $$

Hotel Tierra Maya *(Km 3.5 north,* ☎ *in US 800/480-4505, www. tierramaya.net, restaurant)* is a small, full-service modern hotel that overlooks a beautiful beach. It offers six tastefully decorated rooms with private balconies. Personal attention by the owners makes this a good choice. $$-$$$

Farther north along the beach road from Xcalak is **Sandalwood Villas** *(Km 8 north,* ☎ *983/831-0034, restaurant)*, owned by Andy and Ruth Sanders. Their three beachfront villas are huge, complete with kitchens, but guests have written us to praise the meals served in their palapa restaurant. Electricity is solar-powered. $$$

Near to them is **Sin Dudas Villas** *(Km 8 north,* ☎ *983/831-0006, breakfast included)*, meaning "Without Doubts." Without any doubt, these large villas feature a stunning Maya-inspired décor with comfortable charm. Designed by the architect-owner, emphasis is on beauty, with an ecological edge. Their distance from town is part of their appeal. $$$

Budget travelers can look for the **Xcalak Caribe Hotel** on the beach in town. It has three remodeled rooms with cold-water showers. Another in the basic range is **Hotel Caracol** at the start of the street in town.

The best eats in town – according to almost everyone, including the many signs that say so – is **Conchitas**, along the waterfront. It looks shacky but is pleasant inside, with commendably clean bathrooms, not to mention inexpensive and tasty food. Beachfront **Xcalak Bar Caribe** is also a good hangout, or try some of the individual hotel restaurants. Some good guidance on visiting Majahual and Xcalak can be found at **www.xcalak.info/**.

You can reach the many small places along the beaches of Xcalak and Majahual from Chetumal, on a bus that bumps along the long sand road paralleling the shoreline. It leaves Chetumal's main station at 6 am and 2 pm and takes three hours to reach Xcalak. If you're coming by bus from Playa or Cancún, get off in Limones and hook up with the local bus from Chetumal at about 7:30 am or 5:30 pm, give or take a half-hour. For faster access from Chetumal, catch a *colectivo* bus from the Hotel Ucum, downtown.

There are two minor Maya sites on the peninsula, **Rio Uach** and **Xcalak**. Both the Army and the Navy guard the area against smuggling, so expect to get stopped and possibly searched as you come and go.

Once you're back on the road south to Bacalar, the town of **Pedro Santos** has a small shop where an English-speaking extended Mormon family from nearby Chula Vista sells baked goods and cheese. They formerly hawked their wares out at the *topes* before the road was widened and repaved. Don't blink, you'll pass through the town before you know it.

■ Chacchoben

The newly excavated Maya ruin of Chaccoben is accessed off 307 on the road toward Mérida, south of Limones. The exploration of the site, dating back to Pre-Classic and Early Classic times, began in earnest in 1994. Since then the major buildings have been cleared, including the two main pyramids. Archaeologists believe the site had a combined civil and religious use, affiliated most likely with a larger Maya city in the north of Belize. Eroded hieroglyphs are visible, as is a pictoral representation of the cycles of the sun and Venus. There is plenty of opportunity to walk around the expansive unexcavated portions. Abandoned around 700 AD, it was partially repopulated by the Maya during the Late Post-Classic era. In this period the "Leaning Temple of Chacchoben" was built on the steps of Temple I. If the buses from Puerto Maya cruise ships aren't here, it's totally deserted.

Bacalar – Km 37

*Blue color is everlastingly appointed by the
Deity to be a source of delight.*
~ John Ruskin, English art critic, 1819-1900

Located 38 km (24 miles) northwest of Chetumal, the historic town of Bacalar overlooks Lake Bacalar, also known as the Laguna de Siete Colores, the "Lagoon of Seven Colors." The Maya name, Bak Halal, means

Laguna Bacalar, Lagoon of Many Colors.

"Place Surrounded by Canes." It boasts magnificent water with hues of mauves and blues and greens, great for swimming and is lined on its elevated west bank with summer homes and a few small hotels. The 42-km-long (26-mile) lake is linked to the Hondo River that separates Mexico and Belize by the Chaac Inlet, where traditional regattas are held on and around August 16 each year.

The town of Bacalar itself is not geared for tourists, although the one-story buildings are all of great antiquity. The first Spanish colony settled here in 1545, but by 1652 it was destroyed and abandoned. In 1726, Canary Islanders resettled it, building the thick stone **Fort San Felipe** in 1729 to fend off English pirates who scourged the town. The fort brought protection to the town from attack by water, only to have the city ravaged twice from the inland by the Maya – the second time in one of the most bloody and brutal massacres of the Caste War. Only a handful of people survived the slaughter.

Today's Fort San Felipe commander is Ofelia Casa Madrid, a strong woman with a Masters Degree in Social Anthropology and history teacher in a local high school who works part-time as the fort's caretaker. Be sure to stop and say hello and give her a chance to practice her English.

There are popular, **balinerios**, or swim clubs, along the lake banks near the fort and Navy post. Bring your swimsuit and jump in.

■ Accommodations & Dining

Most tourists skip the multicultural Chetumal downtown and stay along the picturesque Laguna Bacalar, 30-something kilometers north of the city on 307. The choices are fewer than the capital city but generally more appealing. Bacalar is a great place to base yourself for explorations of the Maya ruins in the south of Quintana Roo or to nip into Belize. Here are the accommodations and restaurants in order, north to south:

HOTEL PRICE CHART	
NOTE: Often, one shared bed in a room is cheaper than two. Prices based on cost per night, for two.	
[No $]	Less than US $20
$	US $20 - $40
$$	US $40 - $80
$$$	US $80 - $125

North of Bacalar town, tucked away in a hollow along the lagoon, is **Rancho Encantado** *(Hwy 307, ☎ in US 800/505-MAYA, or 505/758-9790, in Mexico 983/831-0037, www.encantado.com, gift shop, restaurant, group facilities, kayak & windsurfing, spa & jacuzzi, prices are MAP).* The Rancho is the original Lake Bacalar retreat hotel, specializing in luxury accommodations for the body, yoga and holistic health for the mind. Each self-contained casita or palapa bungalow features tropical hardwoods, tile floors, and a tasteful Mexican décor. The private casitas are scattered along the shoreline, where massages are offered in a hut built over the edge of the lake and a huge, impressively tall palapa is used for relaxation, meditation, or meetings. The restaurant serves delicious meat and veggie meals. Encantado also offers small private tours to Maya ruins, including less visited places and one not yet open to the public – El Resbalon. $$$

Puerta Del Cielo *(Hwy 307, ☎ 983/837-0413, pool, restaurant & bar)*. If it wasn't situated between two more noteworthy competitors, the Puerta would merit more consideration. It looks more like a storefront from the road, but in back, 13 basic but brightly painted connected bungalows zig-zag down the hillside toward the lagoon. Each simple room has a view and a tiny patio. The large suite with two beds and kitchenette (#11) has worn, overstuffed furniture and can house two couples. The restaurant and bar are at the water's edge. $

The road that runs along the lake in town is called La Costera and it is peppered with lakefront private homes and villas. Two nice B&Bs have opened there: **Casita Carolina** *(Costera, ☎ 983/834-2334, casitacarolina@aol.com, communal kitchen, $)* is a two-house complex on the lake, just a block south of the fort. The rooms are well-appointed and each is unique. The large backyard of the two homes that constitute the B&B contains a palapa roof cottage that often rents long-term.

There is also **Amigos B&B Bacalar** *(Costera, ☎ 983/834-2093, www.bacalar.net, 3 rooms, fans, $-$$)*, owned by the Kopelman family, who also have a B&B of the same name on Cozumel. There are two pleasant bedrooms upstairs, with a balcony overlooking the lake, and a large one downstairs. Con-

Hotel Laguna sports Mediterranean-style architecture.

tinental breakfast is served on the back terrace and they rent bikes and kayaks. There is a communal sitting room, use of microwave and fridge.

The food pickings are slim but improving in the town Bacalar itself, off to the east of the main highway. You can stop in **Seis Hermanas**, a popular restaurant along the coast road, opposite the swim club (*balneario*). Two blocks west and one block north from the fort is **Restaurante Orizabas**, a decent inexpensive Mexican restaurant in the old Colonial town.

Hotel Laguna *(Hwy. 307, ☎ 983/834-2206, fax 834-2205, restaurant, swimming pool, bar, 27 rooms with fan or 3 bungalows that sleep 5 to 8)*. This hard-to-miss whimsical-style hotel was built in the mid-1970s and is frozen in time. The one-of-a-kind building is white, with tons of turquoise trim and an orange roof. The place grows on you – we think it's very special. All the rooms have white wrought-iron furniture on balconies that face the lake. Thick wooden louvered windows in the tidy rooms allow in the fresh breeze or the light from one of the area's incredible sunrises. Immaculately landscaped walkways and terraces lead from the deep swimming pool down the steep hill to a boat and swimming dock. Sea shells of all shapes and sizes cover the hotel. Truck loads of shells must have been hauled from the Caribbean to create the picturesque décor. Small hand-painted wall tiles with amusing observations and Spanish sayings are also ubiquitous. The only real drawback we found was very slow toilets, which took several flushes to remove waste, but that's a small price to pay for a magical experience. $

Cenote Azul Trailer Park *(Hwy. 307, electric, bathrooms, showers, dump, wash room, no phone)*. A very friendly family runs this convenient trailer and camping area right next to Cenote Azul and the Bacalar Lagoon, less than a mile south of the Hotel Laguna. Flat, quiet, shady and convenient to just about anywhere, it's one of the cheapest campgrounds around. Tenters or hammockers need mosquito netting.

Cenote Azul Restaurant *(Hwy. 307, along the Bacalar Lagoon, no phone)*. Woven wicker covers the support columns and ceiling of this mostly seafood restaurant perched on the edge of a deep turquoise cenote (one of many with the "Azul" name). The cenote is also a local swimming hole. One of the largest in the world, it looks like an oval lake, some several

DINING PRICE CHART	
NOTE: Prices based on a typical entrée, per person, and do not include beverage.	
$	Less than US $5
$$	US $5 - 10
$$$	Over US $10

hundred feet across, with a depth of 300 feet. Fish hang around the edge waiting for food scraps. The seafood or Mexican dishes at the restaurant are tasty (mosquitoes are a problem at dinner), the service friendly and the swimming or snorkeling loads of fun. What's extra-special for daredevils is the opportunity to dive into the cenote from the roof of the restaurant, about a seven-meter (23-foot) drop. Exhilarating. $-$$

Chetumal

Time is a river without banks.
~ Traditional folk saying

On May 5, 1898, the Mexican Navy founded a settlement they called Payo Obispo along the mouth of the Hondo River where it flows into the bay. It was part of an effective military strategy to end the Caste War by cutting off the supply of arms purchased by the Maya from English merchants in Belize and smuggled up the Hondo. In 1936, the name changed back to a version of the area's pre-Hispanic name, "Chechemal." Chetumal became the capital when Quintana Roo became a state and since then the population has grown to nearly 130,000, including suburbs.

A grand sculpture in the center of the traffic circle before town announces Chetumal's heritage and distinction as the "Cuna de Mestija," the Cradle of the Mestizo Race. The children of Gonzalo Guerrero, the shipwrecked Spanish sailor, and his wife, the daughter of the local Maya lord of Chechemal, were the first mixed race children in all of Mexico. See page 41 for full story.

Chetumal was never a tourist destination in itself, but it does have a unique Caribbean feel due to its proximity to breezy Belize. This is a good base for day-trips into southern Quintana Roo and the surrounding countryside offers some pleasing diversions.

Tasty Treats

When Prince Bernhard of Holland visited, local cooks honored him by creating a delicious new regional dish, a hollowed-out ball of Dutch cheese filled with a mixture of ground pork, capers, olives, raisins, tomato, onion and sweet chile, covered in sauce. It's on local menus as **chile relleno**. He was so delighted, he asked for the recipe, took it back, and it's now a favorite dish in Holland. It's a heavy meal, so chances are you'll get only a slice of the cheese ball in restaurants.

A popular local bread, **pan bon**, is based on an English recipe smuggled across the border from Belize.

Some rare eateries in Chetumal and the small villages in the southern Quintana Roo area, including some of those along the lagoon, serve tasty regional dishes such as **wild boar** and **tepescuincle** (*haleb* in Mayan). This large rodent (scientific name, *Agouti paca*) looks a little like a giant chipmunk without a tail. It has short gray to brown fur with four or five rows of buff-colored spots, a buff belly and small ears. It's an intrinsic part of the jungle ecosystem because, like a North American squirrel, it buries seeds and fruits that germinate later, renewing the forests. The animals use bony swellings on their cheekbones as resonating chambers to produce sounds and their calls can be quite loud.

> ### SAVE THE TEPESCUINCLE
>
> Tepescuincles are in danger of extinction. To save them in the wild, breeding farms have been created in Central America and tropical Mexico. Although they are a traditional Maya treat, please decline these if you see them on the menu.

Orientation

■ Getting Around

 To enter the city from the Northwest, follow the signs straight past the airport and into town, or turn left on Av. Insurgentes to the circle then turn right (south) into town.

The long Chetumal Bay waterfront is a great walk, bike ride or drive and a bandstand near the hulking Obelisk features Sunday concerts. The grand pier was built to carry freight, passengers and cars over to Xcalak. But somebody forgot to tell the ocean not to constantly fill up the channel with sand. The ferry service functioned less than a year because the shallows needed constant dredging.

Practicalities

CLIMATE: Chetumal averages 95°F in August and 85° in December. It gets copious amounts of summer rainfall.

EVENTS: The **Fiesta de San Ignacio** in Chetumal is a big fiesta held the last week in July that features reggae, calypso and Mexican music. A big time celebration.

IMMIGRATION PAPERS: If there's a chance you'll be going into Guatemala, you'll need a tourist card, available at the border or the Guatemala Consulate on Av. Obregon (☎ 983/832-1365). To extend your Mexican tourist card you can try to find the immigration office (☎ 983/884-0434 or 884-8487) off Av. Insurgentes, a few blocks south from the sad-to-see zoo, in back of some kind of garage. Bring two copies of everything. If you need only 30 days or less, go hang out in Belize a couple of days, then you'll be issued a new card as you re-enter Mexico from Belize.

MONEY MATTERS: Av. Heroes has several money change booths, but the rates are not as favorable as those at the banks. There are several ATMs in downtown banks.

PHARMACY: Farmacia Social Mechaca (☎ 983/832-0044) is on Av. Indepencia.

POLICE: The police are available at ☎ 983/832-1500, emergency 060.

TELEPHONE EXCHANGE: A *larga distancia* telephone shop is on Obregon at Heroes.

TOURIST INFORMATION: Chetumal tourism information is located on Av. 22 Enero near the corner of Héroes, with the main office in the Palacio del Gobierno, second floor, on Av. Heroes, well north of downtown.

Adventures

■ Sights & Attractions

The city's heart contains an excellent "must-see" museum, the **Museo de la Cultura Maya** (☎ 983/832-1350), on Av. Heroes. Its permanent exhibition introduces visitors to the complex Maya culture. A leafy forest cuts across several floors surrounding a life-size reproduction of a sacred Ceiba, the tree of life. A working clock effectively explains the Maya calendar. If you see only one thing in Chetumal, it should be this museum.

Near the Museum is the **Altamirano Market**, an art deco-style *mercado*, also on Av. Heroes. We shop there.

The **Maqueta Payo Obispo**, a wooden, English Colonial-style building to the northwest of the Legislative Palace, on Av. 22 de Enero, contains an intriguing scale model of the former Payo Obispo, reconstructed from the memories of old residents and built by Luis Reinhard Macliberty. The wooden Caribbean-style town depicted was all but destroyed by Hurricane Janet in 1955. Janet also killed 800 residents. Admission is free.

The **Zoo** in Chetumal is on Av. Insurgentes; you'll pass it on the left if you enter town that way. However, like other zoos in less affluent countries, this one is relatively poorly maintained. But we've had a report that improvements have been made after our last visit, so please let us know. Kids might like the mini-train.

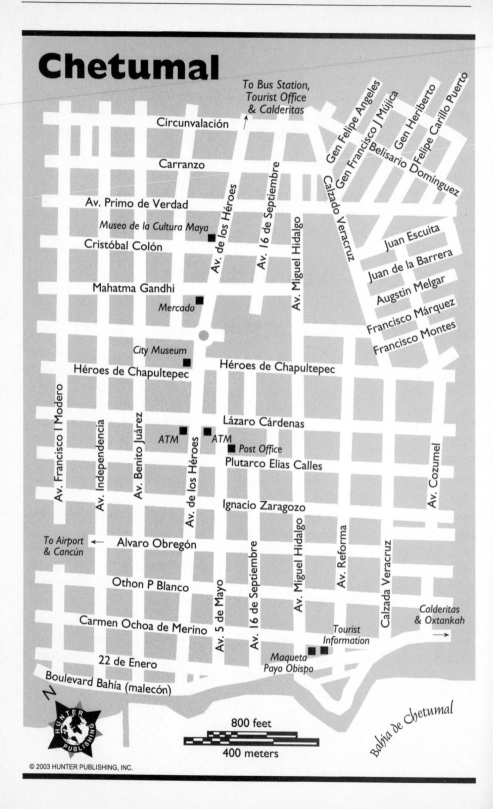

Chetumal

To Bus Station,
Tourist Office
& Calderitas

Circunvalación

Carranzo

Av. Primo de Verdad

Museo de la Cultura Maya

Cristóbal Colón

Mahatma Gandhi

Mercado

City Museum

Héroes de Chapultepec

Héroes de Chapultepec

Gen Felipe Angeles

Gen Francisco J Mújica

Gen Heriberto

Belisario Domínguez

Felipe Carillo Puerto

Calzado Veracruz

Av. de los Héroes

Av. 16 de Septiembre

Av. Miguel Hidalgo

Juan Escuita

Juan de la Barrera

Augstin Melgar

Francisco Márquez

Francisco Montes

Av. Francisco I Modero

Av. Independencia

Av. Benito Juárez

Av. de los Héroes

Lázaro Cárdenas

ATM

ATM

Post Office

Plutarco Elias Calles

Ignacio Zaragozo

To Airport
& Cancún

Alvaro Obregón

Othon P Blanco

Carmen Ochoa de Merino

22 de Enero

Av. 5 de Mayo

Av. 16 de Septiembre

Av. Miguel Hidalgo

Av. Reforma

Calzada Veracruz

Av. Cozumel

Calderitas
& Oxtankah

Tourist
Information

*Maqueta
Payo Obispo*

Boulevard Bahía (malecón)

N

HUNTER PUBLISHING

800 feet

400 meters

Bahía de Chetumal

© 2003 HUNTER PUBLISHING, INC.

■ Eco-Adventures

Without the long Caribbean beaches of Cancún, southern Quintana Roo has lagged far behind its northern half in tourism development. In evaluating the lure of Chetumal, the tourism office adroitly put adventure and eco-tourism high on the list. Encouraged by people such as Ernesto Parra, former Director of Fondo Chetumal, the natural wilds of the sparsely populated area are enticing naturalist adventure tours. On one trip, we kayaked a stream through the jungle until it joined the Rio Hondo along the Belize border. We followed the Hondo to a river crossing that consisted of an overhead cart, strung by wire high over the brown water. We climbed a hill to the crest that overlooked Cenote Crocodile, at the base of a shear white limestone cliff. From here we could see the farmlands in Belize. From the narrow caves in the cliff face came hundreds of thousands of bats on cue at dusk, flying through the trees and enveloping our hill top in a cloud of fluttering wings. A fantastic feeling, like no other we've ever experienced. After camping out, the next day we rappelled the cliff face – down an intimidating 55 meters (180 feet) – and celebrated with a swim in the cenote. There are no crocodiles in the cenote of the same name, but we saw more wildlife in nature on this trip than any other. Contact Ernesto Parro Calderón or his partner, Alejandro Vargas, at their expedition and adventure group, **Mayan World Adventures** (in Hotel Los Cocos, ☎ 983/833-2509, www. mayanworldadventures.com). They offer local cultural and historical tours such as a city tour and guided visits to the ruins of Kohunlich and Dzibanché, as well as Oxtankah. A great way to see the latter ruin is by bicycle and Mayan World has a fun Oxtankah bike tour package. Their other packages include kayaking to Isla Tamalcab, hikes in the rainforest, an expedition to Tres Garantías, as well as the adventure we described above. Best yet is a two-week expedition that features camping, hiking, biking, and kayaking into the jungle to find unexcavated Maya sites. Plus, you eat well when you're traveling with them.

Tres Garantías is a remote area in the low jungles southwest of Kohunlich where local villagers are attempting to combine ecology and tourism by offering a jungle stay with hiking trails and birdwatching. Very rustic and natural. Check with the tourism office or Mayan World Adventure, and bring your own water.

Besides visiting the impressive pre-Hispanic ruins off the highway west toward Xpujil, the surrounding area offers numerous opportunity for day-trips. **Calderitas** is a small weekend getaway north of the city. It boasts a string of wonderful little side-by-side restaurants along the waterfront that make a fun destination for an afternoon. Right next to them is a pleasant public beach. Check out the interesting huge pink and white Oxtincok hotel and restaurant across the street behind a wall of bouganvillea. Follow the coast road out of Chetumal to get here, then continue three km (1.8 miles) from

Calderitas to visit **Oxtankah**, a Maya and Colonial Spanish ruin. Oxtankah's claim to fame is its association with Gonzalo Guerrero, the shipwrecked Spanish sailor who married a Maya princess and fathered North America's first mestizo children. Under the arch next to the ruined baptistry is a period piece of grafitti. Etched into the wall (in a spot that looks as if it was repaired with cement) is the impression of three Spanish ships. Perhaps it was done by a Maya who saw them anchored in the bay, or by a Conquistador, wishing for home.

■ Adventures on Water

Chetumal is a perfect place from which to take a boat trip to Xcalak, Belize, or the nearby **Isla Tamalcab** to see the fuzzy wild capybaras, large native rodents of South America that look like furry pigs, run like horses and swim and float like hippopotami. Tamalcab can also be reached by sea kayak; ask Mayan World Adventures (☎ 983/833-2509, www.mayanworldadventures.com) to make arrangements or try renting your own boat at Cristy's Punta Maya Restaurant (see below).

The small village of **Xul Há**, "Bottom of the Water," up Hwy 307, sits on a circular lagoon that feeds Lake Bacalar through an inlet with a current. Swimming these "rapids" reportedly takes you past some interestingly carved designs in the bedrock.

El Palmar is a tiny village 51 km (32 miles) southwest from Ucum, a bit out of the way. It has a huge crystalline swimming pool fed by a natural spring that is cool and pleasant. They welcome tourists.

■ A Sidetrip To Belize

From Chetumal it's an easy jaunt down to Belice (Belize) for a day or longer. There's no need for a visa to enter Belize, but you will need additional car insurance – your Mexico automobile insurance is no good there.

The road to Belize is outside town and it is a short drive to the border. Before you go you may still need to get your car spray-fumigated at a building set up for that purpose on the left a kilometer or so short of the border. Belize is trying to prevent agricultural cross-contamiation; fumigation takes only a few minutes and costs about US $3. It is required for all cars entering Belize, unless you're going to the Free Zone, a large fenced-in area just across the river that started as a duty-free zone to attract shoppers from Mexico to the usually more expensive Belize. It proved so successful that now a Las Vegas-style casino has opened there to attract Mexican tourists. The **Princess Hotel and Casino** (☎ 501/423-7521) is very popular, especially with the governmental middle class from Chetumal. Because table gambling is illegal in

Mexico, the free zone is drawing tourists from all over Mexico who stay in Chetumal and go across the border to gamble in the Princess. Word has it that another casino is in the works.

Two bus lines serve Belize: **Batty's,** a local service, and **Venus**, which also features a 2 pm express to Belize City. Buses depart near the *mercado* or the main bus terminal two km (1.25 miles) north of the city center.

See more about Belize on page 265 below, or consult the *Belize Adventure Guide*, available from Hunter Publishing.

Accommodations

Making Chetumal City your base means you also have a fair variety of agreeable and inexpensive hotels from which to choose.

HOTEL PRICE CHART	
NOTE: Often, one shared bed in a room is cheaper than two. Prices based on cost per night, for two.	
[No $]	Less than US $20
$	US $20 - $40
$$	US $40 - $80
$$$	US $80 - $125

Hotel Marlon (*Av. Juárez No 87,* ☎ *985/832-9411, fax 985/832-6555, 50 rooms with 2 junior suites, air, TV, pool*). The Marlon is a modern business hotel with a reputation as an excellent value. Downstairs is a lobby/bar with a colorful stained-glass window, the Montecarlo restaurant and an inviting pool in the center courtyard. You get more for less staying here. $

Hotel Principe (*Av. Heroes No. 326,* ☎ *985/832-4799, fax 985/832-5191, pool, restaurant, private parking*). Another modern and clean hotel, set back from the busy main street and a real bargain 12 or more blocks from the bay. $

Holiday Inn Caribe (*Av. Niños Heroes No. 171,* ☎ *985/832-1100, fax 985/832-1676, TV, telephone, pool, private parking, 86 rooms & suites with air*). This hotel, set across the main shopping street from the Museo de Cultura, was remodeled in 1995 and delivers the kind of room quality expected of the Holiday Inn chain. The owner is active in promoting Chetumal tourism and, fortunately, her interest begins with pleasing her guests. This is the best place to stay in .town We liked the rooms very much, but found the restaurant lacking. Private parking and a swimming pool. $$

Hotel Los Cocos (*Av. Niños Heroes No. 134,* ☎ *985/832-0542, 832-0544, restaurant, pool, 70 rooms & 8 suites with air*). Los Cocos is strong competition for the Holiday Inn across the street. This independent "luxury" hotel has good-sized but plain rooms with air-conditioning, an appealing swimming pool and a cool and attractive entryway. We love their streetside restaurant, where the service is the best in the city and the food is delicious (great *sopa de* *limon).* At Christmas time, it is beautifully decorated, with tiny fairy lights all over, and the interior foyer of the hotel should win a prize – really fantastic! $$

Hotel Ucum *(Mahatma Gandhi No. 4, ☎ 985/832-0711).* Its name sounds amusing only if you pronounce it in English instead of Mayan – and you share our sophomoric sense of humor. Basic accommodations in this friendly but not fancy hotel come with fans in rooms set around a massive open courtyard. A clean budget hotel next door to the Holiday Inn. A good restaurant and coffee shop on the same side street is **Pantoja**. A daily *colectivo* for Xcalak leaves from here. $

Explorean Club is a luxury hotel outside town at the Kohunlich ruins. See page 271.

Hotel Ucum.

Dining

Fresh seafood is a major menu item here, as it is in restaurants along most of the long shoreline of the Yucatán Peninsula. What distinguishes it from Cancún, however, are the bargain prices. All the options we list here qualify from budget to moderate. Two well-known seafood restaurants are **Emiliano's**, usually packed for lunch, on Av. San Salvador at Calle 9, and **Mandinga**, on Av. Belice No. 124, revered for its octopus and conch soup. Try the **Café Espreso**, facing the bay, for good coffee and breakfast.

DINING PRICE CHART	
NOTE: Prices based on a typical entrée, per person, and do not include beverage.	
$	Less than US $5
$$	US $5 - 10
$$$	Over US $10

Los Cocos *(Av. Niños Heroes).* This restaurant in front of the Hotel Los Cocos is our all-time favorite place to eat in Chetumal. It's in the middle of everything, near the *mercado* and the museum, and offers excellent Mexican cooking at reasonable prices. Good service, good coffee, and big drinks make it popular with visitors from Belize as well as locals. If you only eat in one place downtown, this should be it. $-$$

Cristy's Ponta Maya *(on the* malecón *at Punta Maya, no phone).* One of Chetumal's most attractive eating places is under a giant palapa among a grove of trees along the edge of the breezy bay. American soft rock plays in the background and local families reserve tables for special occasions. They rent awning-covered motor boats to tour the bay (US $25 hour, seats up to six) or you can spend $90 for a day and go as far away as San Pedro, Belize (which, like the Gilligan's Island, is a three-hour tour). Photocopied navigational maps are provided. $$

Puente al Sol *(Blvd. Bahia at the southern end of the* malecón, *no phone).* Dine or drink under this big palapa-roofed eatery on a wooden deck that goes right out over the water. The open southwest end, facing the water and shaped to resemble the bow of a ship, gives it the name "Bridge to the Sun." Live music every evening. $$

Sergios *(Av. Obregon at Av. Cinco de Mayo).* Sergios is a long-established Italian restaurant on a busy corner downtown. It is very a popular place to get sandwiches, grilled steaks, or pasta – plus they dish up a unique pizza. Very tasty and worth finding for lunch or dinner. Everyone knows Sergios. $-$$

Restaurant El Fenicio *(Av. Niños Heroes & Zaragoza,* ☎ *983/832-0026).* This restaurant in the downtown area offers dependable Mexican cooking at reasonable prices. Open 24 hours a day. With a handy mini-supermarket in back, it's a local favorite. Large open windows face the street, making it a great place to watch people in the heart of the shopping district. $-$$

La Troje de Sergio's *(on the* malecón, ☎ *985/832-7249).* A popular upscale seafood restaurant with an extensive menu that includes Italian dishes. It has a relaxing atmosphere with a great view across the street to Chetumal Bay. $$

Belize

Belize is an eccentric and quirky little English-speaking country wedged between Mexico and Guatemala and the worlds of the Maya, Hispanic, Caribbean and British cultures, as well as that of the US – from where the many dive enthusiasts flock. It was formerly known as British Honduras and

has a checkered past as an important part of the Maya world, Spanish colony, part of Guatemala (it still has a disputed border with them), hide-out of cutthroat pirates, home of rough-neck loggers who carved the mahogany out of the wild jungles, refuge for slaves, and flooded back water country. Today, it is famous first for its fantastic diving off the many quays and offshore reefs and for an active ecological preservation effort. Best places to visit include the Rio Bravo Conservation Area, Cockscomb Jaguar Reserve, Bermudan Baboon Sanctuary, the Maya Mountains, Ambergris Caye and more. Archeological treasures continue to emerge from the inland jungle, the most famous of which is Lamanai.

BARON BLISS DAY

Every March 9, Belizians celebrate Baron Bliss Day. The British baron with a Portuguese title – the "Fourth Baron Bliss of the former Kingdom of Portugal" – died of food poisoning while fishing off the coast in 1926. Though he never physically set foot in Belize, he left the bulk of his estate to the colony. Today, that legacy continues to finance public works and an annual regatta in his name.

For a quick and pleasant day-trip into Belize, head to **Corozal Town**, nine miles south of the border and 96 miles north of Belize City. Originally a private estate on the banks of Corozal Bay, it was settled by refugees from Bacalar during the Caste War. In 1955, Hurricane Janet blew many of the wooden houses akimbo. It's a quaint, easy-going and safe Caribbean town.

Orientation

■ Entering Belize

Entering Belize from Mexico is easy, even on a bus. Stop at the office on the Mexican side, have your passport stamped and hand in your tourist card. On the Belize side, stop in the office and fill out a form of intent and a Customs declaration. If you're driving, be sure to declare your car because they add an additional stamp for it in your passport. Rental cars are not supposed to be taken in, according to your Mexican rental agreement, as the insurance is no good. (But the Belizian officials don't care – you'll be lucky if they stop playing cards long enough to let you pass.)

Money changers conveniently wait outside the border office. You can spend US dollars if you don't want to bother exchanging, especially if you are only going in for a short trip.

Campers and RVers can kip at the peaceful lake just over border on the way to Corozal.

Corozal Town

In the small wooden town hall on Corozal's main square is a lively **wall mural** painted in 1953 by a famous local artist, Manuel Villamore Reyes, depicting the area's history. Older and wiser by 1986, when asked to restore it, he repainted it instead, treating the plight of the Maya in a much more sympathetic light. Using deep natural colors and skillfully weaving scenes together, he connected lives through history – the good and bad, happy and sad.

The main square also houses the **post office**, where you can buy some of Belize's very attractive and colorful stamps. Next door is the magistrate's court and if it's in session you can see judges in the traditionally English white wigs, presiding over trials. Nearby, only the four corners of the old fort that once stood there are still visible.

■ Ruins

Completely ringing Corozal Town are the post-Classic **Santa Rita Maya** ruins, originally explored by British medical practitioner, Thomas Gann, in the late 19th century. The tallest site is a little difficult to find, set among a few homes near the northern edge of town. Wear long pants and insect repellent because no-see-ums are not no-feel-ums.

The **Cerro Maya** ruins are visible as a lump in the trees across the bay from town. The Maya abandoned this important trading center around AD 100. A canal 4,000 feet long, 20 feet wide and six feet deep encloses a pyramid plaza complex that features carved masks and two ceremonial ballcourts within a total of 90 acres. Once planned as a tourist attraction, the Cerro ruins are accessible only by hired boat from Corozal.

One of Belize's most impressive Maya ruins is **Lamanai** ("submerged crocodile"), set along the New River Lagoon within a 950-acre archeological reserve. It was occupied from 1500 BC to the 19th century and is one of the longest-occupied sites in Mundo Maya. The jungle setting and impressive ruins are a worthwhile excursion into the countryside. Although it's not particularly close to Corozal Town, **Henry Menzies** at the Caribbean Village (see below) arranges boat trips up the unspoiled New River to explore the abandoned city. It's an expedition-style adventure and a good day's pleasure, with plenty of wildlife on the overhanging jungle shore. Henry acts as a travel agent and facilitator for any itineraries in Belize, including those awkward connecting flights.

Tea to the English is really a picnic indoors.
~ Alice Walker, The Color Purple

■ Accommodations & Dining

Caribbean Village *(on the bay, PO Box 210, Corozal Town, Belize, ☎ 501/422-2045, fax 501/422-3414, cabins, trailer park & camping).* Despite its pretentious name, the Caribbean Village Resort is a jumbled collection of camping and trailer spots and individual cabins in an ideal location on a palm-covered bulge along the bay south of town. In the center of the horseshoe-shaped complex is an inexpensive family seafood-specialty restaurant run by the Menzies family. Here, locals and friends, as well as guests, enjoy simple but tasty Belizian cooking. The guest cabins are clean and neat and, although not up to resort standards, are very comfortable. The owner, Henry Menzies, is a personable and knowledgeable guy who can arrange bike rentals and boat trips in Belize. $

HOTEL PRICE CHART	
NOTE: Often, one shared bed in a room is cheaper than two. Prices based on cost per night, for two.	
[No $]	Less than US $20
$	US $20 - $40
$$	US $40 - $80
$$$	US $80 - $125

Tony's Inn & Beach Resort *(south end, PO Box 12, Corozal, Belize, ☎ 501/422-2055, fax 501/422-2829).* Tony's Inn is the best place in Corozal Town for quality in accommodations and food. It's set on the water's edge with its own dock and beach. This stylish inn features clean and comfortable deluxe and moderate guest rooms with double or king-size beds, air-conditioning, private bathrooms and cable TV (let's go Cubs!). Their dining area boasts linen tablecloths set in a glassed-in dining room overlooking the bay. If you're looking for a change of pace – a bit of Britain in Belize – stop here. Reasonably priced. $$

Forest of Kings

Those who walk through the roots of life arrive here
with the great lady of the land, who sees and reflects the truth,
to go teach her sons where the only light lies...
~ fragment of an inscription on the Chicanná façade

The southern portion of Quintana Roo and Campeche is rich in spectacular Maya ruins that until recently have been next to impossible to visit. Now, besides the Rio Bec-style ruins at Becán and around Xpujil, several additional sites are open to the public. You have a chance to see ruins in all their magnificence without the crowds of Tulum or Chichén Itzá. One can walk in ancient ruined cities and be the only human there, surrounded by the ghosts of the Classic Maya and watched by the living inhabitants of the jungle – wild animals and birds. This little-explored corner of the Yucatán Peninsula is well worth a close look.

We list the ruins in Quintana Roo state as you head east toward Xpujil on the road to Escárcega. If you're following this route through to Campeche or Chiapas, turn to the Forest of Kings chapter in Southern Campeche State (see page 414). If you're coming from Campeche City or Palenque, read backwards.

The Road to Ruin

Highway 186, between Chetumal and Escárcega, runs past some magnificent Maya cities from the Classical Age. Profiles of some of those ruins are presented below, going from Chetumal heading west. With some hard driving you could visit the more important ruins and still make Campeche or Chetumal in a very long day. An overnight in Xpujil is a good idea if just for driving safety, but is a great idea if you're going to spend time at the rarely visited ruins of the southern zone.

Do not drive this road at night, and use some commonsense precautions, such as tagging along with another vehicle for safety in numbers. There have been rare reports of robberies in the central sparsely populated region. An army post in Xpujil patrols the area.

■ Dzibanché & Kinichna

These two Classic-era ruins are within hiking distance of one another. They were newly opened to the public in 1996 and are a tremendous find. Dzibanché, "Written on Wood," was the most important Maya city of the region. Its name comes from the large lintel made of quebracho wood that bears a glyph date of AD 618. This complex of impressive pyramids and stone buildings will take your breath away, especially early in the morning or late in the afternoon when there is rarely another soul among the

Hidden ruins at Dzibanché.

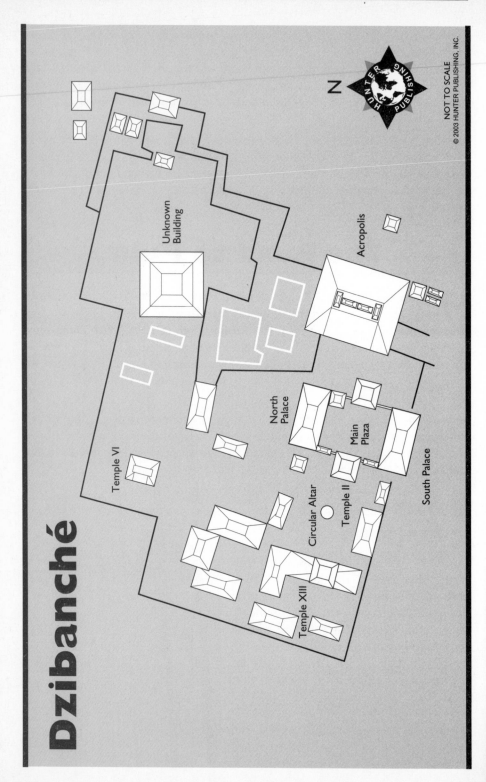

massive structures and tall jungle trees. This site, and its incredible solitude, was one of the best of the Maya ruins we visited, despite the fact it was extensively rebuilt. And if it wasn't the "best," it had the authentic ambiance of a city lost to time and hidden for ages by the verdant forest. Besides its natural water sources, Dzibanché has several chultuns, underground excavations that served as water reservoirs. An important jade pendant dated AD 909 was uncovered here, along with a stairway with four carved steps and a carved stone lintel. Nearby, the Kinichná ruins feature a tall pyramid with a clear view across miles of virgin jungle.

■ Kohunlich

This site is best known for its **Pyramid of the Masks**. The turn for Kohunlich is less than a mile farther west on the Chetumal-Escárcega Highway 186. It flourished from AD 350-900, at the height of the Classic period, and contains an esplanade that served as a base where water flowed down to an artificial lagoon. The most important building is the famous **Los Mascarones**, decorated with various stucco face designs from around AD 500, representing the different ages of the sun. Thatched roofs protect the Olmec-style faces from the elements. Flash photography is prohibited. There are public bathrooms here. The tall jungle as you enter sets the mood for this lost Maya city.

Stone mask at Kohunlich.

INAH, the National Institute of Anthropology and History, is training and employing Guatemalan refugees to work in conserving the archeological zone of Kohunlich. This effort duplicates one at Edzná near Campeche, where the objective is to provide work and social benefits to the displaced Maya who fled political persecution in their own country.

Accommodation

Explorean Club *(Kohunlich ruins, US ☎ 877/397-5672, Mexico ☎ 800/366-6666, www.explorean.com, restaurant, gift shop, health club, pool, all-inclusive)*. You'll see the Explorean's brown thatched roofs rising from the tree tops as you drive toward the Classic-aged ruins. There's no sign for the driveway on the left, but you shouldn't miss this fabulous relaxing retreat set at the top of rolling hills. The lobby is under a gigantic palapa and the nearby swimming pool, a long thin lap pool, is set on the edge of a wall that overlooks the gardens and jungle below. Two igloo-like stone huts are used for dry saunas (with some aromatherapy thrown in for good health) and there's a steam sauna and exercise gym. The resort's suites are in charming palapa villas that spill down the landscaped hillside. Each has a private patio and walled in back yard. Amenities are all first class (typical of its owners, Fiesta Americana) and include king-size beds, fans, air condi-

HOTEL PRICE CHART	
NOTE: Often, one shared bed in a room is cheaper than two. Prices based on cost per night, for two.	
[No $]	Less than US $20
$	US $20 - $40
$$	US $40 - $80
$$$	US $80 - $125

tioning, marble baths, complimentary robes, coffee and tea delivered to your door each morning, designer toiletries and thick cotton towels. Naturalist-led tours are offered, and a bike path leads to the ruins. All-inclusive runs about $235 per person. $$$$

■ Chakambakam

Heading west again from Kohunlich brings you past the village of Caobas, 93 km (58 miles) from Chetumal. Four km (2.5 miles) of unpaved road to the right leads to the ruins, whose name means "Surrounded by Mangroves." The road isn't marked, so you have to ask directions. The Classic-era civic-religious center with a tall pyramid sits on a small peninsula that juts into a lagoon. Stucco and stone sculpture (including Olmec-style masks) have been found here and a *sacbé* leads to the north. Excavations are ongoing and the site was not yet open to the general public as of summer of 2003, but we've included it just in case. If you're following this route through to Campeche or Chiapas, turn to the Forest of Kings chapter in Southern Campeche State (see page 414). Also look at the *Bribes and Scams* section, page 85, to read about the Pemex station, east of Xpujil.

If it weren't for people, life wouldn't be quite so interesting. On the other hand, if it weren't for life, people wouldn't be quite so interesting either.
~ Dave Allhargen

Yucatán

I must learn Spanish, one of these days,
Only for that slow sweet name's sake.
~ The Flower's Name, Robert Browning, 1812-1889

At A Glance

NAME: The name "Yucatán" may have originated from a classic New World misinterpretation. When the Spanish put ashore and asked the native Maya to tell them the name of the land, they replied "u'y than, u'y than," meaning, "We don't understand, what the hell are you talking about?" That was eventually corrupted to "Yucatán" (youk-ah-TAN).

LOCATION: Yucatán is a wedge-shaped state covering most of the northern part of the peninsula. It borders the Gulf of Mexico, where the Gulf meets the Caribbean.

CAPITAL: Mérida.

MAJOR CITIES: Mérida, Motúl, Izamal, Valladolid, Tizimin and Progreso.

POPULATION: 1,500,000 indigenous Maya and Spanish descent.

CLIMATE: Hot and humid inland, ocean breezes cool the coastline. Dry in the winter.

VEGETATION: Scrub forest, mangroves and cattle and farm land.

GEOGRAPHY: Lowland, with many cenotes, Gulf coast beaches and a range of hills (Puuc region).

SIZE: 16,000 square miles (40,000 square kilometers).

WILDLIFE: Pheasant, deer, jaguarundi, flamingos and armadillos.

ECOLOGICAL RESERVES & PARKS: Parque Natural del Flamingo Méxicano de Celestún, Dzibilchaltún, San Felipe, Rio Lagartos and El Palmar.

MAJOR ARCHEOLOGICAL SITES: Chichén Itzá, Ekbalam, Dzibilchaltún, Uxmal, Kabáh, Sayil and Labná.

El oro y amores eran malos de encubrir.
(Gold and love affairs are difficult to hide.)
~ Spanish proverb

Mérida

You are in love with a country where people laugh in the sun
and the people are warm as the sunshine and live and move
easily, and women with honey colored skins and men with
no frowns on their faces sit on white terraces...
~ A.S.J. Tessimond, 1902-1962

It doesn't take long to realize that Mérida is the cultural focal point for the entire peninsula. Even more so since the beginning of 2000, when it was named the Cultural Capital of the Americas. Despite its size and unfortunate urban inconveniences, Mérida is one of the Yucatán's most hospitable and nostalgic cities. Its Colonial center thrives and is full of Maya men and women dressed in traditional country garb; round-faced children with sheepish grins and bright laughs; young, intense college students from the city's several universities; businessmen in *guayaberas* and businesswomen in modern dress; young European tourists bearing backpacks; older North American adventurers in khaki slacks from L.L. Bean; loving Mexican couples strolling the Plaza Mayor; vendors clamoring for sales; and families on their way to church or a *posada*. Mérida seems to be a living, breathing entity.

Mérida's heart is the **Colonial Centro**, much larger than Campeche's walled city. Central to its existence are the venerable old churches, the *mercado*, a meeting place for two cultures, and the unique and delicious Yucatecan cooking.

The Yucatán's largest city was founded as the peninsular capital by **Francisco de Montejo**, El Mozo (the Younger or the Son), at the ancient Maya city of T'Ho (pronounced "Hoe"). Maya in the countryside still use the traditional name, "Place of Five Temples," when referring to Mérida. T'Ho's impressive buildings reminded Montejo of the Roman ruins in the Spanish city of Mérida, sealing T'Ho's fate and its name. He inaugurated the new capital on January 6, 1542, with the words "... I wish to populate [and] construct a city of 100 neighbors.... May Our Lord keep it in His Holy Service for all time."

The blueprint called for a rectangular-shaped city graced by wide avenues and a large *zócalo*, or main square. They began building the city from the ruined Maya pyramids found there, which provided enough stone to create all the edifices bordering the downtown plaza and more. Surrounding the city center, where the Spanish and Creoles lived, were *barrios* – lower-class residential neighborhoods: **Santiago** and **Santa Catarina** in the west for the local Maya; **San Cristóbal** to the east for highland Maya; and **Santa Lucia** in the north for blacks and mulattos. El Mozo began building his own house – Casa Montejo – on the square during the time his wife Andrea gave birth to their daughter, Beatriz, in 1543. The house still stands (now a bank) and its ornate entrance façade features the Montejo coat of arms flanked by gruesome symbols of his power: two Spanish Conquistadors stand with their feet on the necks of two defeated Maya warriors.

The occupation of T'Ho was not easy for the Spanish. Six months after Montejo founded Mérida, thousands of Maya warriors attacked. Somehow, they failed to dislodge the beleaguered Conquistadors. In many ways that fateful battle marked an end to the Maya era and the beginning of a Colonial system, with huge Spanish land holdings upon which the Maya labored as virtual slaves.

A rustic church served the growing capital until 1561 when work began on the huge cathedral at the west side of the *zócalo* using stones from the dismantled T'Ho pyramids. The massive **Catedral de San Ildefonso** was finished in 1598, making it the oldest cathedral on the American continent.

By the late 1800s, henequen was king and *hacendados* (hacienda owners) and wealthy families built opulent homes along the Paseo de Montejo to the north end of town. Mérida is usually referred to as the "White City," due to the large number of white buildings it has. It also became known as the "Paris of the West" because of the French baroque influence of its baronial mansions and its thriving culture.

To enjoy Mérida at its finest calls for time. Time for leisurely lunches under the portales across from the Plaza Mayor. Time for Sunday strolls along the Paseo's leafy green walkway or listening to choral serenades in a park under the stars. Time to watch courting couples or old friends sit in S-shaped cement park seats known as *confidenciales*. Sit in one and absorb the rhythm of life as it reverberates through the park. Or see the city's sights in romantic horse-drawn carriage called a *casela*. There's always something interesting going on in Mérida.

> *The voyage of discovery lies not in finding new landscapes,*
> *but in having new eyes.*
> ~ Marcel Proust

Yucatán

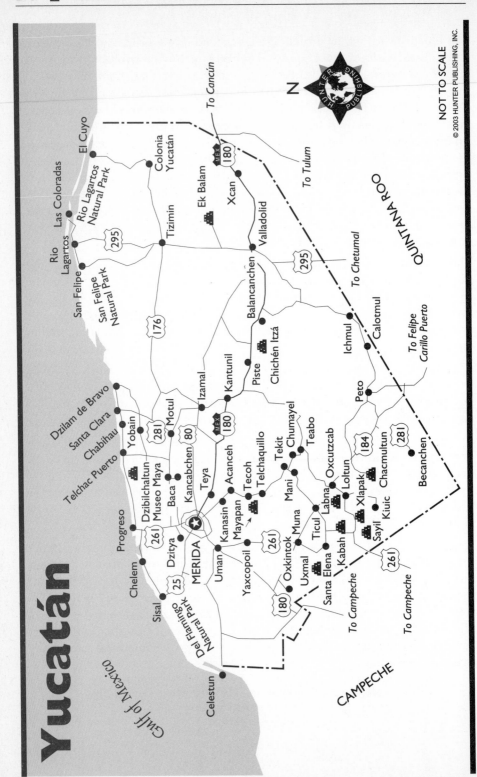

NOT TO SCALE

Cenote Samula, Dzpitnup (see page 320)

Above: Working the salt mountain at Las Coloradas (see page 345)

Below: El Palacio, Sayil – Maya ruins (see page 377)

Detail of the Nunnery Quadrangle, Uxmal (see page 372)

Orientation

■ Getting Around

If you've been out wandering the countryside, Mérida may come as a surprise. It's a big, cosmopolitan city with big city drawbacks: crowded streets and traffic pollution. The very things that make the Colonial Centro so attractive are responsible for some of its worst problems – narrow streets built for horse and carriage were never intended to hold jockeying cars or lumbering buses spewing exhaust. Busy season is in the summer, when Europeans and Mexicans on holiday flock to the city, while Meridaños flee the heat and humidity for the cooler countryside and shore, mainly at Progreso. Still, none of these disadvantages should inhibit your enjoyment of a truly unique city.

All roads in the Yucatán lead to Mérida, 320 km (200 miles) west of Cancún and 190 km (119 miles) from Campeche. Like the hub of a wheel or the center of a spider web, roads spoke out from Mérida in several directions: **Highway 261** north to Progreso and south to Muna; **Highway 180** south to Campeche and east to Valladolid and Cancún; roads west to Celestún and east to Motúl. A **bypass** road (*periférico*) rings the city. Pay close attention to the signs on the bypass to be sure you don't miss your desired exit.

DISTANCES FROM MERIDA	
Acanceh . . . . 30 km/19 miles	Muna. . . . . 62 km/39 miles
Campeche. . . . . 192 km/119 miles	Oxkutzcab. . . . . 138 km/86 miles
Cancún . . . . 306 km/190 miles	Progreso . . . . 33 km/21 miles
Celestún . . . . 85 km/53 miles	Sayil . . . . 110 km/68 miles
Chichén Itzá . . . . 120 km/75 miles	Teabo . . . . 87 km/54 miles
Chumayel . . . . 82 km/51 miles	Tecoh. . . . . 36 km/22 miles
Dzibilchaltún . . . . 15 km/9 miles	Tekit . . . . 66 km/41 miles
Dzilam de Bravo. . . . . . . 107 km/67 miles	Telchac Puerto . . . . 69 km/43 miles
Dzitnup. . . . . 167 km/104 miles	Telchaquillo . . . . 46 km/29 miles
Grutas de Balancanche . . . 122 km/76 miles	Teya . . . . 10 km/6 miles
Grutas de Loltún . . . . . . 138 km/86 miles	Ticul . . . . 84 km/52 miles
Izamal. . . . . 70 km/44 miles	Umán . . . . 17 km/11 miles
Kabáh . . . . 101 km/63 miles	Uxmal . . . . 80 km/50 miles
Labná . . . . 119 km/74 miles	Valladolid . . . . 162 km/101 miles
Maní . . . . 127 km/79 miles	Xlapak. . . . . 116 km/72 miles
Mayapán. . . . . 102 km/64 miles	Yaxcopoil . . . . 33 km/21 miles

Once a walled city like Campeche, Mérida still has three standing Moorish-style gates through which ran *camino reales*, royal roads. They went overland to Valladolid, Campeche and Champotón. The painted red cobblestone vestige of those roads can be found in the southern and western parts of the old city. Left over from Colonial times are the unique and artistic name plaques set into the walls of building corners all over the old city. They are remnants of the Spanish attempt to teach the Maya their language and to provide easy directional reference points for their own illiterate people. For example, a ceramic tile plaque with a picture of a parrot and its name underneath in Spanish, became

Name plaques set in the walls are left over from Colonial times.

the name of the corner. Consequently, people could meet on "Flamingo" corner or could reference their address as between "Monkey" and "Drop of Water." The surviving plaques are protected by building codes that prevent their destruction.

The grid-like construction of Mérida's streets makes finding your way easy. Odd-numbered streets run east and west, with higher numbered streets to the south of the main plaza. Even-numbered streets run north and south, with higher numbered streets to the west. Most of the references we offer in this guide are within walking distance of the *zócalo*, or Plaza Principal, and up the Paseo de Montejo, a Champs-Elysées-like boulevard between Calles 56 and 58. Alternate streets run one-way for vehicular traffic.

> **AUTHOR'S TIP:** *Traffic police control the large amount of traffic clogging the narrow streets in the city center. Be aware they will ticket you for driving infractions, so pay attention to the traffic flow, traffic lights and their hand signals.*

In-town **bus routes** are difficult to figure out unless you're familiar with the names of the neighborhoods. Nearly all the buses that run on the Paseo Montejo, however, get you downtown near the main plaza. Ask someone on the street or a shopkeeper; Meridanos are friendly and helpful folk. Besides walking, **taxis** are the best way to get around, although they can be difficult to find because they're not always roaming the streets looking for passengers. Have your hotel, or any hotel, call for one. Alternatively, there are taxi stands at most of the parks and squares, so you'll usually find one waiting there. Negotiate your fare beforehand, as prices are generally higher in Mérida than anywhere else due to a very strong *taxistas* union. **Bicycles** are probably not a good idea on the narrow inner-city streets.

Mérida has a large airport, but most international passenger service has switched to Cancún. Check with your carrier if you want to fly here. Continental, Aeromexico and Mexicana have connections from Mexico City as well as Cancún. There's also a new international airport near Chichén Itzá.

Many of the long-haul buses into and from Mérida use the new first-class bus depot, **CAME**, on Calle 70 between 69 and 71, about seven blocks southwest of the Plaza Mayor. The second-class terminal, **Autobuses Unión**, is nearby on Calle 69 between 68 and 70. A first-class terminal to Cancún is in the **Fiesta Americana** building, opposite the Hyatt.

The **train** station is at Calles 48 and 55 for the last remaining passenger service in the Yucatán: the Sunday tour train to Izamal.

Practicalities

AA: A group of recovering people have an English-language meeting at the English Library (☎ 999/924-8401), on Calle 53 between 66 and 68, every Thursday at 7 pm.

BICYCLE REPAIRS: There are a couple of motorcycle and bicycle shops in town, notably **Bicimaya** (☎ 999/924-8034) on the corner of 69 and 56 in the *mercado*.

CONSULATES/IMMIGRATION: There is a **US Consulate** in Mérida on Paseo Montejo near the Holiday Inn. The phone is ☎ 999/925-5011. The consul of the **UK** has gone back to Cancún, and **Canadians** have to call either Mexico City or Cancún. Other consulate phone numbers are: **Austria** (☎ 999/925-6386, **Spain** (☎ 999/944-8350), **Germany** (☎ 999/981-2976), **Belgium** (☎ 999/981-1099), **Belize** (☎ 999/928-6152), **France** (☎ 999/925-2886) and **the Netherlands** (☎ 999/924-3122). You can reach the immigration office for tourist card extensions by phoning ☎ 999/928-5823.

HEALTH CLUB: Work out your kinks in **Gym Biceps Mixto** on Calle 62 between 57 and 59 (☎ 999/923-2887). About US $4 per day gets you access to a full line of modern exercise equipment and free weights.

JUST DESSERTS: You can put the fat back on at **Capuchino Cheesecake Deluxe** at the corner of 47 and 64; by its name you know what we mean. Then steam it off again at the Colon Hotel Baths.

LANGUAGE: If you're tired of speaking English, live with a local family and study Spanish in immersion classes at the **Centro Idiomas del Sureste**. It has three locations (one downtown and two in residential areas) close to the city center. Classes of three hours per day run a minimum of two weeks and there's a grueling but effective option for a full five hours of tongue-numbing lessons daily. All levels, from beginners to advanced. We took classes for four weeks in San José, Costa Rica a few years ago and found the experience invaluable. A half-day of class and the balance practicing your new skills is a quick and painless way to speak like a native. Call Charlene Biddulph, their US agent, at Language Studies Abroad, to register (☎ 800/424-5522). *En-tiende*?

LAUNDROMAT: There's a small, inexpensive laundromat, **Lavanderias Automatics**, on Calle 59 near 74. They do a good, dependable job. Another worthwhile laundromat can be found two blocks due west of the Fiesta Americana hotel, on Av. Cupules and Av. 62. They are never open on Sunday. Most operators will separate whites and darks automatically, but it never hurts to ask for *separado*.

LIBRARY: To read more, there is an easy-going English-language library on Calle 53 between 66 and 68.

MEDICAL FACILITIES: The **Red Cross** is good in an emergency, ☎ 999/924-9813. The big hospital in town is the **Hospital O'Horan** on Av. Itzáes (☎ 999/924-4711).

MONEY MATTERS: **American Express** has an office in the Hotel Aluxes on Calle 60.

MUSEUMS: Anthropology & History (Paseo de Montejo, 9 am-8 pm daily, except Monday, 9 am-2 pm). Admission US $2. **City Museum** (Calle 61 and 58, every day 10 am-2 pm). **Popular Art Museum** (Calle 59 and 50, Tuesday through Saturday 9 am-8 pm, Sunday 8 am-2 pm). **Natural History** (Calle 59 and 84, Tuesday through Saturday 9 am-6 pm). **MACAY** Contemporary Art Museum (Calle 60 next to Cathedral, open 10 am-6 pm except Tuesday, US $2.50). **Yucatecan Music Museum**, Calle 57 and 48, open 9 am-5 pm, closed Monday).

POLICE, ETC.: Instead of gun-toting Army patrols to help tourists, Mérida boasts a **Tourism Police Force**, graduates of the Luis Sotelo Regil Police Academy. They patrol the downtown in distinctive white shirts and light brown pants with a Policía Turística patch on their right sleeve. Although not completely fluent in English, the 41 officers are eager to help and can do so. ☎ 999/925-2525, ext. 260. The municipal police are at ☎ 999/925-2555.

The **Green Angels** (for roadside assistance) are at ☎ 999/983-1184.

POST OFFICE: The post office is an elegant building in the middle of the busy *mercado* on Calle 65, near 56. It closes at 1 pm on Saturdays.

SOCIAL GRACES: The international community has a get-together cocktail party and social on the first Friday of every month. In even-numbered months it's hosted at the English Library and in "odd" months by Dennis LaFoy of Yucatán Trails Travel. His venue changes so check with him first. The International Women's Club meets from 9:30 am to noon at the Expreso Maya Train Office at Calle 43 between 46 and 50 on the last Saturday of each month. A great way to meet folks.

TOUR GROUPS: In addition to running an excellent travel agency, **Yucatán Trails Travel** (Calle 62 between 57 and 59, ☎ 999/928-2582, yucatantrails@hotmail.com), Canadian Dennis LaFoy organizes a monthly get-together of the English-speaking community. Send him an e-mail to find out when the next meeting is and hear what it's like to live abroad. Yucatán Trails will make individualized tour and travel arrangements to the ruins and other exciting Yucatecan sights, and will even help you nip over to Cuba. There's a scheduled bus tour to ruins and sights offered by **Turitransmerida** at Calle 55 and 58 (☎ 999/924-1199, www.turitransmerida.com.mx). It runs seven days a week to Uxmal, Chichén, and Celestun; several days a week to Dzibilchaltun and Progreso, Izamal, cenotes, or the Ruta Puuc. The **Nómadas Youth Hostel** also has a good travel agency for economical guided and self-guided tours (see listing under *Accommodations*).

For archeological trips to the ruins, natural and cultural tours, or just all around adventure trips, try Carlos Sosa at his agency, **Balam-Beh Expeditions** (Calle 46 #471-A, ☎ 999/924-1871, balambeh@prodigy.net.mx). Carlos is very personable, bilingual and obviously knows his stuff.

TOURIST INFORMATION: The tourism office is behind thick and tall wooden doors on the corner of the huge Teatro Peón Contreras on Calle 60, two blocks north of the Plaza Mayor.

Festivals & Events

There is no city in the Yucatán that puts on a happier face than Mérida. Check our list of holidays on page 71 for special celebrations during the time you'll be in town, especially January 6, the city's birthday. There's always something to see or do, and every night of the week brings a fiesta, a concert, a show. The added bonus is that the events were never meant for "tourists," but for Meridanos themselves, and they're an integral part of local culture.

One fiesta was hardly ended when another began.
~ John Lloyd Stephens, writing of Mérida, 1841

Traditional dancers, Mérida.

■ Every Day is a Celebration!

Sunday: All day long on Sundays the downtown area around the main *zócalo* (aka Plaza Mayor or Plaza Principal) closes to vehicular traffic and becomes a giant bazaar and outdoor picnic with musical concerts, puppet shows, folk dancing and activities for children. It's all free. At 11 am there's a concert under the arches of the **Palacio de Gobierno**, while the police band strikes it up at the **Santa Lucia Park**. Marimba music makes its mark at the **Parque Hidalgo** on Calle 60 at 59 at 11:30 am. At 1 pm a folklorico ballet recreation of a mestizo wedding occurs in front of the **Palacio Municipal** on the Plaza Mayor. There seems to be music, fiestas and flea markets in every park around town. On Sunday, 10 am to 2 pm, there's a popular browsing bazaar market at the **Parque Santa Lucia**, a good place to buy colorful old stamps. In front of the cathedral you can rent pedal carts with canvas roofs for a fun trip around the traffic-free streets. A Sunday in Mérida is not to be missed.

Monday: **Vaquería Yucateca** takes place at 9 pm (be there early) in front of the **Palacio Municipal** at the Plaza Mayor. This free concert and show features folk dancers and the police band performing traditional jarana dances where the dancers balance trays with bottles and glasses full of beer on their heads as they dance. How do they do it? This celebration is traditional with *vaqueros* (cowboys) who hold a fiesta after the hacienda cattle round-up. Free.

Tuesday: **Musical Memories** is a free concert of familiar and modern music at 9 pm at the **Parque Santiago**, Calle 59. Very popular. Next to the park there is a charming local *mercado* with flower vendors and many little places to eat. It's quieter and less pressured than larger *mercados*.

Wednesday: At 8 pm there's a music and poetry performance at the **Mayab Culture House** on Calle 63 between 64 and 66. The **Retreta**, a concert of music from the 18th century to the present, is performed at 9 pm in **Ermita Park**, the corner of Calles 66 and 77. Both are free.

Thursday: **Serenata Yucateca** at Parque Santa Lucia. This event, first begun on January 14, 1965, is a free showing of folk dance, poetry and musical entertainment and has become one of the most popular traditional evenings for Meridanos and tourists alike. There are plenty of seats under the stars.

Friday: **University Serenade**. Students from the university perform a collection of songs and dances typical of the Yucatán in the college garden of the university's main building. Starts at 9 pm, free admission. **Catholic Mass** in English is held at the Santa Lucia church, facing the park of the same name at 6 pm. The visually stunning **Ballet Folklórico** begins at 9 pm at the **Centro Cultural Universitario**, Calle 60 and 57 (☎ 999/924-6429). It showcases beautiful dress and music from all over Mexico – not to be missed.

Saturday: By far the biggest event in town is **la Noche Mexicana**, held in the little park at the beginning of the **Paseo Montejo** at Calle 47. A concert dance stage is set up for live music and traditional dance from other regions of Mexico. Local artisans show their wares along the cobblestone entryway. This event draws hundreds of people and the quality of the performers, who donate their time, is outstanding. Begins between 7:30 and 8 pm. Sabado is also **la Noche Romántica**, or "Romantic Night," which means that mariachis and musical groups perform in restaurants and bars throughout the town, plus the main square often has a show.

■ Sports

Big name **bullfight** matadors appear only during the "season," January through March, at the **Plaza de Toros**, Paseo de Reforma, near Colon. A **baseball** team, los Leones de Yucatán, plays February through July at the **Kukulcán Sports Center** on Calle 14, next to the Santa Clara Brewery in the south of town. The local **soccer** team, los Venados del Yucatán, is in the second division. Lately they've done very well. They play in the same sports center in the Carlos Iturralde Rivero Stadium. The phone (for both) is ☎ 999/940-0366.

Many hotels have **swimming** pools and **Hotel Colon** (☎ 999/923-4355) has a steam room. Otherwise, Meridanos go to Progreso to swim in the Gulf. The **Hyatt** and the **Holiday Inn** have **tennis courts** and there are several courts at **Club de Golf La Ceiba**, which also has a nine-hole **golf course** (☎ 999/927-0035). The **Club de Golf Yucatán** (☎ 999/924-7525), 16 km (10 miles) north of town on the way to Progreso, offers 18 holes with a par 72.

Shopping

T he peninsula's Yucatecan artisans produce some of the finest handicrafts in Mexico. *Hamacas* (hammocks) are a major item, along with *huipiles* and *guayaberas* (traditional clothing) and *huaraches*, leather hand-tooled sandals. Masks, baskets, pottery, Panama hats made from jipijapa palm leaves, gold and silver jewelry, leather crafts and belts, wood carvings and colorful party piñatas – all can be found in Mérida's major shopping area, the municipal market, south of the Plaza Mayor and on Sundays in the park bazaars.

> **AUTHOR'S TIP:** *Watch your valuables when you're in the crowded* mercado *area. Although theft is not a common occurrence, we once lost a camera to pickpockets here.*

■ Traditional Buys

For more handicrafts, try **Casa de Artesanias** on Calle 63, between 64 and 66. They have a wide selection of folk art and regional crafts. **El Arte Maya** is upstairs on Calle 60 between 63 and 65 facing the plaza. Also try the **Crafts Market** in the green *mercado* building at Calle 67 and 56.

COPAL

When you're in the *mercado* here, or in any country village, pick up some copal, a sticky resin incense in colors ranging from pale yellow to deep amber. Copal was used by the Maya for the last three thousand years. Shave thin slivers off the lump and burn or, even better, place a small amount on a lighted charcoal cone. It gives off an earthy fragrance that is redolent of myrrh, musk and pine. You'll find copal in a stall that sells religious items. See page 116 for a Cancún shop that sells Copal.

Several men's clothing shops are along Calle 59, including the well-known **Jack Guayaberas**, where you can have comfortable *guayabera* shirts made to order.

For jewelry, look in **La Perla Maya** on Calle 60 No. 485, or **Las Palomas**, also on Calle 60, between 53 and 55.

To pick up some of the best coffee from Chiapas and Veracruz, look for the roasting shop of **Frederico Navarro Alfaro**, Calle 58 between 47 and 49.

It's not far from the end of the Paseo. Otherwise, good coffee can be bought by the pound at **La Habana**, Calle 59 and 62, and it's sister restaurant, **El Gran Café**, at the end of Paseo Montejo, a few blocks from Navarro's shop.

Hammock seller in Chiapas.

How to Buy a Hammock

God's blessing on the man who invented sleep.

~ Sancho Panza in Cervantes' *Don Quixote de la Mancha*

Long before Columbus, Yucatecans slept on *hamacas* strung from wall hooks or outside between trees. When Spanish Conquistadors arrived, they quickly recognized the advantages of hammocks and incorporated them into their night life. Comfortable, durable, portable and easy to clean, they make safe cribs for young babies. The best hammocks made in Mexico are from the Yucatán and in Mérida, the heart of hammock industry, where they are sold on almost every street corner. They make great gifts and, once you get used to lying in one, you'll be drilling holes in your bedroom walls for the one you bring home.

Hammocks come in four sizes: *sencilla* (single), *doble* (double), *matrimonial* (queen-size) and *matrimonial especial*, the largest of all. Singles are really for children. Most tourists are amazed at the size of singles and some can be convinced into believing singles are queen-size by an enthusiastic vendor. Genuine matrimonials are about 16 feet long, one third of that being the main body. They should weigh an average of four to five pounds.

To check for a good weave, hold the hammock loosely in your hand and gently spread the strings apart. Spaces between the weaves should be no bigger than two inches or so. Good ones will have double that or, even better, triple string weaves. The hammock should also have a hundred or more pairs of strings (*brazas*) at each end gathered into the hanging loops, and these should be thick and tightly wrapped.

To see if a hammock is long enough for you, grab it at the edge where the body and the end-strings meet and hold your hand level with your forehead. The opposite end of the body should touch the floor. Most of the colorful ones that you see for sale will be nylon (the best choice for function and durability), although cotton and fine silk (so soft) are sometimes available.

The word "hammock" is the only surviving word of the Arawak Indian civilization, which was wiped out from their Caribbean islands by the Conquest.

Hammocks are in great abundance in Mérida and you will almost certainly be approached by a vendor. Despite their aggressive sales pitches, vendors are not all out to cheat you. But don't shop only by price. Quality counts, so always ask to see the best first. You'll probably find a better selection in the *mercado* at slightly higher prices.

Some excellent shops that deal almost exclusively in hammocks allow you to try out the goods before you buy. **La Poblano**, at Calles 60 & 58, has always been highly recommended. It's worth a visit just to see their extensive inventory. Open Monday-Saturday, 8 am-7 pm. Also recommended is the family-run **Hamacas El Aguacate** on Calle 58 at 73. Or you can drive or catch a bus to see hammocks being made in Tixkokob, a Colonial town east of the city whose awkward Mayan name means lyrically "where the nightingale sings." Virtually all the hammocks for sale in the Yucatán are handmade in family workshops. An English-speaking artisan, whose family makes quality hammocks and welcomes visitors, is **Gregorio Tuyub May**. He lives on Calle 21 No 138 between 28 and 30 in Tixkokob (☎ 999/911-0179).

■ American Outlets

A **Sam's Club** is located in the north of town on the continuation of Paseo Montejo on the way to Progreso. The **Costco** store is on Calle 60 north that parallels the prolongation of the Paseo, north of town. There are also two big suburban-style shopping malls, one with a **Liverpool** (a Mexican Bloomingdales) as the anchor store, near the new convention center. **Sears** anchors the other mall called the Gran Plaza. Sears also has a department store downtown on Calle 63, between 56 and 58.

Night Spots

Business was his aversion and pleasure was his business.
~ Maria Edgeworth 1767-1849

 Although Meridanos love their fiestas, their city isn't a late-night party town like Cancún. For some dancing and music, try **Pancho's**, on Calle 59 between 60 and 62, or **Carlos 'n Charlies**, an import from Cancún, on the Prolongación Montejo No. 477. The **Hotel Calinda Panamericana** has a disco on Calle 59 and 52 and so do the **Holiday Inn** and **Hyatt** hotels, side-by-side on Av. Colon off the Paseo.

If you want to see a movie, there are several theaters. We once saw *Schindler's List* subtitled in Spanish – now that was an experience! The **Cine Fantasio** faces Parque Hidalgo and is squeezed between the Gran Hotel and the Hotel Caribe. At the **Cinema 57** on Calle 59 between 68 and 70, Arnold Schwarzenegger once saved the United States while we were away. **Cine Premier** is on Calle 57 and 62. A brand new six-screen cinema with first-run movies is in the new **Siglo XXI Convention Center** north of town. Green buses that run up Calle 60 past the Hyatt stop there (30¢).

Hungry night owls will find their way to **La Habana Restaurant**, at the corner of 59 and 62 (see below), or the Yucatecan **Restaurante Caleca,** at 62 and 61 off the Plaza Mayor, both open 24 hours.

Adventures

Keep moving if you love life, and keep your troubles well behind you.
~ John McCain, US Senator, Arizona

■ Area Adventures

As a base to see and do other adventureous things in the Yucatán, Mérida is ideal. We offer ideas for local excursions along the *Convent Route* (page 380), the Ruta Puuc (page 375) and *For Adventure Guide Readers Only* (page 295). In fact, most of the state is accessible for day-trips so check out the compass point sections to see Uxmal, Chichén Itzá, Celestún, Dzibilchaltún, Izamal, cenotes, and more ruins.

■ Sights

The **Paseo de Montejo** is a wide tree-lined boulevard that begins at Calle 47 and runs north through the fine homes and mansions built in the belle époque-style by wealthy families and hacienda owners who made turn-of-the-century fortunes on the near-monopoly the Yucatán had in henequen. Some of the mansions are still private homes, but many are now used as office space. Still others have been replaced by more modern and garish office buildings. The trolley tour from Santa Lucia Park (see *Organized City Tours*, below) will include other impressive homes in a nearby neighborhood. The Paseo is a popular place to take *calesa*, horse-drawn carriage rides, day and night. Check for them near the Holiday Inn on Av. Colon and the Paseo. North of there, at the circle of the Paseo and 59a, is the monumental **Monumento a la Patria**, created by Colombian sculptor Romulo Rozo, depicting the tumultuous history of Mexico and its 32 states.

The **Museo Regional de Antropologia** (Anthropology Museum) is in the Palacio Cantón (entrance on Calle 43 and Paseo de Montejo, ☎ 999/923-0557). Designed by Enrico Deserti, the Italian architect who did the Teatro Peón Contreras downtown, the opulent museum was built around 1911 as a home for General Francisco Cantón. The home became the official residence of the governor of Yucatán before opening as the rich anthropological showpiece of the Yucatán's historical treasures.

> **AUTHOR'S TIP:** *If you're looking for a good inexpensive dinner along the pricey boulevard, we recommend the **Cafeteria Impala** at the start of the Paseo and 47. Even more native are the eateries surrounding little Parque Santa Ana on Calle 47, a half-block west of the Paseo's beginning. A string of outdoor restaurants there, jammed into the little street, are super-popular for good, inexpensive food and drink. Open early and late.*

Museo Regional de Artes Populares is on Calle 59, between 48 and 50. This free museum displays artwork, textiles and regional handicrafts. It also has a unique gift shop. One block west is the square where you'll find **Los Almendros** restaurant.

Only three gates remain of the 13 that once permitted entrance into Mérida's walled city. The **Arco de Dragones** is on Calle 63 at Calle 50. The **Arco del Puente** is one block south on Calle 61 and 50. Its most interesting feature is the pedestrian tunnel cut into the south side of the arch, connecting sidewalks. It requires one-at-a-time passage while you bend over to fit through its approximate four-foot height. The most attractive gate is the **Arco de San Juan** (Calle 64 at 69) in front of a park of the same name. The buildings to either side used the old wall as part of their construction, and the red cobblestone road, Calle 64, is the former Camino Real (Royal Road) that connected Mérida to Campeche. The narrow street is lined with closely built Colonial homes lit at night by golden yellow streetlights. There's something inexplicably attractive about this little section of town around the old gate. Nearby, under a gigantic shade tree, is the tiny **Ermita de Santa Isabel**

church, where travelers customarily prayed before setting out along the Royal Road into the countryside. It's the smallest house of worship in the city.

The **Cementerio General**, the permanent home of Mérida's citizenry of yore, is south of the Colonial center toward the airport on Calle 66 or Calle 90 off of Av. Itzáes, which is the road to Campeche. We're cemetery freaks so it appealed to us. It's somewhat hard to find, despite its large size. Once there, you'll be struck by the wall-to-wall mausoleums with more angels than there are in heaven. The grave of Felipe Carrillo Puerto and the stone wall where he and his brothers were executed in 1924 flank the little snack bar where the public road bends. Under the pine tree opposite is the grave of his fiancée, American journalist Alma Reed, who pined for him until her death in 1966. Francisco Pancho is the caretaker, but he couldn't help us find Mundaca's grave.

Parque Zoologico El Centerario sits at the intersection of Av. Itzáes and the west end of Calle 59. This large zoo and children's amusement park is filled on Sundays as families jam its shady wooded walkways, picnic area and small lake where they rent rowboats. Free admission. Children will like this better than those boring old ruins you've been dragging them to. Nearby is the Juárez former Penitentiary, a huge yellow building in front of Parque de la Paz.

> **AUTHOR'S TIP:** *If you are out by the zoo there's a very good grilled chicken restaurant nearby on the west side of Av. Itzáes called* **Pollo Brujo**. *This clean and very tasty fast-food eatery is a good place to try pollo asado or pollo carbon.*

Organized City Tours

A pleasant way to get a city overview is the **Discover Mérida** two-hour sightseeing tour offered in an open-sided trolley bus. It leaves Santa Lucia Park at 10 am and 1, 4 and 7 pm daily and costs US $8 (☎ 999/927-6119). A bilingual guide (ours was named Misty Chuc – talk about cross-cultures, a Maya valley girl?) accompanies the run, which stops at a sculpture park, Parque de las Americas, midway, to stretch your legs. Another trip around Mérida, then up to the ruins of Dzibilchaltún, leaves at 9 am, Tuesday through Sunday (US $10). Horse-drawn carriages also tour the downtown and brightly lit Paseo Montejo.

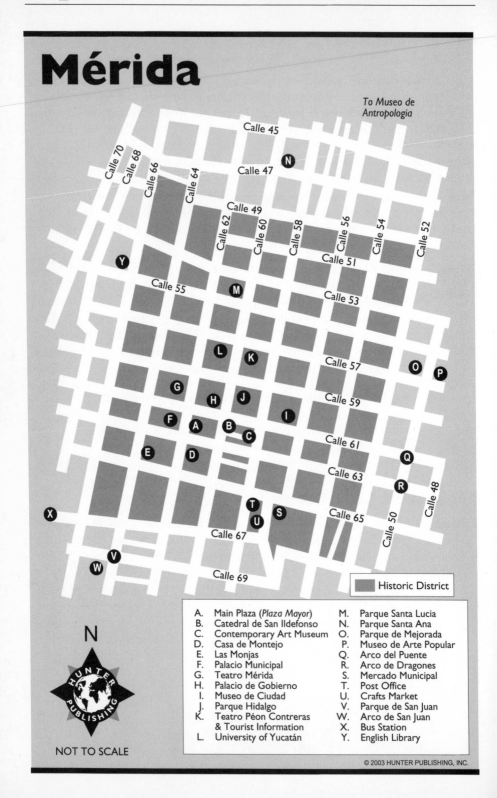

Mérida

To Museo de Antropologia

Historic District

A.	Main Plaza (*Plaza Mayor*)	M.	Parque Santa Lucia
B.	Catedral de San Ildefonso	N.	Parque Santa Ana
C.	Contemporary Art Museum	O.	Parque de Mejorada
D.	Casa de Montejo	P.	Museo de Arte Popular
E.	Las Monjas	Q.	Arco del Puente
F.	Palacio Municipal	R.	Arco de Dragones
G.	Teatro Mérida	S.	Mercado Municipal
H.	Palacio de Gobierno	T.	Post Office
I.	Museo de Ciudad	U.	Crafts Market
J.	Parque Hidalgo	V.	Parque de San Juan
K.	Teatro Péon Contreras	W.	Arco de San Juan
	& Tourist Information	X.	Bus Station
L.	University of Yucatán	Y.	English Library

N

HUNTER PUBLISHING

NOT TO SCALE

© 2003 HUNTER PUBLISHING, INC.

■ Adventures on Foot

Walking Mérida

Most of Mérida's in-town adventures involve absorbing the soul of the city through the soles of your feet. A morning walking tour of Mérida is a wonderful way to see the town. Start at the **Plaza Mayor**, the center of the original walled city. ●A● The plaza went through several names, beginning with the Plaza de Armas, where Montejo's original troops paraded. It still can't make up its mind because it's also known as the Plaza Principal and the Zócalo. The large circular walkway, under shade trees, revolves around a garden and laurel topiaries – a magnificent Mexican obsession. Iron benches and *confidenciales* offer perfect places to people-watch. Friendly Meridanos may approach you to practice their English.

To the east of the park on Calle 60 at 61 is the hulking **Catedral de San Ildefonso** ●B● begun in 1561 with stones from the Maya pyramids at T'Ho and finally completed in 1598. It is the oldest cathedral in North America and considered the finest Colonial monument of the Spanish in the New World. The plain, fortress-like exterior was part of a functional design. The indigenous people of the Yucatán didn't take too kindly to the Spanish invaders and, time and again, churches served as a last line of defensive fortification. Inside the thick walls the interior décor is equally unadorned but the main altar is impressive and supposedly the second-largest in the world. To the side of the altar is the small shrine to the charred crucifix of **Cristo de las Ampollas**. It was carved

Catedral de San Ildefonso towers over the square in Mérida.

from a tree that was struck by lightening and burned all night, but remained unscathed by the flames. A subsequent church fire left it with the blisters that give it its name: "Christ of the Blisters." When church is in service, there are poor and crippled people asking alms just inside the doorways. We can't help but give.

Next door to the Cathedral the "**Ateneo Peninsula**," the former palatial home of the Yucatán's Bishop built between 1573 and 1636, is now the **MACAY**, the Contemporary Art Museum of the Yucatán ●C● (☎ 999/928-3258, US $3). It is open daily and Sundays 10 am-6 pm, closed Tuesdays. The air-conditioned salons where big shots of the Franciscan order once roamed now contain interesting art exhibits that change every three months. In 1916 General Salvador Alvardo, the Mexican commander who put down the Yucatán's bid for independence during the 1915 Mexican Revolution, created a wide pedestrian passage known as the **Pasaje de la Revolution** that separates the cathedral and the museum. Until the 1940s, an extravagant glass roof covered the walkway.

Two former Franciscan monasteries survive in Mérida. **Las Monjas** ("The Nuns") was founded in 1589 for the Conceptionist Order of the Poor Clares. It's on Calle 63 and 64 just west of the main plaza. **La Mejorada** is a monastic retreat for the conservative Observant Franciscan Recollect. It's on Calle 50 and 59, and now serves as the University of Yucatán's School of Architecture. The upper cloister provides access to the church choir and roof for a great view, if they let you go. **Las Monjas** ●E●, with its Moorish-style mirador added in 1648, is one and a half blocks west of the Casa de Montejo at 63 and 64.

The **Casa de Montejo** ●D● is the stately mansion across from the south side of the plaza, built by Francisco Montejo for his family beginning in 1542. Incredibly, his family descendants lived there for 435 years until the late 1970s when Banamex Bank bought and restored the property. The Colonial façade is typically high-walled and plain, but an intricate bas-relief around the doorway reminds the Maya daily of the Conquest and the power of the Montejos. It shows two Spanish knights standing upon the heads of defeated Maya warriors, whose mouths cry out in pain. The stone inscription in Spanish reads, "The Adelante Don Francisco Montejo caused this to be made in the year 1549." The sculpted window frames and doorway were all restored in 2000. You can walk inside to some public areas whenever the bank is open.

On the west side of the plaza is the yellow **Palacio Municipal**, ●F● site of much of Mérida's Sunday entertainment and reportedly the place where the last Maya building was dismantled. It's also the locale for Monday night's Vaquería Yucateca exhibition (see page 282). Next door to it is a modern exposition hall behind a modern Colonial façade. It frequently hosts art shows in salons off its giant round atrium and there is a concert there almost every night at 9 pm. Rumor has it is also scheduled to have a planetarium. A half-block north, on the left, is the new Art Deco-style **Teatro Mérida** ●G●. Gleaming chrome and glass block have transported this former run-down movie house into an Edwardian delight – and a new theatrical and cultural icon for the city. They could film an episode of Hercule Poirot here. Across the street is a small Italian restaurant, **Pan e Vino**, in case the three tenors come to town.

Under the arches along Calle 61 on the northern border of the plaza is the **Palacio del Gobierno ●H●**. It's open to the public and offers a fine collection of paintings depicting the Yucatán's tragic history. The vividly colored murals, upstairs in the Salon de Historia, were completed in 1978 by local artist, Fernando Pacheco Castro. The Salon hosts a performance every Sunday at 11 am. Outside its high French windows are wrought iron balconies with wonderful views of the park and cathedral. In 1999 they installed glass doors that now limit access (and photography) from the balconies. Under the portales that run the length of the building there are several restaurants, including **Pizzeria Bella**, a very tasty pizzeria, and the **Dulcería y Sorbetería** ice cream parlor, where a dreamy assortment of ice creams and sherbets come in exotic tropical flavors. There is also an excellent hairdresser/barber shop next door on Calle 61.

The opposite corner of Calle 61 at Calle 60, along the side of the cathedral, is a good place to pick up a *casela*, a horse-drawn buggy, for touring the town. One block east is the **Museo de la Ciudad ●I●**, a small museum of the city in a former convent chapel.

Back on Calle 60 heading north are several interesting gift stores and on your left is the **Teatro Daniel Ayala**, another professional theater in culture-rich Mérida. On the right is the **Parque Hidalgo ●J●**, where small outdoor restaurants line the way and hammock vendors lie in wait. Next comes the ancient **Iglesia de Jesus**, built in 1618 by the Jesuits. It's one of Mérida's older buildings. This church, with the quiet little Parque de la Madre in front, is a favorite site for weddings and its antique exterior is a great backdrop for photos. The west wall has faint markings of Maya carvings from the stones of the building that stood on this site.

The huge Italianate **Teatro Peón Contreras ●K●** is next with the tourist information center in the corner office. Don't miss a chance to tour the Teatro or, even better, see a theatrical or music production in this jewel of Mérida's architecture. The ornate interior is breathtakingly impressive. On the cobblestone side street is the **Café Peón Contreras**, a romantic sidewalk restaurant that features cappuccino and Cuban coffee. With an inviting atmosphere, it definitely has the best outdoor seating in Mérida. The theater was designed in 1908 by Italian architect Enrico Deserti along the lines of the great European opera houses. The sweeping marble staircase and frescoed dome were restored in the 1980s to their earlier glory. The apogee of culture in Mérida, it attracts international stars.

The **University of the Yucatán ●L●** stands across the street behind black iron gates and big wooden doors. Inside, the courtyard looks up at Moorish-style arches on the hallways surrounding the building that dates from 1711. Site of a Jesuit college, the State University was founded in the 1920s by Felipe Carrillo Puerto. It now holds school offices and a cultural center for students.

Yucatán

The small **Parque Santa Lucia •M•** is rather plain during the day, but is a popular place on Thursday evenings when the **Yucatecan Serenade** occurs. Regulated to a Poets' Corner are busts of some of Yucatán's beloved musicians and poets. A small church across from the park, built in the late 1500s for African and Caribbean slaves that lived in the district, offers an English Mass on Saturday evenings at 6 pm.

Turn left to Calle 56 and return to the square past more beautiful Colonial buildings.

■ Adventures on Wheels

There's a **train excursion** on a special rail car to Izamal, the "Yellow City," and tickets are available at any travel agency or the Cultur office at the Centro de Convenciones on Calle 60 Norte, No. 301. The train leaves 8:15 am every Sunday from Central Station at the corner of 48 and 55. The US $18 per-person price includes transportation in town by Victoria horse-drawn coaches with a lunch and folklore music and dance show at the Parador Turistica. The train leaves Izamal at 3:20 and returns to Mérida at 5:10 pm.

For a "Discover Izamal" **bus tour** every Monday, Wednesday, Friday and Saturday, contact **Transportación Turística Carnaval** at ☎ 999/927-6119, or get in touch with a local travel agent. There's also s scheduled bus tour to ruins and sights offered by **Turitransmerida** at Calle 55 and 58 (☎ 999/924-1199, www.turitransmerida.com.mx). Seven days a week to Uxmal, Chichén, and Celestun; several days a week to Dzibilchaltun and Progreso, Izamal, cenotes, or the Ruta Puuc.

ADS bus lines have a special tour bus that departs Mérida at 8 or 8:30 am (Calle 69) for the Maya ruins at Uxmal, as well as the other important Puuc sites. It returns to town about 4 or 4:30 pm. Check with the bus line at the terminal for schedule changes. There is also second-class bus service that stops along the route, but ask at the main bus station before you board to make sure.

For Adventure Guide Readers Only

Writers and travelers are mesmerized alike by
knowing of their destinations.
~ Eudora Welty, speaking at Harvard, 1984

Exclusively for readers of this book, we've arranged visits to two working henequen/sisal factories to see the how valuable local fiber is grown and used.

The first is **Hacienda San Antonio Tehuitz**, in the suburbs of Kanasin, five km (three miles) east of town from Calle 69. Call Ileana Zapata or Gustavo Baas in the Kanasin city hall between 8 am and 1 pm at ☎ 999/988-0131. The small plant where the fiber is made is open from 5 pm to 11 pm, Monday, Wednesday and Friday. Señor Arsenio Rocha directs the factory.

A second place that will welcome *Adventure Guide* readers is the **Hacienda Chunkanan**, 56 km from Mérida, where they will also take you by truck to several beautiful close-by cenotes, including a fabulously impressive one: Bolon-Cho-Hool. Follow the Convent Route directions to Acanceh (page 380), then continue on the road to Cuzama. A sign in the village directs you to the hacienda on the right. No prearrangements are necessary, they're open during the day.

Try sliding down ropes into deep caverns and mysterious caves with Monica Mora and Fernando Torres of **Deep Rock Adventures** (☎ 999/987-2592, deeprockadventures@yahoo.com.mx). They operate out of Mérida and get into some some very interesting, out-of-the-way caves and cenotes in the Yucatán countryside.

TIE ME UP, TIE ME DOWN

Henequen is one of the most versatile plants in the huge agave family, whose plant leaf fibers are used to make cord and rope. Agaves are also used to produce the alcoholic drink, *pulque*, and tequila is fermented from yet another variety. The pulp of other types is used as food and to produce soap. You'll see rolling fields of the spiny plants behind rock walls all over northern Yucatán. The other name for them is sisal (see-SAL) after the Yucatán port.

The plants have leaves up to six feet long and a flower stalk (which can be 40 feet high). It blooms only once and then dies. They take five to 10 years to mature (lives can be prolonged by cutting some leaves each year). The sword-like leaves are 30 to 60 inches long and four to five inches wide, ending in sharp points. They are cut by hand, trimmed of their top spine and side needles. One person and helper can cut from 3,000 to 5,000 leaves in a day.

Narrow gauge railways were once employed to transport the bundled leaves to a plantation mill. Now trucks and tractors handle most of that task. At the mill, machines beat and scrape the pulp from the fiber, which is then dried in the sun or in drying machines and sorted into grades according to length and quality. Originally used in agriculture balers, the natural fiber has more recently found a home in furniture manufacturing.

During the period the Yucatán was the sole source of henequen, extensive plantations allowed hacienda owners to amass fortunes, leading to an economic boom that transformed the countryside. To provide labor, much of the Indian population was forced into debt peonage, the equivalent of slavery. Today, Tanzania, Brazil and Kenya are the main sources of better quality sisal, though the Yucatán still produces a large amount of henequen.

Accommodations

If some people didn't tell you,
you'd never know they'd been away on vacation.
~ Elbert Hubbard, 1856-1915

 Mérida has the luxury of being the commercial and cultural center of the Yucatán, as well as a tourist destination in itself. In fact, the city's busiest season comes when Mexican tourists vacation here in July and August. The city center's buildings are almost exclusively Colonial relics from the halcyon days when Mérida was know as the "White City" and the "Paris of the West." So it's natural that accommodations here span the range from "contemporary comfortable" and "Colonial rustic" to "Colonial charming." It's the latter that we find most pleasing, as they offer a chance to live in the past with the conveniences of today.

MERIDA'S BUDGET HOTELS

Those of you who normally choose hotels in the "Moderate" category, because of comfort and quality, should still look closely at Mérida's budget hotels, as many of them deliver what you're looking for at a very low price.

■ Hostel Hotels

Nómadas Youth Hostel *(Calle 62 at 51, ☎ 999/924-5223, fax 999/928-1697, www. hostels.com.mx, nomadashostel@hotmail. com, travel agency).* A charming couple, Raul and Geovanna, have opened this finely tuned and sparkling clean youth hostel that, of course, accepts all ages. It was brand new in 2000 and is a step above most hostels we've seen. Private rooms with bath contain two queen beds and are a real bargain. The dorms can sleep 28 in bunk beds, with lockers, shared baths and a kitchen. Nice touches include a washroom, rooftop clothesline, purified drinking water to fill your bottles, microwave, coffee machine, juicer, Internet access, bike rentals and a helpful staff. If you're lucky enough to secure one of the private rooms, it beats many of the plain local hotels. If you're into hosteling, this is the place to stay.

HOTEL PRICE CHART	
NOTE: *Often, one shared bed in a room is cheaper than two. Prices based on cost per night, for two.*	
[No $]	Less than US $20
$	US $20 - $40
$$	US $40 - $80
$$$	US $80 - $125

Rainbow Trailer Park *(Highway 261 north of the city, no phone).* Big enough for RVs, this trailer park in the shadow of the huge Tejidos de Hennequen Yucatán factory offers hot water, showers, electric and a swimming pool. The location doesn't give much of a view, but the park is close enough to town on the road to Progreso to make it worthwhile for camping or parking the rig while day-tripping the entire northern Yucatán area. Mérida has spread so far north that a huge shopping center and the new convention center are very close on the other side of the henequen factory. Buses and combis stop out front for rides into the downtown.

Hotel Oviedo *(Calle 62 No. 515 between 65 & 67, ☎ 999/928-5618, 33 rooms with fans).* The Oviedo is another Colonial mansion converted into a hotel. It's clean but rather spartan. It gives you an idea of what it was like sleeping back in Colonial times as the rooms haven't changed much since Zorro slept here. There's private parking in the center courtyard. Huge old doors open into each room.

Hotel Sevilla *(Calle 62 No. 511 near 65, ☎ 999/928-8360, 28 rooms with fans).* The Sevilla hangs a wooden sign outside, announcing its membership in the Mérida hotel association. It's such an official-looking sign we first mistook the building for government offices. Inside, this very old Colonial hotel is awash in marble and tile. Check out the carved marble lion next to the patio with a very pretty garden in the center. The rooms, which are also traditional Colonial, are very basic. The Sevilla is one of those frustratingly charming places that has the potential to be great, but isn't.

Hotel Trinidad Galeria *(Calle 60, corner of 51, ☎ 999/923-2463, fax 999/924-2319, 31 rooms with fans, pool, 24-hour free coffee, tea, water).* The Galeria has a creative, bohemian "coffee shop" atmosphere. It's the other Mérida hotel of artist Manolo Rivero, in case you couldn't guess from all the artwork on display. *ArtNexus*, a bilingual art magazine, considers both Trinidad hotels in Mérida to be "museums." The big atrium-like entrance is a jungle of plants and sculpture. In the labyrinth of hallways under large overhangs are sculpture, paintings, plants and artwork situated around comfortable sitting areas. More area is dedicated to relaxing than to accommodations. Guests we talked to raved over the ambiance, but were unimpressed with the sleeping quarters. The low-ceilinged rooms have only two small windows but are painted completely white to help lighten them. Unique. $

The Nest Backpackers Hostel *(Calle 67, between 68 & 70, no phone, www.nesthostel.com).* This is brand new and two blocks from the bus station. Air-conditioned dorm rooms, plus double beds for couples. Landscaped gardens and a rooftop beer garden. Hammock heaven for the young at heart.

■ Budget Hotels

Dolores Alba *(Calle 63 No. 464 between 54 & 52, ☎ 999/928-5650, fax 999/928-3163, www.doloresalba.com, 90 rooms with air or fans, pool, TV, phone, restaurant, private parking).* Doña Sanchez and her sons converted their own three-story family mansion into an appealing hotel just up the street from one of the Colonial gates to the city, El Arco del Dragones. Despite its location only two blocks from the busy *mercado* shopping area, the Dolores Alba is quiet and comfortable. In 1999 the hotel built all new superior rooms that surround a large, high-arched courtyard with a sparkling blue pool with the soothing sound of a waterfall, and greenery. The new accommodations are very large, with two queen-size beds, reading lamps, tiled floors and bath. Big mirrored windows facing the central courtyard give more light and space, while still insuring privacy. Private covered parking is available. No credit cards accepted. An excellent value, clean and very popular – for good reason. The Sanchez family, experienced hoteliers, also operate another Dolores Alba in Chichén Itzá, about three km (1.8 miles) from the ruins. $-$$

Posada Toledo *(Calle 58 at 57, No. 487, ☎ 999/923-1690, fax 999/923-2256, hptoledo@finred.com.mx, 23 rooms with air or fans).* The Toledo is a mark above most former Colonial homes converted into hotels. Located close to all the action in the Centro, the Toledo is an oasis of cool green garden in its courtyard and in its high-arched, tiled hallways that grace the western side. It's picture perfect and has everything you think of when you think Colonial mansion. Along the street side, the rooms are more hotel-like, but #25, the upstairs back suite (US $50), is the former master bedroom of the Hernández Guerra family, the hotel's owners. Heavy Spanish wood furniture dominates here, even in the fancy dining room (breakfast only) at the rear of the garden. The hotel is very popular, so reservations are recommended. $-$$

Hotel Montejo *(Calle 57 No. 507,* ☎ *999/928-0277, 22 rooms with air or fans, 1 suite, restaurant, travel bureau).* Two blocks up the street from the Teatro Peón Contreras, the Montejo may be one of the least changed of all the hotels that were once the private homes of wealthy Spanish Colonials. The ambiance is old, from the heavy wooden ceiling beams to the polished wooden doors. Unfortunately, some of the clean bed linen is somewhat old and worn. The center courtyard drips with cool greenery. Doubles have two twin beds. There is an air-conditioned restaurant downstairs where you can charge to your room. A 24-hour public parking lot is just down the street. Noted Maya scholars such as Michael Coe sometimes stay here while they're in town. $

Hotel Trinidad *(Calle 62, between 55 & 57,* ☎ *999/923-2033, fax 999/924-1112, www.hoteltrinidad.com, 19 rooms with fans, 3 share a bathroom, 24-hour free coffee, tea, water).* The Trinidad is one of two bohemian Colonial hotels owned by noted Mexican artist and collector Manolo Rivero. Walk into the Trinidad and enter a stunning world of eclectic art, including huge Colonial mirrors, painted over Picasso-style, and a hotel staff out of the 1940s. If they played music in the lobby it might be Edith Piaf or Segovia; either would complement the time-warp feeling. The entryway has two dark, art-filled sitting areas with dusty overstuffed furniture. Rooms are built around two courtyards. Those around the first courtyard are more appealing – Colonial-styled with high ceilings. A "super artist's suite" with a king-size bed and "luxury" bathroom is also available. Tall trees grow up over the center patio walls so it's cool and quiet. There's a sunny lounge area on the roof. You can pay with a credit card if you pay in advance and can use the pool at the nearby sister hotel. Artsy-funky. 20% discount for students. $

Hotel Santa Lucia *(Calle 55 No. 508 between 60 & 62,* ☎ */fax 999/928-2672, www.hotelsantalucia.com.mx, 51 rooms with air, pool, security safe, TV, secured parking nearby, car rental).* Located just across the road from the happening Plaza Santa Lucia, this Colonial home was expertly altered from mansion to two-story hotel in 1990. Solid wooden doors lead to cheery rooms that have two queen-size beds and clean tiled bathrooms. Three corner rooms have balconies overlooking a small pool and patio and there's a wrought-iron spiral staircase from the pool to the second floor. The Santa Lucia is a good choice if you're into Colonial-era hotel rooms without the dark woods. They also own the Hotel San Juan down the street and the Hotel San Clemente in Valladolid. $

Hotel San Juan *(Calle 55 No. 497A between 60 & 58, ☎/fax 999/924-1742, www.hotelsanjuan.com.mx, 63 rooms with air, pool).* This new (1996) hotel, a half-block up from the delightful Santa Lucia Park, is an attractive conversion of an old Colonial building. It is a sister hotel to the Santa Lucia down the street, but with smaller rooms and slightly higher prices. Rooms have all light woods and white tiles and outside there's a narrow courtyard for sun worshippers and an appealing little pool. Because of its popularity, a third story was added in 1999. $

Hotel María José *(Calle 64, between 53 & 55, ☎ 999/928-7037, 20 rooms, 2 suites, air, cable, parking).* The bright pink María is a modern hotel (July 2002) in an old Colonial building. Although it doesn't have a Colonial ambience, it is a good value, with wide, open hallways and pleasingly clean rooms. Quarters on the left upstairs are a shade larger than those on the right. Breakfast buffet available. $

Hotel Ambassador *(Calle 59 No. 546, corner of 68, ☎ 999/924-2100, fax 999/924-2701, 100 rooms with air, pool, secure free parking, restaurant, TV).* The modern Ambassador has aged better inside than out. Attractive and comfortable rooms with two queen-size beds face a small green courtyard, behind which are a restaurant and inviting pool. Outside, the once intriguing exterior of mosaic tiles that face the side street on each floor is in need of a facelift. Flags out front give it a European flair. Marble-tiled room walls and modern bathrooms are great, but the hot water here is lacking. The small restaurant, **La Luz**, serves good basic Mexican food and very good coffee. Ask about the hotel's excellent value package rate that includes breakfast. $

Casa Bowen *(Calle 66 No. 521-B at the corner of 65, ☎ 999/928-6109, 28 rooms with air or fans, 6 of them with kitchenettes, private parking).* Despite the sometimes surly front desk staff, dollar for dollar the Casa Bowen is one of the better values in town in the budget category. Colorful tile work and marble grace the public areas, where there are many sitting nooks tucked into corners. There's a small lounging area with a TV next to the attractive cool garden that grows in the first courtyard. The rooms are plain but clean and use a lot of frosted glass. It's a comfortable Colonial hotel in two buildings. The building on the side has parking in its courtyard and the upstairs rooms are the ones with kitchenettes. They contain an old fridge, gas stove, sink and a card table for dining; ask for your pots and tableware. Across the street there's an inexpensive small restaurant, which is much loved by budget-minded Italians who stay at the Bowen. The hotel owner also rents a four-bedroom house in Progreso for around US $600 per month. $

Hotel Reforma *(Calle 59 No. 508 at the corner of 62, ☎ 999/924-7922, fax 999/928-3278, 45 rooms with air or fans, pool, travel agency).* The entry hall walls of the old Reforma Colonial hotel feature mosaic tile around a tiny, square courtyard. Upstairs rooms are the nicer, with two queen-size beds in each high-ceilinged, tile-floored room. The clean bathrooms are also an advantage. The perennially popular Reforma is located on a busy corner close to all the action, so choose a room that faces the deep blue pool or the patio. Friendly, helpful staff. $

Hotel Aragon *(Calle 57 #474 between 52 & 54, ☎ 999/924-0242, fax 999/924-1122, info@hotelaragon.com, 17 rooms, 1 jr. suite, air, fans, TV, continental breakfast).* This old Colonial hotel has changed its name and management but retains its value. Each standard room offers two double beds, while the suite has a king-size. The cute little patio around back has five black wrought-iron tables where a free continental breakfast is offered. Complimentary coffee, tea and purified water available 24 hours. $-$$

HOTEL PRICE CHART	
NOTE: *Often, one shared bed in a room is cheaper than two. Prices based on cost per night, for two.*	
[No $]	Less than US $20
$	US $20 - $40
$$	US $40 - $80
$$$	US $80 - $125

Hotel Colon *(Calle 62 No. 483 between 57 & 59, ☎ 999/923-4355, fax 999/924-4919, www.thenettraveler.com/hotelcolon, 53 rooms with air, 12 jr. suites, telephone, TV, pool, restaurant, steam baths & masseur).* The historic Colon was converted into a landmark hotel from an old Colonial mansion way back in 1920. It's been modernized since then, and the rooms are clean, comfortable and very large, with both a shower and a bathtub in each bathroom. It's an old hotel with impressive tile work – some of the ceilings are tin, stamped during the Victorian era – and offers most modern comforts. Fortunately, when it was modernized, they left the gorgeous tiled entry foyer and private steam baths, which local Meridanos have always used – and you can too. Built long before steam baths acquired an unsavory reputation in the States, the individual hot baths here are from a time gone by. Pastoral scenes and colorful patterns hand-painted on tiles make this a must see even if you don't partake of your own private steam bath. The baths are attractive and well lit, and come complete with double shower and a cool in-room swimming pool with, for a touch of scandal, a mirrored ceiling. You can reserve one even if you don't stay here (they are open from 3 pm to 9 pm; bring a decent towel, the ones for rent are thin). Massage may be arranged in advance. Six steam-only rooms have a shower, toilet and tile settee all done in functional plain white tile. The hotel also boasts a pleasing outdoor pool and quiet tropical gardens plus an inexpensive restaurant. Shhhh... this is one of our secret favorites. $-$$

■ Moderate Hotels

Casa Mexilio *(Calle 68 No. 495 between 59 & 57, US ☎ 800/538-6802, Mexico ☎ 999/928-2505, www.mexonline.com/casamexilio.htm, 11 rooms total with air or fans, pool, jacuzzi, rates include full breakfast).* There are some homes in Colonial Mérida – hidden behind centuries-old walls – that are just marvelous inside. This is one of them. Casa Mexilio, an old, multilevel Spanish house, almost defies description. The rooms are individually decorated and woven into a quilt of gardens and patios. We "oohed" and "aahed" at each unique guest room. We wandered across a wooden bridge over a lovely garden and up outside steps to a rooftop patio with a magnificent view of the city at night. Then we dipped down again to a high-walled courtyard garden with a cenote-style swimming pool and jacuzzi. The Casa's American owner has quixotic taste in décor and has filled his intimate hotel with collectibles he has acquired in 20 years of wandering Mexico. A stay here is an experience and a delight. Book ahead for a great boutique hotel experience. $$

Luz en Yucatan (*Calle 55 next to the Santa Lucia Church, ☎/fax 999/924-0035, www.luzenyucatan.com, studio apartments, kitchen, pool, air, spa services*). What began as a health retreat in the middle of the Colonial heart of Mérida, right next to the Santa Lucia church, has matured into an excellent place to spend a longer term – even if you're not interested in their weight loss, holistic health or spa offerings. Well-appointed, one-bedroom studios or two-bedroom apartments have been built in a Colonial building with plenty of comfortable sitting and meditation areas. There's a small backyard pool and an overall feeling of tranquility. Check out the cat's paw prints in the cement steps leading to the second floor. $$

In Ka'an Bed & Breakfast (*Calle 15, between 24 & 26, ☎/fax 999/943-4156, www.inkaan.com, 7 rooms, air, TV, includes breakfast*). Retired Canadians Bill & Bonnie Wrenshall designed their own dream home in 1994 that they now share with weary travelers. ("In Ka'an" means "my heaven.") Two guest houses, with two bedrooms each, flank the impressively large swimming pool and 23-meter lap pool. Each house is fully equipped with kitchen and is ideal for families or longer stays. The low-rise Colonial-style main home has three bedrooms, two with queen-size beds and one with two twin beds, plus they offer two one-bedroom and one two-bedroom apartments. An acre of gardens graces the fenced property in a quiet suburb in the northeast of the city. The B&B is in a *barrio* of Mérida called Colonia Maya, near the *periferica*, so these street directions are not in the downtown. Take a taxi or call ahead for directions. $$

Medio Mundo (*Calle 55, between 64 & 66, ☎/fax 999/924-5472, www.hotelmediomundo.com, 10 rooms, air or fans, pool*). It took only two years for owners Nelson and Nicole to completely restore and convert one of Mérida's old homes into an intimate and immaculate new hotel. But it took much longer searching through Spain and Mexico to find just the right property to fulfill their dream. Painted in a bright hacienda blue, the large comfortable rooms here are super clean with separate washrooms from the bathrooms – a plus. A small kidney-shaped pool, located in the back garden where there's a cantina-like juice bar that also offers a full breakfast (US $7), is very inviting.

Beautiful Talavera tile and attention to every detail, the Medio Mundo does nothing by half. $$

Gran Hotel *(Calle 60 No. 496 at Parque Hidalgo, ☎ 999/923-6963, fax 999/924-7622, 30 rooms with air, 2 suites, restaurant, TV).* The historic Gran Hotel received a 1987 facelift and looks much as it did when it opened originally in 1901. The French Neoclassic design is painted a cool mint green and faces the popular Hidalgo Park, only one block from the main *zócalo.* The rooms are modern, complete with high ceilings and arches, and set in an elegant turn-of-the-century building. This hotel is reminiscent of other "Gran" or "Grand" hotels that grace main squares in many Spanish Colonial capitals. In the cool entranceway there is a small restaurant, El Patio, where you can dine indoors or al fresco. $$

Hotel Caribe *(Calle 59 at Parque Hidalgo, ☎ 999/924-9022, fax 999/924-8733, www.hotelcaribe.com.mx, 42 rooms with air or fans, restaurant, pool).* In the beginning (1876) it was the "Convent de Monjas," a nun's Catholic high school. After that auspicious inauguration, it became the founding site of the University of Yucatán before finally opening as an elegant hotel in 1941. There's a rooftop pool and sun patio and the Hotel Caribe's accommodations make it a worthy competitor to the Gran Hotel next door. Its interior courtyard is part of the El Rincón ("Corner") restaurant, which serves elegant meals at reasonable prices. Rooms run from Colonial to modern in their furnishings, so take your pick. Helpful, courteous staff. $$

Casa Del Balam *(Calle 60 between 57 & 55, ☎ 999/924-2150, fax 999/924-5011, www.yucatanadventure.com.mx, 51 jr. suites, air, pool, cable TV, restaurant & bar).* This was once the opulent Moorish-styled home of Señor and Señora Fernando Barbachano, tourism pioneers in the Yucatán and owners of the Mayaland resorts. This elegant old hotel with much greenery on its cool patio and central courtyard is now run by their daughter, Carmen. Despite its modern amenities, including hair dryers and welcome soundproof windows, the "House of the Jaguar" retains its Colonial charm with marble floors, wrought-iron patio furniture, antiques and carved stone arches. Next door to the Teatro Peón Contreras concert hall/theater. $$

Misíon de Fray Diego *(Calle 61, between 64 & 66, in US & Canada ☎ 866/639-2933, in Mexico ☎ 999/924-1111, http://lamisiondefraydiego.com, 20 rooms, 4 deluxe, 2 suites with jacuzzis, cable, air, restaurant, pool, valet parking).* La Mision de Fray Diego is a beautiful, three-story hacienda-style hotel right downtown, within walking distance of everything. It's easy to miss as you drive by; the front entrance is a plain but tall 17th-century façade wall with a huge carved wooden door. Inside, however, it's an island of peace and serenity, with elegant comfortable rooms surrounding a small key-hole shaped pool in a garden courtyard. Each high-ceilinged bedroom features brightly painted walls and old-fashioned double wardrobes. We enjoyed our stay here immensely because of its deft combination of Colonial ambiance and thoroughly modern amenities. Parking is in a private lot down the street. $$-$$$

■ Expensive Hotels

Fiesta Americana *(Paseo Montejo at the corner of Av. Colon, US ☎ 800/345-5094, Mexico ☎ 999/942-1111, fax 999/942-1112, www.fiestaamericana.com.mx, 350 air-conditioned rooms on 5 floors, 3 phones in each room, including 1 in the bathroom, security safes, TV, pool, sauna, exercise room, non-smoking rooms, shopping mall).* In the battle of luxury hotels in Mérida, the Fiesta Americana is, for our money, the clear winner. Built in a grand belle époque style, it offers all the luxury accoutrements one would expect, including a pool, gym, spa with sauna and steam room, tennis court, beauty parlor, jacuzzi and satellite TV. The rooms have wrought-iron balconies outside and inside overlook a huge atrium, crowned by an impressive stained-glass roof. We went up and down several times in their glass elevators just to admire the view! If you've been out in the hinterlands of Yucatán, it's quite a treat to be pampered here. $$$

Holiday Inn *(Av. Colon, US ☎ 800/465-4329, Mexico ☎ 999/925-6877, fax 999/925-7002, www.holidayinn.com, 213 rooms, air, pool, 2 restaurants, exercise room).* The four-story Holiday Inn is a good value if you're into American comfort and style in a foreign country. Known both as a business as well as a tourist hotel, this Holiday Inn is as pleasing as any in the States or Canada. The outdoor restaurant out front is an enticing place for a romantic night out. It serves up a tempting buffet grill with live Mexican music and soft candlelight. $$-$$$

Hyatt Regency *(Calle 60 at Av. Colon, US ☎ 800/233-1234, Mexico ☎ 999/942-0242, www.hyatt.com, pool, air, cable TV, gym, tennis, 2 restaurants, bar).* This high-rise modern hotel, a little north of the downtown and one block east of the Paseo de Montejo, offers typical Hyatt high quality. The highlight of the open lobby is a tiled waterfall cascading down one wall. Our room had a large, comfy, king-size bed with a multicolored coverlet that picked up the Colonial colors in the room. A big screen TV with cable, minibar, tile bathrooms, desk, reading lamps and overstuffed chair helped make our stay very comfortable. The all-you-can-eat breakfast buffet every morning takes up an entire side of the dining room and is delicious. $$$

■ Haciendas

Several restored haciendas close to Mérida offer tours, meals and accommodations. See pages 97-104 for full descriptions of the following haciendas.

Hacienda Xcanatún *(Km 12, Hwy. 261, in US ☎ 877/278-8018, in Canada 866/818-8342, in Mexico 999/941-0213, www.xcanatun.com, 18 rooms).*

Hacienda Temozón *(Km 182, Hwy. 261, in US* ☎ *888/625-5144, in Mexico 999/923-8089, fax 999/923-7963, www.haciendatemozon.com, 26 rooms & suites, restaurants, air, telephones, tennis).*

Hacienda Katanchel *(Km 26, Route 180, in US* ☎ *800/525-4800, in Mexico 999/923-4020, fax 99/23-40-00, www.haciendakatanchel.com, 39 rooms & suites, pool, restaurant, telephones).*

> *Such hath it been – shall be – beneath the sun*
> *The many still must labor for the one.*
> ~ Lord Byron, 1788-1824

Dining

> *My tummy is smiling.*
> ~ Abigail Trillin, age 4

 The combination of Mérida's cosmopolitan aspirations, Spanish Colonial mindset and its Maya heritage can best be found in the cuisine mix of the old city. Arabic, Italian, French, Mexican, Yucatecan – even American – tastes are all here. What's equally appetizing is that you can eat very well for very little. Remember, most of these places do not have phones and reservations are not necessary.

DINING PRICE CHART	
NOTE: *Prices based on a typical entrée, per person, and do not include beverage.*	
$	Less than US $5
$$	US $5 - 10
$$$	Over US $10

Café Alameda *(Calle 58 No. 474 between 55 & 57).* Old men tend to hang out at this café smoking hand-rolled cigarettes, arguing animatedly and drinking thick Arabic coffee. With its small open-air courtyard behind a peach-colored wall, the Alameda feels like the last bastion of "home" for the Lebanese that flocked to the Yucatán at the turn-of-the-century. You'll probably feel at home and learn to linger here as well. It serves coffee strong enough to stand your hair on end and typical Spanish and Middle Eastern cooking. Try the shish kabob. $

Cafeteria Pop *(Calle 57 No. 501 between 60 & 62).* This is the coffee shop that invented coffee shops in Mérida, and it's open from 7 am to midnight. It's a "cool" place to be, attracting students from the university across the street. Cool because it has a strong air-conditioner and cool because its décor is vintage modern-art 1960s social protest. The haunting images of the three faces on the wall were painted in 1971 by Señor Martel, a local architect. They are a copy of a woodcut by Miguel Bresciano, made for a 1968 album of protest folk songs, *Canciones Para Mi America*, by Uruguayan singer Daniel

Viglietti. Very bohemian. This place is packed with people for dinner, lunch and breakfast. Excellent brewed coffee in bottomless cups. Although it's called a "cafeteria," it's actually a sit-down restaurant with generous servings of well-prepared dishes at inexpensive prices. The rumor is that it shares some high-quality cooking with the pricier Peregrino next door, as they have the same owner. Mundo has been a waiter here since 1971. $

Pizza Bella *(on the zócalo)*. Pizza Bella, on the square across from the main plaza, has very good pizza and offers clean inside eating when it becomes too hot outside. Great for people-watching. $

Vito Corleone Pizza *(Calle 59 No. 508 between 60 & 62,* ☎ *999/923-6846).* The bright yellow tiles of the counter and streetside pizza oven are the signature of this immensely popular hole-in-the-wall pizza parlor. An upstairs dining area adds to the university student hang-out atmosphere. The parlor makes clever use of pottery, which is imbedded in one wall. And the thin-crust pizzas are surprisingly good. If you're stuck in a hotel, order one to be delivered. $

Sigueff's *(Calle 60 between 35 & 37,* ☎ *999/925-5027).* Since 1959, Sigueff's has been the place to go for long breakfasts and lunches typical of the "old days." Although times have changed – they've moved uptown from their original mansion into a lovely hacienda-style place with a bright open-air courtyard – they still serve the same fine international, Yucatecan and Lebanese food. Not all that far from downtown, they're six blocks north of Santa Lucia, one block south of the Fiesta Americana and the Hyatt. Try the Arab sampler platter for around US $9, or the the dish they invented: Huevos Motuleño. Breakfasts and lunches are served until about 6 pm, closed Mondays. This is a Mérida tradition. $-$$

El Cedro de Libano *(Av. Colon & Calle 62 A,* ☎ *999/925-3723).* If you're looking for a bit of Lebanese cuisine for dinner, try the Cedar of Lebanon, a block and a half west of the Fiesta Americana and Hyatt. They feature lamb brochettes, stuffed chicken, traditional raw kibi, and grape/cabbage leaf rolls. Noon to 10 pm. $-$$

Pórtico del Peregrino *(Calle 57 No. 501 between 60 & 62,* ☎ *999/928-6163).* They named this romantic restaurant after a popular folk song about Alma Reed, the American journalist who was the lover of Mexican revolutionary Felipe Carrillo. It offers an enchanting old-world setting in both its dining areas – either al fresco under a clay tile roof (the tiles were brought as sailing ship ballast from Marseilles, France in the 1800s), or inside in the Spanish Colonial dining room. The food at the Peregrino brings diners back again and again. The Mexican and international dishes are fabulous. Try the chicken breast in green salsa. The Pórtico is also a favorite destination for expatriates on a night out. It's an excellent value, offering fine food with flair. Our top choice. $$

Pancho's Restaurant *(Calle 59 No. 509 between 60 & 62)*. Pancho's offers a bit of a "Playa Del Carmen" atmosphere in Mérida. Set well back from busy Calle 59, its entryway is filled with artifacts like a turn-of-the-century horse-drawn carriage and dozens of old photos from the era of Pancho Villa and the Mexican Revolution. Inside there are two bars and three dining areas, two of them outside patios under trees decorated by twinkly lights. The sombrero-wearing, bandoleer-toting *campesinos* running around are waiters. The food is fairly good. Live dance music starts at 11:30 pm and rocks your socks until 2:30 am. $$

El Nuevo Tucho *(Calle 60 #482 between 55 & 57, ☎ 999/924-2323)*. Although the entrance may look like you're going into a disco, El Tucho is a very large family restaurant set back off the traffic of busy Calle 60. An abundance of waiters insures good service for their Mexican/Yucatecan cuisine. The tables, with colorful linen cloths, face a raised bandstand where musical groups perform daily. It's been a family restaurant since 1986 and serves *botanas* with the beers. It has a welcoming touch and a huge dining room. Lunch and dinner. Try their *queso relleno*. $$

La Flor de Santiago *(Calle 70 between 57 & 59)*. When we first discovered La Flor, it was a traditional side-street coffee house that attracted locals and people from the next-door church, park, and *mercado*. It had an ancient brass coffee maker, seemingly designed by Rube Goldberg, that had been in service since the café's opening in 1926. After a long remodeling, it has reopened as a café, restaurant and bakery that features a wood-fired brick oven. If you're out by the Parque Santiago, eat here. $-$$

Restaurant Amaro *(Calle 59 between 60 & 62, ☎ 999/928-2451)*. This is another romantic and intimate restaurant in a Colonial building with an open-air courtyard dining area. However, the Amaro offers more than the same old cuisine –and vegetarians are especially pleased that they add a fair variety of veggie dishes to their Mexican menu. Candlelit tables and live musical troubadours have made it a popular dining experience since 1987. $$

Cafeteria Impala *(Paseo at Calle 47)*. Not a cafeteria in the traditional sense, the Impala's inviting linen-covered tables and dinette chairs from the 60s line the wide sidewalk al fresco at the beginning of the Paseo. A neon sign announces its presence, but it's the smell of coffee and delicious food that make it difficult to walk by without stopping. The mouth-watering *pollo Yucateca* here comes smothered in pickled onions with a few jalapeños for kicks. A good-size menu offers Mexican food at reasonable prices. Try the chocolate in water or milk and drink it like the ancient Maya: strong, unrefined and hot. Open 6 pm to 2 am, daily. $

Yucatán

CHOCOLATE?

Although often attributed to the Mexica/Aztec culture, chocolate as we know it now was most likely introduced to the Spanish by the Maya. Its name originates with the Mayan words "chocol ha," which mean hot water – as that was the way the ancient Maya preferred to drink it. At some point the Nahuatl word, "atl," replaced the Mayan word for water, ha, and it all eventually became the word "chocolate." Whatever it's called, we love it.

Restaurante Express (*Calle 60, across from Hidalgo Park*). This heavily male-dominated restaurant feels like a place where one of Mexico's many revolutions was orchestrated, accompanied by food and beer and flaying hand gestures. Facing the street and shady park, the busy eatery attracts regulars and foreigners with its good food at reasonable prices. Open 7 am to midnight. $

Los Almendros (*Calle 50, between 57 & 59, in Plaza de la Mejorada,* ☎ 999/ *928-5459*). Chef-founder Rubén Gonzalez Gonzalez opened the first Los Almendros in 1962 in Ticul, a small Maya town on the Ruta Puuc, south of Mérida. By 1972 his creative cooking had become so well known that he opened this Mérida location. Cancún's downtown restaurant opened in 1979. The secret of Señor Gonzalez's success is not a secret – he treats traditional Yucatecan food as if it were gourmet cuisine. It was in Los Almendros that *poc chuc*, marinated pork slices topped with onions and grilled, was invented. It's now one of the countryside's most popular (and delicious) dishes. This modern glass and steel restaurant is brightly lit but with the ambiance of a diner. Photos of the menu's dishes line the wall, offering a wide selection of Mexican food, including a sampler of Yucatecan specialties. As with other Almendros restaurants, when they're on, they're on, but when they're not, you wonder what all the fuss is about. Another location in town, **Gran Almendros**, ☎ 999/923-8135, is on Calle 57 at 52. $$

Alberto's Continental (*Calle 64 & 57,* ☎ *999/928-5367*). Alberto Salum, his sister Nery or brother Pepe have been the hosts since 1962 and will greet you personally at this wonderful dinner destination. The corner site of Alberto's was originally a Maya mound, dismantled in 1727 to build the foundation of today's Colonial building. As you might imagine, the interior is rich with ambiance. The dining room's mosaic tile floor was imported from Cuba long ago to replace the original unadorned stone. Curved Moorish arches and red tile floor invite diners to an outdoor patio, enveloped by rubber trees, for a wide selection of Italian, Yucatecan and Lebanese fare. There's a sampler dinner of Lebanese specialties or try their fish "Celestun" – sea bass stuffed with shrimp. The food is excellent. Classically intimate and romantic. $$-$$$

La Cafe Habana (*corner of 59 & 62*). This café/restaurant fills up with students, lovers and others daily, much as it has since 1954. On a recent Thursday evening at 10:30 it was absolutely packed. A very popular place for late diners and snackers. People-watchers come here during the day and sit in the big windows for the best view. Open 24 hours, seven days a week. You can buy good Chiapas coffee in bags here. $-$$

La Habana's owner has a variety of restaurants in town and it's worth mentioning another: **El Gran Café** at Calle 47 and the Paseo Renate at the end of Paseo Montejo. It offers a similar menu, with a weekend buffet. On the open-air terrace above is a bar and grill, **Arriba**, which overlooks the Paseo. $-$$

We don't have enough room to describe all fine dining opportunities in Mérida, especially those not in the Centro. For fabulous seafood lunches, look to **La Pigua** (☎ 999/920-3605) on Calle 33 at Cupules and 62, in the Colonia Alcalá Martín neighborhood. Take a taxi. Sushi can be found at **Campay Sushi** (☎ 999/948-0385), a stylish Japanese restaurant in Colonia Mexico, Calle 19 (a section outside the center of town, so take a cab). Open 1:30 to 11 pm, closed Mondays. Mange Italiano at **Bologna** (☎ 999/926-2505), located at Calle 21 and 28, east of Paseo Montejo, in the Itzimna neighborhood. It has northern Italian owners and romantic terrace dining.

For an authentic hacienda dining experience, look to the agricultural suburbs outside of Mérida. **Hacienda Teya** is the venerable hacienda restaurant east of the city, known for its cuisine. **Hacienda Xcanatún** is a newly opened hacienda hotel, with a gourmet chef, north of the city on the way to Progreso. See page 98 for complete details.

Mundo Maya

All human beings have an innate need to hear and tell stories and have a story to live by.... Religion, whatever else it has done, has provided one of the main ways of meeting this abiding need.
~ Harvey Cox, The Seduction of the Spirit

In a modern secular society, people usually define a spiritual reality based upon their religious values, while they define physical reality by agreed-upon scientific principles. A chair is a chair, held down by gravity. But the ancient Maya lived (as do many of their modern descendants) in a world in which these two planes of existence inextricably interlock – defining the material world as a manifestation of spiritual reality and vice-versa. Their humanity and the worlds of nature and spirituality were and still are, in many ways, all one. The gods of the Otherworld influenced fate: they were capable of bringing drought or rain, disease or health, victory or defeat, life or death. Yet the gods depended on the actions of mortals for their welfare as well (the cosmic crocodile monster of the sky would shed its own blood as rain in response to the

Maya kids.

royal sacrifices from the earth below). Leaving nourishment and sustenance as an offering to departed souls is an ancient custom that continues today.

How The World Works

The Maya conceived their world as having three regions: the bright world of Heaven, the stony Middleworld of earth and the dark water of the Underworld. These worlds were sacred and alive and a part of one another. At sunset, for example, the Underworld rotated with the other worlds to become the starry night sky.

The principal axis of existence was the path of the sun as it blazed across the sky, and each direction of the compass had a god and a color associated with it. **East**, the most important direction because of the sun's birth, was red; while **West**, where the sun died, was black. **South** was yellow and **North**, from where rain came, was white.

 MYSTERIOUS MAYA: In the Maya view of the world east, not north, belongs at the top of maps.

These directions were also seen in relation to the center (blue-green, yax), where a Ceiba tree, known as the World Tree (Wacah Chan), linked all three domains – its roots in the Underworld, trunk in the Middleworld and branches holding up the Heaven.

We divided our adventures in Yucatán state into the four cardinal points of the Maya world, making red (east), where the sun rises, our beginning. Day or overnight trips from Mérida are the best way to get to see the many wonders of the surrounding countryside.

EAST - RED

(Lakin Chac)
Coming from Cancún

Let others hail the rising sun: I bow to those whose course has run.
~ David Garrick, 1717-1779

East of Mérida there's a countryside rich in history. It offers magnificent Maya ruins at Chichén Itzá and Ek Balam; the Colonial heritage of majestic but tragic Valladolid; beautiful religious Izamal. We suspect most readers will approach the world of the Yucatán heading west, toward Mérida from Cancún. So have we arranged the sights in Lakin Chac in that order: Valladolid and Chichén Itzá, then points north, and finally to Izamal, only 70 km (43.5 miles) from Mérida. If you're heading east from Mérida, hold the book upside down and read backwards.

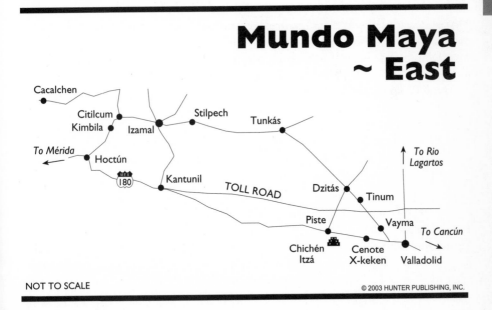

Mundo Maya
~ East

NOT TO SCALE

© 2003 HUNTER PUBLISHING, INC.

Valladolid

Tradition does not mean that the living are dead,
it means that the dead are living.
~ Harold Macmillan, British Prime Minister

Valladolid rests almost in the center of the Yucatán Peninsula, 160 km (100 miles) from Cancún and 159 km (99 miles) from Mérida. It's a Colonial town (pop. 70,000) often overlooked by the rush of tourists heading to nearby Chichén Itzá. This is a great place to spend a night or more if you're exploring the Chichén Itzá and Ek Balam ruins and surrounding countryside.

Tour buses to Chichén are now stopping briefly in Valladolid for a quick shopping trip under the green trees that line the plaza. Maya women sell *huipiles*, hammocks, jewelry and handicrafts there. Harried tourists then re-board the bus, eager to arrive at the Maya ruins before the day gets too hot.

Yet pleasant, provincial Valladolid (pronounced "buy-a-doe-LEED") is not a city to be hurried. Its rhythm and old-world style need to be savored, absorbed over time. Otherwise you miss little discoveries that make a trip special. We were lucky enough to be sitting in a restaurant during mid-January celebrations when the next day's bullfight matadors arrived to a flurry of excitement, proudly wearing splendid suits made of lights. They stopped to pay respect to elderly *hacendados*, dressed in traditional Spanish costume, who were sitting at a nearby table. Soon, the blaring music of a sidewalk fiesta with food and goods lining streets, packed with people, lured us outside. We were two of only a handful of tourists enjoying the festivities. The next day we were the only *Norteamericanos* to attend the bullfight. People welcomed us, encouraged us to take pictures and tried to explain new snack foods. Instead of "hot dogs," stadium vendors sell fresh fruit dipped in chile powder. POW! The weekend experience left us feeling as though we had gone back in time. And what an appropriate place to regress. The elegant Colonial walls of Valladolid have seen much in their long history.

Montejo the Younger and his cousin, Montejo, El Sobrino, overcame truculent Maya resistance to conquer the ancient city of Zací ("White Hawk") early in 1543. On the site of Zací, on May 28 of that year, the Montejos founded Valladolid, whose Colonial coat of arms features a white hawk image and the prophetic slogan, "Heroic City." In the middle of sugar cane and cattle country, but isolated by distance from Mérida, Valladolid matured in relative autonomy and it remained the most "Colonial" of the peninsula's larger cities – more conservative and perhaps more proudly aristocratic than Mérida itself.

Its hubris completely shattered in January 1847, when a Yucatecan secessionist army, using armed Maya soldiers in its ranks, attacked the garrison of

Mexican loyalists. A slaughter of non-Indian civilians resulted. Several months later, an informer named a young Maya, Antonio Ay, in a plot for a new revolution to reduce taxes on the Indian population. To set a stern example and to avenge the January atrocities, a firing squad shot young Ay against the Santa Ana chapel on July 26, 1847. If they were looking to curb Maya passions by executing its alleged leader, they were dead wrong. Antonio Ay's death was the catalyst that began the bloody Caste War, with Valladolid in the heart of it. By mid-March, 1848, a vicious slaughter of Vallísoletaños occurred and surviving residents fought their way out of the city toward Temax, fleeing the ruthless Maya advance.

Valladolid has again returned to peaceful, wonderful city. Don't miss it.

Orientation

■ Getting Around

Heading to Valladolid from Cancún you have a choice of two routes, both known on the maps as Highway 180. The first is the **Mérida Cuota**, the only road west made easy to find from Cancún. It's a toll road with very limited exits and two collection booths, one east of Valladolid and one west of Piste. The road is new and allows cars to zip along at a fast clip. If you're going to Valladolid, Chichén Itzá or Mérida, the Cuota's shortcut through the jungle makes life much easier. For access to the Cuota from Cancún, simply follow the signs for Mérida and Valladolid on Highway 307 South. The Valladolid exit is north of the city. As you drive into town there will be a large, castle-like handicraft market on your right. If you are bypassing Valladolid for Chichén Itzá, a new bypass road takes you to the highway west of town.

The alternative route to Valladolid is **Mérida Libre**, the two-lane road that goes through the heart of the Maya country. For us it has the great advantage of letting you see the "real" Yucatán, and we've had a special adventure of one sort or another every time we've been on it. The road is always interesting, wandering through villages passed by time, but it does require some patience. *Topes* (speed bumps) guard each village and make for a slower journey. However, there's more to life than driving fast, especially in the Yucatán. Private homes along the way sell handicrafts, gifts and bottles of honey.

If you're traveling to Valladolid from Mérida on Route 180, follow the signs at Kantunil for either the Libre or the Cuota. Or, for more fun, you can go through backroads from Izamal to Valladolid, retracing in reverse the escape of the Colonials during the Caste War. Other ways to Izamal from Mérida are west through the hammock town of Tixkokob, or northwest in a loop through historic Motúl.

Yucatán

Finding your way around Valladolid is very straightforward. The city is compact and laid out in the typical Colonial grid of mostly one-way streets. Odd-number streets run east and west, even run north and south. Most of the attractions are close to the main plaza. The free highway, Mérida Libre, becomes Calle 39 through town heading west and Calle 41 heading east.

Practicalities

BAKERY: Don't miss the *panaderia*, **La Especial,** a clean and delicious bakery on Calle 41. Jorge Canul owns it, along with one in Tizimín. It has been a family business since 1916. Be sure to try their *pan cubano*, a sweet bread that is as velvet as pound cake and just as delicious. A cousin, Eduardo Canul, owns La Especial bakery in Bakersfield, California.

BICYCLE RENTALS: The best place to rent bicycles is the sporting goods shop of Antoñio "Negro" Aguilar, the self-proclaimed "King of Baseball," who once played professional minor league baseball in Tennessee for the old Washington Senators. The former chief of police in Valladolid, he and his son are very friendly and they offer a good selection of bicycles (all one-speeds) in excellent condition. They rent, with a lock, for about US $1 per hour; long-term rental is available. From his shop on Calle 44, between 41 and 39 (☎ 985/856-2125), you can ride to X-keken and Samula cenotes (four km/2. 5 miles) or Rio Lagartos, a long 104-km (64-mile) ride. If you want to play some sports in town, see Antoñio. He also has eight very clean rooms for rent (in the budget price range) in a building above a kindergarten nearby. They feature private parking and a small pool and we are very pleased to recommend them. Please say hello from us. Antoñio is a genuine character and he and his family are good people.

FIESTA: Valladolid becomes one big fiesta the last week in January, from around January 26 to February 2. The center of the celebration is in the Candelaria section northwest from the square, and the highlight is a grand bullfight at the ring. Follow the crowd out Calle 33.

LAUNDROMAT: An inexpensive laundromat is in the **Super Maz** supermarket shopping center on Calle 39 near Calle 56, but be sure to specify separation (*separado*) of whites and colors. The shopping center also has a health food store and supermarket.

MEDICAL FACILITIES: The **Red Cross**, for emergency ambulance service, is at ☎ 985/6-24-13. The emergency **hospital** is behind the San Bernardino church, ☎ 985/856-2883, 856-2413.

MONEY MATTERS: Next to the post office is a **Bancomer Bank**, where you should ask for a receipt (*recibo*). There's a **Bital Bank** that sometimes

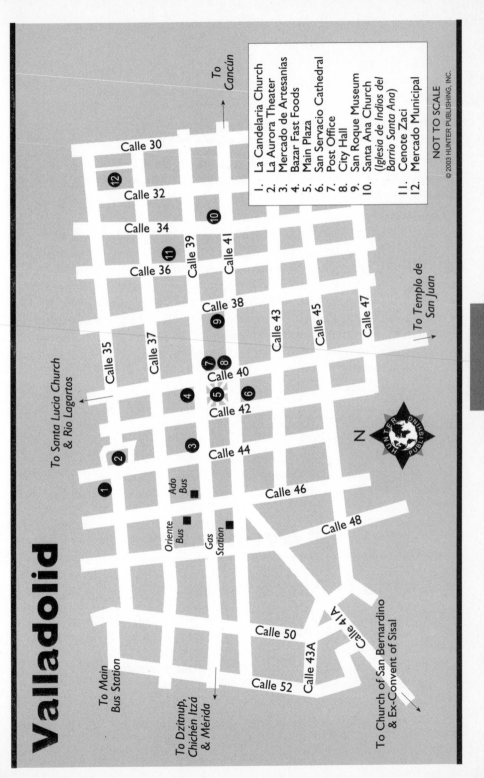

Valladolid

To Santa Lucia Church & Rio Lagartos

To Main Bus Station

To Dzitnup, Chichén Itzá & Mérida

To Cancún

To Templo de San Juan

To Church of San Bernardino & Ex-Convent of Sisal

Calle 30
Calle 32
Calle 34
Calle 36
Calle 35
Calle 37
Calle 39
Calle 41
Calle 38
Calle 40
Calle 42
Calle 44
Calle 46
Calle 48
Calle 43
Calle 45
Calle 47
Calle 50
Calle 43A
Calle 41A
Calle 52

Ado Bus
Oriente Bus
Gas Station

1. La Candelaria Church
2. La Aurora Theater
3. Mercado de Artesanias
4. Bazar Fast Foods
5. Main Plaza
6. San Servacio Cathedral
7. Post Office
8. City Hall
9. San Roque Museum
10. Santa Ana Church (Iglesia de Indios del Barrio Santa Ana)
11. Cenote Zaci
12. Mercado Municipal

NOT TO SCALE

© 2003 HUNTER PUBLISHING, INC.

N

HUNTER PUBLISHING

Yucatán

gives a better rate west on Calle 41 and a **money change booth** (*cambio*) next to the cathedral.

POLICE: Local police are at ☎ 985/856-2100. The highway patrol, ☎ 985/856-2780. Emergencies are at ☎ 060.

POST OFFICE: The post office is on the square, Calle 40.

TOURIST INFORMATION: Tourism information in this friendly town is next to the city hall on Calle 40 at the corner of 41.

TOWN TOURS: A two-hour bus tour in an open trolley-style bus, *La Guagua,* departs every Sunday in front of the cathedral at 9 am and 4 pm (US $5).

TRANSPORTATION: A whispered voice may have said "If you build it, they will come" to optimistic state government officials who spent big bucks in 2000 building a huge new Chichén Itzá International Airport near Káua (pronounced kawa), about half-way between Valladolid and the ruins. They hope that more tourism will result because charter and scheduled flights from Europe will want to land there instead of Cancún or Mérida. Not everyone agrees with the expensive project (US $13.5 million) and its three-km (1.8-mile) runway. Critics argue that the money could have done more good spent on social benefits. So far, that argument is winning – those flights haven't materialized.

Polished and pampered bronze and maroon **taxis** – each city in the Yucatán sports its own individual taxi colors – conveniently hang out along the plaza across from the church. The fare for the half-hour ride to Chichén is around US $20. Local **bus** service is frequent to Chichén Itzá, Cobá, Mérida, Cancún and even Playa del Carmen. The main bus station, on Calle 54 and 37, is a bit of a hike (seven blocks) to the downtown. A local Oriente Bus is on Calle 46, between 39 and 37, and an ADO Bus Terminal is on the corner of 46 and 39.

Adventures

■ Sights & Attractions

Blood and guts are not the only features of Valladolid's history. The **Church of San Bernardino de Siena** and the **Ex-Convent of Sisal**, a religious complex at the corner of Calles 41A and 49 in the Sisal section of Valladolid, are two of the most beautiful buildings of the Colonial period and are the oldest Spanish-built structures in the Yucatán. The huge stone convent complex is similar to but not as grand as the one at Izamal. It was designed by the architect of Mérida's cathedral, Juan de Mérida, in 1552, and built over one of the deepest and most extensive cenotes on the peninsula. For a small donation you can walk through to the peaceful

Convento de San Bernardino.

monastery-like gardens in the back. The old dome-shaped building here is the well/cenote, used first by the Maya and then by the Spanish conquerors for fresh water. A few years ago, a dive team found weapons from the Caste War rusting in its depths, too delicate to retrieve.

Inside the church itself, some of the original 16th-century paintings can still be seen on the walls behind the side altars. The church's former ornate decorations were stripped in the Caste War and Mexican Revolution, never to be replaced (as has been the case in most of the Yucatán's churches).

Approaching the church, in a section of town known as the Calzada de los Frailes, is the prettiest street in all the Yucatán, **Calle 41A**, which leads from a lovely Colonial square to the convent. The road is cobblestone and lined by restored and authentically painted Colonial-era one-story buildings. Huge clay pots filled with exotic green plants have been placed in the narrow street, forcing what little traffic there is to zig-zag around them.

The magnificent baroque **San Servacio Cathedral** stands on the square in town. The original one, consecrated on March 24, 1545 and called San Gervacio, was torn down in 1706 by the order of Obispo Reyes Rios, who had it rebuilt facing north as a "punishment" to the unknown criminals who stole from the altar of the original church. Their mark of shame means that the entrance door does not face east, as do most other Colonial churches in the Yucatán. Valladolid has several other 16th-century churches, including the **Iglesia de Indios del Barrio de Santa Ana**, a chapel built exclusively for Maya Indians, where Antonio Ay was shot, Calles 41 and 34; **Templo de San Juan**, Calles 49 and 40; **Santa Lucia**, Calles 40 and 27; and **La Candelaria**, with a park across the street known as a romantic "lovers' park," at Calles 44 and 35. At the far end of the park you'll find **La Aurora**, a public stage theater. The **San Roque Museum** is set in a chapel built for the former Name of Jesus Hospital. It features a tiny display and a quiet stone memorial park with several benches in the rear. It's at Calles 41 and 38.

The **central plaza** is especially pleasant in Valladolid. At its heart is a water fountain with a painted statute of a Maya woman pouring water from a clay jug. The low brick walk that surrounds it is lined with iron bench seats and romantic *confidenciales* for sitting and relaxing, or maybe getting your shoes shined. The park's trees fill at dusk with hundreds of birds whose combined calls drown out the sounds of traffic. In the evening, wrought-iron lanterns glow yellow under the shadow of the cathedral that presides over strolling lovers, candy vendors, shoe-shine men and mothers with their children, in awe of the tall *touristas*.

> **AUTHOR'S TIP:** *Signs in the plaza caution tourists not to tolerate children begging or asking to watch your car, which they pronounce in English as "wash your car." Instead, refuse (it's unnecessary, Valladolid is very safe) and encourage them to go to school.*

Stop in the **Palacio Municipal**, where the stone steps to the second floor have been worn into hollows by years of use. A coat of arms and an honor roll of the Conquistadors who founded and stayed in the city in 1543 hang on the hall walls. In the upstairs salon, some very impressive historical murals grace the room and portraits of long-dead city fathers and heroes have a place of honor. As in Mérida, window balconies provide a rewarding vista of the cathedral and park.

The **municipal *mercado*** in Valladolid (Calles 37 and 32) is one of our sentimental favorites. It's the town meeting place for Vallísoletaños and plenty of country folk from the surrounding Maya villages. It's open daily, but Sunday is the big market day (best in the morning). Produce and food dominate the eastern and center stalls (the inside meat market, a staple of village *mercados*, is not the kind of place to take your vegetarian friends) while clothes and sundry crafts fill the rest. This is a good place to buy chile powder, anchiote paste, woven plastic shopping bags, fruits and vegetables. Visit the *tortillaria* on the corner and see corn tortillas being made.

There's an indoor **Mercado de Artesanías** on Calle 39 near the corner of 44 that's worth a stop. **La Antigua** gift shop has a wide array of Mexican handicrafts in ceramic, leather, onyx and wood at fair prices. They're on Calle 37 at the corner of 40, a block back from the plaza. Under the big trees in the *zócalo*, Maya women line the sidewalks selling handmade crafts such as *huipiles* – they even make them for Barbie dolls – handkerchiefs, blouses, jewelry and hammocks. If you're not going on to Mérida, this is a good place to buy hand-knotted hammocks (see some hints about quality on pages 285-86).

Maya women who wear *huipiles* will also carry a cotton or silk shawl, called a *rebozo*.

REBOZOS

Many years ago, each village had their own unique pattern and color, but that is no longer true. Around Valladolid, the preference seems to be a clay-brown background with flecks of white. Other available hues include black and white, purple and black, black and red, gray and white or generally earth-tone colors. Long and rectangular, *rebozos* are more like stoles than shawls, fringed at both ends. They contain a fancy woven pattern and either a knotted fringe or a macramé-style trim with tassels.

Rebozos, like hammocks, come in a variety of qualities dependent upon the material and closeness of the weave. They can be gorgeous and eye-catching accessories for an evening or cocktail dress and are a unique gift. You'll find a good selection at **Casa Miranda** on Calle 39, third floor. While it looks like a five-and-dime store downstairs, upstairs there are some quite fashionable women's clothes and accessories at reasonable prices.

Cenote Zací, the ancient Maya city water source, is on Calle 36 between 39 and 37. It's worth seeing if you haven't yet visited a cenote. The somewhat dramatic large open hole has terraced stone steps that lead down to the somber dark water. The owners have built a cool, shady park around the cenote that contains long stone walls, a life-size Chac Mool statue (great for photos), a rounded stone oven, and a large palapa-covered restaurant serving Mexican meals. Unless you're eating in the restaurant, there's a small admission charge. On the high ground above the cenote a local man dives the 26 meters into the deep cenote whenever there is an audience. A friend passes around the hat. This is a spectacular jump. The small zoo there, unfortunately, is pathetic.

Twenty-two km (13.6 miles) due south of Valladolid and two km (1.25 miles) south of Tixcacalcupul, on Highway 295, are the remnants of the 100-km-long (62-mile), Cobá to Yaxuná *sacbé* (white road) of the ancient Maya. A sign says "Mirador," meaning a sight, but there really isn't much to see. The sacred raised roadway looks like a clearing in the trees, but if you look closely in the weeds you'll see the outline of the *sacbé,* made of limestone boulders. We couldn't find it last time we passed. See Felipe Carrillo Puerto in Quintana Roo, page 245, for some fascinating facts about the towns south of Valladolid. There is also a new shortcut to Cobá and Tulum east of town, near Chemax.

■ Adventures on Foot

 A beautiful and truly unique cenote is **Cenote X-Keken** (ISH-ka-ken): two km (1.25 miles) west, on the way to Chichén Itzá, then two km south, toward the village of Dzitnup. The Valladolid city fathers created a four-km (2.5-mile) bicycle or hiking *sacbé* parallel to the road.

Yucatán

This fairly easy ride or walk runs from the edge of town to the cenote, where you are rewarded by a cool swim. (See *Practicalities*, page 314, for bike rental details.)

X-Keken is open from 8 am to 5 pm and is best visited in late morning or early afternoon, when there are fewer people and less chance of tour buses. Bring a bathing suit (*sin* suntan oil) to this truly magical cenote in an underground cavern. Entrance (US $2) requires going down some steep steps carved into the stone (there's a rope to assist you) and walking a short distance until the passage opens into a huge underground cavern. Recessed lights highlight the gigantic stalactite that cascades down from the ceiling into the turquoise water. A hole in the roof of the cavern allows a thick, brilliant shaft of sunlight to stream into the cave, illuminating the water like an electric spotlight. Some rocky alcoves on a ledge above are useful as changing areas. Snorkeling and swimming are possible (there is a changing area), but food, drink, suntan oil and smoking are not allowed. The people of Dzitnup want to keep this enchanting wonder in pristine condition. The interior is quite moist and warm and the rocks can be slippery, so be careful. Handicraft stands with good prices surround the parking lot and a public bathroom is available.

Directly across the street is **Cenote Samula**, which attracts fewer visitors but is just as spectacular as X-Keken. Not for swimming, you stand on a large cliff ledge and look down into the clear blue *agua* to see fish swimming around. From the roof, tree roots have grown down 20 meters (65 feet) to drink the water below. Only in the Yucatán!

■ Adventures in the Water

Just outside town on the road toward Mérida is a new attraction, **Acuatica Waterpark** (☎ 985/856-2070). It's very popular with locals. There are two water slides, a restaurant and snack bar, but no lockers. Open from 11 am to 7 pm, admission US $4. For real adventurers, stop in the village of Káua, halfway to Chichén, and visit the deep cenote Yaxhek, Mayan for "Green Glow," where locals swim. You'll be the only *gringos*, guaranteed.

> **NAVIGATIONAL TIP:** *In the other direction from Valladolid, east toward Cancún, is an alternate route to the ruins of Cobá, either as a side trip or as part of a run to Tulum and the Caribbean shore. Turn south in Chemax and go 45 km (28 miles) to Cobá.*

Accommodations

Hotels in Valladolid are appealing, plentiful and priced right. Most cost well below what you pay in Cancún. For super cheap digs, look either to the hostel below or stop in Antoñio Aguilar's Sport Shop on Calle 44, between 41 and 39, and inquire about his very nice rooms for rent. (See *Bicycle Rentals*, page 314).

Hotel Zaci *(Calle 44 No 491, between 37 & 39, ☎/fax 985/856-2167, 50 rooms with air, cable TV, telephone, breakfast-only restaurant, pool).* The Zaci is magical at night when its two parallel walkways of red tile and white arches are softly lit. During the day it's pretty as well, painted all white with red roof tiles and terra-cotta floors and decorated with a scattering of green plants in clay pots. The one-story hotel becomes three floors in back, curving around a deep blue pool and a tiny restaurant under a striped awning. It's a very pleasant experience. Each room is medium-size with modern bathrooms, two queen-size beds and big closets. $

Maria de la Luz *(Calle 42 at the corner of 41, opposite the zócalo, ☎/fax 985/856-2071, www.mariadelaluzhotel.com, 69 rooms with air, 2 suites, secure parking, pool, restaurant).* Completely remodeled at the end of 1998, the Maria has lots of new rooms and a brand new look in its extremely popular dining room. The medium-size additional rooms have two queen-size beds in each, big closets and pleasing tiled bathrooms. The older Colonial-style rooms have new tile floors and fresh paint, but smaller closets. We still like these, but suggest you get one that doesn't face the street. All the guest rooms wrap around a refreshing kidney-shaped pool. The restaurant serves good meals at reasonable prices and a daily breakfast buffet for around US $4. Say hola to Elio, a waiter here since 1981. The restaurant ambiance is tropical, with comfortable bamboo chairs and stained-glass lampshades. $

Hotel San Clemente *(Calle 42 No. 206, between 41 & 43, ☎ 985/856-2208, 64 rooms with air, TV, restaurant, pool, private parking).* This Colonial hotel across the street from the side of the San Servacio Church at the corner of the *zócalo* has the same owner as the Santa Lucia and San Juan hotels in Mérida. Rooms are large and modern, with good-size bathrooms and comfortable beds; the owners have recently redecorated them. There's a center courtyard and small pool, which the three floors wrap around. The fountain in the center is a copy of the one in the middle of the *zócalo*. The second and third floors offer fantastic views of the church lit up at night. Also home to **Domino's Pizza**. $

Don Luis *(Calle 39 No. 191, between 38 & 40, ☎ 985/856-2024, 24 rooms with fans, pool, secure parking)*. This tropical-looking hotel holds a special place in our heart as it was the first place we ever stayed outside Cancún, many years ago. Unfortunately, it is now more of a choice for backpacking budget travelers. The rooms are clean but spartan (threadbare sheets). Outside, tall coconut trees sway in the breeze around a large oval pool. There's a small independent restaurant, Cupules, which used to be in the San Clemente. The hotel is close to the town square, two blocks from Cenote Zací, four from the *mercado*.

La Candelaria Hostel *(Calle 35 between 42 & 44, ☎/fax 985/856-2267, candelaria_hostel@hotmail.com)*. This is one of the more pleasing youth hostels in Yucatán, set in a long green building facing the quiet Candelaria Park. Rooms are small but spotlessly clean. The walled backyard features a covered eating area, laundry washing area, bathrooms, and hanging hammocks. Comfortable, safe and great for a long- or short-term stay.

Hacienda San Miguel *(outside town on road to Uaymá, Tinúm & Dzitas, ☎ 985/858-1539, 8 cabañas with fans, pool, includes breakfast)*. See page 100 for a full description of this hacienda property.

El Meson del Marquéz *(Calle 39 No. 203, between 40 & 42, ☎ 985/856-2073, fax 985/856-2280, 76 rooms & jr. suites with air, pool, bar, gift shop, restaurant, secure parking, telephones)*. The Meson is rightfully considered the best in town. It was originally the ancestral family home of its owner, Mario Escalante Ruiz, but he converted the large Colonial house into a hotel in 1966 and it has been growing ever since. Quiet and cool, it now boasts 28 rooms and 48 suites in three newer buildings behind the original home. Tall bamboo trees wave in the wind three stories above the well-kept grounds and oval per and thinner, younger even. This professionally run hotel is a leader in promoting Valladolid tourism and it starts by giving guests the royal treatment. The Meson features a romantic candlelit restaurant with fine food in an al fresco patio dining area. Make reservations for your intended stay; they accept American Express cards only. $-$$

Dining

Check the hotel listings for two outstanding restaurants, namely **Maria de la Luz**, where we hang out, and especially **El Meson del Marquéz**.

DINING PRICE CHART	
NOTE: Prices based on a typical entrée, per person, and do not include beverage.	
$	Less than US $5
$$	US $5 - 10
$$$	Over US $10

Plaza Maya *(Calle 41, between 48 & 50)*. This unobtrusive storefront restaurant with a yellow awning leads back to a large palapa-covered dining room decorated with Maya frescoes. The kitchen, visible behind a large glass window, is sparkling clean and the cooking staff all wear chef's whites. Salsa is served in carved stone bowls and, if you ask, they'll bring you a small courtesy glass of Xtabentun ("ISHta-ben-tune"), a Maya liqueur made from anise and honey, as an after-dinner drink. Try their typical Yucatecan/Valladolid platter (US $8), with eight different local dishes, including *longaniza*, a local sausage that tastes like a juicy Slim Jim, and *venado* (deer meat), which we declined. Deer has been a staple of Maya diet since ancient times, but lately it's overhunted in the Yucatán and we didn't want to contribute to the problem. The Plaza Maya has been a dining treasure since 1988. $-$$

Restaurant las Campanas *(Calle 42, at corner of 41)*. This remodeled restaurant, in another old building at the corner of the *zócalo* and the San Servacio Church, serves inexpensive Mexican food and great *horchata*, a refreshing rice milk drink. It's a good example of the incredibly high ceilings typical of the Colonial era. Good service and specials on beer. Live music after 9 pm. $

Restaurant Los Portales *(Calle 41, at corner of 40)*. Los Portales has been here perhaps forever (it's been a restaurant for over 100 years). It opens early and is a good place for a light meal or soft drink. Dine inside or on the tile sidewalk under the portales, a great place to hang out and watch the traffic go by. The entryway to the bathrooms was built for people under five foot tall. For dessert, look up across the street to El Kabah, a coffee house open long hours with a second-story view of the square. $

El Bazar *(Calles 38 & 40)*. In the open building on a corner across from the main square, the Bazar is a non-bizarre collection of family-owned eateries and a few shops. It's the most fun place to eat in town. There are about a dozen little market-style *loncherias* here that open early and close late. Food is inexpensive. El Bazaar is our favorite place for breakfast or lunch when

Yucatán

we're on the move. You'll have more choices of where to sit and what to eat than you can handle. As the babble of languages overheard attests, everybody eats here – tourists and residents alike – sooner or later. If you have the stomach for it, this is the place to try *mondongo*, a Yucatecan haggis-like sausage dish made from beef stomach. Those that try it (and it's very popular) say it has a strong taste and smooth texture. Dinner usually features a simple *comida corrida* that will fill you up without cleaning out your purse. $

Where is the best seafood in the middle of the dry Yucatán jungle? Well that seems to be a topic of discussion in town, so who are we to argue? Our favorite had always been **La Sirenita** on Calle 34 near 31, a few blocks from the *mercado*. This modern spot even offers customers a small swimming pool out front. However, our friend Negro Aguilar swears by a different place, a bar-restaurant called **El Payaso**, on Calle 33 out near the bullring and fairgrounds. A third contender, more in the center of town, is the palapa roof restaurant, **El Caribe**, located on Calle 41, between 50 and 52.

Chichén Itzá

I would rather live in a world where my life is surrounded by mystery than live in a world so small that my mind could comprehend it.
~ Harry Emerson Fosdick, *Mystery of Life*

The enigmatic ruins of Chichén Itzá ("Mouth of the Well of the Itzás," pronounced chee-CHEN-eat-ZA) have intrigued and baffled archeologists and historians since they were first described by Bishop de Landa in the late 16th century. Nineteenth-century books by author and adventurer John Lloyd Stephens and British artist Frederick Catherwood, as well as some by Augustus Le Plongeon and his wife, Alice, fueled imaginations about the mysterious civilization that seemed to have disappeared into the remote jungles of Mexico and Central America.

Today there is no living city known as "Chichén Itzá." The closest town to the ancient ceremonial center is Piste, two km (1.25 miles) west. If you want to stay overnight to see the light show at 7 pm, or just to spend more time at these exceptional ruins, the hotel choices include three in the archeological zone itself, one just outside, and several in Piste. Every travel agency in the Yucatán hawks one-day tours of the ruins and, while it is possible to see them in one arduous day (open 8 am to 5 pm), you may prefer to stay and see the nighttime laser light show. If you do stay overnight it means you can get there early in the day, before the crowds arrive, or hang out in the late afternoon, as shadows begin to fall and the sun's glow illuminates the magnificent restored structures. The site occupies nearly 10 square km (four square miles), so it takes some time to fully appreciate. Guides are available (try

Maya woman

Olmec head, La Venta National Park, Villahermosa (see page 429)

joining or forming a group) at the new visitors center, which has bathrooms, gift shops (with surprisingly reasonable prices), a bookstore, museum and food court.

THIS OLD RUIN

Three main styles named for the regions in which they are predominant characterize Maya architecture in the peninsula. The styles overlap and share characteristics. The blocks of stone you see in restored ruins today were originally covered with plaster, which was often painted with specific designs or in solid colors.

RIO BEC: This Late Classic style is characterized by tall towers that simulate pyramids, intricate roof combs and unusable stairways with faux temples on the second level. Examples can be seen in the southern sites of Xpujil and Rio Bec. Façades feature ostentatious adornments of carved stone.

CHENES: Buildings are typically one story with a central doorway elaborately designed as a monster's mouth, complete with fierce teeth. Chenes and Rio Bec styles were contemporaneous and are close enough to be almost indistinguishable.

PUUC: Named for the Puuc Hills of Yucatán, classic Puuc style features structural corners of ornately decorated masks of Chac and the rain gods. Round columns in rows also distinguish this most impressive of Classical styles. Uxmal is an excellent example.

SACBES: Common features of most Maya sites are elevated causeways called *sacbés* ("White Roads"). These pathways linked ceremonial sites within civic centers, but, more interestingly, they also connected Maya urban centers. *Sacbés* are elevated as much as 4.5 meters (15 feet) above the terrain and are as wide as 18 meters (60 feet), but most are of more modest proportions. Builders edged them with cut stone, filled the core with rubble, then paved them over with a hard white stucco, cambered in the center for drainage. Evidence indicates their use was primarily ceremonial, but their commercial and military advantages are obvious.

The longest single *sacbé* stretches 100 km (62 miles) from Cobá to the minor site of Yaxuná, southwest of Chichén Itzá. Unfortunately, very few of these fascinating white walkways are in good enough condition to function as hiking trails. The rough jungle has long ago reclaimed them.

Everyone is the son of his own works.
~ Miguel de Cervantes

Yucatán

History

The only thing new in the world is the history that you don't know.
~ Harry S. Truman, 1884-1972

The social catastrophe in the ninth century that caused the demise of the southern Classic cities resulted in Chichén Itzá's gradual rise to rule the northern Yucatán. The city is thought to have been settled during the Late Classic period based on the architectural similarities of the "old" part of the city, Chichén Viejo, to the Puuc style. This part of Chichén was abandoned along with the rest of the Classical cities, but was resettled by Chontal Maya, or Itzás, a seafaring tribe who came into the northern Yucatán in the early Post-Classic period. These people, whom the locals considered barbarians, were in turn culturally absorbed by the Yucatecan Maya along with Toltec warriors who came from Tula in the Mexican state of Hidalgo. Prior to the Toltec presence in the Terminal Classic period, influences from central Mexican culture had already permeated Maya culture. One of those influences was the cult of Quetzalcóatl, the king/god whom the Maya called Kukulcán. The building boom over the 300 years of Chichén's dominance resulted in stunning architectural wonders decorated with images of Chac, the rain god, and Kukulcán, the plumed serpent.

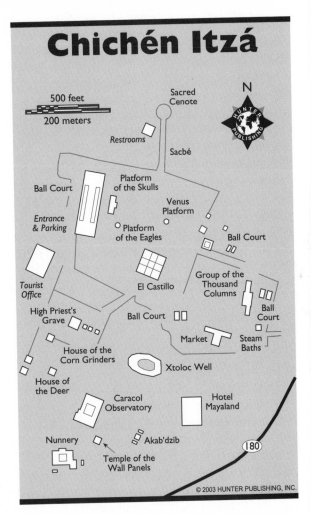

The downfall of Chichén in AD 1221 at the hands of rival city-state Mayapán purportedly involved the kidnapping of the bride of the king of Izamal. The details are unclear but may be related to the legend of Hunac Ceel, who survived a plunge into the sacred sacrificial cenote at Chichén, which was supposed to take its victims directly to the Underworld. Ceel predicted Chac would bring plenty of rain and shortly thereafter became ruler of Mayapán. He may have engineered the kidnapping dispute that pitched Izamal against Chichén and resulted in the downfall of both, bringing about the rise of victorious Mayapán as the new capital of the northern Maya. Religious Pilgrims continued to visit Chichén even after the Spanish Conquest. Montejo briefly tried to found a city here but, luckily for archeology, found local resistance too fierce to make it worthwhile.

 MYSTERIOUS MAYA: The conch was the Maya glyph for zero. The Maya developed a numerical concept long before mathematicians in the Old World.

Exploring the Ruins

EL CASTILLO: The 25-meter-tall (82 feet) Temple of Kukulcán, known as El Castillo, "the Castle," dominates the view as it rises majestically in the apparent center of the ruins. Built before AD 800 (before the Toltec invasion, but in a Toltec style), the pyramid is an eloquent statement of engineering genius and an elegant highlight of a mighty city that stretched at least 25 square km (10 square miles) beyond its wide central plazas. The view from the top is delightful and worth the steep climb.

The impressive structure you are viewing covers a smaller, older one that can still be seen (11 am to 1 pm and 4 to 5 pm) by entering a narrow stairway at the western edge of the north staircase. Inside, archeologists found a Chac Mool (a reclining statue that holds a bowl over its stomach, thought to be where hearts cut from sacrificial victims were offered to the gods) and a red jaguar altar with inlaid eyes and spots of shimmering jade. It is often hot, crowded and humid inside these ruins. Not recommended for those who suffer from claustrophobia.

The construction of this temple brought into play the engineering, mathematical and celestial reckoning abilities of the ancient Maya. In some ways, it is the Maya calendar embodied in stone. There are 364 steps plus a platform to equal the 365 days of a year, 52 panels on each side representing the 52-year cycle of the calendar round, and nine terraced levels on either side of the stairways that total the 18 months of the Maya solar calendar. El Castillo's axis are so perfectly aligned that the sun shadows of the rounded terraces fall on the side of the northern staircase where they form the image of an undulating serpent. During the spring equinox (approximately March 21), the ser-

pent seems to be slithering down the stairs, while in the fall (September 21) it reverses and climbs the pyramid. The clever optical illusionists who built it also made it seem taller than it really is. You'll wonder how such diminutive people as the Maya could climb such tall steps. Coming down is harder than going up and, as you use the rope aid, you may notice you have to walk down almost sideways. Some speculate that the reason the steps are so narrow is so people coming back down could never turn their back on the temple of Kukulcán that crowns the pyramid's top.

According to a well-known North American acoustics expert, if you clap your hands in front of the pyramid's tall staircase it produces an echo (known as the "picket fence effect") that he believes sounds like the Quetzal, a bird sacred to the Maya. He postulates that the sonic effect was consciously designed into the construction by the builders.

> **AUTHOR'S TIP:** *Remember that video cameras at all archeological and museum sites require an extra fee. Tripods are banned and, in most cases, so is the use of a flash.*

BALLCOURT: The largest and best-preserved ballcourt in all Mesoamerica is located here, just northwest of Kukulcán's pyramid. It is one of nine ballcourts built in the city, emphasizing the importance of the ceremonial game the Maya called **Pok-Ta-Pok**. It was a religious rite more than a recreational game. Carvings on both sides of the walls show scenes of players dressed in heavy padding (they struck the ball with their hips and body,

El Castillo.

never their hands or feet). The object was to get the leather ball through one of two carved stone rings placed high on the center of opposite walls. A carved relief also shows a player holding the head of another player kneeling next to him, blood spurting out of the lifeless body. If you stand in the **Temple of the Bearded Man** (at the north end) and speak in normal tones, the fantastic acoustics of the court's design allow you to be heard clearly over 500 feet away at the southern wall. Above the southeast corner of the court is the **Temple of the Jaguars**, with serpent columns and carved panels. Inside the temple are polychrome bas-reliefs recounting a battle with a Maya village and a sculpture of a jaguar, possibly a throne.

TEMPLES: To the right of the ballcourt is the **Temple of the Skulls** (Tzompantili, a Toltec name), where rows of skulls are carved into a stone platform. Here, heads of sacrificial victims were put on a pole for display. Eagles tear the hearts from the bodies in another V-for-violence-rated carving. The platform due north of El Castillo is the **Temple of Venus**. Rather than a voluptuous woman in a diaphanous gown, the Maya depicted her as a feathered monster with a man's head in her mouth. Hmmm. This structure is also named Chac Mool because his image was discovered buried inside.

CENOTE: The sacred cenote, **Cenote of Sacrifice**, is a hike (about a fifth of a mile long) up an original *sacbé* to the north. The well is 200 feet across and over 115 feet deep, and was used for ceremonial purposes, not for drinking. To this end, the Maya paid tribute to Chac with gifts of various artifacts and sacrificial victims. Bones of 50 children, men and women have been discovered here. Original dredging was done in the late 1800s and early 1900s by American Edward Thompson, who owned the Hacienda Chichén. He sent a huge cache to the Peabody Museum at Harvard University, where much of it is still on display. The National Geographic Society and CEDAM, the Mexican diving association, pulled thousand more pieces from the well in the 1960s.

GROUP OF A THOUSAND COLUMNS: The complex east of the pyramid is named after the many rows of columns, once roofed over, that form a colonnade around the courtyard. Almost Greek or Roman in appearance, the imposing **Temple of the Warriors**, a huge three-tiered platform with a temple on top, approached by a staircase on the west, dominates its surrounding buildings. There is a large colonnade of stone pillars carved with figures of warriors at its base and a reclining Chac in the temple at the top. Columns wrapped with carvings of serpents served to hold up the roof, now long gone. The temple was built over an earlier one. The inner temple had pillars sculpted in bas-relief (they retain much of their color) and murals painted on the walls. The courtyard to the south contains the **Steam Bath No. 2**, believed to be a Maya ceremonial sweathouse, undergoing restoration, and a platform at the south end known as the **Market**. Neither of these is in good condition.

SOUTH CHICHEN: The trail south from El Castillo pyramid leads to an area often less crowded with tourists. The first structure you come to is the Ossuary, or **Grave of the High Priest**, now being actively restored. Its design is similar to that of El Castillo, but on a lesser scale. This pyramidal base covers a natural grotto cave in which bones of a man were found. A small temple farther down the trail is the **Red House**, or ChicHan-Chob, meaning "small holes," probably referring to the latticework in the roof comb. This building is in the Puuc Late Classic style, dated by a glyph at about AD 869, and offers a pleasing view of the other structures.

The trail then leads to **El Caracol**, one of the most fascinating structures on site. The name means "snail" or "conch" in Spanish, alluding to the spiral staircase found inside (off limits). The round structure, the only one of its kind at Chichén, is the celestial observatory from where the Maya watched the heavens. The slits in the dome and walls aligned with certain stars and Chac masks over its four doors face the cardinal directions. A path to the northeast leads to Chichén's former water supply, the **Cenote Xtoloc**, "Iguana." Due south is the **Temple of Sculptured Panels**, a good spot for photos of El Caracol.

The Nunnery, or Las Monjas, is next. This impressive structure measures 62 meters (210 feet) long, 31 meters (105 feet) wide and is more than 15 meters (50 feet) high. The construction is Maya rather than Toltec (which was perhaps the residence of royalty). The resemblance of the myriad rooms to European convents gave it its name. A doorway in the Annex next to it forms the open monster mouth associated with the Chenes architectural style. Near the Annex is the tiny **La Iglesia**, whose upper façade and roof comb are a riot of Chac masks and animal gods, *bacabs*. Another building, down a dusty foot trail east of the Nunnery, is the plain **Akab-Dzib**, Mayan for "Obscure Writing," named for some undeciphered hieroglyphics on its lintel.

OLD CHICHEN: A third section of the ruins lies scattered in the brush but connected by trails south of the Hacienda Chichén hotel. Unless you fancy yourself an explorer, it's probably best to have a guide to see these structures. The most noteworthy of these ruins is the **Temple of Three Lintels**, dated AD 879 and built in the Classic Puuc style.

> **AUTHOR'S TIP:** *You might pick up a good local guide, less expensively than at the main ruins, in nearby Piste. Wear slacks, sunscreen and insect repellent; take water and a hat.*

■ Trip to Grutas De Balankanche

The caverns of Balankanche, six km (3.7 miles) east of Chichén's ruins, were a center for the worship of the gods Chac, Tlaloc and Kukulcán during the 10th and 11th centuries. Artifacts, sculpture and pottery are found around the crowning attraction of the caves, a thick stalagmite "Ceiba Tree." Open from 9 am to 4 pm. Guided tours in Spanish, French or English are the only way to see the caves, which are relatively large and open. Spanish-language tours are at 9 am, noon, 2 and 4 pm; in French at 10 am; and in English at 11 am, 1 and 3 pm. If you're early, hang out in their cool and inviting botanical gardens, with flora identification signs in English and Spanish. Admission is about US $5.

■ Cenote Ik-Kil

Across the highway from the Dolores Alba Hotel, about two km (1.25 miles) east of the entrance to Chichén Itzá, is Ik-Kil, a private park with cenote for swimming. This interesting diversion hit the headlines in October 2002 when the roof of the underground cavern collapsed and killed a Japanese couple on their honeymoon. Speculation was that dynamiting for the stairs weakened the natural structure. If you're hot and tired from visiting the ruins and want to swim in a cenote instead of a pool, it's now safe. About US $5 entrance fee.

QUEEN MOO & THE EGYPTIAN SPHINX

An investigation into the history of archeology in the Yucatán will eventually come across Augustus and Alice Le Plongeon, referred to as either crackpots or important contributors to the understanding of the lost Maya.

In 1873, Augustus and his young wife landed in the Yucatán to study and document Maya civilization using glass plate photography. He and Alice first stirred up controversy when, in an effort to protect Uxmal from looters, Augustus placed an advertisement in a Mérida newspaper claiming to have set dynamite booby-traps around the ruins. It was to prevent destruction, Alice later explained to the *New York World*, "not at the hand of Indians, who stand in awe of the effigies of the ancient rulers of the country, but the very administrator who is destroying these monuments, by order of the master, to use the stones in the building of his farmhouse."

Yucatán

The ploy blew up in the face of the Le Plongeons when, although it temporarily stopped the plundering of Uxmal's stones, it became a false but oft-repeated story that he had used dynamite to excavate buildings at Uxmal and Chichén Itzá. But the nail in the coffin of the Le Plongeons' credibility came from their own ill-conceived speculations on Maya history. Augustus and Alice believed the Maya to be descendants of the Atlantis civilization. In their recreation of the story, Queen Móo, leader of the Maya and builder of some of Chichén's marvels, traveled to Egypt, where she was welcomed as the god Isis.

Unfortunately for the Le Plongeons, they were attacked in professional circles by jealous archeologists who ridiculed both the conclusions they reached as well as them personally. Lost in the insults from critics who had never even been to the Yucatán was the Le Plongeons' groundbreaking work and professional methods of excavation – as good if not better than their trained contemporaries – and the important find of Chac Mool at Chichén Itzá. Augustus had a premonition that encouraged him to dig in a certain spot, where he uncovered the famous Chac Mool statue.

A very readable and sympathetic book about them is **A Dream of Maya,** by Lawrence Desmond and Phyllis Messenger, published by the University of New Mexico Press.

He and his wife could only report what they actually found, but it was impossible to be in the presence of so many wonders without doing a little wondering themselves.
~ Manly Hall, writing of the Le Plongeons in *Horizon* magazine, 1948

Accommodations

If you want to stay overnight to see the light show at 7 pm, or just to spend more time at these exceptional ruins, the hotel choices include three in the archeological zone itself, one just outside, and several in Piste.

■ Hotel Zone

Hacienda Chichén Resort *(Hotel Zone, US ☎ 800/624-8451, Mexico ☎ 985/851-0045, fax 985/851-0110, www.haciendachichen.com, 24 rooms, 4 suites, air, pool, restaurants, safety deposit, babysitting).* See our section on hacienda accommodations, page 100, for a full review of this highly recommended property.

Mayaland *(Hotel Zone, US* ☎ *800/235-4079, Mexico* ☎ *985/851-0103, fax 985/851-0129, 92 rooms, bungalows & suites with air, TV, balconies or terraces, 2 swimming pools, 2 restaurants).* The huge, white hacienda-style Mayaland is so close to Chichén that many windows overlook several important ruins. Although it's somewhat ugly from the dead-end road, the interior is lavish and luxurious. The 100-acre gardens contain winding paths amid lush tropical flowering plants.

HOTEL PRICE CHART	
NOTE: Often, one shared bed in a room is cheaper than two. Prices based on cost per night, for two.	
[No $]	Less than US $20
$	US $20 - $40
$$	US $40 - $80
$$$	US $80 - $125

Rooms are tastefully furnished with two big beds, a couch and large dresser, giant closets and hand-blown glass lamps. Bathrooms are not so extravagant. The private bungalows are suite-like in size and feature hand-carved wooden bathroom doors. The two hotel restaurants feature French and international cuisine, with a reputation for excellence. They also offer a buffet lunch and free shuttle to the ruins, but you might as well walk as the pedestrian entrance is just across the parking lot. $$$-$$$$

Villas Arqueológicas - Chichén Itzá *(Hotel Zone, US* ☎ *800/258-2633, Mexico* ☎ *985/856-6000, fax 985/856-6008, www.clubmed.com, 40 rooms with air, pool, tennis, restaurant).* The rooms here were the original ones built for the many archeologists who worked on the restoration of Chichén Itzá. They're somewhat small, with low ceilings and two twin beds snuggled into arched sleeping nooks. It's a warm and cozy use of limited space, like having your own room as a kid. We like the feeling. Closets and bathroom are a good size and done in all natural woods. All the rooms wrap around a big pool, which is dwarfed by a huge palapa bar and restaurant area complete with lazy soft cushions for relaxing. There is a more formal hacienda-style dining room as well. $$

Dolores Alba Chichén *(Km 122 on Highway 180,* ☎ *985/858-1555 but better to make reservations online at www.doloresalba.com, 35 rooms with air or fans, pool, restaurant).* This is the original hotel begun by the Sanchez family, which owns the Hotel Dolores Alba in Mérida. The intricately patterned tiles on the floor of the indoor restaurant were hand-painted specifically for the hotel when it was built around 1955. The three Sanchez brothers now run it with smiles and a good sense of what's important in modern accommodations. Many guests stay two nights, lured by the nightly laser light show at the ruins. Totally remodeled in 1999, the country house-style hotel consists of attached rose-pink cottages in extensive gardens. Each medium-size room is cheerful and pleasant with three windows and a modern bathroom. An inviting palapa provides shade for the outdoor restaurant and for several hammocks swinging peacefully near the pool. Their new second pool is one of the best we've ever seen. The bottom is natural stone, complete with

a swim-through cavern, just like a sparkling cenote. Free transportation from the Alba is offered to the ruins. Walk back or negotiate a taxi fare (should be about US $5; ask first). Reservations can be made through the Dolores Alba in Mérida at ☎ 999/928-5650. $

■ Piste

There are several *posadas* with cheap rooms in the strip mall-like town, such as the basic **Posada Chac Mool**, as well as the upscale **Chichén Itzá Hotel**, in the strip mall-like town of Piste. Taxis can run you to the ruins, which are also reachable via a long walk. Inexpensive eateries line the roadway. One, **Las Redes**, also has a mini-supermarket for your camping and RV supplies.

> **AUTHOR'S TIP:** *The express buses to Cancún or Mérida run only twice a day through Piste so, unless you relish the four-hour trip to either place on the local bus, plan accordingly. The bus station, located next to the Posada Novelo, is less than a kilometer from the road into the ruins.*

Piramide Inn *(Km 118 Highway 180,* ☎ *985/856-2671, 34 rooms with air or fans, pool, restaurant).* Adequate rooms, a good restaurant and a large pool mark this hotel/motel along the highway in the closest town to the ruins. The original owner started the semi-famous "Explorer's Club" here, but since his death the Club has been lost. Camping is available. $

Posada Novelo *(Km 118 Highway 180,* ☎ *985/851-0275, 10 rooms with fans).* The Novelo has the same owner as the Stardust, below, and guests can use the the larger hotel's pool and restaurant. Rooms here are very basic: no toilet seats, worn bedspreads, but clean. The owner also offers a trailer park with full hook-ups in the back. $

Stardust Inn *(Km 118 Highway 180,* ☎/*fax 985/851-0275, 57 rooms with air, pool, TV, restaurant).* No relation to the Las Vegas landmark – although the owner has been to Nevada. The Stardust boasts a huge central pool framed by picturesque coconut palms. The rooms are fairly large, modestly furnished and carpeted upstairs. Show the convivial owner a copy of our book and ask for a discount. It's a friendly establishment, with a good restaurant. If we stay in Piste, this is usually our choice for value. $$

Dining

The pleasant **Cafetería Ruinas** on the Chichén grounds does a fairly good job offering Mexican meals to weary tourists. In Piste, a few minutes by car, **Restaurant Los Parajos** is popular because of

its attractive palapa-laden atmosphere and fair food. **El Carrousel**, across the street serves regional meals inexpensively. The big **Restaurant Xaybe'h** and **La Fiesta** are both good – air-conditioned, but more expensive – handling a fair number of tour bus diners. **La Casa del Mayab**, opposite the Pyramid Inn, serves a tasty all-you-can-eat buffet. The Stardust, above, serves tasty

DINING PRICE CHART	
NOTE: Prices based on a typical entrée, per person, and do not include beverage.	
$	Less than US $5
$$	US $5 - 10
$$$	Over US $10

Yucatecan/Mexican food and seafood. Both of the latter offer a cool swim in their pool. Seafood can be caught at **Restaurant Las Redes**. **Restaurant Las Mestizas** is worthwhile, offering homemade regional cooking and a palapa decorated with butterflies and parrots. You'll find a *panadería*, bakery, on the west end of town.

AUTHOR'S TIP: *If you've gone out for lunch, keep your admission ticket to reenter the ruins the same day. You may have to pay twice for parking (US $3).*

Side Trip to Yaxcaba

For Colonial church and history buffs the village of Yaxcaba ("Clear Turquoise Water") is an interesting side trip from Piste. Its opulent church, built in the 1700s by the more secular Episcopal clergy after they gained control of the mission from the austere Franciscans, is considered one-of-a-kind in the Americas. The three tower western façade rivals that of Mérida in scale but is even more ornate. Adjoining buildings include an arcade chapel, the old atrium wall, and a Moorish-style cemetery gate. Additionally, the Chapel of Santa Cruz overlooks the grotto and deep cenote that gives the town its name. Facing the cenote is the "House of the Wizard," an 18th-century Colonial merchant's house.

At its zenith back in the 18th century when farming times were good, Yaxcaba was home to 4,000 people, most of them of Spanish descent. In 1761, drunken troops from the town's garrison brutally attacked a Maya fiesta in a nearby settlement to break up a minor fight there. In the scuffle Tiburcio Casgaya, the soldiers' overzealous commander, was killed. A plaque announces he is buried in the church atria. Sparked by the unfortunate confrontation, a widespread Maya rebellion ensued. Its leader, Jesuit-educated Jacinto Uc, declared himself "Canek," the ancient king of the Itza, returned to liberate his people from their oppressors. The popular uprising was quickly subdued and Uc was drawn and quartered in Mérida's square. The long memory of the Maya called for retribution against the Yaxcaba garrison when the Caste War began 86 years later. Nearly 5,000 Maya, dressed in cap-

Yucatán

tured uniforms, surrounded the town and taunted the Yucatecans before overwhelming them in a determined frontal assault.

To get there, go west from Piste for 23 km, turn left at Libre Unión and follow the narrow road south. Not too far down that road is a left for a cool deep cenote, **Xtogil**. It boasts hand-hewn steps that snake down to its depths, and overhanging vegetation. Used for ceremonies by the ancient Maya, there's a tiny ruined Spanish chapel built on the hill nearby. It's a wonderful place to camp or picnic. The unexcavated Maya ruin of **Ikil** is not too far from here, but is too hard to find without a guide.

> *For the best appreciation of the large number of Colonial mission churches built by the Spanish, read **Maya Missions**, by Richard and Rosalind Perry, published by Espandaña Press. The book is rich in historical detail, architectural descriptions and pleasing pen and ink illustrations. A must-have title for Yucatán travel.*

About 40 km (25 miles) west of Piste and Chichén toward Mérida is **Cenote Holca**, which features a memorable underground river cenote. You've got to make your way swimming and walking about 125 meters in a cave until you get to the clear cenote pool. Not for the claustrophobic, but fun for others, just to say you did it. Popular for divers. Admission around US $3.

The Road to Rio, Rio Lagartos

The real meaning of travel, like that of a conversation by the fireside, is the discovery of one's self through contact with other people.
~ Paul Tournier, *The Meaning of Persons*

The road north from Valladolid, Highway 296, passes over the toll road from Cancún to Mérida. It's a broad, flat and straight run to Tizimín, a Colonial city in the center of Yucatán's cattle country, then directly up to Rio Lagartos, a working fishing village inside the Rio Lagartos National Park. The 104 km (65 miles) could be a satisfying bike trip if you have the equipment and energy.

WINDMILL WORLD

In the agricultural countryside, you may be surprised by the number of windmills on metal towers with vanes advertising their manufacturer, Aermotor Chicago. Galvanized metal windmills were first introduced into the Yucatán by Edward Thompson in 1887, when he imported two from the States and extolled the virtues of the lightweight wind-driven pumps for water. Wells in the Mérida area averaged 30 feet deep and were hand-dug through limestone. By 1903 there were 1,200 American-made windmills whirling above the city. The venerable Aermotor company is still making windmills today in Conway, Arkansas.

Ek Balam

It ended...with his body changed to light,
A star that burns forever in the sky.
~ from the Aztec story, Flight of Quetzacóatl

The fabulous ruin at Ek Balam ("Black Jaguar") is the first stop along the way, 13 km (eight miles) north of the Cuota. Follow the sign on the right. Scholars believe that this large site was the center of an agricultural area. At the parking lot follow a *sacbé* 100 meters (330 feet) to the closely clustered ruins enclosed by four km (2.5 miles) of low stone walls. You are entering from the south, where a bullet-shaped arch from the Terminal Classic period greets

Yucatán

Pyramid at Ek Balam.

you atop its small platform with a steep climb. The building to the right, with rounded corners, is called **Las Gemelas**, "the Twins," because of its two identical buildings on top. The platform to the east features the statue of a headless torso, apparently a captive, and there are broken stelae. To the west is a ceremonial. But the most obvious building – attracting all the attention – is **Structure 1**, a huge and impressive 30 meters high by 150 meters long and 60 meters wide (100 x 495 x 200 feet) on the north side of a larger, open field courtyard. We climbed it in 1997 before it was excavated with the aid of a rope tied to a tree on top.

For years, Ek Balam was thought to be an agricultural hub, but not a particularly important religious center. Before excavations in earnest resumed in 1999, scholars had dated the city to the Terminal Classic period, the zenith of Puuc architecture, though little of that building style was apparent. Further complicating the issue were ceramic samples that dated occupation as early as the pre-Classic period. When they began digging away the rubble covering Structure 1, which had been a mountain of dirt overgrown with trees, the theories changed.

The excited archeologists discovered a wall built in front of an intricate and outstandingly well-preserved façade that the Maya had filled in with dirt long before the Conquest. Apparently, the religious leaders deliberately abandoned the ceremonial site. But rather than have their work exposed, they preserved it so that the inevitable renewal of Ek Balam's importance would allow future generations to uncover the sacred symbols. Now it looks as if Ek Balam may even rival Chichén in importance because of its spectacular architecture. The western side of the steep great staircase, whose height indicates the building is taller than Chichén Itzá's famous Castillo pyramid, is the best preserved. With the discovery of a large Chene's style mouth entrance to the interior, flanked on each side by magnificent carvings, and the unearthing of a chamber behind, archeologists are anticipating the possibility of one or more burial tombs, possibly complete with valuable artwork. A faded painting is visible on one of the portal doorways.

The ongoing work restricts access and so far entrance into the interior is forbidden, except for the lower rooms along the massive base. But you can climb the stairs where the views of the surrounding dry jungle are absolutely majestic. From the top you can see the tallest pyramid at Cobá, nearly 48 km (30 miles) away. Two tall mounds that look like mountains (but are in reality are more unexcavated pyramids) flank the courtyard to either side. Five *sacbés* leave Ek Balam toward the north, south, east, west and southwest.

In 1597, Conquistador Juan Gutiérrez Picón, who had a land grant that included the ruins, wrote a treatise, *Relación de Ek Balam*, for the King of Spain that extols the site's significance. Now, nearly 500 years later, Gutiérrez's belief in the importance of Ek Balam is vindicated. This is a site not to missed. Open 8-5 pm.

Three hundred meters from the Ek Balam ruins is a rustic but attractive, eco-friendly little hotel called **Genesis Retreat** (☎ 985/852-7980, www.genesisretreat.com). It features Maya-style cabañas in a garden setting, with a cenote-style pool, hot water showers, small restaurant, and customized tours. One cabin is air-conditioned. Interact with locals, ride a mountain bike, get a massage, or lie in a hammock and read a book or two

Tizimín

Tizimín, Mayan for "Place of Tapir," 50 km (31 miles) north of Valladolid, holds little interest for travelers unless it's fiesta time (it's a great town for a fair) or as an alternative to staying overnight in Rio Lagartos. But a new bypass road will speed you around the downtown if you're just heading north. Tizimin is the center of the Yucatán's ranch land. There's an airstrip in town, built for a visit by the Queen of England but not too active lately. The last time we were there we drove across it on a well-used shortcut, while several head of cattle grazed along its weed-choked shoulder. A sad zoo also exists on Calle 51, but there is an appealing restaurant nearby, **Las Flamboyanes**. The restaurants, bakeries and accommodations in Tizimín (pop. 50,000) are all quite adequate and the lack of tourists means they're also very low-priced.

A quick stop could be the grand Colonial church, the **Convento de Los Tres Reyes Magos** (Monastery of the Three Wise Kings) that presides over Tizimín's shady main square. If you're just passing through and want a snack, try **La Especial bakery** on the corner of the little pedestrian lane off the plaza and Calle 55. Owner Jorge Canul's family has been baking in Tizimín since 1916 and has expanded to Valladolid. A cousin, Eduardo, owns a bakery in Bakersfield, California. Don't miss *pan cubano*, the equivalent of pound cake, sweet and smooth. There is a hard-to-find Internet café, **Servicinet**, on Calle 52 #368.

The annual *Feria de los Tres Reyes*, **Three Kings Fair**, in Tizimín is reknowned throughout the Yucatán. It begins just after New Year's with a street fair of handicrafts and games in the central square, and runs for two weeks. Its highlight is a celebration of All Kings Day, Epiphany, January 6, when Christmas gifts are traditionally exchanged. Shops and bakeries throughout Mexico sell *rosca*, a round cake with a miniature doll baked inside. The person who receives the slice with the doll hosts another party on Candlemas, February 2. The big attractions that draw rural Maya farmers, cowboys, and ranch owners into town are the religious processions and festivities, and the hugely popular bullfights that occur each afternoon. Olé.

Whether we're on Tizimín side streets or stretches of lonely roads in the countryside, we can't help but be impressed with the graceful elegance of Maya women sitting side-saddle on bicycles. Just another of our Mexican memories.

Yucatán

■ Accommodations

San Carlos *(Calle 54 No. 407 near 51, 28 rooms with air or fans, parking).* On a back street only a block from the main square, the V-shaped, two-story San Carlos is easy to mistake for an office building from the front. Run under the auspices of a senior Señora, it's the quietest hotel in town. There's a wild green garden growing in the filled-in swimming pool. The rooms downstairs are a little dark so choose one upstairs. $

HOTEL PRICE CHART	
NOTE: Often, one shared bed in a room is cheaper than two. Prices based on cost per night, for two.	
[No $]	Less than US $20
$	US $20 - $40
$$	US $40 - $80
$$$	US $80 - $125

Posada Pastora *(Calle 51 No. 413, between 52 & 54, no phone, 19 rooms with fans, TV, private parking).* A half-block off the main square, this new hotel has big rooms but no closets or toilet seats. They use a lot of frosted glass and black wrought-iron doors that give a feeling of even more open space. It's Tizimín's newest hotel and well worth checking out or even checking in. $

San Jorge *(Calle 53 No. 412 on the* zócalo, *34 rooms with air or fans, pool, private parking).* Beige and white, this Miami Beach-like hotel has clean, medium-size rooms with tile bath and very big closets. You can't be more conveniently located than this, right on Tizimín's central square. Regular hotel rooms, quite reasonably priced. They don't always fill the triangular swimming pool in winter. $

■ Dining

Tres Reyes *(on the* zócalo, ☎ *986/ 863-2106).* A pleasing corner restaurant run by big "Willy Canto." The Three Kings offers good Yucatecan and Mexican cooking, which Willy claims is the best in the world. He offers a varied menu of meats, poultry and fresh fish, all at excellent prices. Order a cold beer and get a great *bocadillo*, an appetizer of pickled cabbage and onions. This is the town's most memorable eatery. $-$$

DINING PRICE CHART	
NOTE: Prices based on a typical entrée, per person, and do not include beverage.	
$	Less than US $5
$$	US $5 - 10
$$$	Over US $10

La Michocana *(on the* zócalo)*.* La Michocana is a chain of ice cream parlors. The one in Tizimín is particularly clean and welcome on a hot day. Try an exotic flavor (of their umpteen choices) and savor it on a shaded bench in the park. $

Rio Lagartos

*In sleep, every dog dreams of food,
and I, a fisherman, dream of fish.*
~ Theocritis

The road to the fishing port of Rio Lagartos has finally been upgraded to actual pavement rather than rutted *sacbé* and is now fine and fast. It takes just 40 minutes to cover the 53 km (33 miles) from Tizimín. Named for the alligator river that no longer contains alligators, the Lagartos is really an inlet to the Caribbean that opens into a huge estuary/lagoon east of town. That lagoon is the home to millions of **pink flamingos** who come each year in the spring to breed in cone-shaped mud nests. The gawky but graceful birds are brilliant white, pink and salmon colors. Boat trips out to see them are the big attraction here.

When they recognized the importance of the flamingo colonies, the Mexican government set aside 118,000 acres in 1979 as a national park to protect the 212 species of native and migratory birdlife. During the summer months, April through August, the colony breeds and tourist access to their breeding area, at the far eastern part of the lagoon, is strictly forbidden. But the areas where they feed are accessible year-round and even during the winter months you'll see huge flocks blanketing the shallow mud flats in a coat of pink and white.

Don't be put off when you enter Rio Lagartos. Some dilapidated housing rests in the mangrove swamp south of town, but the community itself is a typically

Fishermen checking their nets.

Caribbean/Mexican fishing town. As you pull toward the river front, hawkers may approach and ask if you want to see the flamingos. These young entrepreneurs are legitimate, but check the price quoted with the cooperative kiosk along the *malecón*.

Another attraction of Rio Lagartos is a fabulously photogenic brilliant blue cenote, **Cenote Chiquilá**. It's a cool relaxing swim or snorkel and a great place to camp for free (no facilities) or have a picnic. Located about a half-mile out of town, follow the waterfront to the right (east), past the summer homes that dot the harbor, along the dirt road to a palapa-roofed, open-sided shed. Next to a baseball diamond.

Adventures

FLAMINGO TOURS: Flocks of flamingos dine at several locations along the estuary and lagoon and prices for boat rides out to view them depend upon how far you travel. Boats are available on the *malecón* from the fisherman's cooperative. The lagoon begins to widen east of the wooden bridge over the river and it's about 30 minutes to the first feeding spot, **Yoluk**, or Yolv'i (US $30 to get there). This trip takes about two hours total and can include another smaller colony nearby, **Najochin**. Adding the **Chiquilá** colony boosts the price to US $35. The next option takes about three hours total to reach the larger colony of **San Fernando** (US $50-60). Larger again is the one at **Punta Meco**, a four-hour round trip for about US $75. (Note that all these prices are subject to change.) On all trips, the guide will point out a "white mountain" visible on the barrier peninsula. That's a mountain of salt at Las Coloradas, where it has been mined by the Maya for over 2,000 years!

BACK TO NATURE: Hikers, campers and beachcombers can arrange with local fishermen to be dropped off and picked up later, even the next day, on the virtually deserted peninsula. Ask one of the knowledgeable village youth about the access to the peninsula across the way. While some of it is appealing deserted beaches, other parts are brushy and wild with mangrove swamps along the edge that force you to walk in the water. You should be able to plan a day's hike or a camp with some help from the locals. Plenty of solitude, wildlife and nature (including mosquitoes). There's also a good area on the peninsula across from San Felipe, the village to the west, at the mouth of the river.

Accommodations & Dining

Rio Largartos doesn't seem to attract many overnight visitors, and the lack of hotels may be why. That's a shame because early morning is the best time for birding. There is one good place in town, however, and another favorite of ours in nearby village of San Felipe (see below).

Villa de Pescadores *(on* malecón, *no phone).* The Villa de Pescadores is the best place to stay overnight in Rio Lagartos. It's a sturdy, new, two-story hotel facing the harbor, right next to the bar/restaurant Torreja. The best rooms are upstairs; they are large and have a balcony and view of the water. Quarters are clean with welcome window screens and an interesting décor that features one wall made of stone in each room. The Villa has a spiral staircase with a crow's nest viewing platform on top. Early morning, 5-7:30 am, are the best hours to see and hear the wide variety of birds or to take a boat to see the flamingos. $

La Torreja *(on the* malecón *near the Rio Lagartos lighthouse, no phone).* Look! Under the big palapa! It's a bar! No, it's a restaurant! Either way it's big on fresh fried fish and bottled beer. $

La Isla Contoy *(Calle 19, on the waterfront, no phone).* Only fishing boats tied up along the beach sit between you and the *rio* in this screened-in palapa restaurant. With a great view and a rustic décor, their menu is mostly fresh fish, but they're one of the few seaside places to also offer meat and chicken. Enjoy a fish fillet stuffed with shrimp for about US $5 or the fillet in salsa *à la Veracruzano*. Diego, the manager, offers free tourist information and can arrange trips to see the flamingos or a day of fishing. $

Los Negritos *(Calle 10 No. 135, no phone).* This large restaurant on the way into town doesn't have the ambiance of the riverside but may still have the best seafood in town. Owner Gilmer Pacheco, whose nickname provided the inspiration for the restaurant's name, has a photo menu posted inside and individual wooden fish-shaped menus list the items and prices. His *comida casera* (daily special) is either meat or chicken, but everything else is seafood. Appetizers of ceviche come with every drink and the house specialty is a large broiled lobster tail for about US $10. (Mexicans love it with mayonnaise, so if you're not

HOTEL PRICE CHART	
NOTE: *Often, one shared bed in a room is cheaper than two. Prices based on cost per night, for two.*	
[No $]	Less than US $20
$	US $20 - $40
$$	US $40 - $80
$$$	US $80 - $125

DINING PRICE CHART	
NOTE: *Prices based on a typical entrée, per person, and do not include beverage.*	
$	Less than US $5
$$	US $5 - 10
$$$	Over US $10

Yucatán

sure you do, ask for it on the side.) We loved the *mojo de ajo* (fillet broiled in garlic butter). Saturday night from 10:30 pm to 2:30 am the tables are pushed back and the restaurant becomes the Titanic Discotheque, a hip place to go down with the ship. $

San Felipe & Las Coloradas

Love the sea? I dote upon it – from the beach.
~ Douglas Jerrold, 1803-1857

Two seaside villages flank Rio Lagartos, and both are accessible from the crossroads at the never-seems-to-be-staffed Rio Lagartos National Park Information Center, two km (1.25 miles) south of town. San Felipe has a more picturesque harbor than Rio Lagartos and if you're into the sea and quiet fishing villages, this is a very attractive alternative. Camping is available nearby and the town even offers a modern hotel.

An interesting route to San Felipe is to turn left just outside the tiny village of Ki-Kil, north of Tizimin. Look for the ruined church on the right and make the next left after the bend in the road.

Hotel San Felipe de Jesus *(Calle 9 between 14 & 16,* ☎ *986/862-2027, 18 rooms with fans, restaurant).* Opened in 1996, the Hotel San Felipe is very attractive and modern with a restaurant that shares a view of the river and

The harbor at San Felipe.

Gulf of Mexico. This is a much-needed hotel near the increasingly popular flamingo-viewing stop in the Rio Lagartos Reserve. Surprisingly, rates for a boat to go and see the flamingos are a little lower here than they are in Rio Lagartos, even though it's an additional 15 minutes each way in travel time. For swimming and beachcombing, there's a shady shore across the river where Rio Lagartos opens into the Gulf. The deserted public beach there is fabulous. Local fishing boats will ferry you across for about US $2 and will pick you up at a pre-arranged time. For a little over US $15 per hour you can rent a boat to take you on a tour up and down the coast. Ask about fishing as well. Upper rooms in the hotel have an extra *mirador* balcony on the roof (up funky interior stairs) that overlooks the appealing harbor. From there (or any of the rooms that face the water) watch the fisherman shrimp fishing by night, their flashlights, miners' hats or lanterns glowing in the dark, bobbing up and down as they jockey for the best location. Magical. $

We can't speak for the name of San Felipe's inviting waterfront restaurant, **El Popular Vaselina** (Favorite Grease Spot?), but it is very popular. No surprise here, fish is the specialty. Its building is new, large, clean and palapa-covered and it overlooks an idyllic harbor. What more could you ask for?

The brilliant white **salt mountains** at Las Coloradas are fascinating, but there's little to do or see in the village itself. Its fine sandy beach is full of fishing boats flying colorful flags in the strong breeze. Fishing is one of two main occupations at this Maya outpost. The other is salt, gathered here for over 2,000 years. The ancient Maya used it as a trading commodity through all the stages of their civilization. Salt is collected by filling large ponds with saltwater which is then evaporated, leaving the salt. Mineral deposits make the concentrated ponds gleam purple and red, hence the name of the village. You can try stopping in the modern salt production facilities and ask to look around. At least keep your eye out for wildlife in the low brush that lines the dusty white road. Please don't drive too fast here. We found a rare jaguarundi's burrow and sat watching him (or her) watch us for five minutes. This area is rich in all kinds of wildlife.

The wooden bridge you cross on the way often has fishermen net-fishing from the top, but if you stop to talk or take pictures, be sure to wear either slacks and long sleeves or insect repellent; mosquitoes here love fresh blood.

Izamal

At nine o'clock we entered the suburbs of Izamal....
It was the last day of the fiesta of Santa Cruz....
But amid this gay scene the eye turned involuntarily to immense mounds rising
grandly above the tops of the houses...
proclaiming the power of those who reared them and destined, apparently, to
stand when the feebler structures
of their more civilized conquerors shall have crumbled into dust.
~ John L. Stephens, *Incidents of Travel in Yucatán,* 1843

Izamal is known as the "Yellow City," and all the homes within it are painted yellow or gold. This indicates a religious symbolism, but no one seems to remember exactly why or even when (1960s?) the houses changed color. It is a real treat to drive into an authentic Colonial city that gets more religious pilgrims than tourists. The huge gold-painted monastery in Colonial Izamal is built over an Early Classic Maya religious center where pilgrims have come to worship the supreme god, Itzamná, and Kinich Kakmó, a manifestation of the sun god, Kinich Ahau, for a thousand years. A dozen temples were once in the ceremonial city that lost influence and fell to Mayapán in the Terminal Classic period. Its long occupation and use lasted through the Spanish Conquest. Izamal's holiness among the Maya was based on the legend of a priest-god Zamná (Itzamná), whose body was cut up and buried in the principal temples in town. The religious significance of Izamal to the Maya might explain why the Franciscans chose it as the location for their enormous monastery in the center of town, now one of the two main tourist attractions of this pleasant Colonial anachronism.

Victoria cab in front of Izamal's monastery.

One way to enjoy the city's flavor is to tour town in a nostalgic Victoria, a horse-drawn carriage that continues to serve as a mode of transportation for visitors and locals alike. Many of the brightly decorated carriages look as though they've been lovingly cared for since the time of Queen Victoria, for whom they're reportedly named.

Orientation

■ Getting Around

There are numerous ways to get to Izamal, depending, of course, on where you're coming from and how pressed you are for time. Whether you're coming from Mérida or Valladolid, Izamal can be reached from the town of Kantunil on **Route 180**. From Mérida, turn off 180 at either Hóctun or Kantunil. Or go by way of Motúl, a slower way through many small Maya villages. From Valladolid, take 180 to Kantunil, or the back road that retraces the retreat of the Caste War refugees through Tinúm, Dzitas, Quintana Roo, Tunkas and Stilpech (we loved this route). The road forks (you go right) as you leave town. A **train** runs daily to Izamal from Mérida with an "Izamal by Train" excursion on Sunday. A "Discover Izamal" bus tour leaves Monday, Wednesday, Friday and Saturday.

Buses serve the city from either direction. Be sure to ride in a Victoria horse-drawn hansom in Izamal (found in the nearly shadeless park next to the convent).

Practicalities

GIFT SHOPPING: Handicrafts are special at **Hecho a Mano** ("Made by Hand") at Calles 31 and 38. Owned by Americans Jeanne Hunt, a photographer, and Hector Garza, a collector of unique folk art, this is a pleasant stop to shop, and is one of Yucatán's best handicraft outlets. It's well worth a visit for those hard-to-find gifts.

The **Parador Turístico** on Calle 30, No. 22, has various Maya vendors and puts on cultural shows, including the Sunday show (worth catching even if you aren't with the Mérida train excursion). It starts at about 1 pm. If you go and there is no one there, walk around the corner to Tumben-Lol restaurant, which plays host to smaller groups.

The cottage-industry village of **Kimbilá** is 12 km (7.5 miles) east of town, where El Milagro de Dios and Creaciones Addy are noteworthy shops for *huipiles*.

Yucatán

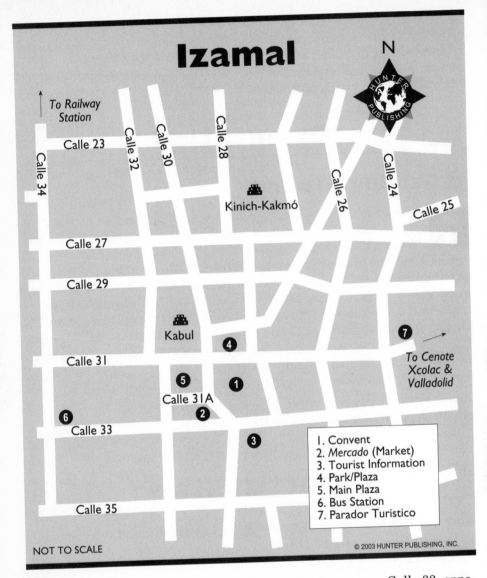

Izamal

N

To Railway Station

Calle 23

Calle 34

Calle 32

Calle 30

Calle 28

Kinich-Kakmó

Calle 26

Calle 24

Calle 25

Calle 27

Calle 29

Kabul

④

⑦

Calle 31

⑤

①

To Cenote Xcolac & Valladolid

Calle 31A

②

⑥

③

Calle 33

1. Convent
2. *Mercado* (Market)
3. Tourist Information
4. Park/Plaza
5. Main Plaza
6. Bus Station
7. Parador Turistico

Calle 35

NOT TO SCALE

© 2003 HUNTER PUBLISHING, INC.

PHARMACIES: There are at least two pharmacies, one on Calle 33, opposite the municipal market, and the other inside the municipal market across from the convent.

TOURIST INFORMATION: There's a tourist information room at the corner of Calles 33 and 30.

TRANSPORTATION: The **train station** is on Calle 30 and the **bus station** is on Calle 32, No. 302. There are three easy-to-find gas stations in town.

Adventures

■ Sights & Events

The gargantuan golden yellow structure that commands a view of the city and the lives of the people in Izamal (Mayan for "Dew of Heaven") is the **Convento de San Antonio de Padua**. In 1533 the Spanish Franciscan order had the colossal Maya temple Ppal-Hol-Chac ("House of Heads and Lightening") demolished down to its base, 180 meters long and 12 meters high (590 x 39 feet). With the discarded stones, architect Fray Juan de Mérida began the first monastery in the New World, which was completed by Fray Francisco de la Torre in 1561. Climbing the long stone steps of the convent leads to the graceful arcade with 75 arches. The strolling covered walkway encloses a grand courtyard, the Atrium. At 8,000 square meters, it is the largest in Mexico and second in size only to the Vatican in the Catholic world. Pope John Paul II spoke in the Atrium here on August 11, 1993, and met here with representatives of Latin America's indigenous peoples.

A number of paintings thought to date from the 16th and 17th century were recently found on the walls of the church entrance and cloisters when a thick layer of whitewash was removed. One of the most beautiful of the frescoes is dedicated to fourth-century martyr Saint Barbara.

The church interior is relatively stark except for the magnificent gold-leaf *retablo* (altar back) and the statue of the Virgin carved by Friar Juan de Aguirre and transported from Guatemala in 1558. She resides in a side alcove surrounded by oil paintings of Yucatecan bishops. The statue has miracles attributed to it, including becoming too heavy for thieves from Valladolid who tried to spirit her away to their town.

Apart from the pagan and religious festivities in honor of the Virgin, held on December 10-ish, the biggest celebration in Izamal is the procession of the **Black Christ of Stilpech**. At dawn on October 18, inhabitants travel to Stilpech to find the statue that they bring back about 7 am, heralded by the sounds of hymns, prayers and firecrackers. Then there's an all-day fiesta. Izamal is worth a stop on any Yucatán adventure.

■ Adventures on Foot

At the height of its Early Classic glory, Izamal boasted a plaza surrounded by the pyramids of Kabul ("House of the Miraculous Hand"), Itzamatul ("Dew That Falls From Heaven"), Ppal-Hol-Chac ("Lightning House") and Kinich Kakmó ("Fire Macaw With the Face of the Sun"). The gigantic 35-meter (115-foot) pyramid of **Kinich Kakmó** is visible

as you drive into town and from the main plaza, so it should be easy to find, right? Wrong. Once you set out on foot, the base disappears in the maze of modern buildings. We felt foolish to have lost it. The base of the monstrous mound is 195 meters by 174 meters (640 x 570 feet) – a big city block. A stairway has been restored so it's an easy, but hot, climb. Since the stairway rises from the street, the full size of the pyramid is not apparent until you reach the first terraced level and discover a second bulky pyramid of another 17 meters (56 feet) rests on top of it. Bishop de Landa described it as "a building of such height and beauty that it astonishes me."

We finally found it by hiring a horse-drawn Victoria cab to take us there, but you can get there on foot. Walk north on Calle 30 from the front of the convent to Calle 27 and turn right (east) to Calle 28.

■ Adventures on Water

About 14 km (nine miles) east of town on the road to Stilpech (follow Calle 31) is the **Cenote X-Kolac**, which makes for a cool and refreshing swim. It has some facilities.

Accommodations

Macan Ché (*Calle 22 between 31 & 33, ☎/fax 988/954-0287, www. macanche.com, 12 cottages with fans, pool, rates include breakfast*). Izamal's most attractive accommodations are here at Macan Ché, where your host is an American, Diane Dutton. On a quiet side street near the El Conejo ruins, the hotel is a short walk to the center of town or the Parador Turístico. Crushed stone paths trail back to individual cabañas scattered around her jungle-like tropical garden. Each is tastefully decorated in a different theme: Mexican, African, Colonial, etc. Rooms are large and comfortable. There's an English-language reading library. The surrounding trees provide cool shade and the sounds you hear all day are sweet songbirds, while at night neighborhood dogs sometimes serenade. Full breakfast is served in the palapa-covered dining room. There is private parking. Access to horseback riding is only a few blocks away at Diane's ranch, where she rents three more private casitas as well as camping spots. Ms. Dutton, who is active in local community affairs (organizing dance classes and hosting Piñata parties

HOTEL PRICE CHART	
NOTE: Often, one shared bed in a room is cheaper than two. Prices based on cost per night, for two.	
[No $]	Less than US $20
$	US $20 - $40
$$	US $40 - $80
$$$	US $80 - $125

for children), also owns **Hacienda San Antonio Chalante**, 11 km away outside of Sudzal. See page 99. $-$$

Green River Hotel *(Avenida Zamná, ☎ 988/954-0337, 11 rooms with air, pool, minibar, TV)*. According to local folklore there once was a river near the site of this little hotel so it kept the area's traditional name: Rio Verde. Out of the town center by about six blocks, the Green River is a clean, modern one-story building on a wide boulevard of flamboyane shade trees. All the rooms are pleasant and adequately sized with closets and new bathrooms, and there are four larger rooms available with three beds. Quiet and very peaceful, and only a short walk or carriage ride to the convent and ruins. Manager Herbert Sosa is friendly and helpful and speaks fairly good English. If you make reservations, he'll pick you up downtown. $

Hotel Canto *(Calle 31, on the square, no phone, 15 rooms with fans)*. The Canto is a tremendous disappointment because the entryway in the row of Colonial buildings that front the main square is quite inviting. It has beautiful tile work, a green courtyard garden and a locally popular tiny restaurant. But the dingy small rooms haven't been improved, except perhaps for grungy bathrooms, apparently since John L. Stephens slept here in 1842. This is a place for extreme backpacking hammock-sleepers only. However, the restaurant is cheap and you can go out the back and climb the unexcavated pyramid, "Kabul," that abuts the rear of the building.

Hacienda San Antonio Chalante *(Sudzal, ☎/fax 988/954-0287, www. macanche.com, 9 rooms & suites, 2 pools, horseback riding, bar)*.

Hacienda San José *(Km 30 Tixkokob-Tekantó Rd, Tixkokob, in US ☎ 888/ 625-5144, in Mexico 999/910-4617, fax 999/923-7963, www.luxurycollection. com, 15 rooms & suites, restaurant, pool)*.

See pages 99-100 for a full description of these two hacienda properties.

Dining

 Kinich Kakmó *(Calle 27 No. 299, between 28 & 30, no phone)*. Fifty meters (165 feet) down the street from the Kinich Kakmó pyramid is this intimate and inviting restaurant, one of Izamal's most popular with tourists. The dining area rests in back under a large palapa roof, hidden behind a Colonial front. It is pleasingly decorated with clay pottery and Maya artifacts. You're invited to wander along a stone path in the garden where two Maya women hand-make tortillas the traditional way in their

DINING PRICE CHART	
NOTE: Prices based on a typical entrée, per person, and do not include beverage.	
$	Less than US $5
$$	US $5 - 10
$$$	Over US $10

Yucatán

very smoky (too smoky for their health) open kitchen. The attentive staff in the Kinich restaurant offer a varied menu. Browse the tiny, reasonably priced gift shop that shares the front of the restaurant. Best eats in town. $

Tumben-Lol *(Calle 22 No. 302, between 31 & 33, no phone)*. Around the corner from the new Parador Turístico and up the street from El Conejo ruins is the Tumben-Lol, a large palapa-covered, red-tiled restaurant. It has a smaller menu than the Kinich Kakmó, but slightly lower prices to match. It boasts impressive polished wood entrance doors and a small attractive walled garden at the edge of the palapa. Clean and cool. The restaurant's name in Mayan means "New Flower," and each of the handmade chairs has a flower carved in the top. The restaurant hosts the Sunday folk show and dance when there are not enough tourists on the train to open the Parador. $

El Toro Restaurant *(Calle 30 No. 303, at Calle 33, no phone)*. Across from the *mercado* and *Convento*, near the Tourist Information office, is this clean and appealing little Mexican/Yucatecan restaurant named "The Bull." The owner, Norma Rosado, is attracting tourists to Izamal with good food, low prices, and clean bathrooms.

The next compass direction of the Maya world is West, or black, where the sun dies. This is the area we will explore next.

WEST - BLACK

(Chikin - Ek)

Celestún

Over the long haul of life on this planet it is the ecologists and not the bookkeepers of business, who are the ultimate accountants.
~ Stewart L. Udall, former US Secretary of the Interior

There are two ways to reach Celestún and the fabulous flamingo flocks that feed there. Before Hurricane Gilbert in 1988 these birds flocked only to Rio Lagartos, but after the damage done to the lagoons and estuaries, they changed their feeding habits and visited new grounds. Flamingos eat standing in groups of hundreds on mud banks in Celestún's shallow estuary. They force the muddy water through the serrated edges of their bill and strain the edible animal and vegetable matter for nourishment. The pink coloring comes from the red pigment found in shrimp-like animals that are an important part of their diet. Without this, their feathers would turn a dull buff color. The Yucatán's shrimp make for spectacular colors and, as a result, the birds at

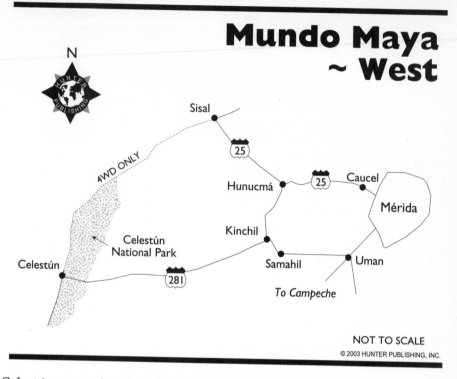

Mundo Maya ~ West

N

Sisal

25

4WD ONLY

25 Caucel

Hunucmá

Mérida

Kinchil

Celestún
National Park

Celestún

Samahil

Uman

281

To Campeche

NOT TO SCALE

© 2003 HUNTER PUBLISHING, INC.

Celestún are an electric pink and rose salmon. Over on the Gulf beach (besides good swimming in the warm soft surf) Celestún is a beachcombers delight. Tons of shells wash up. We spend hours collecting exotic specimens only to leave them in piles in the sand.

The first route to Celestún is the one more clearly marked: Route 281 through **Hunucmá**, then 64 km (40 miles) to the bridge over Celestún's untroubled water. The second way is faster, more interesting and much narrower. Go south to **Umán** and follow the signs toward Celestún, through Samahil, then Kinchil, where you connect with Route 281, straight east to Celestún. Note: If you ask directions anywhere in the Yucatán, forget asking where highway number blah-blah is; Yucatecans don't think of these roads by route numbers.

The road to Celestún makes a good but long bike ride if you brought your own. Most guidebooks recommend viewing the birds early in the morning, but we found the late afternoon sun, with its golden-red glow, perfect for photography. Midday is hot.

In 1979, the Mexican government set aside the surrounding 15,000 acres of beach and mangrove jungle as a bird and nature sanctuary and its popularity as an ecological tourism destination increases each year. If you're planning to spend the night (not a bad idea), go straight to the beach and book a room.

The beachfront is where all the town's hotels and restaurants are located. Remember to bring cash, as there are no banks or ATMs in Celestún.

Adventures

■ Eco-Tours (Flamingos)

 As you cross the bridge over the estuary, 25-foot launches with outboard motors line the banks and wooden pier on the far side. These canvas-roofed boats take tourists out into the shallow waters to see the flamingos, native and migratory birdlife (304 species have been identified) and a cenote in the mangrove jungle. The large reception center, called the **Unidad Turistica Celestún**, has a snack bar and very welcome public bathrooms. Buy your boat tickets here. Launch pilots no longer scare up the flocks for photographs, so don't ask. It disturbs their feeding patterns, putting unnecessary stress on the colony.

The tour (one hour) begins at the bridge and covers two or three massive flocks before stopping at a swimming cenote (sometimes at an "extra" charge) on the way back. The boats, whose prices are set by a unionized cooperative, take four to six people for about US $45 per boat plus $2 each person. Because the water is very shallow and the flamingos are at their best during the dry winter season, boats with four to six people can't always get as close as those with only two people. We rented a launch for just the two of us. It cost extra but we got our money's worth.

A second flamingo-bound route leaves from the beachfront on the Gulf, where you ride south in the surf along the pencil-thin peninsula and see an additional flamingo group, then around the point for a stop at Tampeten, a "petrified forest," near the entrance to the estuary. These boats then go on to the first large colony of flamingos north of the bridge, stop at the jungle cenote and return. It takes about three hours and costs around US $80 plus $20 per person. You can also arrange for these boats on the beach, as well as at the Tourism Center.

The Gulf beach at Celestún is good for swimming, shell-collecting, fishing, beachcombing or watching the frigate birds drift overhead while sitting in one of the many beachfront restaurants that spill out onto the sand.

Celestún's natural beauty makes it a natural for eco-tours. Feliciano Pech, a local fisherman with a concern for the ecology, and David Bacab, a native of Celestún and trained conservationist, have teamed up to open **Celestún Expeditions** (☎ 988/916-2049, celexp@diariol.sureste.com) on Calle 10 between 9 and 11. They offer bilingual guided expeditions on land and sea around northeastern Yucatán for ecological, cultural, birding, and natural history. Well north of the town, out of sight along the rutted sand road, there

is a **lighthouse** with a good view of the mangrove forests. It is a great place for birding, best only with four-wheel-drive and guide.

Take the sand road out of town to the south to explore the ruins of **Hacienda Real de Salinas**, an abandoned and sacked hacienda. Follow the road along the inner harbor, past the dump and into the woods. History, adventure, and birding in one. Or take a trip through the lagoons just across the

Flamingos in flight.

border into Campeche State to the nature reserve **Kanbalan.** (Celestún is on the border between the two states and the local fishermen are fierce rivals.) Kanbalan is a pristine area with flamingos, parrots, monkeys, fish, and even a crocodile or two. You can rent a canoe (about US $35 a day) with a map of the area at **El Lobo** restaurant. They'll also do a nice boxed lunch for you. If you'd prefer a guide ask at El Lobo or at Celestún Expeditions (above).

Accommodations

Hotel María del Carmen *(Calle 12, ☎ 988/916-2051, 15 rooms with fans, 4 rooms with air)*. New in 1992, the beachfront complex added a third story in 1997. All the quarters are the same, with small balconies facing the Gulf, tile floors and bathrooms that have hot water (a seaside luxury). A very popular hotel. Get an upper floor with a view of the ocean; they are the better rooms. $

Eco Paraíso Xixim *(Km 9 on the dirt road north from Celestún, ☎ 988/916-2100, fax 988/916-2111, www.ecoparaiso.com, 15 cabañas with fans, beachfront, safety boxes, pool, tours, restaurant, bike rentals, rates includes breakfast & dinner)*. Seems to be a serious effort to balance the ecological impact of a hotel with its natural surroundings and still turn a profit. Xixim means "sea shell."

The hotel markets itself as "state-of-the-art" ecological. To save on water and waste, guests have the option of not having their sheets and towels changed daily – a painless and effective way to conserve. Electricity, which comes from a distant generator, is restricted to certain hours. Organic vegetables are

HOTEL PRICE CHART	
NOTE: Often, one shared bed in a room is cheaper than two. Prices based on cost per night, for two.	
[No $]	Less than US $20
$	US $20 - $40
$$	US $40 - $80
$$$	US $80 - $125

Yucatán

grown on the 280-acre grounds of the former coconut grove, using composted waste as fertilizer. They even recycle waste water here after it undergoes treatment. Most of the guests at Xixim (pronounced "Shi-shim") are Europeans on package tours that include scheduled trips to the Celestún Biosphere, Uxmal and other Maya ruins, as well as some haciendas and cenotes. If the hotel's not full you can buy a package or just take a bungalow for a while. There's a three-mile beach and reservations strongly suggested. You'll need to slather on eco-friendly mosquito repellent, which they sell at reception. Check out their turtle preservation efforts.

The cool, screen-windowed palapa guest cottages are new (the hotel opened in December of 1996) with two double beds, seafront porches and gorgeous turquoise-tiled bathrooms. $$$$

Hospedaje Sofia *(Calle 10, no phone, 5 rooms)*. The back of this newish motel is next to Celestún Expeditions (see page 354). Very serviceable, very plain, with two queen-size beds and no toilet seat. Fan, hot water – all at a low price. This is a best basic budget buy. Secure parking. $

Hotel Sol y Mar *(Calle 12 between 11 & 13, ☎ 988/916-2166, 17 rooms, air, fridge, restaurant, cable TV)*. If this upstairs/downstairs motel looks as if it's been transplanted from South Florida, that may be because a former Floridian and Cuban-American, Geraldo Vasquez, is half-owner. New in 1999. Rooms are large with two queen-size beds, TV and a fridge. Upstairs have fans only but are more breezy, offer a sea view and are slightly cheaper. Rooftop deck patio. One block off the beach, across from La Palapa restaurant. $

Ecohotel Flamingo Playa *(beachfront, north end, ☎ 988/916-2133, drivan@sureste.com, 6 rooms, air, cable, pool)*. This six-room hotel is a welcome addition to Celestún's short list of hotels. It's on the beach, at the end of the row of streetlights. Facing the sea are two rooms that cost more than the four others that face the veranda under Moorish arches. It's unusual looking. A pleasantly large square pool of cool water lies between the hotel rooms and the sandy beach on a cement patio. The family that takes care of it is friendly, and parking and rooms are secure. Basic décor with two matrimonial beds, hot water, fans, and air conditioning. Good value, comfortable and clean. $$

Hostel Ria Celestún *(Calles 12 & 13, # 104a, no phone, www.trav.com)*. This is a new and welcome clean hostel in the middle of the village. Bunk beds, shared bath and hammocks on a pleasant patio. Also has small private bedrooms. Full kitchen, TV area, book exchange and bikes for rent. Cash only.

Dining

 La Palapa Restaurant has become a tour-bus stop since its inception in 1998. It features a wooden boat bar and numerous tables under an overhang on the beach. It has attractive hand-painted

wooden chairs and good food, but you'll pay more. The **Restaurant Celestún** gets crowded with fisherman families chomping on fried fish. Murals of the sea decorate the walls. The cheapest place on the sand is **Restaurant La Boya**, where many locals hang, eating fish and drinking *cerveza*. Just inland across the street is a good, very inexpensive family restaurant, **Chivirico**. At **Restaurant La Playita** on the beach, owner Pedro "Pete" Avila Canul runs a tight ship serving delicious seafood to hungry hordes. We became addicted to *mojo de ajo*, fish grilled with garlic and butter. Superb.

DINING PRICE CHART	
NOTE: *Prices based on a typical entrée, per person, and do not include beverage.*	
$	Less than US $5
$$	US $5 - 10
$$$	Over US $10

El Lobo *(south corner of the square, no phone).* A Dutch couple with wanderlust found Celestún too good to leave and opened a charming little pizza shop that opens at 8 am for breakfast and early lunches until noon. When the sun goes down, Luisa and Rob reopen for tasty dinners. Eat upstairs in a breezy wooden-roofed patio or downstairs in the Colonial building graced with an original painting on the wall and a fun planter made from an old mannequin wearing a pair of worn jeans. Very good food. Dutch-style pancakes, pizzas, breakfast at any time, and the best coffee in town. Say hello from us. $

Sisal

In 1810, when Mérida needed another port for transportation and shipping closer than their rival Campeche, they chose Sisal, which quickly became a humming little seaport. An 53-km (33-mile) escape corridor from Mérida to the port was kept open during the siege of the Caste War. Surrounded by Maya warriors, the Governor of the Yucatán had already decided to evacuate the city and flee to Sisal when, in the middle of the battle, the time came to plant corn. The Maya armies picked up and went back to their fields, snatching defeat from the jaws of victory. But it soon became apparent that Sisal, along the shallow Gulf of Mexico, could no longer fulfill Yucatán's growing need for a deepwater port to handle the increased export of henequen from the haciendas. When the port of Progreso opened in 1872, Sisal, which gave its name to henequen fiber, sank back into oblivion. Today, it's a forgotten little sleepy fishing village where you can do nothing, because there's nothing to do. The red-and-white lighthouse is now a private home that you can ask to see (don't forget a tip). A cement pier at the end of the road juts into the Gulf, good for fishing, swimming, taking photos or hanging out with the ever-present kids. A beachside restaurant and bar at the foot of the pier welcomes strangers as friends to this historically rich, backwater village. If it's hot in Mérida and you need beach, this makes a quiet alternative to Progreso. Bus service is available from the downtown station. To drive, take the road (Rt. 281) off the

periférico (the loop road around Mérida) to Hunucmá (pottery, gasoline and yet another Colonial church), 29 km (18 miles), then follow the signs for Sisal, another 24 km (15 miles). The road to Hunucmá is also one of two ways to get to Celestún.

Moving on around the Maya compass, we now head to the north, from where rain came – and still does.

NORTH - WHITE

(Xaman - Zac)

The big loop (Mérida to Progreso, along the coast to Dzilam de Bravo, then back through henequen plantations to Motúl and home to Mérida) may be a bit much to appreciate in one day. You might consider doing the ruins and Progreso one day and the coastal route and inland Colonial cities on another. If you do go for the whole circuit, leave early. If you're still shopping for that

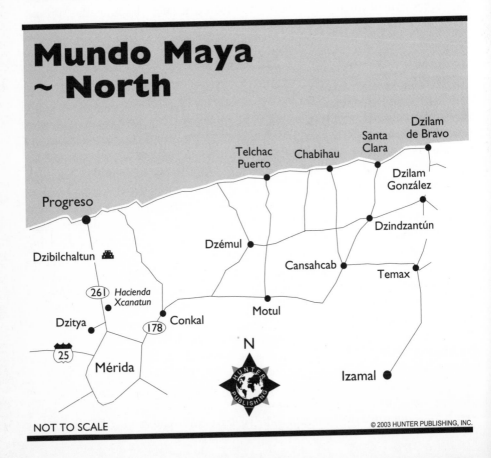

Mundo Maya
~ North

NOT TO SCALE

© 2003 HUNTER PUBLISHING, INC.

artisan's special gift, try stopping a few miles north of Mérida in **Dzitya**, to visit the shops where craftspeople work in cement, stone and wood. Stop at the side of the church to ring the stones. The stones that hang on what looks like a metal rug rack were reportedly used by the Conquistadors to communicate with the Maya villagers, and perhaps even before that. A unique tradition.

Dzibilchaltún Ruins

The Paseo de Montejo becomes a major highway from Mérida north to the time-worn port of Progreso. The road is a wide, four-lane highway past the giant henequen factory and the flatlands of the north. Despite clearing the land for successive boom-and-bust plantings of sugar cane and henequen, the large Maya ruined city of Dzibilchaltún (tsee-beel-chahl-TOON), where some 20,000 people once lived, was not "discovered" until 1941. Although the interest to casual visitors isn't intense, it is an important archeological site, continually occupied from 800 BC until after the Spanish Conquest.

The Mexican Government spent a large amount of money on the new **museum** at Dzibilchaltún ("Where There is Writing on Flat Stones"). Along with collected stelae and figures found at the site, the museum features a reproduction of a Maya village where attendants demonstrate traditional folk arts and crafts. It's worth a visit while you're here. The museum closes on Mondays.

The most interesting area of the spread-out ruins (8,400 rubble structures in 19 square km/7.6 square miles) includes the famous **Temple of the Seven Dolls**, as well as a small Terminal Classic building (**Structure 38**) and a **stone chapel** built by the Spanish, circa 1590. Seven clay figurines, each with some deformity, were placed under the temple floor, thereby giving it its name. Possibly these "dolls" were used in ceremonies to cure illness, but no one really knows.

Temple of Seven Dolls.

The long *sacbé* that leads through the open fields to the temple is a very crunchy white road, not to be walked in the heat of the day. Several nature trails have been cut into the scrub forest around the site and they make a great alternative to the *sacbé* that leads to the temple or a worthy shady hike

Yucatán

on their own. Pick up the booklet, available in the museum, about birds and plants along the trail, which ends at a pleasant cenote not far from the entrance. The 40-meter-deep (132 feet) **Cenote Xlacah** goes down at a slant and is now a public swimming hole and pleasing picnic area. A National Geographic expedition once recovered nearly 30,000 Maya ceremonial artifacts from its cool waters. "Wear a swimsuit," advises a sign.

Tours and taxis will fetch you at the cenote (it's 15 km/9.3 miles, north of Mérida and four km east). The bus to the village of Chanculob (close to the ruins) leaves from the terminal downtown at Calle 62 between 65 and 67.

Progreso

Why can't the captain of a vessel keep a memorandum of the weight of his anchor, instead of weighing it every time he leaves port?
~ George Prentice, 1802-1870

The long pier at Progreso.

If it weren't for the hordes of Meridaños escaping the summer heat in town, Progreso might have descended into another sleepy Gulf coast village. Founded in the late 1800s to replace the port of Sisal, which proved inadequate for the booming Yucatecan henequen trade, the port prospered until the decline in demand for the fiber at the end of the First World War. Like Sisal and Campeche before it, the long limestone shelf under Progreso's harbor inhibits its ability to function as a deep-sea port.

Today, the shallow harbor can't accommodate the deeper draft of many modern ships, although Progreso is able to export sisal, honey, cement, fish and

salt in smaller freighters. To continue its role as a shipping port and to attract cruise ships, the government has built a long pier (*muelle*) seven km (4.3 miles) out into the Gulf. This is one of the longest wharves in the world, and on a hazy day it's hard to see the end from the shoreline. It makes a great walk or bike ride, although big trucks occasionally rumble by. There isn't a stitch of shade, so don't go out during the sunny midday. Even with the pier, the Gulf waters are still too shallow for the gigantic cruise ships that float into Cozumel.

Scheduled for fall through spring weekly sailings from Tampa, Florida, is the **Yucatán Express** (☎ 866/670-3939, www.yucatanexpress.com), a combination passenger cruise ship and car ferry. We hope it continues to call in Progreso as the town has cleaned up a lot to greet the cruisers and it offers a convenient way to get to the Yucatán. Great rates and super sailing.

Shopping

For unique shopping, check out the bright blue clapboard **Mundo Marino**, "Marine World," gift shack on the corner near the *mercado*. It's a fun place where you can buy shark jaws and teeth, stuffed fish, shells, nets, and just about anything having to do with the sea. There's a busy supermarket, **San Francisco de Asis**, in town. Across the street from the San Francisco is a bank with ATM, and the bus station is two blocks from the main square.

Sights & Adventures

You can observe a lot by watching.
~ Yogi Berra

 SIGHTS: Besides sea and surf, Progreso does not offer too much for an extended vacation. In an effort to attract more tourists, they have cleaned up the town, especially around the center, but the tourist information is in an awkward spot: Calle 30 and on the way out of town! The beach and *malecón* are groomed. The best view of the city is from the old white *faro* (**lighthouse**), built around 1890 and now open to the public. Tip the keeper or whoever lets you up.

Not too far down the coast from Progreso is **Chuburna**, where we heard there's an interesting abandoned hacienda and unexcavated Maya ruins. Take a taxi from the front of the San Francisco and let us know.

WATERSPORTS: The shallow waters that restrict shipping make for great swimming in warm, protected waters. You can walk out into the gentle surf for a great distance before the water reaches your waist. The wide beach is a

favorite spot for Progreso's many fiestas. The *malecón*, which runs east from the *muelle*, is a broad boulevard, home to several good restaurants and a seawall with sidewalks for walking and people-watching.

Just before you enter town on the right, the lagoon has been upgraded to host **sculling and rowing races**. National competitions are held here and a team from Mérida practices for the Olympics.

Accommodations & Dining

 Hotel pickings in the city are skimpy, but we can rave about the **Casa Quixote** (*Calle 23 between 48 & 50*, ☎ *969/935-2909, www.casaquixote.com, 4 rooms plus a 2-bedroom apartment, cable, pool, breakfast included, parking*). One of the first things that strikes you as you enter this former seaport summer home of one of Mérida's Lebanese merchant aristocracy is the fabulous tile work on the floors. Turn-of-the-century and earlier homes like this one

HOTEL PRICE CHART	
NOTE: Often, one shared bed in a room is cheaper than two. Prices based on cost per night, for two.	
[No $]	Less than US $20
$	US $20 - $40
$$	US $40 - $80
$$$	US $80 - $125

feature the most magnificent tile floors, made in patterns that create the illusion of room-sized area rugs. The Harris family from Texas bought and restored this impressive house, a half-block from the beach, into a wonderful little B&B. This is the kind of luxury accommodations previously lacking in Progreso. If you're tempted – especially in summer or Easter week – make reservations ahead. Beautifully decorated. Don't miss the weekly Saturday night Texas BBQ, even if you're not staying here. $$-$$$

Try the **Hotel San Miguel**, Calle 78, a decent place with rooms for about US $20, or the basic and clean **Hotel Progreso**, Calles 29 and 78. Several other hotels along the *malecón* are worth looking at, especially **Hotel Real del Mar** on Calle 19. It is in back of the new palapa-covered seafood restaurant, Pelicanos. **Hotel Tropical Suites** is across the street (room 20 on the 3rd floor is the best). Both of the latter cost around US $40.

As you take the coast road out of town into Chicxulub and beyond, there's **Margarita's Ville**, a small family hotel (Margarita and Cappy) on the beach in San Miguel, 15 km (nine miles) east.

Across the street from the lighthouse in Progreso is an interesting and busy *mercado*, where we often eat in a corner stand, **Loncheria El Angelito**, family-owned for 16 years on the corner of Calles 80 and 27. Another favorite is **Riko's Restaurant and Pizza**, nearby on 80. The absolute cleanest place in town is **Riko's Loncheria** (must be many Rikos here), Calle 68 and 29,

four blocks off the beach and three blocks east of the big Telemex microwave towers. Along the *malecón* there are several good seafood restaurants that look better than the places in town. The one with the best ambiance is **Le Saint Bonnet**, which offers a good seafood menu, but hardly French food.

The Coast Road

As refuge from the harsh cold of Canada and the US in the winter, many *Norteamericanos* own homes or condominiums outside Progreso on the warm waters of the Gulf. They're known as "snowbirds." A 74-km (46-mile) paved road scoots along the northern coast of the Yucatán from Progreso east to Dzilam de Bravo, then turns inland.

It's a fun day trip from Mérida to go through some places most tourists never see. For the first part of the coastline you have to do as we did: critique the architecture, from garish to superb, of the many expensive homes that line the shore. When you smell the sea breeze across some of the long deserted beaches away from Progreso, stop, take off your shoes, and wander the shore – the shells here are incredible.

Sights en Route

 Chicxucub Puerto is the first town you reach, seven km (4.5 miles) east of Progreso. The entire northern coastline was hard hit in 2002 by Hurricane Isadora, which dumped a record amount of rainfall there as well as inland through Mérida. That's why the road you're on is new, the old one washed away.

Heading east you'll pass through several villages as the expensive homes begin to peter out and wildlife and sea birds take their place. The community of **Uaymitun** (25 km/15 miles) east of Progreso) has built a wooden tower to see the pink flamingos feeding in the shallow lagoon, Laguna Rosada, just off the road. Admission is free and they will loan you powerful binoculars at no cost. On the far side of the inland lagoon are the **Xcambo** ruins.

The next towns are **Telchac** and **Telchac Puerto**, a fair-sized village with several fish restaurants on the *malecón*. There's a little harbor where a commercial fishing fleet is based, its boats packed like sardines, tightly woven together (good photo op). When the boats head out to sea, it's for 15 days at a time. **Palula Beach Camping**, just after Telchac and before the village of Chabihau, has clean and appealing beachfront primitive tent spots. You might prefer a room in the house. They have five available on a B&B basis.

The deserted beaches all along this route are great for beachcombing and swimming. If you started in Mérida, about now you're hungry again. **Santa Clara** is a charming little fishing village with an appealing inexpensive beachfront hotel, **Hotel Playa Azul** (look for a little sign) and a tiny seafood restaurant, **Restaurante La Morena**. Latin rock and roll accompanies some great-tasting ceviche, served as a free *antojito* (appetizer) if you're having beer. You can order a ceviche meal (enough for two). The other menu item is whole fried fish accompanied by tortillas and a tasty cabbage salad. A local hang-out for fisherman and locals, this makes a welcome break. The beaches are fine for swimming here.

The coast road ends in the fishing village called **Dzilam de Bravo**, where the infamous pirate Jean Lafitte is allegedly buried, along with his brother, Pierre, in the local cemetery. According to legend, Jean was buried under a wooden grave marker found with his name inscribed, although there is no record of his return after he left the Yucatán in 1826. His brother Pierre, however, really is buried there. Both pirates were popular with local fishermen because of their kindness – kind of like Robin Hoods of the sea. There's a **lighthouse** at the end of town. If you're out for more than a day-trip, launches hired from Dzilam will take passengers along the coast into the Parque Natural San Felipe to see *ojos de agua*, as well as awesome flocks of pink flamingos and waterbirds galore.

The narrow paved road south from Dzilam leads inland through huge henequen plantations and cattle ranches. This area is chock-full of ancient haciendas, some ruined, others still working. We spent some time on this trip chasing chimneys through the underbrush to find old abandoned haciendas.

The crescent of the limestone shelf here in the north is the Yucatán's "**Zona de Cenotes**." Scientists believe the preponderance of cenotes (set in a crescent shape) delineate the edge of the Chicxulub meteor crater, the one that many theorize caused the extinction of the dinosaurs. A preliminary survey of the state counted over 600 cenotes.

 MYSTERIOUS MAYA: The name Chicxulub means "wound of an arrow." Did the Maya know of the meteor strike at that time, 65 million years before?

In the crossroads town of **Dzilam González** (with a tasty bakery, La Rosita Panaderia), you can turn right to the Colonial town of **Dzindzantún**, with a detailed 16th-century church and ex-convent, or go straight south to the larger town of **Temax**, a center for hand-embroidered *huipiles*. Either way, the road back to Mérida is then through **Cansahcab**, another Colonial town with a rich folk history. New highways bypass the small towns for faster regress.

An even richer history and a fascinating city on its own (worth visiting if you're not too tired by now), is **Motúl**. This Colonial city, 51 km (32 miles)

northeast of Mérida, is predominately populated by Maya. It is the birthplace of Felipe Carrillo Puerto, the Socialist reform governor of the Yucatán, assassinated at the behest of reactionary *hacendados* (hacienda owners) before his planned wedding to American journalist Alma Reed. Read their story on page 49. Motúl retains some of the tragic romanticism of that story.

The town is very clean and well maintained. The airy main plaza features a freshly painted white and green **Palacio Municipal** (a museum dedicated to Carrillo located in his former home), several restaurants and beautifully decorated **horse-drawn carriages** that serve as the town's taxis. Motúl's annual celebration for their patron saint, Juan Bautista, is held on July 16. The **Hotel Motúl**, on the square above the Bital Bank, seemed suitable for a night's stay.

We found at least one strong reason for a stop in Motúl: **Cenote Sambula** (Calle 43, eight blocks south of the *zócalo*), became a public park in 2003 with a good palapa-roofed restaurant, but the cenote below it – where you can swim for free – has been around for eons. Changing cubicles are provided. The cenote is in a cave, with broad Colonial-style cement steps down to a solid cement floor. Legend holds that it once hid Felipe Carrillo and his supporters when the federales were searching for him during the Mexican Revolution. The clear green waters disappear farther into the cave and brave swimmers can venture inside where there is light from another opening. Did we mention that the food at the restaurant above is Yucatecan, delicious and cheap? There are plenty of signs around town advertising this newly popular eatery.

If you spend the night in Motúl or plan a separate visit you could include the Maya ruins at **Aké**, south of Motúl through Tixkokob and Ekmul. This sleeper of a ruin, the last one to be visited by Stephens and Catherwood in their second trip of 1842, is hardly ever seen by tourists. It's an Early Classic city in an open field, best known for Structure 1, a pyramidal base supporting a platform with 36 standing stone pillars. Some of the massive stone blocks on the 150-foot-wide stairway from the ancient plaza are over 6.6 feet long and as many wide. How were these enormous heavy blocks quarried, moved and put in place? Mysteries of the Maya.

There's a henequen factory nearby. If you're visiting Aké specifically, there is perhaps a more convenient turnoff, with a large sign, at Km 40.5 on Route 180 east from Mérida, near Kantunil. The ruins are 11 km (seven miles) up the stone side road.

SOUTH - YELLOW

(Kan - Nohol)

*It is no surprise that the good old days seem better than the present,
they've spent more time in editing.*
~ Texas Wilson, in the cartoon, *Ziggy*

There are three basic routes into the Yucatán's Kan Nohol with its Maya sites, natural wonders and Colonial architecture: **Route 180** south toward Campeche, where you can cut over to Muna and Uxmal and the Ruta Puuc; directly south on **Route 261** through Muna to Uxmal; or meandering down the **Convent Route** through Colonial towns to Oxkutzcab and the Ruta Puuc. Best choice? Do them all.

Umán & Oxkintoc

Seventeen km (10.6 miles) southwest of Mérida, at the end of a wide road through an industrial area, is the Colonial city of Umán, on Route 180 to Campeche. Here you'll find the massive domed 16th-century church of **San Francisco de Asis**. From Umán there are two choices south: to Muna and Uxmal direct, or south for 48 km (30 miles) toward Maxcanú and a new highway past the ruins of Oxkintoc, retracing the route John Lloyd Stephens followed to Uxmal in 1841. If you're coming up from Campeche, this road, along the base of the Puuc hills, is now the fast route to Uxmal. Follow the signs. Oxkintoc will be on your right, and the little village of Calcehtok will be on your left, down a narrow road.

Oxkintoc, which means "three day flint," was a large and important Maya city occupied for 1,400 years between 300 BC and AD 1100. The 11 large temple mounds spread over many acres are just being excavated by INAH, so you may see workers under the supervision of Mexican archeologists. One of the largest temples, from the Early and Late Classic periods, is called the "Labyrinth." When John Lloyd Stephens (who seemed to be everywhere first) went to visit a "cave" near Maxcanú, he was led to this Oxkintoc mound whose subterranean construction had a "marvelous and mystical reputation." Stephens went on to explain that, "The universal belief was that it contained passages without number and without end." He became the first to realize that these passages and chambers were man-made, not natural. Entrance is on the west side. Bring a flashlight, water and a sun hat. Some of the material found at the site is now displayed in the Mérida Museum.

Rogerio Cuy is the man to have as a guide to the caves that Stephens missed: the **Grutas Calcehtok** (the Mayan name, Xpokil). At the end of the paved road, only one or two km past the turn into the ruins, is a parking area and turn-around where a marked path leads to a big hole in the ground. A metal ladder descends into a secret oasis of banana trees and jungle plants, all hidden seven meters or so below the rocky limestone ground. At one end of the depression is a large, rock-strewn cavern that slants down to another, deeper oasis, where shafts of light from openings above are like spotlights on

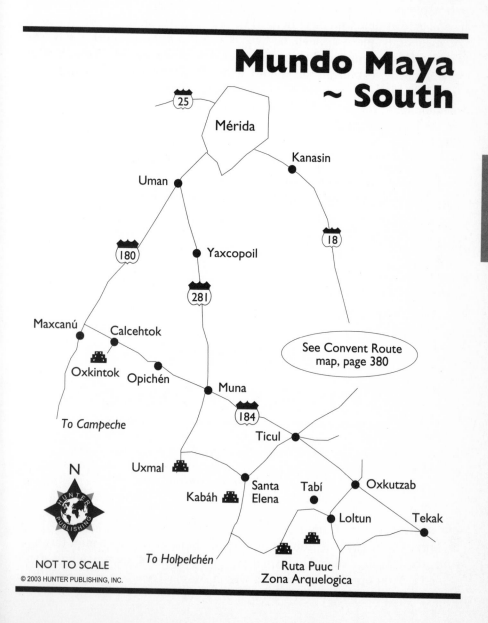

Mundo Maya
~ South

Mérida

Kanasin

Uman

Yaxcopoil

Maxcanú

Calcehtok

Oxkintok   Opichén

To Campeche

Muna

See Convent Route
map, page 380

Ticul

N

Uxmal

Kabáh   Santa
Elena   Tabí

Oxkutzab

Loltun   Tekak

NOT TO SCALE

To Holpelchén

Ruta Puuc
Zona Arquelogica

© 2003 HUNTER PUBLISHING, INC.

Yucatán

the dark floor. At the foot of this cave, natural tunnels lead off into as much as eight km (five miles) of underground blackness. The cavern is so large that to see the entire length takes about six hours; the first hour of exploration can be done walking upright. Deep inside, there are the petrified skeletal remains of an ancient Maya (INAH has taken the other two mummies, dated around AD 800) and 1,200-year-old hieroglyphs on the cave walls. We were happy simply to climb down the ladder and peek inside.

Rogerio, whose father Roger was once the caretaker for Oxkintoc and an early explorer of the *grutas*, usually hangs out near the entrance, waiting to show people around and be of help. If he is not there, or you're looking for a good meal and a place to sleep, he lives close by and can be contacted by the **Parador Restaurant and Cabañas** back down the road in Calcehtok. This appealing little restaurant (no phone), with its primitive but clean overnight cabañas (hammock sleeping) and cool swimming pool, is hoping to lure visitors stopping at the ruins. There are no facilities at Oxkintoc, so the friendly Parador is a very welcome way station. The beer here is ice cold and the Yucatecan food is delicious.

Continue past Opichén to Muna, then south to Uxmal or north back to Mérida, or perhaps straight toward Ticul and Loltún.

If you want to stay overnight in high style near the Oxkintoc ruins, try the elegant **Hacienda Santa Rosa** *(Km 129 Hwy 180 near Maxcanu, reservations in US* ☎ *800/625-5144, in Mexico 999/910-4852, www.luxurycollection.com, 11 rooms, restaurant, pool).* This small GHM hacienda is intimate, its ambience like a private home. $$$$+

Another possibility is the historic **Hacienda Blanca Flor**, just south across the border in Campeche State. Reservations are required. See page 102.

Uxmal & The Ruta Puuc

... I had seen seven different places of ruins, memorials of cities which had been and had passed away – such memorials as no cities built by Spaniards in that country could present.
~ John Lloyd Stephens, on his way to revisit Uxmal, 1841

The direct route to Uxmal, perhaps the most striking and beautiful ruined Maya city in the Yucatán, runs south on Route 261 from Umán through Muna, then straight ahead to Uxmal. About one-third of the way along is the hacienda, **Yaxcopoil** ("Place of the Green Alamo Trees"), a restored 17th-century sisal hacienda converted into a museum that re-creates life as it was

for wealthy *hacendados*. The same family has owned it for generations since 1864, and the décor is still in that period. The vast estate grew henequen and the museum shows how it was worked into fiber. Also on the grounds are the Maya ruins of the same name, with original furniture and kitchen utensils inside. The exterior of the main house has a decidedly French influence and it's not surprising that, with its tall, distinctive, Moorish-style double entry arch, it has been used as a film set. About 15 km (9.3 miles) south of Umán, it's a worthwhile diversion. *(US $5 admission, open Monday through Saturday, 8 am-6 pm and Sunday from 9 am-1 pm, www.yaxcopoil.com.)*

Farther south is the **Hacienda Ochil**, a restored henequen hacienda along the route to Uxmal. It features a very good restaurant in the former main house and handicraft shops scattered in the outbuildings. A small museum shows how sisal is harvested and, for fun, a narrow-gauge rail circles the lovely gardens. No entrance fee.

A new road now bypasses the Colonial town of Muna by climbing the steep Puuc hills to the west of town. If you take the old route through town, **Restaurant Chun Yaax-Che** brags that it serves the "best food in the Yucatán." It's located up a side street before the central plaza and serves good cooking on linen tablecloths. It's mainly used by tour bus groups during lunch, and specializes in *pollo pibil*, chicken wrapped in banana leaves and baked in a pit grill. It has an artisan workshop of renowned reproduction artist, Rodrigo Martine.

As you leave Muna on the old road and climb the steep Puuc Hill that dwarfs the town, **Hacienda Ahal** *(☎ 997/971-0195)*, with rustic accommodations but beautiful gardens, will be on your right. When you reach the crest of the hill, stop at the art shop, **Chac Nah** ("Red House"). It offers public bathrooms with beautifully carved wooden doors and a lookout tower (*mirador*) with a spectacular view of the surrounding countryside and the ruins of Uxmal rising above the jungle. Chac Nah is the workshop of a talented artist and craftsman in wood, stone and clay. He is planting an ambitious cactus garden, but his livelihood has been stymied by the bypass road, which terminates past the summit. Continue downhill to the Uxmal ruins.

After Uxmal and nearby Kabáh, there are a series of ruined Maya cities along a route referred to as the "Ruta Puuc," named after its proximity to the Puuc hills. In combination, these spectacular ruins represent some of the most provocative examples of Classic Maya architecture in the rococo Puuc style.

Uxmal

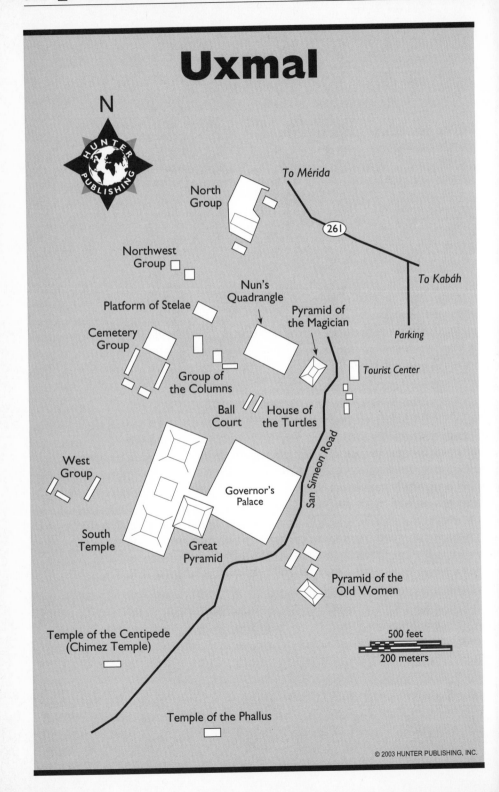

N

To Mérida

North Group

Northwest Group

261

To Kabáh

Nun's Quadrangle

Platform of Stelae

Pyramid of the Magician

Parking

Cemetery Group

Group of the Columns

Tourist Center

Ball Court

House of the Turtles

San Simeon Road

West Group

Governor's Palace

South Temple

Great Pyramid

Pyramid of the Old Women

Temple of the Centipede (Chimez Temple)

500 feet

200 meters

Temple of the Phallus

© 2003 HUNTER PUBLISHING, INC.

Uxmal

From its front doorway I counted 16 elevations with broken walls, mounds of
stones and vast, magnificent edifices which,
at that distance, seemed untouched by time and defying ruin.
I stood in the doorway when the sun went down, throwing from the buildings a
prodigious breadth of shadow, darkening the terraces, presenting a scene
strange enough for a work of enchantment.
~ John L. Stephens, describing the vista from the top
of the Pyramid of the Magicians, 1840

Uxmal (oosh-MAL) means "Three Times Built," although there is evidence that there were five building periods. This is one of the peninsula's most beautiful ruined Maya cities. Not quite as grandiose as Chichén Itzá, Uxmal is more magnificent in an ornate Puuc style. Finely shaped limestone veneers, applied to lime-based concrete over block, characterize Puuc architecture. The lower façades of Puuc buildings are typically plain, but intricate mosaics decorate the elaborate upper façades. Among the most common motifs are criss-cross lattices, geometric designs, monster serpents and masks.

The city reached its peak of grandeur during the Late and Terminal Classic periods as a contemporary of the great southern city-states of Palenque and Tikal. Unlike many of the Maya ruins, the existence of Uxmal never faded from collective memory. Its existence was first recorded by Europeans when a Spanish priest, Diego López de Cogullado, wrote about it only 15 years after the Conquest. The imposing ceremonial city had been abandoned by the Maya in the late 10th century, with a brief resurgence in the Terminal Classic period by either Toltecs or Itzá Maya or a combination. One persistent theory about Uxmal holds that its location – in a very dry area – was eventually responsible for its downfall. Uxmal is one of the few Classic Maya cities not built near a cenote, but the people overcame that severe disadvantage by building **chultuns**, cistern-style reservoirs that held rainwater. Chac, the rain god, was understandably important to the residents of these arid hills and his image appears frequently.

Uxmal's showpiece ruins have added a 45-minute sound and light show during the winter months, one in Spanish at 7 pm and one at 9 pm in English. You can rent audio translators. We found the experience worthwhile. Colored lights highlight intricate façade features in the Nunnery Quadrangle and color spotlights illuminate the hill-top Governor's Palace and Great Pyramid. The background music adds a regal ambiance. However, in recreating the myths of the Maya and Uxmal, the storyline becomes somewhat disjointed, so we found it possible to see the show in Spanish and still enjoy it.

THE PYRAMID OF THE MAGICIAN: El Adivino is the first majestic structure you'll come across after entering through a new visitors center. The

dwarf-sorcerer in Maya folklore who built the pyramid that bears his name was a mythical figure who hatched from an egg and grew to maturity in one year. The pyramid has a unique shape with a base that appears oval but is actually rectangular, with severely rounded corners and steep sides up to its 100-foot height. What you see now is the fifth construction, each building period adding to and covering the previous. The climb to the top is difficult, but offers a stupendous view. If you venture up, climb down the other side. Interesting Chac masks flank the fourth level stairway on the west side.

THE NUNNERY QUADRANGLE: This building got its name from a 16th-century priest who thought its 70-odd cell-like rooms reminiscent of an austere convent. Four rectangular buildings flank a compact courtyard. The smaller structure on the east bears a painted capstone with a date of AD 907 and the name of Lord Chac, believed responsible for building the Nunnery Quadrangle, the Ballcourt and possibly the Governor's Palace. The detail on the second-story structure is incredible and is where you see the 1,000-year-old depiction of traditional *naj* houses.

A complex of buildings on a rise south of the Quadrangle includes the compact **Turtle House**, a little temple with decorations of turtles along its façade. Turtles were associated with the god Chac because both man and turtles need rain to survive.

THE GOVERNOR'S PALACE: Overlooking the Turtle House, this palace is a masterpiece of Maya architecture. The exquisite structure, originally three connected buildings, is built upon a natural platform high above the surrounding city. From here a *sacbé* runs to Kabáh, one of the nearby cities believed to be under Uxmal's influence. That *sacbé* was first considered to be the reason the building is at a slight angle to the others, but it has been found that the large central doorway, with its elaborate carvings on the lintel, is in perfect alignment with the planet Venus. The upper façade of this well-preserved building, woven with corner Chac masks, lattice work designs, and human figures in detailed headdresses, make its décor truly magnificent. When Stephens saw it he wrote: "... as the stranger ascends the steps and casts a bewildered eye along its open and desolate doors, it is hard to believe that he sees before him the work of a race in whose epitaph – as written by historians – they are called ignorant of art. If it stood... in Hyde Park or the Garden of Tuileries, it would form a new order... not unworthy to stand side by side with the remains of Egyptian, Grecian and Roman art."

THE GREAT PYRAMID: This structure has been partially restored and gleams against the green jungle. Although not as impressive as other structures at Uxmal, it's a great spot for photography. View the well-preserved step mask in the interior temple and the corner Chac masks in its profusion of decorations, including depictions of the sun god. Below it is the House of the Doves and a plaza layout similar to the Nunnery Quadrangle, but not as well preserved.

■ Accommodations & Dining

Villas Arqueológicas *(next to the ruins of Uxmal, 40 rooms with air, in US* ☎ *800/624-8451, in Mexico* ☎*/fax 997/976-2020, www. clubmed.com, pool, restaurant, tennis courts)*. A duplicate, approximately, of its lovely sister hotels in Cobá and Chichén. All the Villas are Club Med properties, all make your stay pleasant, and none is all-inclusive. Only a few steps from the ruins, cozy and very appealing. See our review of Chichén Itzá's hotel, page 333. $$

HOTEL PRICE CHART	
NOTE: *Often, one shared bed in a room is cheaper than two. Prices based on cost per night, for two.*	
[No $]	Less than US $20
$	US $20 - $40
$$	US $40 - $80
$$$	US $80 - $125

Lodge at Uxmal *(next to the ruins,* ☎ *997/971-2102, fax 997/976-2102, www.mayaland.com, 40 rooms, air, cable TV, minibar, 2 pools, 2 restaurants)*. The Lodge is the premier hotel among the close-knit accommodations community, located exactly opposite the entrance to Uxmal. Their "all-master" bedrooms are very large, and the end units of the two-story giant thatched-roof bungalows feature rounded walls, a traditional Maya design. Ask for an end unit upstairs on the wooden veranda. The bedroom doors are intricately carved wood and natural wood vertical blinds cover the windows. Bathroom doors and windows feature hand-crafted stained glass. Rooms have coffee makers. The tile bathrooms are as big as some rooms we've stayed in. When you're done with the ruins, arrange a two-hour horseback ride to Hacienda San Simone de Péon for about US $30. $$$

Misión Uxmal *(Km 78, Hwy. 261,* ☎ *997/976-2022, fax 997/976-2023, 70 rooms with fans, 2 suites, restaurant, pool)*. The three-story hacienda-style Misión has rooms with large balconies or patios that look out to the Uxmal ruins about a half-mile away. We feel the balcony railings are a little too low and it's a long drop to the ground. Very dangerous.

The huge teardrop-shaped pool is magnificent, perhaps the best we found in the Yucatán. There's little to do in the evening except sleep – if only the mattresses weren't so torturously hard. Local woodworker, Carlos Cancino Baaz, sells his carving and native art wares near the pool. If you're seeking out-of-the-way places nearby, ask him about serving as your guide. He knows his way around but speaks only Spanish or Mayan. $$-$$$

Hacienda Uxmal *(at the turnoff for the ruins Hwy. 261, US/Canada* ☎ *800/ 235-4079, Mexico* ☎ *997/971-2102, www.mayaland.com, 80 rooms, 2 suites, air, 2 pools, restaurant, tennis)*. Big curved arches grace the covered tiled hallways of this two-story Mayaland luxury hotel, a two-minute walk from the ruins entrance. Hand-painted tile and a generous use of hardwood trim complement the hacienda-style architecture. Rooms are in two wings facing a

Yucatán

central courtyard with a large pool. A walking/jogging trail winds through their botanical garden. Past guests include Queen Elizabeth and Prince Philip of Great Britain, Princess Grace and Prince Rainier of Monaco, and Jacqueline Kennedy Onassis and Henry Kissinger of the United States (they had separate rooms). $$$-$$$$

Rancho Uxmal *(Km 70 Highway 261, no phone, ☎ 997/977-5293, fax 997/977-6254, 20 rooms with air or fans, pool, restaurant).* If you're not into the bigger bucks of Uxmal's big three hotels, stay here. It's about three km (1.9 miles) up the road and half the price. Pleasant plain rooms in this simple hacienda-style hotel are perfectly acceptable for a night, or you can camp in back where there are electrical hookups. $

Sacbé Bungalows & Camping *(Santa Elena, ☎ 985/858-1281, sacbehostel@hotmail.com, 16 km/10 miles south of Uxmal, 7 km/4.3 miles north of Kabáh, 5 bungalows, hostel dorm, private baths, communal kitchen, tent & trailer sites, restaurant).* An excellent alternative to staying at Uxmal is the next town south, Santa Elena (once known by its Mayan name, Nohcacab). Shortly south of the turnoff to the town is this facility, with several attractive guest cabins as well as a camp area. In 1990, Edgardo Portillo and his French wife, Annette, cleared the land for their dream business, a family campground. They created the most pleasant and tidy campground we have found in the Yucatán. But what pleases most guests are their small bungalows with bathrooms. Very appealing. Flowering cactus and plants accent level lawns and the private bungalow *casitas* are immaculately clean. Up the street on the corner from Sacbé and Flycatcher is **Chac Mol**, a good little eatery. In the heart of the Ruta Puuc, between important ruins, Sacbé makes an ideal base for explorations. Edgardo is full of information and can direct you to cenotes and ruins that tourists never see. A true best buy. Buses stop out front. To visit the Maya ruins of Sacbé (Mascarón) or to see the overgrown Uxmal-Kabáh *sacbé* that runs behind the campground, ask for guide Emilio Santos Camal in Santa Elena.

Flycatcher Inn B&B *(Santa Elena, www.mexonline.com/flycatcherinn.htm, flycatcherinn@yahoo.com, 5 rooms, breakfast included).* Years ago we heard about an American woman living in tiny Santa Elena but couldn't find her. When we finally did she turned out to be the charming Kristine Ellingson who, with her Yucatecan husband Santiago, has opened this lovely bed and breakfast just a few meters north of Sacbé Bungalows. The bedrooms in the house, up a rise from the road, are large with window screens and attractive wrought iron furniture designed and forged by Santiago. The pretty hand embroidered wall hangings in the rooms are for sale and benefit a local women's handicraft co-op. Spotlessly clean. The name "flycatcher" refers to a small local bird with yellow stripes that eats insects (Xtakay in Mayan). Guided tours to the unexcavated ruins of Naohpat and Mulchik are possible. A stay here makes you want to stay longer. Say hello from us. $

SANTA ELENA

Santa Elena's fine old Colonial church (with rare portable carved folk-art altars) sits on top of long steps, high on a hill. Nearby is the burned out ruins of an old ossuary described by John L. Stephen: *Death was all around us. Adjoining the church... was a great charnel house, along the wall of which was a row of skulls. Within the enclosure was a promiscuous assemblage of skulls and bones several feet deep. The floor of the church was interspersed with long patches of cement that covered graves. In the choir of the church were rows of skulls all labeled on the forehead and containing startling inscriptions. I took up one and staring me in the face were the words: 'I am Peter Moreno: an Ave Maria and Paternost for God's sake brother.'*

The skeletons no longer remain in the ruined ossuary, but the mummified corpses of several sacrificed children were unearthed a few years ago in front of the church altar. Alongside the church is a small museum (please donate generously) that displays a pre-Columbian Maya skelton and mummifed children, plus artifacts from Colonial times. It's worth a visit. There's a good view too from the church steeple which they may allow you to go up inside (ask them to open the door). If you're not going to the other Ruta Puuc ruins, there is a shortcut back to Ticul from here.

Ruta Puuc

Man himself is a visitor who does not remain.
~ anonymous statement in proposed
environmental legislation in the USA

KABAH: Straddling both sides of the highway south of Santa Elena are the ruins of Kabáh, which means "He of the Strong Hand." All the ruins are close to the road, with the majority of buildings on the east side (the left if you're traveling south). The best of this interesting site, connected by the *sacbé* to Uxmal, is the **Palace of Masks** or Codz Poop ("Coiled Mat"), a Mayan name referring to the resemblance between the curled snouts of the Chac masks (that also serve as steps to the inner rooms) and a rolled-up sleeping mat. The 148-foot-long building rests on a high terrace platform and absolutely bursts with 300 Chac masks, all with hooked noses. So many identical masks would seem to show a baroque ostentation, as if Kabáh's architects wanted to one-up larger Uxmal. Other buildings on the east side near the Codz Poop are the **Temple of Columns**, famous for rows of semi-columns on the upper part of the façade, and **El Palacio**, the Palace. Across the street on the west side you'll pass the rubble mound of the Principal Teocalis, or Great Temple. Climbing is not recommended because of loose stones. Farther up the dirt path is a restored vaulted stone arch that it marks the end, or the begin-

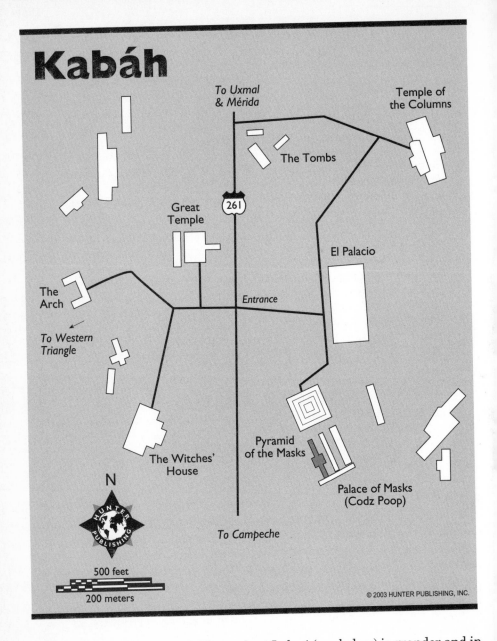

Kabáh

To Uxmal & Mérida

Temple of the Columns

The Tombs

261

Great Temple

El Palacio

The Arch

Entrance

To Western Triangle

Pyramid of the Masks

The Witches' House

Palace of Masks (Codz Poop)

N

To Campeche

500 feet

200 meters

© 2003 HUNTER PUBLISHING, INC.

ning, of the *sacbé* to Uxmal. The arch at Labná (see below) is grander and in better shape.

AUTHOR'S TIP: *If you're planning to spend the night at Uxmal or Santa Elena to see Uxmal's light and sound show, you may prefer to do this route in re-*

verse, starting at the Loltún caves for their first tour (9 or 9:30 am), then following the ruins route backwards. To reach Loltún from Mérida, first, drive Hwy. 261 to Muna. Turn left on 184. It's about 65 km (40 miles) to Oxkutzcab. Follow the signs to Loltún. Or even better, make it a two-day trip by combining the Ruta Puuc with the Convent Route itinerary (see page 380).

SAYIL: The "Place of the Ants," Sayil, offers a fair number of standing structures stretching back on well-cleared paths as much as three-quarters of a mile from the road (although the best places are close). The left turn for the Puuc Highway is south of Kabáh and Sayil is about four km (2.5 miles) on the right, after the turn. The most impressive building by far is a three-tiered palace mounted on a pyramidal base. **El Palacio** is considered another masterpiece of Maya architecture. The Classical-Greek-looking structure rises an impressive three stories and features a wide central staircase that divides the 280-foot length into two wings. You'll need a wide-angle lens to get a complete picture of this breathtaking building. The wide doorways are supported by thick, free-standing columns, with a frieze above showing images of the descending god (the Bee God), which Stephens described as a "figure of a man supporting himself on his hands, with his legs expanded in a curious, rather delicate attitude." At the northwest corner is a chultun that held as much as 7,000 gallons.

From the palace, an elevated *sacbé* filled with large stones stretches through the open field to **El Mirador**, currently under excavation and restoration by archeologists. Next to it is the elaborate but ruined **Temple of the Lintel**, with carved glyphs that decorate its façade. Sayil reached its peak (9,000 residents) in the Terminal Classic period. Check out the phallic stone idols lined up along the small structure near the palace or on the stelae beyond El Mirador.

If you read Stephens' colorful book he mentions the Well of Chac, near Sayil, and tells of his harrowing descent to the water level of this deep cavern, depended upon as a community water source as late as the 1950s. The ropes and ladders to the vertical shaft part have rotted away. Extremely curious people will find the well 500 feet southeast of the Km 30 marker on the road, up a rough foot trail. To go beyond the opening to the vertical shaft would be foolhardy.

> **AUTHORS TIP:** *A good guide to the area is **Emilio Santos Camal**, in Santa Elena. Ask local residents where to find him.*

XLAPAK: This is a small site, about six km (3.75 miles) past Sayil, has only one building worth seeing – Structure I, also called the "Palace." There are

sets of three Chac masks on the corners of the upper façade, with their noses curled up, while each Chac mask above the doorways has proboscis that curls down. The name in Mayan means "Old Walls."

LABNA: Labná is best known for its magnificent arched portal, once connected to a structure that separated two quadrangle courtyards, each of which was surrounded by buildings (now rubble). The corbeled arch (10 x 19 feet) rests on a small platform flanked by two doorways into small side rooms. The west face features decorative moldings of undulating zig-zags and above these are depictions of thatched-roof Maya huts (*najs*) with lattice work accents. In the niche doorways, seated figures are thought to have existed.

The **Palace** is the first building you come to when you enter. It was built during the Late Classic period around AD 850. It has a built-in second-story chultun and a sculpture of a serpent gripping a human head in its gaping jaw at the eastern corner. There are 60 chultuns in and around Labná – "Old House of Women" – and archeologists believe that 3,000 Maya once lived here.

There are several other interesting sites in the area, including **Chuncatzim I**, **Huntichmul** and **Sabacché**, but these are for die-hard amateur archeologists. See "Authors Tip" on the previous page for the names of two local guides if you want to retrace Stephens' visits.

TABI: As the Puuc Highway snakes away from the cluster of ruins toward Cooperativa, orange groves flank the roadway. Approximately 14 km (15 miles) after Labná is a small sign for Tabi, an astonishing hacienda hidden way back on a nature preserve behind the orange groves and anchiote trees. There is now a dirt road next to that sign that declares the Tabi Forest Preserve. It is a route best taken in a four-wheel-drive if the ground isn't completely dry, although we did it in a Nissan sedan. To go the old way, enter the orange groves, turn right and then left. You may have to ask for directions from agricultural workers because it is not well marked (we got lost). Despite the difficulty in finding it, it's worth the effort. Just before you give up, the entrance appears on a bumpy road into a tall forest. After creeping along the driveway with slits of light slicing between the trees, you come to an amazing sight – an absolutely huge golden yellow hacienda across several acres of lawn in the middle of nowhere. There's not a sound except for the forest birds and hot breeze in the leaves. See page 101 for a detailed description about this unique accommodation option.

Nobody visits here and that's both a blessing and a shame. It's a fabulous place to explore, one that still breathes history. If you visit, the caretaker will show you the property with its ruined chapel (a massive brown beehive hangs in the wooden eaves), a tall furnace chimney you can walk inside, and old sugar cane machinery. Please remember to tip. There is also a cenote and a small Maya ruin down a cattle trail in the back. Tabi is a total experience not to be missed. Once back on the roadway, turn left for Loltún and Oxkutzcab.

GRUTAS DE LOLTUN: So far, scientists know the history of the people of the Yucatán began here at Loltún Cave (Loltún means "Rock of Flowers"), where stone tools and animal remains were radiocarbon dated to 2200 BC. It also contains some of the earliest ceramics on the peninsula, dating from around 700 BC. Besides the fascinating natural underworld formations there are cave paintings and stone carvings, including a crude imitation Olmec-style head. There are several glyph-carved door jambs and an erect stone phallus on display outside, but it's the splendid natural stalactites and stalagmites inside that capture the imagination. There's a restaurant and bathrooms. Tour guides sell snacks and water in the reception area. Tours (about US $10), the only way to see the caves, run at 9:30 and 11 am, and 12:30, 2 and 3 pm, but double-check with the office upon arrival. Closed Mondays.

Where you made a left into the caves of Loltún, a right would take you through Cooperativa, then a left to Kancab and a right to **Chacmultún**, a sleeper of a Maya ruin near Tekax that might prove attractive to can't-get-enough ruin enthusiasts. Its name means "Mounds Made of Red Stone," and its low, compact buildings, though not as impressive as Labná or Sayil, are fairly interesting. About 27 km (17 miles) from Loltún.

OXKUTZCAB: This bustling and clean Maya town is in the heart of Yucatán's agricultural district and the fertile soil in the area grows a large percentage of the peninsula's oranges. During the last week of October and first week of November the town erupts in **Orange Festival** fun, when every day is a fiesta in the town square. The 16th-century church on the plaza is yet another beautiful Colonial relic. If you're finishing up the Ruta Puuc or the Convent Route and you're hungry, **Su Cabaña Suiza** restaurant on Calle 54 is open until 6:30 pm. This family-owned eatery specializes in Mexican and Yucatecan food prepared over charcoal fires. The smell of delicious grilled meats should get your juices flowing before you even enter the palapa-covered dining room. Tables and chairs outside also beckon. It's very inexpensive.

The only hotel we know of in Oxkutzcab is **Los Tucanes Hotel** on Calle 64. Reportedly, archeologists working the ruins sometimes stay here. See *Ticul*, page 386, for good hotels and the scoop on the three-wheeled bicycles, *triciclos*, that ply the narrow streets.

The Ruta Puuc and the next itinerary, the Convent Route, are arranged so that each can be completed in a day (albeit a long one). You may prefer to stay somewhere along the line and combine the two into a giant loop. A night in Ticul, Santa Elena, Uxmal or even Tabi takes the pressure off seeing and doing everything and still getting back to Mérida for the night. By doing the Ruta Puuc in reverse, you can stay the night at Uxmal to see the evening light and sound show.

The Convent Route

Hunting God is a great adventure.
~ Marie De Floris OSB, to novice nuns making their vows

The third way from Mérida into the south of Yucatán is the new road marked as **Route 18** on older maps. Following this off-the-beaten-path itinerary takes you past ancient churches, convents, courtyards and cenotes. If you leave early, this makes a pleasant day trip by car. Or you can stay overnight somewhere along the Ruta Puuc for a great combination of Maya and Colonial past.

The Convent Route road was upgraded in 1999 so that it now bypasses each of the villages we describe below, making visits into each small town optional.

From downtown, take Calle 67 east and rejoin 69 where it's two-way, then go over the bypass highway (*periférico*) and follow the signs for Kanasin to Acanceh. The scrub forest you may pass is the Cuxtal Ecological Preservation Zone. The first time we tried to take this route we got on the wrong road to begin with (by following Calle 42 south) and went through tiny towns, such as Tahdzibilichén and Tekit de Regil. Along the way we found some fascinating diversions, played soccer with local youth on the grounds of one of the several abandoned haciendas and didn't even realize we were lost until we rejoined the "route" in Tecoh. We definitely prefer this to the faster direct road. It proves there is much to discover on the little roads around Mérida, even if you

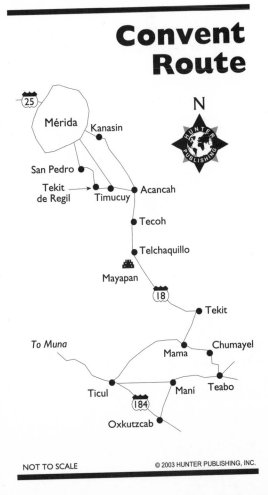

Convent Route

N

NOT TO SCALE   © 2003 HUNTER PUBLISHING, INC.

don't have an entire day. These side roads make great bike trips too.

The first village on the main route, 10 km/6.25 miles after Kanasin, is **San Antonio Tehuitz**, a working henequen plantation town (see *For Adventure Guide Readers Only*, page 295, for the special offer). A few miles later is another sisal hacienda town, **Tepich**. Then it's off to Acanceh.

ACANCEH: The central plaza in the busy small village of Acanceh ("Moan of the Deer") hosts an uninteresting Colonial church as well as an interesting Maya ruin called the **Grand Pyramid**, an early classic giant from sometime around 300-600 BC. Its five sculpted face stone masks were uncovered in 1998, but unfortunately their noses were put out of joint. Work is ongoing on a smaller building next to it. The caretaker looks for foreigners to show around and may approach your car and show his INAH identification card to introduce himself.

About four blocks away are more ruins, including the **Temple of the Stuccoes**, with visible glyphs. Ask someone for directions; if they take you, tip 10 pesos or so. Acanceh is a total of 22 km (13.75 miles) from Kanasin. For a possible side trip from here to **Chunkana**, a working hacienda, see *For Adventure Guide Readers Only*, page 295.

TECOH: This town ("Place of the Puma") has a very ornate church and convent complex dedicated to the Virgin of the Assumption, built on the base of a very large Maya pyramid. The carved stones, altar, carved statues and paintings are impressive. In 1562, two young boys were sacrificed here on the altar in a grotesque combination of Maya and Catholic practices. Maya priests cut their hearts out and threw the bodies into the local cenote (which, by the way, does have interesting caves). Eight km (five miles) from Acanceh.

In 1562, two young boys were sacrificed here on the altar at Tecoh.

TELCHAQUILLO: Drive slowly or you'll miss this tiny village. The central plaza has an austere, photogenic Catholic church, with carved blocks from the ruined city of Mayapán used to build its walls. Ancient designs on the block are still visible where the stucco has worn off the exterior. The little square across the street has a cenote with carved steps down into it. Stephens commented that during his first visit, "Women, with their water jars, were constantly ascending and descending; swallows were darting through the cave in every direction and

Yucatán

the whole formed a wild, picturesque and romantic scene." Kids now swim there.

MAYAPAN: Only a few kilometers farther along and you'll come to the historical Maya city of Mayapán. The walled city is the size of Chichén Itzá and has 4,000 mounds. It once ruled the northern Yucatán with an iron fist. Legend says that the great Kukulcán from Chichén Itzá founded it around AD 1000. The dynasty that resulted was the Cocom family, who joined in a federation with Chichén until a war between the two city-states resulted in Mayapán conquering the Itzás in 1221. Buoyed by their victory, the Cocom extracted tribute from other Maya cities and for two centuries consolidated their power. One method was to force members of the rival royal families to live as captives in Mayapán. This included the Xiú family from Uxmal, who finally led a general revolt and successfully sacked the city in the mid-1400s. It was immediately abandoned and never occupied again. The Xiú family founded a new capital at Maní but continually battled the surviving Cocoms for the next 100 years. Their mistrust of one another prevented them from driving out the European invaders. When Montejo successfully defended T'Ho (Mérida) in 1542, the Xiú ruler made a fateful alliance with the Spanish to once-and-for-all wipe out their ancient rivals, the Cocoms. Only too late did it become apparent to the Xiú that the price the Spanish would extract was subjugation of all Maya 100 years later.

Restoration is intense here because the ruins were really ruined. Recent digs have uncovered paintings and promise even more surprises. A visit here is a

Mayapan was once a very important city.

chance to see an ongoing archeological dig. With few tourists, Mayapán is a lonely site, as if the ruins themselves harbor a heavy heart over their role in the demise of the Maya.

TEKIT: Tekit, 30 km/19 miles beyond Mayapán, is a larger and more prosperous village. The Moorish-styled 16th-century parish church contains wall niches that house ornate statues of saints and there's an impressive wood *retablo* (altar).

MAMA: Next on the route, 7 km (4.3 miles) down the road, is Mama ("Abode of the Water Goddess"), a small village even your mother would appreciate. Its famous bell-gabled church, thought to be the oldest on the route, features a large garden, a well with a famous closed atrium over top (one of two surviving in the Yucatán), frescos and a baroque altar. The celebration called the "Battle of the Flowers" – the highlight of Carnival – occurs here the day before Ash Wednesday. As you pass through the village, notice the number of little houses that have Corinthian columns holding up front porches. The columns were a mark of status. If you've had enough, from Mama you can turn right through Chapab straight to Ticul and the fast road back to Muna and Mérida. There's an abandoned hacienda about 12 km (7.5 miles) down the road. But you don't want to miss the end of the trip at a truly beautiful and tranquil spot, so take the turn left instead to complete the Convent Route through Chumayel and the historical town of Maní.

CHUMAYEL: This is the village where the important Maya document Chilam Balam was written. One of the highlights of these books chronicles the rise of Chichén Itzá. **Teabo** is four km (2.5 miles) past Chumayel, and is well known for its hand-embroidered *huipiles* and stately 17th-century temple. There are vestiges in the village of an important Maya cemetery. Next comes **Tipikal**, a "tipikal" Maya village with a beautiful parish church and the ex-Convento of the Virgin of Magdalen. Check out the carved steps. The last church on the Convent Route, and the major attraction, is Maní, another 12 km (7.5 miles).

Maní

There is in the town of Maní, a deep well....
[At the well] there is an old woman who sells [enchanted] water.
And the Feathered Serpent is there too, where the water will be sold.
The old woman will demand a small boy for every cup of water.
These things are coming to pass, the days draw close.
~ A.F. Allen, Epoch of Miracles

We've saved the best stop – the tragic town of Maní – for last. Here, in a devil's bargain, the Maya Xiú family dynasty surrendered to Montejo and joined the Spanish in fighting the Cocom clan. Almost immediately Montejo's Franciscan missionaries began building a massive church and

Rooftop bells on Maní's monastery.

monastery using 6,000 Maya slaves. Under Fray Juan de Mérida's direction, workers completed the huge complex in 1549, in only seven months. The thick stone monastery contains a working church (San Miguel). On our last visit, a choir composed of young Maya girls, some in *huipiles*, filled the temple with song. In a juxtaposition of the past and present, their sweet voices were accompanied by a modern electric piano and synthesizer that recorded them on multiple tracks. This played back as they sang, making them seem like a huge choir. The haunting sound followed us as we wandered through a labyrinth of cloistered rooms and delightful pocket gardens. The remnants of colorful religious paintings and faded graffiti from hundreds of years past can be seen on the plaster walls. Inscribed on the wall in a cubbyhole that leads to the bell gable are names of people long forgotten – perhaps a wayward Conquistador looking for immortality, an earlier tourist far from home, or a courting couple searching for privacy. Who knows? The walls remain silent. Silent witness as well to the 200-some townspeople slaughtered within when the Maya rebelled during the Caste War.

It was in Maní in July of 1562 that the zealous Bishop Diego de Landa rid the city of important Maya documents and statues during the Franciscan movement of converting the indigenous people to Christianity. He gathered and destroyed some 5,000 idols, 13 altars, 27 scrolls on deer skin and 197 vases with hieroglyphs that, in combination, represented the history of the Maya. These were the first "books" of the New World, older than any of Europe. He later regretted some of his destructiveness and wrote all he could remember in a book, *Relation of Things in the Yucatán*, the most important contemporary single source of Maya culture and history we have today. Only four works survived the Friar's furious onslaught, but legend maintains that a Maya king buried historical documents in Uxmal, rather than see them destroyed. If they exist, they've never been found.

Near the monastery, in a low-walled depression just off the corner of the central plaza, is a cave/well that by Maya legend is connected through the underground back to the cathedral in Mérida. The ancient legend claims that this cave is one end of a twisted rope, a living umbilical cord full of blood, that connects the natural and supernatural worlds.

There are several connecting passages and cave pools that are inhabited by white, freshwater shrimp, often caught for food by local children. Stephens

visited it in 1841 and pottery excavated in 1958 revealed its use as far back as 800 BC. If the gate is locked, the key is in the little grocery *tienda*.

From Maní you can drive to Oxkutzcab or Ticul for a good meal or a night's sleep.

> *For thou desirest no sacrifice, else would I give it thee;*
> *but thou delightest not in burnt offerings.*
> ~ Christian Prayerbook, ca. 1662

FAHRENHEIT 451

Few Maya writings survived the religious zeal of Fray Diego de Landa. In an effort to convert the Maya into Christians, the good friar destroyed virtually all of their "pagan" texts. A few surviving documents give a glimpse of how the ancient Maya saw themselves.

Popul Vuh is considered to be the most important primary source on Maya mythology. It was preserved through oral tradition until written, anonymously, around 1544 in the Quiché Maya language and Latin. The first four chapters deal with the creation of the world and the creation of man and woman from corn. The middle relates the adventures of young demigods; moral lessons about the consequences of doing evil; and the hubris of Vucub-Caquix, who wanted to be both the sun and the moon. The final part, less literary than historical, lists the kings and conquests of the Quiché Maya up to shortly before the Spanish Conquest.

The **Rabinál Archí** is an historical drama and the only surviving example of pre-Hispanic theater in North America. The plot involves the capture of the Prince of Quiché by warriors from rival tribes. The prince refuses to humiliate himself to avoid death. The audience knows what's coming and, in the end, he is sacrificed.

Anales de los Cakchiqueles is a work translated from Cakchiquel Mayan language. It's a 96-page legal document that some Cakchiquel nobles used to recover privileges lost during the Colonial period. It contains the genealogy of the Xahil family and the history of the Cakchiquel tribe.

Another very important work, **Libros de Chilam Balam**, written after the Conquest, is composed of religious texts (Maya and Christian), historical texts, medical writings, astrology and rituals. Several fragments of Maya song lyrics also survive in the Songs of Dzitbalché, including one to accompany a "sacrifice by arrows" rite.

Poignantly, a recently discovered Maya ceramic vessel from between AD 600 and 900 (covered with glyphs and text) proves that written "books" existed in North America more than 600 years before Columbus arrived.

TICUL: Ticul is the home to a thriving pottery industry and many of its small workshops (*fábricas*) fill its neighborhoods. Artisans are also famous here for their embroidered cotton *huipiles* and these and other craft wares can be found in the *centro mercado* downtown, just off the plaza. Ticul presents you with some strange Maya-like statuary on the main drags into town and yet another ubiquitous old church, this time a grand fortress-like 18th-century cathedral with an older Colonial monastery attached. The busy part of this busy town is around the market, whose surrounding streets are awash in *triciclos*, the three-wheeled bicycles that serve (quite well) as people-powered taxis – you'll see a small family crammed onto the seat over the two front wheels – or as carriers, hauling everything from manufactured goods to fire wood, vegetables or reeds cut as fodder for farm animals. If you stay in Ticul, or just pass through and want to see the sights, park your car away from the *mercado* and walk or hire an inexpensive *triciclo*. Be the Sydney Greenstreet of Mexico.

Ticul is also noted for its cottage-industry shoe manufacturing (buy 'em here). With so much commerce, it has a life of its own besides tourism. Perhaps that accounts for the lack of good tourist amenities. Ticul is ideally situated as a base to visit Maya ruins, cenotes and old haciendas, and now has some good hotels downtown. For example, the **Hotel Plaza** (Calle 23 at 26, ☎ 997/972-0484, *www.hotelplazayucatan.com, air*), new in 1998, has large modern upstairs rooms in a Colonial building overlooking the square. The rooms with floor-to-ceiling windows face all the activity in the plaza, including the long line of Maya women who gather to crochet and sew under the former Municipal Palace's shady portico. The bells ring the hours at night. $

The inexpensive **Hotel Sierra Sosa**, a half-block away on Calle 26 #199A, has 17 respectable and clean rooms with HBO on the tube. What more could you ask for?

The latest addition to Ticul's fledgling hospitality industry is **Hotel San Antonio** (*Calle 25-A, facing the park near the church,* ☎ 997/972-1893, *27 rooms, restaurant, air, TV*). This modern hotel in a remodeled Colonial-style building offers clean and attractive hotel rooms overlooking a corner of the park. Its restaurant, with French windows that open to tiny balconies, features typical Yucatecan and Mexican food at low prices. Opened in mid-2002. $

Los Almendros Restaurant got its start in the early 1960s in a big Colonial house. The venerated restaurant, on Calle 23 No. 27, has grown into a chain of semi-successful Yucatecan eateries. Try the *poc chuc, pollo ticuleño* or *papadzules*, egg-filled tortillas covered in a spicy sauce. Eating in at least one of Los Almendros' locations is a requirement for any visit to the Yucatán, but many other restaurants throughout the peninsula are also "cooking good."

Along with varied arts and local crafts, Ticuleños also weave Panama hats in some of the numerous caves of the area; some workrooms are even hand-dug. The craft shop of **Bonan K'at** is under the Municipal Palace, where the Maya women gather to embroider, sew and gab on weekends. But it is pottery that attracts the most attention. **Arte Maya**, on the way out of town toward Muna, is a high-quality shop and gallery that makes Maya reproductions and original stone, ceramic and clay pieces. The entryway itself looks like a Maya ruin. Some of their work is fantastic and considered to be of museum quality. More fabulous *fábricas* are found on Calle 23 as you enter or leave town.

> *Every moon, every year, every day, every wind,*
> *Move on by and also pass away.*
> ~ Book of Chilam Balam

Yucatán

Campeche

Spanish language dictionaries define *campechano* as cheerful, good-hearted, genial and generous.

At A Glance

NAME: "Campeche" (cam-PAY-chay) derives from the name of the former Maya trading town of Ah-Kin-Pech. Close to where the Maya repulsed the initial attempt to conquer the peninsula, it later became the stronghold of the Spanish colonists in the Yucatán.

LOCATION: In the southeastern corner of the Yucatán Peninsula, bordering Quintana Roo and Yucatán states to the north and east; Guatemala and the Mexican state of Tabasco to the south; and the Gulf of Mexico to the west.

CAPITAL: Campeche City.

MAJOR CITIES: Campeche City, Ciudad del Carmen, Escárcega, Champotón, Calkiní and Hopelchén.

MAJOR INDUSTRIES: Oil and commercial fishing.

POPULATION: 650,000.

CLIMATE: Tropical, hot and humid. Coastline cooled by soft winds. Rain in the summer. Average year-round temperature, 27°C/81°F.

VEGETATION: Jungle, mangrove swamps and savanna.

GEOGRAPHY: Lowland, hilly in some areas, lagoons, Gulf coast beaches.

SIZE: 20,325 square miles (50,812 square kilometers).

WILDLIFE: Iguanas, parrots, monkeys, deer, jaguars, tapirs, and *mucho* water birds.

ECOLOGICAL RESERVES: Calakmul Biosphere, Laguna de Terminos.

ARCHEOLOGICAL SITES: Edzná, Calakmul, Xpujil, Becán, Chicanná, Balamku and Hochob.

TOURISM OFFICE: In Plaza Moch-Couoh, Avenida Ruíz Cortines s/n, 24000 Campeche. Open Monday to Friday, 9 am to 2 pm and 4 to 7 pm. ☎/fax 981/816-6767.

Campeche

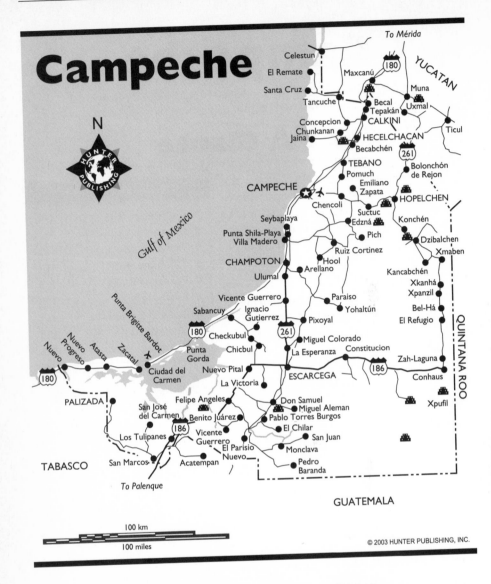

Campeche

N

Gulf of Mexico

To Mérida

Celestun
El Remate
Santa Cruz
Maxcanú
180
YUCATAN
Muna
Tancuche
Becal
Tepakán
Uxmal
Concepcion
Chunkanan
Jaina
CALKINI
HECELCHACAN
Becabchén
Ticul
TEBANO
261
Pomuch
Bolonchón
de Rejon
CAMPECHE
Emiliano
Zapata
HOPELCHEN
Chencoli
Suctuc
Edzná
Konchén
Seybaplaya
Pich
Punta Shila-Playa
Villa Madero
Ruiz Cortinez
Dzibalchen
Xmaben
CHAMPOTON
Hool
Arellano
Kancabchén
Ulumal
Xkanhá
Xpanzil
Vicente Guerrero
Paraiso
Bel-Há
Sabancuy
Ignacio
Gutierrez
Yohaltún
El Refugio
QUINTANA ROO
Punta Brigitte Bardot
180
Checkubul
Pixoyal
261
Miguel Colorado
La Esperanza
Constitucion
Zah-Laguna
Nuevo
Progreso
Atasta
Zacatal
Punta
Gorda
Chicbul
186
Conhaus
180
Ciudad del
Carmen
Nuevo Pital
La Victoria
ESCARCEGA
PALIZADA
Felipe Angeles
Don Samuel
Miguel Aleman
Pablo Torres Burgos
Xpufil
San José
del Carmen
Benito Juárez
El Chilar
186
Vicente
Guerrero
El Parisio
Nuevo
San Juan
Los Tulipanes
Monclava
TABASCO
San Marcos
Acatempan
Pedro
Baranda
To Palenque
GUATEMALA

100 km

100 miles

© 2003 HUNTER PUBLISHING, INC.

Campeche City

*The history of Campeche, written in stones, fortresses,
gates and walls, tells us of the past; of Maya warriors,
Spanish seafarers and fearsome pirates.*
~ Roman Piña Chan, Campeche historian

Campeche is like a venerable old lady seated on the shore of the Gulf of
Mexico, resplendent in a coat of many colors. The old port city, built on

Typical street in Campeche City.

the site of the early Maya center of Ah-Kin-Pech ("Priest of the Tick,") is one of the peninsula's most Colonial, and most colorful, cities. The entire town has recently been painted in authentic shades of yellow and gold, pastel greens and blues, turquoise and pinks, and hacienda red. Famous for its hospitality, it is quiet and reserved yet vibrantly alive with a culture that's unique. In 2000, UNESCO (United Nations Educational, Scientific and Cultural Organization) named Campeche a World Heritage Site, a significant honor of which the city is justifiably proud. To be declared a World Heritage Site means the city will receive funding for further restoration of its Colonial heart. But the honor also comes with the responsibility of maintaining the magnificent and profound heritage reflected in its Maya-Spanish-Campechano architecture.

What makes Campeche (cahm-PAY-chay) doubly attractive to *Adventure Guide* travelers is that it is bypassed by most tourists to the Yucatán. Their loss and our gain – off-the-beaten-trail attractions of the countryside make for a great uncrowded vacation.

Situated on the warm and shallow Gulf of Mexico and guarded by flanking forts, the city was officially founded in October of 1540, though its first attempt at settlement came in 1517. It became the main Spanish port and the city from which roots of Colonial influence spread over the Yucatán. Perhaps because of its importance – and certainly because of its location – Campeche fell prey to constant attacks by pirates and plunderers, many of whom based themselves at Ciudad del Carmen. In 1663, pirates massed a savage attack

and overran the vulnerable settlement, butchering its men and raping and enslaving its women. Then, in 1685, the pirate Lorencillo occupied the city for 56 torturous days.

Finally, after 130 years of continuous harassment, the city had enough of being pillaged by the likes of Francis Drake, John Hawkins, Peg-leg the Pirate, Henry Morgan and Bartolomé the Portuguese. They hired French engineer Louis Bouchard de Bocour to build a huge, hexagonal fortress with walls 2.5 meters thick (eight feet), guarded by eight towers (*baluartes*), to repulse the buccaneers. On the bluffs either side of the city, forts armed with cannon could put attackers in a withering crossfire. The defenses stopped the bloody pirate attacks, but Campeche's walls were employed again when Maya armies regained the peninsula in the 1840s and drove survivors inside the bulwarks, saving the lives of thousands of Campechanos from slaughter. Lacking Campeche's battlements, the government in the old corsair hang-out of Ciudad del Carmen – where the last of the buccaneers were finally routed in 1717 – hired ships from the Republic of Texas, before Texas became a state, to protect it from Maya attack in the Caste War.

Today, Campeche (population 175,000) extends inland and north and south from the confines of its former defenses. Unfortunately, in the 1960s the city fathers implemented a modernization plan that filled in the waterfront from the old gates and seawall out into the Gulf to accommodate new buildings. That, combined with the fact that several large portions of the wall were destroyed over the years in the growth of the town, makes us wonder how majestic the old city must have been when it was completely enclosed. Still, the inner city's charming cobblestone streets and ancient Colonial buildings enchant and inspire. And recently, the government rebuilt the seafront, adding both walking and bicycle paths, "friendship" parks with sitting areas and fountains, pedestrian crosswalks and parking. Now the magnificent new *malécon* is full of people enjoying themselves day and night, and especially at sunset.

CELEBRATIONS IN CAMPECHE

If you're lucky enough to be in Campeche for **Christmas** you're in for a visual treat. Colorful Christmas lights enhance the romantic atmosphere along the cobblestone streets and it is even more enchanting with the restoration and painting of the Colonial downtown. Fairs and public celebrations are common in the city center, but **Carnaval**, held in February before Lent, is extraordinary. Campeche's celebration, considered to be the oldest and most traditional in all of Mexico, has taken place annually without interruption since 1583 – over 420 years!

Provincial Campeche is a perfect base from which to explore and a rewarding place to simply stay and enjoy. Look for it online at **www.campechetravel. com**.

DISTANCES FROM CAMPECHE	
Becán . . . . 250 km/155 miles	Escárcega . . . . 150 km/93 miles
Calakmul . . . . 360 km/224 miles	Mérida . . . . 192 km/119 miles
Cancún . . . . 494 km/307 miles	Palenque. . . . . 366 km/227 miles
Ciudad del Carmen . . . 212 km/132 miles	Palizada . . . . 360 km/224 miles
Champotón. . . . . 65 km/40 miles	Sabancuy . . . . 130 km/81 miles
Chetumal . . . . 422 km/262 miles	Seybaplaya. . . . . 32 km/20 miles
Chicanná . . . . 270 km/168 miles	Villahermosa . . . . 450 km/280 miles
Edzná . . . . 65 km/40 miles	Xpujil . . . . 290 km/180 miles

Orientation

■ Getting Around

Campeche City was originally divided into several *barrios*, including **Guadeloupe** and **San Francisco** to the north, where the Maya population lived; **San Román** in the south, where *mestizos* and mulattos lived; and the **Walled City**, where the Spanish elite resided. This separation of races was typical of Colonial times and contributed to the Caste War uprising many years later. Those distinctions are no longer a part of Campeche's make-up, but the neighborhoods each have their own distinctive personality.

Monument to the Maya, South Entrance to Campeche City.

The city rests on the edge of the Gulf of Mexico, its shallow harbor port facilities long since unusable for large modern ships. The main routes in and out of town run north and south. The southern road splits at Champotón, due south for Escárcega or southwest along the coast for Ciudad del Carmen, the "economic engine" that powers the state economy. The way north to Mérida also splits into long- and shortcuts. **Route 180** takes you 175 km (110 miles) directly to Mérida, while **Route 261** loops east then north past the deep underground caverns of Xtacumbilxuna, near Bolonchén, as well as the famous Maya ruins at Uxmal and Kabáh.

Campeche

A road known as the **Circuito Baluartes** rings the walled city's exterior. Odd-number streets run east-west, perpendicular to the sea, and even-number streets run north-south. Although you may have arrived in Campeche by car, vehicles are a liability in the Colonial part of town. The streets are exceedingly narrow and parking is at a premium. If your hotel doesn't have private parking and you find a space on any of the criss-cross one-way streets, leave your car there. Old Campeche is a city made for walking.

Practicalities

COMMUNICATIONS: A *larga distancia* is **Intertel** on 57th, and Internet cafés are springing up everywhere, including one on Calle 12 at the Circuito Baluartes.

IMMIGRATION: Renew your tourist card at the **immigration office**, Secretaria de Relaciones Extenores, at the corner of Calle 12 and 53, ☎ 981/811-3524.

LAUNDROMAT: A good laundromat/dry cleaners in the heart of the Colonial section is **Lavandería La Antigua**, Calle 57 (8-4 pm, Monday-Saturday).

MEDICAL FACILITIES: The **General Hospital** is at ☎ 981/816-4233.

MONEY MATTERS: The banks with ATMs are **Bancomer** and **Atlántico** on Av. 16 de Septiembre; **Banamex** on Calle 53 and 10; and **Serfin** on Calle 18 No. 102.

POLICE: The police can be reached at ☎ 981/816-3635. Emergencies, dial 060.

POST OFFICE: The post office is in the Federal Palace building on Av. 16 de Septiembre.

SWEET STUFF: The **Panificadora NuevaEspaña** is a sweet-smelling bakery on Calle 10, between 59 and 61. It has a large selection of delicious goods, fresh out of the oven. Got a sweet tooth? So do Campechanos. Try the mouth-watering marzipan at **Dulces y Mazapanes** in the Colonial Carmelo suburb, Privada de Santa Barbara No 5 upstairs (☎ 981/815-1509). A San Francisco de Asis **supermarket** is one block north of the Hotel del Mar, along with a sports complex.

TOURIST INFORMATION: Tourist information is available in English at Casa Seis ("6") on Calle 57 between 8 and 10. See the walking tour, page 398, for more details on the magnificent Moorish-style *casa* that houses a museum and tourist office. Guides can be engaged at the office on Calle 49, between 10

and 12. The tourism phone is ☎ 981/811-3989 and the State Tourism is 981/811-9255.

TRANSPORTATION: The ADO **bus** station is on Av. Gobernadores in the Santa Ana District, 2 km (10 long blocks) northeast of the Sea Gate. The *mercado*, on Circuito Baluartes near the Baluarte de San Pedro, is the place to catch local buses. Ask a merchant for help figuring out which goes where.

Nightlife

The nocturnal pleasures of Campeche revolve around the dinner/nightclub **Lafitte's** in the Hotel del Mar, where you walk a plank to enter. If that's too mundane, find the best disco in town at **KY8**, on Calle 8 near the Sea Gate There's a **pool hall** on Calle 55 just around the corner from Los Portales and a **juice bar** hang-out on Calle 57.

Shopping

Several craft stores with some great regional and national crafts are in the Colonial downtown. One of the best is **Tukulná**, on Calle 10 No. 333 (☎ 981/816-9088), between 59 and 61. See page 411 for details.

Other worthwhile artisan and handicraft places include **Veleros Boutique** in the Ah Kin Pech Plaza, stand 119, **Arte Mexicano** on Calle 59, 9B, plus **Típica Naval**, on Calle 8 near the Baluarte de la Soledad. Another fortress town (*baluarte*), **San Pedro**, has a regional handicraft exhibit and sells arts and crafts. It guards the town's lively *mercado* across the street.

For traditional shirts, dresses or linen cloth to make your own, try **Wilma**. People come for miles to her shop on Calle 59 between 16 and 18.

Campeche

MODEL SHIPS

A traditional handicraft of Campeche – now imitated throughout the state – is building scale models of sailing ships out of wood. It began around 1965 when David Perez Noceda, a native Campechano, naval officer and shipwright carpenter, built his first model ship while at sea. He retired from seafaring to establish Artesanía Tipica Naval and Veleros. Two generations later the family craftsman use only native Campeche material: precious woods, jippi, bull's horn, stone, red and black coral, and shark skin.

Adventures

Campeche is a garden of fancy, That is an invitation to dream.
~ Campeche, a popular song

■ Adventures on Foot

Campeche's colorful Colonial buildings and confined spaces make a walking tour (or two) a wonderful way to appreciate the city. Though it's a diminutive city, seeing its points can require a long walk. Wear comfy shoes and don't plan on walking around during the hottest part of the day. An afternoon siesta or a long leisurely lunch is called for. Fortunately, dusk and the early evening are magical times downtown.

My land is a poem of the moon, My land is a Sultana,
Bewitched by a fairy....
~ Las Torres de Catedral (Cathedral Towers), popular song

In the late 1990s, an ambitious program was begun by the people of Campeche to restore their historical heritage and the beauty of their Colonial downtown. Under the direction of architect José Beunfil, 1,600 façades were rehabilitated to their former glory using authentic Colonial-era colors – 1,200 buildings in the center and the rest in the original quarters of San Román, Guadeloupe and San Francisco. A walking tour of Campeche is a vivid pleasure not to be missed.

Start at ●A● the **Puerta del Mar**, the Sea Gate, on Calle 8 where it meets Calle 59. This was one of the four main entrances into the walled defenses built to stop pirate attacks. Walk north on 8 past Restaurante Marganzo and the Artesanía Tipica Naval to the Parque Principal. You could start your visit across the street at the **Baluarte de la Soledad** ●B●, a fortified part of the wall that contains the Museo de Estelas Maya, the **Museum of the Maya Steles** (open 8 am-2 pm and 5-8 pm daily). Besides Maya records carved in stone, the museum contains some Colonial-era artifacts. The fountain next to it lights up in the evening.

Campeche's small but pretty **Parque Principal** ●C● is the life center of the old town, the place where couples stroll and families gather on Sundays. The dominant gazebo, a former bandstand in the park's center, was converted into a romantic evening restaurant, El Kiosko. There were once circular paths surrounding the gazebo that were formal walking areas in the 1800s. Children and the elderly used the inner circuit, while young people used the middle one (young ladies on the outside, gentlemen on the inside) and the general public used the outer circuit.

A. Puerta del Mar
B. Baluarte de la Soledad:
   Museo de Estelas Maya
C. Parque Principal
D. Casa Seis
E. Catedral de la Concepción
F. Baluarte de Santiago:
   Botanical Garden
G. Mansion Carvajal
H. Teatro de la Ciudad
I. Baluarte de San Pedro
J. San Francisquito Church
K. Casa de Teniente del Rey
L. Puerta de Tierra
M. Baluarte de San Juan
N. Ex-Colegio de la Misericordia
O. Baluarte de Santa Rosa
P. Instituto Campechano,
   Ex-Templo de San Jose
Q. Baluarte de San Carlos
R. Church of San Román
S. Palacio Municipal
T. Tukulná

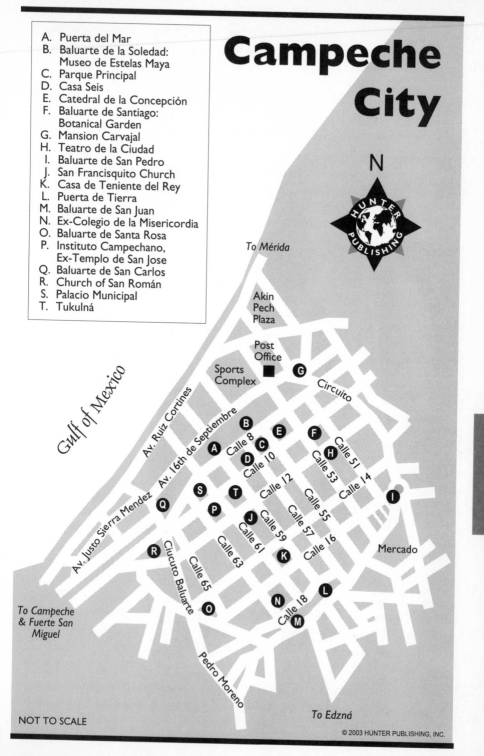

Campeche City

N

To Mérida

Akin Pech Plaza

Post Office

Sports Complex

Gulf of Mexico

Circuito

Av. Ruiz Cortines

Av. 16th de Septiembre

Av. Justo Sierra Mendez

Calle 8
Calle 10
Calle 12
Calle 51
Calle 53
Calle 14
Calle 55
Calle 57
Calle 59
Calle 61
Calle 63
Calle 16
Calle 65
Calle 18

Ciucuto Baluarte

Mercado

Pedro Moreno

To Campeche
& Fuerte San
Miguel

To Edzná

NOT TO SCALE

© 2003 HUNTER PUBLISHING, INC.

Campeche

A stop in ●D● **Casa Seis** ("House 6") on Calle 57 is required for any visitor to Campeche. The fabulously restored Moorish building is a museum that features living rooms with authentic furniture and ornamentation from Campeche's Colonial heyday. The massive muralist painting in the conference room was done by artist Ricardo Chavez. Marble floors and opulent décor show just how much wealth passed through Campeche in the years it dominated trade on the peninsula. The cultural center serves as the city's main tourist information office and offers a cool, quiet coffee shop. Open 9 to 9.

Los Portales arched façade faces the park on the east. It boasts an excellent restaurant, called **Casa Vieja**, above the stores. The area to the Calle 57 side is known as El Cuauhtemoc. In 1865, Empress Carlotta was a guest here when she toured the peninsula. Enter the building on 57 to find inside a quiet tiled courtyard with wrought-iron garden tables and a small snack bar.

The cathedral took 150 years to finish.

The massive but plain façade of the **Catedral de la Concepción** ●E● (open mornings and evenings) dominates the plaza. A church was built on this location by Montejo in 1541, almost as soon as the Spanish had established themselves in the peninsula, but the cathedral that replaced it – begun in 1639 – wasn't finished for a century and a half. One of its spires is known as the "Spanish Tower" because it was completed during Colonial rule in 1760. The other is "La Campechana," which was finished in 1850.

Farther down Calle 10 is the **Mansion Carvajal** ●F●. This stately building has rich marble floors, undulating Arabic arches and a sweeping staircase. It was the former home of Don Fernando Carvajal Estrada, one of Campeche's richest hacienda owners. The magnificent Moorish-styled mansion now houses government offices and handicraft shops, open daily except Sunday. On the corner of 10 and 51 is the former home of Juan José de León y Zamorano, the Spanish king's lieutenant between 1815 and 1820. Some of the other good areas for substantial Colonial homes are on Calles 55, 57 and 59, in the heart of the Centro.

Turn left on the Circuito Baluartes to reach the **Baluarte de Santiago** ●G●, which is filled with a tiny but exotic *jardín botánico*, a botanical garden refuge from the city traffic. Also called X'Much-Haltun, the garden nurtures 150-plus species of regional flora. English-language tours are given and ad-

mission is by donation. *Baluarte* means tower or bastion. Besides the two gates, only six of the eight bastions survive from the original fortifications built in 1686.

Walk east up either the Circuito or Calle 51 to Calle 12, where you'll find the **Teatro de la Ciudad ●H●** between 51 and 53, also known as the Theatro de Francisco de Paula Toro. The magnificent neoclassic theater opened its doors to the public on the 15th of September in 1834. It was built by French engineer Teodoro Journet, and was remodeled in 1916 and 1990. Inside the ornate theater is impressive, three floors high with railed balconies. If you find an opportunity to attend a performance while you're in Campeche, be sure to go! Most of the next block south is taken up by the side of the **Iglesia del Dulce Nombre de Jesús** – Church of the Sweet Name of Jesus – built in 1663. If you're hungry already, head over to Calle 55, between 10 and 12 and stop at La Parroquía bar and restaurant for an inexpensive lunch. Maybe a siesta at your hotel?

If you're not yet hungry, you have a choice. Walk west up Calle 51 to the northern end of the walled city where the **Baluarte de San Pedro ●I●** stands sentinel. (Across the *circuito* here is Campeche's main *mercado*.) Or you can push directly on south on Calle 12 to the corner of 59 where the **San Francisquito Church ●J●** (San Roque) sits next to the impressive Cultural Institute. The church was built in the 1700s as a refuge for friars whose monastery to the south was threatened by pirates. The **Cultural Institute** was once the Franciscan Hospital del San Roque.

Now wander east up Calle 59 to the **Casa de Teniente del Rey ●K●**, on Calle 59 between 14 and 16 (not to be confused with the hotel of the same name). The Colonial building is the former mansion of another king's lieutenant, and is open 8-2 and 5-8 pm. It contains a regional museum collection of Maya artifacts and stone carvings, as well as an example of the wooden contraption that deformed baby's skulls by flattening the forehead. A flat forehead was a mark of beauty to the ancient Maya, as were tattoos, where the skin cut and infected so that the resulting scars made the design. Also housed here is the companion jewelry to the jade mask found in Structure VII in Calakmul, on display at Fuerte San Miguel.

On Calle 59, notice the names of saints above the door lintels as you get near the famous **Puerta de Tierra ●L●**, "Land Gate," perhaps Campeche's best-known symbol. The land gate saw thousands of refugees pour through its heavy fortifications when the Maya rebelled in the Caste War. The enormous thick door made of jabin wood is the original from 1732, when the gate was built. A drawbridge adds further protection to the entrance. The stone fortress has preserved almost all its original 18th-century gun emplacements, gunpowder store rooms, sight holes and tower. Open for inspection Tuesday to Saturday from 8-2 and 4-8. A **Light and Sound Spectacular** is held every Tuesday, Friday and Saturday at 8:30 pm, which explains – through the

Campeche

Pirate fights are popular with children and adults alike.

use of spotlights, slides and actors – the history of Campeche. Simultaneous translation in English or French is provided. As part of the show you're invited to walk the ramparts of the wall from the Puerta to the **Baluarte de San Juan ●M●**, where an authentic-looking pirate "spirit" fights it out with a noble Spanish solider below. A folk dance is also performed. Diorama rooms within the stone walls portray life in the fortress during those days. Arrive early to get tickets.

Still walking? Right near the San Juan Baluarte is the recently remodeled **Ex-Colegio de la Misericordia ●N●**, on Calle 63, distinguished by the semi-circular bump next to the entrance. This former school was transformed into the town jail in 1845, and remained so as late as 1983. The building now houses the Municipal Archives.

If you follow the circuit toward the waterfront you'll next pass the **Baluarte de Santa Rosa ●O●**. It hosts a small art gallery.

Two blocks farther on Calle 10 is the city's university, **Instituto Campechano ●P●**, built in 1756. The site began as a Jesuit religious residence and has a magnificent central patio. The attached church is the **Ex-Templo de San Jose ●P●**. When the Jesuits were expelled in 1761, after a failed Maya rebellion lead by the Jesuit-educated Jacinto Canek, work on the temple was suspended until 1799 when the Franciscan "Third Order" finished the construction in 1809. The church has an intricate mosaic façade of Talavera tile and, appropriate to Campeche's importance as a seaport, its south tower was converted to lighthouse in 1858.

Around the corner is the **Baluarte de San Carlos ●Q●**, named after Carlos II, the last King of Spain of the Hapsburg dynasty. This bastion – the first one built (1686) of the eight original bastions – faced 12 cannon toward the city's most vulnerable side. There once existed a tower for meteorological observation above the ramparts. Inside, the powder room, guard room and jail room still exist. The Baluarte houses the **City Museum**, with a fascinating collection of old maps and a scale model of the Colonial walled town. Open Tuesday-Saturday from 8 to 8 and Sunday from 9 to 1 pm.

About four blocks south on Calle 10 is the **Church of San Román ●R●**, constructed in the 16th century and home of the Cristo Negro de San Román –

the "Black Christ" – carved from ebony hardwood. The Aztec who accompanied Montejo lived in this neighborhood, so perhaps it is no coincidence that they had worshipped Tezcatlipoca, the "black god of war," a cult the Spanish tried to eradicate by substituting the image with one of Christ, which had to be black to be accepted. One of the miracles attributed to the statue occurred when an attempt to move it to another church resulted in the statue raising its arms high enough to make it impossible to get out the door. There is no record of whether they tried turning it on its side, but it still resides in San Román.

Returning north on Calle 8 you'll pass the **Palacio Municipal •S•**, a huge Colonial building with wrought-iron gates that began as a hospital in 1846. Across the street are the garish modern government buildings that include the "UFO," as Campechanos have nicknamed the clam-shaped silver building that houses the State Congress.

Turn right up Calle 61 to 10th and find the city arts building, **Tukulná •T•**, on Calle 10 No. 333, between 59 and 61. Formerly known as the Handcraft House, it was extensively remodeled inside as well as out. This is a beautiful Colonial building with an exposition area, handmade crafts from the surrounding Maya villages, traditional music and the services of a bilingual guide (make an appointment in advance). Several small tables in an indoor courtyard are available for refreshments, coffee and soda.

In the Guadeloupe Barrio on Calle 8, which becomes Av. Miguel Aleman, is the old **Church of Guadalupe**, built in 1660 and located about five blocks north of the Baluarte Santiago. Two or so blocks east are the **Los Portales de San Francisco**. Where the old Camino Real crossed the neighborhood is the mercantile arches of San Francisco, a corner building surrounding a stone courtyard with a "Neo-Romantic" style clock tower.

Just past the Guadalupe church begins the former Maya neighborhood and its famous brick-red church, **San Francisco de Campeche**. It was built on the site of the first mass held on firm land in the New World (an earlier one was held on Cozumel island), when Córdoba landed here on St. Lazarus Day, February 15, 1517.

Don't forget to stroll the inviting **waterfront**, which is especially beautiful at sunset. And if you're an early riser, go to the **fisherman's pier** north of the downtown in Barrio San Francisco about 6 am to see the fishing boats either returning or setting out, depending on the season.

■ Sights

My pride is to have been born in the Belle of the Seas,
Old Colonial land... The Cathedral Towers.
~ Las Torres de Catedral (Cathedral Towers) popular folk song

Campeche has two formidable forts flanking the old city. The **Fuerte San José El Alto** – built not to stop pirates but Spain's Colonial rivals, England – is a few kilometers north of town on a bluff overlooking the city. Inside is an exposition entitled "Boats and Arms." The fort offers a great view of the nearby giant statue of Benito Juárez, the Mexican hero.

Corner turret of San Miguel Fort.

Campeche's pride and joy, however, is the **Fuerte San Miguel**, about four km (2.5 miles) south of town atop a steep hill. It's above an industrial waterfront section, just past the huge statue of a Maya with his arm holding a torch entitled "The Resurgence of Campeche." The stone fort is in excellent condition and from its parapets one can sense the power and security this fort must have given those under its protection. At sunset, alone on the rampart with only the black-barreled cannon, purple sky and blue water, your senses are overwhelmed. Evoke history by crawling around the sentry towers and imagine firing cannon down upon the ruthless pirates – be a kid again. It's even got a moat!

In the stone floor interior there is a magnificent little museum that boasts some incredible Maya pottery and stonework and the priceless and breathtaking jade mask recovered from Calakmul. An intricately carved ship's prow in the graceful and sleek shape of a greyhound, recovered from the mud of the Champotón River, is also on display. This is a stunning place to visit at sunset (but don't try to walk it; take a cab or drive). No flash photography is allowed in the museum rooms.

Those looking beyond the city to real adventure expeditions into the Southern Campeche wilderness should try **Expediciones Ecoturísticas** (Calle 12 #1684, ☎ 981/816-0197, www.campeche. com/aventura). This experienced agency offers hard or soft eco-tourism and natural and cultural explorations – in off-road vehicles, mountain bikes, on horseback, on foot, camping and kayaking. For local archeological tours in the Forest of Kings, or overnight expeditions into the Calakmul Biosphere, contact Leticia or Fernando at the **CIIT** in Xpujil (☎ 983/871-6064). They are excellent and knowledgeable (see page 419).

■ Adventures on Wheels

It's fun to take the **trolley tour** (US $3) of town on the *Tranvia* that leaves on the hour daily from Parque Principal. The guide's explanations are all in Spanish. The trip gives a great overview of Campeche – especially of the San Francisco neighborhood north of the city wall, where there are elegant Colonial buildings and churches. *El Guapo*, "The Handsome One," a second trolley, includes visits to the forts outside the city.

A new **luxury train ride/tour** runs from Mérida to Campeche to Palenque and includes stops at the ruins. For details, turn to page 428.

If you've got a car, try a circular **half-day excursion** into Campeche's Maya and Colonial past. See an abandoned hacienda 10 km (six miles) away at **Hobomo**, once Campeche's richest. About midway are the spectacular ruins of **Edzná**. With some extra effort you could also include the archeological ruins of Tixmucuy. The suggested loop includes the towns of China, Cholul, Pocyaxuma, Nohacai, Edzná, Cayal, Tikinmul, Castamay and back to Campeche. Don't worry about getting lost, we did and lived to tell about it.

Maya Ruins

*The act of writing requires a constant plunging back
into the shadow of the past where time hovers, ghost-like.*
~ Ralph Ellison

Campeche's southern zones of enigmatic Maya cities center around Xpujil and the Calakmul Biosphere.

The north-central part of Campeche features several Maya city sites, the most notable, Edzná and Hochob, are detailed below. Another, **Isla de Jaina**, off the coast north of Campeche city, is a partly man-made island. It has little of interest to tourists, but archeologists were thrilled at the discovery of an elite Maya burial ground here, the largest known necropolis in the Americas.

The site has yielded clay figurines (on display in the Camino Real Museum in Hecelchakán and in Mexico City) representing the deceased Maya nobility, a quarter of whom were female. Visits can be arranged in advance with INAH and you can rent a boat from the small fishing village near Punta Arena.

■ Edzná

Ruins at Edzná.

The best of Campeche's central and northern abandoned Maya sites is Edzná, which means "House of Grimaces," an easily accessible and magnificent ruin about 50 km (31 miles) southeast of the capital. A long-hidden jewel in the ring of Maya cities, the European and American explorers and archeologists that swarmed over the Yucatán in the late 19th century failed to find the lost city of Edzná. It wasn't until 1927 that the ruins were "discovered" by Nazario Quintana, although local Maya knew of them for years.

Occupied from around 400 BC to AD 1500, the huge ceremonial center's significant standing architecture is all within easy walking distance. Evidence indicates that a population of 70,000 may have lived there during its apogee in the Late Classic period between AD 600 and 900.

Unique to Edzná is the archeo-astronomical phenomenon that occurs around May 1 to May 3 and again, August 7 to 9, about 5 pm, when the sun's golden rays illuminate a stela in the sanctuary of the five-story Main Temple pyramid. The significance of the May date is that the gods were declaring it time to plant corn. Every year there is a organized celebration at the ruins; check with the tourism office.

Its new entrance is under the trees and gives you a bit of a natural jungle feeling. The first building inside the complex is the 20-room residence, the **Platform of the Cuchillos** (Knives), named for the rich find of obsidian knives discovered there.

One important aspect hidden from the casual observer in Edzná is the great hydraulic works that provided irrigation and perhaps drinking water through 12 canals and a series of reservoirs. One canal travels eight miles in a southerly direction.

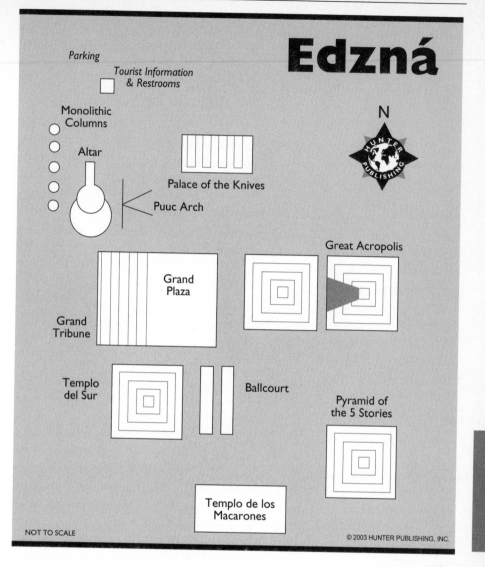

Parking

Tourist Information & Restrooms

Monolithic Columns

Altar

Palace of the Knives

Puuc Arch

N

Great Acropolis

Grand Plaza

Grand Tribune

Templo del Sur

Ballcourt

Pyramid of the 5 Stories

Templo de los Macarones

NOT TO SCALE

© 2003 HUNTER PUBLISHING, INC.

Campeche

South of the platform is **Nohoch Na** ("Great House"), which appears to be bleachers for the Grand Plaza (525 feet long and 330 feet wide). Its function may well have been for viewing tremendous ceremonies on the Grand Plaza and excavations indicate it covers an earlier building. The south end has the Petén-style **Templo del Sur** and small ballcourt with a surviving ring (the goal) in the middle of the west side. On a long flat platform east of the Grand Plaza is another magnificent complex known as the **Great Acropolis**, anchored by the monumental Late-Classic **Temple of Five Stories**, which absolutely overwhelms the impressive buildings that surround it. Twice a year the sun illuminates the holy chamber through the doorway on the top. Check

out the vaulted arch beneath the stairway on the first two levels. It is at least 1,300 years old and still standing. Best photos come in the afternoon.

Many of the restoration workers today are Guatemalan refugees, displaced Maya from across the border. If you're in Campeche, Edzná is a sight not to be missed. Some people even come down for the day from Uxmal and the Puuc ruins to see it.

DIRECTIONS: There are two ways to reach the ancient city from Campeche. The most common way is east on **Highway 180** to the cutoff for Edzná on the right (Route 188). Our *Adventure Guide* way is out from the Land Gate on Calle Pedro Moreno through the little town of China (chee-na). Our guide, Erik, calls it "Bump Town" because of the numerous *topes* in town.

A tour to Edzná with a bilingual guide is offered by several travel agencies and hotels in town with an option of stopping here. Departures are at 9 am and 2 pm (about US $30).

ACCOMMODATIONS: There are no accommodations at Edzná, but you could splurge big time on the nearby **Hacienda Uayamón** *(Km 20 Uayamón-China-Edzná Hwy, reservations ☎ 981/829-7526, fax 999/923-7963, http://promo.starwood.com/worldwideleisure/americas, 12 rooms, pool, restaurant)*. See page 103 for a full description of this delightful property.

■ Hochob

This site is harder to reach, set well off the beaten trail. Hochob (Mayan for "Maize Storage Place") is a small but interesting Late Classic Chenes-style site. Several structures are arranged around a plaza, the most interesting of which is the **Principal Palace**, decorated with an intricate monster mouth mask doorway and Chac corner masks. Pottery found at the site indicates it was still occupied when the Spanish landed.

On the road from Hopelchén to Dzibalchén you'll have passed El Tabasqueño ruins, a Chenes site not yet excavated. A guide to Hochob is the caretaker Hortensio Camál Ku, who lives in Chencoh near the ruins. Ask for him there or at Hochob. Other bilingual guides are José Williams and William Chan Cox, both residents of Dzilbalchén and experienced guides to Campeche's ruins. They are well known; ask anyone in town.

Accommodations

There are hotels around old Campeche and also in the suburbs, but we prefer to stay close to the Colonial center. Because so few tourists crowd the narrow streets of Campeche, rooms cost a fraction of what

they do in Cancún and are even lower than Mérida. Most people stay only one or perhaps two nights in Campeche and that's a shame – it's a good place to relax and enjoy. After all, in two days you can eat only six times – in a town where they have over a hundred ways of cooking pompano fish. Don't discount all the budget hotels, some of which offer wonderful accommodations.

<table>
<tr><td colspan="2">**HOTEL PRICE CHART**</td></tr>
<tr><td colspan="2">*NOTE: Often, one shared bed in a room is cheaper than two. Prices based on cost per night, for two.*</td></tr>
<tr><td>[No $]</td><td>Less than US $20</td></tr>
<tr><td>$</td><td>US $20 - $40</td></tr>
<tr><td>$$</td><td>US $40 - $80</td></tr>
<tr><td>$$$</td><td>US $80 - $125</td></tr>
<tr><td>$$$$</td><td>US $125 - $200</td></tr>
</table>

■ Budget Hotels

Hostal Campeche *(Calle 57 & 10, ☎ 981/811-6500, www.hostalcampeche.com, 40 beds, kitchen, laundry, Internet, air, breakfast included).* The peninsula's newest hostel is one of the Yucatán's more appealing ones. Located next to Casa Seis, with balconies facing the street and park, it's right in the heart of the city, where almost all festivities begin. An added plus for guests are the numerous restaurants very close by. The hostel, with a stylized monkey as a logo, offers a shuttle service to the ruins. This clean facility will be far more popular than the older youth hostel out by the University Sports Complex, especially now that Europeans, tired of the crowds along the coast of Quintana Roo, have discovered lovely Campeche. $

Samula Trailer Park *(Samula, no phone, full hook-ups, camping, showers).* Take Av. Jose Lopez Portillo east at the Pemex station, past the university and around some curves past a large shopping center. Go up a small hill and look for a tiny sign on your right. Good luck. The campground and Anita, the woman who runs it, were immortalized (more or less) in *Temple of the Jaguar*, by Donald Schueler, a fascinating book about his cathartic wanderings around the Yucatán. $

Hotel Castlemar *(Calle 61 No. 2, ☎ 981/816-2886, fax 981/811-0524, 18 rooms with fans).* The airy front rooms facing the narrow street are the better ones in this small hotel that looks like a castle in the southern part of the old city. Ornate tile work, balconies, interior courtyard – all say "Colonial." Some of the bathrooms are showing age, but a lot of character. $

Hotel Campeche *(Calle 57 No. 2, ☎ 981/8166-5183, 32 rooms with fans, restaurant).* This hotel, converted from a huge private mansion in 1939, is on a convenient corner of the park square. It's unadorned, with two aged, tiled open-center courtyards. Some rooms (relatively small) have short crooked doorways – built for people under 5'4" – so you know it's authentically Colonial. The mattresses are foam rubber and the pillows are tiny, but the rooms are clean and it's definitely a step up from the dark Reforma. Usually fills up

Campeche

with European tourists. Economical restaurants are downstairs on the corner. $-$$

Hotel America *(Calle 10 No. 252,* ☎ *981/816-4588, fax 981/816-0556, www. hotelamericacampeche.com, 52 rooms with fans or air, telephone, TV).* Travelers who enjoy staying in a Spanish-styled hotel in the heart of the oldest part of town often opt for the America, one block south of the main plaza. It's big and white with a dark wood trim. Rooms surround a tiled open courtyard, complete with hacienda artifacts such as wooden carts and farm tools. Arches face the courtyard and checkerboard tiles line the walkways. Parking anywhere in the Centro is scarce, but there's private parking here. $-$$

Colonial Hotel *(Calle 14 No. 122,* ☎ *981/816-2222, 30 rooms with fans, some with air).* This distinguished hotel in the middle of the Centro has been operating since 1946. A century before that it was the private home of the King of Spain's former Colonial Governor – Brigadier Don Miguel de Castro y Araos – and his wife. The family-run hotel is friendly and well kept, with tropical plants and a communal sitting area next to its tiled center courtyard. The rooms are small, with typical high ceilings and intricately designed tile floors. It's gracefully old and simple, with a strong appeal all its own. $

■ Moderate Hotels

Baluartes *(Av. Ruíz Cortines,* ☎ *981/816-3911, fax 981/816-2410, www. baluartes.com.mx, 104 rooms with air, restaurant, parking, pool).* The boxy Baluartes sits next to Hotel del Mar along Campeche's park-like waterfront. It's less expensive than its brand-name neighbor. Renovated rooms are comfortable, although the common areas are a little lacking. Good points include a bright and friendly café/restaurant, La Almena, and a swimming pool in the shape of a bow-tie that can be used by non-guests for a small fee. Excellent location. $$

Hotel del Mar *(Av. Ruíz Cortines No. 51,* ☎ ☎ *981/811-9191, fax 981/811-1689, delmarcp@prodigy.net.mx, 148 rooms & suites with air, pool, jacuzzi, cable TV, secured parking, nightclub, gym, sauna).* The staff at the del Mar is absolutely first rate. The hotel has long been acknowledged as the best in the city for both business travelers and tourists. It's the kind of place where they make you feel at home by remembering your name. All the rooms have private balconies that face the tranquil Gulf of Mexico and, although slightly worn around the edges in some of the public areas, the guest rooms are pleasing and comfortable. The popular restaurant, Café Poquito, is frequently full of Campechanos as well as hotel guests – and for good reason. The reasonably priced food and service are excellent and the Sunday buffet brunch is particularly popular. The glass-enclosed sunny dining area is also one of the largest non-smoking sections we've seen in Mexico. **Lafitte's Restaurant** and bar

in the hotel is also a local favorite. Check out the illuminated glass mural on the café's wall – what is that Maya handsignal? $$-$$$

Sir Francis Drake Hotel *(Calle 12 at 65, ☎ 981/811-5626, fax 811-5627, www.hotelfrancisdrake.com, air, cable, restaurant, inside parking, mini-bar).* The Francis Drake, named after the famed English sea admiral and one-time pirate who is said to have once raided Campeche city, is a new (11/2002) luxury hotel in a Colonial building in the historic center. Rooms are modern, with a well-appointed restful décor, big comfy beds, and high standards. We stayed here when it first opened and absolutely loved it. Although it's a bit formal, this is the type of hotel that should entice tourists to stay longer in Campeche and enjoy all it has to offer. $$-$$$

Dining

The feminist movement has helped open minds and kitchens to the notion that men can be at home on the range.
~ Ren_ Veaux, chef, Lasserre restaurant, Paris

Seafood is Campeche's specialty and there are several good restaurants along the waterfront south in the San Román neighborhood. Shrimp cocktails were invented here and all the signs you see advertising *cocteles* are not for mixed drinks, but shrimp. Ironically, mixed drinks are also said to have been invented in the saloons of Colonial Campeche and the combi-

PRICE CHART	
NOTE: Prices based on a typical entrée, per person, and do not include beverage.	
$	Less than US $5
$$	US $5 - 10
$$$	Over US $10

nation of two drinks was called *campechana* – cheerful and happy. You can't beat the care and pride Campechanos put into their gastronomy, nor will you find better prices. Reservations are not necessary. ("Key Ha Na" is phonetic Mayan for "good tasting food," so compliment the chef!)

Marganzo Regional Restaurant *(Calle 8 No. 267).* The Marganzo is situated almost in front of the Puerta del Mar. The elegant restaurant, with starched white table linens and waitresses dressed in colorful Mexican folk dresses, has always been special to visitors and residents alike. It offers the best of Mexican cooking with seafood specialties, such as stuffed pompano and *pan de cazón* (layered tortilla, shark and tomato sauce). This moderately priced restaurant is worth every peso. Open from breakfast until late at night. $$

Miramar *(Calle 8 on the corner of 61).* The Miramar has been serving seafood and regional specialties to both Campechanos and visitors for over 45 years, so they must be doing something right. It has a Colonial atmosphere with

high ceilings and long open windows. Ask for a recommendation. The waiters know their menu inside and out; many of them have worked here a long time. It's on the corner facing the Government Palace. $-$$

Casa Vieja *(upstairs on Los Portales facing the park)*. Follow the painted tile risers and red clay steps to the inviting entry to this easy-to-see but hard-to-find restaurant (its entrance is the doorway next to the Modatelas store under the arches). Climb to the second-floor foyer, decorated with old photos of Campeche and an eclectic collection of artifacts on the wall, then through the interior rooms, which are like homey old living rooms, to the outside tables. Casa Vieja, "Old House," has a romantic ambiance with meals served on the veranda overlooking the park above Los Portales. Cuban food. $$

La Pigua *(Malecón Miguel Aleman No. 197A)*. A pigua is a small crustacean similar to the shrimp, so you know this famous eatery's specialties are from the sea. The chef, Darío Chi Jesús, developed a Campeche-style "caviar" that is now imitated in many other restaurants. La Pigua is often packed for leisurely lunches, its customers encouraged by the excellent food served in sunroom-style dining room with glass windows and a profusion of tropical plants. Open for lunch until 5 pm. $-$$

Restaurant Bar Familiar La Parroquía *(Calle 55 between 10 & 12)*. If one restaurant says "Campeche" and everything about it, it's La Parroquía. All at once it's a family restaurant, a pub, a hangout and a meeting place for old men reliving their glory days or young lovers whose best is yet to come. Open 24 hours a day, this immensely popular spot serves up regional dishes and typical Mexican food in a large fan-cooled open dining area at prices that barely lighten the wallet. This is one of the few places whose atmosphere is created by people rather than murals on the wall. $

Campeche has earned a well-deserved reputation among gourmets as a great place to eat regional food. Besides dining opportunities in the historical center – including economical spots such as **Restaurant Campeche**, Calle 57 on the square, or the artsy, bohemian coffee shop, **Juice Garden**, a block up the street – there are also a large number of excellent eateries outside the old city walls.

Just a block to the north of the old city is La Pigua, reviewed above, as well as **Cenaduria Portales** *(Calle 10 in the barrio de San Francisco, ☎ 981/811-1491, $-$$)*, that specializes in regional food. Open seven days, 6 pm until midnight, the Portales family restaurant is a good place to try *antojitos* (appetizers), such as *panuchos* (a tortilla stuffed with bean, egg and meat). This well-known restaurant is about 10 blocks north of the historic center.

To the south of the town wall there is a stretch of restaurants along the waterfront in San Román, including the super seafood spot, **El Navegante** (☎ 981/816-9326, $-$$) and the extremely popular **Cactus** (☎ 981/811-1453, $-$$), which serves up heavy duty American-cut steaks. A little farther south

on Av. Lopez Mateos, where it meets the *malecón*, is a row of good spots, including **Pioneros** (☎ *981/816-5579, $-$$*), a Western steak and international restaurant. Around the corner on the waterfront is **La Palapa** (☎ *981/816-5918, $-$$*), known for seafood and swimming in their *balneario*. Next to Palapa is **Chez Fernando** (☎ *981/816-2125, $-$$*), with an excellent French and international menu.

Northern Campeche

When you come to a fork in the road, take it.
~ sage advice from Yogi Berra, baseball player and manager

There are two routes south from the Yucatán into Campeche – the Fast Route and the Slow Route. As you travel either the slow or fast way, you'll pass numerous Maya villages where the inhabitants still earn their livelihood in agriculture. The fast route requires you to get off the highway in order to see these villages. For the reader ,we are listing most things here from north to south, although it is just as common to find Adventure Guiders traveling the circuit the other way.

The Fast Route

Haste maketh waste.
~ old English proverb

The direct route between Mérida and Campeche is the *corta*, or shortcut. Opened in 1540, it was the first overland road laid by the Spanish, who called it the *Camino Real*, Royal Road. A superhighway now zips past many of the towns that dotted the route from the two capitals. If you take the highway, it bypasses the northern town of **Becal** and rejoins the old highway farther south. If you're thinking of seeing this village, follow the road signs.

The tiny town of Becal (from the Mayan, Bec Ha, meaning "Path to Water"), just below the border of Yucatán, is the center of Panama hat making on the peninsula. This distinctive headgear is made in some 2,000 subterranean workshops (some are natural caves, most are hand-dug) where skillful craftsmen hand-weave the delicate leaves of the jipijapa palm tree into wonderful hats. The damp air keeps the fibers moist and pliant, essential for the tight weave needed in a top-quality hat. The finer the weave, the more supple and softer the feel – and the more wear-resistant and better looking it is. Nearly everyone in town has a *gruta* and works in the family cottage industry. Ask around and you'll be welcomed into a workshop cave to watch the hat-makers

at their craft. Or look up **Rita María Calán Tuyub**, who organized Unión de Artesanas de Bec Há. She lives on Calle 34 Number 222. Call her at ☎ 943/431-4130.

It's amazing to see the amount of effort that goes into creating a hat that is fancy enough for dress but versatile enough to roll up in your suitcase then massage back to shape when you reach your destination. We have found that gently unfolding our crushed hat, spraying it with water and placing over an inverted bowl helps return the headpiece to its original shape. Then, the brim should be placed on a flat surface, shaped and left to dry. When you're buying a hat, it's important to choose the highest quality you can afford. The artisans will thank you and you'll thank them for the many years of use. If you don't get to Becal, you'll find plenty of these hats for sale in Campeche city.

In the town of **Calkiní** ("Power of the Sun") there are plenty of artisans that make distinctive pottery. **Ceramics Calkiní** on Calle 22, on the road north of the center, have great fired ceramics at cheap prices. It is also the home to hammock makers. Check out their showroom at Km 82 on the highway. In town, the green and white Municipal Palace in the Centro has colorful murals on its walls. The church on the plaza is the Franciscan **San Luis Mission**, which features an outstanding principal altar and a park in front. The mission was founded in 1549 by a Franciscan cleric, Fray Luís de Villalpando, who built an unusual, huge open-air chapel atop the main Maya temple platform. Over the years two churches were built around the chapel. The Mission is home to the Franciscan Order of the Poor Clares. The exterior has masonry resembling an inverted clam shell over the entrance doorway. The outstanding interior feature is the huge "folk-baroque" *retablo* rising an astonishing 35 feet above the altar.

The Maya city of **Hecelchakán** ("Divided Savanna") contains an 18th-century church and the **Museo Arqueológico del Camino Real**. The golden-color museum displays some of the fantastic clay burial figurines found on Isla de Jaina, as well as representative pieces from all of Campeche's archeological zones. It boasts an indoor display as well as an outdoor corridor and garden area. Find it opposite the basketball court. The imposing church features two large bell towers and an enormous 18th-century dome that rises above the nave. A very pleasant stop with several outdoor eating stands in the central plaza.

If you're thinking of staying, you can't do much better locally than the historic **Hacienda Blanca Flor** *(reservations ☎ 999/925-8042, hblanca@prodigy.net.mx, 14 jr. suites, 6 casitas, pool, includes breakfast by reservation only).* Find this well-known hacienda hotel from Mérida by turning off Rt. 180 at the sign for Pocboc. From Campeche and Hecelchakán, take the road toward Santa Cruz and watch for the ruined church on the left; the hacienda is opposite. See page 101 for a complete description of this property and its fascinating history.

Along the highway outside of the village of **Pomuch** (Po-MOOCH), there's a small bakery shop under a palapa roof. Be sure to stop for *Pan de Pomuch*, a unique bread stuffed and baked with ham, cheese, and jalapeños. We can taste it now – mouth watering!

Seventeen km (10 miles) or so north of Campeche is **Hampolol**, a nature reserve. The reserve is crossed by the Rio Verde and has some cenotes with water lilies. Several adventure activities are available here: hikes, canoeing, horseback riding and exploring the ruined Hacienda Dos Rios.

After the small village of **San Francisco Koben**, just before the turn for Campeche, is a series of roadside shops selling gifts, especially wooden ship models – a signature handicraft of the state – and *nance* (nan-SAY), a sweet fruit soaked in a sugar liquid with a touch of Xtabentun, an anise-and-honey liqueur. The delicious small orange and black fruit is arranged in bottles, looking like eyes. A traditional Maya treat. Both sides of the road are lined with shops, so a stop should be worthwhile.

The Slow Way

It is impossible for a man to learn what he thinks he already knows.
~ Epictetus

The long way south follows Highway 261 from Uxmal for 264 km/165 miles, but is perhaps more visually interesting than the shorter route. This way is best known for its northern Maya sites across the state line in Yucatán, which include Uxmal, Kabáh and other Puuc ruins.

A cement arch announces the border between Yucatán and Campeche. Sometimes an army checkpoint hassles travelers on the Yucatán side. The drive south is long and uneventful, with few signs of civilization until you arrive in the tiny village of **Bolonchén** ("Nine Wells"), where the **Gruta de Xtacumbilxuna** ("Cave of the Hidden Girl") lies.

When John Lloyd Stephens visited the seven natural cenotes in the cavern between 1841 and 1842, he described it this way: "Gigantic stalactites and huge blocks of stone assume all manner of fantastic shapes and seemed like monstrous animals or deities of a subterranean world.... The fame of the Cueva of Bolonchén extends throughout the Yucatán." While it is true the cavern is huge and impressive, it is not as attractive as it could be because of exposed orange cables that carry electric for the lighting and some clutter on the steps and path down. Still, it is an impressive gigantic cave to the underworld. The young boy who guided us threw a stick into the black hole crossed by a wooden bridge inside and it took about 10 seconds before it hit bottom. What looks like bats flying above appear to be martins who make mud nests

in the entrance roof. The cave is maintained by the city so it is open seven days a week.

Two roads to the **Xtanpak** ruins are marked on the left, the first is a dirt road (32 km/20 miles long) just south of Bolonchén. A second and more main road (36 km/22 miles long) is three km/1.9 miles north of Hopelchén.

Hopelchén ("Five Wells") is a Colonial town with a colorful country Maya market. **Los Arcos Hotel**, on the square, has a restaurant and inexpensive rooms. Incidentally, if you're into folk art, some of the best wood carvers in Campeche, called **Uchben Cuxtal**, can be contacted through that hotel. From the main square, an improved road zigs 63 km (40 miles) southeast to **Dzibalchén** and the ruins of Hochob. From there you can drive straight to Xpujil in the south. But you're going on to Campeche, so follow the route as it bends east past ranch after ranch.

Forest of Kings

A people without history is like the wind on the grass.
~ Sioux saying

This section continues from the Road to Ruin section in the Quintana Roo chapter, page 269. We pick up at the western border of Campeche and presume you're heading east from Chetumal. If you're coming from Campeche or Palenque, you'll have to read backwards. The ride between Chetumal and Escárcega is a long one, six hours or so. Consequently, even if you're not into the ruin route, an overnight in Xpujil might be a good idea. That's especially true if you're driving straight from Chiapas to Chetumal. There are very few accommodations or sights to recommend in Escárcega, a dusty highway crossroads town (see the listing on page 420). Xpujil, on the other hand – located on the border of Campeche and Quintana Roo – is a welcome stop and an ideal base from which to explore the many ruins in the area or the Calakmul Biosphere.

The lively little town offers a *larga distancia* telephone, an Internet office, and several clean hotels and restaurants. Read the caution about the town's only Pemex station in our *Bribes & Scams* section, page 85.

Xpujil

Xpujil (also spelled Xpuhil), pronounced ISH-poo-HEEL, is becoming a mecca for tourists visiting the Maya ruins. Many of them are taking ad-

vantage of experienced guides to the area, although none is necessary to find the larger sites.

The easiest way to get a knowledgeable guide and information about the many fascinating ruins around Xpujil and southern Campeche is at the **Tourist Information Office** (☎ 983/871-6064), located in a small building at the eastern end of Xpujil. The team of Leticia Valenzuela and her husband, Fernando, do a wonderful job of offering guided tours by the hour, day, or more extensive explorations. Both natural and archeological tours are available. Stop in even if you're passing through – they sell cool local crafts like the carved hardwood bat that we hung from our car's rearview mirror for good luck. Other reliable area guides can be arranged at any of the larger restaurants in town.

North and south of Xpujil, two million acres of the vast Calakmul Biosphere stretch on either side into the jungle. South of Xpujil on the way to Rio Bec ruins is the active *ejido*, **20 de Noviembre** (BAYN-tae day Novi-EM-brey.) An *ejido* is a land cooperative created to benefit *campesinos*. For those interested in off-the-beaten track adventures and contact with an authentic Mayan community, this is a community – with rustic amenities – anxious to attract eco-archeological tourists. Stop in and ask "bash kawa leek?" (what's happening?). Spanish-speaking guides available to the area's ruins. You can even stay there and interact with a traditional Maya village.

The road north eventually leads to Hopelchén, from where you can travel on to Campeche City or continue through Uxmal to Mérida. Just a short distance north of Xpujil, however, is the community of **Zoh Laguna**, headquarters of the **Bosque Modelo Calakmul** (Model Forest Calakmul). Stay overnight at Mercedes Cabañas in town. Well to the north of Xpujil lies Hopelchén, from where you can travel on to Campeche City or continue through Uxmal to Mérida.

■ Accommodations & Dining

Chicanná Ecovillage *(Highway 186 just across from the turning for Chicanná ruins, reservations taken at Hotel del Mar:* ☎ *981/811-9191, fax 981/811-1618, delmarcp@prodigy.net.mx, pool, restaurant).* This property has been hacked out of the jungle in the rich archeological area along the Campeche-Quintana Roo border in the hopes of attracting tourists to the under-visited Maya sites nearby. Each enticing thatch-roofed building of stucco, stone and tile, with polished hardwood houses four large guest rooms. It's very Polynesian looking. Terraces and balconies with rustic leather tables and half-round chairs (known as *equipales*) look over manicured lawns and landscaped gardens. Putting the "Eco" in "Ecovillage" is the design for the rooms' air circulation, which eliminates the need for air-conditioning, and the solar hot water heaters, which mean not-so-hot water on cloudy days. The property includes a quality restaurant, where guests hang

out in *equipales* on the front veranda drinking and socializing. Tasteful furnishings include Maya painted table lamps, and the property is immaculately clean. $$$

Mirador Maya Hotel & Restaurant *(Highway 186, ☎ 983/822-9163)*. At the far western end of town, Mirador Maya sits under a giant palapa roof. The cabins behind it are rustic but tidy and the meals in the restaurant are substantial and tasty. A daily special for around US $4 makes it a "must-stop" for long-haul truckers. The manager, Moises Carreón, is an approved and knowledgeable guide.

HOTEL PRICE CHART	
NOTE: Often, one shared bed in a room is cheaper than two. Prices based on cost per night, for two.	
[No $]	Less than US $20
$	US $20 - $40
$$	US $40 - $80
$$$	US $80 - $125
$$$$	US $125 - $200

Hotel and Restaurant Calakmul *(Km 153 Highway 186, ☎/fax 983/832-9162)*. Doña Maria Cabara Dominquez offers a big smile to all who come into her pleasant little restaurant and hotel on the edge of dusty little Xpujil, approximately halfway along the Chetumal-Escárcega highway. The food is excellent: generous, delicious and economical. It's a good place to stop if you're tired of driving. The 13 modern rooms with private bath and shower in a new hotel addition are clean and neat. There's also eight wooden palapa-topped cabañas that share a communal bath for about $15 a night. Good bilingual guides to the Maya ruins can be arranged here. $

Road To Ruin

Ultimately, magic finds you – if you let it.
~ Tony Wheeler, Fast Company

The ruins of southern Campeche are spectacular and worth all the effort it takes to reach them. The concentration of sites means you can make quick visits to the easily accessible ones along your route, or dig deep into Maya history and present ecology with off-road sites such as Rio Bec and Calakmul. We list the ruins from east to west.

■ Xpujil

The tall towers of the Xpujil ruins, derived from the Mayan for "Place of Cattails," are typical Rio Bec-style. Mask panels flank doorways to lower rooms. Although weather-worn, the small set of ruins is worth a good look. The tall, twin-towered ruins are located at the eastern edge of town. Very clean outhouse-style bathrooms are outside the welcome center.

■ Rio Bec

The ruins collectively known as Rio Bec are actually five separate sites. You might not want to see all five, and they're difficult to reach, but a guide can take you to Rio Bec B, Structure I, to see one of the best preserved buildings in the region. Discovered in 1906 – then lost again until 1973 – the magnificent site contains an aura of intrigue and romance. If Rio Bec B were easier to reach, it would attract many more admirers with its serpent monsters on 55-foot towers. The façade features huge face masks and the interior boasts Maya graffiti on the plaster walls. Follow the signs from Highway 186 about 13 km/eight miles west of Xpujil, south through the Maya village of 20 de Noviembre. The town has a small crafts shop and two tiny corner stores for provisions. Ask for Margarita Cauich, president of the women's craft committee. She can arrange for a home-cooked Maya meal when you return. Rustic cabaña lodging on a hill overlooking the forest is also available in this eco-tourism-conscious town. The road to the ruins becomes dirt for 13 km/eight miles and it's best to hire a guide from the village, such as Humberto Dzib Tun, as the road branches frequently without good signs. Also of interest if you have the time (and a guide) is **Hormiguero**, Spanish for "Anthill," a small but fascinating site from the Late Classical period.

■ Becán

About seven km (4.4 miles) east of the town of Xpujil are the impressive ruins of Becán, visible on the right. Surrounded by a long moat-like fortification, its name means "water-formed gorge," even though it never was. The seven causeways that cross the earthen fortification are believed to have led to the seven cities under Becán's authority. Built on an outcropping of limestone, its massive towers and enclosed plaza are magnificent. The best time to take photos here is the late afternoon when the golden-red light of the setting sun causes the east-west facing structures to glow.

■ Chicanna

Down the road on the left, nearly opposite the entrance to the Chicanná Ecolodge, is the short road to the Chicanná ruins, most notable for the busy and elaborately carved Chenes-style monster mouth doorway. Chicanná, which means "House of the Mouth with Snakes," has a well-preserved building that features the wide doorway into the distinctive slack-jawed monster's mouth.

The Chenes-style mouth doorway at Chicanna makes a great photo op.

■ Calakmul Biosphere & Ruins

To the legions of the lost ones, to the cohorts of the damned.
~ Rudyard Kipling

Calakmul, the ancient "City of Adjacent Mounds," was once a victorious rival against Tikal across the border in Guatemala and perhaps the largest city of its time. Its area of influence is now part of a huge nature preserve (almost 13% of Campeche state) that borders another reserve in Guatemala. Explorer Cyrus Longworth Lundell discovered the remarkable ruins in the jungle in 1931, and recent excavation of this important city has yielded some incredible precious-stone pieces, including the fabulous jade mask now on display in Fort San Miguel at Campeche. Numerous steles are among the 7,000 buildings (most mapped so far are small and unnoteworthy for tourists) and 70 square kilometers (27 square miles) that make up the site. A guide is very helpful here, but not absolutely necessary. Road conditions make it difficult to reach during the rainy season. The turnoff is clearly marked (near Km 97) and there's a guard house with a gate where a local man collects the US $5 toll. The ruins are about 62 km (38 miles) down a paved but narrow and twisting road. Ask at the guard house if anyone else has gone in before you, so you can beware of head-on collisions along the sharp curves.

There is a new rustic cabana hotel opened just inside the gate, hidden by the trees. **Hotel Puerta Calakmul** *(Km 98.5 Escarcega-Chetumal Hwy, no*

Sketch of the fabulous jade mask found at Calakmul.
© *Joyce Kelly,* An Archeological Guide to Mexico's Yucatán Peninsula,
published by the University of Oklahoma Press.

phone, 13 single cabins, 2 double cabins, fans, swimming pool, camping area, restaurant). Set on 115 hectares, the Calakmul is a needed lodging to bring more tourists to the southern ruins. The comfortable rooms come with two double beds. They are simple, but very attractive. Each has a bathroom with hot-water showers. There are several hiking trails into the surrounding bush and the camping area offers electric (but no dump station) for RVs. The Calakmul makes a good base for exploring the area ruins in depth. $-$$

Mexico's largest preserve, the **Calakmul Biosphere**, was created in 1989 in a rainforest that stretches as far as the eye can see both north and south of the roadway. In its vast area, spider monkeys, ocelots, tapirs, peccaries and deer are still the prey of Señor de la Selva, lord of the jungle – the jaguar. Botanists estimate over 800 plant species call Calakmul home.

Some guided naturalist and archeological activities can be arranged in Xpujil. Approved guides from different local *edijos* (communal villages) take visitors on hikes, mountain biking, horseback riding, even kayaking – and some overnight camping is available as part of the longer trips. The tours include archeological and naturalist activities in the "zone," as well as cultural interaction with local Maya communities. They are designed to suit small groups, and can incorporate individual itineraries. Contact Leticia or Fernando at the **Tourist Information Office** in Xpujil (☎ 983/871-6064). An excellent and experienced expedition and tour agency in Campeche is **Expediciones Ecoturísticas** (Calle 55 #36, ☎ 981/816-0197). They offer

Campeche

hard or soft eco-tourism and natural and cultural explorations, including bouncing around in off-road vehicles, mountain biking, horseback riding, hiking/camping and kayaking.

■ Balamku

Balamku – rescued from looters in 1990 – is an excellent and undiscovered (at least by tourists) Maya ruin in the jungle of Campeche. Local people, who call the site Chunhabil, fortunately reported the looting activity to INAH before too much damage was done. Its most impressive feature is the bas relief stucco façade, which is well preserved with some visible remains of the yellow, red and black paint that once covered it. A stylized jaguar graces the center of a main panel. Sitting on a zig-zag border, the powerful animal with an apparently skeletal head wears a belt, bracelets, a collar and pectoral. The figure gives the site its archeological name, "Jaguar Temple." The façade is in the interior of the pyramid temple, so don't miss it. Tripods and flash are, as always, not allowed. To take a photo you'll need very fast film. Monopods are okay. At Km 93.3, turn at the dirt road cutoff, two km (1.25 miles) west of the village of Conhuas (1.6 km/one mile west of the Km 95 sign).

Escárcega

There's little to attract tourists to the crossroads bus-stop town of Escárcega, 150 km (93 miles) south of Campeche and 300 km (186 miles) from Villahermosa, at the junction of Highways 186 and 261. Most people who stay overnight are on the long trip between Palenque and Chetumal. Xpujil is about two hours east; Campeche 1½ hours; and Palenque is a little over three hours. The big lagoon about 50 km (32 miles) east of Escárcega is the **Laguna Silvictuc**, with a village of the same name. Rich in flora and fauna, the lagoon had been tagged as a possible site for a resort. The region has sea bass, white turtles, a clam hatchery and, reportedly, interesting caves called "Montebravo."

There is a big Pemex at the intersection for Palenque and Chetumal highways and a brand new station well west of town at Km 51 near Silvictuc.

Accommodations & Dining

If it's getting late, the best hotel in town is **Hotel Escárcega** on the main drag, west of the downtown. It has 66 rooms around a new gazebo bar and pavilion. If you're on a super-tight budget, you could

stay at the **Posada Escárcega** on Calle 25, a half-block north of the Pollos y Huevos fast-food shop on the corner. It offers private parking in a center courtyard and costs about US $10 for a double, with air. Basic but quiet. **Hotel Maria Isabel** on Av. Justo Sierra, a topiary-lined street parallel to 186, is better than its restaurant. Decent rooms and a green courtyard. These places are never full, so reservations are not necessary.

The restaurant at **Hotel Escárcega** serves respectable food. There are many small eateries on 186 near the train tracks and in the surrounding *mercado*, including the **Pollos y Huevos** (Chicken and Eggs) a decent place down the main street on the corner of Calle 25. Unfortunately, there is nothing out of the ordinary in town.

Coastal Campeche

God made the world round so we would never be
able to see too far down the road.
~ Isak Dinesen

Thirty-three km (20 miles) south of Campeche city, along the road that hugs the shoreline, lies **Seybaplaya**, the coast's first good swimming beach. The road offers great scenery and it's fun to drive the hairpin turns, but it's a real bugger if you get behind a smelly truck or bus. There is no passing. A new toll road direct between Campeche and Champotón bypasses the torturous and hilly coast road that used to be the only route south from Campeche. To follow the coast road, simply head south from the waterfront. To reach the toll road, drive east on Central Ave. from the Land Gate.

Seybaplaya's fishing boats are picturesque. Colorful flags, denoting the boat's registration, flap in the breeze. A dirt road north from the port around the big hill leads to a pleasant secluded rocky beach, a popular spot for locals. South of Seybaplaya is a hotel that looks like an old fort, **Hotel Tucan Siho Playa** *(Km 35 Champoton Coastal Highway,* ☎ *982/823-1200, pool, restaurant, air)*. The stately hotel incorporates the main building of a 19th-century hacienda with both modern and Colonial wings full of rooms. Perched abreast the rocks along a slight bluff facing the sea, the Siho Playa offers an unusual and relaxing retreat, 30 minutes from Campeche or 40 from Edzná. Check out the chapel in the chimney even if you're just passing. First established to grow henequen, the Siho Playa hacienda turned to sugar cane and, for a brief while, made the area a major rum and candy source. The sweet tooth stuck and Campeche is still known for its candy.

Champotón is a historically significant fishing town with some decent restaurants that face a charming harbor where the river curls around before en-

tering the Gulf. It has almost an English village look to it, though the climate is a wee bit warmer. It was in Champotón where a Maya ambush repulsed the first invading Spanish soldiers, discouraging them from the staying in the Yucatán. North of town there's a series of palapa seafood restaurants on the beach. All looked inviting and are extremely popular after work. Follow the seabirds all along the Gulf seafront south to basketball-court-size cement areas where local fishermen's families dry minnows for *charalitos*, a crunchy snack food for sale in the *mercados*. There is a school for artisans in town know as X-maha Nah ("House of the Butterfly") on Calle 32 in the Preparatoria Nocturna (night school) building.

The coast road south skirts miles and miles of open empty beaches, ideal for beachcombing and exploring. Unfortunately the idyllic dunes, once shaded by swaying coconut palm trees, are now lined by tall leafless tree trunk skeletons, victims of a combination of yellowing disease and Hurricane Roxanne. But life goes on. The beautiful sand beaches here are the favorite nesting area for hawksbill turtles. There's also a turtle research center, about halfway between Champotón and the fishing village of Sabancuy, where you can stop and see any babies they're holding for release.

Sabancuy isn't on the long sand dune of the coast road; it's about 500 meters (1,600 feet) inland, across the bridge over the northern end of the Laguna de Terminos. It's a pleasant little town with a Colonial church and swimming in the lagoon is refreshing here. Snorkeling and diving are good in the northern part of the lagoon. There are several inexpensive restaurants in the center and the road inland from here connects with the one to Escárcega. Just south of the turn for Sabancuy is a big, shady, thatch-roofed restaurant, Viaductoplaya, at Km 77.5. Along with its main dining area, numerous small tables under individual shade palapas line the white Gulf coast beach offering an unbeatable view of the water. Moderate prices, a specialty in seafood and its large size mean that buses often a stop here. Unless your mother warned you about waiting an hour after eating, the swimming along the white sandy beach is excellent. The coral reefs offshore, Los Bajos, are alleged to be good for diving. Stay in town at the **Sabancuy Plaza** (☎ *982 / 825-0081*).

Ciudad del Carmen

At the tip of a long sliver of sandbar island between the huge Laguna de Terminos and the Gulf of Mexico sits Ciudad del Carmen – or "Carmen," as everyone calls it. The Maya fished from here for a thousand years and the tradition continues with the city's large but rusted fishing and shrimping fleet.

History

In the 17th and 18th centuries, seafaring pirates used the lagoon's protected waters as their lair. From here they attacked merchant vessels taking cargo back to Spain. It was also from here that they sacked the city of Campeche numerous times. Legend has it that during this time the citizens of Carmen developed a curious defense against pirate abductions: only men went shopping in the *mercado*, reportedly dressed as women.

Spanish naval attempts to dislodge the pirates failed until 1717, when forces from Campeche finally killed the remaining corsairs in a surprise attack. Though they never again had a stranglehold in Carmen, pirate ships continued to shelter in the Laguna whenever they could.

The burnt-orange French clay roofing tiles made by Frères Martin (Martin Brothers) were brought as ballast in sailing ships in the 1800s and protect many of Carmen's oldest roofs. In the center of the town's old *zócalo*, three concentric paths circle the bandstand, used for the segregation of society women, gentlemen and the peasants and workers. This vestige of social order is evident in other town plazas throughout the Colonial world.

Mixing Oil & Water

Today the social order is supported by wealth flowing from the offshore oil rigs of Pemex, the national petroleum company. Carmen is heavily populated by American and Mexican workers and executives allied with the oil industry. Rush hour is a tough time to get around town because of the resulting proliferation of automobiles. Traffic crawl is also related to the preponderance of potholes the size of moon craters in streets built upon shifting sands.

The state of Campeche is trying to develop tourism in its southern region and it hopes to make Carmen and Laguna de Terminos the focal point. Certainly hiring a fishing boat for fishing or touring the lagoon is worthwhile, but the city of Carmen is too spread out and generally too commercial to be a destination of its own. There is great potential, however, in the surrounding countryside and getting to Carmen is an experience that makes the trip worthwhile in itself.

The land completely enclosing and including the giant lagoon has been declared a nature preserve because of its wealth of plant and wildlife. Someday, the Laguna de Terminos' rich ecological attractions will be more fully exploited for low-impact visits. Dolphins reproduce in numbers there and the surrounding jungles and rivers offer countless opportunities for ecological

Campeche

tourism. Campeche state also has the largest wild bird reserves in North America.

In Carmen, look or ask for launches that will take you out for a tour to see the dolphins or manatees. Perhaps someone will soon get it together to offer an organized ecological adventure. Across the lagoon the Palizada River and the small town of **Palizada**, reached from the road to Palenque, offer some fascinating fishing and exploration opportunities – including seeing the prehistoric *pejegarto*, a crossbreed between a fish and alligator. The undeveloped southern area near the Tabasco border is particularly wild and beautiful. Much of both can be seen in boats hired in Carmen.

The **Casa de la Cultura** features a new museum in a restored Colonial building with beautiful arches. It displays Maya art and artifacts from the areas surrounding Carmen and features an interactive section dedicated to ecology, oil production and piracy. Are they all related? Open Tuesday through Sunday from 9 am to 7 pm at Calle 26, between 45 and 43, near the waterfront. Other local attractions include the **Botanical Garden and Ecoparque Fenix/Cocodrilario**, located near each other on the lagoon side to the southeast before town, where the *periferica* splits north to the airport. The big church in Carmén is the **Iglesia de Nuestra Señora del Carmén**, at the intersection of Calle 26 and 35.

The Chedraui supermarket is located on Calle 31 opposite the big Pemex building and, if you're desperate, a McDonald's is not too far away, across from the University. More fast food can be found at Calle 31 and the *perifierica* (bypass) that circles the city. Vaquero Mexican Fajitas and Tex-Mex food is across from a KFC.

Bridges have replaced the ferries that used to bog down travelers in Carmen going to or coming from **Villahermosa**, **Tabasco**, but watch your speed, the police are vigilant on the bridge. If you do stop in Carmen, expect prices to be a lot higher than Campeche because it's a business town.

Accommodations

Hotel Acuario *(Calle 51 No. 60, ☎/fax 938/382-3947, 54 rooms & suites, air, TV, gym room, restaurant).* This hard-to-find hotel is an appealing place to stay, halfway between the best beach (Playa Norte) and downtown. Its customers are mostly middle executives in town on business and its owner, former lawyer Pedro Fonz, is a jovial host. Ask him about eco-tours. The modern three-story hotel offers secure parking on a quiet residential street and has a small pool and jacuzzi. The excellent little restaurant, facing a verdant courtyard with a stone fountain, specializes in fresh seafood and shrimp cocktail. $$

Eurohotel Best Western *(Calle 22 No. 208, ☎ 938/382-3044, www.bestwestern. com.mx, 80 rooms with air & 12 suites, pool, restaurant, bar, disco).* Located in the heart of Colonial downtown. Accommodations are modern and comfortable in a tall, bright-white building surrounding a deep blue pool. The hotel offers twice-a-day free shuttles to Carmen's busy airport. There's a good restaurant, serving Sunday brunch – the place to be. $$

Hotel Del Parque *(Calle 33 between 20 & 22, ☎ 938/382-56766, 24 rooms with air, TV, restaurant).* This business hotel is centrally located right next to Carmen's main *zócalo*. Modern rooms, all of which face south, have big windows and large balconies. The rooms are huge, with two queen-size beds in each. $

PRICE CHART	
NOTE: Often, one shared bed in a room is cheaper than two. Prices based on cost per night, for two.	
[No $]	Less than US $20
$	US $20 - $40
$$	US $40 - $80
$$$	US $80 - $125
$$$$	US $125 - $200
$$$$$	Over US $200

Eli Gar Hotel *(Calle 35 between 30 & 32, ☎ 938/382-0602).* Since 1972 the Eli Gar has been filling the needs of travelers looking for basic and inexpensive accommodations in a relatively pricey town. Plain but clean. $$

Lossandes *(Periférica Norte No. 67, ☎ 938/382-2388, 95 rooms, pool, restaurant, air, cable, tennis).* No, it's not a misspelling, although we keep thinking of this pleasant new hotel near the river and airport as, "Los Andes," when it should be "Los Sandies." A great big pool is flanked by two stories of motel-like rooms. $$

Lli-Re *(Calle 32 & 29, ☎ 938/382-6408, 73 rooms & 3 suites, restaurant).* We call this modern hotel in the Colonial area off Calle 31 the Lilly Ray. Lots of Talavera tile work and good prices. $-$$

Hacienda Real *(Calle 31 No. 106, ☎ 938/381-1700, 94 rooms & 12 suites, pool, restaurant, cable).* The brand new Hacienda Real is the premier hotel in Carmen and a favorite of oil executives with business at the Pemex offices, three minutes away. The rooms here are beautiful, comfortable and elegant, decorated with antique and Spanish-style furniture. $$$

Dining

Los Robles *(Calle 26 No. 157).* In what was once their house, the Robles family serves Saturday and Sunday meals. A stylish conversion with good food. Try the lamb Barbacoa. $-$$

Campeche

La Flama *(Calle 35 No. 39).* One of Carmen's newest restaurants, La Flama brags about its filet fajitas accompanied by vegetables sautéed in butter and their American meat cuts. $-$$

San Carlos "El Chelo Baeza" *(Av. Periférico Norte No. 20).* This simple restaurant is well known for its excellent seafood. Pompano, delicate *pan de cazón* and a bouillabaisse with a touch of butter are among the house specialties. Reportedly, even some other restaurant owners recommend the San Carlos. $-$$

DINING PRICE CHART	
NOTE: Prices based on a typical entrée, per person, and do not include beverage.	
$	Less than US $5
$$	US $5 - 10
$$$	Over US $10

Palenque (Chiapas)

> *They'll like you because you're a foreigner.*
> *They love foreigners, it's just strangers they hate.*
> ~ Jonathan Raban, British scholar and author

The ride into Tabasco and Chiapas from Escárcega is a long (216 km/135 miles) but straight foray past what's left of the jungle, cleared for cattle ranching by slash-and-burn technique. As you come into Tabasco the vegetation becomes more lush and verdant; it is still hot and humid here. The troubles of Chiapas, namely the Zapatista upheaval, have not affected the area around Palenque and the road from Escárcega is secure. The underlying problems, however, remain – abject poverty as well as a justifiable distrust of the military and judicial system – along with its associated tension. In spite of that, Chiapas' natural beauty continues to attract visitors, including us.

As a ruined Maya city, Palenque ("Place of the Sun's Death") has to be seen to be believed. If you're this far south and have the time, it's well worth a visit. There's a new visitors center and museum where guides to the ruins are available.

The Ruins

The staggering structures, surrounded by the rainforest of the Palenque National Park, feature extraordinary bas-relief sculpture and magnificent well-preserved details. Perhaps the best time to see them is in the ethereal early morning rainforest mist. The **Temple of the Inscriptions** – which makes a great climb, 69 steps, steep and tall – is where the crypt of the King Pacal was uncovered in 1952. Carry a flashlight for the steps down inside. The

impressive structure, known as the "Palace," rests on a plot the size of a full city block, highlighted by an architecturally rare (for the Maya) four-story tower. Inside there's a labyrinth of hallways and tunnels ripe for your exploration. Or you can hike paths in the surrounding jungle (wear mosquito repellent) and discover new ones.

Late in 1999 a new chamber discovered in **Temple XX** revealed painted murals on the walls, the first such display in Palenque. When the Ground Penetrating Radar loaned from National Geographic Society picked up some anomalies, archeologist Maureen Carpenter had workmen remove a stone that revealed a five-meter-deep (16-foot) pit into a chamber with murals of God K, 11 intact vessels and lots of jade ornaments. Earlier that year, another exciting discovery was made in **Temple XIX** – a stunning limestone bench, depicting three seated figures, two of them facing each other and the third facing a panel of 32 glyphs. The end figures are connected by a 12-foot sculpted rope. Glyphs date it to AD 736 Digging continues and rumors are flying that a major discovery is to be announced soon.

Palenque ruins.

Nearby Attractions

One of two luxuriant attractions in the nearby countryside is **Misol Há**, Mayan for "Waterfall," about 20 km (12.5 miles) down on the road toward Ocosingo. Falls plunge steeply into a large sparkling pool, perfect for

Misol Há waterfall.

swimming. Underneath is a stream in a cave that young guides will lead you into. Remove your shoes or wear water sandals. This is a peaceful natural place to hang out. Attractive, almost Adirondack-like cabins staggered under the big pine trees on the hill above the river are available for rent. Cabins are fully equipped (☎ 934/345-1210, about $30).

Another 45 km (28 miles) on the Ocosingo road leads to a right turn for **Agua Azul** (Yax Há, or "Blue Water") National Park. Cascading waterfalls of celadon streams rumble over huge boulders with white foam and fine soft mist. The atmosphere is mystically magical. Hiking, camping, swimming, even whitewater rafting, are spellbinding adventures here. This can be a day-trip in itself – roundtrip combi buses leave from Palenque's downtown daily. Our whitewater raft trip was thrilling but involved lots of getting out and leaping down waterfalls into the pools below because of the rapids' steep angles. We recommend it, but only if they've improved the safety measures – our headgear was baseball batting helmets. Insist upon at least one kayaker to accompany your rafts. Check with your hotel or with a local travel agency for more information on these trips.

Palenque has an airport served from the Yucatán, especially Cancún, and there are air hops from here to the other big Maya sites nearby, **Bonhampak** and **Yaxchilán**. Or you can still take the fascinating river trip Yaxchilán, escorted by armed forces. See a travel agent. Another important ruin accessible from Palenque is **Tonina**. "Place Where Sculptures of Stone Were Made in Honor of Time."

You can also opt to travel in luxury and style in restored 1940s vintage railroad cars on a new private train ride from Mérida to Campeche to Palenque. Tourist or deluxe classes are available, with optional guided tours to Uxmal, Edzná, Palenque, Aqua Azul and the Olmec heads at La Venta. See page 295 for details on the Expreso Maya.

SPEAKING STONES

One of the most spectacular late discoveries at Palenque was a royal tomb with a well-preserved skeleton inside. The bones are presumed those of a queen, thought to be either the mother or grandmother of the powerful ruler, Pacal. Two companions were also buried with the queen (a common practice in Mesoamerica), and archeologists also found a jade mask within. The tomb, unlike other royal burial areas, is a simple stone vault, devoid of fancy decorations. Pacal, whose tomb was found in the Temple of the Inscriptions in 1952, was buried in a much more ornate manner with a sarcophagus decorated with hieroglyphics and beautiful stone carvings. Seven companions accompanied him to the Otherworld, a sign of his exalted status in the dynasty. His tomb also contained a false chamber, built to foil grave robbers.

The discovery of the Queen's tomb began during a visit to Palenque, when a French psychic sensed strong "energies" coming from Temple 13, next to the Temple of the Inscriptions. She informed archeologists of a tomb inside and told them they must ask the permission of the queen to enter. Remembering that psychic energy also accounted for a discovery at Chichén Itzá (Augustus Le Plongeon) the skeptical scientists began to dig.

Over all the world men move unhomeing and eternally
concerned: a swarm of bees who have lost their queen.
~ Christopher Fry, English writer

Accommodations & Dining

The town of Palenque, a relatively short distance from the jungle-enshrouded ruins, has a plethora of small hotels for budget stays. If money is tight, in town rooms are your best bet. **La Posada** (☎ 916/345-0437) off Calle Merle Green (aka Calle Hidalgo) behind the Maya Tulipanes Hotel is a decent choice. Or the cabañas are good at **Hotel La Cañada** (☎ 916/345-0102), located down the same street in a shady spot. Five hundred meters (1,600 feet) from the ruins is the **Maya Bell** (☎ 916/348-4271), a youth hostel with all the pluses and minuses of dorm living. Ask for recommendations for other low price places at the tourist information office in the **Casa de la Cultura** on Calle Jiménez.

PRICE CHART	
NOTE: Often, one shared bed in a room is cheaper than two. Prices based on cost per night, for two.	
[No $]	Less than US $20
$	US $20 - $40
$$	US $40 - $80
$$$	US $80 - $125
$$$$	US $125 - $200
$$$$$	Over US $200

Campeche

Also in the quiet *barrio* of La Cañada find more comfortable digs at the **Maya Tulipanes** (☎ 916/345-0201, $$), a very pleasant mid-scale hotel with a lovely freeform swimming pool. Restaurant and room service too! The nearby **Maya Palenque** (☎ 916/345-0780, $$) is a four-story hacienda-style hotel affliated with Best Western, so you can predict its quality and service.

The former Day's Inn is now the **Tulija Casa Inn** (☎ 916/345-0104, $$), about eight km (five miles) from the airport, on the road to the ruins. With 48 rooms and 28 villas, we liked the free Chiapas coffee in room. One of the best full-service hotels is the **Mision Palenque** (☎ 916/345-0241, $$) on Rancho San Martin, one km east of the *Zocálo* downtown. We enjoy staying here and sneaking down to the natural mud baths in the forest below the hotel. Hot showers, a sauna, and a good restaurant.

Near the ruins is the **Hotel Maya Tucán** (☎ 916/345-0290, $$), a sister hotel to the intriguing one in Campeche. It boasts a natural lake, beautiful gardens and plenty of nature. The **Hotel Nututun Palenque** (☎ 916/345-0100, $$) has colorful casitas that overlook the river. We also like the surrounding jungle environment of the large resort, **Chan-Kah Ruinas** (☎ 916/345-1100, $$), three km (1.9 miles) south toward the ruins. It features individual bungalows, a big palapa restaurant, and lagoon-style swimming pools. Impressive gardens and floor-to-ceiling windows enhance the view, but cut privacy.

For eats, most tour groups dine close to the ruins in **La Selva**, which balances a pleasing ambiance with good food. An excellent Mexican bar and restaurant is **La Jabita II**, on the Periférica Norte. For good regional food, bring your tummy to **Restaurante Maya** on the plaza, where Independencia meets Av. Hidalgo. **Café y Arte** is a coffee shop that sells books and food on Calle Independencia.

There's a supermarket, **Supermercado Central**, on Av. Juarez, where you can stock up on essentials.

AUTHORS' FAREWELL

No matter where you go or what you do, we hope you enjoy Mexico as much as we have. We've tried to organize and evaluate the attractions of this fabulous land in a way that you'll find useful. And we hope to provide both seasoned and fresh adventurers with new activities in a destination we're sure you'll want to visit again and again. See you on the road!

For memory has painted this perfect day
With colors that never fade,
And we find at the end of a perfect day
The soul of a friend we've made.
~ Carries Jacobs Bond, 1862-1946

Appendix

Hollywood vs. Mexico

The country due south of La-La Land was never ignored by Tinsel Town's movie moguls, although their portrayal of Mexican culture and history should be taken with a grain of salt. In fact, take several grains of salt on the rim of your margarita as you sit back and enjoy one of these videos.

- *Night of the Iguana:* Ava Gardner and Richard Burton slither around in Puerto Vallarta. Directed by John Huston. The movie transformed the sleepy fishing village into a jet-set getaway.

- *Under the Volcano:* Albert Finney drinks his way down, in and through 1930s Cuernavaca.

- *Like Water for Chocolate:* A dreamy tale of delicious love and romantic food, from Laura Esquivel's bestseller. Good movie, great book.

- *Treasure of the Sierra Madre:* Bogie and Huston feud over their greed in steamy Tampico. In Gold We Trust.

- *Juárez:* Paul Muni as Benito Juárez with Bette Davis as Carlota and Mexico as itself.

- *The Mexican: Quien esta el Mexicano,* you ask? A pair of cursed pistolas with fancy handles mean big trouble and luke-warm reviews for Brad Pitt and Julia Roberts.

- *Born in East LA:* Cheech Marin proves he's no dope as he struggles to get back to the US after being mistakenly deported to Tijuana as an illegal alien.

- *Against All Odds:* Jeff Bridges and James Woods chase Rachel Ward around Cozúmel and the Maya ruins of Chichén Itzá.

- *Captain from Castille:* Stars Cesar Romero as Hernan Cortés, with Tyrone Power and Jean Peters in an epic recreation of the Spanish Conquest of Mexico. Somewhat true to history, *mas o menos.*

- *Villa Rides:* Yul Brynner – with hair – as Pancho Villa. Charles Bronson and Robert Mitchum also have hair.

- *Viva Zapata:* Marlon Brando portrays Emiliano Zapata as Marlon Brando.

- *10:* Dudley Moore, Julie Andrews and Bo Derek. Bo started a craze for beachside beaded hair and undulating pectorals.

- *Fun in Acapulco:* Elvis Presley dives off the cliffs at La Quebrada in Acapulco and still lives!
- *Old Gringo:* Carlos Fuentes' novel about Ambrose Bierce was filmed in Zacatecas. Gregory Peck plays the crusty old *gringo* who gets the young girl. Lucky stiff.

Made in Mexico (but depicting other areas!)

- *Clear and Present Danger:* Tom Clancy's bestseller about drug-crazed South American bad guys was filmed in the Mexican states of Veracruz and Morelos.
- *Predator:* Arnie fights a slippery illegal alien outside Puerto Vallarta.
- *Unforgiven:* Clint Eastwood directs then shoots stuntmen in this noir-western. We think *The Outlaw Josie Wales* was his best work.
- *Romancing the Stone:* One of our all-time favorite romantic comedies features Kathleen Turner as a novelist and Michael Douglas as a dreamer searching for a sailboat in the "Columbian" jungle. Features NJ native, Danny Devito.
- *African Queen:* Some scenes were filmed at Coyuca Lagoon outside Acapulco.
- *Herbie Goes Bananas:* Walt Disney's Puerto Vallarta-filmed movie about a loveable Volkswagen may explain why the Beetle is still manufactured in Mexico to this day.
- *Total Recall:* Recall Arnold Schwartzenegger dreaming about a vacation on Mars? Well, he went to Mexico instead – it's cheaper.
- Additionally, parts of *Titanic*, *Pearl Harbor*, the original *Planet of the Apes*, *Traffic*, *Tomorrow Never Dies*, *Close Encounters of the Third Kind*, *Free Willy*, and even *Romeo & Juliet* were filmed south of the border. And why not? Didn't the Aztecs invent popcorn?

Lazy Day Reading

There is no Frigate like a book, To take us lands away.
~ Emily Dickinson, 1830-1886

■ CULTURE & PEOPLE (fiction)

Consider This, Señora, Harriet Doerr
Stones for Ibarra, Harriet Doerr
Aztec, Gary Jennings
The Underdogs, Mariano Azuela
Idols Behind Altars, Anita Brenner

Like Water for Chocolate, Laura Esquivel
Rain of Gold, Victor E. Villaseñor
Where the Air is Clear, Carlos Fuentes
The Plumed Serpent, D.H. Lawrence
Pedro Páramo, Juan Rulfo
Mornings in Mexico, D.H. Lawrence
The Old Gringo, Carlos Fuentes
The Treasure of the Sierra Madre, B. Traven
Under the Volcano, Malcolm Lowry

■ CULTURE & HISTORY (non-fiction)

Maya Missions, Richard and Rosalind Perry
Archaeological Guide to Mexico's Yucatán Peninsula, Joyce Kelly
The Caste Wars of the Yucatán, Nelson Reed
Incidents of Travel in the Yucatán, John Lloyd Stephens
The Modern Maya, Macduff Everton
Mexico, Michael D. Coe
A Dream of Maya, Lawrence Desmond & Phyllis Messenger
Labyrinth of Solitude, Octavio Paz
The Children of Sanchez, Oscar Lewis
Tepoztlán, Robert Redfield
Distant Neighbors, Alan Riding
The Ancient Past of Mexico, Alma Reed
The Temple of the Jaguar, Donald Schueler
Mexico, Adventures in Nature, Ron Mader

Phonetic Mayan Glossary

We don't pretend to have the spelling correct in the following glossary of Mayan phrases, because we wrote them down phonetically. The Maya are tickled when you greet them in their own language. Try it out on your taxi driver! Everyone we spoke to was pleased at our attempts and they all wanted to help us learn more. Remember an "x" in Mayan is pronounced "ish" or "sh."

¿Bash kawa leek?	Hello, what's happening?
Mish baa	Nothing much
Maa lo ben	I am well
Bish ah oh?	How are you?
Maa lo	OK or good
Me nan	None
Ma	No
Hey-eley	Yes
Sama	Tomorrow (see you tomorrow)
Too la Kin	See you another day

Appendix

Dios bo teak . . . . Thank you (or, literally, God will thank you)
¿Tush ka bean? . . . . Where are you going?
Inka bean a Ho . . . . I am going to Mérida
Ine kash tich in bay... . . . . I am looking for the road to...
¿Bish aka ba? . . . . What's your name?
¿Tush ka tah? . . . . Where are you from?
Tush ka ka tah . . . . Where do you live? (can be used as above)
Tech schan. . . . . To you also
Koe-osh. . . . . Let's go, *Vamos*
¿Bash le baa'la? . . . . What is this?
¿Ba hooush? . . . . How much does this cost?
Key ha nah. . . . . Good food
Dzoe Key. . . . . Finished (you might say this is to a waiter)
Otoch or Naa . . . . House
Pack ha'al or Cheena . . . . An orange
¿Bish uc akab ley catala? . . . . What is the name of this place?

Good luck, and let us know how you do!

Spanish Vocabulary

■ DAYS OF THE WEEK
domingo . . . . Sunday
lunes . . . . Monday
martes . . . . Tuesday
miercoles . . . . Wednesday
jueves . . . . Thursday
viernes. . . . . Friday
sabado . . . . Saturday

■ MONTHS OF THE YEAR
enero. . . . . January
febrero. . . . . February
marzo. . . . . March
abril . . . . April
mayo . . . . May
junio . . . . June
julio . . . . July
agosto . . . . August
septiembre . . . . September
octubre. . . . . October
noviembre . . . . November
diciembre . . . . December

■ NUMBERS

un	one
dos	two
tres	three
cuatro	four
cinco	five
seis	six
siete	seven
ocho	eight
nueve	nine
diez	ten
once	eleven
doce	twelve
trece	thirteen
catorce	fourteen
quince	fifteen
dieciséis	sixteen
diecisiete	seventeen
dieciocho	eighteen
diecinueve	nineteen
veinte	twenty
veintiuno	twenty-one
veintidós	twenty-two
treinta	thirty
cuarenta	forty
cincuenta	fifty
sesenta	sixty
setenta	seventy
ochenta	eighty
noventa	ninety
cienone	hundred
ciento uno	one hundred one
doscientos	two hundred
quinientos	five hundred
mil	one thousand
mil uno	one thousand one
mil dos	two thousand
un millón	one million
mil millones	one billion
primero	first
segundo	second
tercero	third
cuarto	fourth
quinto	fifth
sexto	sixth
séptimo	seventh

octavo . . . . eighth
noveno . . . . ninth
décimo . . . . tenth
undécimo . . . . eleventh
duodécimo . . . . twelfth
último . . . . last

■ CONVERSATION

¿Como esta usted? . . . . How are you?
¿Bien, gracias, y usted? . . . . Well, thanks, and you?
Buenas dias. . . . . Good morning.
Buenas tardes.. . . . . Good afternoon.
Buenas noches. . . . . Good evening/night.
Hasta la vista. . . . . See you again.
Hasta luego. . . . . So long.
¡Buena suerte! . . . . Good luck!
Adios.. . . . . Goodbye.
Mucho gusto de conocerle. . . . . Glad to meet you.
Felicidades. . . . . Congratulations.
Muchas felicidades. . . . . Happy birthday.
Feliz Navidad. . . . . Merry Christmas.
Feliz Año Nuevo. . . . . Happy New Year.
Gracias. . . . . Thank you.
Por favor. . . . . Please.
De nada/con mucho gusto. . . . . You're welcome.
Perdoneme. . . . . Pardon me.
¿Como se llama esto? . . . . What do you call this?
Lo siento. . . . . I'm sorry.
Permitame. . . . . Permit me.
Quisiera... . . . . I would like...
Adelante. . . . . Come in.
Permitame presentarle... . . . . May I introduce...
¿Como se llamo usted? . . . . What is your name?
Me llamo... . . . . My name is...
No se. . . . . I don't know.
Tengo sed. . . . . I am thirsty.
Tengo hambre. . . . . I am hungry.
Soy norteamericano/a . . . . I am an American.
¿Donde puedo encontrar...? . . . . Where can I find...?
¿Que es esto? . . . . What is this?
¿Habla usted ingles? . . . . Do you speak English?
Hablo/entiendo un poco . . . . I speak/understand a little Spanish.
  Español
Hay alguien aqui que . . . . Is there anyone here who
  hable ingles?   speaks English?
Le entiendo. . . . . I understand you.

No entiendo. . . . . I don't understand.
Hable mas despacio por favor.. . . . . Please speak more slowly.
Repita por favor.. . . . . Please repeat.

■ TELLING TIME

¿Que hora es? . . . . What time is it?
Son las.... . . . . It is...
... cinco.. . . . . five oíclock.
... ocho y diez. . . . . ten past eight.
... seis y cuarto. . . . . quarter past six.
... cinco y media. . . . . half past five.
... siete y menos cinco. . . . . five of seven.
antes de ayer.. . . . . the day before yesterday.
anoche. . . . . yesterday evening.
esta mañana.. . . . . this morning.
a mediodia.. . . . . at noon.
en la noche. . . . . in the evening.
de noche. . . . . at night.
a medianoche. . . . . at midnight.
mañana en la mañana.. tomorrow morning.
mañana en la noche.. . . . . tomorrow evening.
pasado mañana.. . . . . the day after tomorrow.

■ DIRECTIONS

¿En que direccion queda...? . . . . In which direction is...?
Lleveme a... por favor.. . . . . Take me to... please.
Llevame alla ... por favor.. . . . . Take me there please.
¿Que lugar es este? . . . . What place is this?
¿Donde queda el pueblo?. . . . . Where is the town?
¿Cual es el mejor camino para...? . . . . . . Which is the best road to...?
Malécon.. . . . . Road by the sea.
De vuelta a la derecha. . . . . Turn to the right.
De vuelta a la isquierda.. . . . . Turn to the left.
Siga derecho.. . . . . Go this way.
En esta direccion.. . . . . In this direction.
¿A que distancia estamos de...? . . . . How far is it to...?
¿Es este el camino a...? . . . . Is this the road to...?
Es.... . . . . Is it...
¿... cerca? . . . . near?
¿... lejos? . . . . far?
¿... norte? . . . . north?
¿... sur? . . . . south?
¿... este? . . . . east?
¿... oeste? . . . . west?
Indiqueme por favor. . . . . Please point.
Hagame favor de decirme . . . . Please direct me to...
    donde esta...

... el telefono. . . . . the telephone.
... el bano. . . . . the bathroom.
... el correo. . . . . the post office.
... el banco. . . . . the bank.
... la comisaria. . . . . the police station.

■ ACCOMMODATIONS

Estoy buscando un hotel... . . . . I am looking for a hotel that's...
... bueno. . . . . good.
... barato. . . . . cheap.
... cercano. . . . . nearby.
... limpio. . . . . clean.
¿Dónde queda un buen hotel? . . . . Where is a good hotel?
¿Hay habitaciones libres? . . . . Do you have available rooms?
¿Dónde están los baños/servicios? . . . . Where are the bathrooms?
Quisiera un.... . . . . I would like a...
... cuarto sencillo. . . . . single room.
... cuarto con baño. . . . . room with a bath.
... cuarto doble. . . . . double room.
¿Puedo verlo? . . . . May I see it?
¿Cuanto cuesta? . . . . What's the cost?
¡Es demasiado caro!. . . . . It's too expensive!

Index